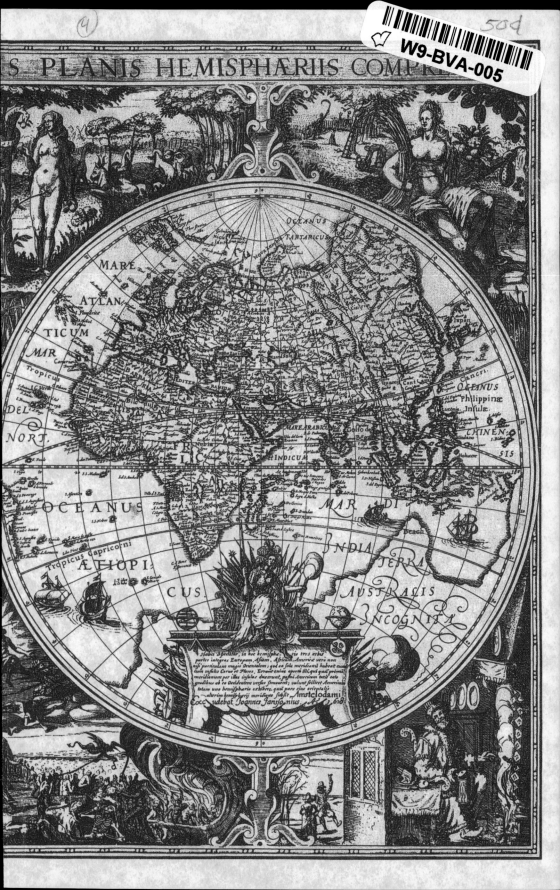

UNCOMMON GROUNDS

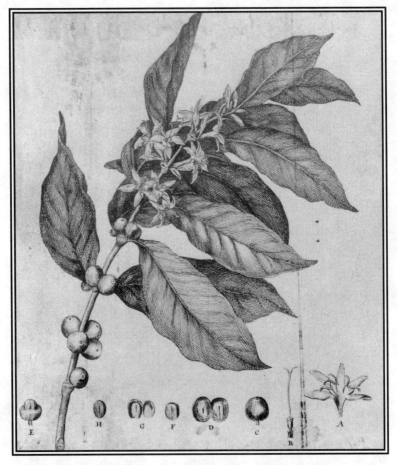

This detailed engraving was one of the first accurate portrayals of the exotic coffee plant, published in 1716 in Voyage de L'Arabie Hereuse

UNCOMMON GROUNDS

*The History of Coffee
and How It
Transformed Our World*

MARK PENDERGRAST

BASIC
BOOKS

A Member of the Perseus Books Group

Published by Basic Books,
A Member of the Perseus Books Group

FIRST EDITION

Designed by Heather Hutchison

A CIP catalog record for this book is available from Library of Congress.
ISBN 0-465-03631-7

98 99 00 01 02 ❖/RRD 10 9 8 7 6 5 4 3 2 1

To Alfred Peet,
coffee curmudgeon supreme

CONTENTS

Part Three
Bitter Brews

Part Four
Romancing the Bean

Photographs appear following pages 138, 266, and 394

The voodoo priest and all his powders were as nothing compared to espresso, cappuccino, and mocha, which are stronger than all the religions of the world combined, and perhaps stronger than the human soul itself.
—**Mark Helprin,** *Memoir from Antproof Case* (1995)

Prologue
THE *ORIFLAMA* HARVEST

Guatemala, January 1997. Picking coffee berries (known as *cherries*) for the first time, I struggle to keep my balance on the precipitous hillside. My basket, or *canasta*, is tied around my waist, and I try to position myself so that the cherries fall directly into it as I pull them off. As Herman, my *caporal* (supervisor), requested, I try to pick only the rich red cherries, but sometimes I accidentally knock loose a green one. I'll have to sort them later.

I pop the skin of a ripe coffee cherry open in my mouth and savor the sweet mucilage. It takes a bit of tongue work to get down to what at first I take to be the bean. Instead, I find that it is the tough-skinned *parchment* protecting each bean. Like peanuts, coffee beans usually grow in facing pairs. Spitting out the parchment, I finally get the two beans in my mouth, which are covered by a diaphanous *silver skin* resembling tissue paper. In some cases where the supporting soil lacks sufficient boron, I might have found only one bean, called a *peaberry*, considered by some to possess a slightly more concentrated taste. After a while, I spit out the seeds, which are too hard to chew.

I hear other harvesters—whole families of them—chatting and singing in Spanish. This is a happy time, when the year's hard work of pruning, fertilizing, weeding, tending, and repairing roads and water channels comes down to ripe coffee. I don't know Spanish, so instead I sing an old song, "Spanish Is a Loving Tongue," which at least has a few phrases: *mi amor, mi corazón.*

When I stop, I hear giggles and applause. Unwittingly, I have attracted a group of kids, who now wander off to resume picking or pestering their parents. Children begin helping with the harvest when they are seven or eight. Though many *campesinos* keep their children out of school at other times for other reasons, it's no coincidence that school vacation in Guatemala coincides with the coffee harvest.

I am 4,500 feet above sea level on *Oriflama*, the coffee *finca* (plantation) owned by Betty Hannstein Adams. Betty's grandfather, Bernhard Hannstein ("Don Bernardo") arrived in Guatemala over a hundred years ago, one of many German immigrants who pioneered the country's coffee production. Bernhard's son, Walter (Betty's father), eventually took over management. *Oriflama*, which contains over 400 acres, is half of the original farm, which was called *La Paz.*

Most of the coffee trees are *caturra* and *catuai*, hybrids that are easier to harvest because they are shorter and more compact than the older *bourbon* variety. Still, I have to bend some branches down to get at them. After half an hour I have picked half a *canasta*, about 12 pounds of cherries that, after processing to remove the pulp, mucilage, and parchment, will produce 2 pounds of green coffee beans. When roasted, they will lose as much as 20 percent more in weight. Still, I have picked enough to make several pots of fine coffee. I'm feeling pretty proud until Herman, who stands just over five feet and weighs a little over 100 pounds, shows up with a full *canasta* and gently chides me for being so slow. I am big, he says, and don't have as far to reach.

The farm is almost intolerably beautiful, covered with the green glossy leaves of the coffee trees, prehistoric tree ferns and Spanish daggers along the roadside (to prevent erosion), rolling hills, invisible harvesters singing and calling to one another, laughter of children, birds chirruping, clouds rolling over tops of hills, big shade trees dappling hillsides, springs and streams. As in other high-altitude coffee-growing areas, the temperature never strays far from 75° F.

In the distance I can see the volcano, Santa María, and the smoke from the smaller cone, Santiago, where in 1902 a side eruption exploded, burying *Oriflama* under a foot of ash and killing all the songbirds. "Oh God, what a sight," wrote Betty's grandmother, Ida Hannstein, soon after. "As far as the eye could see everything was blue and gray and dead, like a mammoth cemetery."

It is difficult to imagine that scene now, as I stand in the midst of what seems to be a paradise. The nitrogen-fixing shade trees—*inga, poro*, and others—along with the cypresses and oaks that stand in majestic groves and the macadamia trees grown to diversify output, provide a much-needed habitat for migratory birds. At breakfast I had melon, cream, and honey that came from the plantation; also black beans, rice, and of course, coffee.

By 4:00 P.M. the harvest day is over, and everyone brings bulging bags of coffee cherries to the *beneficio* (processing plant) to be weighed. Most laborers and their produce are picked up by trucks along the network of roads throughout the plantation, but the first to arrive on foot, like me, were picking nearby. In other parts of Guatemala the Mayan Indians are the primary harvesters, but here they are local *ladinos,* whose blood combines an Indian and Spanish heritage. Like Herman, my *caporal,* they are all very small, probably owing to their ancestors' chronic malnutrition. Many wear secondhand American T-shirts that appear incongruous here, one sporting a picture of Alf (an old TV character) and another from the Kennedy Space Center.

Tiny women, perhaps four foot five inches, can carry amazingly large bags, twice their 80 pound weight. Some of the women carry babies in slings around front; after they dump their loads, they rearrange the babies on their backs. The child harvesters also are remarkably strong and capable. They bring in loads that would kill me, dump them onto the scale, wait anxiously for the weight to be announced, then turn away smiling broadly with a piece of paper indicating their pay. A good adult picker can harvest over 200 pounds of cherries and earn $8 a day, more than twice the Guatemalan minimum daily wage.

In Guatemala, the contrast between poverty and wealth is stark. Land distribution is lopsided, and those who perform the most difficult labor do not reap the profits. Yet there is no quick fix to the inequities built into the economic system, nor any viable alternatives to coffee as a crop on these mountainsides. The workers are in many ways more content and fulfilled than their counterparts in the United States. They have a strong sense of tradition and family life.

I am confused. As the workers bring in the harvest, I ponder the irony that, once processed, these beans will travel thousands of miles to give pleasure to people who enjoy a lifestyle beyond the imagination of these Guatemalan laborers. Yet it would be unfair to label one group "villains" and another "victims" in this drama. I realize that nothing about this story is going to be simple.

I donate my meager harvest to the kid with the Alf T-shirt and turn once again to look at the valley and volcano in the distance. Back at my home in the United States, I have already begun to accumulate books, interview transcripts, and mounds of photocopies that threaten to swamp my small office, where I will write this history of coffee. But now I am living it, and I can tell that this experience, this book, will challenge my preconceptions and, I hope, those of my readers.

Introduction

PUDDLE WATER
OR PANACEA?

O Coffee! Thou dost dispel all care, thou are the object of desire to the scholar. This is the beverage of the friends of God.
      —**"In Praise of Coffee," Arabic poem** (1511)

[Why do our men] trifle away their time, scald their Chops, and spend their Money, all for a little base, black, thick, nasty bitter stinking, nauseous Puddle water?
      —*Women's Petition Against Coffee* (1674)

It is, after all, only a berry, encasing a double-sided seed. It first grew on a shrub—or small tree, depending on your perspective or height—under the Ethiopian rain forest canopy, high on the mountainsides. The evergreen leaves form glossy ovals and, like the seeds, are laced with caffeine.

Yet coffee is the second most valuable exported legal commodity on earth (after oil), providing the largest jolt of the world's most widely taken psychoactive drug. From its original African home, coffee propagation has spread in a girdle around the globe, taking over whole plains and mountainsides between the Tropics of Cancer and Capricorn. In the form of a hot infusion of its ground, roasted seeds, coffee is consumed around the world for its bittersweet bouquet, its mind-racing jump start, and social bonding. At various times it has been prescribed as an aphrodisiac, enema, nerve tonic, and life-extender.

Coffee provides a livelihood (of sorts) for over twenty million human beings. It is an incredibly labor-intensive crop, with all but a tiny percentage requiring the individual human hand. Calloused palms plant the seeds, nurse the seedlings under a shade canopy, transplant them to mountainside ranks, prune and fertilize, spray for pests, irrigate, harvest, and lug 200-pound bags of coffee cherries. Laborers regulate the complicated process of removing the precious bean from its covering of pulp and mucilage. Then the beans must be spread to dry for several days (or heated in drums), the parchment and silver skin removed, and the resulting green bean (*café oro*, or "golden coffee," as it is known in Latin America) bagged for shipment, roasting, grinding, and brewing around the world.

The inescapable irony of the coffee industry is that the vast majority of those who perform these repetitive tasks work in the most beautiful places on earth, with tropical volcanic peaks as backdrop in a climate-controlled heaven that rarely dips below 70°F or tops 80°–and these laborers earn an average of $3 a day. Most live in abject poverty without plumbing, electricity, medical care, or nutritious foods. The coffee they prepare travels halfway around the world and lands on breakfast tables, offices, and upscale coffee bars of the United States, Europe, Japan, and other developed countries, where cosmopolitan consumers routinely pay half a day's Third World wages for a good cup of coffee.

The list of those who make money from coffee doesn't stop in the producing countries. There are the exporters, importers, and roasters. There are the frantic traders in the pits of the coffee exchanges who gesticulate, scream, and set the price of a commodity they rarely see in its raw form. There are the expert cuppers and liquorers (equivalent to wine tasters) who spend their day slurping, savoring, and spitting coffee. There are the retailers, the vending machine suppliers, the marketers, the advertising copyrighters, the consultants.

Coffee is an extraordinarily delicate commodity. Its quality is first determined by essentials such as type of plant, soil conditions, and growing altitude. It can be ruined at every step along the line, from fertilizer and pesticide application to harvesting methods to processing to shipping to roasting to packaging to brewing. A coffee bean greedily absorbs odors and flavors from a host of nauseating companions. Too much moisture produces mold. A too-light roast produces undeveloped, bitter coffee, while overroasted coffee resembles charcoal. After roasting, the bean stales quickly unless used within a week or so. Boiling or sitting on a hot plate quickly reduces the finest brew to a stale, bitter, mouth-turning cup of black bile. In addition, it can be adulterated with an astonishing array of vegetable matter, ranging from chicory to figs.

How do we judge coffee quality? Coffee experts talk about four basic components that blend to create the perfect cup: aroma, body, acidity, and flavor. The *aroma* is familiar and obvious enough–that fragrance that often promises more than the taste delivers. *Body* is a more subjective quality and refers to the feel or "weight" of the coffee in the mouth, how it rolls around the tongue and fills the throat on the way down. *Acidity* does not refer literally to a pH level but to a sparkle, a brightness, a tang that adds zest to the cup. Finally, *flavor* is the evanescent, subtle taste that explodes in the mouth, then lingers as a gustatory memory. Coffee experts, like wine connoisseurs, become downright poetic in describing these components. For example, Sulawesi coffee possesses "a seductive combination of butter-caramel sweetness and herbaceous, loamy tastes," coffee aficionado Kevin Knox writes.

A good cup of coffee can turn the worst day tolerable, provide an all-important moment of contemplation, rekindle a romance. And yet, poetic as its taste may be, coffee's history is rife with controversy and politics. It has been banned as a creator of revolutionary sedition in Arab countries and in Europe. It has been vilified as the worst health destroyer on earth and praised as the boon of mankind. Coffee lies at the heart of the Mayan Indian's continued subjugation in Guatemala, the democratic tradition in Costa Rica, and the taming of the Wild West in the United States. When Idi Amin was killing his Ugandan countrymen, coffee provided virtually all of his foreign exchange, and the Sandinistas launched their revolution by commandeering Somoza's coffee plantations.

Beginning as a medicinal drink for the elite, coffee became the favored modern stimulant of the blue-collar worker during his break, the gossip starter in middle-class kitchens, the romantic binder for wooing couples, and the sole, bitter companion of the lost soul. Coffeehouses have provided places to plan revolutions, write poetry, do business, and meet friends. The drink became such an intrinsic part of Western culture that it has seeped into an incredible number of popular songs: "You're the cream in my coffee"; "Let's have another cup of coffee, let's have another piece of pie"; "I love coffee, I love tea, I love the java jive and it loves me"; "Black coffee, love's a hand-me-down brew."

The modern coffee industry was spawned in late nineteenth-century America during the furiously capitalistic Gilded Age. At the end of the Civil War, Jabez Burns invented the first efficient industrial coffee roaster. The railroad, telegraph, and steamship revolutionized distribution and communication, while newspapers, magazines, and lithography allowed massive advertising campaigns. Moguls tried to corner the coffee market, while Brazilians frantically planted thousands of acres of coffee trees, only to see the price decline catastrophically. A pattern of worldwide boom and bust commenced.

By the early twentieth century, coffee had become a major consumer product, advertised widely throughout the country. In the 1920s and 1930s, national corporations such as Standard Brands and General Foods snapped up major brands and pushed them through radio programs. By the 1950s, coffee was the American middle-class beverage of choice.

For good or ill, coffee's modern saga explores broader themes as well: the importance of advertising, development of assembly line mass production, urbanization, women's issues, concentration and consolidation of national markets, the rise of the supermarket, automobile, radio, television, "instant" gratification, technological innovation, multinational conglomerates, market segmentation, commodity control schemes, and just-in-time inventories. The bean's history also illustrates how an entire industry can lose focus, allowing upstart microroasters to reclaim quality and profits—and then how the cycle begins again, with bigger companies gobbling smaller ones in another round of concentration and merger.

The coffee industry has dominated and molded the economy, politics, and social structure of entire countries. On the one hand, its monocultural avatar has led to the oppression and land dispossession of indigenous peoples, the abandoning of subsistence agriculture in favor of exports, overreliance on foreign markets, destruction of the rain forest, and environmental degradation. On the other hand, coffee has provided an essential cash crop for struggling family farmers, the basis for national industrialization and modernization, a model of organic production and fair trade, and a valuable habitat for migratory birds.

The coffee saga encompasses a panoramic story of epic proportions involving the clash and blending of cultures, the cheap jazzing of the industrial laborer, the rise of the national brand, and the ultimate abandonment of quality in favor of price cutting and commodification of a fine product in the post–World War II era. It involves an eccentric cast of characters, all of them with a passion for the golden bean. Something about coffee seems to make many coffee men (and the few women who have made their way into their ranks) opinionated, contentious, and monomaniacal. They disagree over just about everything, from whether Ethiopian Harrar or Guatemalan Antigua is the best coffee, to the best roasting method, to whether a press pot or drip filter makes superior coffee.

Around the world we are currently witnessing a coffee revival, as miniroasters revive the fine art of coffee blending and customers rediscover the joy of fresh-roasted, fresh-ground, fresh-brewed coffee and espresso, made from the best beans in the world.

Coffee has assumed a social meaning that goes far beyond the simple black brew in the cup. The worldwide coffee culture is more than a culture—it is a cult. There are usenet newsgroups on the subject, along with innumerable sites on the World Wide Web, and Starbucks outlets populate every street corner, vying for space with other coffeehouses and chains.

And after all is said and done, it's just the pit of a berry from an Ethiopian shrub.

Coffee. May you enjoy its convoluted history over many cups.

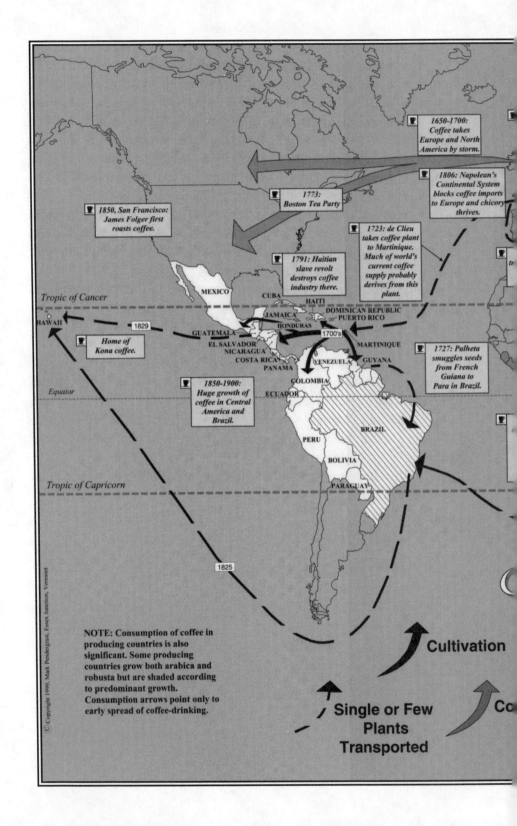

1650-1700: Coffee takes Europe and North America by storm.

1806: Napolean's Continental System blocks coffee imports to Europe and chicory thrives.

1773: Boston Tea Party

1850, San Francisco: James Folger first roasts coffee.

1723: de Clieu takes coffee plant to Martinique. Much of world's current coffee supply probably derives from this plant.

1791: Haitian slave revolt destroys coffee industry there.

Tropic of Cancer

MEXICO CUBA HAITI
JAMAICA DOMINICAN REPUBLIC
1829 HONDURAS PUERTO RICO
HAWAII GUATEMALA MARTINIQUE
EL SALVADOR 1700's
NICARAGUA VENEZUELA GUYANA
COSTA RICA PANAMA
COLOMBIA
ECUADOR

Home of Kona coffee.

1727: Palheta smuggles seeds from French Guiana to Para in Brazil.

1850-1900: Huge growth of coffee in Central America and Brazil.

Equator

BRAZIL
PERU
BOLIVIA

Tropic of Capricorn

PARAGUAY

1825

© Copyright 1999, Mark Pendergrast, Essex Junction, Vermont

NOTE: Consumption of coffee in producing countries is also significant. Some producing countries grow both arabica and robusta but are shaded according to predominant growth. Consumption arrows point only to early spread of coffee-drinking.

Cultivation

Single or Few Plants Transported

Co

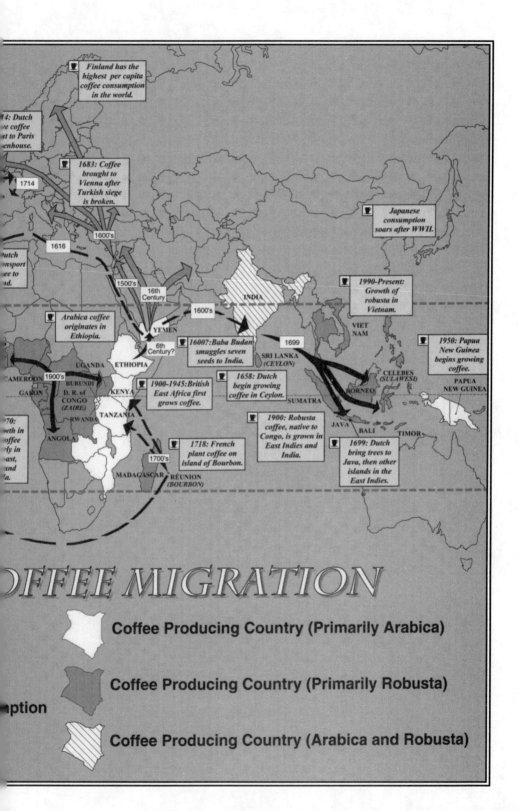

Finland has the highest per capita coffee consumption in the world.

14: Dutch
e coffee
t to Paris
enhouse.

1683: Coffee brought to Vienna after Turkish siege is broken.

1714

Japanese consumption soars after WWII.

1600's

1616

utch
nsport
ee to
d.

1500's

16th Century

Arabica coffee originates in Ethiopia.

1600's

INDIA

1990-Present: Growth of robusta in Vietnam.

YEMEN

6th Century?

1600?:Baba Budan smuggles seven seeds to India.

1599

VIET NAM

1950: Papua New Guinea begins growing coffee.

UGANDA

ETHIOPIA

SRI LANKA (CEYLON)

CELEBES (SULAWESI)

PAPUA NEW GUINEA

CAMEROON

1900's

BURUNDI

KENYA

1900-1945:British East Africa first grows coffee.

1658: Dutch begin growing coffee in Ceylon.

SUMATRA

BORNEO

GABON

D. R. of CONGO (ZAIRE)

RWANDA

TANZANIA

70:
wth in
offee
ly in
ast,
and
a.

ANGOLA

1900: Robusta coffee, native to Congo, is grown in East Indies and India.

JAVA

BALI

TIMOR

1699: Dutch bring trees to Java, then other islands in the East Indies.

1700's

1718: French plant coffee on island of Bourbon.

MADAGASCAR

RÉUNION (BOURBON)

OFFEE MIGRATION

Coffee Producing Country (Primarily Arabica)

Coffee Producing Country (Primarily Robusta)

ption

Coffee Producing Country (Arabica and Robusta)

~ *Part One* ~

SEEDS OF CONQUEST

According to folklore an Ethiopian goatherd named Kaldi
discovered the joys of coffee when his goats ate the berries and
became so frisky that they "danced." Kaldi soon joined them.

~ 1 ~

COFFEE COLONIZES
THE WORLD

Coffee makes us severe, and grave, and philosophical.
–Jonathan Swift, 1722

[Coffee causes] an excessive state of brain-excitation which becomes manifest by a remarkable loquaciousness sometimes accompanied by accelerated association of ideas. It may also be observed in coffee house politicians who drink cup after cup ... and by this abuse are inspired to profound wisdom on all earthly events.

–Lewis Lewin, ***Phantastica: Narcotic and Stimulating Drugs*** (1931)

Possibly the cradle of mankind, the ancient land of Abyssinia, now called Ethiopia, is the birthplace of coffee. Situated at the conjunction of the African and Arab worlds known as the Horn of Africa, the mountainous country, split down the middle by the earthquake-prone Great Rift Valley, has a biblical quality–and little wonder. Across the nearby Red Sea, further to the north, Moses led his people to freedom. The Queen of Sheba later descended from the Ethiopian mountains to join King Solomon in Jerusalem, and, according to legend, she founded the Axum dynasty that established its rule in the first century A.D. (a monarchy that continued, with a hiatus between 572 and 1270, until 1974, when Haile Selassie was deposed).

Always relatively poor, the Abyssinians were nonetheless a proud, independent people, most of them adopting a cloistered, orthodox form of Christianity when no other African indigenous people held

3

that faith. "Encompassed on all sides by the enemies of their religion," the historian Gibbon noted, "the Ethiopians slept near a thousand years, forgetful of the world by whom they were forgotten." Likewise forgotten—or not yet discovered—was the beverage we now call coffee.

The Puzzled Boy and His Mad Goats

We do not know exactly when or by whom coffee was discovered. Of the various Ethiopian and Arab legends, the most appealing involves dancing goats. A goatherd named Kaldi, a poet by nature, loved following the wandering paths made by his goats as they combed the mountainsides for food. The job required little of him, so he was free to make up songs and to play his pipe. In the late afternoon, when he blew a special, piercing note, his goats scampered from their browsing in the forest to follow him back home.

One afternoon, however, the goats did not come. Kaldi blew his pipe again, fiercely. Still no goats. Puzzled, the boy climbed higher, listening for them. He finally heard bleating in the distance.

Running around the corner of a narrow trail, Kaldi suddenly came upon the goats. Under the thick rain forest canopy, which allowed the sun to sift through in sudden bright splotches, the goats were running about, butting one another, dancing on their hind legs, and bleating excitedly. In winded wonder, the boy stood gaping at them. *They must be bewitched*, he thought. *What else could it be?*

As he watched, one goat after another chewed off the glossy green leaves and red berries of a tree he had never seen before. It must be the trees that had maddened his goats. Was it a poison? Would they all die? His father would kill him!

The goats refused to come home with him until hours later, but they did not die. The next day, they ran directly back to the same grove and repeated the performance. This time, Kaldi decided it was safe for him to join them. First, he chewed on a few leaves. They tasted bitter. As he masticated them, however, he experienced a slow tingle, moving from his tongue down into his gut, and expanding to his entire body. Next, he tried the berries. The fruit was mildly sweet, and the seeds that popped out were covered with a thick, tasty mucilage. Finally, he chewed the seeds themselves. And popped another berry in his mouth.

Soon, according to legend, Kaldi was frisking with his goats. Poetry and song spilled out of him. He felt that he would never be tired or grouchy again. Kaldi told his father about the magical trees, the word spread, and soon coffee became an integral part of Ethiopian culture. By the time Rhazes, an Arabian physician, first mentioned coffee in print in the tenth century, it probably had been deliberately cultivated for hundreds of years.

It is likely that, as in the legend, the beans and leaves of *bunn,* as coffee was called, at first were simply chewed, but the inventive Ethiopians quickly graduated to more palatable ways of getting their caffeine fix. They brewed the leaves and berries with boiled water as a weak tea. They ground the beans and mixed them with animal fat for a quick-energy snack. They made wine out of the fermented pulp. They made a sweet beverage called *qishr* out of the lightly roasted husks of the coffee cherry, a drink now known as *kisher.* Finally, probably in the sixteenth century, someone roasted the beans, ground them, and made an infusion. Ah! Coffee as we know it (or a variety thereof) finally came into being.

Ethiopians still serve coffee in an elaborate ceremony, which often takes nearly an hour. As charcoals warm inside a special clay pot, guests sit on three-legged stools, chatting. As your host talks with you, his wife carefully washes the green coffee beans to remove the silver skin. The beans, from your host's trees, have been sun-dried, their husks removed by hand. The hostess throws a little frankincense on the coals to produce a heady odor. Then over the coals she places a flat iron disk, a bit less than a foot in diameter. With an iron-hooked implement, she gently stirs the beans on this griddle. After some minutes they turn cinnamon, then begin to crackle with the "first pop" of the classic coffee roast. When they have turned a golden brown, she removes them from the fire and dumps them into a small mortar. With a pestle she grinds them into a very fine powder, which she deposits in a clay pot of water set atop the coals to boil. Along with the pulverized coffee, she also throws in some cardamom and cinnamon.

The smell now is exotic and overwhelming. She pours the first round of the brew into small 3-ounce cups, without handles, along with a spoonful of sugar. Everyone sips, murmuring appreciation. The coffee is thick, with some of the grounds inevitably suspended in the drink. When the cup is drained, however, most of the sediment remains on the bottom.

Twice more, the hostess adds a bit of water and brings the coffee to a boil for more servings. Then the guests take their leave.

Coffee Goes Arab

Once the Ethiopians discovered coffee it was only a matter of time until the drink spread through trade with the Arabs across the narrow band of the Red Sea. It is possible that when the Ethiopians invaded and ruled Yemen for some fifty years in the sixth century, they deliberately set up coffee plantations. The Arabs took to the stimulating drink. (According to legend, Mohammed proclaimed that under the invigorating influence of coffee he could "unhorse forty men and possess forty women.") They began cultivating the trees, complete with irrigation ditches, in the nearby mountains, calling it *qahwa*, an Arab word for wine–from which the name *coffee* derives.

At first the Arab Sufi monks adopted coffee as a drink that would allow them to stay awake for midnight prayers more easily. While coffee was first considered a medicine or religious aid, it soon enough slipped into everyday use. Wealthy people had a coffee room in their homes, reserved only for ceremonial imbibing. For those who did not have such private largesse, coffee houses, known as *kaveh kanes*, sprang up. By the end of the fifteenth century, Muslim pilgrims had introduced coffee throughout the Islamic world in Persia, Egypt, Turkey, and North Africa, making it a lucrative trade item.

As the drink gained in popularity throughout the sixteenth century, it also gained its reputation as a troublemaking social brew. Various rulers decided that people were having too much fun in the coffeehouses. "The patrons of the coffeehouse indulged in a variety of improper pastimes," Ralph Hattox notes in his history of the Arab coffeehouses, "ranging from gambling to involvement in irregular and criminally unorthodox sexual situations."

When Khair-Beg, the young governor of Mecca, discovered that satirical verses about him were emanating from the coffeehouses, he determined that coffee, like wine, must be outlawed by the Koran and he induced his religious, legal, and medical advisors to agree. Thus, in 1511 the coffeehouses of Mecca were forcibly closed.

The ban lasted only until the Cairo sultan, a habitual coffee drinker, heard about it and reversed the edict. Other Arab rulers and religious leaders, however, also denounced coffee during the course of the 1500s. The Grand Vizier Kuprili of Constantinople, for example, fearing sedition during a war, closed the city's coffeehouses. Anyone caught drinking coffee was soundly cudgeled. Offenders found imbibing a second time were sewn into leather bags and thrown into the Bosphorus. Even so, many continued to drink coffee in secret, and eventually the ban was withdrawn.

Why did coffee drinking persist in the face of persecution in these early Arab societies? The addictive nature of caffeine provides one answer, of course; yet there is more to it. Coffee provided an intellectual stimulant, a pleasant way to feel increased energy without any apparent ill effects. In an elaborate social ritual, coffee was brought to a boil three times in the *ibrik* (a small conical copper pot with a long handle) before the viscous drink was dispensed into small cups, the pourer carefully shaking his hand so that a little *wesh,* or froth, topped each cup. Coffee-houses allowed people to get together for conversation, entertainment, and business, inspiring agreements, poetry, and irreverence in equal measure. So important did the brew become in Turkey that a lack of sufficient coffee provided grounds for a woman to seek a divorce.

Smugglers, New Cultivation, and Arrival in the Western World

The Ottoman Turks occupied Yemen in 1536, and soon afterward the coffee bean became an important export throughout the Turkish empire. The beans generally were exported from the Yemeni port of Mocha, so the coffee from that region took on the name of the port. The trade route involved shipping the coffee to Suez and transporting it by camel to Alexandrian warehouses, where it was picked up by French and Venetian merchants. Because the coffee trade had become a major source of income, the Turks jealously guarded their monopoly over the trees' cultivation in Yemen. No fertile berries were allowed to leave the country unless they first had been steeped in boiling water or partially roasted to prevent germination.

Inevitably, these precautions were circumvented. Some time during the 1600s a Moslem pilgrim named Baba Budan smuggled seven seeds out by taping them to his stomach and successfully cultivated them in southern India, in the mountains of Mysore. In 1616 the Dutch, who dominated the world's shipping trade, managed to transport a tree to Holland from Aden. From its offspring the Dutch began growing coffee in Ceylon in 1658. In 1699 another Dutchman transplanted trees from Malabar to Java, followed by cultivation in Sumatra, Celebes, Timor,

Bali, and other islands in the East Indies. For many years to come, the production of the Dutch East Indies determined the price of coffee in the world market.

During the 1700s *Java* and *Mocha* became the most famous and sought-after coffees, and those words are still synonymous with the black brew, though little high-quality coffee currently comes from Java, and Mocha ceased operation as a viable port in 1869 with the completion of the Suez Canal.

At first Europeans didn't know what to make of the strange new brew. In 1610 traveling British poet Sir George Sandys noted that the Turks sat "chatting most of the day" over their coffee, which he described as "blacke as soote, and tasting not much unlike it." He added, however, that it "helpeth, as they say, digestion, and procureth alacrity."

Europeans eventually took to coffee with a passion. Pope Clement VIII, who died in 1605, supposedly tasted the Moslem drink at the behest of his priests, who wanted him to ban it. "Why, this Satan's drink is so delicious," he reputedly exclaimed, "that it would be a pity to let the infidels have exclusive use of it. We shall fool Satan by baptizing it and making it a truly Christian beverage."

In the first half of the seventeenth century, coffee was still an exotic beverage, and like other such rare substances as sugar, cocoa, and tea, initially was used primarily as an expensive medicine by the upper classes. Over the next fifty years, however, Europeans were to discover the social as well as medicinal benefits of the Arabian drink. By the 1650s coffee was sold on Italian streets by *aquacedratajo*, or lemonade vendors, who dispensed coffee, chocolate, and liquor as well. Venice's first coffeehouse opened in 1683. Named for the drink it served, the *caffè* (spelled *café* elsewhere in Europe) quickly became synonymous with relaxed companionship, animated conversation, and tasty food.

Surprisingly, given their subsequent enthusiasm for coffee, the French lagged behind the Italians and British in adopting the coffeehouse. In 1669 a new Turkish ambassador, Soliman Aga, introduced coffee at his sumptuous Parisian parties, inspiring a craze for all things Turkish. Male guests, given voluminous dressing gowns, learned to loll comfortably without chairs in the luxurious surroundings, and to drink the exotic new beverage. Still, it appeared to be only a novelty.

French doctors, threatened by the medicinal claims made for coffee, went on the counterattack in Marseilles in 1679: "We note with horror that this beverage . . . has tended almost completely to disaccustom people from the enjoyment of wine." Then, in a fine burst of pseudo-science, one young physician blasted coffee, asserting that it "dried up the cerebrospinal fluid and the convolutions ... the upshot being general exhaustion, paralysis, and impotence." Six years later, however, Sylvestre Dufour, another French physician, wrote a book strongly defending coffee, and by 1696 one Paris doctor was prescribing coffee enemas to "sweeten" the lower bowel and freshen the complexion.

It wasn't until 1689 when François Procope, an Italian immigrant, opened his Café de Procope directly opposite the Comédie Française, that the famous French coffeehouse took root. Soon French actors, authors, dramatists, and musicians were meeting there for coffee and literary conversations. In the next century the café attracted notables such as Voltaire, Rousseau, Diderot, and a visiting Benjamin Franklin. Coffee also provided a living for fortune-tellers, who claimed to read coffee grounds. A long line indicated a long journey. A circle forecast a birth. A cross meant eventual death.

The French historian Michelet described the advent of coffee as "the auspicious revolution of the times, the great event which created new customs, and even modified human temperament." Certainly coffee lessened the intake of alcohol while the cafés provided a wonderful intellectual stew that ultimately spawned the French Revolution. The coffeehouses of continental Europe were egalitarian meeting places where, as the food writer Margaret Visser notes, "men and women could, without impropriety, consort as they had never done before. They could meet in public places and talk."

Increasingly they did so over coffee that was not nearly so harsh a brew as the Turks made. In 1710, rather than boiling coffee, the French first made it by the infusion method, with powdered coffee suspended in a cloth bag over which boiling water was poured. Soon they also discovered the joys of sweetened "coffied milk" or "milky coffee." The Marquise de Sevigne declared this form of coffee "the nicest thing in the world," and many French citizens took to *café au lait*, particularly for breakfast.

French writer Honoré de Balzac did not trifle with such milky coffee, though. He consumed finely pulverized roasted coffee on an empty stomach with virtually no water. The results were spectacular. "Everything becomes agitated. Ideas quick march into motion like battalions of a grand army to its legendary fighting ground, and the battle rages. Memories charge in, bright flags on high; the cavalry of metaphor deploys with a magnificent gallop." Finally, his creative juices flowing, Balzac could write. "Forms and shapes and characters rear up; the paper is spread with ink—for the nightly labor begins and ends with torrents of this black water, as a battle opens and concludes with black powder."

Kolschitzky and Camel Fodder

Coffee arrived in Vienna a bit later than in France. In July 1683 the Turkish army, threatening to invade Europe, massed outside Vienna for a prolonged siege. The count in charge of the Viennese troops desperately needed a messenger who could pass through the Turkish lines to reach nearby Polish troops who would come to the rescue. Franz George Kolschitzky, who had lived in the Arab world for many years, took on the job, disguised in a Turkish uniform. On September 12, in a decisive battle, the Turks were routed.

The fleeing Turks left tents, oxen, camels, sheep, honey, rice, grain, gold—and five hundred huge sacks filled with strange-looking beans that the Viennese thought must be camel fodder. Having no use for camels, they began to burn the bags. Kolschitzky, catching a whiff of that familiar odor, intervened. "Holy Mary!" he yelled. "That is coffee that you are burning! If you don't know what coffee is, give the stuff to me. I can find a good use for it." Having observed the Turkish customs, he knew the rudiments of roasting, grinding, and brewing, and he soon opened the Blue Bottle, the first Viennese café. Like the Turks, he sweetened the coffee considerably, but he also strained out the grounds and added a big dollop of milk.[1]

Within a few decades, coffee practically fueled the intellectual life of the city. "The city of Vienna is filled with coffee houses," wrote a visitor early in the 1700s, "where the novelists or those who busy themselves with newspapers delight to meet." Unlike rowdy beer halls, the cafés provided a place for lively conversation and mental concentration.

Coffee historian Ian Bersten believes that the Arab taste for black coffee, and the widespread European (and eventually American) habit of taking coffee with milk, owes something to genetics. The Anglo-Saxons

---

[1]Some Viennese were undoubtedly familiar with coffee prior to Kolschitzky's exploits, since the Turks established an embassy in Vienna in 1665.

could tolerate milk, while Mediterranean peoples–Arabs, Greek Cypriots, and southern Italians–tended to be lactose-intolerant. That is why they continue to take their coffee straight, if sometimes well-sweetened. "From the two ends of Europe," writes Bersten, "there eventually developed two totally different ways to brew this new commodity–either filtered in Northern Europe or espresso style in Southern Europe. The intolerance to milk may have even caused cappuccinos to be smaller in Italy so that milk intolerance problems could be minimized."

Lovelier Than a Thousand Kisses

Coffee and coffeehouses reached Germany in the 1670s. By 1721 there were coffeehouses in most major German cities. For quite a while the coffee habit remained the province of the upper classes. Many physicians warned that it caused sterility or stillbirths. In 1732 the drink had become controversial (and popular) enough to inspire Johann Sebastian Bach to write his humorous *Coffee Cantata*, in which a daughter begs her stern father to allow her this favorite vice:

> Dear father, do not be so strict! If I can't have my little demi-tasse of coffee three times a day, I'm just like a dried up piece of roast goat! Ah! How sweet coffee tastes! Lovelier than a thousand kisses, sweeter far than muscatel wine! I must have my coffee, and if anyone wishes to please me, let him present me with–coffee![2]

Later in the century, coffee-obsessed Ludwig van Beethoven ground precisely sixty beans to brew a cup.

By 1777 the hot beverage had become entirely too popular for Frederick the Great, who issued a manifesto in favor of Germany's more traditional drink: "It is disgusting to notice the increase in the quantity of coffee used by my subjects, and the like amount of money that goes out of the country in consequence. My people must drink beer. His Majesty was brought up on beer, and so were his ancestors." Four years later the king forbade coffee's roasting except in official government establishments, forcing the poor to resort to coffee substitutes, such as

---

[2]"Oh, Daddy, don't be such a drag," a modern librettist translates the cantata. "If I don't get my coffee fix three times a day, I'll die!"

roast chicory root, dried fig, barley, wheat, or corn. They also managed
to get hold of real coffee beans and roast them clandestinely, but government spies, pejoratively named *coffee smellers* by the populace, put
them out of business. Eventually coffee outlived all the efforts to stifle it
in Germany. *Frauen* particularly loved their *Kaffeeklatches*, gossipy social
interludes that gave the brew a more feminine image.

Every other European country also discovered coffee during the
same period. Green beans reached Holland by way of Dutch traders.
The Scandinavian countries were slower to adopt it–though today they
boast the highest per-capita consumption on earth. Nowhere did coffee
have such a dynamic and immediate impact, however, as in England.

The British Coffee Invasion

Like a liquid black torrent the coffee rage drenched England, beginning at Oxford University in 1650, where Jacobs, a Lebanese Jew,
opened the first coffeehouse for "some who delighted in noveltie." Two
years later in London, Pasqua Rosée, a Greek, opened a coffeehouse
and printed the first coffee advertisement, a broadside touting "The
Vertue of the *COFFEE* Drink," described as

> a simple innocent thing, composed into a Drink, by being dryed in an
> Oven, and ground to Powder, and boiled up with Spring water, and
> about half a pint of it to be drunk, lasting an hour before, and not Eating
> an hour after, and to be taken as hot as possibly can be endured.

Pasqua Rosée made extravagant medicinal claims; his 1652 ad asserted that coffee would aid digestion, cure headaches, coughs, consumption, dropsy, gout, and scurvy, and prevent miscarriages. More
practically, he wrote: "It will prevent Drowsiness, and make one fit for
business, if one have occasion to *Watch*; and therefore you are not to
Drink of it *after Supper*, unless you intend to be *watchful*, for it will hin-
der sleep for 3 or 4 hours."

Coffee and coffeehouses took London by storm. By 1700 there were
more than two thousand London coffeehouses, occupying more
premises and paying more rent than any other trade. They came to be
known as *penny universities*, because for that price one could purchase a
cup of coffee and sit for hours listening to extraordinary conversations–
or, as a 1657 newspaper advertisement put it, "PUBLICK INTER-

COURSE." Each coffeehouse specialized in a different type of clientele. In one, physicians could be consulted. Others served Protestants, Puritans, Catholics, Jews, literati, merchants, traders, fops, Whigs, Tories, army officers, actors, lawyers, clergy, or wits. The coffeehouses provided England's first egalitarian meeting place, where a man was expected to chat with his tablemates whether he knew them or not.

Edward Lloyd's establishment catered primarily to seafarers and merchants, and he regularly prepared "ships' lists" for underwriters who met there to offer insurance. Thus began Lloyd's of London, the famous insurance company. Other coffeehouses spawned the Stock Exchange, the Bankers' Clearing-house, and newspapers such as *The Tattler* and *The Spectator*.

Before the advent of coffee the British imbibed alcohol, often in Falstaffian proportions. "What immoderate drinking in every place!" complained a British commentator in 1624. "How they flock to the tavern! [Here they] drown their wits, seeth their brains in ale." Fifty years later another observed that "coffee-drinking hath caused a greater sobriety among the nations; for whereas formerly Apprentices and Clerks with others, used to take their mornings' draught in Ale, Beer or Wine, which by the dizziness they cause in the Brain, make many unfit for business, they use now to play the Good-fellows in this wakefull and civill drink."

Not that most coffeehouses were universally uplifting places; rather, they were chaotic, smelly, wildly energetic, and capitalistic. "There was a rabble going hither and thither, reminding me of a swarm of rats in a ruinous cheese-store," one contemporary noted. "Some came, others went; some were scribbling, others were talking; some were drinking, some smoking, and some arguing; the whole place stank of tobacco like the cabin of a barge."

The strongest blast against the London coffeehouses came from women, who unlike their Continental counterparts were excluded from this all-male society (unless they were the proprietors). In 1674 *The Womens Petition Against Coffee* complained, "We find of late a very sensible *Decay* of that true *Old English Vigour*. . . . Never did Men wear *greater Breeches*, or carry *less* in them of any *Mettle* whatsoever." This condition was all due to "the Excessive use of that Newfangled, Abominable, Heathenish Liquor called *Coffee*, which . . . has so *Eunucht* our Husbands, and *Crippled* our more kind *gallants*. . . . They come from it with nothing *moist* but their snotty Noses, nothing *stiffe* but their Joints, nor *standing* but their Ears."

The *Women's Petition* revealed that a typical male day involved spending the morning in a tavern "till every one of them is as Drunk as a Drum, and then back again to the Coffee-house to drink themselves sober." Then they were off to the tavern again, only to "stagger back to *Soberize* themselves with Coffee." In response, the men defended their beverage. Far from rendering them impotent, "[coffee] makes the erection more Vigorous, the Ejaculation more full, adds a spiritualescency to the Sperme."

On December 29, 1675, King Charles II issued *A Proclamation for the Suppression of Coffee Houses.* In it he banned coffeehouses as of January 10, 1676, since they had become "the great resort of Idle and disaffected persons" where tradesmen neglected their affairs. The worst offense, however, was that in such houses "divers false malitious and scandalous reports are devised and spread abroad to the Defamation of his Majestie's Government, and to the Disturbance of the Peace and Quiet of the Realm."

An immediate howl went up from every part of London. Within a week, it appeared that the monarchy might once again be overthrown—and all over coffee. On January 8, two days before the proclamation was due to take effect, the king backed down.

Ironically, however, over the course of the eighteenth century the British began to drink tea instead of coffee. Most of the coffeehouses turned into private men's clubs or chop houses by 1730, while the huge new public tea gardens of the era appealed to men, women, and children alike. Unlike coffee, tea was simple to brew and did not require roasting, grinding, and freshness. (It was also easier to adulterate for a tidy additional profit.) In addition, the British conquest of India had begun, and there they concentrated more on tea than coffee growing. The British "Honourable East India Company" pushed tea through its monopoly, and smugglers made tea cheaper. Also, the British had never learned to make coffee properly, and the milk they added to it was foul. Thus, while the black brew never disappeared entirely, its use in England diminished steadily until recent years.

The Legacy of the Boston Tea Party

As loyal British subjects, the North American colonists emulated the coffee boom of the mother country, with the first American coffeehouse opening in Boston in 1689. In the colonies there was not such a clear distinction between the tavern and the coffeehouse. Ale, beer, coffee, and tea cohabited, for instance, in Boston's Green Dragon, a coffeehouse–tavern from 1697 to 1832. Here, over many cups of coffee and other brews, John Adams, James Otis, and Paul Revere met to foment rebellion, prompting Daniel Webster to call it "the headquarters of the Revolution."

By the late eighteenth century, as we have seen, tea had become the preferred British drink, with the British East India Company supplying the American colonies with tea. King George wanted to raise money from tea as well as other exports, however, and attempted the Stamp Act of 1765, which prompted the famous protest, "No taxation without representation." The British parliament then repealed all the taxes—except the one on tea. Americans refused to pay the tax, instead buying tea smuggled from Holland. When the British East India Company responded by sending large consignments to Boston, New York, Philadelphia, and Charleston, the Boston contingent rebelled in the famous "tea party" of 1773, tossing the leaves overboard.

From that moment on, it became a patriotic American patriotic duty to avoid tea, and the coffeehouses profited as a result. The Continental Congress passed a resolution against tea consumption. "Tea must be universally renounced," wrote John Adams to his wife in 1774, "and I must be weaned, and the sooner the better." Of course, the pragmatic North Americans also appreciated the fact that coffee was cultivated much nearer to them than tea and was consequently cheaper. Increasingly, over the course of the nineteenth century they would rely on coffee grown due south in their own hemisphere.

Coffee Goes Latin

In 1714 the Dutch gave a healthy coffee plant to the French government, and nine years later an obsessed French naval officer, Gabriel Mathieu de Clieu, introduced coffee cultivation to the French colony of Martinique. After considerable court intrigue, he obtained one of the Dutch offspring plants from the Jardin des Plantes in Paris and nursed it during a perilous transatlantic voyage, later referring to "the infinite care that I was obliged to bestowe upon this delicate plant." After avoiding capture by a corsair and surviving a tempest, de Clieu's ship floundered in windless doldrums for over a month. The Frenchman protected his beloved plant from a jealous fellow passenger and shared his limited supply of water with it. Once it finally set down roots in Martinique, the coffee tree flourished. From that single plant, much of the world's current coffee supply probably derives.[3]

Then, in 1727, a mini-drama led to the fateful introduction of coffee into Brazil. To resolve a border dispute, the governors of French and Dutch Guiana asked a neutral Portuguese Brazilian official named Francisco de Melho Palheta to adjudicate. He quickly agreed, hoping that he could somehow smuggle out coffee seeds, since neither governor would allow the seeds' export. The mediator successfully negotiated a compromise border solution *and* clandestinely bedded the French governor's wife. At Palheta's departure, she presented him with a bouquet of flowers—with ripe coffee berries disguised in the interior. He planted them in his home territory of Para, from which coffee gradually spread southward.

Coffee and the Industrial Revolution

Coffee's growing popularity complemented and sustained the Industrial Revolution, which began in Great Britain during the 1700s and spread to other parts of Europe and North America in the early 1800s. The development of the factory system transformed lives, attitudes, and eating habits. Most people previously had worked at home or in rural craft workshops. They had not divided their time so strictly between work and leisure, and they were largely their own masters. People typically ate five times a day, beginning with soup for breakfast.

With the advent of textile and iron mills, workers migrated to the cities, where the working classes lived in appalling conditions. As women and children entered the organized workforce, there was less time to run a household and cook meals. Those still trying to make a

---

[3]The Dutch stock from which de Clieu's tree sprang was known as *typica*. The French were responsible for another important coffee variety. In 1718 in Bourbon on the island of Réunion (in the Indian Ocean) they successfully planted seeds from Mocha, giving rise to the strain known as *bourbon*. Though his tree was seminal, de Clieu was not the first to bring coffee to the Caribbean. The Dutch had introduced coffee into their colony of Dutch Guiana in South America, while the French grew it to the east in French Guiana.

living at home were paid less and less for their work. Thus, European lacemakers in the early nineteenth century lived almost exclusively on coffee and bread. Because coffee was stimulating and warm, it provided an illusion of nutrition.

"Seated uninterruptedly at their looms, in order to earn the few pennies necessary for their bare survival," writes one historian, "[workers had] no time for the lengthy preparation of a midday or evening meal. And weak coffee was drunk as a last stimulant for the weakened stomach which—for a brief time at least—stilled the gnawing pangs of hunger." The drink of the aristocracy had become the necessary drug of the masses, and morning coffee replaced beer soup for breakfast.

Of Sugar, Coffee, and Slaves

By 1750 the coffee tree grew on five continents. For the lower class it provided a pick-me-up and moment of respite, although it replaced more nutritious fare. Otherwise its effects seemed relatively benign, if sometimes controversial. It aided considerably in the sobering of an alcohol-soaked Europe and provided a social and intellectual catalyst as well. As William Ukers wrote in the classic *All About Coffee*, "Wherever it has been introduced it has spelled revolution. It has been the world's most radical drink in that its function has always been to make people think. And when the people began to think, they became dangerous to tyrants."

Maybe. Yet increasingly, as the European powers brought coffee cultivation to their colonies, the intensive labor required to grow, harvest, and process coffee came from imported slaves. Captain de Clieu may have loved his coffee tree, but he did not personally harvest the millions of its progeny. Slaves from Africa did.

Slaves had initially been brought to the Caribbean to harvest sugarcane, and the history of sugar is intimately tied to that of coffee. It was this cheap sweetener that made the bitter boiled brew palatable to many consumers, and that added a quick energy lift to the stimulus of caffeine. Like coffee, sugar was popularized by the Arabs, and its popularity rose along with tea and coffee in the second half of the seventeenth century. Thus, when the French colonists first grew coffee in San Domingo (Haiti) in 1734, it was natural that they would require additional African slaves to work the plantations.

Incredibly, by 1788 San Domingo supplied *half* of the world's coffee. The coffee, therefore, that fueled Voltaire and Diderot was produced by the most inhuman form of coerced labor. In San Domingo the slaves lived in appalling conditions, housed in windowless huts, under-fed, and overworked. "I do not know if coffee and sugar are essential to the happiness of Europe," wrote a French traveler of the late eighteenth century, "but I know well that these two products have accounted for the unhappiness of two great regions of the world: America [the Car-ribean] has been depopulated so as to have land on which to plant them; Africa has been depopulated so as to have the people to cultivate them." Years later a former slave recalled treatment under French mas-ters: "Have they not hung men with heads downward, drowned them in sacks, crucified them on planks, buried them alive, crushed them in mortars? Have they not forced them to eat shit?"

It is little surprise, then, that the slaves revolted in 1791 in a struggle for freedom that lasted twelve years, the only major successful slave revolt in history. Most plantations were burned to the ground and the owners massacred. By 1801, when black Haitian leader Toussaint Louverture attempted to resuscitate coffee exports, harvests had de-clined 45 percent from 1789 levels. Louverture instituted the *fermage* system, which amounted to state slavery. Like medieval serfs, the workers were confined to the state-owned plantations and forced to work long hours for low wages. At least they were no longer routinely tortured, however, and they received some medical care. But when Napoleon sent troops in a vain attempt to regain Haiti from 1801 to 1803, the coffee trees were once again abandoned. Upon learning of his troops' final defeat in late 1803, Napoleon burst out: "Damn cof-fee! Damn colonies!" It would be many years before Haitian coffee once more affected the international market, and it never regained its dominance.

The Dutch jumped into the breach to supply the coffee shortfall with Java beans. Though they did not routinely rape or torture their labor-ers, they did enslave them. While the Javanese pruned trees or har-vested coffee cherries in the sweltering tropical heat, "the white lords of the islands stirred only for a few hours every day," according to coffee historian Heinrich Eduard Jacob.

Little had changed by the early 1800s, when Dutch civil servant Ed-uard Douwes Dekker served in Java. He ultimately quit in protest to write the novel *Max Havelaar*, under the pen name Multatuli. Dekker wrote:

> Strangers came from the West who made themselves lords of his [the native's] land, forcing him to grow coffee for pathetic wages. *Famine?* In rich, fertile, blessed Java–*famine?* Yes, reader. Only a few years ago, whole districts died of starvation. Mothers offered their children for sale to obtain food. Mothers ate their children.

Dekker excoriated the Dutch landowner who "made his field fertile with the sweat of the labourer whom he had called away from his own field of labour. He withheld the wage from the worker, and fed himself on the food of the poor. He grew rich from the poverty of others."

All too often, throughout the history of the coffee industry, these words have rung true. But small farmers and their families, such as Ethiopians tending their small coffee plots in the highlands, also make their living from coffee, and not all coffee workers on estates have been oppressed. The fault lies not with the tree or the way coffee is grown, but with how those who labor to nurture and harvest it are treated.

Napoleon's System: Paving the Way for Modernity

In 1806, three years after going to war against Great Britain, Napoleon declared France self-sufficient and enacted what he called the Continental System, hoping to punish the British by cutting off their European trade. "In former days, if we desired to be rich, we had to own colonies, to establish ourselves in India and the Antilles, in Central America, in San Domingo. These times are over and done with. Today we must become manufacturers." *Tout cela, nous la faisons nous-memes!* he proclaimed: "We shall make everything ourselves." The Continental System spawned many important industrial and agricultural innovations. Napoleon's researchers succeeded, for instance, in extracting sweetener from the European sugar beet to replace the need for cane sugar.

The Europeans could not, however, make coffee for themselves, and settled on chicory as a substitute. This blue-flowered European herb (a form of endive) had a long white root with a bitter juice. When roasted and ground, it produces a substance that *looks* somewhat like coffee.

When brewed in hot water, it produces a bitter-tasting, dark drink that some might take as a coffee substitute, but without the aroma, flavor, body, or caffeine kick of coffee. Thus the French developed a taste for chicory during the Napoleonic era, and even after the Continental System ended in 1814 they continued to mix the herb root with their coffee. The Creole French of New Orleans soon adopted the same taste.[4]

From 1814 to 1817, when Amsterdam once more resumed a central place in coffee trading, the price ranged from 16 cents to 20 cents a pound in U.S. money—quite moderate compared to the $1.08 a pound it had been in 1812. Growing consumer demand throughout Europe and the United States, however, jacked the price back up to 30 cents or more for Java. As a result, coffee farmers planted new trees, and in areas such as Brazil entirely new coffee areas were carved from the rain forests.

A few years later in 1823, just when these new plantations were coming into production, another crisis loomed. War between France and Spain appeared imminent. Coffee importers throughout Europe rushed to buy. They assumed that the sea routes would shortly be closed again. The price of the green bean rose sharply. But there turned out to be no war, at least not immediately. "Instead of a war," wrote the historian Heinrich Jacob, "something else came. Coffee! Coffee from all directions!" Beans arrived from Mexico, Jamaica, the Antilles. For the first time, a major Brazilian harvest loomed. Prices plummeted. There were business failures in London, Paris, Frankfurt, Berlin, and St. Petersburg. Overnight, millionaires lost everything. Hundreds committed suicide.

The modern era had commenced. Henceforth coffee's price would swing wildly due to speculation, politics, weather, and the hazards of war. Coffee had become an international commodity that, during the latter part of the nineteenth century, would completely transform the economy, ecology, and politics of Latin America.

---

[4]Chicory had been used as a coffee adulterant as far back as 1688, but the French habit became ingrained during the Napoleonic era.

~ 2 ~

THE COFFEE
KINGDOMS

You believe perhaps, gentlemen, that the production of coffee and sugar is the natural destiny of the West Indies. Two centuries ago, nature, which does not trouble herself about commerce, had planted neither sugarcane nor coffee trees there.
                                                    −**Karl Marx, 1848**

By the time Marx uttered these words, coffee cultivation in the West Indies already was declining. However, over the next half century—before 1900—non-native coffee would conquer Brazil, Venezuela, and most of Central America (as well as a good portion of India, Ceylon, Java, and Colombia). In the process, the bean would help shape laws and governments, delay the abolition of slavery, exacerbate social inequities, affect the natural environment, and provide the engine for growth, especially in Brazil, which became the dominant force in the coffee world during this period. "Brazil did not simply respond to world demand," observes the coffee historian Steven Topik, "but helped create it by producing enough coffee cheaply enough to make it affordable for members of North America's and Europe's working classes."

Yet coffee did not make much of an impression in Brazil or Central America until the colonies broke away from Spanish and Portuguese rule, in 1821 and 1822. In November 1807, when Napoleon's forces captured Lisbon, they literally drove the Portuguese royal family into the sea. On British ships the royal family found its way to Rio de Janeiro, where King John VI took up residence. He declared Brazil to be a kingdom and promoted agriculture with new varieties of coffee, grown experimentally at the Royal Botanical Gardens in Rio and distributed as seedlings to planters. When a revolution in Portugal forced John VI to return to Europe in 1820, he left behind his son, Dom Pedro, as regent.

Most Latin American countries, sick of the colonial yoke, soon broke away, led by Venezuela, Colombia, and Mexico, followed by Central America, and finally, in 1822, by Dom Pedro in Brazil, who had himself crowned Emperor Pedro I. In 1831, under pressure from populists, Pedro I abdicated in favor of his son Pedro, who was only five. Nine years later, after a period of rebellion, chaos, and control by regents, Pedro II took over by popular demand at the age of fourteen. Under his long rule, coffee would become king in Brazil.

Brazil's Fazendas

Brazil has become so closely identified with coffee that many people believe the plant originated there. What happened in Brazil exemplifies the benefits and hazards of relying heavily on one product. Coffee made modern Brazil, but at an enormous human and environmental cost.

At over three million square miles, Brazil is the world's fifth-largest country. Beginning just south of the equator, it occupies almost half of South America, knocking against 4,600 miles of the Atlantic on the east and the upthrusting Andes to the west, stretching north to the Guiana Highland and the Plata Basin in the south. The Portuguese, who discovered, exploited, and subjugated Brazil, were initially enchanted with the country. In 1560 a Jesuit priest wrote, "If there is paradise here on earth, I would say it is in Brazil."

Unfortunately, the Portuguese proceeded to destroy much of that paradise. The sugar plantations of the seventeenth and eighteenth centuries had established the pattern of huge *fazendas* (plantations) owned by the elite, where slaves worked in unimaginably awful conditions. It was cheaper to import new slaves than to maintain the health of existing laborers, and as a result, slaves died after an average of seven years. Growing cane eventually turned much of the northeast into an arid savanna.

As sugar prices weakened in the 1820s, capital and labor migrated to the southeast in response to the coffee expansion in the region's Paraiba Valley. While Francisco de Melo Palheta had brought seeds to

Para in the northern tropics, coffee grew much better in the more moderate weather of the mountains near Rio de Janeiro, where it had been introduced by a Belgian monk in 1774. The virgin soil, the famed *terra roxa* (red clay), had not been farmed due to a gold and diamond mining boom in the eighteenth century. Now that the precious minerals were depleted, the mules that once had carted gold could transport beans down already-developed tracks to the sea, while the surviving mining slaves could switch to coffee harvesting. As coffee cultivation grew, so did slave imports to Rio, rising from 26,254 in 1825 to 43,555 in 1828. By this time well over a million slaves labored in Brazil, comprising nearly a third of the country's population.

In order to placate the British, who by then had outlawed the slave trade, the Brazilians made the importation of slaves illegal in 1831 but failed to enforce the law. Slavery's days were clearly numbered, however, and so the slavers, attempting to take advantage of the time left to them, increased the number of slaves imported annually from twenty thousand in 1845 to fifty thousand the following year and to sixty thousand by 1848.

When British warships began to capture slave boats, the Brazilian legislature was forced to pass the Queiroz Law of 1850, truly banning importation of slaves. Still, some two million already in the country remained in bondage. A system of huge plantations, known as *latifundia*, promoted a way of life reminiscent of the slave plantations of the Old South in the United States, and coffee growers became some of the wealthiest men in Brazil.

In 1857 the American clergyman J. C. Fletcher wrote of his visit to the 64-square-mile coffee *fazenda* of Commendador Silva Pinto in Minas Gerais. "He lives in true baronial style," Fletcher commented appreciatively. In the huge dining room three servants came, bearing "a massive silver bowl a foot and a half in diameter." Later he listened to fifteen slave musicians playing an overture to an opera, after which the black choir sang a Latin mass.

A few years later a traveler in the Paraiba Valley described a typical slave schedule. Though not the same plantation visited by Fletcher, the conditions under which the slaves labored were probably similar:

> The negroes are kept under a rigid surveillance, and the work is regulated as by machinery. At four o'clock in the morning all hands are

called out to sing prayers, after which they file off to their work. . . . At seven [P.M.] files move wearily back to the house. . . . After that all are dispersed to household and mill-work until nine o'clock; then the men and women are locked up in separate quarters, and left to sleep seven hours, to prepare for the seventeen hours of almost uninterrupted labor on the succeeding day.

Although some plantation owners treated their slaves decently, others forced them into private sadistic orgies. Beatings and murders were not subject to public scrutiny, and slaves were buried on plantations without death certificates. Slave children were frequently sold away from their parents. Constantly on guard against slave retaliation—a scorpion in the boot or ground glass in the cornmeal—owners always went armed. "On this plantation," one owner proclaimed, "I am the pope." Slaves were regarded as subhuman, "forming a link in the chain of animated beings between ourselves and the various species of brute animals," as one slaveholder explained to his son.

 Brazil maintained slavery longer than any other country in the Western hemisphere. In 1871 Pedro II, who had freed his own slaves more than thirty years earlier, declared the "law of the free womb," specifying that all newborn offspring of slaves from then on would be free. He thus guaranteed a gradual extinction of slavery. Even so, growers and politicians fought against abolition. "Brazil is coffee," one Brazilian member of parliament declared in 1880, "and coffee is the negro."

War Against the Land

In his book *With Broadax and Firebrand: The Destruction of the Brazilian Atlantic Forest* the ecological historian Warren Dean documents the devastating effect that coffee had on Brazil's environment. During the winter months of May, June, and July, gangs of workers would begin at the base of a hill, chopping through the tree trunks just enough to leave them standing. "Then it was the foreman's task to decide which was the master tree, the giant that would be cut all the way through, bringing down all the others with it," Dean writes. "If he succeeded, the entire hillside collapsed with a tremendous explosion, raising a cloud of debris, swarms of parrots, toucans, [and] songbirds." After drying for a few weeks, the felled giants were set afire. As a result, a permanent yellow pall hung in the air at the end of the dry season, obscuring the sun.

"The terrain," Dean observes, "resembled some modern battlefield, blackened, smoldering, and desolate."

At the end of this conflagration, a temporary fertilizer of ash on top of the virgin soil gave a jump-start for year-old coffee seedlings, grown in shaded nurseries from hand-pulped seeds before being transplanted. The coffee, grown in full sun rather than shade, sucked nutrition out of the depleting humus layer relatively quickly. Cultivation practices–rows planted up and down hills that encouraged erosion, with little fertilizer input–guaranteed wildly fluctuating harvests. Coffee trees always take a rest the year after a heavy bearing season, but Brazilian conditions exacerbated the phenomenon. When the land was "tired," as the Brazilian farmer put it, it was simply abandoned and new swaths of forest were then cleared. Unlike the northern arboreal forests, these tropical rain forests, once destroyed, would take centuries to regenerate.

How to Grow and Harvest Brazilian Coffee

The Brazilians quickly learned the rudiments of coffee growing and harvesting, much of it universal to the plant wherever it grows. Their agricultural methods required the least possible effort and emphasized quantity over quality. The general way Brazilians grow coffee remains largely unchanged over a hundred years later.[1]

Coffee thrives best in disintegrated volcanic rock mixed with decayed vegetation, which describes the red clay, the *terra roxa*, of Brazil. Once planted, it takes three or four years for a tree to bear a decent crop. In Brazil each tree produces delicate white flowers three and sometimes four times a year (in other areas of the world there can be only one or two flowerings). It is common in many parts of the world to see blossoms, green berries, and ripe cherries all on the same tree. The white explosion, which takes place just after a heavy rain, is breathtaking, aromatic, and brief. Most coffee trees are self-pollinating, allowing the monoculture to thrive without other nearby plants to attract honeybees.

The moment of flowering, followed by the first growth of the tiny berry, is crucial for coffee growers. A heavy wind or hail can destroy an

---

[1]Most Brazilian coffee is still stripped rather than selectively harvested, then "dry" processed. Some things have changed, however: mechanical harvesting is now possible on flat Brazilian farms, different types of trees now grow there, and many huge *fazendas* have given way to smaller lots.

entire crop. Arabica coffee (the only type known until the end of the
nineteenth century) grows best between 3,000 and 6,000 feet in areas
with a mean annual temperature around 70°F., never straying below
freezing, never going much above 80°. The high-grown coffee bean, developing slowly, is generally more dense and flavorful than lower
growths.

Unfortunately for Brazil's coffee, 95 percent of the country rests below 3,000 feet, so that Brazilian beans have always tended to lack acidity and body. Worse, Brazil suffers from periodic frosts and droughts,
which have increased in intensity and frequency as the protective forest
cover has been destroyed. Coffee cannot stand a hard frost, and it
needs plenty of rain (70 inches a year) as well. The Brazilian harvest begins soon after the end of the rains, usually in May, and continues for
six months. Because Brazilian coffee is cultivated without shade, it
grows even more quickly, depleting the soil unless artificially fertilized.

Coffee trees usually are pruned on a regular basis. Still, most trees in
the early Brazilian *fazendas* required ladders for the harvest. Trees will
produce well for fifteen years or so, though some have been known to
bear productively for as long as twenty or even thirty years. When trees
no longer bear well, they can be "stumped" near the ground, then
pruned so that only the strongest shoots survive. On average–depending on the tree variety and growing conditions–one tree will yield five
pounds of fruit, translating eventually to one pound of dried beans.

Coffee is ripe when the green berry turns a rich wine red (or in odd
varieties, yellow). It looks a bit like a cranberry or cherry , though it is
more oval shaped. Growers test a coffee cherry by squeezing it between thumb and forefinger. If the seed squirts out easily, it is ripe.
What is left in the hand–the red skin, along with a bit of flesh–is called
the *pulp.* What squishes out is a gummy *mucilage* sticking to the *parchment.* Inside are the two seeds, covered by the diaphanous *silver skin.*

The traditional method of removing the bean from nature's multiple
wrappings, known as the *dry method,* is still the favored method of processing most Brazilian coffee. Both the ripe and unripe cherries, along
with buds and leaves, are stripped from the branches onto big tarps
spread under the trees. Then they are spread to dry on huge patios.
They must be turned several times a day, gathered up and covered
against the dew at night, then spread to dry again. If the berries are not
spread thinly enough, they may ferment inside the skin, developing unpleasant or "off" tastes. When the skins are shriveled, hard, and nearly

black, the husks are removed by pounding on them. In the early days the coffee was often left in its parchment covering for export, though by the late nineteenth century, machines took off the husks and parchment, sized the beans, and even polished them.

The dry method often yielded poor results, particularly in the Rio area. Since ripe and unripe cherries were stripped together, the coffee's taste was compromised from the outset. The beans might also lie on the ground for so long that they would develop mold or absorb other unpleasant earthy tastes that came to be known as a *Rioy* flavor (strong, iodinelike, malodorous, rank).[2] Some Rio coffee, however, was handpicked, carefully segregated, and gently depulped. Called *Golden Rio*, it was much in demand.

From Slaves to Colonos

By the late nineteenth century the Rio coffee lands were dying. The Rio region was "quickly ruined by a plant whose destructive form of cultivation left forests razed, natural reserves exhausted, and general decadence in its wake," wrote Eduardo Galeano in *Open Veins of Latin America.* "Previously virgin lands were pitilessly eroded as the plundermarch of coffee advanced." As a result, the main coffee-planting region moved south and west to the plateaus of São Paulo, which would become the productive engine for Brazilian coffee and industry.

With prices continually rising throughout the 1860s and 1870s, coffee monoculture seemed a sure way to riches.[3] The new coffee men, the Paulistas of São Paulo, considered themselves progressive, modern businessmen compared to the old-fashioned baronial lords of Rio coffee. In 1867 the first Santos railway to a coffee-growing region was completed. In the 1870s the Paulistas pushed for more technological change and innovation—primarily to advance the sale of coffee. In 1874 Pedro II dictated the first message to Europe on a new submarine cable, facilitating communication with a major market. By the following year 29 percent of the boats entering Brazilian harbors were powered by steam rather than sail.

---

[2] Some consumers got used to the Rioy flavor, however, and came to prize it.

[3] Coffee was a "monoculture" as an export crop. In fact, *colonos* frequently grew subsistence crops between the coffee trees.

Railroads quickly replaced the mule as the preferred method of transporting beans from the interior to the sea. In 1874 there were only 800 miles of track; by 1889 there were 6,000 miles. The lines typically ran directly from coffee-growing regions to the ports of Santos or Rio. They did not serve to bind regions of the country together; rather, they deepened dependency on foreign trade.

After 1850, with the banning of slave importation, coffee growers experimented with alternative labor schemes. At first the planters paid for the transportation of European immigrants, giving them a house and assigning a specific number of coffee trees to tend, harvest, and process, along with a piece of land so that they could grow their own food. The catch was that the sharecroppers had to pay off the debt they incurred for the transportation costs, along with other advances. Since it was illegal for the immigrants to move off the plantation until all debts were repaid—which typically took years—this amounted to debt peonage, another form of slavery. Thus it was no surprise when Swiss and German workers revolted in 1856.

The Paulista farmers finally gained enough political clout in 1884 to persuade the Brazilian government to pay for immigrants' transportation costs, so that the new laborers did not arrive with a preexisting debt burden. These *colonos*, mostly poor Italians, flooded São Paulo plantations. Between 1884 and 1914 more than a million immigrants arrived to work on the coffee farms. Some eventually managed to secure their own land.[4] Others earned just enough to return to their homelands, embittered and discouraged. Because of the poor working and living conditions, most plantations maintained a band of *capangas*, armed guards who carried out the planter's will. One much-hated owner, Francisco Augusto Almeida Prado, was hacked to pieces by his *colonos* when he strolled through his fields unprotected.

The Brazilian Coffee Legacy

The Brazilian coffee farmers did not think of themselves as oppressors, however; on the contrary, they considered themselves enlightened and progressive, wishing to enter the modern world and to industrialize

---

[4]Indeed, Francisco Schmidt, a German immigrant in the 1880s, eventually came to own twenty huge *fazendas* with sixteen million coffee trees, a private railway and phone system, and thousands of *colonos*.

with the profits from coffee. After concluding that the *colono* system produced coffee much more cheaply than slavery, the Brazilian coffee farmers led the charge for abolition, which occurred when the aging Dom Pedro II was out of the country. His daughter, Princess-Regent Isabel, signed the "Golden Law" on May 13, 1888, liberating the remaining three-quarters of a million slaves. A year later the planters helped oust Pedro in favor of a republic that for years would be run by the coffee planters of São Paulo and the neighboring province of Minas Gerais.

Unfortunately, the liberation of the slaves did nothing to improve the lot of black workers. "Everything in this world changes," a popular verse went, "Only the life of the Negro remains the same: / He works to die of hunger, / The 13th of May fooled him!" The planters favored European immigrants because they considered them genetically superior to those of African descent, who increasingly found themselves even more marginalized.

In the coming years under the *colono* system, coffee production would explode, from 5.5 million bags in 1890 to 16.3 million in 1901. Coffee planting doubled in the decade following abolition, and by the turn of the century over 500 million coffee trees grew in the state of São Paulo. Brazil flooded the world with coffee. This overreliance on one crop had a direct effect on the well-being of most Brazilians. A contemporary writer observed that "many articles of ordinary food required for the consumption of the [Brazilian] people, and which could easily be grown on the spot, continue to be largely imported, notably flour.... Brazil is suffering severely for having overdone Coffee cultivation and neglected the raising of food products needed by her people."

Guatemala and Neighbors: Forced Labor, Bloody Coffee

At the same time that Brazil led the coffee boom, Central America came to rely on the same imported plant, with similar results. Except for Costa Rica, where coffee paired with a more egalitarian ethos, the new crop spelled disaster for the indigenous people while it enriched the rising coffee oligarchy. The history of Guatemala exemplifies that of the entire region.

In contrast with land-rich Brazil, Guatemala is slightly smaller than Tennessee, tucked between Mexico and Belize to the north and Honduras and El Salvador to the south. Known as "the Land of the Eternal

Spring," Guatemala is one of the most exquisite places on earth, as one visitor wrote in 1841:

> The situation was ravishingly beautiful, at the base and under the shade of the Volcano de Agua, and the view was bounded on all sides by mountains of perpetual green; the morning air was soft and balmy, but pure and refreshing.... I never saw a more beautiful spot on which man could desire to pass his allotted time on earth.

Beautiful, but troubled. Below all of Central America, tectonic plates grind against one another, occasionally spewing lava into the air through one of the innumerable volcanoes in the region, or shaking the earth to remind humans that the world—at least this part of the world—is not a stable place. A great deal of the man-made problems, however, stemmed from the way the region's coffee economy developed in the late nineteenth century.

After declaring independence from Spain in 1821, the Central American states united in an uneasy alliance until 1838, when a revolt led by Rafael Carrera in Guatemala led to its demise and the countries of Central America permanently split.

Carrera, part Indian himself, was the charismatic peasant leader of the indigenous Mayan Indians, who had been harshly treated by the "Liberal" Mariano Gálvez government.[5] In Central America the Conservatives generally supported the Catholic church and the old-guard Spanish descendants, while protecting Indians in a paternalistic manner. Liberals, on the other hand, favored the rising middle class, challenged the church's power, and sought to "civilize" the Indians.

Under Gálvez, lands that had been held in common by indigenous villages increasingly were confiscated, forcing Indians to become sharecroppers or debt peons. Many Indian children were taken from their parents and assigned to "Protectors," who often treated them as indentured servants. As a result of these policies, the Mayans retreated higher into the mountains and the *altiplano*—the high plateau—where the land is not so desirable.

---

[5] The Mayan Indians were not—and are not—a homogeneous group. There are some twenty-eight peoples, including the Quiche, Cakchiquel, Kekchi, Ixil, and Mam. While scattered throughout Guatemala, most reside in the western highlands.

Carrera, who aligned himself with the Conservatives, effectively ruled from 1839 until his death in 1865. Although a dictator who amassed a personal fortune, he was extremely popular with the indigenous peoples. He respected native cultures, protected Indians as well as he could, and tried to incorporate them into his government.

In the 1840s Guatemala's export economy was based on cochineal—a dye produced by a small insect that fed on a cactus. The dried insects yielded a brilliant red that was much in demand in Europe. Carrera encouraged agricultural diversification, however, away from the monoculture of cochineal. He was more concerned about the internal self-sufficiency of Guatemala than with an excessive reliance on foreign markets. When Europeans invented synthetic analine dyes in 1856, and it became clear that cochineal's days were numbered, Carrera approved of the growth of coffee instead. Three years earlier, coffee beans had appeared among the country's official exports for the first time. But the president also encouraged cotton and sugar.[6]

By the time of Carrera's death and for the few years following, during the rule of Vicente Cerna (1865–1871), the profits from coffee continued to grow. The sides of Guatemala's volcanoes—particularly on the Pacific side—proved to be perfectly suited for growing the coffee. There was just one hitch. In many cases the steeply sloped hillsides where coffee grew best, previously considered worthless, were occupied by Indians. The *ladino*[7] coffee growers needed a government that would allow them to take this land and guarantee them a cheap, reliable supply of labor.

In 1871 the Liberals overthrew Cerna, and two years later General Justo Rufino Barrios, a prosperous coffee grower from western Guatemala, assumed power. Under Barrios, a series of "liberal reforms" were instituted, making it easier to grow and export coffee. The amount of coffee exported from Guatemala grew steadily, from 149,000 quintales (1 quintal = 100 kilograms) in 1873 to 691,000 by

---

[6]Coffee as an export crop developed relatively late in Central America because square-rigged ships, then in use, could only travel downwind easily. The trade winds from the Atlantic blew ships westward toward the coast of Central America, but there was no easy way to sail back east. The advent of clipper ships, which could sail closer to the wind, and then steamships, made coffee exports more feasible.

[7]A *ladino* in Guatemala generally refers to someone with mixed European and Indian blood, or a *mestizo*. Pure-blooded Indians could also become *ladinos*, however, if they adopted Western dress and lifestyles.

1895, and over a million in 1909. Unfortunately, these "reforms" came at the expense of the Indians and their land.

Throughout Central America and Mexico at this time the Liberals took power, all with essentially the same agenda: to promote "progress" in emulation of the United States and Europe, always at the expense of the indigenous populations. In *Nostromo*, his 1904 novel about Latin America, Joseph Conrad exclaimed, "Liberals! The words one knows so well have a nightmarish meaning in this country. Liberty, democracy, patriotism, government—all of them have a flavour of folly and murder."

Guatemala—A Penal Colony?

The Mayans had little sense of private property, preferring instead to share their agricultural space with one another, but they resented being displaced from their traditional lands. Through a series of laws and outright force, the Barrios government began to take prime coffee lands away from the Indians. Often they tried to placate the Mayans by giving them other marginal land.

The Liberal government encouraged agricultural development by defining all lands not planted in coffee, sugar, cacao, or pasture as "idle" (*tierras baldías*), then claiming them as national property. In 1873 nearly 200,000 acres in the western piedmont regions of Guatemala were divided into lots up to 550 acres and sold cheaply. Any required payment automatically excluded peasants from ownership.

Like the Brazilians, the Guatemalans tried to attract immigrant labor, but these attempts largely failed.[8] They had to rely on the Indian, who had little incentive to work. As much as Liberals may have wished to apply the "North American solution"—that is, simply eliminating the "inferior" race—they could not afford to do so. They needed their indigenous population as virtual slave labor. Living in self-sufficient villages, however, most Mayans were loath to work other than briefly for a little money.

---

[8]From 1890 to 1892, twelve hundred laborers from the Gilbert Islands of the Pacific were brought by *blackbirders*, or slavers, to work on the coffee plantations of Guatemala. Less than eight hundred survived the trip, and a third of these died in the first year. The last of the survivors were finally returned to the Gilbert Islands in 1908.

The Liberal government solved the problem through forced labor (*mandamiento*) and debt peonage. For an Indian the only alternative to being dragged off to work on a farm (or to the army or gang labor on a road) or to go into debt to a coffee farmer was flight.

Many Indians in fact did flee. Some sneaked across the border to Mexico. Others took to the mountains. To maintain order the Liberals instituted a large standing army and militia. As Jeffrey Paige observed in his book *Coffee and Power*, "Guatemala had so many soldiers that it resembled a penal colony because it *was* a penal colony based on forced labor." Thus, coffee money funded a repressive regime that fostered smoldering resentment among the Indians. Sometimes they rebelled actively, but such attempts only resulted in Indian massacres. Instead they learned to subvert the system by working as little as possible, by taking wage advances from several farmers simultaneously, and by running away.

The Indians sometimes petitioned the *jefe políticos* (governors) for help. Their plaintive appeals are heartrending, even at the remove of a hundred years. One laborer alleged that "Don Manuel, the brother of my actual employer, beat me without motive . . . as well as my wife and our baby, with the result that they both died." A man over eighty wrote that through "all the flower of my youth the patron exploited my labor," but now, sick and crippled, he was to be released to "die slowly in the fields as do the animals when they become old and useless."

The forced Indian migration down from the *altiplano* to the coffee harvest also resulted in Mayans contracting diseases such as influenza and cholera, then bringing them back to their home communities, where deadly epidemics swept entire villages.

From the grower's perspective, securing a reliable labor supply was difficult. Indians ran off. Other planters stole their workers. Competition was so fierce that some growers bid on someone described as "a bum, who once was imprisoned for a wounding, always has been lazy and is full of tricks." Another farmer wrote hopelessly to the *contratista* to whom he had given money to secure workers: "You have forgotten your promises and obligations. . . . The coffee is falling off the trees, workers are required, and all I have is your telegram."

Thus, the coffee economy of Guatemala, as well as that of nearby El Salvador, Mexico, and Nicaragua, frustrated everyone in one way or another. Above all, however, it relied on the forced labor and misery of the indigenous population. With this unhappy foundation a future of inequity and violence was all but assured.

The German Invasion

Into this mix came a new kind of immigrant, full of energy, self-assurance, and a willingness to work hard. Mostly they were young Germans seeking their fortune in this exotic clime. In order to attract such entrepreneurial outsiders, in 1877 the Liberals passed a law to help foreigners obtain lands, granting a ten-year tax exemption and a six-year holiday from import duties on tools and machines. The Barrios government signed contracts with foreign firms for major construction and colonization projects. During the last two decades of the 1800s enterprising Germans, many fleeing Bismarck's militarism, flocked to Guatemala–and to the rest of Central America. By the late 1890s they owned over forty Guatemalan coffee *fincas* and worked on many others. Soon German coffee growers in the Alta Verapaz region of Guatemala got together to solicit private capital from Germany to build a railroad line to the sea. This was the beginning of a trend in which the Germans brought capital and modernization to the Guatemalan coffee industry.

By 1890, two decades after the Liberals took over, the largest Guatemalan *fincas*–over one hundred of them–represented only 3.5 percent of the country's coffee farms but accounted for over half of the total output. While foreigners ran many large plantations, others were still owned by the Spanish descendants of the original conquistadors. In 1890, for instance, the largest coffee grower in Guatemala was General Manuel Lisandro Barillas, the president of the country and owner of five coffee *fincas*, along with a 70,000-acre plot in the highlands where his Indian laborers lived.

These large-scale operations typically had their own processing machinery and were diversified enough to grow their own food. Small, marginal coffee farms of only a few acres, usually owned by poor, illiterate peasants, had to rely on the larger farms for processing. They and their children were sometimes subjected to forced labor on the bigger farms. In some cases the dominant farms deliberately sabotaged their smaller neighbors, as *finca* agents burned their *milpas* (small subsistence plots, usually of corn) and destroyed their coffee bushes.

Securing credit was always a major problem for the coffee farmer, whether large or small. Typically, European or North American banks would loan to coffee import houses at 6 percent. The import houses in turn would loan to export houses at 8 percent, who then loaned to large growers or *beneficios* (coffee processing plants) at 12 percent. The small farmer would have to pay the *beneficio* 14 to 25 percent, depending on the perceived risk. Most entrepreneurs starting a plantation found themselves deep in debt before their first crop matured four years later. The Germans had an advantage, since they frequently arrived with capital and maintained ongoing relations with German brokerage firms that gave them lower interest rates. They also had recourse to diplomatic intervention and maintained close ties to foreign-controlled export and import houses. Nonetheless, the coffee industry of Latin America has never resolved the credit problem satisfactorily.

Many of the Germans who came to make their coffee fortunes in Guatemala were not wealthy men when they first reached the country. Bernhard Hannstein, born in Prussia in 1869, left Germany "to get away from the military habits of Germany, to flee the tyranny of [my] eccentric father and to be a free man." In 1892 Hannstein found work at La Libertad, one of the huge coffee plantations owned by ex-president Lisandro Barillas, where he received $100 a month plus free room and board—many times more than the Indians.

It apparently did not trouble the German—used to harsh Prussian work conditions—that Indians were virtual slaves. "Indians," he wrote in a letter, "are small, dumpy figures who occupy the lowest rung on the plantation, the so-called *mozo*, or worker, and eke out an existence on one mark a day." He described the debt peonage system without any judgmental emotion. "The only way to make an Indian work is to advance him money, then he can be forced to work. Very often they run off but they are caught and punished very severely." The very next sentence Hannstein commented, without apparent irony, "The owners of the land have a very different viewpoint; if they don't earn 120 percent on something they don't consider it worth the trouble to plant it or build it."

A few years later Bernhard Hannstein fathered a child by a Mexican woman with whom he lived and was appalled by the child's dark color and resemblance to him. Quickly he bought a piece of land for the woman, installed her there, and went back to Germany to find Ida Hoepfner, a proper wife. He eventually worked his way up the hierarchy and came to own Mundo Nuevo and other plantations.

Meanwhile, to the north in Alta Verapaz, young Erwin Paul Dieseldorff, another German, slowly assembled the largest privately owned coffee plantations in the area. At first he lived among the Indians, ate their food, and learned their language and culture. Eventually Dieseldorff became an expert on Mayan archeology, folklore, and herbal medicine. As long as the Indian laborers obeyed him, Dieseldorff treated them with paternal kindness. Yet he too paid the Indians a pittance and kept them bound to him in a feudal system of debt peonage. He summed up his and other Germans' philosophy when he observed, "The Indians of the Alta Verapaz are best handled as if they were children."

How to Grow and Harvest Coffee in Guatemala

Although it took some trial and error to establish the custom, coffee in Central America has traditionally been grown under shade trees of various types to protect the coffee from sun, promote automatic mulching, and prevent the coffee trees from overproducing and exhausting themselves and the soil. These shade trees usually are pruned yearly to allow the proper amount of sunlight to pass through; the wood then can be used for fuel.

Unlike the Brazilian bean, the coffees of Central America were harvested by the "wet" method—so named because it requires a huge amount of water—invented in the West Indies and popularized in Ceylon and Costa Rica. According to most coffee experts this system yields a superior bean with fewer defects, producing a drink with bright acidity and full, clean flavor. It is also far more labor-intensive, requires more sophisticated machinery and infrastructure, and needs an abundant supply of fresh running water at each *beneficio*, or processing facility. The mountainsides of Guatemala provide plenty of water, and the German farmers brought much technical know-how.

As the coffee industry developed during the late nineteenth century, importers began to refer to two types of coffee: *Brazils* and *milds*. The Brazilian coffee gained a reputation for lower quality—often, but not always, deserved. Most other, more carefully processed arabica coffees were known as milds because they were not as harsh in the cup as the Brazils.

While the Brazilian laborers can simply strip the branches, the Guatemalan harvesters must pick only the ripe berries, which are depulped by machine, then left in water-filled fermentation tanks for up to forty-eight hours. As the mucilage decomposes, it loosens from its sticky binding on the parchment and in the process lends a subtle seasoned flavor to the inner bean. From the fermentation tank the beans bump along a long channel, where the loosened mucilage washes off with the waste water. Still covered in parchment, the beans then are spread out to dry in the sun or are dried artificially in huge rotating cylinders heated by dried parchment from previous batches, along with coal, gas, or wood pruned from shade trees. Women and children hand sort the dried coffee, removing broken, blackened, moldy, or overfermented beans.

Since the actual coffee bean constitutes only 20 percent of the weight of the cherry, this whole process produces an enormous amount of waste product. The mounds of wet pulp are often recycled as smelly fertilizer, if the *beneficio* is located on the farm. Allowed to float downstream, the mucilage causes massive pollution problems.

Women and Children as Laborers

Women (and children in the old days) always did the tedious sorting in Guatemala and elsewhere, primarily because they traditionally have been paid even less than their husbands. While the men performed most of the physically demanding jobs such as clearing, planting, pruning, and digging irrigation ditches, women and children did much of the harvesting as well.

On a good farm, harvest time is a relaxed, joyous occasion. The pay may not be great but it is higher than any other time of the year, and no one forces children to work any set schedule. In the late nineteenth century, however, women and children were often forced to work long hours in the fields along with everyone else. One observer in 1899 described the "ragged, tattered pickers, large and small, father and mother and a brood of partially clothed children" on their way to pick coffee.

> The father and mother salute you with the deference born of generations of training. Later, from the depths of every thicket comes the chant of singing voices, and the chorus is feminine, the woman of poverty, somehow, knowing how to be happier than the man. The little children gather all the low berries which may be reached by their tiny hands. [At dusk,] the sleepy, tired tots stumble along, with all the brightness of life gone out, for that day, from their worn-out little souls. It is no uncommon sight to see a mother carrying a sleeping child, besides all her other load.

Occasionally, however, Guatemalan women forgot how "happy" they were in their poverty, and they somehow overcame the "deference born of generations of training." Men sometimes took wage advances to be worked off by their wives or children, virtually selling their labor. Juana Domingo wrote from jail to the *jefe político* of Huehuetenango in 1909, for instance, because she refused to work after she was "sold by my own father, which is the custom among our race." Women were routinely subjected to sexual exploitation by overseers. Sometimes complaining backfired, as when the *finca* administrator for one woman added the cost of capturing her rapist to her debt.[9]

Coffee in Guatemala thus brought a reliance on a fickle foreign market, the rise of a coercive police state, gross social and economic inequality, and the virtual enslavement of the indigenous peoples. The pattern was set. Large *fincas*, owned by *ladinos*, Germans, and other foreigners who earned huge profits in good years, were worked by migrant labor forces forced down from the adjacent highlands. In years to come this coffee legacy would lead to repeated uprisings, discontent, and bloodshed in one of the most beautiful countries in the world. "The strategies of government in Guatemala," writes one Latin American historian, "can be briefly summarized as: censorship of the press, exile and prison for the opposition, extensive police control, a reduced and servile state bureaucracy, matters of finance and the treasury in the hands of interrelated members of the large coffee-growing families, and benevolent treatment of foreign companies."

Stealing the Land in Mexico, El Salvador, and Nicaragua

The pattern set in Guatemala was echoed in neighboring countries, except that the size of the typical coffee *finca* was smaller. To the north, in Mexico, Porfirio Díaz attracted American capital to his "liberal" regime (1877–1880, 1884–1911), where laborers on the sugar, rubber, henequen (a plant used to make rope), tobacco, and coffee plantations

---

[9]Of course, not all *finca* owners abused their laborers. On many plantations in Brazil, Guatemala, and elsewhere, enlightened owners treated workers as humanely as possible, paid higher than standard wages, and provided some medical care. Even in such cases, however, the Indians remained poor peons, with little hope of upward mobility, while the owners lived in relative affluence.

were little more than slaves. A labor agent, known as an *enganchador* (snarer), would supply unwary laborers through lies, bribes, or outright kidnaping. The mortality rate for the workers on the henequen farms of the Yucatan or the tobacco plantations of the infamous Valle Nacional was horrendous. Conditions were somewhat better on the coffee *fincas* in southern Mexico in the mountains of Chiapas, since migrant labor had to find it sufficiently attractive to return every year.

In El Salvador, the small but densely populated Pacific Coast country to the south of Guatemala, the disenfranchisement of the Indians was even more violent. While in Guatemala the Mayans lived primarily above the coffee regions, in El Salvador the majority lived in areas suitable for coffee growing. Land expropriation began in 1879, and legislation in 1881 and 1882 eliminated the indigenous system of common lands and communities. The Indians revolted throughout the 1880s, setting fire to coffee groves and processing plants. The government responded by creating a mounted police force to patrol coffee sectors and squelch rebellions. A famous group of fourteen families—with surnames such as Menéndez, Regalado, de Sola, and Hill—came to own most of the coffee plantations of El Salvador, and through a well-trained militia they maintained an uneasy peace, punctuated by coups that replaced one authoritarian military regime with another.

In Nicaragua, to the south of El Salvador and Honduras, coffee cultivation began early, but it did not dominate the economy as in Guatemala and El Salvador, and the Indian resistance in Nicaragua was not so easily broken. Coffee cultivation began in the southern uplands in earnest during the 1860s, where the transition from other commercial agriculture took place relatively smoothly. But the prime coffee-growing lands turned out to be in the north central highlands, where Indians owned most of the land, and the familiar process of disenfranchisement took place. In 1881 several thousand Indians attacked government headquarters in Matagalpa, in the heart of prime coffee-growing regions, to demand an end to forced labor. The national army finally put down the revolt, killing over a thousand Indians. Nonetheless, peasant resistance remained strong, even after Liberal General José Santos Zelaya, the son of a coffee planter, took over in 1893. He ruled Nicaragua until 1909, creating an effective military and successfully promoting coffee, despite continued agitation, including the assassination of the largest coffee grower in the country.

Coffee in Costa Rica: A Democratic Influence?

Coffee-rich Latin American countries have been routinely racked by revolution, oppression, and bloodshed. The singular hopeful exception to
this rule, on the whole, has been Costa Rica. In his thought-provoking
1994 book *States and Social Evolution: Coffee and the Rise of National Governments in Central America*, Robert Williams argues that the way coffee land
and labor evolved in the late nineteenth century helped determine the
shape of Central American governments, setting patterns that continue
to this day:

> Along with the expansion of coffee came changes in trading networks, in-
> ternational financial connections, patterns of immigration and investment,
> and international political relations, but coffee also reached back into the
> structures of everyday life of ports, capital cities, inland commercial cen-
> ters, and the countryside, altering the activities of merchants, moneylen-
> ders, landowners, shopkeepers, professionals, bureaucrats, the urban poor,
> and the peasantry. . . . A careful look at this single commodity affords a
> lens through which to view the construction of Central American states.

In Guatemala and El Salvador, as we have seen, coffee cultivation led
to explosive growth, social inequality, huge plantations owned by a
wealthy elite, and mistreatment of the indigenous population. In Costa
Rica, however, reliance on coffee resulted in democracy, egalitarian relations, smaller farms, and slow, steady growth. Why did cultivation of the
same tree lead to such different results? The primary reason appears to
be the lack of a ready labor force. Most of Costa Rica's Indians, never
very numerous, had been killed off by early Spanish settlers or by disease. Consequently, by the time the Costa Ricans began serious cultivation of coffee in the 1830s, they could not establish the huge *latifundia*
that later developed in Brazil and Guatemala. Small family farms were
the norm.[10] As a result, Costa Rica's coffee industry developed gradually,
without the need for repressive government intervention.

---

[10]Costa Rica had no dye industry (indigo or cochineal) because during the colonial period the
Spanish would not allow it. Costa Rica thus had motivation to try coffee before Guatemala, and it
was Costa Rica that pioneered new growing and processing techniques. Where Indians did remain in Costa Rica, however, as in Orosi, they were dispossessed of their land just as in
Guatemala.

In addition, Costa Rican coffee production commenced in the rich highlands of the Central Valley, near San José, and spread outward from there. For years to come, an ever-expanding frontier would allow new coffee entrepreneurs to establish farms in virgin lands. Because of this opportunity, fewer fights developed over land. During harvest season families helped one another, in the same spirit as barn raisings in the United States. The farmers themselves performed the hard physical labor and felt close to the land. Thus, a relatively egalitarian national ethos developed.

The conflict within Costa Rica developed between small growers and owners of the *beneficios*, which processed the coffee. Because the farms were generally so small, they could not afford their own wet processing mills. As we have seen, the coffee cherry must be processed very soon after harvest, or it will ferment. The *beneficio* owners therefore had a great deal of clout and could set artificially low prices, reaping most of the profits. While this inequity did cause tension, the Costa Rican state managed it peacefully, on the whole. This small Central American country has had its share of revolution and bloodshed over the years, but nothing to compare to its neighbors. The reason can probably be traced directly to how the coffee industry developed there.

The British initially dominated foreign trade with Costa Rica, but Germans quickly moved in as well, so that by the early twentieth century they owned many of the *beneficios* and larger coffee farms in the country. Still, unlike Guatemala, Costa Rica offered opportunities for the hard-working native poor to join the coffee social elite. For example, Julio Sanches Lepiz began with a small farm, and through accrued investments in coffee farms he became the largest coffee exporter in the country. Though his success was extraordinary, other relatively poor Costa Rican farmers also built impressive holdings.

Indonesians, Coolies, and Other Coffee Laborers

Java and Sumatra, like many other coffee-growing regions, possess astonishing natural beauty. This scenery, however, directly contrasted with the "contempt and want of consideration with which the natives are treated," as Francis Thurber observed in his 1881 work *Coffee: Plantation to Cup*. Each family of natives had to raise and care for six hundred fifty coffee trees and to harvest and process them for the Dutch government. "The price received by the natives from the government is placed at a figure low enough to leave an enormous margin of profit to the government," Thurber noted. The Dutch thereby "have maintained a most grinding despotism over their miserable subjects, levying forced loans and otherwise despoiling those who . . . have accumulated anything beyond their daily subsistence."

The situation in India was no better. In 1886 Edwin Lester Arnold, an Englishman who owned coffee plantations there, described how to secure laborers in his book *Coffee: Its Cultivation and Profit.* A planter would journey to the country's lowlands and hire *maistries*, or head men, who in turn would bribe coolies (peasant laborers) with advances. The head men then would arrive in the jungle, "each at the head of his gang of coolies, all heavily loaded with earthen 'chatties' or cooking pans, native shawls, supplies of dried fish, curry stuffs, etc.; and 'salaaming' to the European." They would build huts and begin to work off their advances. It was best not to treat them too harshly, Thurber observed, "for in that case they would bolt."

The work day for the coolies described by Thurber began at 5:00 A.M., with men sent with axes and crowbars to cut and move logs for a new road, while women and children were dispatched to weed the coffee. "No sooner are they clear of the settlement, and winding along the narrow jungle paths, than they make all sorts of attempts to escape." Men were paid five annas a day—a pathetic amount—while women received only three. "Even the little children came up, ducked their small shaven heads in comical homage to the great white sahib, and held out very small brown hands for the price those hands were supposed to have earned at the rate of a penny a-day."

At the same time, Arnold observed with satisfaction, "the profits derived from healthy Coffee are so large, that were it not for many enemies which hamper the planter's struggles and stultify his best efforts, his occupation would be one of the most profitable in the world." The author then listed various coffee pests, ranging from elephants, hill buffaloes, cattle, and deer to jackals, monkeys, and the coffee rat. (Fortunately the coolies enjoyed coffee rat fried in coconut oil, considered a delicacy.) Also there were grubs, mealy bugs, scaley bugs, borers, and weevils to contend with.

"All these drags on the planter's prosperity, however, sink into insignificance by the side of a minute and consequently intangible fungus." Arnold was referring to *hemileia vastatrix*, the dreaded coffee leaf rust, that first appeared in Ceylon in 1869 and virtually wiped out the coffee industry of the East Indies within a few years—ironically, just as Latin America was flooding the market with beans.

Vastatrix Attacks

Even the name, *hemileia vastatrix*, sounds monumentally ominous, and it continues as a plague to this day. Called *rust* because of its initial yellow-brown stain on the underside of the coffee leaf, it eventually turns black, producing the spores of pale orange powder that rub off and spread. The blotches gradually enlarge until they cover the entire leaf, which then falls off. Finally, the entire tree is denuded and dies. The first year it appeared, the rust did substantial damage in Ceylon, but then it seemed to go into remission, alternating between good and bad years. Scientists from all over the world advised the beleaguered coffee growers. The planters tried chemicals. They tried stripping the diseased leaves. Nothing worked.

Various theories held that the rust was caused by the shade trees (*dadap*) commonly in use, or that too much dampness encouraged the disease. It does appear in fact that the fungus thrives in moist environments. The real villain, however, is monoculture. Whenever man intervenes and creates an artificial wealth of a particular plant, nature eventually finds a way to take advantage of this abundant food supply. The coffee tree is otherwise rather hardy. Plants containing mind-altering alkaloids such as caffeine and cocaine almost all grow in the tropics. Indeed, one of the reasons the tropical rain forest provides so many unique drugs is that the competition for existence is so fierce, there being no winter to provide a respite from the battle for survival. The plants developed the drugs as protective mechanisms, just as tropical poison dart frogs have chemical self-protection. The caffeine content of coffee probably evolved as a natural pesticide to discourage predators. Nonetheless, with acres and acres of coffee trees growing, it was inevitable that some nasty little bug or fungus would specialize in the bonanza.

"Now it seems but a question of time for Coffee to be as great a failure in Java as it has turned out to be in Ceylon," wrote Edwin Arnold in 1886. "In many estates the trees display nothing else but branches full of berries, which are still fresh-looking and green, but have become partially black and have dropped off." Arnold was correct. That bastion of traditional coffee soon switched primarily to tea.

One effect of the coffee rust epidemic was a frantic search for more resistant coffee species than the prevalent arabica strain. *Coffea liberica*, found native in the African country of Liberia, seemed promising at first, but it too succumbed to the rust, yielded less than *Coffea arabica*, and never gained in popularity, despite producing an acceptable cup. *Coffea canephora*, chewed by Ugandan natives, "discovered" by whites in the Belgian Congo and named *robusta* by an early promoter, turned out to be resistant and prolific, and it grew at lower altitudes in moister, warmer conditions. Unfortunately, this hardy strain of coffee tasted harsh in the cup and contained twice the caffeine of arabica. Nonetheless, it was destined to play an important role in the future.

The American Thirst

Despite the devastating effects of *hemileia vastatrix*, however, the world coffee supply would continue to grow, stimulated in large part by the seemingly bottomless American coffee cup. While the British sipped tea, their rebellious colonies gulped a stronger black brew, destined to fuel the remarkable American entrepreneurial spirit. By the end of the nineteenth century the United States would consume nearly half of the world's coffee.

3

THE AMERICAN DRINK

We have joined in many a march in old Virginia, when the days were long and hot, and the power of the soldiers to endure the fatigue of the march and keep their places in the ranks was greatly enhanced by an opportunity to brew a cup of coffee by the wayside.

–Captain R. K. Beecham,
Gettysburg: The Pivotal Battle of the Civil War

The American thirst for coffee was slow to develop in a young country whose rambunctious citizens preferred booze. "Most colonial drinking was utilitarian, with high alcohol consumption a normal part of personal and community habits," observe the authors of *Drinking in America*. "In colonial homes, beer and cider were the usual beverages at mealtime.... Even children shared the dinner beer." Many colonists considered coffee and tea poor substitutes for strong alcoholic brews. Thus the first Continental Army ration, established by Congress in 1775, contained no coffee, only a daily allowance for spruce beer or cider.

Still, coffee was popular enough to cause over a hundred angry Boston women to raid a food warehouse in 1777. During the Revolutionary War, dealers took advantage of scarce supplies to hoard coffee beans and jack up prices. As Abigail Adams described to her husband, John, "there is a great scarcity of sugar and coffee, articles which the female part of the state is very loath to give up, especially whilst they consider the great scarcity occasioned by the merchants having secreted a large quantity." She then described how the women raided the warehouse, while "a large concourse of men stood amazed, silent spectators."

Throughout the first half of the 1800s the American taste for coffee swelled, particularly after the War of 1812, which temporarily shut off access to tea just when all things French, including coffee drinking, were stylish. By that time Brazilian coffee was closer and cheaper anyway—and perhaps price counted even more than political ideology or fashion statements when Americans came to choose their favorite caffeinated beverage. Per-capita consumption grew to three pounds a year in 1830, five and a half pounds by 1850, and eight pounds by 1859. Although there were urban coffeehouses, most Americans drank coffee at home or brewed it over campfires while headed west. By 1849 coffee had become the "great essential in a prairie bill of fare," according to one surveyor of the time. "Give [the frontiersman] coffee and tobacco, and he will endure any privation, suffer any hardship, but let him be without these two necessaries of the woods, and he becomes irresolute and murmuring."

Once introduced to the black brew, Native Americans adopted it as well. The Sioux called it *kazuta sapa*, or "black medicine." Indeed, the Indians attacked many wagon trains specifically to get coffee—along with sugar, tobacco, and whiskey. On the other hand, white traders took advantage of the Indians, trading one cup of coffee for a buffalo robe.

Home Roasting, Brewing, and Ruination

In the predominantly rural United States of the mid-nineteenth century, people bought green coffee beans (primarily from the West or East Indies) in bulk at the local general store, then roasted and ground them at home. Roasting the beans in a frying pan on the wood stove required twenty minutes of constant stirring and often produced uneven roasts. For the affluent there were a variety of home roasters that turned by crank or steam, but none worked very well. The beans were ground in a manufactured coffee mill or a mortar and pestle.

Housewives usually brewed coffee just by boiling the grounds in water. In order to clarify the drink, or "settle" the grounds to the bottom, brewers employed various questionable additives, including eggs, fish, and eel skins. One popular cookbook contained the following recipe: "To prepared coffee, put two great spoonfuls to each pint of water; mix it with the white, yolk and shell of an egg, pour on hot, but not boiling water, and boil it not over ten minutes." If eggs were not available, creative coffee brewers could use cod. The consequent brew must have possessed a fishy off taste—yet it still gained in popularity from year to year, and coffee "experts" repeated the same advice.[1]

The routine American ruination of coffee must have surprised sophisticated European visitors. During the first half of the nineteenth century there was a veritable explosion of European coffee-making patents and ingenious devices for combining hot water and ground coffee, including a popular two-tier drip pot invented around the time of the French Revolution by Jean Baptiste de Belloy, the Archbishop of Paris.

In 1809 a brilliant, eccentric expatriate American named Benjamin Thompson—who preferred to be known as Count Rumford—modified the de Belloy pot to create his own drip version. Rumford also made a correct brewing pronouncement: Water for coffee should be fresh and near boiling, but coffee and water should never be boiled together, and brewed coffee should never be reheated. Unfortunately for American consumers, however, Rumford's pot and opinions did not travel back across the Atlantic. Nor did the numerous, elegant brewers from France and England—notably those designed in the 1840s by Madame Vassieux and James Napier—that relied on a partial vacuum to draw hot water through ground coffee.

Typical North American coffee of the period was boiled until it was a bitter brew badly in need of milk and sugar to make it palatable.

The Antebellum Coffee Industry

After the coffee crisis and glut of 1823[2] prices tumbled to around 11 cents a pound in 1825 from a high of 21 cents in 1821. For the next thirty years prices remained low (usually below 10 cents), as increasing production continued to overtop burgeoning consumption. Java and Ceylon pumped out more and more coffee, as did Brazil. Costa Rica

---

[1]Nonetheless, at least early American coffee was fresh roasted. "To have it very good, it should be roasted immediately before it is made," wrote Eliza Leslie in an 1837 cookbook, "doing no more than the quantity you want at that time." Another 1845 writer advised, "Do not let it boil," but she was a voice crying in the wilderness.

[2]See the end of chapter 1 for a description of the 1823 coffee crisis.

had begun to export as well. At the same time, coffee harvests from the islands of the West Indies, so important until the late eighteenth century, tailed off due to low prices, political disturbances, and labor scarcity. Many neglected plantations became overgrown, while in the lowlands, sugarcane, now far more lucrative, dominated.

The low prices that were hurting the coffee growers contributed to the growing popularity of the drink among the lower classes, particularly in continental Europe and the United States. In 1833 James Wilde imported the first commercial coffee roaster to New York from England. By the middle of the 1840s, at least in urban areas, a coffee-roasting industry had developed. In Germany, England, and the United States, multiple patents for large-scale roasters were taken out. The most popular roaster in the United States was the Carter Pull-Out, invented by James W. Carter of Boston in 1846, which featured huge perforated cylinders that turned inside brick ovens. Once the coffee was roasted, workers had to haul the gigantic cylinder out horizontally, accompanied by suffocating smoke, and dump the beans into wooden trays, where laborers stirred them with shovels. Sweating in a factory along the row of Carter Pull-Outs resembled labor in the lower range of Dante's Inferno amidst smoke, stress, and burned beans. By 1845 there were sufficient facilities around New York City to roast as much coffee as was then consumed in the entirety of Great Britain.

The Union (and Coffee) Forever

The Civil War (1861–1865) reduced coffee consumption in America, as the Union government levied a 4-cent duty on imported beans and blockaded Southern ports, preventing the rebels from receiving any coffee. Until the war, production had dwindled, discouraged by years of low prices, while consumer demand gradually grew. Now producers, encouraged by huge price hikes caused by the war, redoubled their efforts. In 1861 the price for Brazilian coffee increased to 14 cents a pound. In the ensuing war years it rose to 23 cents, then 32 cents, and finally 42 cents a pound before falling back to 18 cents after the war. Since the U.S. Army was a major purchaser, each Union victory spurred active trading and price hikes. By 1864 the government was buying 40 million pounds of green coffee beans.

The Civil War gave soldiers a permanent taste for the drink. Each Union soldier's daily allotment included one-tenth of a pound of green coffee beans that, translated into annual consumption, was a whopping 36 pounds per capita. "Coffee was one of the most cherished items in the ration," wrote one historian. "If it cannot be said that coffee helped Billy Yank win the war, it at least made his participation in the conflict more tolerable." The book *Hardtack and Coffee*, written in 1887 by former Massachusetts artilleryman John Billings, described the overwhelming importance of the coffee ration:

> Little campfires, rapidly increasing to hundreds in number, would shoot up along the hills and plains and, as if by magic, acres of territory would be luminous with them. Soon they would be surrounded by the soldiers, who made it an almost invariable rule to cook their coffee first, after which a large number, tired out with the toils of the day, would make their supper of hardtack and coffee, and roll up in their blankets for the night. If a march was ordered at midnight, unless a surprise was intended it must be preceded by a pot of coffee.... It was coffee *at* meals and *between* meals; and men going on guard or coming off guard drank it at all hours of the night.

Because coffee was such an important ration constituent, the method of dividing it fairly (after the coffee had been pooled for grinding) developed into quite a ritual. "The lieutenant's rubber blanket lay on the ground," Stephen Crane wrote in one of his Civil War short stories, "and upon it he had poured the company's supply of coffee.... He drew with his sword various crevices in the heap, until brown squares of coffee, astoundingly equal in size, appeared on the blanket." In order to assure fairness, the officer in charge of dividing the coffee then would turn his back while one of the men called out, "Who shall have this pile?" and the officer would read a name from his roster.

Since ground coffee stales quickly, soldiers preferred to carry whole beans and grind them as needed. Each company cook carried a portable grinder. A few Sharps carbines were designed to hold a coffee mill in the buttstock of the gun, so that the soldier could always carry his grinder with him.

The soldiers usually took their hard-boiled coffee black. One of Sherman's veterans later described the coffee as "black as the face of a plantation, strong enough to float an iron wedge, and innocent of lacteal adulteration." Many soldiers boasted of their capacity for the brew. One claimed he drank two or three quarts a day, while another said he sometimes imbibed six quarts. Coffee was more than a pick-me-up; it also proved useful in other ways. Each box of hardtack biscuits carried a label suggesting the soldier boil his coffee, crumble the biscuits into it, and skim off the weevils.

The poverty-stricken, undernourished Confederates meanwhile had to drink coffee substitutes made from acorns, dandelion roots, sugar-cane, parched rice, cotton seed, peanuts, wheat, beans, sweet potatoes, corn, rye, okra, or chicory. Real coffee was so scarce in the war-torn South that it cost $5 a pound in Richmond, Virginia, while one Atlanta jeweler set coffee beans in breast pins in lieu of diamonds. While the typical New Englander had better access to coffee, it cost a fair amount there too, so that many substitutes found a market up North as well. "All manner of mixtures were sold with high-sounding names," one contemporary recalled, "often bearing an endorsement from persons possessed of a national reputation."

The Civil War marked a watershed in American history in several ways—this terrible internecine conflict also catalyzed American indus-trial invention. The carnage made possible by the Gatling gun and the ironclads presaged a new age in which the steamship, the railroad, and the telegraph would transform the American landscape. From the ashes of the conflict the United States would rise to create the most dynamic capitalistic society in the world—inventive, boisterous, cantankerous, self-made, and fueled by a flood of coffee, much of it preroasted, pack-aged, and branded.

Jabez Burns, Inventor

During the Civil War two inventions revolutionized the nascent coffee industry, both developed to take advantage of the war economy. The first, created for peanuts in 1862, was the inexpensive, lightweight, and durable paper bag—an unheralded event at the time. The second, in-vented in 1864 by Jabez Burns, was the self-emptying roaster. Burns, who emigrated to the United States from England in his teens, was the nephew of his namesake, a famed British Baptist preacher. From the evangelist he inherited a revulsion for hard liquor, boundless self-assur-ance and self-righteousness, and a devotion to coffee, the temperance beverage.

The industrious younger Jabez Burns created a string of inventions, including a primitive adding machine, the "Addometer," in 1858. Seeing an opportunity during the war, he quit his job as bookkeeper for a coffee mill to pursue an improved roaster. He now called himself simply Jabez Burns, Inventor. "During the war," he later wrote, "every known method or machine" was tried for roasting. "It was for the writer to invent the principle now most generally in use." Using a clever double-screw arrangement, Burns's invention pushed the beans uniformly up and down a chamber as the cylinder turned. Best of all, when the operator opened the door of the roaster, the beans neatly tumbled out into a cooling tray.

Over the next fifteen years Burns sold hundreds of his roasters as the United States, with amazing rapidity, developed into a consumer society that relied on convenient, mass-produced products. Every town of any size had its own roaster, which introduced a measure of uniformity to coffee roasting that was a sign of things to come. Soon after, a Pittsburgh grocer named John Arbuckle would revolutionize the nascent coffee industry by showing how standardization, branding, and marketing could sell cheap goods.

Arbuckles' Ariosa: The People's Coffee

Just before the Civil War, in 1860, two young brothers, John and Charles Arbuckle, joined Duncan McDonald—their uncle on their mother's side—and another friend named William Roseburg to form the wholesale Pittsburgh grocery business of McDonald & Arbuckle. Though they dealt in most foods, twenty-one-year-old John Arbuckle decided to specialize in coffee, which he correctly perceived as a commodity with a future. Four years later, when Jabez Burns invented his roaster, Arbuckle bought one for his Pittsburgh plant, where he began selling preroasted coffee in one-pound packages. Others in the trade mocked him at first for selling coffee "in little paper bags like peanuts," but Arbuckle's product was an immediate success.[3] He employed fifty girls to pack and label, then later secured the rights to an automated packaging machine that performed the work of five hundred human packers. Arbuckle also applied an egg-and-sugar glaze, purportedly to

---

[3]The New York roaster Lewis Osborn was actually the first to sell packaged coffee. Osborn's Celebrated Prepared Java Coffee came on the market in 1860, but it disappeared three years later, killed by the war economy.

prevent his roasted beans from staling and to help in "clarifying" the coffee.

John Arbuckle proved to be a marketing genius. He knew that in addition to his innovative concept of providing conveniently preroasted coffee, the most important selling point would be a distinctive brand name and label. He tried out various names, including Arbuckles, Fragar, and Compono, before hitting on Ariosa, which became his flagship brand. ("A" probably stood for Arbuckle, "Rio" for coffee coming from Rio de Janeiro, and "Sa" for Santos, another Brazilian port, or South America, or *Sociedade Anonima*, the Brazilian equivalent of "Incorporated.") Much Rio coffee was (and still is) noted for its distinctively moldy off taste, and, while it had its adherents, was one of the least acceptable beans in the trade. Santos had a better reputation.

Arbuckle enjoyed a good scrape with competitors. He started immediately by issuing a handbill with a woodcut illustration of Dilworth Brothers' coffee establishment. Various bugs and filth appeared in the coffee barrels. "No wonder I have been sick," a man observed. "I see what killed my children," a nearby woman cried. A bitter feud ensued, though no legal action resulted.

In 1871, with sales exploding in Pittsburgh, John Arbuckle left his brother Charles to open a factory in New York. Before the Civil War, New Orleans had been the major point of entry for coffee in the United States. A war blockade had closed the port, however, and New York had become the hub of the American coffee trade. By this time the uncle had departed, and they renamed the firm Arbuckle Brothers.

The following year Arbuckle printed a brightly colored handbill showing a disheveled housewife at her wood stove lamenting, "Oh, I have Burnt my Coffee, again." Her well-dressed, seated guest advises her: "Buy Arbuckles' Roasted, as I do, and you will have no trouble." The text continued with the claim that "every grain is evenly roasted," flatly asserting, "You cannot roast Coffee properly yourself."

The names *Arbuckle* and *Ariosa* soon became household words throughout the East Coast and the frontier, while John and Charles Arbuckle became multimillionaires. Already demonstrating a desire to enter all aspects of the business, the Arbuckles had purchased a printer to make their own labels and were also doing job printing for others.

In the 1880s John Arbuckle established branches in Kansas City and Chicago, with over a hundred additional stock depots across the country. He ventured to Brazil to establish green bean exporting offices in

Rio de Janeiro, Santos, and Victoria, the three main Brazilian ports, as well as several branches in Mexico. Arbuckle even owned his own shipping fleet. The Arbuckle plant along the Brooklyn waterfront occupied a dozen city blocks and stabled two hundred draft horses. Arbuckle started his own barrel factory after he got into the sugar business. The barrels were made from Arbuckle-owned timber stands in Virginia and North Carolina. The Brooklyn plant had its own hospital and dining room for employees. In the days before "vertical integration" became a buzzword, Arbuckle had mastered the concept.

Out in the American West, strong, boiled Ariosa became the cowboy's coffee of choice. "Cookie, pour me a cup o' that condensed panther y'u call coffee," a macho cowpoke would say. "This is the way I like it, plum barefooted [black]. None o' that dehorned stuff y'u get in town cafes for me."

The son of a Scottish immigrant, Arbuckle combined a pragmatic gruffness with a more tender side. Stubborn and independent, he also maintained a firm notion of right and wrong. "I say anything that is not right can be changed," he once asserted, adding that "it is my nature to make kindly feelings." Yet Arbuckle did not brook opposition if he felt he was in the right. In years to come he would become embroiled in a titanic, prolonged battle for control of the coffee industry.

In his latter years he spent a great deal of money on philanthropic ventures–enterprises such as his "poor man's yachts," three ships Arbuckle had fitted up to haul impoverished New Yorkers out to sea for a night. At one point he said that his "life had been saved" by a sea voyage. "I realized what a boon the cool, salt air of the ocean is to the sweltering, overworked people of the crowded cities." He converted another boat to the Riverside Home for Crippled Children, and he founded an 800-acre farm at New Paltz, New York, as a fresh-air getaway for city children. Later he funded a home for the aged.

Mr. Chase Meets Mr. Sanborn

Farther north, in Boston, another coffee dynasty took shape after the Civil War. Growing up on Cape Cod, Caleb Chase worked in his father's grocery store until he was twenty-four, then moved to Boston to work for a leading dry goods house. In 1864, the same year Jabez Burns invented his roaster, Chase, then thirty-two, went into business for himself as a coffee roaster with two partners. In 1867 James Sanborn, four

years younger than Chase, moved to Boston from his native Maine.
Having working in a machine shop, then sold garden seeds, he now set
up as a coffee and spice man. In 1878 the two men joined forces under
the name of Chase & Sanborn, specializing in coffee and tea.

They established a reputation for their high-grade Standard Java
brand, shipped in sealed tin cans of their own manufacture. In 1880
Chase & Sanborn expanded to Chicago, and two years later they
opened a Canadian branch in Montreal. By 1882 they were selling over
100,000 pounds of coffee a month from their seven-story factory on
Boston's Broad Street. They hired some twenty-five thousand local selling agents in nearly every city and town in the South, West, and
Canada, giving each exclusive sales privileges in his defined market
area. With such aggressive expansion profits grew quickly, never falling
below a million dollars a year after 1880.

Chase, Sanborn, and their junior partner, Charles Sias, were master
marketers as well as expert coffee men. The first to use sealed cans in a
vain effort to avoid staling from oxygen (the air was sealed in too), they
made much of their Seal Brand Java & Mocha, trademarking it with the
Chase family seal (a lion rampant over four crosses) along with the Latin
inscription, "Ne cede malis," meaning roughly, "Yield not to evil."

They did, however, yield somewhat, as one of their longtime employees revealed years later. Their Java & Mocha brand contained very
little coffee from either origin. When Swift & Company, charged with
misrepresentation for using the term *Pure Leaf Lard*, lost their case, the
Boston coffee roasters dropped the geographical terms and simply
called their coffee Chase & Sanborn Seal Brand. At the same time, the
firm put out a variety of second- and third-tier coffees with appealing if
nondescriptive names: Sanrika, Crusade, Esplanade, Golden Glow,
Good Fellow, Buffalo Brand, Bonita, and Dining Car Special. All of
these were packed in parchment-lined paper bags.

Chase & Sanborn were among the first to use premiums to market
their coffee. They spent $20,000 a year on advertising, much of it in the
form of educational color booklets such as *The History of the American
Flag, North American Birds*, or *The Story of the Pilgrim Fathers*. Other giveaways included blotters, novelty cards, and store displays. At one point
they mounted giant coffeepots on fifty of their horse-and-wagon delivery teams, complete with steam pouring out of the spout.

Realizing the importance of establishing rapport with their customers, the owners sought salesmen who had the "personal touch." If a

customer fell ill, the Chase & Sanborn man would call on him. In hard times, such as the Vermont flood of 1927, all debts owed to the company were canceled entirely. In the cash-strapped South, cotton was sometimes accepted in payment. The firm invariably sent holiday greeting cards to every customer.

One Chase & Sanborn advertisement from 1892 showed a sweet grandmother peering into the bottom of a coffee cup, with her daughter and granddaughter peering over her shoulder. "What vision, dear Mother, in your cup do you see?" asked the caption. "The whole world drinking Chase & Sanborn Coffee and Tea." An accompanying card explained how to tell fortunes from coffee or tea grounds in the bottom of a cup. The same year, Chase & Sanborn issued *Chunks of Gold*, an amplified booklet of endorsements accompanied by the explanation that such customers "buy our Teas and Coffees EXCLU-SIVELY, simply because they are proven THE BEST." They boasted that their buying agents, located at strategic points in the producing countries, bought mostly from private plantations, securing the "choicest selections."

It is likely that this hyperbolic advertising came from Charles Sias, a younger and more flamboyant partner who had joined the firm in 1882. Caleb Chase and James Sanborn exemplified the old-line Yankee aristocracy, with a dignified pragmatism and dry sense of humor. Chase invariably asked an associate how business was going each day, because, he explained, it would help him decide whether to order steak or beans for lunch. Sanborn displayed his diplomacy one day when a woman asked him for his advice on the best way to make coffee. He asked her how she brewed it, then said, "My word, madam, I don't know any better way to make coffee."

Despite such deference to customers' taste, the two senior partners did indeed know their coffee. And they took pains to make sure they bought the best for the price they paid. They always roasted a sample by hand, then ground it fine, weighed it carefully, and compared it in the cup to another coffee with a fine reputation, known to give "complete satisfaction." While the tea buyers had "cup tested" in this fashion for many years, Chase & Sanborn were coffee pioneers in the early 1880s, though they noted that "this process is pursued by comparatively few," indicating that others had also adopted the practice. They added, correctly, that "it takes years of careful application and general adaptability to succeed as a coffee expert."

Jim Folger and Gold Rush Coffee

In the meantime another coffee dynasty, founded by James Folger, had begun in San Francisco, though the path to it wound from the faraway island of Nantucket, where the Folgers were a whaling clan. In *Moby-Dick*, Melville referred to "a long line of Folgers and harpooneers."[4] But by 1842 the sperm whale had been hunted almost to extinction. In 1849, when word of California gold reached Nantucket, fourteen ships of hopeful young men sailed away in search of the glittering metal rather than whale blubber. Among them were three of the Folger boys—Edward, twenty, Henry, sixteen, and James, fourteen—on a ship bound for Panama.

After a harrowing trip they made it to the chaotic boomtown of San Francisco in May 1850. Only two years earlier the town had held eight hundred people. Now forty thousand would-be millionaires tramped through the mudslides that passed for streets. The city's principal businesses were saloons, gambling establishments, and whorehouses, where bags of gold dust bought women's favors. While his brothers ventured into mining country, young Jim joined twenty-seven-year-old William Bovee in the Pioneer Steam Coffee and Spice Mills—named somewhat wishfully, since there was no steam engine to run anything yet. The roaster had to be turned by hand, probably by the fourteen-year-old Folger.

Though undoubtedly stale by the time it was brewed, the coffee proved an instant success among the miners, too frantic searching for gold to waste time stirring their green beans over a campfire. In 1851 Bovee bought a steam engine and moved to larger quarters. Meanwhile Jim Folger's older brothers returned from their not terribly successful mining venture. Henry, the middle brother, booked passage for the East, but Edward set up a whale oil business next door to his brother's coffee roasting establishment.

For a time Jim Folger, by now eighteen, left to open a store to service gold miners at a spot called "Yankee Jim." One miner's 1852 diary from the area noted, "The young man from Nantucket, Jim Folger, is most courageous—at his tender age he has more sense than most of us."

---

[4] Abiah Folger was Benjamin Franklin's mother.

Soon, however, Folger sold out and rejoined Bovee, now as a clerk and traveling salesman. The same miner's 1858 diary entry noted that Folger was "in business for himself down in Frisco and selling coffee to every damned diggings in California."

By the time he was twenty-four Folger was married and a full partner in the firm, along with Ira Marden, who had bought out Bovee. For a time the business flourished, then foundered in the general economic collapse following the Civil War. The firm went bankrupt in 1865, and Jim Folger bought out his partner, determined to revive the business and pay off his debts, which took him nearly a decade. "This payment being unexpected, I hereby gratefully acknowledge the honorable transaction of a noble merchant," one grateful creditor wrote on an 1872 receipt to Folger. It helped when he found a wealthy German partner, Otto Schoemann, who brought $10,000 to the partnership.

Renamed J. A. Folger & Co., the firm thrived during the 1870s. In 1875 the Dun credit agent reported that Folger had paid off half of his debt and intended to pay the rest. "They are doing an excellent business and gaining right along." In 1877 August Schilling, age twenty-seven, who had been clerking with the business, bought Schoemann's share. He was later to branch off with his own coffee enterprise. At decade's end Folger was sending his salesmen as far afield as Montana, Oregon, and Washington.

By the late 1870s there were similar success stories in most major cities of the United States, as well as throughout Europe. Most roasters grew out of wholesale grocery businesses whose owners had the foresight to see that specializing in coffee could make their fortune. The time was ripe for a trade publication to admonish, titillate, lecture, and instruct this growing industry.

Jabez Burns, Editor:
Keeping Coffee and Women in Their Place

In 1878 Jabez Burns commenced publication of *The Spice Mill*–the first trade journal to cover coffee, tea, and spices–though the majority of its pages were devoted to coffee. It was a quirky publication given over entirely to the opinions of its editor. "We call our paper the *Spice Mill*," he wrote in the first issue, "because we intend to deal in a spicy way with the spice of active manufacturing business life." He added that he wanted to deal not only with facts and figures but also to reduce "*habits, tricks*–and *frauds*–to powder."

Jabez Burns loved the art of roasting. "Coffee," he wrote, "you develop, and by skill and judgment change from caterpillar to a butterfly, as it were–you bring out a hidden treasure." He recommended sample roasting small batches of beans before buying them (a recent innovation at the time), rather than judging them solely on their looks. He endorsed a swift, hot roast rather than a slow bake, warning that "the very best coffee in the market may be made insipid trash for the want of sufficient roasting." When coffee is roasted it doubles in size, but it loses anywhere from 15 to 20 percent of its weight as the water is driven off. In order to reduce this weight loss, many roasters resorted to extremely light roasts that produced bitter, undeveloped cups of coffee.

Burns denounced "the abuse of water [and] the plastering on of compounds of every variety in the shape of glaze." When the beans were dumped out to cool, many roasters sprayed the beans to "quench" them quickly–still a common practice. There is nothing wrong with this, so long as the quick spray simply halts the roasting process, the water hissing off as steam. Some roasters (then and now) applied an overabundance of water, however, adding weight and waterlogging the beans. Others put on glazes made with egg, sugar, butter, or other compounds, purportedly to preserve freshness. This may well have been the case, but others abused the practice simply in order to add weight or to hide defective beans from view.

When he strayed from coffee, Jabez Burns revealed a less appealing side, spicing his *Spice Mill* with racist jokes and slurs. He also disapproved of the fight for women's rights. He lamented "our agitating women of the present day," urging businessmen never to employ women because "it pains us to see a woman out of her sphere." Burns emphasized that he was only trying to protect the ladies from "the insult of the rude strange youth, the cunning of unprincipled employers, and the immorality of the vicious men she must meet in nearly every department of manufactory or shop work." Besides, women were taking away men's jobs. Burns may have invented a labor-saving roasting machine, but he clearly thought that females should not be allowed to operate it.

In other words, coffee *men* were all right, but not coffee *women*. Burns's attitude was not unusual. Front Street, the New York bastion of the green coffee importers, was for years an all-male enclave. Women who entered the business had to claw their way through the prejudice of the industry.

On another trade issue, however, Burns disagreed with other coffee men who descried any adulteration of coffee with other substances. Burns preferred his coffee mixed with chicory. "There are a number of prepared coffees, well-understood mixtures of course, that are really superior in flavor and appearance to the bean itself." As long as the public knew that it was not buying pure coffee, and that the price was consequently lower, he saw no problem. "The competitive spirit of the age" would assure quality, since "every grocer is aware that the goods he sells are compared with those of his neighbor."

Unfortunately, this competitive spirit did not always work to the benefit of the public. Some U.S. manufacturers produced fake whole coffee beans made from rye flour, glucose, and water. "Sometimes the retailer is deceived," a contemporary *Scientific American* article noted, "but nine times out of ten he is the one who introduced adulteration. The ground article is very easily produced in the proper color, and an aroma is infused by using strong decoctions of coffee essence." The sale of coffee essence itself was usually a con job, made with black-strap molasses, chicory, and perhaps a dash of genuine coffee extract.

"The adulterations of coffee are so great," groused one 1872 consumer, "that pure coffee is rarely to be had except in private families where the head of the house attends in person to the preparation of the precious cup." Three years later a letter in the *New York Times* complained, "In this City, veritable coffee has become almost extinct." In his classic *Coffee: From Plantation to Cup*, Francis Thurber observed, "The adulteration of coffee and the vast scale on which it is practiced, are well-known facts," which is one reason he suggested each family grind its own beans. Unlike Burns, Thurber despised chicory and repeated with relish the story of a coffee lover who asked at a restaurant, "Have you any chicory?"

"Yes, sir."

"Bring me some." After the waiter brought a small can of chicory the guest asked, "Is that all you have?"

"We have a little more."

"Bring me the rest." The waiter brought another can.

"You have no more?"

"No, sir."

"Very well. Now go and make me a cup of coffee."[5]

Chicory was not the only coffee additive. The list of coffee adulterants indeed is amazing: almonds, arrowhead, asparagus seeds and stalks, baked horse liver, barberries, barley, beechmast, beetroot, box seeds, bracken, bran, bread crusts, brewery waste, brick dust, burnt rags, burrs, carob beans, carrot, chickpeas, chicory, chrysanthemum seeds, coal ashes, cocoa shells, comfrey roots, cranberries, currants, dahlia tubers, dandelion roots, date seeds, dirt, dog biscuits, elderberries, figs, gherkins, gooseberries, haws, hips, holly berries, horse chestnuts, Jerusalem artichokes, juniper berries, kola nuts, lentils, linseed, lupine, malt, mesquite, monkey nuts, mulberries, parsnips, pea hulls, pumpkin seeds, quaker-grass roots, rice, rowan berries, sand, sassafras, sawdust, sloes, sunflower seeds, swedes, turnips, vetch, wheat, whey, wood chips—and more. Even used coffee was employed to adulterate coffee.

At least none of those myriad items would kill anyone, unlike some of the coloring agents applied to beans. "Very dangerous powders or mixtures are used to color the beans," Thurber noted, "the practice being resorted to in order to meet the prejudices of consumers in certain sections for a bright yellow, black, or olive-green colored bean." An 1884 headline in the *New York Times* blared, "POISON IN EVERY CUP OF COFFEE." An investigation revealed that Guatemalan and Venezuelan coffee had been "taken to two mills in Brooklyn, and had there been treated with coloring matter, so as to make them resemble Government Java. This deception has been going on for years." The coloring matter contained arsenic and lead. "A careful analysis led to the conclusion that every cup of coffee made from the colored beans, which are put upon the market as Java, contains one-sixtieth of a grain of arsenious acid, which is a virulent poison." Rio coffee was also polished and colored to produce a handsome green rather than a dull gray. Chemists asserted that "it requires an almost white heat to destroy the arsenic, but even then the lead will still remain."

John Arbuckle, always ready to take advantage of a competitor, printed an Ariosa ad in which the text read: "Help us drive out of the market the poisonous Coffees that are now being so largely sold;

---

[5]Coffee adulteration was also prevalent in Europe. While traveling on the continent in 1878, Mark Twain objected to European coffee that "resembles the real thing as hypocrisy resembles holiness."

3,000,000 pounds of Coffee have been colored during the past year with *Arsenic, Venetian-Blue, Chrome-Yellow* and other ingredients."

The swift rise of Brazilian coffee explains the popularity of the poisonous coloring. Owing to Brazil's climate and soil conditions, its beans produced inferior coffee to the traditional Java and Mocha, and sold at a considerable discount. Consequently many retailers passed off beans from Brazil or other parts of Latin America as coming from Arabia or Indonesia, particularly Old Government Java, which referred to coffee held in *go-downs,* or storehouses, by the Dutch government for seven years or longer. During this process coffee beans age, mellow, and turn a shade of brown. This coffee, like fine old wine, commanded a premium price and was worth imitating.[6]

The Indispensable Beverage

For fifteen years following the Civil War, coffee prices remained high as consumption and production raced to match one another worldwide. As a result, coffee cultivation exploded in Central America, Java, Sumatra, Ceylon, Venezuela, and Brazil.

By the 1870s, according to Robert Hewitt, Jr., coffee had become "an indispensable beverage" to citizens of the Western world—especially to Americans, who consumed six times as much as most Europeans. In his 1872 book *Coffee: Its History, Cultivation, and Uses,* Hewitt added that: "There is scarcely any other item of commerce that has made more rapid progress in the world, or gained for itself more general acceptation with all classes." As a *Harper's* commentator put it in the same year, "The proud son of the highest civilization can no longer live happily without coffee.... The whole social life of many nations is based upon the insignificant bean; it is an essential element in the vast commerce of great nations." The coffee industry had become Big Business, as Thurber observed in 1881:

> After leaving the plantation and before reaching the consumer, it has paid tribute to the transporter, to the shipping bankers of that country; to

---

[6]Few agree about whether aged beans taste better or not. Generally, aging reduces the acidity, or brightness, of a cup of coffee. Aging therefore is usually considered inappropriate for the snappy high-grown coffees of Central America or the blander Brazils, but it enhances the heavy body of a Sumatra or Mysore.

the ships which carry it abroad; the custom-houses of importing countries, to their stevedores, storage warehouses, insurance companies, and
bankers; to the brokers who sample and sell it, the weighers who weigh
it, and the wholesale merchants who buy it. Then comes its cartage or
lighterage, its roasting and sale to retail merchants, and its transportation
to the point where it is finally distributed and consumed. Twelve hundred millions of pounds of coffee annually pass through this routine, and
probably a hundred millions of people, besides the consumers, are directly or indirectly benefited. Factories have been brought into existence
to manufacture the machinery required in the cultivation and preparation of this staple; great mills work throughout the whole year on the
bagging required for the packages; warehouses worth millions have been
provided for its storage; mighty fleets of vessels are created and maintained for its carriage on the sea, and railroads for its transportation on
land.

By 1876 the United States was importing 340 million pounds of coffee annually, accounting for nearly a third of all coffee exported from
producing countries. Of all the coffee consumed in the United States
nearly three-quarters came from Brazil, where coffee had not even
been a meaningful export crop two generations earlier. As the steady
flow of Brazilian beans became a flood, three powerful American coffee barons—known as the Trinity—struggled to maintain their lucrative
domination of the market.

~ 4 ~

THE GREAT
COFFEE WARS OF
THE GILDED AGE

Speculation seeks to discount the future in hope of much and rapid gain, and strengthens the popular tendency to wrestle with scarcely calculable forces, and to enter blindly upon ventures in which rational foresight sees but little hope of eventual good.

—Richard Wheatley,
"The Coffee Exchange of the City of New York" (1891)

The coffee market has always been volatile. Rumors of Brazilian frosts cause price hikes, while surprisingly large harvests produce dreadful declines, along with misery for farmers and laborers. Market forces, complicated by nature and human greed, have resulted in extended cycles of boom and bust that continue to this day. Since coffee trees take four or five years to mature, the general pattern has been for plantation owners to clear new lands and plant more trees during times of rising prices. Then, when supply exceeds demand and prices fall, the farmers are stuck with too much coffee. Unlike wheat or corn, coffee grows on a perennial plant, and a coffee farm involves a major commitment of capital that cannot easily be switched to another crop. Thus, for another few years, a glut ensues. All of this is complicated by the effects of plant disease, war, political upheaval, and attempts to manipulate the market.

As the coffee industry boomed during the 1870s, large importing firms made huge profits, but at substantial risk. One syndicate of U.S.

importers that dominated the coffee scene, comprised of three firms known as the Trinity: B. G. Arnold and Bowie Dash & Co. of New York, and O. G. Kimball & Co. of Boston. It was headed by B. G. Arnold, known as "The Napoleon of the Coffee Trade" and typical of the new breed of green coffee man, described by one trade insider as "a born trader, a fighter, commercial wizard, an experienced merchant in politics, weather and geography." For ten years, according to a contemporary, Arnold had "ruled the coffee market of this country as absolutely as any hereditary monarch controls his kingdom."

The firm of R. G. Dun assessed business credit risk during the Gilded Age, and its agent's annotations on Arnold's firm, approaching the fateful end of 1880, tell their own story:

> *Jan. 6, 1872*: Concern is said to have made fully a million during the past year, having a monopoly of the coffee trade. . . . Their business is mainly speculative.
>
> *June 5, 1875*: Estimated worth at least 1.5 million dollars. In the long run have made a large amount of money in their coffee operations. Occasionally the market will go against them but it is more than made up by after rise.

Then, in 1878, it became clear that the Brazilian state of São Paulo was going to flood the market with coffee. "This year marked a new era in the coffee trade," wrote Francis Thurber three years later. "Then it was that the large crops made it apparent that the time . . . when the production would exceed consumption had come." The Trinity struggled to maintain its stranglehold on the market, but the tide had turned. Two years later the Dun agent wrote:

> *Nov. 20, 1880*: The firm are known to have lost heavily lately, yet they are not seriously affected.

The syndicate of B. G. Arnold, Bowie Dash, and O. G. Kimball had artificially held up the price of Java coffee for many years. As vast amounts of Brazilian beans began to flood the market, the Trinity increasingly had difficulty holding so much of the available stock that they could demand favorable prices. Whereas they had heretofore specialized in quality Java beans, they now began to buy Brazilian beans in a desperate bid to boost prices. In October one coffee importer failed, but it was known to be overextended. On November 25 a tea importing firm went bankrupt. Front Street (shorthand for the coffee district) tensed for the next blow.

A Coffee Suicide?

On Saturday, December 4, 1880, O. G. Kimball died in Boston. Only forty-two, Kimball had no known health problems. He played cards on the fateful Saturday night of his death, making "a great effort to appear unusually cheerful," according to a friend. He retired before his wife at 10:00 P.M. She found him dead on his bed an hour later. The news hit the New York coffee market hard the following Monday. "The fact that his death practically dissolved his firm caused considerable uneasiness among his creditors to learn the exact condition of his affairs," wrote a *New York Times* reporter on December 8. "It also inflicted a blow to the credit of B. G. Arnold & Co." The newspaper that day attributed the death to "congestion of the lungs," but added that "his death was hastened by the anxiety and reverses of the past few months."

Rumors of suicide flew on the street—though Kimball's friends denied that he would have done away with himself. Regardless, his death spelled the end for his two cohorts in the Trinity.

On December 8 the New York *Journal of Commerce* reported on the suspension of B. G. Arnold & Co. with incredulity. "At first the report was not credited," the reporter wrote, "as the house had always borne the highest reputation for financial stability, and its dealings have been on a gigantic scale. But about noon the announcement was officially made." Later it came out that the firm was left owing over two million dollars. Similarly, the *New York Times* wrote: "Business men of every calling were astonished and shocked yesterday at the announcement that B. G. Arnold & Co., the largest coffee house in the United States . . . had failed."

The following day, December 9, no one could sell coffee at all. "There was no attempt to do business, everyone being suspicious of his neighbor," recalled Abram Wakeman, a veteran coffee man, in his reminiscences. Two days later Bowie Dash & Co. suspended business transactions, with liabilities of $1,400,000. The losses for coffee amounted to nearly $7 million in 1880, with $3 million more lost the following year. "The history of the trade for the twelve months [of 1880] is a record of loss and disaster such as never was experienced before in the coffee trade in the United States," observed Francis Thurber.

Creating the Coffee Exchange: No Panacea

Some who had been worst hit by the ruinous 1880 collapse decided to begin a coffee exchange. Though complex in execution, a coffee exchange is a simple concept. A buyer contracts with a seller to purchase a certain number of bags at a specified time in the future. As time goes by, the value of the contract changes, depending on market factors. Most real coffee men would use the contracts as *hedges* against price changes, while speculators would provide the necessary *liquidity*, since every contract requires a willing buyer and seller. While a speculator may profit, he also may lose his shirt. Essentially he provides a form of price risk insurance for coffee dealers.

"It was contended," recalled Abram Wakeman, "that had there been an Exchange . . . the crash would not have taken place. Also, roasters wishing to have a certain price to figure on could, by buying futures, tell just what the coffee would cost." Besides, it would be good for New York, concentrating the trade there. The exchange could arbitrate disputes and police the growing trade abuses. Those in favor of a new coffee exchange also argued that, with fixed standards for grades of coffee, outsiders and bankers would take an interest in coffee, carrying additional quantities that would help the market.

Others argued against a coffee exchange, predicting that it would be a "bucket shop" where speculators would push out real coffee men—a charge that has since been repeated many times. Nevertheless, the exchange was duly incorporated on December 7, 1881, exactly a year after B. G. Arnold & Co. had gone bankrupt. Benjamin Arnold was one of the incorporators and became the first president. For quite some time no one trusted the exchange, which became "the laughing stock of the trade, very little business being done," as Abram Wakeman recalled. Eventually, however, it became a frenzied scene of buyers, sellers, and speculators yelling and screaming at one another in the pit. Rather than discouraging attempts to corner the market, however, the exchange only added new wrinkles to the power play, as the ticker tape became the heart-stopping center of attention, spitting out price symbols.

A great boom occurred in 1886–1887, for instance, on news of a Brazilian crop failure. Several large houses in Brazil, Europe, New Orleans, Chicago, and New York—led by Tammany boss Joseph J. O'Donohue—joined forces to bull the market (i.e., artificially raise prices by purchasing stock or future contracts) up to a target of 25 cents a pound for December options. O'Donohue took his profits at 17.5 cents by selling his position, but a Brazilian bull syndicate, represented by B. G. Arnold, continued to boom the market up, with December futures closing above 21 cents in June 1887. On Monday, June 13, hundreds flocked to the exchange to witness "the slaughter of the bulls," as the December option price plummeted to 16 cents.

"Collapse was inevitable and precipitated panic," wrote contemporary journalist Richard Wheatley. "Immense quantities of coffee were thrown overboard by holders unable longer to carry them." The bears themselves came to the rescue, however, buying huge amounts of cheap coffee. Tammany boss O'Donohue joined with Hermann Sielcken, of W. H. Crossman & Brother, and calmly bought 100,000 bags at declining prices. For this they were "loudly cheered for their bravery." Of course they also made money on both ends of the market swing. Sielcken, a brilliant German immigrant, would soon become a major force within the coffee world—feared, respected, and loathed by many in the trade. At this point, however, Sielcken was the hero who saved the market, bidding the price back up to 17 cents.

The Most Speculative Business in the World

By century's end technology had made worldwide communication virtually instantaneous. Coffee exchanges in major European ports corresponded rapidly with New York. "Silently the submarine cable ticks off the news that supple fingers chalk and print of steamers leaving Rio and Santos on certain days, and with what cargoes," wrote Richard Wheatley in 1891. The New York Coffee Exchange tracked the day's price of coffee for delivery in each of the following eleven months, comparing it to the price of the previous year. Traders could ascertain the stocks of coffee at eight principal European ports in each month of the two past business years. "These facts and conditions, comparisons and symptoms, of the world's commerce in coffee daily, weekly, and yearly, are under the eye of the broker," Wheatley continued, "and guide his judgment in the contracts made so explosively on the floor of

the Exchange. To the uninitiated most of the superscriptions are mysterious as algebraic formulae, but to the experienced are significant as the
movement of hands on a dial." Despite such sophistication—or perhaps
due to it—speculation and attempts to outguess or corner the coffee
market continued unabated.

In ensuing years the coffee drama repeated itself many times, in different unpredictable permutations, with rumors of over- or underpro-
duction, war, disease, and manipulation. With the era of larger and
larger Brazilian crops, especially since 1894, prices dropped for several
years, down to a miserable 4.25 cents a pound for Brazilian beans in
November 1898. Then in 1899 Brazil was quarantined due to a serious
outbreak of bubonic plague. Turning bullish, the coffee men, rejoicing
in the sorrows of others, called it the "bubonic plague boom," as coffee
advanced (temporarily) to 8.25 cents.

John Arbuckle, the coffee magnate, summed it up succinctly when he
took the stand to testify in an antitrust case in 1897: "There will be a
failure of the crops . . . in Brazil, and the price will run way up; they will
have a big crop and it goes way down; the fact is, since I have been in
the business here, since 1870, nineteen or twenty of the men have failed
on that account . . . there appears to be no help for it; coffee is the most
speculative business in the world."

The wild gyrations of the coffee market captured the popular imagination, and in 1904 novelist Cyrus Townsend Brady penned *The Corner
in Coffee*, a melodramatic tale of love, betrayal, bears, bulls, and coffee
speculation. He conducted research by interviewing coffee dealers,
brokers, and members of the Coffee Exchange. "I acquired enough information about speculation in coffee to cause me to make a solemn
resolution never to touch it except as a beverage," Brady wryly noted
in his preface. In the book the original mastermind behind a coffee corner reverses himself in order to save his girlfriend's money. He helps to
break it in the most dramatic scene of the book:

> The corner was breaking, it was broken!
> He . . . forced his way through the great crowds until he reached the
> floor of the Exchange. Around the coffee pit pandemonium reigned. It
> was the centre, the vortex, of a seething maelstrom of passion. One sale
> succeeded another, and the market was going down. Down, down,
> down! . . .

Screaming men were frantically shaking their nervous hands aloft before Drewitt, the junior partner of Cutter, Drewitt & Co., who was selling as imperturbably as he had bought. The Exchange was in a perfect roar. . . . Clothes were torn, a man fell and was trampled by the maddened crowd. . . . Coffee fell 20 cents a pound in two hours.

Eventually, by the turn of the century, it became more and more difficult to manipulate the overwhelming volume of beans that flooded the market. The crops of 1901–1902 came in at fifteen million bags—much bigger than anyone predicted—and demoralized the coffee market throughout the world. "The position of the coffee-producing countries was pitiful," Abram Wakeman wrote, "they being dependent on the coffee crops for their livelihood.. . . Many were ruined. This was especially so in the mild coffee districts, located at great distances from the ports of shipment."

The Great Coffee–Sugar War

In the meantime, as the nineteenth century roared to its climactic end, business titans John Arbuckle and H. O. Havemeyer clashed. It started when Arbuckle decided to diversify from coffee into sugar. After all, he used an enormous amount of refined sugar for his coffee glaze. Why not package sugar in one-pound packages, just as he did his coffee? At first he simply ordered refined sugar, mostly from the American Sugar Refining Company, owned by H. O. Havemeyer, the king of the sugar trust.

Known as a predatory businessman, Havemeyer already had driven most competitors out of business. Outspoken, gruff, and dictatorial, Havemeyer once complained: "There is a prevailing hostility to wealth. This is perfectly illogical. Everyone wants money. It is the abuse of money, not its possession, which is opposed to public interest." Havemeyer saw nothing wrong in predatory pricing to drive out competition, but he was of course happy to allow Arbuckle to sell sugar, as long as the coffee magnate bought his product.

Then Arbuckle, who had always sought vertical integration (control of a business at every stage of production), decided to build his own sugar refinery and go into competition with Havemeyer. Late in 1896 Havemeyer summoned coffee broker Hermann Sielcken. "He asked me in which way he could do a large business in roasted coffee,"

Sielcken recalled later. Sielcken told Havemeyer that he needed to buy
a preexisting brand. "I told him that the brand had to be known, principally to the women, who are usually the buyers of coffee." Asked for
such a product, Sielcken suggested the Lion brand, owned by Ohio-
based Woolson Spice Company, which had been paying 100 percent
dividends per year.

Havemeyer said that he had heard rumors that Arbuckle was going
into the sugar business, and that he would not wait for that to happen.
"If Arbuckle Brothers had the intention of going into the sugar business," Sielcken said, "he would go into the coffee business." As a result
of that conversation, Hermann Sielcken traveled secretly to Toledo,
Ohio, where he purchased 1,100 out of 1,800 outstanding shares of the
company for Havemeyer, then made a second trip, where he purchased all but 61 shares that the owners refused to sell.

Many years later John Arbuckle recalled how he learned of Havemeyer's purchase of the Woolson Spice Company: "We were surprised
one morning to hear that the Woolson Spice Co. had reduced their
[coffee] price, I think a cent a pound, if I remember right; and we did
not see any reason, because green coffee was not any lower; and we
were very much surprised. Later in the day we heard that they had
bought the controlling interest in the Woolson Spice Co. Then we
knew it was war."

Just as Havemeyer got into the coffee game, overproduction hit and
prices slid. Determined to drive Arbuckle under by slashing prices,
Havemeyer directed Hermann Sielcken to buy the cheapest Brazilian
beans and to undercut Arbuckle's prices, even at the risk of losing
money.

It became clear to John Arbuckle by the beginning of 1897 that "no
matter at what price we might put our coffee they would put a lower
price; they intended to drive us out of the market." He added, "If we
would say today that we would stop building our [sugar] refinery, I
think they would stop roasting coffee." Arbuckle had no intention of
backing down, however, and a battle of mammoth proportions commenced.

Cutting the Thing Wide Open

H. O. Havemeyer sent word that he wanted to see Arbuckle. They met
at Havemeyer's New York home. Getting right to the point, Have-

meyer told him, "I want to buy 51 percent of your [sugar] refinery." Arbuckle shot back, "Mr. Havemeyer, as long as I live and have my senses, you will never own a dollar's worth of it. But this world is big enough for all of us."

"Well, I have got 11,000 stockholders to take care of," Havemeyer answered, "and I have got to take care of them."

"You could take care of them a good deal better by treating others in a more kindly way," Arbuckle observed. The meeting ended in stalemate, and the war continued.

Arbuckle countered by pouring more money into sugar production. "We went to work and increased our refinery, and now it is between 7,000 and 8,000 barrels of sugar a day—we can run to 8,000 barrels a day. But it is probably not profitable to do that. When you strain a thing, you do not get the best results." Nonetheless, Arbuckle had to "strain" things in the fierce price wars with the sugar trust. "Yes, at times we would sell at a loss. . . . We started the refinery in 1898, and there was a loss that year; I think there was a loss the next year, and . . . a profit the year following; and then there would be a fight started . . . and sometimes we would not make a penny."

Arbuckle was philosophical about cutthroat capitalism. While he preferred to call on "kindlier feelings," Arbuckle knew that "moral suasion did not appear to have very much effect" on Havemeyer. Consequently, as Arbuckle said, "we would get our temper up, and then cut the thing wide open."

Havemeyer and Sielcken discovered that an Arbuckle crony owned the outstanding stock in Woolson when they were slapped with a lawsuit, brought by the minority stockholder, Thomas Kuhn. The suit alleged that the sugar trust had bought Woolson for the purpose of "crushing of the Arbuckle Brothers and compelling them to abandon their intention of engaging in the sugar business." In order to do so, Woolson had repeatedly dropped prices for coffee. As a stockholder, Kuhn asked for an injunction, alleging that Woolson was losing $1,000 a day. The court ruled in favor of the sugar trust, refusing to grant the injunction, and a subsequent appeal was denied.

At that point John Arbuckle brought suit in his own name against the Woolson Spice Company, demanding as a stockholder to see the books of the company and to receive the transfer of stock he owned. He wanted to know why no dividends were ever paid, when they had been so generous prior to the Havemeyer takeover. On February 18, 1901, three judges concluded that Woolson was in contempt of court for refusing to obey the court order to hand over the books. The sugar trust had until March 5 to file a petition in error. A secret legal settlement was worked out shortly, however, and the lawsuit was dropped. Arbuckle apparently never got to look at the Woolson books.

In the meantime Havemeyer and Sielcken moved behind the scenes in Ohio. Because the Woolson Spice Company contributed so much to the state's economy, they persuaded Joseph E. Blackburn, the Dairy and Food Commissioner for Ohio, to single out Ariosa Coffee as adulterated, hoping to erode its legal customer base. In the words of Blackburn's affidavit:

> "Ariosa" consists of a cheap and inferior grade of coffee which is coated and covered with glutinous mixture, for what purpose, affiant deems it unnecessary to state, but with the manifest result that by such glutinous coating and covering, the inferiority of said coffee is concealed, and it is made to appear better and of greater value than it really is.

On February 5, 1901, Blackburn issued a circular to the grocery trade about the "coffee situation," stating that "the only firm that has refused and still refuses to accept the ruling of this department . . . is Arbuckle Bros., of New York."

Although Blackburn's action did not constitute an outright ban on Ariosa, it hurt business and outraged John Arbuckle, who immediately instituted a lawsuit to make Blackburn take back his allegations. He lost all the way through the Supreme Court in 1902, but he did make an impressive case for himself. Harvey Wiley, the chief of the Division of Chemistry for the U.S. Department of Agriculture and the country's most renowned consumer watchdog, testified that he had inspected the Arbuckle plant and found it to produce "as near as possible a perfect product." Wiley described the process of roasting and glazing in some detail. "It does not conceal inferiority," he asserted. "It [glazing] does not add a cheaper to a dearer substance. On the contrary, this added material is wholesome and digestible. It assists in the clarification of the coffee when the beverage is made; it preserves the aroma and flavor of the roasted berry, and prevents the absorption of moisture which would take place on long standing in the air."

Despite such testimony, the courts simply refused to enter a state regulatory matter. Ariosa apparently continued sales in Ohio, regardless of

Blackburn's opinion—and indeed took over the greater share of the market. Arbuckle sold about a million bags a year when the total U.S. consumption was between four and five million. Thus his firm alone sold nearly a quarter of all American coffee.

The Arbuckle Signatures

Perhaps the main reason for Ariosa's outstanding success, aside from name recognition and a standardized, reliable product, was Arbuckle's premium program, begun just before the coffee–sugar war commenced. In a distinctive script, "Arbuckle Bros." appeared on each package, along with the printed statement, "CASH VALUE ONE CENT." By collecting a sufficient number of these signatures, customers could redeem them for an impressive array of items in the Arbuckle catalog, ranging from toothbrushes and suspenders to clocks, wringer-washers, guns, and jewelry. For sixty-five signatures, women could buy window curtains. For only twenty-eight, men could secure a razor.

In a typical year the Arbuckle Notion Department was flooded with over one hundred million signatures, for which consumers received four million premiums. "One of our premiums is a wedding ring," observed one company official. "If all the rings of this pattern serve their intended purpose, then we have been participants in eighty thousand weddings a year." The catalog was extremely popular in the West. In Santa Fe it was printed in Spanish. The company also began to insert a stick of sugar candy—from their own refinery—into each package of Ariosa.

Havemeyer tried to strike back with his own premium plan, but it failed to make a dent in Arbuckle's sales. The only time Ariosa was challenged was when the Woolson Spice Company salesman told Indians in New Mexico and Arizona that owing to the picture of the lion on its package, drinking the coffee would give them the strength of a lion. Mose Drachman, the local Arbuckle salesman, quickly countered this rumor by assembling the local Indian chiefs. Didn't they see the picture of the angel floating on the Ariosa package? Didn't they know that an angel was stronger than ten thousand lions? The problem was solved. "If Lion wants to beat my angel," Drachman told his wife with satisfaction, "they'll have to put on their label a picture of God himself."

In the West, where Ariosa dominated almost completely, the wooden crates in which the coffee was packed were used for innumerable functions. Entire buildings were made from them. A Navajo baby would be rocked in a cradle made of Arbuckle crates. One reservation physician recalled, "I have seen adults buried in many a coffin built of wood from Arbuckles boxes, and more often than not a package of coffee would be put into the coffin along with other personal effects to ease the trip to the Happy Hunting Ground."

John Arbuckle included beautifully lithographed trading cards in his coffee for many years and offered albums in which they could be displayed. While these were quite attractive and generally educational—showing biblical scenes, state maps, birds, and peoples of the world—they also revealed the racism of the times. "The American Negro is a child of nature, and one of the most entertaining, interesting and happy of beings....'Possum hunting is much practiced in the warmer portions of this country by the Negroes. The opossum is the daintiest of dishes to their taste." The card went on to discuss the cakewalk, banjo, tambourine, and bones, "rude and elementary as they are."

On the flipside of the Ariosa cards were, of course, advertisements for the coffee and its egg-sugar glaze. "*BEWARE* of buying low-grade package coffee," the ad continued, taking aim at Lion brand, "falsely purporting to be made of Mocha, Java and Rio; this being a cheap device, employed by the manufacturers, to deceive unwary consumers."

The cards made lifelong impressions on eager young collectors. In his 1926 memoir *Trail Blazers of Advertising*, adman Chalmers Pancoast recalled that as a schoolboy he knocked on every neighborhood door, urging housewives to buy Ariosa so that he could collect the travel and history cards. "I had the first complete set of Arbuckle's Coffee cards and . . . became the envy of the school yard."

Coffee–Sugar Ceasefire

Despite the cutthroat competition, John Arbuckle and H. O. Havemeyer developed a kind of grudging respect for one another. Although Havemeyer was a "man of very, very aggressive temperament," Arbuckle also saw another side of him. "You would go up to his house and find a very accomplished gentleman of refined tastes and good company." He was astonished to find that Havemeyer was a sensitive and accomplished violinist. "Mr. Havemeyer," he told him, "you can not be as bad a man as they think you are, a man who produces such beautiful music as that." Arbuckle observed him to be "lovely in his family; he had his good qualities, and, of course, he had his bad." Havemeyer was proud of saying that he had no friends below 42nd Street—in other words, in the business district. "I think he took an erroneous idea about business," Arbuckle observed, "that a man in business had to fight everybody, and all that.. . . The fellow that wants to own the world does not always get it."

Although Arbuckle insisted that "there never was any armistice," the great coffee–sugar war really lasted only from 1897 until 1903, when Havemeyer essentially gave up trying to put Arbuckle out of either the coffee or sugar business. Arbuckle asserted that they never came to a formal agreement, but it is clear from many comments he made that he was extremely careful not to be accused of price fixing. At one point, presumably in 1903, Arbuckle admitted writing a note: "Mr. Havemeyer, you know more about sugar than I do, and I know more about coffee than you do. Of course, we are losing a lot of money"—in other words, *let's call off this insanity.* "I have had a good many fights in coffee, and so forth, and I found it paid to have things right no matter what it cost." And with this rather subtle rapprochement the price wars essentially ended. "Kindlier feelings prevailed, and that is what I was working for," Arbuckle recalled. "I knew there could not be any [formal] agreement; but the keynote was always kindlier feelings. 'The world is big enough for us all.'"

By the time Havemeyer gave up trying to drive Arbuckle out of business he had lost $15 million. Arbuckle Brothers, having lost a mere $1.25 million, clearly came out the winner in the great battle. Havemeyer had been bested. In the era of the robber barons it seemed that for once the less rapacious personality triumphed in the world of coffee, where a man's word was better than a signature. John Arbuckle typified many coffee men of that day: gruff but honest and well-intentioned.

By 1905, wishing that he had never tried to make any money on a crazy, unpredictable commodity such as coffee, Havemeyer sought in vain for a purchaser for the ailing Woolson Spice Company, a thriving business he had virtually destroyed in less than a decade. Two years later H. O. Havemeyer died. In 1909 Hermann Sielcken bought the Woolson Spice Company for its cash value of $869,000—quite a bargain compared to the excess of $2 million that Havemeyer had paid in

1896. Like John Arbuckle, Sielcken was a gruff coffee man, but his cut-throat style echoed Havemeyer's.

Indeed, Sielcken managed to turn the coffee misfortunes of others to his own benefit repeatedly. During this same period, in the early 1900s, he would "save" the Brazilian coffee industry while making himself a millionaire many times over.

~ 5 ~

HERMANN SIELCKEN
AND
BRAZILIAN
VALORIZATION

Planters and producers have been lulled into a sense of security in the belief that the present crisis, like the preceding ones, would be dispelled after short duration.

–El Salvador Delegate to 1902 Coffee Conference

If the United States makes a law that the merchant should not speculate, it decrees the merchant to be a shoemaker or a tailor, and shoemakers and tailors are not fit to make the country great.

–Hermann Sielcken

The coffee industry in all its facets was an enormous, interconnected global economic force by the turn of the century. Of necessity, bankers in New York, London, and Hamburg were vitally interested in Brazilian harvest projections, which loomed ever larger, threatening to swamp the world with too much caffeine. Just as it appeared that the tottering financial coffee structure would collapse of its own weight, Hermann Sielcken came to the rescue. In the process he would nearly land in prison.

For many years preceding the crisis period, coffee spelled prosperity. From 1888 to 1895 coffee consumption, fueled by improved standards

77

of living and coffee-loving immigrants, rose with production. The big trading houses kept on hand buffer stocks of some two to four million bags of coffee (132 pounds per bag), insurance against a small crop caused by frost or drought. Known as the *visible supply*, these buffer stocks, which kept well for several years, could then be sold during periods of smaller crops when the price edged upward. Until 1895 wholesale prices remained high, fluctuating between 14 cents and 18 cents a pound on the New York market, leading to vastly increased coffee plantings. There seemed no end to the good times.

Then in 1896 the coffee crisis of Brazil commenced. Planters flooded the world market with too many beans. Supply finally and definitively outstripped demand. The average price per pound for green beans fell below 10 cents and stayed there for years, initiating a boom–bust coffee cycle that continues to this day.

At first the planters were not unduly concerned. The fiscal philosophy followed by Brazil's New Republic government, after the deposition of Pedro II in 1889, called for money—lots of it, quite literally. The Brazilian government cranked up the printing presses. The short-term result of this inflationary policy was an enormous economic boom during the years 1890 and 1891.

While the constantly devalued Brazilian milreis eventually spelled disaster for internal markets, it helped the coffee grower for a few years, since he paid his local expenses in Brazilian currency while receiving his income in the currency of consuming countries. Even if coffee prices fell, *fazenda* owners did not suffer as long as the exchange rate also fell.

In 1897 world production increased dramatically, to sixteen million bags, and prices fell to 8 cents a pound. The world's visible supply jumped to 5.4 million bags, which hung over the market like a price-suppressing sword of Damocles. The following year Joaquim Murtinho, Brazil's new finance minister, reversed the inflationary policies. Murtinho saw that repeated devaluation of the milreis had made it increasingly difficult to service the federal government's debt to foreign creditors. Meanwhile lower coffee prices also led to an unfavorable balance of trade payments. As the value of the milreis rose, the coffee growers' profits, already narrow, dwindled.

A confirmed social Darwinist, Murtinho believed that in business and coffee only the fit would survive. The free market would produce optimal results, and if that meant a few failed plantations, so be it. That would leave the industry "in the hands of those better organized for the struggle."

In 1901 a bumper crop, the result of plantings five years earlier, shot total world production up to nearly twenty million bags, over half of which flowed through the port of Santos. The world consumed only fifteen million bags or so, leaving a surplus of almost five million. The visible supply jumped to 11.3 million bags—over two-thirds of the entire world consumption that year! The price of a pound of coffee fell to 6 cents.

The First International Coffee Conference

Not only Brazil but all the Latin American coffee-producing countries finally recognized that the coffee crisis was not going to resolve itself. In October 1902 most Latin American producers sent representatives to the first International Congress for the Study of the Production and Consumption of Coffee, held at the New York Coffee Exchange, to address "the lack of profit and ruinous price paid for the commodity to the producer." The chairman of the event, Percy B. O'Sullivan, head of the New York Coffee Exchange, expressed collegiality toward the producing countries. "As Americans, anything that binds you closer to us we look upon with favor. . . . We are all coffee men."

That they all made their living from the bean did not mean, however, that they could agree on meaningful action. The producing countries of course wanted high prices for their coffee, while the consuming nations hoped to pay as little as possible. In addition producers bickered with and recriminated one another, each unwilling to sacrifice for the good of the other. Eventually, however, the delegates concurred on a few innocuous proposals: they suggested banning export of the worst grade of coffee, known as *triage*, along with a reduction of European coffee import taxes (the United States had abolished its coffee tax in 1873).[1] They urged "a constant propaganda spoken or written" to increase the use of coffee. Finally, they sought some mechanism to limit coffee exports so that the visible stock remained at a reasonable three

---

[1]The tax reduction was worded vaguely due to Puerto Rican concerns. After Puerto Rico became an American protectorate in 1898, its coffee industry suffered terribly—not only from a devastating cyclone in 1899, but because the former Spanish colony could no longer export its beans duty-free to Spain. For years the Puerto Ricans, as well as the Hawaiians—where coffee cultivation began in 1825—lobbied U.S. politicians to impose a protective tariff on all other "foreign" coffee, in order to encourage the "domestic" coffee industry. They never succeeded.

million bags, and prices would rise—but the conferees could not agree on how to implement such a quota system.

The committee on the cause of the crisis pointed out that during boom years planters spent extravagantly and "made excessive use of their credit, so that when the crisis came about most of them were in debt." Desperate for cash, they rushed their crops to market, thereby increasing the glut and further lowering the price. Furthermore, "coffee lends itself admirably to become the object of syndicates, trusts, speculation of various kinds [and] to the advantages of a few middlemen." Indeed, the giant import-export houses of the consuming countries in Europe and North America simultaneously acted the part of banker (to the farmer), exporter (from the principal shipping ports), carrier, importer, and lastly, distributor. "This is what in plain language is called monopoly."

On the final day of the conference J. F. de Assis-Brasil, the Brazilian representative, offered an astute summary of the coffee boom–bust cycle based on human nature and the fact that it takes five years or so for a coffee seedling to turn into a producing tree. "It seems that each ten years a climax of too high or too low prices must manifest itself," he observed, predicting that prices would peak again in 1912. The reason? "Too high prices are inducements for extending unreasonably the plantations; as a consequence there comes an overproduction." With supply outstripping demand, prices fall. "Many plantations are abandoned; the harvests begin to shrink, while consumption follows its regular expansion." A new shortage prompts new growth, and the cycle repeats itself. "It is an endless chain," he said, "and I could say an endless chain of evils." The cycle could only be broken through "the combined efforts of the interested governments."

One delegate noted acerbically that the overproduction all stemmed from Brazil, which at this point accounted for fully 80 percent of the world's coffee. Assis-Brasil answered defensively that "it is not Brazil's fault that its land be more fertile than others. . . . The evil is common; their remedies must also be taken in common."

The conference ended with plans for a second, more definitive meeting the next year in São Paulo, but the meeting never occurred.

São Paulo Goes It Alone

The international coffee conference had accomplished nothing and the São Paulo planters vented their frustration. At a January 1903 meeting they denounced the Brazilian government for its indifference to their plight. In reporting on the meeting the *Brazilian Review* observed: "Frustrations that are now simmering . . . may boil over at any moment." In response the Brazilian president imposed on any new coffee plantations a tax of $180 an acre, which amounted to a ban on new planting for the next five years. The effect of the law would not be felt until 1907 or 1908, however, since trees planted prior to 1902 would be coming into production until then.

While the plight of plantation owners was bad, the effect on workers was worse, as owners reduced fringe benefits, took over land previously allotted to laborers for subsistence plots, and cut wages. As a result, one Brazilian paper reported, "The exodus of the Italians is critical. They return to their homeland poor and disillusioned." The Italian foreign minister responded by banning subsidized emigration after March 1902.

A late 1902 Brazilian frost reduced production for the next three years, and the visible supply shrank accordingly. Still, low prices persisted and the crisis continued. Growers who had lost trees to the frost replaced them with new seedlings. Meanwhile the milreis continued to strengthen, which hurt the coffee farmer's pocketbook.

Rather than blaming overproduction, many Brazilian planters pointed the finger at foreign coffee monopolies, asserting that short sellers (those betting on declining prices) and speculators were conniving to depress green bean prices. While the foreign firms could not be held responsible for the crisis, there was some truth to the allegations of price manipulation. The twenty biggest firms exported nearly 90 percent of the coffee, and the five largest accounted for over 50 percent. Theodor Wille & Co. of Hamburg, at the top of the heap, exported nearly a fifth of Santos' coffee.

In 1903 Alexandre Siciliano, a wealthy Italian immigrant to Brazil, suggested a valorization scheme (the term *valorizacao* came to mean maintaining the price of a commodity) in which the government would enter into a long-term contract with a private syndicate of merchants and financiers to buy up surplus Brazilian coffee and store it until prices rose. The success of the plan relied on the utter dominion of Brazilian coffee, however. If São Paulo held its surplus coffee back, would the other coffee-growing countries simply rush in to fill the gap? Would Brazil then lose its dominant position in the world market?

To answer these questions the São Paulo secretary of agriculture sent Augusto Ramos on a 1904–1905 fact-finding mission to other Latin

American coffee-producing countries. In his extensive report Ramos concluded that Brazil had little to fear from these countries. They were simply no match for São Paulo in terms of capitalization, efficiency, and productivity. They too were hit hard by low coffee prices and were in no position to expand their production to offset any surplus held back by São Paulo.

In August 1905 representatives of Brazil's major coffee states—São Paulo, Rio de Janeiro, and Minas Gerais—met with federal officials to discuss valorization. As the fall progressed it became clear that the upcoming crop would be of unprecedented size. The three presidents of the coffee-growing states met in Taubate, São Paulo, on February 25, 1906. They produced a signed document, agreeing on a valorization scheme to buy surplus coffee and keep it off the market, asking for federal aid, and requesting that the government stabilize the milreis exchange rate.

The federal government refused to become involved, other than voting to stabilize the exchange rate. On August 1, 1906, the Disconto Gesellschaft Bank of Berlin, through its Brazilian subsidiary, loaned São Paulo £1 million for a year. Ironically, the deal had been brokered by Theodor Wille & Co., the largest German exporter—one of those hated "monopolists" who controlled the coffee market.

The initial £1 million loan was a pittance. To finance the purchase of a decent amount of coffee, São Paulo needed much more capital, and quickly. The state sped a special delegation to Europe to drum up support. But when the London Rothschilds refused, the Paulistas realized that no major bank was liable to help them. The huge 1906 crop loomed, threatening to bring the price of coffee down to a few pennies a pound.

Hermann Sielcken to the Rescue

The desperate Paulistas found help from an unexpected source: Hermann Sielcken, noted for his ruthless treatment of competitors, market manipulation, and attempts to corner coffee.

Sielcken, a ham-faced business titan, spoke excellent English with a slight German accent and not the slightest trace of humor or humility. A graying mustache slightly turned up at the ends sat atop lips set in a grim line. As a contemporary article observed, he was "one of the most feared and hated men in the Coffee Exchange." Sielcken was enormously powerful. "Kaiser Wilhelm is monarch of Germany, but his rule is limited to the German Empire. Hermann Sielcken is a monarch of commerce and his rule extends the world over."

Sielcken left Germany in 1868 before he was twenty-one to work for a German firm in Costa Rica. A year later he ventured to California, where he worked as a shipping clerk. Having learned decent English, he secured a job as an itinerant wool buyer. During his travels he was nearly killed in a train wreck, which left him with a slight stoop.

In 1876, thanks to the Spanish he had picked up in Costa Rica, Sielcken found employment at W. H. Crossman & Son, an import-export firm that dealt in coffee on a commission basis. Venturing to South America, he proved to be a wonderful salesman of "axes and shovels and spades and silverware and everything else," while soliciting commission products for the house. For half a year every mail brought new Sielcken business.

Then suddenly all communication ceased. Weeks, months passed, with no word from Sielcken. Crossman feared his star South American salesman had caught a tropical fever and died. Then one day Sielcken appeared with a large package under his arm. "Gentlemen," he said, "I have given a large amount of business to you, far more than you expected, as the result of my trip." He went on to explain that he had a great many more orders in the package. "I think any person who has worked as hard as I have . . . deserves a partnership in this firm." So he was made a junior partner, then senior, and in 1894 the name was changed to Crossman & Sielcken. Eventually the coffee king also ventured into steel and railroads and bought a sumptuous estate in Baden-Baden that included four villas, a bathhouse for guests, a rose garden with one hundred sixty-eight varieties on twenty thousand bushes, an orchid greenhouse, and elaborately landscaped grounds kept manicured by six professional gardeners and forty assistants.

The Brazilians turned to Sielcken because early in August 1906 he had written an open letter to Brazilian newspapers defending valorization. As a result, a mission made a pilgrimage to Hermann Sielcken's Baden-Baden estate. Sielcken admonished the Brazilian delegation that "if you raise another crop like this there is no financial assistance coming from anywhere. . . . The rest of the world is not going to sit up all night drinking coffee just because São Paulo raises it all day." Assured that smaller crops would be forthcoming owing to the ban on new plantings, Sielcken promised to do what he could.

Hermann Sielcken put together a consortium of German and British banks and coffee merchants. In the first week of October 1906 the São Paulo government and the syndicate authorized the syndicate to begin buying green beans in the Santos export market at an average price of 7 cents a pound. The financiers agreed to pay for 80 percent, with the state of São Paulo providing the other 20 percent. If the free-market price of coffee rose above 7 cents, valorization purchases would suspend. This arrangement meant that syndicate members never paid more than 5.6 cents a pound (80 percent of 7 cents) for coffee, and often considerably less. Not only that, the money advanced by the syndicate was technically a loan charging the Brazilians 6 percent interest, with the coffee itself serving as security. The beans were shipped to syndicate warehouses in Europe and New York. São Paulo, still nominally the legal owner, was to pay annual storage costs as well as a 3 percent commission for initial handling.

By the end of 1906 the syndicate had purchased about two million bags, each holding 132 pounds of coffee. Since the year's bumper crop amounted to twenty million bags, taking such a small amount off the market had relatively little effect. But São Paulo had run out of money and couldn't come up with its 20 percent for more. In addition, the £1 million loan would come due in August 1907.

On December 14 the Paulistas were bailed out by a new £3 million loan from J. Henry Schroeder & Co. of London and the National City Bank of New York. Hermann Sielcken represented the U.S. bank and reputedly covered $250,000 of its loan with his own money. After paying off the million-dollar loan São Paulo now had £2 million to continue buying valorized coffee. By the end of 1907 over a million bags of valorized coffee had been warehoused in the ports of Hamburg, Antwerp, Havre, and New York, with lesser amounts in minor ports such as Bremen, London, and Rotterdam. There the beans remained, waiting for prices to rise sufficiently so that the syndicate could get rid of them at a profit. In the meantime the state of São Paulo continued to owe interest and storage charges. The small 1907–1908 crop allowed some of the valorized coffee to be sold off, but São Paulo remained in dire financial condition.

Late in 1908 Sielcken helped to arrange a mammoth £15 million ($75 million) consolidation loan. By this time the syndicate had sold off some million bags of valorized stock, leaving nearly seven million bags still in the warehouses. These were placed under the control of a committee of seven, only one of whom represented the São Paulo government. Hermann Sielcken was, not surprisingly, one of the committee members. Thus São Paulo lost control of the valorization coffee without ending its financial obligations. By manipulating the stocks and selling them quietly, the syndicate members had managed a virtual corner on the market. It was, as Hermann Sielcken candidly admitted at a congressional hearing a few years later, "the best loan I have ever known."

At first, after the committee took over the valorized coffee, the price per pound remained relatively stagnant at 6 or 7 cents a pound. But in the fall of 1910 the coffee price began to rise. By December it had run up to nearly 11 cents a pound. Throughout 1911 it continued to rise, jumping to over 14 cents.

The United States Howls over Coffee Prices

A howl went up from American consumers and politicians. Never particularly concerned about the plight of the Brazilian farmer during the coffee crisis years, suddenly United States citizens were righteously indignant that their morning coffee price had risen a few pennies. Addicted to their caffeine kick, North Americans apparently regarded cheap coffee as their birthright.

Buried in the U.S. National Archives outside Washington, D.C., is a thick file of correspondence kept by the Department of Justice covering valorization. It provides a fascinating chronology from the end of 1910 to the spring of 1913 showing how and why U.S. Attorney General George Wickersham gradually built a legal case against Hermann Sielcken and his valorized coffee. It also includes Wickersham's polite battle with Philander C. Knox, the secretary of state, over the matter, and an occasional memo to and from President William Howard Taft.

"Brazil has simply mortgaged herself to this syndicate," a small U.S. roaster wrote to Wickersham in December 1910, "and they in return are holding back this coffee to allow the syndicate to sell the 600,000 bags at 4 cents a pound more than they got last year."

A few months later in March 1911 Nebraskan Representative George W. Norris sponsored a congressional resolution asking the Attorney General to investigate "a monopoly in the coffee industry." Wickersham replied that he indeed was conducting an ongoing investigation.

In April, Norris lambasted the coffee trust from the floor of the House, summarizing the valorization loan process. He concluded that "this gigantic combination [has been able] to control the supply and the sale of coffee throughout the civilized world. [They] sold only in such quantities as would not break the market." Frustrated by Brazil's involvement, he observed that when a conspiracy to monopolize a product involved a domestic corporation, it was termed a trust and could be broken. "But if the combination has behind it the power and influence of a great nation, it is dignified with the new term 'valorization.' Reduced to common language, it is simply a hold-up of the people by a combination."

Norris suggested as a solution that the United States put a duty on all Brazilian importations—about $70 million in 1910—"until she should cease giving her support to the valorization scheme." He wanted to allow coffee from other countries to enter freely, however. Though George Norris regarded himself as a crusading idealist, he often antagonized party regulars. As a consequence, his denunciations of the coffee trust did not immediately produce legislation.

In the meantime the newspapers had taken up the cause, arousing general public indignation. "It would be far better to go without coffee than to be openly fleeced by the Government of Brazil," stormed the Albany, New York, *Argus*. "It is about time for the Department of Justice at Washington to take a look at this interesting band of robbers," another New York editorial intoned. By June 1911 George Wickersham was getting rafts of personal letters. "The coffee that is used to make [the poor's] miserable slop," wrote an Ohio businessman, "has been raised in price more than 100 percent." The famed naturalist John Muir wrote to express his "indignation upon this coffee imposition." He referred to "this iniquitous conspiracy between a foreign nation and an American citizen [Hermann Sielcken]," and asked, "Why should not this Trust be broken up?"

Restrictive sales were indeed the mechanism used by Sielcken and Arbuckle Brothers, which had joined the profit-making scheme. Together the two firms controlled the majority of the valorized coffee. In order to keep prices high they sold the coffee directly to roasters, often in the South or West, with the stipulation that none be resold on the exchange. Since they sold the coffee at a slight discount to the exchange price, the deal appealed to roasters. It circumvented, however, the natural functioning of the Coffee Exchange. In addition, Arbuckle Brothers bought enormous quantities of coffee from the exchange to raise the price then sold it, along with the valorized coffee, in secret private sales, insisting that it not be resold on the exchange. The old antagonists, Sielcken and Arbuckle, thus found common cause in making money from the valorization scheme.

The attorney general appointed William T. Chantland as his special assistant to look into coffee valorization. Chantland quickly proved himself a dogged opponent of the coffee trust and in July 1911 suggested prosecuting Hermann Sielcken. In a September memo he noted that the United States consumed nearly half of the world's coffee, and 80 percent of the Brazilian crop. Americans consequently were more affected by valorization than any other nationality. "In plain English," he wrote, "this whole thing looks like a plan devised in the apparent interest of São Paulo and Brazil, but, in fact, carried out to the great glory and financial profit" of bankers and coffee merchants such as Hermann Sielcken, "the financiers and the committee members who now seem to be juggling the supply to suit themselves and to enhance their fortunes."

Chantland singled out Sielcken in particular. "He is the illegitimate trustee of the operations in this country of the illegal agreement or its results.... His acts must stand by themselves as misdemeanors." He recommended "seizure and condemnation proceedings on the first valorization coffee to move in interstate commerce."

Goaded by George Norris and William Chantland, Attorney General Wickersham gradually came to the conclusion that he should prosecute Sielcken and the coffee trust, and he leaked such rumors to the press. The affair split the new National Coffee Roasters Association at its first convention in November 1911, where roaster Thomas J. Webb excoriated valorization as "the greatest grafting scheme the world has ever seen." Keynote speaker Hermann Sielcken defended valorization, asserting that there was no coffee trust, no corner. He claimed that he had only bought goods with his own capital, then resold them legitimately. "The newspapers never consider anything to be natural; they must make it mysterious, and they love to talk about millions and millions, and impress upon your mind the wicked New Yorkers and the capitalists."

Sielcken Snaps His Fingers

On May 16, 1912, Hermann Sielcken appeared as the first witness before the "Money Trust Investigation" congressional subcommittee.

Arrogant and unrepentant, he did not back down an inch, claiming that the valorized coffee had no effect whatsoever on the price.

During these hearings Sielcken and committee lawyer Samuel Untermyer crossed swords repeatedly. Untermyer asked Sielcken, "The idea was to keep that surplus [of coffee] off the market, was it not?" Sielcken answered, incredibly: "No; I was always trying to sell it. It was not kept off the market." When the coffee baron made such brazenly false statements, it was obvious that Untermyer could barely keep his lawyerly composure. He elicited from Sielcken that there were some four million bags of valorized coffee sitting in warehouses in the United States and Europe.

UNTERMYER: And coffee is selling at nearly 14 cents a pound, is it not?
SIELCKEN: Yes.
UNTERMYER: More than twice what it was selling at when the scheme went into effect?
SIELCKEN: Yes.
UNTERMYER: And you gentlemen were so anxious to sell that coffee that you have still got it, have you not?
SIELCKEN: We are anxious to sell it.

Little wonder that Untermyer interrogated Sielcken with strangled politeness and scarcely veiled sarcasm. "I suppose the purpose of making these elaborate provisions [to valorize coffee] had nothing to do with an attempt to limit the supply of coffee, had it?" the lawyer asked. "It had only to do with the equalization of the supply; not with the control," Sielcken parried. He meant that it would "equalize" the supply by transferring the large surplus of one crop into the next, but he was clearly engaging in semantic subterfuge.

Sielcken then made an outrageous statement: "If the amount of coffee held by this valorization in the United States today was sold tomorrow, it would not make *that* much difference in the market," he said, snapping his fingers.

"Then the fact that the price of coffee has gone from 5 cents a pound to 14 cents a pound has not anything to do with the fact that you gentlemen kept these millions of bags off the market?"

"Not *that* much," Sielcken replied, snapping his fingers again.

Later the coffee king actually lectured the committee. "
icize or give an opinion upon what the Brazilian Governmer
do I think it proper that this committee should ... express the
upon the action of another government, upon which we have no
to express an opinion." Untermyer replied between clenched teeth,
think this committee will take care of itself, and so will the Government."

Despite his prevarications, Sielcken ultimately appeared much more knowledgeable and reasonable than his interrogator. He explained that without the valorization scheme "there would have been a revolution in São Paulo." Untermyer responded with astounding insensitivity: "Do you think that would have been a worse condition than that we should pay 14 cents a pound for coffee?"

The frustrated Sielcken finally was allowed to make a long statement. His review of Brazilian coffee prices and history was cogent and convincing. Historically, coffee had cost over 20 cents a pound back in the 1870s and averaged 15 cents from 1886 to 1896, before the years of overproduction. He pointed out that even with valorization the price did not materially rise for nearly four years, until 1910. Then, he asserted, the price went up due to smaller crops, not valorized coffee. (The price indeed went up precisely when Assis-Brazil had predicted back in 1902; it peaked in 1912.)

Sielcken asserted that without valorization the price of coffee would have been *higher* in 1912. He reasoned that in 1906 and 1907 the prices would have dropped to such disastrous levels that planters would have been driven out of business, and subsequent crops would have been smaller and smaller. "In case the plantations had been neglected, we might have had crops of two, three, and four million bags, and a price for coffee of 25 cents."

The government's attitude was unfair and ethnocentric, Sielcken asserted. "I question the propriety of the United States criticizing or going into the details of the action of another country. Supposing that in this country we had a deal on cotton in the South, and Brazil should say, 'Well, we want to look into that.'" As he pointed out, "any foreign government or any foreign party that would act in that way would be thrown out of this country." He said that the American attitude amounted to saying to the Brazilians, "You shall sell your products always at the lowest, and we ours at the highest [price]. You must not

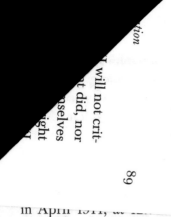

ny nature or form. That is a conspiracy if
es.... I challenge the Attorney General in
er in this country to tell me that as a coffee
to accept consignments."

ged virtually unscathed from the hearings.
le fabulous amounts of money from the val-
a broker he could buy it himself, then resell
stage. When coffee was at its highest point

in April 1911, at ___ nts, he said "I bought it and sold it." Untermyer asked, "Do you mean that you sold it for the committee or
bought it yourself?" Sielcken refused to divulge the details, answering
simply: "I made a profit on that deal."

The Lawsuit Against Sielcken

The day after Sielcken's testimony, Attorney General George Wickersham proceeded with his plans for a lawsuit, writing a crudely ciphered
message (apparently to prevent Sielcken or the Brazilians from spying)
on May 17, 1912, to a subordinate: "Appears Taeidzyil will probably
misapplying julhest. Defamed osirify homomorph teal," which meant,
"Appears Sielcken will probably leave Monday. Bill must be filed tomorrow." Shortly thereafter the attorney general petitioned for a temporary restraining order, enjoining the removal of the nine hundred
thousand bags of valorized coffee held in New York, and levying formal charges against Hermann Sielcken, the New York Dock Company,
and the foreign members of the valorization committee.

The U.S. Secretary of State, Philander Knox, found himself caught
between the attorney general and the Brazilian government, which
protested that the coffee warehoused in New York was the property of
the State of São Paulo, security for a loan, and that the United States
had no right to confiscate it. On May 29 William Chantland wrote to
an assistant U.S. attorney that "the Attorney General is very much interested and [is] in the fight to the finish." Two days later Wickersham
wrote a not-for-publication letter to a New York newspaper editor, stating his case in strong language. He objected to "a foreign government
[going] into partnership with a group of international bankers," noting
that "an increase of one cent a pound in the price of coffee means ten
million dollars on the amount used in the United States. . . . They practically took from seventy to eighty million dollars out of the pockets of

the American people." Wickersham also wrote a long memo to President Taft justifying the case.

The court nevertheless refused to sanction a preliminary injunction to confiscate the coffee. The government then narrowed its suit, focusing on Hermann Sielcken. Negotiations between Sielcken, his lawyer, Crammond Kennedy, and Attorney General Wickersham commenced. Wickersham wanted Sielcken to release all nine hundred thousand bags of coffee in return for dropping the suit; Sielcken promised to release only seven hundred thousand bags, the amount held in the United States at the beginning of the suit. In a telegram to his lawyer the coffee king pointed out that it was in his own best interest to sell as much as possible—he was only trying to protect the Brazilian government's interest by limiting the amount sold. In June, Sielcken warned that if a settlement were delayed, it "may force Brazil to measures totally destroying all good will and commerce between the two countries."

The fight over seven hundred thousand versus nine hundred thousand bags continued throughout the summer of 1912. Sielcken promised to sell the seven hundred thousand bags by April 1913. Apparently some compromise was reached, but when Wickersham returned from a September camping vacation, he exploded when he found that "the Brazilians are unwilling to enter into the arrangement suggested." He insisted that "the Department is prepared to submit the facts in the case to a grand jury, and I have no doubt that the indictment of Mr. Sielcken, and possibly some others, would follow."

The secretary of state's office tried to convince Wickersham to moderate or delay his case in the interests of smoothing over international relations. Wickersham repeatedly delayed the hearing. As 1912 wound to a close, George Norris introduced a bill to force the sale of valorized coffee. In response the National Coffee Roasters Association (NCRA) passed a resolution denouncing the bill, which would create "an element of uncertainty and danger." Other coffee men wrote to Wickersham to assure him that the meeting was "packed by Green Coffee interests" and did not represent the true feelings of the roasters.

William Ukers, the influential and well-informed editor of the *Tea & Coffee Trade Journal* (a competitor of *The Spice Mill* since 1901), wrote Wickersham to say that "the valorization interests organized the Coffee Roasters Association for the express purpose of throttling any movement calculated to interfere with their plans." In his journal, Ukers editorialized that "just because the Brazilians were so stupid as to keep on year after year producing more coffee than the world needed," why should the American consumer foot the bill? He added that Representative Norris might be jeopardizing his political future by fighting the big-money interests and "the Great Hermannus."

Sielcken attacked the Norris bill as being "so ambiguous that I personally cannot understand it." He scoffed at the politician's interference with a legitimate business transaction. "If Mr. Norris means that he wishes to prevent the price of coffee from ever advancing, he must make laws to prevent droughts, frosts, and unseasonable weather of any kind."

As the new year turned, Sielcken and the Brazilian government suddenly changed their proposed settlement. Rather than selling the valorized coffee by April, they now wanted the entire year. Wickersham accused them of "entirely lacking in good faith." In a letter to Knox he proposed to go forward with his lawsuit immediately. Knox once again wrote to beg that he accommodate the Brazilians.

Then, on January 21, Knox wrote that the minister of foreign affairs for Brazil had informed him that all of the valorized coffee in the United States had been sold to some eighty purchasers in several different states. Wickersham did not believe it. "I should be inclined to think that there was no truth in the statement, and that it was simply made for the purpose of diverting attention from the operations of the syndicate." The attorney general could be forgiven for being skeptical, since the Brazilians had just asked for a year's extension and since they refused to reveal who had bought the coffee. It is likely, however, that most of it truly had been sold.

On February 27 a very frustrated Wickersham wrote to George Norris at the House of Representatives. "I have several times felt very much like ordering a criminal prosecution of Hermann Sielcken, but the international questions involved have prevented [it], and I fear I shall not be able to do anything about it before I go out of office."

In the meantime the Brazilians retaliated against the pending lawsuit by rescinding a 30 percent tariff preference for American flour, causing flour exporters to write their senators, complaining about the valorization suit. "A very large proportion of the export business of the United States to Brazil is threatened with absolute extinction," one such exporter wrote on March 28, 1913. William Jennings Bryan also weighed in on the side of the Brazilian government.

By April the United States had a new attorney general, J. C. McReynolds. William Chantland, Wickersham's special assistant, wrote a strong memo to McReynolds informing him that Hermann Sielcken was "manipulating the coffee situation to suit himself," and urging McReynolds not to dismiss the suit until Sielcken or the Brazilian government provided details of precisely who had bought the valorized coffee. McReynolds ignored Chantland and wasted no time in dropping the controversial valorization suit in April. Sielcken was finally off the hook.

The first phase of valorization was nearly complete. Some 3.1 million bags of coffee remained in European warehouses, the last of which was sold in 1916. Nearly two million bags were sold after World War I commenced, the proceeds deposited with a Berlin banking house as the German government embargoed the funds. In the Versailles Treaty ending the war the Brazilians successfully lobbied for restitution. In 1921 the Germans paid over 125 million marks to Brazil, and the books were finally closed on a highly effective price manipulation.

There is no question that the valorization scheme benefited Hermann Sielcken and his associates more than the farmers or government of Brazil. It did prevent mass bankruptcies, foreclosures, and possible revolution, however. Unfortunately, its perceived success encouraged Brazil to pursue further valorization schemes of one sort or another for the next few decades. In the euphoria of 1912, with coffee prices going up, the Brazilian politicians abandoned the tax on new plantings, allowing overproduction a few years later. Over time it also became clear that Brazil was not immune to competition from other coffee-growing countries. The result: Brazil's domination of the world coffee industry (nearly 80 percent in the early twentieth century) would slowly erode.

Hermann Sielcken's Final Years

For septuagenarian Hermann Sielcken everything seemed to be going well. As the valorization suit finally was dismissed early in 1913, his partner George Crossman died, leaving him a million-dollar bequest. It turned out that Crossman and Sielcken, about the same age, had made a kind of bet on who would live longer: Each had included the other for a million dollars in his will. (Crossman's son received only $300,000.)

Soon afterward the seventy-three-year-old Sielcken, widowed seven years previously, married Clara Wendroth, forty years his junior. They sailed for Germany in October 1914, just before the outbreak of World War I. Sielcken, the astute internationalist who could predict Brazilian harvests so well, apparently refused to believe that war actually would transpire.

In 1915 the *New York Times* reported a rumor that Sielcken was being detained in Germany, where the government was extorting large amounts of money from him. In fact, however, as the article reported, Sielcken had always been "very pro-German in his opinions." The money he donated to German war relief was purely voluntary. In 1915 he secretly furnished $750,000 to purchase the New York *Evening Sun,* which promptly supported the German cause. The fired editor bitterly reported that his replacement's office was known as "Little Germany."

As Sielcken's health failed in 1917, so did his fortunes. Only days before his death in October his U.S. property, worth over $3 million, was seized under the Alien Property Act. It took four years for Sielcken's widow to prove that he had been a naturalized American citizen. The government then returned the money.

Litigation over Sielcken's estate, valued at over $4 million, continued to keep his name alive for years. After his death two women with whom he apparently had been romantically involved came forward. The Woolson Spice Company, controlled by Sielcken at his death, passed into other hands. After examining the books the new managers sued the estate for $800,000. It seems that in 1913, when the government suit had pressured Sielcken into selling the valorized coffee, he had dumped some twenty-three million pounds of Brazilian coffee into the warehouses of the Woolson Spice Company, for which he had charged the company the prevailing high prices. Shortly thereafter, when the valorized coffee was sold, the price dropped substantially. Sielcken's executor settled the case out of court for around $250,000.

The Caffeine Kicker

While coffee dominated the world's breakfast table, however, its very ubiquity and effectiveness drew criticism. By the turn of the century many reformers were convinced that coffee was an evil drug whose immoderate use could lead to insanity or even death. As a result, pure food faddists such as John Harvey Kellogg and C. W. Post produced "healthy" coffee substitutes, and another aspect of the coffee wars commenced.

~ 6 ~

THE
DRUG DRINK

The drug, caffeine, in coffee keeps many persons awake nights when they ought to be asleep. If you've found only that one annoying fault with coffee (there are others) isn't it time to quit it and use POSTUM? ... "There's a Reason"

—**1912 advertisement for Postum**

The high prices that accompanied valorization may have infuriated American consumers and politicians, but they delighted Charles William Post. As the inventor of Postum, America's favorite coffee substitute, Charley Post, or C.W. (as he preferred to be addressed formally), profited handsomely whenever green bean prices soared and people sought cheaper alternatives. Taking advantage of a new national health consciousness and adopting a scientific patter, Post promised that by drinking Postum, his coffee substitute, consumers would be on the "road to Wellville," as he put it. His folksy but negative approach to advertising revolutionized modern marketing while appalling everyone in the coffee industry.

Even an admiring contemporary journalist described Post as "powerful, restless, nervous, ambitious, opinionated, prejudiced, with ego plus." With his ubiquitous advertising, self-righteousness, posturing grandiosity, and propaganda against "coffee nerves," Post was the opponent coffee men loved to hate. And they did, vilifying him in the pages of the *Tea & Coffee Trade Journal* as "the cereal slush king" and worse. By 1900 there were half a dozen other Battle Creek, Michigan, firms producing "healthy" coffee substitutes. During the valorization

period, several other cereal firms marketed coffee substitutes or exten-
ders. Postum, however, was by far the most successful. With Grape-
Nuts cereal, it made Post a multimillionaire even before the valorization scheme.

Born in 1854 in Springfield, Illinois, Charley Post quit school at fifteen. He made up for his short attention span with inventive fervor and
entrepreneurial energy. While still in his teens he started a hardware
store in Independence, Kansas, selling it a year later for a profit. He
worked for a while as a traveling salesman of farm implements, then invented and manufactured farm equipment on his own, obtaining
patents for a seed planter, sulky plow, harrow, hay stacker, and various
cultivators. He also invented a smokeless cooker and a water-powered
electric generator.

Post's extraordinary inventiveness did not come without cost, however. By 1885 he had developed neurasthenia, a fashionable "disease"
of the era. Named and popularized by Dr. George Beard, neurasthenia
supposedly involved an exhaustion of the body's limited supply of
"nervous energy." Many overworked businessmen and oversensitive
upper-class women believed that they suffered from this ailment. "The
combined effects of work with stimulants and narcotics," Post said later,
"produced a nervous breakdown."

After a brief recovery, Post took his wife, Ella, and young daughter,
Marjorie, to California in 1888, then to Texas, where he took to a
wheelchair owing to his supposedly weak nerves, while simultaneously
managing a woolen mill, selling land and homes, and representing several electrical motor manufacturers. He also invented a player piano,
an improved bicycle, and "Scientific Suspenders," which could not be
seen when worn under a coat.

Despite his entrepreneurial fervor, Post hadn't yet made a decent living, and the financial strain caused digestive disorders and another
breakdown in 1890. He moved his family to Battle Creek, Michigan,
to seek care at the famed Sanitarium, or "San," of Dr. John Harvey
Kellogg.

Kellogg, a combination of quack and genius, had turned the San into
a national phenomenon. A diminutive, bearded dynamo, he made
himself the impresario of health faddism, and one of his particular dislikes was coffee. "The tea and coffee habit is a grave menace to the
health of the American people," he intoned, adding that they caused

arteriosclerosis, Bright's disease, heart failure, apoplexy, and premature old age. "*Tea and coffee are baneful drugs* and their sale and use *ought to be prohibited by law.*" He even alleged that "insanity has been traced to the coffee habit."

Mind Cure and Postum

Post's nine months at the San failed to cure his indigestion or nervous disorder. "I think you should know," Dr. Kellogg gravely informed Ella Post, "that C.W. has very little time left. He is not going to get well." In desperation Ella took up the study of Christian Science with her cousin, Elizabeth Gregory. Mrs. Gregory told the ailing Post that he should simply deny his illness, that it was all in his mind, and that he could eat whatever he pleased. Obeying her suggestion, he began to feel better, left the San, and moved in with his new healing guru.

By 1892 Post had recovered sufficiently to open his own Battle Creek alternative to Kellogg's Sanitarium, which he christened La Vita Inn. Mrs. Gregory provided mental treatments for a slight extra charge. A couple of years later Post published a book, *The Modern Practice: Natural Suggestion, or, Scientia Vitae*, which he reissued the next year with the catchier and more egotistical title *I Am Well!* In it Post claimed miraculous cures for himself and those who stayed at his inn, espousing "New Thought" or "mind cure." All disease was simply the result of "wrong thinking."

In 1895 Post first manufactured Postum, a grain-based coffee substitute that bore a suspicious resemblance to Kellogg's Caramel Coffee (served at the San).[1] In October 1896 he transferred $37,000 of the inn's assets to provide start-up capital for Postum Ltd. When his new drink proved profitable, Post abandoned his therapeutic practice at the La Vita Inn and modified his views to fit his new product. In *I Am Well!* he had written that all disease stemmed from "mental inharmony" and could be cured through right thinking. Soon, however, he was advertising an easier method: "Remember, you can recover from any ordinary

---

[1]Kellogg may not have liked coffee, but he liked Post's rip-off even less. "Most coffee substitutes consist of cereals in some form combined with molasses and roasted, [which] develops in these substitutes poisonous phenolic and other smoke products the same as are produced in ordinary coffee." He complained later that Post had "made some millions by the sale of a cheap mixture of bran and molasses."

disease by discontinuing coffee and poor food, and using Postum Food Coffee."[2]

Post turned out to be a natural salesman. A tall, slim, square-shouldered man with chiseled good looks, he impressed both men and women with his charismatic, persuasive presentations. In 1895 he took a portable stove along with Postum samples to Michigan grocers. At each store he would prepare a pot, boiling the prescribed twenty minutes, all the while praising the drink's medicinal and mouth-watering properties. "When well brewed," he proclaimed, "Postum has the deep seal brown of coffee and a flavor very like the milder brands of Java."

The first Grand Rapids grocer Post visited wasn't moved, since he had a large supply of Kellogg's Caramel Coffee on hand, gradually turning stale. Post convinced the grocer to take Postum on consignment, promising that advertising would create a demand. Then the industrious entrepreneur visited the editor of the *Grand Rapids Evening Press*, brewed more Postum, and served it. The editor remained dubious until he noticed Post's stationery, with a red dot in one corner and the legend below, "It makes red blood." Impressed by Postum's health claims, he gave Post $10,000 worth of advertising credit.

In the late nineteenth century, advertising agents usually acted only as brokers, placing ads written by clients. Post always enjoyed writing his own copy anyway; he clearly understood the benefits of advertising before most other food manufacturers. By mid 1895 he was spending $1,250 a month on advertising. In 1897 the figure had risen to $20,000 a month. Over his entire career he spent well over $12 million to promote his products, 70 percent in local newspapers, the balance in national magazines. Post remained convinced that such gigantic advertising outlays were fully justified, creating demand for a mass-produced and widely distributed product. Through economies of scale he could lower the cost of goods to the consumer despite his ad expenditures.

Within a few years, the nondescript barn in which Post first brewed Postum was surrounded by pristine white factory buildings, known as the White City. The most impressive building served as his "temple of propaganda," as one journalist put it, where Post's advertising men dreamed up new slogans for him to approve or amend. It was, accord-

---

[2]Post wrote in *I Am Well!* that "whisky, morphine, tobacco, coffee, excessive animal passions, and other unnatural conditions" contributed to ill health. Post knew about "animal passions," bedding an associate's wife and siring two children by her in 1894 and 1896.

ing to the writer, "the most unique and sumptuously furnished office building in the world."

Post's Fierce Attacks

Post believed in appealing directly to the consumer rather than relying on salesmen to convince grocers and wholesalers to stock his product. With such "pull" advertising, consumers would *demand* his products.

The Postum ads used a vernacular sometimes described as "farmer's English" to appeal to the common man; the ads "must use plain words, homely illustrations, and . . . the *vocabulary of the customer*," Post emphasized. One of his best-known advertising lines, "If Coffee Don't Agree, Use Postum Food Coffee," drove the coffee men *and* grammarians wild, but it sold Postum. At the end of every ad Post added a tag line: "There's a Reason." It was never quite clear what this sentence meant. Regardless, the phrase found its way into the popular culture of the time, as surely as "Just do it" and other catchphrases have become imbedded in modern parlance.

By May 1897 sales were booming, largely due to scare ads that depicted harried, desperate, and dissipated people hooked on caffeine. They warned of the hazards of "coffee heart," "coffee neuralgia," and "brain fag." Abstaining from coffee and drinking Postum would effect the promised cure.

An interviewer told Post, "Your advertising . . . has this element of combat in it. It always carries a chip on its shoulder, as it were, and goes straight for the other fellow's eyes." Indeed, Post's ads almost literally hit consumers between the eyeballs. "Lost Eyesight through Coffee Drinking," one headline blared. "It is safe to say that one person in every three among coffee users has some incipient or advanced form of disease." Coffee was a "drug drink" that contained "a poisonous drug— caffeine, which belongs in the same class of alkaloids with cocaine, morphine, nicotine, and strychnine." One ad featured coffee spilling slowly from a cup, accompanied by an alarming text: "Constant dripping wears away the stone. Perhaps a hole has been started in you. . . . Try leaving off coffee for ten days and use Postum Food Coffee."

Other ads resorted to personal intimidation. "Is your yellow streak the coffee habit?" Post's copy asked. "Does it reduce your work time, kill your energy, push you into the big crowd of mongrels, deaden

what thoroughbred blood you may have and neutralize all your efforts
to make money and fame?"

When he wasn't frightening his readers Post buttered them up, appealing to their egos. He addressed an ad to "highly organized people,"
telling them that they could perform much better on Postum than on
nerve-wracking coffee. Post also addressed the modern man, asserting
that Postum was "The Scientific Way To Repair Brains and Rebuild
Waste Tissues." Coffee was not a food but a powerful drug. "Sooner or
later the steady drugging will tear down the strong man or woman, and
the stomach, bowels, heart, kidneys, nerves, brain, or some other organ
connected with the nervous system, will be attacked."

Post has been given credit for first adapting patent medicine come-
ons—with their exaggerated health claims, appeals to snobbery and
fear, bogus scientific jargon, and repetitive incantations—for a beverage,
thus paving the way for modern consumer advertising. In fact he may
have learned from Coca-Cola, first offered in 1886 as a "brain tonic,"
and also destined to play an important role in coffee history.

Tapping the Paranoia

Post, a man of his times, tapped into a fin-de-siècle American fear. The
pace of change—with telegraphs, electricity, railroads, ticker tapes, economic booms and busts—seemed overwhelming. In addition, the typical American diet, heavy with grease and meat, was guaranteed to
cause indigestion—dyspepsia was the most frequent medical complaint
of the age. This heavy food was usually washed down with an ocean of
poorly prepared coffee. By the turn of the century the typical U.S. citizen used an average of 12 pounds of coffee annually—nothing compared to the Dutch, the world leaders at 16 pounds per capita, but a
great deal of coffee nonetheless. People frequently sought drug-laced
patent medicine remedies for their stomach problems.

In this turbulent atmosphere Post's new national product advertising,
cleverly adopting much of the scientific patter and overblown claims of
the patent medicines, was extraordinarily effective. Regional coffee advertisers, with the exception of the Ariosa and Lion brands, could not
compete. Their local messages, stressing familiar themes such as aroma
and good taste, were no match for Post's sophisticated pitches. Worse,
in the face of the Postum onslaught, many coffee ads became defensive,

saying that *their* coffee (as opposed to others) lacked poisonous substances and tannins.

Post further infuriated coffee men by writing inflammatory, pseudo-scientific letters directly to consumers. "Coffee frequently produces indigestion and causes functional disturbances of the nervous system," he wrote in one such letter. He asserted that caffeine attacked "the pneumogastric nerve (the tenth cranial or wandering nerve, the longest and most widely distributed nerve of the brain)," often leading to paralysis. "Coffee is an alkaloid poison and a certain disintegrator of brain tissues."

The fact that Post himself continued to drink the evil brew did not soften his attacks on coffee. According to his daughter, Marjorie, Post would drink coffee "for a few days and be sick, and he'd drink Postum for a few days and be well, and then he'd go back to coffee." He even did so in public. One newspaper reporter noted that at a dinner, Post imbibed "oh, horrors, some of that terrible, nerve-destroying beverage, the deadly coffee," despite being "the champion of the coffeeless nerve."

Finding that Postum sales were seasonal—peaking in the winter—Post invented Grape-Nuts cereal in 1898 to round out the year, calling it "The Most Scientific Food in the World." Postum sales also swelled, by 1900 reaching $425,196, nearly half of which was pure profit. In 1908 Postum accounted for over $1.5 million in sales, though it was topped by Grape-Nuts and Post Toasties by that time.

Monk's Brew and Other Ploys

Post sold Postum boxes for 25 cents retail and a case of a dozen boxes to grocery wholesalers for $2, leaving a slim profit margin for retailers. The product was in such demand, however, that merchants had little choice but to carry it. Inevitably, competitors sprang up, offering a similar coffee substitute at a substantially reduced price. Post responded to these challenges by creating a new drink, Monk's Brew, pricing it at only a nickel a package, and marketing it aggressively in towns where underpriced competitors were making inroads. Once Monk's Brew wiped out the competing brands, Post withdrew it from the market. "The imitators were ruined," Post chortled. "It was one of the most complete massacres I have ever seen." The wily Post took the returned

Monk's Brew and repackaged it as Postum—quite legitimately, in fact, since it *was* precisely the same product.

Although Post rolled in money, he was stingy with his own employees. The packing room women received 0.3 cents for each box of Postum they filled but were fined a full 25 cents for each box they accidentally tore. Even though they were paid on a piecework basis, workers' pay was still docked when they showed up late for work. In addition, Post was rabidly antiunion, spending much time and money in his latter years writing and distributing right-wing diatribes against the evils of organized labor.

Over time Post left the day-to-day manufacturing process to his managers, while he pursued a restless, nomadic life among homes in Washington, D.C., Texas, California, New York City, London, and at his married daughter's home in Greenwich, CT. He conducted much of his business by mail. While delegating most aspects of his fabulously successful enterprise, however, Post continued to pay personal attention to advertising copy. He often kept a piece of copy in his pocket for weeks, adding a new touch daily, aware that each word would reach some thirty million readers. "I have never been able to get anybody to write our advertising better than I do myself," Post observed, "and have never been able to teach anyone to write it my way."[3]

He observed with satisfaction that dozens of Postum competitors had fallen by the wayside. "It is fairly easy to make a good palatable and pure food and quite another thing to sell it." Post was among the first advertisers to approach his subject psychologically. "Observe the acts of men day by day," he said, "their habits, likes, dislikes, methods, hopes, disappointments, bravery, weakness, and particularly study their needs."

Post solicited testimonial letters by placing ads in popular magazines, promising "Many Greenbacks." Post selected the best and rewrote them to make them more punchy. "I was a coffee slave," began one such edited letter. "I had headaches every day." When the woman quit coffee and imbibed Postum, all her troubles vanished. "The rheumatism is gone entirely, blood is pure, nerves practically well and steady, digestion almost perfect, never have any more sick headaches."

---

[3]In his later years Post left the invention of new products to others. His cousin, Willis Post, who headed the British outpost, invented instant Postum in 1911, obviating the need to boil the drink for twenty minutes.

A nurse from Wilkes Barre, Pennsylvania, wrote: "I used to drink strong coffee myself, and suffered greatly"—until she switched to Postum, of course. "Naturally, I have since used Postum among my patients, and have noticed a marked benefit where coffee has been left off and Postum used. I observe a curious fact about Postum used among mothers. It greatly helps the flow of milk."

A St. Joseph, Missouri, man attested: "About two years ago my knees began to stiffen and my feet and legs swell, so that I was scarcely able to walk, and then only with the greatest difficulty, for I was in constant pain." His problem? Coffee. The solution? Postum.

The independent Post eventually fired his advertising broker and in 1903 created the Grandin Advertising Agency, named after Frank C. Grandin, his employee in charge of advertising. Grandin's only client was Postum. Later Post acquired his own newspaper in Battle Creek, which he used as a platform for disseminating his rather quirky views, as well as advertising Postum, Grape-Nuts, and Post Toasties.

Post was not alone in damning coffee. Most doctors of the era warned against the beverage's habitual use. In 1906 a London doctor—perhaps more loyal to tea—stated, "Coffee drunkards, as I may call them, are greatly increasing in number." He added that the coffee habit produced "palpitations of the heart, an irregular pulse, nervousness, indigestion and insomnia." One Dr. Leszynsky observed in 1902: "I have seen victims of the coffee habit among commercial travelers, brokers, merchants, actors, writers, and men connected with the news departments of the daily papers." According to Leszynsky, such addicts suffered everything from flatulence to "general tremulousness and diminished muscular power."

Even American physicians such as Dr. George Niles had harsh words for the drink so beloved by his countrymen. True, he thought that "strong coffee, either alone or with a little lemon juice, is often useful in overcoming a malarial chill or a paroxysm of asthma." But he went on to warn that "it is easy to form a coffee habit, which, yielded to, may lead into muscular tremors, palpitation, a feeling of praecordial oppression, tinnitus aurium, hyperesthesia, muscular lassitude, vertigo, heartburn, vague symptoms of indigestion, constipation and pronounced insomnia." On the whole, coffee came in for an inordinate amount of criticism in the first two decades of the twentieth century.

The Coffee Merchants React

C. W. Post had amassed a fortune more quickly than any other American of his era. At the beginning of 1895 he was only a struggling mind-cure innkeeper who had just made his first batch of Postum. Seven years later he was a millionaire.

By 1906 resentment over the success of Postum had reached fever pitch among coffee men. William Ukers, editor of the *Tea & Coffee Trade Journal,* wrote a nasty editorial upon the marriage of Marjorie Merriweather Post. "It is interesting to note," wrote Ukers, "[that] it was announced . . . the fond father had settled $2,000,000 on his daughter and had carefully drilled her in business methods. . . . But what's $2,000,000 to Post, who every year spends a million and a half in advertising alone? My, what a commentary on the gullibility of the American public!"

Many coffee advertisements of the era only made matters worse. "*I TOLD YOU TO BRING ARBUCKLE'S PACKAGE,*" one ad read, showing a wife socking her husband on the jaw and spilling a bag of coffee. "Be real angry if they send you a substitute," read the ad copy, "which is not as good, and may in time ruin your digestion and nerves." Such a come-on may have been good for Ariosa in the short run, but it conveyed the impression that most other coffee was harmful. Another ad for Dern Coffee asserted that "if coffee makes havoc with your nerves and digestion, it is because you are not using a fresh roasted, thoroughly cleansed, correctly cured coffee." Consequently Dern Coffee "gives you the strength and aroma of the coffee without its nerve-destroying qualities."

Similarly, many defensive articles on coffee wound up damning it with faint (or no) praise. A May 1906 piece in the *Tea & Coffee Trade Journal* by John G. Keplinger entitled "The Healthfulness of Coffee" began with the assertion that "almost any nonsense makes an impression on the public mind if only reiterated often enough in print." Well and good. But then Keplinger proceeded to admit that "without doubt coffee has been the cause of much discomfort, headache, sour stomach, blurred vision, etc." The reason? Coffee was harmful, according to this author, if diluted with milk and sugar; it should only be drunk black.

Apparently unaware that he failed to practice what he preached, Keplinger went on to advise coffee advertisers to emphasize positive attributes, rather than stating that *their* brand of coffee did not produce headache, constipation, dyspepsia, or nervous trouble. Some people may never have heard such negative comments about coffee. For such innocents, the mere suggestion of these ills might be enough to induce them.

Keplinger then offered sample advertisements of which he approved. The very first headline was: "Is Coffee Harmful?" It is difficult to understand how the author could fail to take his own advice. His other ads approached the absurdity of vintage patent medicine claims. "Coffee is a valuable remedial agent, or rather a preventive, when there are epidemics of typhoid fever, cholera, erysipelas, scarlet fever and the various types of malarial fever." Another headline suggests that "Good Coffee Soothes the Nerves" because it is "a non-reactive stimulant, as has been proved time and again by the sphygmograph and as a brain stimulant it may be termed an intellectual drink."

One of the favorite ploys of coffee boosters throughout the first part of the century was to cite anecdotal stories to illustrate the drink's beneficial effects on longevity. On her ninety-second birthday, for instance, Mrs. Hannah Lang nimbly performed a set of folk dances. "It is the proud boast of Mrs. Lang that she has never been sick a day in her life. . . . About the only health rule she follows is to drink four cups of strong coffee every day." Mrs. Christine Hedin of Ironwood, Michigan, celebrated her hundredth birthday by "drinking coffee all day long," as was her normal habit (from four to ten cups daily). A centenarian Frenchman was told that coffee, which he drank to excess, was a poison. "If it is poison," he said, "I am a fine example of the fact that it is a very slow poison."[4]

In July 1906 *Tea & Coffee Trade Journal* editor Ukers offered a call to arms:

Here and there manufacturers and dealers are waking up to the fact that the substitute beverage-makers have stolen a march on them and now they are determined to regain the lost ground. . . . The Postum Company certainly have had a wonderful opportunity and have made the most of

---

[4]In eighteenth-century Sweden twin brothers were sentenced to death for murder. King Gustav III commuted it to life sentences in order to study the then-controversial effects of tea and coffee. One brother drank large daily doses of tea, the other, coffee. The tea drinker died first, at eighty-three.

it. The retail coffee dealers of the country did nothing to upset their plans. . . . The advertising of this substitute for coffee has attacked coffee strenuously and bitterly and with consummate skill, and the result is that thousands of people who have been in the habit of drinking coffee regularly have given it up.

Clearly C. W. Post's advertising was far more effective than any for coffee. Frustrated and baffled by the challenge, the coffee men even considered hiring Post clandestinely to write copy for them, though the plan never materialized, which was just as well, said Post. "Could I advertise coffee as I advertise Postum? No! I believe in Postum, and have no such belief in coffee."

It would take another decade or two before coffee advertisers learned Post's lesson that a positive image was at least as important as taste.

The Collier's Libel Flap

A prominent national periodical, *Collier's Weekly*, pointedly refused questionable patent medicine ads after printing Samuel Hopkins Adams's widely read 1905 muckraking series "The Great American Fraud," which lambasted misleading ads and contributed to the passage of landmark food legislation the following year. Yet, as one outraged reader complained later that year, *Collier's* ran Post's ads, which invariably touted medicinal cures. Stung, the magazine's advertising manager wrote to Post, explaining that he could no longer print such ads. In 1907 the magazine published an editorial criticizing Grape-Nuts advertising for claiming that the breakfast cereal could cure appendicitis. "This is lying, and potentially, deadly lying." The article called Postum testimonials by physicians and health officials "mythical."

Post responded with a venomous $18,000 article-advertisement campaign run in newspapers across the country in which he asserted that the author of the *Collier's* article had "curdled gray matter." Post had the nerve to assert that it was *he* who had refused to advertise in the magazine, and that he had been attacked as a result. Moreover, he defended his testimonials. "We have never yet published an advertisement announcing the opinion of a prominent physician or a health official on Postum or Grape-Nuts when we did not have the actual letter in our possession."

In 1907 *Collier's* filed a libel suit against Post. When it finally came to trial three years later, Post had to defend his earlier writings such as *I Am Well!* in which he claimed miraculous healing powers for, among other things, a molar abscess and a wheelchair-bound invalid. "And now you've reached the point where you propose to relieve pains, not by the use of mental suggestion, but by Grape-Nuts and Postum?" the prosecuting attorney asked. "At fifteen cents a pound?" Post: "Yes." The lawyer got Post to admit that he gave prizes for good testimonials and that he did not have time to investigate whether all were genuine.

In his final arguments the plaintiff's attorney dramatically pointed at Post and begged the jury, "Help us to make this man honest." They complied, finding Post guilty of libel and fining him $50,000. Eventually the trial verdict was reversed by the New York Court of Appeals, but Post had learned his lesson. From then on he moderated his claims. Within a few years Postum was advertised to cure constipation rather than brain fatigue or appendicitis.

Dr. Wiley's Ambivalence

"If some isolated case is found where a man has sold roasted peas and chicory as coffee, a terrible howl goes up," editor William Ukers observed in spring 1906. "And yet when Millionaire Post proceeds to offer burnt cereals as coffee nobody says a word. And where is Dr. Wiley all this time?" Harvey Wiley, who was then lobbying hard for the new pure food act that would pass the next month, had become an enormously influential spokesman for truth in advertising and labeling. Wiley mounted a *moral* crusade against fraud and vice. "The injury to public health," he said, "is the least important question . . . [and] should be considered last of all. The real evil of food adulteration is deception of the consumer."

Wiley's obsession with deceit rather than health issues was reflected in his legislation. The Pure Food and Drugs Act did not make poisonous substances illegal; it simply said that they had to be identified on the label. Caffeine was not placed on the list of poisonous substances that had to be so labeled. With twelve pounds consumed by every man, woman, and child, coffee was the most popular beverage in America; most coffee men therefore must have felt that they were relatively safe and hoped that Wiley would direct his attention to the mislabeling of products such as Postum.

Eventually he did, forcing Post to remove the word *Coffee* from his label and advertising. With obvious satisfaction, Ukers printed the new and old labels side by side, demonstrating that the hastily deleted word left a gaping white hole in the copy. But the pure food law also caused trouble for coffee men. If government agents found chicory or other substitutes in coffee, they prosecuted. If they found "black jack" beans—that is, discolored or moldy from blights or improper processing—being imported, they put a stop to it. Over the next few years, scores of coffee prosecutions cleaned up the coffee and coffee substitute industry.

While such enforcements were salutary, other prosecutions seemed merely bureaucratic, malicious, or stupid. Although Brazilian and Central American beans had been widely misrepresented as Java coffees, this term was traditionally and correctly applied to coffee coming not only from the island of Java itself but any of fourteen nearby islands. Nonetheless the Board of Food and Drug Inspection ruled the same year that coffee grown in Sumatra had to be labeled Sumatra coffee rather than Java. No one in the industry could see the harm in such long-standing practices, but the government did.

Since Harvey Wiley had championed the pure food law that had helped police their industry, Ukers and other coffee experts wanted to believe that Wiley was on their side. Yet in 1910 the crusading chemist got carried away in a speech reported by the newspapers. Wiley asserted that "coffee drunkenness is a commoner failing than the whiskey habit. . . . This country is full of tea and coffee drunkards. The most common drug in this country is caffeine."

The coffee men should have known that at best Wiley harbored mixed feelings toward caffeine and coffee. Soon after the pure food law passed he instituted an attack on Coca-Cola. Wiley disapproved of caffeinated beverages but felt that coffee and tea were safe from legal assault since they *naturally* contain caffeine, just as peaches and almonds naturally contain hydrocyanic acid. Coca-Cola, however, was consumed regularly by both children and adults, and caffeine was deliberately added to it. Wiley therefore persuaded his reluctant superiors to allow him to seize forty barrels and twenty kegs of Coca-Cola syrup that had crossed state lines.

Bringing Coca-Cola to trial in 1911 at Chattanooga, the government charged that the drink was adulterated, defined by the pure food law as containing a deleterious added ingredient. The government consequently had to prove that caffeine was both harmful and an added ingredient under the law. Coffee men must have watched the dramatic trial with mixed feelings. On the one hand, they squirmed when expert witnesses attacked caffeine as poisonous. On the other hand, they recognized that the popular soft drink was beginning to erode their own market.

Despite their impressive credentials, most expert witnesses relied on flawed experiments highly colored by their own opinions. Harry and Leta Hollingworth's groundbreaking double-blind experiments on caffeine's effects on humans—still-cited classics of the literature—were the exception. The experiments indicated that caffeine, in moderate amounts, improved motor skills while leaving sleep patterns relatively unaffected.[5]

Coca-Cola eventually won the case, though not on any scientific grounds. All of the testimony proved irrelevant. Judge Sanford issued his opinion from the bench, ordering the jury to return a verdict in favor of Coca-Cola. Without deciding whether caffeine was a poison or not, Sanford said that it was *not* an added ingredient under the law, but had been an integral part of the formula since the drink was invented. The trial had an impact on Dr. Wiley as well. His superiors, looking for any excuse to ditch the bullheaded chemist, accused Wiley of having illegally paid a witness too much for his testimony. Wiley resigned in March 1912, at the height of his national popularity.

That same year the coffee men, hopeful that Wiley would support them, paid him to deliver the keynote address at the National Coffee Roasters Association on the topic, "The Advantages of Coffee as America's National Beverage." In his opening remarks the truculent chemist told them that pure *water* should be the national drink. In his rambling speech he reserved his primary venom for Coca-Cola, but he also lambasted coffee and caffeine. The southern soft drink was "a first artificial cousin of coffee, because the dope that men put in Coca-Cola is the dope the Lord puts in coffee—caffeine." He went on to say, "I would not give my child coffee or tea any more than I would give him poison."

Wiley shamefacedly admitted that, like C. W. Post, he drank coffee himself. "I know it does not do me any good; I know it is harmful, that

---

[5]For an assessment of coffee's effect on health see chapter 19.

it makes many dyspeptics, and many other nervous wrecks by the hundreds of thousands, yet I sit down every morning and drink my coffee. I like it."

The Birth of Decaf

Owing to the very public contemporary controversy over caffeine, entrepreneurs began to look for a naturally caffeine-free coffee. Four varieties were identified, mostly in Madagascar. Unfortunately, the drink produced from their roasted seeds was bitter and unpalatable. The famed agronomist Luther Burbank opined that a decent-tasting hybrid was certainly desirable and might indeed be possible, but it would involve years of experiments in the tropics. "It would be absolutely impossible for me to pay any attention to the coffee plant, as it would require removing to another climate." He added another important question: "Would coffee be used, except for the exhilaration accompanying the caffeine? I think it would, but this is for someone else to decide."

Soon Burbank's question could be answered with a very qualified Yes. Convinced that his father, a professional coffee taster, had died prematurely as a result of too much caffeine intake, Ludwig Roselius, a German merchant from Bremen, succeeded in extracting caffeine from green beans by superheating them with steam, then flooding them with the solvent benzol. He patented his process and incorporated his company in 1906. Within a few years his decaf coffee was available in Germany as Kaffee Hag; in France as Sanka (*sans caffeine*), and in the United States, from the Merck drug company, as Dekafa. Competitors sprang up on both sides of the Atlantic. Robert Hübner, another German, introduced his Hübner Health Coffee in 1911 to the American market, claiming to extract the caffeine through a pure-water process without using a chemical solvent. The next year two brands of "instant" coffee–the condensed particles of a regular brew–went on sale.[6]

Post's Last Act

The decaffeinated and instant coffees made only a small dent in regular coffee consumption and did not unduly disturb the coffee men. At least

---

[6]See chapter 8 for a detailed account of the G. Washington brand, the most successful early instant coffee.

they were *coffee*, unlike Postum, whose ads continued to malign their product. C. W. Post regularly appeared in the *Tea & Coffee Trade Journal* as the Antichrist of Coffee.

In January 1914 Post suffered a nervous and physical collapse. The newspapers duly reported that he had fled to his Santa Barbara ranch "for a complete rest," along with his personal physician and his wife, Leila. In the pages of the *Tea & Coffee Trade Journal,* editor William Ukers couldn't resist pointing out that Post, who warned constantly of "coffee-slugged nerves," had succumbed to a nervous breakdown himself. "We would not appear to gloat over his misfortune," Ukers wrote, doing just that. "Indeed, if his breakdown is in any measure due to his drinking Postum all these years, he has our deep sympathy." Ukers wished the millionaire a speedy recovery, suggesting that a nurse "slip him a cup of coffee now and then during his convalescence."

In March, Post's doctor diagnosed him with appendicitis—ironic, since only four years earlier Post had declared repeatedly during the *Collier's* trial that Grape-Nuts prevented or cured appendicitis. Admitting that he needed an operation must have created a crisis of faith for the man who had written: "Sickness, Sin, and Disease are creations of the human intellect, and exist only in a mesmeric or abnormal state."

Post took a private train from California to Minnesota, where Mayo Clinic doctors would operate on him. The press wrote breathlessly of his "race with death," but after routine, successful surgery Post returned to Santa Barbara, where he fell into a deep depression, seldom leaving his bed. "There is a taste of Heaven in perfect health," Post once observed, "and a taste of Hell in sickness." On May 9, 1914, Post sent his wife Leila to conduct some business. He told his nurse, "I am very nervous. My mind is perfectly clear but I cannot control my nerves." Then, at the age of fifty-nine, C. W. Post, the multimillionaire health guru, dismissed his nurse, placed a shotgun in his mouth, and pulled the trigger.

Some believed that Leila, nearly thirty years younger than Post, had been unfaithful and that Post had committed suicide upon discovering it. More likely the man who was worth $20 million upon his death chose to exit the world due to a bruised ego. Mental discipline, Postum, and Grape-Nuts had not made him well, as his book title so brazenly had proclaimed him to be. Post died, but his fortune, and Postum's anticoffee advertising, survived him. His daughter, Marjorie Merriweather Post, and her second husband, the financier E. F. Hutton, were to continue the business and expand it substantially—creating General Foods, and ironically, purchasing Maxwell House Coffee in 1928. Post must have rolled over in his grave—or perhaps laughed with glee that his daughter was making money from the drug drink he secretly enjoyed.

~ *Part Two* ~

CANNING
THE BUZZ

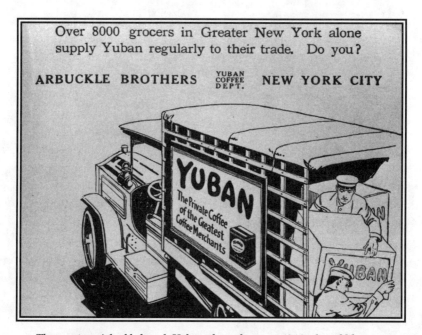

The premium Arbuckle brand, Yuban, shown here in a 1916 ad, could have revived the ailing coffee giant's fortunes. But because it refused to pay for a national campaign, Arbuckles' faded from view, eventually selling Yuban to General Foods.

～ 7 ～

GROWING PAINS

[By 1915], the sheer excitement of expanded consumption, the new rituals of buying and selling—universalized by name brands, national trademarks, and chain stores— became characteristic of everyday life in which millions, regardless of place or position, shared. Materialism became Americanism.

–Thomas J. Schlereth,
Victorian America: Transformations in Everyday Life, 1876–1915

The seeds of the modern U.S. coffee industry grew along with an increasingly urban, industrialized country. Before coffee, many other consumer products—Ivory Soap, Coca-Cola, Listerine—claimed a national market, with the help of sophisticated advertising strategies. Coffee, however, was difficult to distribute widely. Once roasted, it staled quickly, thus discouraging aggressive national campaigns. Nevertheless, a few visionary coffee companies—Folger's, Hills Brothers, Maxwell House, Chase & Sanborn, Arbuckle Brothers—learned Postum's advertising lessons, while hundreds of other coffee roasters struggled to survive in an increasingly competitive, fractious market before the onset of the First World War.

Brand Proliferation

The battle for coffee market share was waged primarily on a regional level in the pre–World War I era. Even so, a coffee marketing revolution would take place in a remarkably short period of time. In 1908 an advertisement appeared in the *Tea & Coffee Trade Journal* picturing a "New Case for Bulk Coffee," with four bins already labeled Ext. Fine

Santos, Old Gov't Java, Arabian Mocha, and Golden Rio. Ten years later such an ad would have been completely anachronistic. Branded coffee rapidly replaced the bulk coffee of the traditional country store.

Looking back over a thirty-year career, retailer J. C. Reid observed in 1915, "I have seen the transition or partial transition from selling crackers, rice, currants, raisins, spaghetti, macaroni, rolled oats, corn meal, borax, baking soda, coffee, etc., out of a box, barrel or sack to being sold in . . . packages under trade-mark brands." True, he noted, there was a trade-off. Consumers got a little less for their money than when they purchased in bulk, but they received similar quality and quantity, protected by a moisture-proof package. Coffee no longer smelled (and tasted) of the pickle barrel sitting next to the bulk bin, and the blend's flavor was generally consistent in every package.[1]

Many grocers were unhappy that their customers could buy the same brand of packaged coffee at a competing store. One grocer told Reid that he pushed his bulk coffee because he could get it fresh-roasted in small batches from his local roaster and blend to suit his customers—snaring a 40 percent profit, much more than the net from branded coffee. Even this grocer had to admit, however, that the percentage of coffee he sold by brand was increasing.

Another contemporary grocer favored brands, though. "Quality talks," he wrote. "Best results are obtained by handling a good, advertised line in package or cans. [I] am now selling about twice as much since settling down to one line. Our coffees now run uniform, and when we find a blend a customer likes, we have no more trouble." In the "modern grocery store," Reid concluded, "you can readily see that there are scarcely any articles of merchandise that they sell that are not already wrapped and packed in neat, easily, economically handled, germ-proof, trade-mark, quality-speaking packages."

In 1915 a survey of some 5,500 coffee drinkers revealed that 86 percent bought their coffee prepackaged. Together they listed over a *thousand* different brands—not that surprising, since a concurrent survey conducted by the National Coffee Roasters Association came up with 3,500 American coffee brands. It was, as one observer noted, a "Package-age."

---

[1]"The air was thick with an all-embracing odor," wrote Gerald Carson in *The Old Country Store*, "an aroma composed of dry herbs and wet dogs, or strong tobacco, green hides and raw humanity." Bulk roasted coffee absorbed all such smells.

Whether coffee came in a package or not, the American consumer continued to ruin the brew by boiling it. Now, however, they could do it conveniently with a pumping percolator. While *percolation* literally refers to a simple drip method, in North America it came to refer to a pot with a central tube and glass cover. When the water heated sufficiently, it perked up through the tube, spraying the coffee back over the grounds repeatedly. In the early twentieth century these pumping percolators were electrified and became standard kitchen appliances. Because the percolators produced an overextracted brew—leaching unpalatable components from the grounds—economical housewives were almost sure to get a bitter cup, either too weak or too strong, depending on the amount of coffee and water they used.

In 1908 German housewife Melitta Bentz began a revolution in coffee brewing when she punched holes in the bottom of a tin cup, lined it with her son's blotter paper, and created a superior once-through drip brewing method that quickly spread through Europe and created a dynasty for the Melitta brand. The same year in the United States I. D. Richheimer introduced his drip Tricolator, a pot with a filtered midsection; and three years later Edward Aborn invented a superior drip brewer called the Make-Right, but neither of them achieved widespread popularity. It would take the rest of the century for most Americans to learn the virtues of drip brewing.

A & P Grinds Its Own

Although American brands were proliferating, they faced stiff competition from two sources: price-cutting chain stores and door-to-door peddlers.[2] Of the nascent chains by far the greatest threat came from the Great Atlantic and Pacific Tea Company, otherwise known as the A & P. Founded in 1859 by George Francis Gilman, the company initially sold animal hides. Yet within a few years, under the codirection of clerk and subsequent partner George Huntington Hartford it was christened the Great American Tea Company, specializing in tea, with over a dozen stores in Manhattan. Soon they added coffee as well. Gilman and Hartford eliminated middlemen, buying coffee and tea on the docks straight off the clipper ships. In 1869 the Great American Tea Company became

---

[2]Mail order houses also made incursions into the retail coffee market. The 1897 *Sears Roebuck Catalog*, for instance, offered green, whole-roasted, or roast-ground coffees.

the Great Atlantic and Pacific Tea Company, ostensibly in honor of the completion of the transcontinental railroad that year. It also signaled the company's plans for expansion beyond the east coast of the United States. In 1871, in the aftermath of the Chicago Fire, the company sent staff and food, staying to open stores in the Midwest.

In 1878 Hartford officially took over the operation, while Gilman retired to enjoy a lavish lifestyle. Hartford expanded, supervising over two hundred stores by 1901, in addition to sending over five thousand peddlers in standardized red-and-black A & P wagons to deliver directly to the home. Gradually, under the direction of George H. Hartford's sons George L. and John, the company offered other groceries as well. Aping Arbuckle, the A & P offered premiums and trading stamps to lure consumers. By 1907 A & P's sales had reached $15 million a year.

The older, more conservative brother, "Mr. George," as he was known by employees, minded the books. He also cupped the coffee and tea samples every afternoon at 3:00 P.M., continuing this task into his nineties. The flamboyant "Mr. John" drove the company's marketing and expansion. It was he, for instance, who sent out red and gold coaches drawn by a team of eight horses decorated with spangled harnesses and gold-plated bells. The local citizen who came closest to guessing the correct weight of the team won $500 in gold.

In 1913 John Hartford broke with traditional practices and introduced the company's first "Economy Store," which was strictly cash-and-carry—no deliveries, no phone orders, no premiums. By cutting out wholesalers the A & P could sell quality food at low prices with no frills. In an incredible entrepreneurial burst, John Hartford opened seventy-five hundred such stores (approximately three a day) between 1914 and 1916—and then weeded out over half of them. Seeking a kind of brand recognition for the stores themselves, he standardized their architecture and layout so that he could reputedly find the coffee in any store blindfolded. Each store required only one employee—manager. At a time when most city dwellers spent nearly half their salaries on food, the new A & P's were wildly successful.[3]

After a run-in with Cream of Wheat, which refused to sell to A & P if the chain sold it below the retail price, John Hartford increasingly re-

---

[3]The patriarch of the business, George Huntington Hartford, died in 1917 at the age of eighty-four. George Gilman died in 1901.

lied on the firm's own brands, some known as Ann Page products. Through a wholly owned subsidiary, the American Coffee Corporation, he placed his own coffee buyers in Brazil, Colombia, and elsewhere, purchased directly, roasted the beans, and provided grinders in each store, where he sold Eight O'Clock Coffee, along with Red Circle and Bokar, his premium grade.

The Premium Peddlers

While the A & P wagon men gradually gave way to that firm's economy chain stores, other door-to-door salesmen, particularly those of the Jewel Tea Company, challenged branded coffee. In the late nineteenth century quite a few small-time businessmen eked out a living by delivering bulk-roasted coffee by horse-drawn wagon. These "wagon men" plied their trade primarily in major cities, where deliveries could be made close to one another. In 1899, when Frank Skiff, having saved $700, quit his regular sales job in order to deliver tea, coffee, and spices on his own, he was just one of several hundred such peddlers serving Chicago and its suburbs. Nor was his Jewel Tea Company unusual in offering premiums to customers, who earned a certain number of coupons with each purchase and could eventually trade these for selected household goods.

The next year Skiff's brother-in-law, Frank Ross, joined him at Jewel. Then in 1901 the enterprising Ross had a fateful encounter with a Mrs. Scannon, who answered the door with a hot tea kettle in hand. Ross barely got to begin his sales pitch. "Get off my porch or I'll scald your eyes out!" she threatened. It turned out that Mrs. Scannon had saved coupons for nearly a year in order to earn a coveted rug. But just when she was ready, her wagon man went out of business. Consequently she held a low opinion of such schemes.

Thinking quickly, Ross yelled from the safety of the sidewalk, "What would you say if I told you I'd leave these beautiful Haviland plates today and you could be using them while you traded them out?" Thus began the phenomenally successful "advance premium" program. In 1916, fifteen years after offering its first advance premium to Mrs. Scannon, the Jewel Tea Company, now selling a variety of household goods, went public with a $16 million capitalization. The company boasted eight hundred fifty thriving wagon routes serving two million families, a huge coffee roasting plant in Chicago, and an elaborate sales hierarchy based on the frontline wagon men who visited each customer every two weeks. About half of the company's income stemmed from its coffee sales.

The company's success inspired imitation and competition. By the time Jewel offered common stock to the public there were four hundred similar firms; ten of them, like Jewel, had gone national. *The Interstate Grocer* estimated in 1915 that the "peddlers," as retailers contemptuously called the wagon men, had snagged 60 percent of their coffee business.

The coffee roasters were just as unhappy as the retail grocers, since the Jewel Tea Company and its imitators roasted their own coffee, thus capturing a major portion of the trade. In 1916 speaker Paul Haserodt horrified his audience at the National Coffee Roasters Association annual convention by dramatizing a typical Jewel house visit:

SOLICITOR: Mrs. Jones, where do you buy your coffee?
MRS. JONES: I buy it of my grocer.
SOLICITOR: What do you pay for your coffee?
MRS. JONES: Thirty cents a pound.
SOLICITOR: That's just what we charge for ours, but I have something special today. I give you this electric iron. . . . It's yours. All I ask you to do is to buy 60 pounds of coffee. You don't take the coffee any faster than you need it. Our driver will deliver you two pounds every two weeks, and you pay for it as you get it.
MRS. JONES: Well, I should like that iron, but how about the coffee? Is it good?
SOLICITOR: I guarantee it. If you don't like it, you don't have to keep it.

The Jewel solicitor told his customers that they were earning "profit-sharing credits." When Mrs. Jones—or "Mrs. Average Housewife," as the Jewel literature preferred to call her—had nearly earned her electric iron, the driver brought another enticing item. In this way, Haserodt explained to his roaster audience, "he keeps her tied up indefinitely."

The Institutional Niche

Those who retailed their coffee directly to consumers received the greatest publicity and battled for grocery or pantry shelf space. But other regional roasters specialized in providing coffee for hotels, hospitals, restaurants, private clubs, and steamship lines. Known as institutional roasters, they too were fiercely competitive. Frederic A. Cauchois of New York, for example, provided his freshly roasted Private Estate Coffee daily by a wagon route in dated bags. Any beans that remained after two weeks were taken back in exchange for fresh product. Cauchois preached the drip brewing method and provided his clients with fine Japanese paper filters and urns that were inspected once a week. By 1904 he had established roasting plants in Philadelphia, Washington, Pittsburgh, and Chicago, in addition to New York City.

In contrast to Cauchois, many other institutional roasters learned to cut corners in order to maximize profits. Russian immigrant Philip Wechsler thrived by loaning money to others who wanted to open delis or groceries—on the condition that they buy his coffee at his price. Legend has it that the sign over his desk read, "Give 'em sawdust."

In Chicago, Harry and Jacob Cohn, two Lithuanian immigrants, founded their own competing coffee companies in the first part of the century. Older brother Harry founded Superior Tea & Coffee Company in 1908 with his cousin Walter Katzoff. After working at Superior for a while, Jacob Cohn started Continental in 1915. While his older brother specialized in home deliveries, Jacob chose the institutional route, delivering to restaurants and cafeterias. He sold restaurant owners brewing equipment virtually at cost and gave them free urn bags and cleaners. Superior, too, eventually switched to restaurant service, and the companies became fierce institutional competitors, expanding from the country's center in an effort to best one another. In California, Roy and Frank Farmer started Farmer Brothers.

Sexy Coffee?

The stodgy coffee men were slow to learn from the razzle-dazzle salesmanship of competitors such as Jewel and Postum. By 1907 it was clear that advertising and salesmanship had become increasingly important components of any thriving American business. The *Tea & Coffee Trade Journal* ran an editorial, "Search for a Man," about the difficulties in locating good salesmen. "There are men with the indescribable knack which enables them to sell anything from a gold brick to a cake of soap, but there is no outward sign by which they may be told."

Yet an article a few years later in the same journal criticized exactly such a coffee salesman, who admitted that he knew nothing about his product. "I have never made a cup of coffee in my life. . . . What I do is sell labels, cans, [and] canisters–but most emphatically do I not sell coffee." A former insurance salesman, this man knew human nature, even if he didn't know beans about coffee. "I pick up a label," he continued, "and tell about it being a thing of beauty and a joy forever, and I get the name on the dotted lines and get out." If a dealer had the temerity to request a sample of the coffee, the salesman would "gently but firmly insinuate that it is presumptuous on his part to request to see samples of my world-renowned and old-established brands."

It is of course understandable that true coffee men would be horrified by such a cavalier attitude. Without a decent product this flash approach would not produce a loyal customer. Yet in this infancy of modern capitalism, as the twentieth century advanced with all the speed of its newly discovered electricity, the coffee men needed to embrace the new hucksterism in order to sell their brown beans.

Most coffee roasters struggled to understand new marketing methods. They observed, for instance, that milk sales went up at a Boston sales counter when the drink was poured by a sexy young woman. "She was a comely, buxom lass with brown hair, liquid brown eyes and a complexion which would make a ripe peach want to hide itself," a coffee journal reported. Yet few coffee ads attempted any form of sex appeal for the traditional, dignified beverage. One that did, albeit in an awkward, school-boyish fashion, was widely criticized. A 1912 ad for Satisfaction Coffee depicted a can with female legs fleeing from a pursuing male. "Worth running after any time," read the text. "Always pure. Never sold in bulk." This ad was, noted a trade journal, "in questionable taste."

In 1909 Sigmund Freud and Carl Jung arrived at Clark University in Massachusetts to deliver lectures that had a profound effect on the American psyche. Soon coffee men were wondering how to "get into people's minds" to influence their buying decisions. Five years later Dr. Hugo Muensterberg, a Harvard psychology professor, lectured on the topic "Applying Psychology to Business." He made extraordinary–and frightening–claims. "Business men will eventually realize that customers are merely bundles of mental states and that the mind is a mechanism that we can affect with the same exactitude with which we control a machine in a factory."

When advertising experts from outside the industry tried to tell the roasters what to do, the coffee men didn't listen. At their 1915 convention the roasters heard from "sales counselor" St. Elmo Lewis, who told them that a negative, defensive campaign never worked. "You won't get far by calling the substituters liars." Instead he wanted the roasters to promote cooperative advertising. They should create a substantial ad fund to bring the industry out of the "stone age of advertising."

The next year H. H. Clark, an advertising man, wrote an incisive article for a coffee trade journal. He emphasized that the retailer could no longer be held responsible for pushing a particular brand. "It is sold to the consumer not by a man behind the counter, but by a chap sitting in some office possibly a thousand miles removed from the actual sale—plotting the advertising." Clark pointed out that American per-capita consumption had dropped from nearly thirteen pounds a year in 1901 to less than ten pounds. "The present situation is simply the result of . . . a policy of let things alone—let the grocer alone, let the soap clubs and wagon route men alone, let competition alone, just fight among each other for the remaining business." He too exhorted them to band together for cooperative advertising.

Clark pointed to Postum's success. C. W. Post had begun with all the odds against him, trying to sell a coffee substitute universally despised as the "war coffee" of the 1860s. Yet Post had succeeded through consistent, persistent advertising. Even though coffee was "a product with a strong natural demand," the coffee men still could not take advantage of it! Clark then outlined a specific campaign, including a seal of quality from the National Coffee Roaster Association to be sold for a tenth of a cent each to raise funds for cooperative advertising that would include billboards, street car placements, dealer displays, newspaper ads, and direct mail fliers.

Clark's article elicited only a letter to the editor indicating how right he had been. In New Orleans roaster Ben Casanas told of a retailer who had complained to him, "I am selling too many articles; go out and create a demand for your stuff, and I will sell it." Rather than taking his advice, Casanas huffed, "Think of it! He will sell it if the quality is no good, simply because we create a demand for it." With local roasters sticking to such provincial attitudes, cooperative advertising appeared to be doomed. Only the bigger roasters with broader vision and an ambition to achieve national distribution actually mounted effective ad campaigns. These roasters and their brands—Hills Brothers, MJB,

Folger's, Cheek-Neal's Maxwell House, Chase & Sanborn, Arbuckle—
were destined to dominate the U.S. coffee trade.

Hills Brothers Fills a Vacuum

With Arbuckle controlling cowboy country and most of the East, three
brands, all located in San Francisco, sparred for control of the Pacific
Coast's coffee business. While James Folger had secured a head start in
1849, Hills Brothers and MJB were challenging the older roaster by the
turn of the century.

Like the Folgers, the Hills brothers came from New England. Their
father, Austin Hills, Sr., born in Rockland, Maine, in 1823, built clipper
ships. In 1863 he joined several other Maine friends in search of the fa-
bled California gold. Failing to strike it rich, he settled for a job as foreman of a San Francisco ship building company. He left his wife and two
sons back in Maine, fetching them only in 1873, when his older son and
namesake, Austin Herbert Hills, was twenty-two, and Reuben
Wilmarth Hills was seventeen.

Three years later the siblings went into partnership as Hills Brothers
in a stall at San Francisco's Bay City Market, selling butter, eggs, and
cheese. In 1881 they bought a retail coffee store, the Arabian Coffee &
Spice Mills. They roasted coffee in front of the store, knowing that the
drama and smell would lure customers. A handbill the next year proclaimed their product "THE FINEST COFFEE in the WORLD!"
adding, "Our Coffee is Roasted on the Premises Every Day, in Full
View of the Customer." In addition to coffee they sold tea, spices, and
flavoring extracts. Reuben took charge of the coffee side of the business, while his older brother Austin continued to sell dairy products.

The 1880s brought high coffee prices, and A.H. and R.W. (as the budding businessmen preferred to be called) took full advantage. By 1884
they had abandoned retail sales in favor of the wholesale business.
Around 1886 R.W. adopted cup testing, which had been pioneered on
the Pacific Coast by fellow San Francisco coffee man Clarence Bickford.
Like a wine taster, the coffee cupper slurped in an explosive burst,
swirled the beverage thoughtfully in his mouth, then spit it into a nearby
spittoon. This cupping ceremony survives to this day as one of the more
serious—and humorous to observe—rituals in the trade.

In 1897 an itinerant artist stopped by the Hills Brothers store. R.W.
suggested that he draw a figure to represent their Arabian Roast Coffee,

as it was known then. The resulting figure, a turbaned, bearded Arab in a flowing robe, has sipped Hills Brothers Coffee ever since, even though Mocha as a preferred brand had begun to fade by the turn of the century, and most of the Hills Brothers beans arrived from Central America and Brazil.

During the Spanish-American War, Hills Brothers sold huge amounts of butter to the U.S. Army for use in the Philippines. Preserved in brine, its taste left a good deal to be desired. In 1899 R.W. stopped in Chicago during a transcontinental trip to ask Norton Brothers, who made their retail dispensers for bulk coffee beans, if they could suggest a better method for packing butter. It happened that Norton Brothers had just perfected a vacuum-packing process. It worked, preserving butter without having to pickle it.

R.W. knew that once roasted, coffee staled quickly due to exposure to air. Would vacuum-packing work for coffee too? It did. Hills Brothers quickly negotiated a contract for exclusive rights to the Norton process on the Pacific Coast for a year. It would be another thirteen years, however, before another San Francisco firm adopted the vacuum pack, and the rest of the country took much longer.

It is odd that no other coffee firm took swift advantage of the new technology. The original Hills Brothers vacuum pack, marketed in July 1900, bore the exaggerated claim that its Highest Grade Java and Mocha Coffee would "KEEP FRESH FOREVER IF SEAL IS UNBROKEN." Though this claim wasn't true, vacuum packing did distinctly improve the quality and freshness of the product. "Coffee packed in an ordinary tin, even if hermetically sealed, always contains sufficient air to oxidize the essential oil and cause the coffee to become stale," wrote R.W. on the side of the vacuum can. "The only way to prevent this is to remove the air from the package."

The vacuum pack allowed Hills Brothers coffee to spread far more quickly throughout the Pacific Coast area, arriving just in time to service another gold rush generation in the Klondike. Soon Hills Brothers Coffee had reached virtually everywhere west of the Rocky Mountains.

The Hills brothers recognized early on the importance of promotion and advertising. At an 1898 "pure food" show in San Francisco, for instance, R.W. had a sample Burns roaster installed, instructing the staff to "roast it full up" for the aroma. R.W. and Mr. Snell, the firm's first advertising director, wrote alliterative copy for a 1910 poster, enticing customers with the "peculiar, penetrating, persistent flavor of skillfully blended, rare, old coffee." Around that same time they began to keep a scrapbook of their ads, along with those of competitors. The scrapbook also contained an inspirational newspaper article that announced, "I Am Your Worst Enemy. I am the ruler of retail reverses. I am the lord High Potentate of Failure." After a daunting list of further disasters the culprit at last was identified: "I am the direct and proximate cause, the germ and the genesis of unsuccessful merchandising. . . . *I am the unadvertised product.*"

R.W. chose the color red as the most attractive and attention grabbing, naming it Red Can Brand, his top-of-the-line ground coffee. By 1912 the firm also packed brands named Caravan (Mocha), Santola (Mocha substitute), Timingo (East Indian), and Saxon (peaberry).[4] At the 1915 Universal Exposition, Hills Brothers mounted an impressive exhibition in which visitors could see coffee roasted, poured into packages, and vacuum packed, all through a glass port.

An unassuming, taciturn man, R. W. Hills believed in delegating responsibility and encouraging his employees to invent better machinery and packing methods. He trusted his motivated employees to work hard. But R.W. also suffered from periodic bouts of depression, and his tendency toward what he termed "the blues" apparently kept him from reveling in the success of his company. "It is wonderful the way the business is growing," a happy employee once commented. "Yes, but it means we must watch our step," the boss replied. "We can lose it easier than we can get it." Nor did Hills ever boast unduly of his accomplishments. "I believe that success in business is fifty per cent judgment and fifty per cent propitious circumstances."

MJB: Why?

A third San Francisco coffee firm soon battled for supremacy with Hills Brothers and Folger's. In 1850 seventeen-year-old Joseph Brandenstein fled Germany, avoiding military conscription while seeking his fortune

---

[4]Like most coffee firms of the era, Hills Brothers had to compete in every niche. Blue Can, packed without a vacuum, used lower-grade ground beans. Mexomoka combined Mexican coffee beans with cereal. Royal, Vienna, Solano, Pacific, and Tremont were all names for coffee–chicory mixtures. Royal Roast, a glazed whole roast coffee, competed directly with Arbuckles' Ariosa. The firm also produced "private label" coffee for other brands. Hills Brothers even packed coffee into lunch boxes for California children.

in California's gold fields. Instead he was robbed in the mining country and wound up in San Francisco with a partner selling leaf tobacco and cigars. He had eleven children (by his wife, that is—he also had a mistress). His three oldest sons, Max, Mannie, and Eddie, joined forces in 1899 to form a tea, coffee, and spice firm, with younger brother Charlie joining later. M. J. Brandenstein & Co. (named for Max) was truncated to MJB to minimize sibling ego conflicts and identification with their Jewish-German origins. The firm quickly shot to prominence in the California coffee world under Mannie's astute leadership.

As his daughter, Ruth, later described Mannie Brandenstein, he was a "super-salesman, raconteur, and would-be actor." A short, slight, prematurely bald man, Mannie appeared to be the exact opposite of R. W. Hills in many ways. While Hills traced his American roots to the Pilgrims, Brandenstein was a loud, brash, second-generation immigrant whose toupee had a tendency to slip sideways when he became excited. Both men, however, knew their coffee. In 1913 Mannie was the first to adopt the vacuum can pioneered by Hills Brothers.

Brandenstein christened his first brand Climax Coffee. A large four-color poster featured a sultry young woman reclining in bed, holding her morning cup of coffee, with a contented, satisfied smile on her rosebud lips. Below her was printed the single, bold word *CLIMAX*. During the raunchy mining era such a racy approach might have been appropriate, but Brandenstein soon toned it down. He had to come up with something else to grab the public's attention for the blandly named MJB Coffee. Taking his cue from C. W. Post, whose mysterious "There's a Reason" sold Postum, Brandenstein made MJB famous with the simple word "*WHY?*" that ended every advertisement. "Why the *WHY?*" asked his daughter. "What's the difference, as long as people ask?" her father answered. "That makes sales."[5]

Brandenstein used electricity to highlight his shop window displays in 1906, the letters MJB pulsing with light and messages such as "**M**ost **J**uvenating **B**lend" and "**M**ost **J**oyous **B**reakfast." By 1909 Brandenstein was placing ads in national coffee trade journals emphasizing the firm's "special pride in importing and handling the best cupping coffees procurable."

---

[5]Mannie Brandenstein also befriended and hired the legendary Albert Lasker, head of the Lord & Thomas agency and chief exponent of the popular "reason why" school of advertising, to handle the MJB account.

Brandenstein astutely picked a force of salesmen, many of whom drank too much but who could nonetheless sell coffee. On July 3, 1910, Mannie Brandenstein took one such eighteen-year-old salesman, Sandy Swann, to Reno, Nevada, where a much-publicized prizefight attracted huge crowds lusting to see the "Great White Hope," Jim Jeffries, beat the upstart black fighter, James Johnson. The night before the Fourth of July bout, Brandenstein and Swann painted "MJB COFFEE WHY?" in white lettering on hundreds of Japanese fans. Then, late at night, they painted giant green footprints leading from the railroad station to the arena. Between the steps were big white question marks and the mysterious letters MJB. The fight proved anticlimactic. Johnson easily defeated the out-of-shape Jeffries. Fortunately for Brandenstein it was a very hot day, so a sea of fans waved in the audience asking, "MJB COFFEE WHY?"

Using reverse psychology, Brandenstein often would bring in three grades of coffee beans on trays for a prospective customer. He would put the most expensive grade on a simple tray on a shelf in the corner of his office. He put the cheaper beans on a fancy tray. "I put the cheapest on my desk practically under his nose," Brandenstein explained to his daughter. "Then I point to the fancy tray on my desk and tell him here are beans that will suit his price." Immediately, the customer's eyes would wander to the other trays. "How about those beans?" he would ask. "Oh, those are top quality beans, way beyond your price." And of course those were the beans the customer bought.

Though he enjoyed racy jokes and advertising, Brandenstein refused to use racial stereotypes in his ads, even though ethnic and racial slurs were common and acceptable in that era. One of his salesmen suggested a coffee billboard depicting a black boy lying in a four-poster bed with only his head poking out from the white covers. The slogan was to read, "A Small Black," with a picture of a demitasse and the letters MJB. Mannie explained to his daughter that "we want to sell our coffee to as many people as possible, and you won't do it that way. But there's a more important reason. You and I belong to a minority and we should be the last to poke fun at another minority. . . . Jokes like these are a mean disguise for prejudice."

With enterprise, energy, and showmanship, along with a quality product, Mannie Brandenstein thus earned MJB Coffee a firm place in the West Coast coffee world.

The Great San Francisco Earthquake

All this time the San Francisco firm pioneered by Jim Folger in the 1850s continued to thrive, despite the increasing competition. In 1889 Folger had died at fifty-one of a coronary occlusion. His son, James A. Folger II, twenty-six, who had been working for the firm for seven years when his father died, took over. Under his direction Folger's specialized in bulk roasted coffee, delivered to grocery stores in sacks or drums. To attract more business he included a wooden measuring spoon in sacks of his Yosemite brand. Seeking to enhance the premium's value, he switched to metal spoons, prompting a flood of protests and lawsuits. Many grocers had not noticed the wooden spoons and had been grinding them together with the coffee beans, but the metal items broke their coffee mills.

In 1898 Folger hired Frank P. Atha, who soon became the company's top salesman. In 1901 Atha suggested a Folger's coffee outlet in Texas, where he faced the difficult task of introducing an unknown, relatively expensive product. Freight charges from the west to the east were higher than the other way round, and Arbuckle's Ariosa already held a dominant position in Texas. Atha decided to push his highest-quality Golden Gate Coffee, offering an exclusive dealership to a grocer in each area. He made a virtue of the fact that he could not afford to compete with the Arbuckle premiums, coining the slogan, "No prizes—no coupons—no crockery—nothing but satisfaction goes with Folger's Golden Gate Coffee." Frank Atha perched on the high seat of the grocer's delivery wagon, chatting with housewives and giving away free coffee samples. He also designed and installed window displays for stores. By his third year he had hired two additional salesmen.

Meanwhile in San Francisco James Folger II built a five-story factory near the piers. Completed in 1905, it was held in place by pilings driven deep into the muddy Bay floor, since it rested on newly created land, once part of Yerba Buena Cove. The next year, in the early morning hours of April 18, 1906, the Folger building was the only coffee structure to survive the famous earthquake and fire. While the rest of San Francisco burned, U.S. Marines set up headquarters in the Folger building and pumped water from the Bay. Folger's maintained "a rushing business during and just after the great conflagration," according to a contemporary account. To his credit, James Folger maintained his old prices, though he could have taken advantage of the situation.

Hills Brothers and MJB were not so fortunate. Both of their factories burned to the ground, but they quickly rebuilt and commenced roasting again. MJB received an advance payment of nearly $15,000 for an order from Kamikowa Brothers, a local Japanese-owned firm that showed its faith in the beleaguered coffee company. "Japanese understand earthquakes," their telegram read.

Chase & Sanborn: Tally-Ho

On the East Coast, Chase & Sanborn continued aggressively marketing its Seal Brand. Caleb Chase and James Sanborn, then in their sixties, retired in 1899, passing the reins to partner Charles Sias, who had worked for them since 1882.[6] Sias, the "Barnum of Coffee," loved a spectacle. A tall man, he wore a long purple coat that flowed behind him in the wind as he drove to work in his tandem horse-drawn buggy, known as a tally-ho. When automobiles later took over, Sias bought a fleet of foreign cars, including a Renault manned by a footman and chauffeur. Although Chase continued to stop into the Boston office every day until the long illness leading up to his death in 1908, the irrepressible Sias clearly enjoyed his turn at the helm.

In 1900 Charles Sias issued a little booklet, *After Dinner Tricks and Puzzles With Your Seal Brand Coffee*, an ingenious collection of thirty-six brainteasers. How many hard-boiled eggs can a hungry man eat on an empty stomach? Answer: One only, for after eating one, his stomach would no longer be empty. The same booklet featured a racist illustration of a black man with huge lips and one eye closed in an exaggerated wink, holding a scroll advertising Chase & Sanborn, "the aristocratic coffee of America, surpassing all others in its richness and delicacy of flavor." An even worse caricature from 1898 showed an old black man with gaping mouth and various missing teeth saying, "My missus says dar's no good coffee in these yer parts. Specs she'll change 'er mine when she drinks SEAL BRAND."

Sias also appealed to the sexism of the era–an approach to selling coffee that would set a tone for the century. He praised the housewife

---

[6]Chase had no children. Sanborn had two sons and two daughters, but while one son had worked for the firm, he apparently didn't take to coffee.

as "the chiefest charm and ornament" of the dinner table, because "a meal is always a feast with a lovely woman at the head of the table." And what better way to guarantee the crowning success of the meal than with Chase & Sanborn coffee—"delicious, aromatic, the odor of which is as of some rare incense from unseen censers swinging through the room." Following this religious reference, the copywriter waxed even more biblical: "Verily, the woman who can make a happy table for her husband is not only a housekeeper—she is a husband-keeper as well."

Chase & Sanborn, which already had roasting plants in Boston, Montreal, and Chicago, thrived in the first decades of the twentieth century without having to resort to giveaways. Still, over half of the firm's sales derived from their cheaper brands. In 1906 Chase & Sanborn's Western trade expanded, in part owing to the influx of coffee-loving Scandinavians. The following year Chase & Sanborn erected a new Montreal factory, to be run entirely by electricity. Business was expected to triple.

Joel Cheek Creates Maxwell House

Joel Owsley Cheek, a latecomer to the national coffee scene, was born in the rural hamlet of Burkesville, Kentucky, on December 8, 1852. After attending college he went to Nashville, Tennessee in 1873 to seek his fortune. Hired as a traveling salesman, or *drummer*, for a wholesale grocery firm there, he moved back to Kentucky to open new territory, generally riding on horseback from one general store to another.

Young Cheek made his first sale to a grocer—a relative—who asked him which coffee was best. In this rural area in the 1870s people still bought their coffee beans green for home roasting. The salesman naturally recommended his most expensive brand, though he didn't really know anything about the relative merits of the beans he sold. That night, his conscience bothering him, Joel Cheek roasted samples of each type on his mother's kitchen stove and decided that one of the cheaper brands yielded a more flavorful brew. The next day he went back to the grocer and explained why he would send the less expensive variety instead.

Experimenting with coffee samples, Cheek discovered that some origins offered superior body, others flavor, and still others "kick" (acidity). By mixing them he sought to find an optimal blend. The years slipped by, with the drummer a welcome visitor in the isolated Kentucky valleys, where he provided news and gossip along with groceries. Married in 1874, Cheek eventually spent enough time at home to sire eight sons and one daughter.

In 1884 the growing family moved to Nashville, where the successful salesman became a partner in the firm, now called Cheek, Webb & Company. There he met and befriended Roger Nolley Smith, a British coffee broker who had operated a plantation in Brazil and could reputedly distinguish between Colombian, Mexican, or Brazilian coffee simply by sniffing the unroasted beans. Together, Cheek and Smith worked on a three-country blend, with the cheaper Santos providing a base and two milds lending more flavor and acidity.

By 1892 Cheek believed he had found the perfect blend. He approached a Mr. Bledwell, the food buyer for the Maxwell House, a prestigious Nashville hotel. Cheek persuaded him to take twenty pounds free on a trial basis. After several days the coffee was gone, and the hotel went back to its former brand. When Bledwell heard complaints, he asked the chef whether there had been any change in brewing methods. No, the chef said, Cheek's blend was just better coffee. From then on, the Maxwell House bought Cheek's beans, granting his request to name the blend after the hotel following a six-month trial.

Inspired by his success, forty-year-old Joel Cheek quit his job in 1893, going into partnership with John Norton to begin a wholesale grocery firm specializing in coffee. In 1900 they were joined by John Neal, a fellow-Kentuckian who had once sold for Cheek. The following year Norton departed. Cheek and Neal formed the Nashville Coffee and Manufacturing Company, specializing in Maxwell House Coffee. They eventually changed their corporate name to the Cheek-Neal Coffee Company and established a highly successful business throughout the Nashville area. In 1905 they opened a roasting facility in Houston, Texas. Five years later they built a new plant in Jacksonville, Florida, followed by another in Richmond, Virginia, in 1916. One by one, six of the eight Cheek sons joined the firm.

The elder Cheek proved to be a promotional and advertising genius, as his push to associate his coffee with a socially prominent landmark indicated. Beginning in 1907 his ads used plenty of white space with tasteful illustrations. One spot featured a coffee cup at the top with steam wafting out of it, labeled "The Cup of Quality." The main copy read: "EVERY HOUSEWIFE who has a knowledge of coffee value will appreciate the rare quality of **Maxwell House Blend**. It is marketed strictly on its merits and is backed by one of the most complete coffee establishments in the world." The snob appeal of a high-quality brew worked particularly well to differentiate Maxwell House in the South, where cheaper blends cut with Rio and cereal traditionally predominated.

That same year, returning from a bear hunt in the Mississippi canebrakes, President Theodore Roosevelt visited the Hermitage, the famed Nashville resort, where he had a cup of Maxwell House Coffee. "Good," the ebullient Roosevelt supposedly pronounced, "Good to the last drop." Years later Joel Cheek would make the slogan synonymous with Maxwell House Coffee. In 1908 an ad appeared in the Nashville City Directory boasting that the coffee "was served to President-elect Taft and a thousand guests at Atlanta" in addition to refreshing Teddy Roosevelt at the Hermitage. To hammer home the socially upscale message the advertisement showed a gigantic woman in an evening gown serving herself an outsized cup of coffee from the top of the Maxwell House Hotel.[7]

Unlike most other coffee roasters, Cheek noted the article on the "comely, buxom lass" who sold so much milk. He hired Edna Moseley, a soft-spoken Southern belle, to demonstrate the virtues of Maxwell House Coffee at state fairs below the Mason-Dixon line. "Miss Moseley," noted the *Tea & Coffee Trade Journal*, "seems to have a happy faculty of making friends as well as customers of all visitors to her booth."

Like its competitors, the Cheek-Neal Coffee Company also put out many lower grades of coffee—over fifty brands—including chicory blends. In 1910 the company was fined for "adulteration and misbranding" of coffee containing 10 percent chicory. There *was* a strip label across the lid reading "Golden Hours Blend, coffee and chicory," but the print was minuscule, whereas the principal label proclaimed in large type, "Cheek & Neal Cup Quality Coffee."

The legal loss had little effect on the firm, however. By 1914 the sixty-one-year-old Joel Cheek, a tall, slender, active man with a well-kept beard, had become a very wealthy man. He was elected vice president

---

[7]Teddy Roosevelt probably never uttered the words "Good to the last drop." If he had, why didn't this 1908 advertisement use the phrase? The first Maxwell House Coffee ad to feature the slogan apparently appeared in the 1920s. Coca-Cola had called *its* beverage "good to the last drop" in 1908.

of the National Coffee Roasters Association (NCRA), which he had joined at its inception. It is easy to see why he was a successful salesman. Amidst all the pompous, back-biting, and long-winded speakers at the annual conventions, his voice stands out for its passion and generosity. Cheek made it clear that he favored honesty but that his famous blends didn't always cost him all that much. "The various grades of coffee you roast can be made to yield certain results in the cup that will cheapen the cost," he explained. "If you don't know that, you ought to get busy and learn it, because if you don't, you will have a hard road to travel."

While Cheek believed in the profit motive, he claimed not to extort money at the expense of others. "Any transaction between me and my fellow man that has not the moral in it on my part to profit him, is an immoral transaction." He conveyed what appeared to be a real concern for the traveling salesman, explaining that he had been on the road himself for twenty-eight years. "Bear with him in his weaknesses and shortcomings. Encourage him as much as you can. Two of the very best men I had were going to the devil from strong drink, and I saved them by treating them kindly, talking to them and pleading with them and for them, and I am proud of that record."

In his 1915 NCRA speech Cheek encouraged his audience to find "hearts in us big enough to feel that we want to help everyone, even to the porter in the basement, or the fellow on the top roasting floor." He reiterated that it wasn't enough simply to employ people. "You love them, you love their families, you are part of them." Cheek said that he cherished as his greatest compliment the time an employee stood up at a meeting and said, "We have no boss, we have a father sitting down there at the end of the table, and you all know it."

Cheek echoed the paternalism of his era of course, but among all the coffee men's speeches of that period his words stand out for their seeming sincerity. A deeply religious man, he regarded the coffee bean as a blessed object:

> We believe that this great Creator has created nothing in vain, that everything that he has caused to grow on this old earth of ours he has provided for some good and useful purpose. . . . There is not a single nation under the sun but what has in their blood a desire . . . for a stimulant of some character. It must and will be satisfied. We believe that this article that we prepare for the people is God-given. We are sure that what

we have to offer is for the good of mankind, for the great masses, for the soldier in the trenches, for the tired, weary laborer, for the poor, and for the toiler everywhere—it is almost everywhere a boon and a blessing.

Gift, Guest, or Yuban?

In 1910 Arbuckle Brothers still unquestionably dominated the national coffee scene. Its Ariosa brand accounted for one out of every seven pounds sold in the United States. But old John Arbuckle and his nephew, Will Jamison, recognized that their market share was eroding, due to increased competition from other brands. Most major competitors offered a cheap glazed coffee in direct imitation of Ariosa. Like Arbuckle, the wagon men offered premiums. People seemed to want the convenience of preground coffee rather than the whole bean. In addition, the national taste in coffee was improving, eschewing Rioy blends such as Ariosa with the reputation of a "harsh, crude, hard-drinking coffee," as one contemporary noted. Even aggressive promotions to reinvigorate Ariosa sales failed.

In March 1912, having worked right to the end, the patriarchal John Arbuckle died at the age of seventy-four, leaving an estate valued at $20 million. A pragmatist, Arbuckle, who looked more like a country farmer than an industrial titan, had respected hard work above all else. "Only workers with hand and brain are worthy of respect," he once said. "All else is chaff and rubbish." Yet he also had provided his "floating hotels" for the homeless, brought "fresh air" children from New York City to his New Paltz farm, and planned a refuge for the handicapped, along with numerous other philanthropies. Arbuckle died without a will—surprising for such a pragmatic businessman. The business, along with his New Paltz farm, eventually devolved to his nephew, Will Jamison, and to Arbuckle's two sisters, Mrs. Robert Jamison and Christina Arbuckle.[8]

Jamison recognized that something had to be done about the erosion of Ariosa's market share. As a stopgap measure he came out with a

---

[8]Although purely speculation, it is not beyond possibililty that Arbuckle left his considerable fortune to charity, and that the will conveniently disappeared. There is no question, however, that Arbuckle's sisters moved quickly to close his floating hotels, despite heartfelt pleas from its occupants: "This is the only home the majority of us possess, most of us being orphans."

ground coffee, but he also decided on a more radical departure. Like Joel Cheek, he would offer a high-end coffee, a top-quality brand to appeal to refined tastes. Cautiously, the firm approached an advertising firm for help in naming and launching the new brand. Up until this time Arbuckle Brothers had relied primarily on word-of-mouth, cheap prices, and premium coupons to sell their coffee.

After months of flirtation and courtship Jamison and his executive, G. H. Eiswald, finally hired the J. Walter Thompson Agency (JWT), where dynamic young creative types sought to bring research, psychology, and a "scientific" approach to advertising. In 1912 JWT's Stanley Resor and his top copywriter, Helen Lansdowne, arrived from the company's Cincinnati branch to take over the Manhattan operation. One of their first tasks was to create a campaign for the new Arbuckle blend. It was not really new, they learned, but had been the preferred personal drink of John Arbuckle, who traditionally had given the blend as a Christmas gift to a limited circle of acquaintances.

In November 1912 Resor wrote a fourteen-page letter outlining the JWT approach to the campaign for what he provisionally called Aro Coffee. Could Aro dominate the national coffee market, just as Ivory Soap, Crisco, Royal Baking Powder, Uneeda Biscuit, Cream of Wheat, and Baker's Chocolate had already done? What were the characteristics of those brands? Resor ticked off five factors. Such a product featured (1) high quality, (2) absolute uniformity, (3) an easily remembered name and trademark, (4) wide distribution, and as a result, (5) the product's purchase becomes "an unconscious act—a national habit."

The new Arbuckle offering apparently would have no problem with the first two items. Arbuckle already had an excellent distribution network, though Resor acknowledged that the finer grocers, such as Park & Tilford, and chain stores such as A & P would resist Aro, preferring their own brands. "The only force which can overcome this resistance of the dealer is consumer demand in large enough volume," the adman noted. Unfortunately, although the Arbuckle offering might be superior, "the product itself lacks any radically different features." Therefore the *advertising* must prompt the crucial consumer demand; it must appeal to emotions more than intellect. Resor quoted the philosopher-psychologist William James: "Our judgments concerning the worth of things, big or little, depend on the feelings the things arouse in us."

Resor recognized that the ads must appeal primarily to *women*, who bought most food and coffee. "Even before a woman tastes it, she will have made up her mind that it is unusually good and that it is the coffee she has been looking for." Coffee offered a fertile field for such advertising, Resor argued. "The fact that people spend an amount of money for coffee out of proportion to their incomes . . . in spite of the high costs and the sensational advertising done by Postum" boded well for Aro.

Addressing the all-important "*name that will wear*," the Arbuckle men suggested that the new brand be called Arbuckle's Christmas, Gift, or Guest Coffee, but Resor and his colleagues convinced them that such a generic name would never do. Besides, few people asked for Ariosa. Because the coupons were signed "Arbuckle Bros.," most consumers thought of the cheap brand as "Arbuckle's" and JWT didn't want the new brand to cannibalize Ariosa sales or be pulled down by its low-class image. How they finally arrived at *Yuban* isn't clear. One story has it that it was a truncation of "Yuletide Banquet." It is likely, however, that it was simply created as an aristocratic-sounding nonsense title.

Resor next outlined the qualities of the container. It should be attractive, distinguished, and memorable. "The air-tight, sealed package, which is broken by the woman herself," would help by "creating the idea the coffee contained inside is absolutely untouched and fresh." He capped his appeal on the final page. "Advertising is an economical selling method that has been evolved to meet new merchandising conditions. Placing merchandise on the dealers' shelves is *not selling*." Rather, newspapers, magazines, billboards, streetcars, and other advertising media offered ways to make a direct appeal to the consumer. The time was ripe for a national coffee campaign, as evidenced by "the growth of the package idea in all lines and even the intermittent, irregular advertising done by coffee roasters."

During the summer of 1913 the Arbuckle management tested JWT, approving a $74,000 ad campaign for the metropolitan New York market for newspaper ads, billboards along commuter railways, and subway signs. Over Thanksgiving the first double-spread advertisements hit twelve New York, New Jersey, and Connecticut papers. Yuban was touted as "The Private Coffee of the Greatest Coffee Merchants," the blend formerly reserved "for their personal and gift use" at Christmas. Yuban produced "the choicest, most delicious cup of coffee which can be secured, *regardless of cost*." The ad ended with the promise that by December 1 "your grocer will be prepared to supply you with this famous coffee."

JWT printed a newspaper list of some twenty-five hundred retail outlets that had already agreed to supply Yuban, inviting the public to call
on these grocers. Any dealer who ordered at least twenty-four pounds
of the new coffee could supply JWT with names and addresses of one
hundred fifty regular customers who then received a direct-mail appeal
for Yuban, listing that grocery outlet. Twenty-five well-trained salesmen
fanned out to sell the trade on "Yuban–The Arbuckle Guest Coffee," as
the coffee-colored label identified it. They carried handsome leather
portfolios of the same muted brown in which they presented the attractive advertising plan for the dealer, including point-of-purchase items
to be used in each store. For the special introduction, Arbuckle made it
possible for the retailer to sell Yuban for 35 cents a pound, about the
same price as higher-class bulk coffee.

With this well-planned campaign swinging into gear, the new brand's
sales were phenomenal. Within ten weeks Yuban outsold any other
packaged coffee in New York. In February 1914 JWT ran a full-page ad
in the New York papers boasting that over five thousand grocers in the
metropolitan area stocked Yuban. The artwork depicted three high-so-
ciety women, complete with ostrich-feather hats, taking coffee at a din-
ing-room table. "Your guests will be quick to appreciate Yuban," the
caption noted. "Its distinct individuality, its liquor, its aroma, its flavor
make it stand out from all other coffees." Customers reported, the ad
continued, that "Yuban is coffee as they have imagined it–that it has
the flavor they have wanted for years." Then JWT rolled out a similar
campaign in Chicago, with equally gratifying results.

As a reporter noted with admiration, the newspaper copy, streetcar
signs, bill posters, and window displays were carefully designed to convey "this Yuban atmosphere of refinement and 'class.'" Yet it soon became clear that snob appeal wasn't limited to the upper crust. Within a
week of Yuban's first advertisement, grocers in African-American sections of Brooklyn were breaking down 35-cent pound packages into 10-
cent units–all that the customers could afford.

The (Slow) Rise of Women

While Stanley Resor took most of the credit for the phenomenally successful Yuban campaign, he did not write the copy. Helen Lansdowne
did. In fact, the enterprising young woman from Covington, Kentucky,
had written *all* of his ads back in Cincinnati, where she had begun her

After coffee spread from Ethiopia to Yemen, the Arabs adopted it as a way of life. This early-18th-century engraving shows a cross-legged Arab sipping coffee that he poured from the ibrik on the floor.

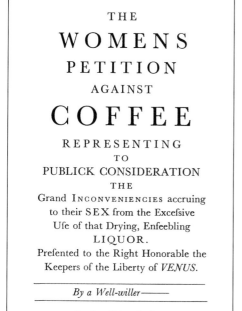

THE

WOMENS

PETITION

AGAINST

COFFEE

REPRESENTING
TO
PUBLICK CONSIDERATION
THE
Grand INCONVENIENCIES accruing
to their SEX from the Excefsive
Ufe of that Drying, Enfeebling
LIQUOR.
Prefented to the Right Honorable the
Keepers of the Liberty of *VENUS.*

By a Well-willer———

London, Printed 1674.

THE

Mens Anfwer

TO THE

Womens Petition

AGAINST

COFFEE:

VINDICATING
Their own Performances, and the Vertues of
their Liquor, from the Undeferved
Afperfions lately Caft upon
them, in their
SCANDALOUS PAMPHLET

LONDON, Printed in the Year 1674.

By 1674, London coffeehouses had become such a craze that women—who were excluded from imbibing there—protested in this pamphlet, claiming that coffee made their men impotent. The men defended their drink, saying it made "the erection more vigorous."

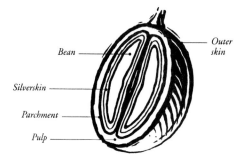

Cross-section of a Coffee Cherry

Nature has protected the coffee seed with several layers: the red outer skin, the sweet mucilage, sticky paper-like parchment, and fine silverskin. In the "wet method," the mucilage is allowed to ferment in vats so that it washes off easily.

Entire families have always harvested coffee. This picture was taken in Guatemala in 1915.

French lieutenant Gabriel Mathieu de Clieux nursed his coffee seedling, sharing his own water ration, to bring it to Martinique in 1723. From that single plant, much of the world's current coffee supply probably derives.

Sweating in a factory along the row of Carter Pull-Outs (invented in 1846) resembled labor in the lower range of Dante's Inferno amidst smoke, stress, and burned beans.

In a marketing war, Lion Coffee claimed that its coffee imparted the strength of a lion, but an Arbuckle salesman insisted that angels were stronger.

Arbuckles' Ariosa package and its floating angel became a universally recognized trademark in the late 19th century.

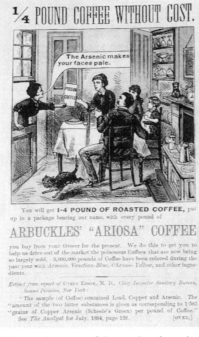

"Help us drive out of the market the poisonous Coffees that are now being so largely sold," the text below this Arbuckle ad read, referring to the widespread use of poisonous coloring agents used on other coffees.

Pittsburgh grocer John Arbuckle revolutionized the nascent coffee industry by showing how branding and marketing could sell cheap goods. Gruff but good-hearted, Arbuckle funded philanthropies such as his "floating hotels."

The Brazilian coffee industry was built on the backs of slaves imported from Africa.

An illustration from the 1904 novel *The Corner in Coffee*: "The crowd of brokers heaved and surged and swayed like a human wave. The place was like a battle-field in the tense emotions in the air, the awful passions it evoked."

The dreaded coffee leaf rust, *hemileia vastatrix*, appeared in Ceylon in 1870 and virtually wiped out the coffee industry of the East Indies within a few years. A hundred years later, it appeared in Latin America.

This 1875 photograph of bare-breasted Mayan coffee workers revealed sullen aquiescence to forced labor.

Joel Cheek, creator of Maxwell House, understood the virtues of snob appeal and advertising. He also treated his employees decently. "Put your arms around them and talk to them like you were not simply interested in them for the dollar you get out of them."

Hermann Sielcken, the arrogant Coffee King who made millions through the Brazilian valorization scheme.

In the United States, women performed the menial tasks in this 1911 coffee factory (*top*), just as Central American women sorted processed coffee beans in 1913 (*bottom*). Similar photographs could still be taken today throughout Asia, Africa, and Latin America.

Since the late nineteenth century, coffee "cuppers" have slurped, savored, and spat their favorite brew all day long—as in this 1909 scene—in an important ritual to assess body, aroma, and acidity.

U. S. Senator George Norris took on what he called the "Coffee Trust," attacking Hermann Sielcken and the valorization scheme. Here, a contemporary cartoonist depicts Norris as a David against the coffee Goliath.

C. W. Post, the brilliant, irascible inventor of Postum, was a marketing genius who called coffee a "drug drink" and ended his ads with the slogan, "There's a Reason." After claiming that his products were cure-alls, Post committed suicide when in poor health.

Reason
Ultimately Rules!

Coffee wrecks some persons

If you are steering for good, sound health and ability to "do things"— change from coffee to

POSTUM

Postum ads such as this 1910 effort, with its dramatic claim that "coffee wrecks some persons," should have alerted coffee men to effective advertising techniques. Instead, they simply fumed.

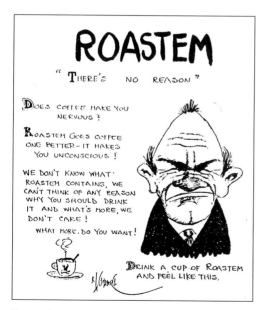

ROASTEM

" There's   no   reason "

Does coffee make you nervous ?

Roastem goes coffee one better—it makes you unconscious !

We don't know what Roastem contains, we can't think of any reason why you should drink it and what's more, we don't care !

What more do you want !

Drink a cup of Roastem and feel like this.

Postum's negative ads drove the coffee men wild. In this 1910 satirical cartoon, they fought back.

To combat health worries, coffee men loved to find consumers such as Mrs. Melinda P. Kyle, shown here in 1912 at 114 years old. She drank 3 cups of coffee every day, beginning at age fourteen.

Teddy Roosevelt supposedly proclaimed Maxwell House Coffee to be "good to the last drop"—used here in a 1921 ad—though Coca-Cola used the phrase first. It is likely that ad men made it up.

This cartoon from a Jewel Tea newsletter illustrates the lure of the "gift" percolator, a premium offered for coffee sales.

The "wagon men" of the Jewel Tea Company delivered coffee door-to-door, giving out "advanced premiums" to lock housewives into purchase plans.

advertising career in 1904 at the age of eighteen. Resor made sure she followed him to the New York office. There, she noted years later, "I supplied the feminine point of view. I watched the advertising to see that the idea, the wording, and the illustrating were effective for women." In 1911 she had been the first woman to attend a Procter & Gamble board meeting, to discuss the marketing of Crisco. "The success of the J. Walter Thompson Company has been in a large measure due to the fact that we have concentrated and specialized upon products sold to women," she said. "In grocery stores, department stores, and drug stores, the percentage of sales to women is especially high."

In 1917 Stanley Resor married Helen Lansdowne. No doubt they truly loved one another, but the union also must have eased any anxiety the groom may have had about his career. As JWT copywriter James Webb Young later observed, Resor himself "had no real flair for advertising," whereas Mrs. Resor "was an A-number 1 advertising man." She also hired other women—Ruth Waldo, Augusta Nicoll, Aminta Casseres—as JWT copywriters.

On one level these advertising women made their living by appealing to the sexism of the era, convincing women that their social status and marriage depended on using the correct brand of coffee, facial cream, or cooking oil. On another they clearly represented a new breed of woman who stood for her rights. Mrs. Resor marched in the huge 1916 Suffragette Parade along with several other JWT women.[9]

While Lansdowne and her colleagues were making their mark on coffee advertising and marketing, however, women were far slower to break into the coffee business itself, other than as overworked, underpaid menial labor. Until 1917 the Hills Brothers factory, run by the kindhearted R. W. Hills, paid male factory workers 50 cents an hour, while women received 23 cents. At the turn of the century they worked ten-hour days, six days a week, with one week of annual vacation.

At least two women did, however, break into the roasting world. In 1911 Indianapolis-based Sarah Tyson Rorer's stoic middle-aged visage stared from packages of Mrs. Rorer's Own Blend Coffee. For a brief period she advertised heavily in trade journals. "Instead of asking you to

---

[9]"Hixson's Suffragette Coffee" in 1913 featured a pretty young woman and the message, "We dedicate this coffee to the suffragette, with the hope and expectation that as we look for all that is pure, noble and uplifting in woman, her sphere of influence for good may be given broader and wider scope through suffrage."

sell *Mrs. RORER's COFFEE* in place of some other, we'll show you how to sell it where you're not selling anything now." If grocers would "just make up your mind to PUSH it," they would find it profitable. For a time Sarah Rorer's coffee achieved decent distribution in the East and Midwest, but without the marketing clout of an Arbuckle her "coopera-tive" plan failed, and her coffee and face soon disappeared.

Alice Foote MacDougall, on the other hand, achieved wealth and fame through her perseverance as a coffee roaster and, eventually, cof-feehouse owner. In 1888 she married Allan MacDougall, fourteen years her senior and an up-and-coming coffee importer on New York's Front Street. Over the next nineteen years he sank slowly into "a slink-ing, pathetic fear and a slow relinquishment, not alone of responsibility, but of all happiness and joy," as Alice MacDougall wrote in her 1928 autobiography. Her husband died of throat cancer in 1907, leaving the forty-year-old mother with three young children and $38 in the bank.

Standing less than five feet tall, afflicted by insomnia, an aversion to food, and what she herself called "hysteria," she decided to forge ahead in coffee, since she knew something about it and considered it a clean, self-respecting business. She leased a small office at 129 Front Street and had stationery printed for A. F. MacDougall. "I did not deem it ex-pedient to proclaim myself a woman by my full signature." Even so, she couldn't hide her gender on Front Street, where she encountered overt hostility. The first importer she approached refused to sell coffee to her. Still, she later admitted, "there was a certain zest in invading this very special district where men ruled supreme and where the mighty pulse-beats of a world at work could be distinctly felt."

At last she secured a supply, mixed her blend, and wrote five hun-dred letters to friends and relatives explaining her troubles and asking them to purchase her coffee. As she gradually built the business, she sent out one hundred new letters every day. Her insomnia came in handy, since she frequently rose at six and didn't arrive home until 8:30 P.M. By 1909 she was grossing $20,000 a year, but her net profit was only 4 cents a pound. Still she persevered. "I believe the only way to conquer is to walk where the battle rages most fiercely, and fight, fight, fight until you win," she wrote in her autobiography. "It is this kind of determination that man has acquired through long generations, and the woman who is to conquer in the business world must acquire it too if she is to succeed."

She also needed discerning taste buds, a lively imagination, and sales instinct. Determined to train her palate, MacDougall cupped samples, slowly learning to distinguish "the flavor of flat-bean Santos, of Peaberries, of Maracaibos old and new, Buchs, and Bogotas, and my eye at the same time was learning the differences in appearance of the green berries." She delighted in promoting her Emceedee brand (M.C.D. for MacDougall). "Are you entirely contented with your present dealer?" she queried. "Is his aim to make money for himself, or to protect *your* best interests? Does his quality always satisfy? MINE DOES." She explained that her price was set barely above cost. "No middlemen, no commissions. I buy here at first hand and deliver to you direct. . . . I buy green coffee. I know just how to blend it, just how to roast it, just how to ship it to you, so as to give you a more delicious drink at the price you want to pay than anyone else." She offered a money-back guarantee.

Her private and mail-order customers had a disheartening way of going South for the winter and to Europe in the summer, so MacDougall turned to institutions: clubs, hotels, hospitals, and colleges. Determined to sell to a well-known sanitarium on the outskirts of New Haven, she arranged to go there with an old man who owned a horse-drawn carriage. Once out in the open country, he stopped the horses, pressed close to her, and "began to make love," as she put it. She grabbed the whip from its socket and screamed at him. She never made it to the sanitarium, but she arrived back in New Haven unharmed. "That was all it was, an episode of a business day. It did me no harm. I laughed over it the next day. . . . This is the kind of thing that happens to women in business. This is the price one pays for emancipation." Indeed, she repeatedly had to fend off lechers. At one point the steward of a gentleman's club locked her in his tiny office, their knees almost touching. "A sardonic smile was on his lips. His small black eyes glistened in a quite tormenting way, and for several minutes he plied me with questions, personal and impertinent." Angry, she demanded—and got—his coffee order and her freedom.

Modern readers naturally may assume that Alice Foote MacDougall was an ardent feminist. After all, she dedicated her book "To Women— Whom I Love and Would Help," then added in the text: "It is futile to ask women not to go into business. . . . One cannot stop world movements." Curiously, however, this indomitable, tiny woman called herself an "anti-feminist." She did not think women should be allowed to vote. And her ultimate advice to women who wanted to go into business was: Don't do it. It's too hard. "If I had my way, all women would be ornamental," she declared. Nonetheless she decided to "utilize the great wave of feminine emotion" called forth by the women's movement and in 1912 began using her full name, Alice Foote MacDougall. When her son, Allan, who had joined her in the business, left to fight in World War I she employed fifteen people.

By the time of the Great War the world's attitudes and ways of doing business were swiftly changing. The conflict, though failing to make the world safe for democracy, hastened other changes—women's suffrage, alcohol prohibition, industrialization, automation, corporate mergers—and it proved to be a catalyst for change in the coffee industry as well.

~ 8 ~

MAKING
THE WORLD SAFE
FOR COFFEE

Take a carefully blended, full-bodied, highly aromatic coffee and brew it carefully ..., obtaining a heavy, delicate, enjoyable beverage. Give it to the average coffee-drinker and he will say, "This is no good." Then take the same coffee, boil it until all its delicate characteristics have disappeared and a lye-like drink has been produced and give it to the same man, who will accept it joyfully, exclaiming, "Ah! That is coffee!"

—Charles Trigg, coffee researcher, 1917

In many ways World War I marked the beginning of the modern world. It introduced technological slaughter and the term *shell shock* but also accelerated a global outlook and increased international commerce. For coffee men, the war shifted the focus of Latin America northward to the United States as its most reliable customer, while imprinting coffee drinking—often in the form of stale, inferior beans—as a regular habit among a generation of veterans.

While Europe suffered through its first modern mass carnage, U.S. roasters took full advantage of a favorable business situation created by the war. Until the conflict, the ports of Hamburg and Havre, and to a lesser degree Antwerp and Amsterdam, had commanded over half of the world's coffee. Because German coffee growers and exporters dominated much of Latin America, German importers traditionally had received the prime growths. Europeans also were willing to pay more for good coffee, leaving Americans with lower grades. With the outbreak of the World War in August 1914, however, that situation changed.

Until then most of the coffee brought to U.S. ports arrived in foreign bottoms. Legislation to bolster the virtually nonexistent American merchant marine had languished, leaving America dependent on other countries' ships. With the declaration of hostilities, every vessel flying the flag of a warring nation had to remain in harbor to avoid being sunk. A quickly enacted stopgap law permitted American registry of foreign-built ships. Firms that had never before transported coffee—such as W. R. Grace & Company, which had made its fortune shipping guano (bird dung fertilizer) from Latin America—jumped at the new business.

In the confused wartime economy, the New York Coffee Exchange closed its doors for four months. In September 1914 an editorial in a coffee trade journal called for American coffee men to act. "South American commerce, rightly ours by virtue of proximity," had been largely controlled by European capital. "Only now, when most of the nations comprising Europe are fighting for the preservation intact of their home territories and independence, have they been compelled to neglect established trade in South America." The time was ripe for aggressive American salesmen. Moreover, coffee prices were bound to decline, since the United States now represented the only major market for the beans.

"New York has become, temporarily at least, the financial and commercial center of the world," a banker informed U.S. roasters in 1915. England gave way to America as the clearinghouse for the world's business, and New York's National City Bank swiftly established new branches in Buenos Aires, Montevideo, Rio de Janeiro, Santos, São Paulo, and Havana, with the United States developing a favorable trade balance.

Latin American planters complained bitterly that while their coffee commanded lower prices, their costs for imported machinery to help process their beans and other items had doubled with the war's onset. Richard Balzac, a coffee expert who specialized in importing Colombian coffee, urged that "the thinking manufacturer of coffee" remember that he needed healthy Latin American plantations. Brazil, already suffering a financial crisis, was seeking another £25 million loan in Europe when the war broke out. Planters desperately requested that the government intervene with a second valorization scheme, but it did not act until near the end of the war. The Brazilians called the war era the *quinquenio sinistro*, the five disastrous years.

Importer J. Aron, based in New Orleans and New York, gleefully advertised, "The war has upset business to such an extent that coffee producers are being forced to market their product at prices below the cost of production. This offers an opportunity for buyers to anticipate future needs and take advantage of the present low prices." Although Brazil remained neutral throughout most of the war, hoping to sell its coffee to both sides, European consumption steadily dwindled. Shipping for a "nonessential" such as coffee was scarce. The British established a relatively firm blockade of the route from Latin America. From the highs of 1912 and 1913, coffee prices dropped precipitously in the first year of the war.

Still, a great deal of coffee did flow through to the warring countries, much of it by way of the United States. "Ordinarily, the English troops would drink tea, but it is said that coffee is being substituted, because of its more stimulating effect. The other nations are also furnishing coffee to the soldiers in large quantities," noted an American roaster. In 1915 the British impounded twelve thousand bags of coffee from thirteen different steamers shipped by the American firm of J. Aron & Company, charging that it was intended for German consumption.

Two years earlier the United States had reexported less than 4 million pounds of coffee. By 1915 that figure shot up over 1 *billion* pounds, virtually all of it headed overseas. Much of it landed in Scandinavian countries, where imports increased tenfold, then eventually found its way to German roasters.

At the same time more U.S. consumers were discovering the snappy full flavor of Guatemalan, Colombian, and other "mild" coffees of Latin America. "For a time," a reporter wrote from Guatemala in June 1915, "the outlook did seem somewhat gloomy, for Germany had always taken about two-thirds of the republic's coffee crop." Now, however, California had become the largest purchaser of Guatemalan coffee.

For many Germans in Latin America, the war proved to be a nightmare. Fearing a Teutonic uprising, the Brazilian federal government suppressed German-language newspapers and interned a number of prominent Germans. American neutrality wore thin in the face of German submarine attacks such as the one that sank the *Lusitania* in 1915, with the United States entering the war in April 1917. Brazil also went to war with Germany, but only after the United States promised to purchase a million pounds of coffee for its expeditionary forces.

The United States quickly passed legislation calling for the confiscation of "alien property" and pressured coffee-producing countries to do the same. In February 1918 Guatemala passed a similar law. Prior to the war German growers in Guatemala, who owned 10 percent of the coffee plantations, had accounted for 40 percent of the total harvest, and Germans controlled 80 percent of the country's beans. Now, under pressure from the United States, control of many German-owned coffee plantations was put under the supervision of Daniel Hodgson, a U.S. citizen living in Guatemala. The U.S. government insisted that nearly two-thirds of the German-owned plantations qualified as "enemy property." Guatemalan dictator Estrada Cabrera took advantage of the situation to enrich his own real estate holdings.

Coffee and the Doughboy

With the American entry into the war, jingoistic fervor quickly turned Germans into monsters in the popular mind. "It is a solemn time, big with destiny," intoned the editor of a coffee trade journal. "Yet the struggle between autocracy and democracy, now world-wide, must go on [for the] preservation of human freedom and civilization." These noble sentiments did not stop American coffee firms from reexporting coffee to the Scandinavian countries, however, knowing that most of the beans would end up in Germany. The same day that Woodrow Wilson declared his intention of making the world safe for democracy, coffee prices on the exchange shot up on the assumption that peace would now come quickly, along with higher prices spurred by renewed European demand.

The war did not end quite so quickly. Instead it provided a demand for even more coffee—over 29 million pounds requisitioned by the Quartermaster-General's Department for 1917. Coffee was, as a contemporary journalist noted, "THE most popular drink of the camp," imbibed at every meal.

Unfortunately, most army coffee—low-grade Santos to start with—was roasted and ground in the United States, then poorly packed. By the time it reached the troops "over there" it was guaranteed to be stale. Also, army regulations called for using only 5 ounces of coffee for every gallon of water. The grounds were to be left in the pot until the next meal, when water was added, along with another 3 ounces of coffee to each gallon of water. The result, servicemen complained, was a "flat, stale and unprofitable mess which resembled nothing so much as dishwater." E. F. Holbrook, a New Hampshire grocer assigned to the Quartermaster's Department to purchase all the military coffee, vowed to modify the hideous instructions for brewing military coffee and to set up roasters behind the lines. If bread could be fresh-baked locally, he argued, then coffee should be roasted nearby as well.

Holbrook lobbied the military, pushing the fact that shipping green beans would save considerable space, since coffee expands when roasted. General Pershing cabled authorization for roasting and grinding machinery to be sent overseas, along with professional roasters and green coffee. By the time the war ended, the U.S. Army was roasting 750,000 pounds of green beans daily.

At first the war demanded little sacrifice from the coffee roasters beyond switching to fiber rather than tin containers. Then early in 1918 cotton speculators entered the coffee market. Alarmed, Herbert Hoover's Food Administration decided to take over the coffee market and freeze the price to prevent speculation. Many importers objected, pointing out that coffee prices had actually declined during the war, whereas other consumer goods cost more. In a letter to Herbert Hoover the entire green coffee trade asserted, "If the regulations are not withdrawn, it must ultimately result in the ruination of our business." Hoover remained unmoved.

A Cup of George for the Boys

The war provided a substantial boost for the new soluble or "instant" coffees. In 1906, while living in Guatemala, a Belgian named George Washington–purportedly an indirect descendant of the first American president–conceived the idea of refining coffee crystals from brewed coffee.[1] By 1910 Washington, now an American citizen living in New York, came out with his G. Washington's Refined Coffee. Although it

---

[1]There are other claimants for the invention of soluble coffee. As far back as 1771 the British granted a patent for a "coffee compound." In the late nineteenth century, R. Paterson & Son of Glasgow invented Camp Coffee, a liquid "essence." In 1900 Tokyo chemist Sartori Kato introduced a group of Chicago coffee men to his version, sold at the 1901 Pan American Exposition and patented in 1903. Around 1906, while sitting in the Faust Cafe, St. Louis roaster Cyrus F. Blanke noticed a dried drop of coffee on his plate and invented Faust Instant Coffee. German-Guatemalan Federico Lehnhoff Wyld independently developed an instant coffee as well, eventually setting up a French soluble business just before World War I sent it into bankruptcy.

did not possess the aroma, taste, or body of coffee brewed from freshly roasted beans, this miraculous instant version did taste perceptibly like the real thing, and it provided the same warmth and caffeine content. Through persistent advertising and clever promotions, the instant coffee made its mark even before America entered the war. Still, prewar instant coffee had appealed primarily to campers and small families in search of convenience.

In the summer of 1918 the U.S. Army requisitioned the entire G. Washington output, which fact the company promptly advertised: "G. Washington's Refined Coffee has gone to WAR." The instant coffee found grateful consumers. "I am very happy despite the rats, the rain, the mud, the draughts, the roar of the cannon and the scream of shells," wrote one doughboy from his 1918 trench. "It takes only a minute to light my little oil heater and make some George Washington Coffee. . . . Every night I offer up a special petition to the health and well-being of [Mr. Washington]." Another soldier wrote, "There is one gentleman I am going to look up first after I get through helping whip the Kaiser, and that is George Washington, of Brooklyn, the soldiers' friend." The doughboys frequently called for a cup of "George" rather than coffee, and they sometimes drank it cold, not for the flavor, but for the kick.

Other coffee roasters scrambled to create their own instant coffees, and several new firms, such as the Soluble Coffee Company of America, sprang into existence. By October 1918 the army was calling for 37,000 pounds of instant coffee a day, while the entire national production was only 6,000 pounds. Then the war ended in November 1918, abruptly eliminating the market for soluble coffee and driving many of its producers out of business. Though G. Washington survived, it never established a large following, and it would take another world war to revive the fortunes of instant coffee.

Peace brought temporary prosperity to coffee producers, but not to American roasters. As it became clear that the war would end soon, Brazilian traders, anticipating renewed European demand, drove Santos futures prices to unprecedented heights. At the same time, the U.S. Food Administration ordered the liquidation of all futures contracts to avoid runaway price inflation. Aggrieved coffee men telegraphed Hoover: "Prices in producing counties are soaring and our merchants are unwilling to import because there is no free market in which they can hedge their purchases." They asked for a "contract absolutely free from restrictions." Again, Hoover remained adamant. When the war ended, the confused, frozen U.S. coffee market did not participate in the celebration. Only G. Washington's Coffee smugly announced that it had "come back from the war where it has been doing its Duty in the Trenches."

The United States Expeditionary Forces had used 75 million pounds of coffee during the war, and the American Army of Occupation in Germany continued to require 2,500 pounds of coffee every day. While the war did not make the world safe for democracy, it had addicted veterans to coffee. "It shall not be forgotten," a coffee roaster gloated, "that a good cup of coffee is one of the vital blessings of their every-day life which should not and must not be denied to them, our boys, the unbeatable, happy warriors of a coffee-loving nation!"[23]

Meanwhile, Back on the Fazenda . . .

The Great War exacerbated a trend that would continue for the next few decades: Brazil, while maintaining its overwhelming dominance of world coffee production, faced stiffer opposition from other producing countries, particularly those of Central America and Colombia. While Brazil struggled with chronic overproduction of its lower grades, the so-called mild coffee countries gradually increased their output, all of which they could sell for a premium above the price commanded by Santos.

Hit with disastrously low wartime prices, the Brazilians financed a second valorization in 1917, holding three million bags off the market. The following year, prices skyrocketed when the war ended, driven by news of a severe Brazilian frost, limited shipping space, speculators, and U.S. Food Administration restrictions. The Brazilian government quickly sold its second consignment of valorized coffee for a tidy profit.

For forty years its coffee had accounted for over half the value of all Brazilian exports. Now in 1918, despite the valorized coffee profits, it fell to a third, partly due to increased Allied demand for other agricultural essentials such as beans, sugar, and beef. In addition, Brazilian industrialization, which had lagged far behind that of the United States, doubled under the impetus of the war and tripled by 1923. Nearly six thousand

---

[2]As the war ended late in 1918, a deadly flu epidemic killed forty million people on every continent. Some believed that coffee cured the flu, but the port of Rio de Janeiro shut down with huge coffee shipments sitting on the docks, because the coffee-drinking stevedores were dying of the flu.

new industrial enterprises—mostly foodstuffs and textiles—sprang up between 1915 and 1919. While much of the capital for these ventures derived from São Paulo coffee growers, this trend signaled the gradual decline of the absolute political power of the traditional coffee barons.

Colombia Comes of Age

While advertisements featuring the mythical Juan Valdez have made Colombian coffee famous in the United States, only after World War I did Colombian coffee exports have an appreciable impact on the market. While Brazil repeatedly held back part of its crop, Colombian production increased, despite almost insurmountable odds.

Although its volcanic landscape suited it for coffee growing, Colombia's geography also made it almost impossible to get the beans to market. The best coffee-growing regions were virtually inaccessible except by way of the shallow, rapid-strewn Magdalena River. "The region is fit for settlement [only] by madmen, eagles and mules," an exasperated early Spanish explorer had observed. Besides, Colombians seemed intent on murdering one another rather than growing coffee. There were civil wars in 1854, 1859–1861, 1876–1877, 1885, 1895, and the Thousand Days War of 1899–1903, which left the country in ruins. "When we aren't in a revolution we are waiting for it," one Colombian coffee grower lamented in the late nineteenth century.[3] "Colombia still disposes of vast lands for coffee culture," Brazilian investigator Augusto Ramos observed in 1905, "but for all that the coffee industry is doomed."

Once at peace, however, Colombia turned toward coffee with the battle cry, *"Colombianos a sembrar café!"* loosely translated as "Colombians, plant coffee or bust!" When coffee prices doubled in 1912 and 1913, one Colombian writer noted "a veritable fever which is populating our lands with coffee trees." While larger plantations, called *haciendas*, dominated the upper Magdalena River regions of Cundinamarca and Tolima, penniless but determined peasants staked new claims in the mountainous regions to the west, in Antioquia and Caldas. Due to a

---

[3]Colombia of course was not alone in suffering repeated military disruptions. Many Latin American countries—particularly those where coffee had created great wealth alongside abject poverty—suffered such upheavals. "Many of the countries where coffee is grown," wrote one commentator in 1914, were "where revolutions are always hatched and brewing." Indeed, he reported, bullets were sometimes literally exported—perhaps not so accidentally—along with the coffee beans.

labor shortage, these small landowners, who became the majority of Colombian coffee growers, frequently helped one another during harvest time. This custom of *la minga*, common among the Indians, called for the host farmer to feed his guest worker, entertain him in the evening, and then reverse roles to harvest his neighbor's *finca*.

On the larger *haciendas* of the upper Magdalena River (twenty thousand trees or larger), tenant farmers lived on small plots where they could grow their own food. Although conditions were never as bad as those in Brazil, Guatemala, and El Salvador, the tenant farmers grew increasingly unhappy on the larger plantations. Conflicts focused on tenant contracts, working conditions, and the right to sell crops grown on workers' plots. Gradually, larger plantations declined as small family coffee farms proliferated. Each farm generally depulped and dried its own coffee but sold its beans to large processing plants for the final removal of the parchment.

Even during periods of coffee price declines, the tenacious Colombian farmer maintained faith in his traditional crop, and coffee became so enmeshed in the mountain culture that sprigs with red berries and glossy green leaves were used to decorate family graves. In 1915 one Colombian coffee grower prophesied: "It is necessary . . . to shove along the planting of coffee, because in that blessed berry *lies salvation.*"

In a symbiotic relationship, new railroads, relying on coffee for profits, allowed more coffee to be grown and transported, though much of it still found its way from the farther mountainous reaches on muleback. With the opening of the Panama Canal in 1914, coffee also could be exported from Colombia's previously unreachable Pacific Coast, and its Buenaventura port assumed increasing importance, taking trade from the traditional Atlantic outlet of the Magdalena River.

A contemporary visitor spoke glowingly of the Antioquia coffee region. "Far as the eye can sweep stretch those undulating slopes of deep, rich green, starred with shading banana trees of lighter emerald. The spacing between the coffee bushes is ever the same, and the ground . . . tilled and weedless. . . . Think of the care, anxiety and multitudinous energies it all means in a soil of fierce fertility, where weeds invade and assault like foaming breakers!"

In 1905 Colombia exported only five hundred thousand bags of coffee. Ten years later, exports had more than doubled. In the ensuing years, while Brazil desperately tried to control its overproduction, Colombian crops continued their steady expansion as the country's high-grown, flavorful beans found favor with American and European consumers.

While World War I closed most European markets, it provided an enormous boost to American consumption of Colombian, Central American, and other mild coffees. In 1914 Brazil had supplied three-quarters of U.S. coffee imports with 743 million pounds, but by 1919 it provided barely half, with 572 million pounds. Meanwhile Colombian imports had increased from 91 million to 121 million pounds. American consumers, noted the *Saturday Evening Post* in 1920, had become accustomed to the finer grades of coffee. "Regardless of price these consumers might never again use the Santos–Brazilian–coffee in prewar quantities." Colombian coffees named for particular localities–Bogotá, Bucaramanga, Cúcuta, Santa Marta, Manizales, Armenia, Medellin– achieved fame among coffee connoisseurs and even run-of-the-mill consumers. Within a few years Maxwell House would mention Bucaramangas and Manizales in its commercial pitches.

During the same period Central American exports to the United States had risen from 40 million to 158 million pounds. In Guatemala business returned to normal after the war, as dictator Estrada Cabrera sold most of the confiscated German farms back to their former owners, who resumed their traditional domination of the coffee industry. (The dictator also continued to hold weekly auctions to sell coffee beans confiscated from German properties.) Haiti, recovered from the long-ago slave insurrection that had ruined its coffee industry, provided 48 million pounds to the United States by the end of the war, up from virtually nothing. Even the Dutch East Indies–principally Java and Sumatra–had recovered sufficiently from the leaf rust plague to increase exports to the United States.[4]

Robusta or Bust

By 1920, 80 percent of Java's coffee crop consisted of robusta beans, the high-caffeine, disease-resistant alternative that had been discovered in the Belgian Congo in 1898, just as the leaf rust *hemileia vastatrix* was

---

[4]The U.S. coffee import figures for 1919 do not represent total U.S. consumption, however, since the United States reexported nearly 78 million pounds of coffee that year. The Haitian coffee crop previously had gone primarily to France.

decimating the East Indies' arabica crop.[5] Unlike its more delicately flavored arabica cousin, robusta—so named for its hardy growth—thrived anywhere from sea level to 3,000 feet and produced its small berries in far greater abundance. It also began bearing in its second year, earlier than arabica. Its only disadvantage lay in the cup: even the best robusta brew tasted harsh, flat, and bitter. It had to be used in a blend with arabicas, to the detriment of the latter. The Dutch, who supervised robusta's growth amidst the rubber trees of Java and Sumatra, nonetheless developed a taste for it, particularly during World War I, when its consumption in the Netherlands surpassed that of Brazilian arabica.

In 1912 the New York Coffee Exchange appointed a three-man committee to study robusta. They concluded that, even in comparison to low-grade Santos, robusta was "a practically worthless bean," and they banned it from the exchange. They were particularly concerned that Javanese robusta might be labeled *Java*, which traditionally meant the finest arabica growths.

Although some robusta plants briefly were exported to Brazil, that country swiftly moved to ban them, fearing the importation of the leaf rust spore, which had yet to reach the Western Hemisphere's coffee. Elsewhere, however, particularly where *hemileia vastatrix* had rendered other coffee problematical, robusta plantations popped up, since the Dutch provided a market for the beans. In India, Ceylon, and Africa, the sturdy robusta plant thrived on abandoned tea or coffee plantations, or in hot lowlands where coffee had never grown before.

Between Cancer and Capricorn

Ethiopia, the birthplace of coffee, now exported a negligible amount of the bean, largely due to graft and corruption extending from King Menelik down to the country's customs agents, and the situation in Yemen wasn't much better. Harrar and Mocha still produced some of the world's best beans, but they were notoriously variable in quality. By this time Jamaica's Blue Mountain coffee was famed for its full-bodied flavor. Although the British consumed mostly tea, they also appreciated

---

[5]In 1862 white explorers had observed Ugandan native use of robusta, but no one thought of using it commercially then. Members of the Baganda tribe separated two robusta beans from the same berry, smeared them with their blood, and thereby declared blood brotherhood.

the finer coffees of the world, taking most of the Blue Mountain as well
as a majority of the high-quality Costa Rican crop. Americans as well
as Europeans prized the sweet, rich flavor of the coffee grown in the
Kona district of Hawaii.

Gradually coffee reached other mountainous regions around the
world, located between the Tropics of Cancer and Capricorn. The
British encouraged the infant industry in British East Africa, soon to be
known as Kenya and Uganda. It is ironic that coffee had to come full
circle, back to Africa. Even though arabica coffee originated in nearby
Ethiopia, the seed was imported by missionaries from the island of
Réunion (formerly Bourbon) in 1901, followed by imports of Jamaican
Blue Mountain stock. Despite the arrival of the dreaded leaf rust in
1912, the coffee exports from British East Africa doubled each year until World War I delayed developments. After the war, Kenyan and
Ugandan planters–all white–continued to expand coffee growth, encouraged by new British-built railways.

Brazil nonetheless continued to dominate the coffee industry. Regardless of local conditions, the São Paulo weather report determined
coffee prices worldwide. Nervous Colombian peons sang as they
picked coffee beans:

> *Cuando está verde, está a cien;*
> *Cuando maduro, está a mil.*
> *Cuando vamos a ogerio–*
> *Grand cosecha en el Brasil.*

"When it is green, it's at a hundred; / When ripe, it's at a thousand. /
When we go to pick it– / A big harvest in Brazil." In other words, no
matter how hard the Colombians worked or how high the quality of
their beans, a large Brazilian harvest drove their coffee prices down.
Their frustrations and fears were undoubtedly echoed in other lan-
guages around the coffee-growing world, ranging from Amharic to
Hindi, as the coffee trade nervously faced the world following the
Great War.

~ 9 ~

SELLING AN
IMAGE IN
THE JAZZ AGE

Professor Prescott speaks of the influence of coffee as a 'beneficent exhilaration' and as tending to increase the power to do muscular work as well as the power of concentration in mental effort. . . . In a sad world, and especially in a country like ours, recently and constitutionally deprived of wine . . . the function of coffee in bringing serene delight is an important one.
—*Boston Transcript* [newspaper], 18 October 1923

While Brazil and other coffee growing countries vied to supply their share of caffeine to the industrialized countries of the north, the jazzed-up North Americans entered a golden age of hustle in which business, advertising, and consumption defined a decade. Coffee emerged as a widely accepted drink, the scourge only of the most ardent health faddist, and it fueled the energetic decade of the twenties.

Prohibition and the Roaring Twenties

National prohibition raised the hopes of coffee producers and roasters around the world. During World War I the American temperance movement had persuaded Congress that the use of grain to make alcohol was an unpatriotic waste of potential food. Along with long-term pressure from the temperance movement, this argument pushed the legislature to pass the Eighteenth Amendment to the Constitution in

1917, prohibiting the manufacture and sale of alcoholic beverages in the United States. In January 1919 the amendment was ratified by the states and went into effect the following year, along with the Volstead Act to enforce it.

Most coffee men rejoiced, assuming that their beverage would replace booze as the preferred pick-me-up on social occasions. "I believe there are great possibilities in coffeehouses succeeding the saloon as a community center," one roaster said hopefully. Another penned doggerel to celebrate the event:

> *When there's such a drink as this,*
> *Liquor never need we miss.*
> *All its virtues we repeat:*
> *"Coffee! Coffee! That's the treat!"*

Coffee consumption in fact did climb slowly throughout the 1920s. "Prohibition has created a situation favorable to increased consumption of coffee," wrote William Ukers in the *Tea & Coffee Trade Journal.* "Many users of alcoholic stimulants who seldom drank coffee before now use it regularly. While the coffeehouse idea has not expanded as rapidly as some anticipated, nevertheless coffee cafes and lunch counters have supplanted hundreds of saloons."[1] Changing eating habits also helped, as light midday meals at luncheonettes and soda fountains brought requests for a sandwich and a cup of coffee. Some factories began to offer free coffee as a work incentive. As Americans became ever more mobile on expanding roadways, they chose coffee as the drink for driving. The truck stop meant the coffee stop. "The 2,000,000 American soldiers who went overseas," Ukers continued, "and there had their coffee three times a day, learned to have a keener appreciation of coffee's benefits, and since returning to civilian life are using it more than ever before."

Yet the most positive influence was probably the first national advertising campaign. Funded by the Brazilian growers via a domestic tax on every exported bag but executed by N. W. Ayer, an American advertis-

---

[1]A Chicago journalist wrote a satirical piece about "The Face on the Coffeehouse Floor" in which "the bartender . . . can tell by your trembling hand and your shaken nerves that you are after coffee."

ing firm, the campaign got under way in 1919 with spots in popular weekly magazines. Most of the ads were bland and predictable. "Your Uncle Sam provided his boys with COFFEE." Coffee was "the drink of intellectuals." All ended with the slogan, "Coffee–*the Essential Drink.*"

After a New York roaster complained that the ads were "spineless, supine and too damned dignified" the copy became a bit more aggressive, fighting back at Postum and other coffee bashers. "It is so easy to get false notions, *but–of course* COFFEE *is Healthful.*" Ads were placed not only in women's magazines but also in medical journals. "Don't Take the Joy Out of Breakfast," the coffee men begged doctors. "Yet isn't that just what you are doing when you unreservedly rule Coffee from the dietary of every patient?" The joint advertising committee even produced generic ads meant to help individual roasters. "Good coffee means _____ brand of coffee. It is fresh and clean–with a fine full body and a rare, rich fragrance. You'll be much taken with the taste!"

The content of the advertising probably didn't make as much difference as its repetition and visibility. At least there finally *was* national advertising for coffee–even if financed by growers in another country. The first year, the Brazilians paid $250,000 for the magazine and newspaper spots, while the U.S. coffee men contributed only $59,000, enough to finance a film, *The Gift of Heaven*, depicting coffee cultivation and consumption, which was shown in some two hundred theaters across the country and donated to colleges and high schools. They also developed a kit aimed at fourth, fifth, and sixth graders–for suggested use in geography, history, foods and cookery, school assemblies, and even English composition–hoping to indoctrinate young children with coffee's virtues. A *Coffee Club* monthly newsletter presented the latest-breaking (favorable) coffee news, along with a cartoon featuring the exploits of Kernel Koffee, a combination tycoon–Southern gentleman. "Men of affairs talk business over their coffee," he explained. "It gives them inspiration."[2]

The national advertising campaign undoubtedly helped boost coffee's image and sales but did cause some problems initially. The Brazil-

---

[2]The *Coffee Club* newsletter sometimes strained for illustrations. On a 1924 cover three bored-looking young men dressed in suit and tie stare into space over their coffee cups, with the caption: "A corner of the Yale Club … with a coffee party in full blast."

ians objected that although they were paying for the ads, none so much as mentioned Santos or Rio coffees. Brazil thereafter began receiving plugs in the promotional copy, even though that country's coffee generally lowered the quality of a blend. In addition, few roasters donated money toward the campaign, even though it benefited them. In an effort to punish nonparticipating roasters, newspaper ads were limited only to regions whose roasters had contributed money. Consequently, ads appeared in only thirty-six states in 1921. The desperate joint publicity committee of the National Coffee Roasters Association drafted an appeal to the much-hated peddlers, chain stores, and mail-order coffee companies. "This campaign is yours as much as any other coffee interest's. You have shared in its benefits."

The twenties also witnessed the coffee industry's first effort to sway public opinion with commissioned scientific research. In 1921 the National Coffee Roasters Association hired MIT professor Samuel C. Prescott to review existing studies on coffee's health effects, as well as to conduct his own experiments. After three years his "dispassionate study of the vast literature on the subject," combined with his "long-continued studies," led him to conclude (not surprisingly) that "for the overwhelming majority of adults, Coffee is a safe and desirable beverage." Prescott also asserted that coffee "whips up the flagging energies [and] enhances the endurance." It was useful as an antiseptic, and "an encourager of elimination." The association's joint publicity committee trumpeted Prescott's conclusions (omitting mention of coffee's diuretic effects) in newspaper ads that reached fifteen million readers countrywide. Reporters and food writers across America picked up the Prescott story, often adding favorable editorial comments.

One indication of just how much the public attitude toward coffee had changed in twenty years was the decline in Postum sales. Vicious anticoffee ads in the grand tradition of C. W. Post no longer worked. In 1924 Postum hired the Erwin Wasey Agency (a young spinoff from Lord & Thomas) to take over from the old in-house agency. New ads featured radiantly healthy, happy people enjoying the drink. "It is not an imitation of coffee or anything else," the 1924 copy proclaimed in the *Saturday Evening Post.* "It is an excellent drink in its own right." At the same time, account executive John Orr Young junked the old "There's a Reason" slogan as old-fashioned and silly. The new ads temporarily halted Postum's sales decline, but the drink would never again challenge coffee's supremacy.

The Coffeehouse Resurgence

Owing to Prohibition, positive publicity, and a public eager to socialize, coffeehouses opened throughout the twenties in major U.S. cities. A 1923 *New York Times* feature article announced a "Coffee-Drunken New York." The subtitle explained, "That's Why It Is So Relentlessly Tense, or, So to Say, Jazzed Up." Coffee officially entered—and helped to create—the jazz age. "Men who drank one cup of coffee before prohibition take two now," the article stated. "The number of men and women who breakfast on nothing but coffee is increasing. And there is an all-day call for coffee as a pick-me-up after moments of stress in business."

That same year the U.S. per-capita consumption of coffee rose to thirteen pounds—the figure had hovered around ten or eleven pounds for years—with Americans consuming half of the world's supply and proud of it. When one New Jersey man read that the average American drank 500 cups of coffee a year, he wrote to Secretary of Commerce Herbert Hoover that he drank twelve cups a day (except on Sundays) for a total of 3,764 a year. "Do I win the prize?" he asked. In 1927 barbershop porter Gus Comstock of Fergus Falls, Minnesota, set a new record by consuming 85 cups of coffee in a little over seven hours. "You're the cream in my coffee," crooned a popular 1928 love song. "You will always be my necessity, I'd be lost without you." By that time coffee indeed had become a staple of American life.

Alice Foote MacDougall published her autobiography the same year. Having clawed her way into the man's world of coffee roasting, she made her fortune during the twenties with her coffeehouses. Just before Christmas 1919 she opened the Little Coffee Shop in Grand Central Station. At first, in her tiny twelve-by-sixteen-foot space, she sold only whole coffee beans—and not very many of them. Then she added a huge electric percolator to entice potential buyers with the aroma. Seeking to create "a place of rest and beauty, a little haven to entice the weary commuter to sit down," she began to sell coffee by the cup at tiny tables.

Then one blustery February day in 1921 MacDougall had an inspiration. "As I entered the Grand Central, I found the huge corridors packed with a damp mass of miserable humanity." She called her apartment and ordered her waffle iron and ingredients, and placed a small sign in the window, WAFFLES. She gave them away, charging for the coffee only. The following Saturday she tried it again but this time charged for the waffles. "Almost before we realized it, we were serving coffee and waffles every day, and all day, and turning people away by carloads."

In 1922 MacDougall opened a second coffeehouse on Forty-third Street and served two hundred fifty customers the first day. She hired black women to cook the waffles at each table, "suggesting the Southern-waffle, colored-mammy, log-cabin idea."[3] Soon she added sandwiches and then "all the delicious foods we could think of."

By March 1923 MacDougall's coffeehouse was serving three full meals to capacity crowds, but she was exhausted from eighteen-hour days and took a much-needed European vacation. "Soon the beauty of Italy and of the gentle laughing Italian people overflowed my senses and life began anew." Back in New York MacDougall rented an adjoining store, doubling her seating capacity less than a year after opening. The new space was narrow, long, and eighteen feet high. Inspired by Italian walls, "broken and crumbling with age . . . every crack filled with tiny vines or baby flowers," MacDougall transformed the high wall of the annex, and the space below became a small Italian courtyard, or *cortile*, which is what she renamed the restaurant. She made her coffeehouses "places of rest for New York, as Italy had been a soul-reviving experience for me."

At the end of the year, with business booming, MacDougall opened a third coffeehouse, the Piazzetta, on West Forty-third Street, based on a little square in Naples. The fourth, the Firenze, opened on Forty-sixth Street in 1925, imitating Florence. Here she created a little Italian street, providing quiet nooks where "lovers or near lovers can enjoy themselves detached from the crowd" while sipping coffee and eating. In 1927 she opened her fifth and largest coffeehouse, the Sevillia, on West Fifty-seventh Street, signing a million-dollar lease for the property ($50,000 a year for twenty years). By the time she published her book in 1928, MacDougall's coffeehouses employed seven hundred people, served six thousand customers a day, and grossed $2 million a year. The following year she opened her last coffeehouse on Maiden Lane. While Alice Foote MacDougall's extraordinary success was unusual,

---

[3]The author's mother, an Atlanta native, credits the Alice Foote MacDougall coffeehouses with saving her life when she was a little girl visiting New York with her mother in the twenties. "I was scared to death of white waiters, whom I had never seen. I would only eat at the coffeehouses where blacks served the food."

many other coffeehouses also opened in major American cities during the decade.

Eight O'Clock Rocks and Jewel Shines

While coffeehouses thrived during the twenties, so did direct coffee sales to consumers, with A & P leading the way. During World War I John Hartford opened hundreds of stores. After the war the pace quickened, with *thousands* of new stores. Overall sales rose dramatically, from $193 million in 1919 to $440 million in 1925, by which time there were fourteen thousand A & P stores across the United States.

A & P had become the largest chain of stores in the world. The Hartford Brothers decentralized into six divisions, each with its own president and staff organization. A central purchasing office oversaw subsidiary corporations. Berent Johan Friele ran the American Coffee Corporation, the coffee-buying arm of the company. A German-schooled Norwegian, Friele was raised in his family's coffee business. While working on the export side in Brazil, he did some work for A & P on the side. In October 1919 at the age of twenty-four he was hired full time to supervise A & P purchases in Brazil. Over the next two decades Friele became the most powerful and knowledgeable coffee buyer on earth. By 1929 A & P sold over a billion dollars' worth of groceries, with coffee—ground fresh at the checkout counter—its best seller.

The wagon men for the Jewel Tea Company also thrived during the twenties, though the company nearly had gone bankrupt at the beginning of the decade. In 1916, with eight hundred fifty wagon routes and a net profit of $1.4 million the previous year, the company had embarked on a major expansion program, more than doubling the number of wagon routes and opening three new coffee-roasting plants. Just after the gigantic Hoboken plant—intended to supply most of the coffee for Jewel—went into operation, the U.S. War Department commandeered it for war production. At the same time, with so many young men at the front, Jewel had difficulty finding appropriate new wagon men.

In 1918 profits fell to a mere $700,000, and in 1919 the company lost $1.8 million. Jewel drivers went on strike for higher wages, since most were earning no commission. With the company failing, founders Frank Skiff and Frank Ross retired, and thirty-six-year-old John M. Hancock, who had served as a naval purchasing agent, led a financial retrenchment. In 1922 Hancock, newly elected president, hired his old navy buddy, Maurice H. Karker, as the Jewel general sales manager.

Hancock and Karker lit an inspirational fire under the company. Net profits grew to $624,000 in 1923 and $855,000 in 1924. That year Hancock left to join Lehman Brothers, and Karker, a heavyset, round-faced executive with slicked-back hair, took over. By 1926 he had pushed profits to $1.2 million, and the last horse-drawn wagon had been replaced by a delivery truck.

Perhaps more than any other coffee business, Jewel profited from the motorization of America, though during the twenties the incredible transformation wrought by the automobile affected every business. Whereas villages once had prospered only along railroad tracks, they now formed at the confluence of roadways. Along these newly paved roads sprung up filling stations, hot dog stands, coffee shops, restaurants, and campgrounds—all more places to buy and drink coffee. A more mobile nation could drive more easily to a chain store for bargains, even if it meant spending more on gas; but the better roadways and growing suburbs also allowed Jewel drivers to cover new fertile ground.[4]

In 1929 construction began for Jewel Park, the future company headquarters, on 200 acres in Barrington, a rural community near Chicago. A planned community would surround the plant, with low-cost homes for Jewel employees. By the end of the decade Jewel had rebounded brilliantly, with $7 million in assets, 1,200 motor routes, 2,400 employees, and nearly a million faithful customers. Coffee provided over half of the sales for the company, with the gigantic Hoboken roasting plant capable of turning out 150,000 pounds a day. Jewel had become a fixture in the lives of loyal customers, while every employee was indoctrinated in the "Jewel Way," exhorted to think like the salesman who said, "If I can get to the point where somebody will refer to me as a typical Jewel man, I'll feel perfectly satisfied."

---

[4]The rise of the automobile affected the coffee industry of Venezuela as well. Located at the top of South America, east of Colombia, Venezuela's mountains provided ideal coffee-growing conditions. In 1920 coffee provided two-thirds of the country's exports, but during that twenties rich oil deposits offered a more lucrative alternative, and coffee cultivation declined.

The West Coast Brands Move East

In San Francisco, which now specialized in the higher-quality Colombian and Central American mild coffees, Hills Brothers, Folger's, and MJB continued to battle for supremacy while expanding their sales territories toward the east. Following Hills Brothers, MJB and Folger's finally had adopted the vacuum can. Folger's Golden Gate Coffee even began to appear in a red can like Hills Brothers. "These red containers make a striking display. They attract attention," a 1920 Folger's letter to dealers advised. The memo itself attracted the attention of H. G. "Gray" Hills, the son of original founder, A.H. "Some nerve," wrote Gray Hills in the margin of the letter he pasted into the Hills Brothers scrapbook.

Hills Brothers had emerged as the leading regional coffee, outselling other brands in half of all grocery stores. The two aging Hills brothers, A.H. and R.W., still monitored the business but their children had taken over the day-to-day decisions. Prior to World War I Hills Brothers Red Can vacuum-packed coffee was sold throughout the seven western states, part of Montana, and Alaska. In 1920 it moved into New Mexico, Colorado, Wyoming, and the rest of Montana. Throughout the rest of the twenties the company steadily marched east, systematically saturating every new area with newspaper ads while salesmen set up window displays in local retail outlets.

Meanwhile at MJB a family rift threatened to pull apart the Brandenstein brothers. Fearful of German-bashing superpatriots during World War I, Mannie Brandenstein and his brothers Eddie and Charlie had "neutralized" their name to Bransten, angering Max and the other siblings, who refused to abandon their real surname. The brothers united after the war when a poor investment in rice threatened to bankrupt the company. The crisis broke Mannie's ebullient confidence and he died soon afterward, but the family company revived after his death by concentrating again on coffee.

The original Jim Folger's son, James A. Folger II, in the meantime continued to lead the oldest San Francisco coffee firm. Folger himself sent word early in 1921 to the troubled Brandenstein–Bransten firm that he would help to bail them out if necessary; but on July 5, 1921, Folger, like his father, died prematurely of a heart attack at fifty-seven. Ernest R. Folger, his younger brother, now assumed the presidency of both Folger companies (in Kansas City and San Francisco). When James A. Folger III graduated from Yale in 1922 with a degree in physics and economics, he joined the family business in the new advertising department. In Kansas City, Frank Atha's sons, Russell and Joseph, also joined the firm.

Under the new management Folger's newspaper ads boasted, "We Go 10,000 Miles for Coffee," taking advantage of the distance the beans traveled from plantation to roaster, and stressing the uniform flavor of its blend. The ads also played up the insecurity of housewives, for whom a good after-dinner coffee meant social status. Folger's billboards offered "A Word to the Wives . . . Folger's Coffee," while a sexist 1922 ad explained, "It's a Vital Matter, Madam—to the Men." If the coffee lacked flavor, "It's a *brand's* fault, not yours."

Struggling to recoup from the Cuban rice disaster, MJB, now under the leadership of Mannie's bellicose brother Max Brandenstein, targeted the lower price range. "Which Coffee is the MOST ECONOMICAL? In a Coffee with the flavor and great strength of M.J.B. you use half as much as of inferior grades." Such a claim was preposterous, leading only to a watered-down brew—but it did sell coffee.

Hills Brothers at the same time hired N. W. Ayer to design their advertising campaigns. In 1921 they placed Red Can spots in every streetcar west of the Rocky Mountains. "Rich flavored and full bodied: Selected from the finest plantations and vacuum packed." That September Eddie Hills, R.W.'s son, wrote to his uncle that "we have been going very strong this month. [For two weeks] we were obliged to run the factory until ten o'clock at night. . . . Things have been running very smoothly with no complications."[5]

Yet things soon *did* become complicated. To boost sales, the spreading chain grocery stores sometimes sold brand-name coffee below their own cost. The small grocer could not compete. Led by Hills Brothers, several coffee firms instituted a "minimum resale price" to protect the traditional retailers. Beginning in fall 1920 Hills Brothers refused to sell to any firm that did not resell their coffee for *at least* a nickel more than the wholesale price, which allowed approximately an 11 percent markup—usually just enough to cover overhead and give a small profit

---

[5]Things may have run smoothly under the direction of the second generation, but the generous treatment of employees was eroding. In 1922, according to a company memo, "the practice of distributing coffee gratuitously to employees" was discontinued.

to the grocer. The rapidly growing Piggly Wiggly chain balked, vaunting the fact that it sold only at cut-rate prices. "No Hills Coffee," its headline advertising read. "Shall the Consumer Be the Goat? No! Never! A thousand times No!" The ad explained that Hills Brothers insisted that the chain raise prices 1 cent per pound.

For its stand Hills Brothers became an instant hero to smaller retailers. The California trade journal, the *Retail Grocers Advocate*, urged readers to "boost Hills Bros. Coffee at every opportunity—morning, noon and night." The editor praised Hills Brothers for standing up to Piggly Wiggly, "this mire-wallowing, squealing, price-cutting outfit."[6] He blasted MJB, Folger's, and Schilling as "outlaw roasters" for selling to the chains and not enforcing a minimum retail price. A Hills Brothers executive declared it "a war, not a battle," and vowed a fight to the finish.

Despite the minimum resale price, the chains' triumph appeared inevitable. Ironically, it was hastened by the Federal Trade Commission, which had been created in 1914 for the purpose of insuring fair competition. In 1925 the FTC sued Hills Brothers for price fixing and constraint of trade. In vain the Hills Brothers briefs pointed out that their minimum resale policy effectively *promoted* competition by protecting the small corner grocery against predatory price cutting. The FTC ruled against the minimum resale price plan.

The legal setback did not stop Hills Brothers' aggressive drive toward the east. By 1925 the firm sold nearly half its coffee outside of California, and that percentage would increase substantially in the next few years. Their ad copy played up their rugged Western origins. "The robust West *loves its vigorous drink*," copy read, while an illustration showed a bronco rider. Another ad portrayed a mountain scene with "Gorgeous heights and deep ravines . . . and Hills Bros. Red Can Coffee." Out in this territory "a canyon is a *canyon*—dizzy-deep and awesome. And coffee is *coffee!*"

By 1926 Hills Brothers was spending a quarter of a million dollars on advertising, mostly in California, Oregon, Missouri, and Utah newspapers. In 1927 the firm opened a sales division in Minneapolis, quickly establishing itself as the leading brand in the Twin Cities area. In

---

[6]Other trade journals, however, roasted Hills Brothers. "The lousy nickel margin which Hills pretends to maintain is worse than no protection." The margin was not enough to allow for a decent profit. "We believe that Hills Bros. don't care a tinker's damn about the retail grocer only in so far as they can capitalize it to their own pocketbook."

December of that year N. W. Ayer conducted an industry survey of over two hundred towns in the Midwest. The emerging portrait showed an industry in transition, ripe for a major advertising campaign. Nationally advertised brands such as Chase & Sanborn and Maxwell House frequently appeared, but rarely as the leading brand; usually a local brand predominated. In fifty-five stores in Aurora, Illinois, for instance, the survey found eighty different brands. In addition, unbranded bulk coffee still outsold the brands in a sizable minority of the stores. Grocers in the rural areas reported that the Jewel Tea peddlers had grabbed as much as 20 percent of the entire coffee business.

In 1928 Hills Brothers opened a Chicago office. For two years they systematically canvassed areas around the big midwestern city in preparation for the big push in Chicago itself. To encourage sales, Hills Brothers began a "sampling campaign," giving away half-pound cans to everyone in a targeted small town, while installing store displays and placing full-page newspaper ads in the local papers. The results often were spectacular. In Milwaukee, when the campaign began in October 1928, Hills Brothers was virtually unknown; two months later it was the best-selling public brand of coffee in the city, though A & P's private Eight O'Clock brand still held the lead.

No longer content with batch-roasted coffee, Hills Brothers' engineers created a long roaster through which beans continuously passed on a conveyer belt. This assembly-line approach assured a uniform roast but destroyed the art of the individual roast master, who fine-tuned each batch to the needs of the particular beans. Hills Brothers nonetheless made their new "controlled roast" the focus of their 1929 advertising, touting it with clever cooking analogies: "To thoroughly bake a hundred-pound fish would be a whale of a job," a headline read, along with an eye-catching illustration of a housewife attempting to do just that. Similarly, the ad explained, coffee had to be roasted just a bit at a time, in a continuous process. For those who didn't know much about roasting coffee, the ads were effective. More important, they were relentless and ubiquitous.

At the end of the decade Hills Brothers was an exceedingly well-managed company. Although still family-owned, the firm was run by second-generation professional managers with near-military precision. Indeed, war analogies surfaced frequently in sales bulletins. "The guns are loaded, men–firing has commenced–the ammunition piles are huge and handy—there will be no let-up in the battle from now on, until the Hills Bros. flag flies from the topmost height." At company conventions employees sang their allegiance to the revered old brothers, A. H. and R. W. Hills: "Hail to you our honored Chieftains! / Staunch, untiring, loyal Captains! / Success was won by constant effort, / 'Red Can' goes marching on."

The Decline of Arbuckles'

While Hills Brothers and other brands demonstrated the wisdom of aggressive expansion and massive advertising campaigns, the incredibly swift decline of the house of Arbuckle provided a cautionary tale. In 1921, as executive M. E. Goetzinger wrote in a brief history of the firm, Arbuckle was "the world's greatest coffee business." Its Jay Street Terminal in Brooklyn was equipped with its own freight station, locomotives, tugboats, steam lighters, car floats, and barges. It owned motor trucks and horses, a gigantic printing press for coffee wrappers and circulars, and a barrel factory, in addition to massive roasters and a sugar refinery. "A more self-contained plant plan than ours it would be hard to imagine," Goetzinger bragged. On staff were physicians, chemists, steamboat captains, chauffeurs, teamsters, wagon makers, harness makers, machinists, draughtsmen, blacksmiths, tinsmiths, coppersmiths, coopers, carpenters, masons, painters, plumbers, riggers, typesetters, pressmen, chefs, and waiters. There were engineers of every description: mechanical, civil, electrical, chemical, railroad.

After John Arbuckle's death in 1912, his nephew, Will Jamison, had successfully launched the high-quality Yuban brand with his mother, Mrs. Catherine Arbuckle Jamison, and aunt, Christina Arbuckle, as financial partners. According to Goetzinger, the two elderly sisters took "the keenest interest in all our more important problems," but they did not take part in active management.

In 1921 Arbuckle Brothers made a fateful decision. The J. Walter Thompson advertising men, jubilant over the swift ascendancy of Yuban in New York and Chicago, wanted to take the brand national. On April 30 they presented a comprehensive 33-page report documenting "the opportunity for a nationally advertised coffee, and none is in so ideal a position to take advantage of it as Yuban." The agency suggested a major full-page advertising campaign in the *Saturday*

Evening Post, Ladies' Home Journal, and *Pictorial Review.* The five-year campaign would cost Arbuckle Brothers approximately 1.5 cents per pound of coffee.

But Arbuckle Brothers rejected the plan. A JWT memo offers only one sentence of explanation: "After consideration, they decided that the effort and cost of going national was too great for them." It is surprising that Will Jamison would not have recognized the wisdom of the campaign, since he had been responsible for Yuban's triumphant 1912 introduction. Although it is only surmise, it seems likely that his mother and aunt, who owned the majority of the stock, vetoed what appeared to them to be an expensive and perilous undertaking.

Whatever the reason, Arbuckle Brothers stopped growing. Within the next few years the two elderly women died. Then in 1928 Will Jamison also died, leaving the company to his two sisters, Margaret and Martha Jamison, who neither married nor took much interest in the coffee business. By the end of the twenties the once-mighty Arbuckle empire still owned the Jay Street Terminal, but its brands had been largely pushed off the shelves by nationally advertised brands. The frustrated J. Walter Thompson men gave up the Arbuckle account and began to look for another coffee that they could promote in popular consumer magazines.

The Corporate Monsters Swallow Coffee

In the summer of 1929, within months of one another, two new corporate giants came into being, signaling a new age in the production of consumer goods and the ultimate death of family businesses. In February Royal Baking Powder Company snapped up Chase & Sanborn Coffee, whose gross sales now topped $12 million annually. A few months later the Fleischmann Company bought Royal, along with Chase & Sanborn, and reincorporated as Standard Brands. Already delivering perishable yeast twice a week to grocers, the new management put coffee on the same trucks, adding the packaging date. "It's dated," ads announced, supposedly assuring Chase & Sanborn's freshness.[7]

---

[7]Fleischmann's Yeast provided 86 percent of Standard Brands' profits. The J. Walter Thompson ad agency sold it not only as a food product but as a medicine to cure acne, constipation, fatigue, rheumatism, headache, old age, and the common cold. The JWT men paid European doctors to vouch for the yeast's magical effects.

In July 1929 Postum, which had already swallowed Maxwell House Coffee, renamed itself General Foods. Maxwell House had been a very attractive acquisition. Under the leadership of Joel Cheek and his numerous offspring it had continued to expand throughout the twenties. In 1921 Maxwell House had entered New York, building a gigantic roasting plant in Brooklyn and running ads that showed flappers sipping from dainty cups, "Good to the Last Drop." In just over two years Maxwell House had overtaken Yuban to become Manhattan's top brand.

The Southern coffee's successful invasion of New York City naturally attracted the attention of the J. Walter Thompson admen, whose national ad proposal had been turned down the year before by Arbuckle Brothers. In 1922 JWT executive John Reber approached Frank Cheek, who managed the Brooklyn plant, but he couldn't shake the Maxwell House allegiance to its little-known advertising agency, Cecil, Berreto, and Cecil. After two years of courtship the JWT men finally won the cherished Maxwell House contract. The coffee firm had just opened a new roasting facility in Los Angeles. "An important factor in our favor proved to be our having a going California office," a JWT memo noted.

Another factor may have been the Thompson agency's increasingly sophisticated manipulation of potential consumers through a combination of surveys and psychology. Although Walter Scott Dill had written *The Psychology of Advertising* in 1913, his approach had been quite simplistic. Now the psychologists promised amazing results based on "scientific" principles.

In 1921 the J. Walter Thompson agency hired John B. Watson, famed as the father of behaviorism, a new school of psychology emphasizing how positive or negative stimuli could shape behavior. According to Watson, humans responded best to stimuli that evoked fear, rage, or love. "Tell [the consumer] something that will tie [him] up with fear, something that will stir up a mild rage, that will call out an affectionate or love response." Once surveys revealed which buttons to push, "any object or person in the world can be made to call out a love response."[8]

---

[8]John Watson was not the only one who made such observations. In 1922 the novelist Sinclair Lewis created George Babbitt, the quintessential American consumer for whom "standard advertised wares ... were his symbols and proofs of excellence; at first the signs, then the substitutes, for joy and passion and wisdom." Every morning the insecure Babbitt "gulped a cup of coffee in the hope of pacifying his stomach and his soul."

He sought "such proficiency in our science that we can build any man, starting at birth, into any kind of . . . being upon order."

When Watson arrived at J. Walter Thompson, he spent nearly a year in a kind of advertising boot camp. "Yubanning is a strenuous job," Watson wrote to a friend. "We are up at 6:30 A.M., have a meeting at 7:45 and by 8:15 we are on the trail of the grocer." By 1924, when JWT snared the Maxwell House account, Watson had risen to vice president and become the ad agency's "chief show piece," as a snide contemporary journalist put it.

Though Watson did contribute to the Maxwell House campaign, it was run by another famed JWT account manager, James Webb Young, whose youthful experience included evangelical door-to-door Bible sales in the South. A surprising number of early copywriters with a religious background were attracted to the secular advertising pulpit. "Business had become almost the national religion of America," Frederick Lewis Allen observed in *Only Yesterday*, his classic book on the twenties. "So frequent was the use of the Bible to point the lessons of business and of business to point the lessons of the Bible that it was sometimes difficult to determine which was supposed to gain the most from the association."

Young conducted surveys of San Francisco and Chicago housewives, along with home tests of Maxwell House. Coffee, he wrote in an internal memo, was "one of the most intensively competitive fields in the world," where Maxwell House had to counter "the aggressive sales and advertising attacks of competitors who in most cases had the advantage of working in their own home territory." Moreover, the surveys revealed that 87 percent of the housewives cited *flavor* as the important factor in their brand choice. Yet "it is extremely difficult for the average person to make clear distinctions where flavor is concerned." Young concluded that while women might *think* they were buying flavor, they really sought social status.

As a traveling Bible salesman, Young had stayed at the old Maxwell House in Nashville several times. He knew how potent stereotyped Southern charm could be, since by that time he had invented Aunt Jemima to sell pancake mixes. Now he sent copywriter Ewing Webb to Nashville to stay in the hotel and soak up the ambiance. Webb wrote compelling copy that positioned Maxwell House Coffee as the aristocratic drink of the Old South. Henry Raleigh, a "high society" illustrator, spent several weeks sketching in Nashville.

J. Walter Thompson then launched its color ads–"A Carnival of Southern Hospitality"–in the *Ladies' Home Journal, Woman's Home Companion, Good Housekeeping,* and the *Saturday Evening Post.* Many Cheek-Neal salesmen and plant managers were appalled, since the Maxwell House Hotel was a "rather shabby relic of its former glory." Yet image, not reality, was what mattered. The ads bent history to make Maxwell House Coffee sound more venerable than it was. "Over this coffee the North and South pledged the new brotherhood years ago." Joel Cheek in fact had invented it in 1892. Sales increases in 1925 over the previous year were gratifying: some months jumped over 100 percent. The Maxwell House ads soon were expanded to show the coffee served at other prestigious hotels around the country.

Letters of praise for the campaign poured in. "I'm going to try Maxwell House Coffee and see if it's as good as the advertising," wrote one consumer. The moral was clear to the men at J. Walter Thompson. "Coffee may be advertised just as coffee–a drink which pleases the palate," wrote James Webb Young in a company memo. "[But] we know that beauty, romance and social prestige mean more than almost anything to a woman," he continued. "The outstanding modern hotels are considered absolute arbiters of correct social usage, particularly with regard to foods." It appeared that the JWT team had, as John Watson suggested, refined its techniques so that "when you go out on the firing line with your printed message you can aim accurately and with deadly execution." To Watson's three stimuli of fear, rage, and love, the advertisers had added a fourth: a yearning for social prestige.

The Roaring Twenties ushered in a new era in advertising. Along with the professional corporate manager and public relations man, the scientific adman had arrived. "It has all changed so rapidly it is astonishing and bewildering," an old-fashioned advertising man groused in 1926. "No business is more serious. It is based on facts." He yearned for the good old days. "Remorseless research data have destroyed all the color, adventure and romance so prevalent in the old advertising game." As one 1927 social commentator noted, "The composition of the air has changed. To the oxygen and nitrogen we breathe we have to add Advertising. . . . Now it surrounds us, envelops us, it is intimately mingled with our every step, in our activities, in our relaxation." The consumer, noted the critic Stuart Chase, "is under mounting pressure . . . to buy, buy, buy."

In 1927 Maxwell House opened a new roasting plant in Chicago, a direct result of the JWT surveys and ad campaign there. A monoplane, the *Miss Maxwell House*, flew across the country to push the coffee, while a new electronic sign in New York's Times Square flashed "Good to the Last Drop." That year Joel Cheek's coffee netted a profit of $2.7 million and became the leading national brand. The coffee also caught the eye of Edward F. Hutton, "Lucky Ned," the millionaire stockbroker who had become Marjorie Merriweather Post's second husband and, in 1923, CEO of the Postum Cereal Company.

With Hutton at the helm and Marjorie Post's financial advisor, Colby M. Chester, Jr., installed as president, Postum's headquarters were moved from Battle Creek to New York City. Without diverging from the path set by C. W. Post, Postum had continued to generate cash but wasn't growing. Hutton, Chester, and other executives made a list of some thirty companies that would fit their criteria. They wanted to buy consumer brands that were already well-advertised, nationally prominent, and profitable. In 1925 they commenced with Jell-O, followed by a string of other acquisitions during the rest of the twenties.

In 1928 Hutton made his biggest purchase, paying $42 million for the Cheek-Neal Company—half in cash, half in stock.[9] Joel Cheek split the proceeds with his nine children and two nephews, making all of them instant millionaires. The following year Hutton reincorporated the firm, calling it General Foods. In a supreme irony C. W. Post's anti-coffee business now had become the purveyor of the country's most prominent coffee brand.

By the time E. F. Hutton and Marjorie Post purchased Maxwell House in 1928 American capitalism had come of age. Until the 1920s most successful corporations and businesses were still essentially family-owned affairs. Eventually the second or third generation, lacking that fire in the belly, sold out, and steely eyed financiers, cynical advertising men, and professional managers took over. Surveys and statistics replaced intuition. The public relations man, he of the firm handshake and perpetual smile, prowled corporate halls.

---

[9]The year before, in 1927, Postum acquired the U.S. rights to market Sanka, a decaffeinated coffee. A Southern black "mammy" graced the label, clearly attempting to cash in on the same Southern associations that sold Maxwell House.

The Great Stock Market–Coffee Crash

Only a few months after the formation of General Foods and Standard Brands, the American stock market crashed, on October 29, 1929, signaling an end to the delirious economic expansion that had made increasing prosperity seem infinite, not only in the United States but in many other areas of the globe, including Brazil. Yet coffee itself had given an ominous warning signal only two weeks prior to the crash.

Throughout the decade Brazilian coffee men had coped with overproduction by holding millions of bags off the market. In 1921 they financed a third valorization with a joint British-American loan totaling £9 million, with security provided by 4.5 million bags of coffee held in Brazil, London, and New York. When coffee prices obligingly doubled by mid-decade, the Brazilians sold most of the coffee, paying off the loan. The planters and politicians of Brazil recognized, however, that storing coffee overseas involved added expenses. President Artur da Silva Bernardes, elected in 1922, ordered the construction of eleven huge São Paulo warehouses, capable of holding 3.5 million bags. He then instituted a policy of shipping just enough coffee to the ports to meet market demand. The planters now would be responsible for financing the retention of their own crops.

The middlemen–exporters, importers, traders, speculators, and roasters–hated the new policy, since they now had little idea how much coffee was lurking in the interior warehouses, waiting to deluge the market at an inopportune time. As prices rose in early 1924, importers and roasters tried to break the system by a policy of heavy buying, hoping to lure the surplus into the open, but they failed. As usual, the rise of coffee prices provoked an outcry in the United States. At the end of June, Emmet Beeson, a New York coffee broker, published a scathing *New York Times* article about the situation, headlined "American Coffee Drinker at the Mercy of Brazil." He suggested that the United States increase the use of the Hawaiian and Puerto Rican coffee grown by its own possessions. "In the final analysis, it would seem that Brazil's greedy tactics will serve to encourage the development of vast areas of coffee lands that are now going to waste in different parts of the world."

In 1925 a delegation of coffee men representing the National Coffee Roasters Association (NCRA), the chain stores, and wholesale grocers, including Berent Friele of A & P, called on Secretary of Commerce

Herbert Hoover, asking that a permanent American commission be installed in São Paulo to monitor Brazilian coffee production and warehoused stocks. Although no friend of the Brazilian coffee growers, Hoover could ill afford to antagonize the government by making such demands. In January 1926, however, Hoover attacked international commodity schemes before Congress. Identifying a "growing menace in international commerce and relations," he complained of price-fixing efforts that constituted an "intrusion of governments into trading operations on a vast scale." Nine raw products were subject to such agreements, but the focus was on rubber (whose price affected the automobile-mad United States) and coffee.

Julius Klein, Hoover's director of the Bureau of Foreign and Domestic Commerce, testified about coffee, emphasizing the secrecy of the warehouse stockpiles. "There is a vast quantity of coffee there that might suddenly be turned loose at almost any moment or under any contingency—political or otherwise." Hoover himself conceded that "if all these combinations had been content with fair returns," he might not object so strenuously; but due to the "inherent quality of all monopolies," speculators inevitably took over to drive prices to unreasonable levels.

Hoover's high-profile pronouncements at the hearings made front-page banner headlines in the *New York Times*: HOOVER WARNS WORLD OF TRADE WAR. Yet there was little else he could do about Brazil's coffee other than prevent American bankers from continuing to finance Brazil's coffee retention scheme. Thumbing its nose at Hoover, the São Paulo government sought a £4 million ($19.2 million) loan in London. British bankers rushed to supply the money, and the bonds were oversubscribed within five minutes on January 6, 1926–the same day Hoover testified before the congressional committee. The rubber problem eventually was solved by the invention of synthetic rubber, but no one could duplicate the lowly coffee bean in a laboratory.

The Brazilians were infuriated with Hoover's grandstanding. Shortly after his speech a Brazilian journalist protested that Americans shouldn't talk, with their "Sugar Trust, Petroleum combines, cigar and tobacco monopolies, Metal Mining and refining combination, United Drugs and Cold Drinks monopolies, meat packers, [and] Motion Picture Trust." U.S. cotton and wheat growers had a system of bonded warehouses; why not the Brazilians? Besides, the major markup on coffee occurred after export. Why did American consumers have to pay 50 cents a pound for coffee imported at 20 cents?

With its newly borrowed money the São Paulo Coffee Institute opened its own bank, the Banco do Estado do São Paulo, and began loaning money based on real estate (primarily coffee plantations), warehouse receipts, and coffee bills of lading. With the 1926 presidential election of Washington Luís Pereira de Sousa, a Paulista, the coffee growers were assured of continued federal support. Although the 1926–1927 crop had been relatively small, the institute decided to carry over more stock in an attempt to bolster sagging prices. The warehouses now bulged with some 3.3 million bags. The following year a bumper crop totaling nearly 30 million bags surprised everyone. In 1927 the São Paulo Coffee Institute called two conferences with other Brazilian coffee-growing states, who agreed to join their retention scheme by limiting coffee sent to the ports.

By the end of 1927 it appeared that the institute could do no wrong, securing a £5 million line of credit for a year from Lazard Brothers in London, followed by a £5 million gold mortgage loan to the Banco do Estado. Even with the bumper crop coffee prices rose. In 1928 Lazard renewed its loan for another twenty years.

Amidst general euphoria, however, there were a few Brazilians who expressed concern about the one hundred million new São Paulo trees about to begin bearing. The Paulistas also were uneasy about the possibility that their archenemy Herbert Hoover might be elected the U.S. president.[10] On the whole, however, the Brazilian coffee planters were optimistic about the future. They argued that the new production would be offset by declining fertility on old plantations, aging of other trees, and continued increase in world consumption. Besides, there had never been two bumper crops in consecutive years. "There is no crisis in the coffee industry," stated Sebastiao Sampaio, the new Brazilian consul general, at the end of 1928.

In the buoyant mood of the twenties, only a few Brazilians protested the continued decimation of their rain forests. During that decade forest destruction in São Paulo proceeded at the rate of 3,000 square kilometers a year. Yet most Brazilians didn't care that the forest was being destroyed. It was only "an unimaginable surfeit of climbing plants, a

---

[10]Herbert Hoover, who objected to the artificial prosperity of the coffee growers, failed to see any parallel to the U.S. economy, inflated by speculative stock buying. "We in America today are nearer to the final triumph over poverty than ever before in the history of any land," he stated in a stump speech. "We shall soon, with the help of God, be in sight of the day when poverty will be banished from this nation."

tragic disorder of trunks [in which] man [is] imprisoned in the laby-
rinth of demented vegetation," according to one commentator. Another literary figure extolled the "aligned beauty of the tree that yields
gold, [the] Green Wave of Coffee." At a typical Brazilian Arbor Day
celebration schoolchildren often planted non-native coffee trees, which
one cynic observed was similar to eulogizing chickens during a wildlife
celebration.

Still the coffee kept coming, and the Brazilians built more warehouses. Herbert Hoover, newly elected president, warned that "Brazil
is carrying the umbrella for the other coffee producing countries," allowing them to expand and profit at Brazil's expense. On a visit to São
Paulo, Berent Friele urged the government there to release more coffee
and lower the price to encourage greater exports to the United States.
The prosperous Brazilian planters ignored Friele and Hoover, despite
signs of trouble. Credit became tighter. Nervous foreign banks refused
to send capital into the country.

But the coffee kings could not be bothered. Many were now millionaires and had settled into a luxurious lifestyle, spending six months on
their plantations and splitting the rest of their time between Paris and
their mansions in the capital. They sent their children to American universities. They had proven their ability to control the world's coffee
crop and prices. Why should they worry?

Under the umbrella provided by Brazil's retention plan Central
American coffee planters prospered. The region's stability, important
to North American businessmen, was guaranteed by the "dollar diplomacy" that sent U.S. Marines into Haiti and Nicaragua to protect
American business interests.[11] In 1929 American professor Parker
Thomas Moon complained of "American imperialism," objecting to
the American habit of "confusing altruism with Wall Street and naval
strategy." Two years later, retired General Smedley Butler admitted
that he had spent the past three decades as a "muscleman for big busi-

---

[11]In Nicaragua dictator José Santos Zelaya received U.S. government support, as Americans
hoped to negotiate a canal through his country. After 1903, however, when the United States en-
gineered a coup in Panama and secured rights to a canal there, Zelaya's fights against U.S. business interests proved more difficult, and in 1909 he was forced to resign. From 1909 until 1933,
with the exception of a brief period in 1926–1927, the U.S. Marines established a protectorate in
Nicaragua to insure the domination of American interests there. North Americans controlled the
banks, the military, and the coffee growers. As a consequence the Nicaraguan coffee economy
stagnated in comparison with its Central American neighbors.

ness" while serving as a U.S. Marine. "I helped in the rape of a dozen Central American republics for the benefit of Wall Street." Although few U.S. businesses owned coffee plantations, many American banks provided credit for the coffee industry. Thus it is relevant that Butler spoke of helping the "National City Bank boys."

In general the U.S. support of the Latin American status quo did provide a beneficial business environment, particularly for coffee farmers. The famous "fourteen families" of El Salvador (by now more like forty), along with growers in Guatemala and Costa Rica, thrived during the twenties. "The coffee barons lived in great splendor, collecting chorus girls in Manhattan, tall blondes by preference, and became familiar figures at the baccarat tables of the Riviera," one historian noted. Regardless of the owners' prosperity, however, the workers made the same 15 cents a day. Even James Hill, one of the founders of an El Salvador coffee dynasty, acknowledged the inequities. "The working people . . . say, 'We dig the holes for the trees, we clean the weeds, we prune the trees, we pick the coffee. Who earns the money then? We do.' Yes, there will be trouble one of these days."

Against this uneasy backdrop the prosperity of the Roaring Twenties fell apart. The 1928–1929 Brazilian crop was much smaller than that of the previous year, coming in at 10.6 million bags. Yet the warehouses still overflowed with coffee, and a vigorous flowering in July 1929 from new trees indicated that a huge crop would arrive in 1930, unless some natural disaster prevented it. By September the planters finally started getting nervous. Rumors spread that they soon would move a million bags of coffee toward foreign markets, and that they were negotiating with Berent Friele and other American buyers to contract for ten million bags, though knowledgeable coffee men were skeptical that so much coffee could ever be absorbed into the market without causing a major price slump.

Lazard Brothers, which had renewed the old loan in July, informed the Paulistas, when they sought another £9 million, that no more money would be forthcoming. Now frantic, the Brazilians sought help from the Rothschilds. No dice. Nor could they expect loans from American banks, especially not with Hoover in the White House.

On October 11, 1929, the Santos Bolsa, the country's coffee exchange, opened as usual. Trading was moderate. The São Paulo Coffee Institute's broker sat silently in his chair all morning. No one paid much attention. In the afternoon, when he still failed to buy, sellers offered much lower prices, yet he never bought. The terrible secret was out. The institute was bankrupt. Coffee prices plummeted. In a desperate attempt to reassure the New York Coffee Exchange, Consul General Sebastiao Sampaio lied outright, denying that Brazil had ever applied for a loan and boasting of Brazil's large gold reserves. The coffee market rallied temporarily. Then on October 29 the New York stock market crashed, and all hope with it.

It is no coincidence that coffee crashed two weeks before the U.S. stock market. By that time coffee was a "canary in the coal mine," since it was so intimately tied to international commerce. Like their prosperous business counterparts in the United States, the arrogant Brazilian coffee kings thought that the prosperity party would never end. As late as October 17 an American economics professor stated that stock prices had reached "a permanently high plateau." Similarly, the Paulistas deluded themselves into thinking they were invincible. As their warehoused coffee commanded higher and higher paper prices, they used it as collateral for ever-higher loans, just as U.S. investors bought on margin. In the end it all came crashing down, buried under the weight of all that coffee. The worldwide Great Depression of the 1930s ushered in years of lower prices for coffee and just about everything else, along with massive unemployment. But no one stopped drinking the black brew.

BURNING
BEANS, STARVING
CAMPESINOS

Coffee is our national misfortune.
–Brazilian coffee grower, 1934

The world's interlocking economic system pulled everyone down when it crashed in 1929, and coffee people—several million of whom relied on the plant and its berries for a livelihood—were no exception. The story of how coffee growers, importers, and roasters survived the Great Depression offers a microcosmic look at how the economic chaos affected the globe. For some the crisis created opportunity; for others it meant bankruptcy, despair, or even death. But for billions of Brazilian coffee beans it meant a holocaust.

The Coffee Inferno

The worldwide economic slump of the thirties spelled disaster for coffee producers. In Brazil the crash signaled the end of the country's Old Republic and the unquestioned domination of the coffee oligarchy. In 1930, after a rigged election put Julio Prestes in power, an October military coup replaced him with Getúlio Vargas, a politician from southern Brazil. Surprisingly, even the coffee kings of São Paulo welcomed the revolt, since the faltering government had failed to rally around coffee valorization at all costs. The price of coffee tumbled from 22.5 cents a pound in 1929 to 8 cents two years later. In 1930, twenty-six million bags of coffee sat in Brazilian warehouses–a million bags more than the entire world had consumed the previous year. In such a desperate situation, any change seemed better than continuing along the same path.

Vargas, a short, stocky lawyer with a ready smile and a pragmatic bent, was to rule Brazil for an unprecedented length of time. Chewing contemplatively on his ever-present cigar, he presented the facade of a calm, friendly listener who genuinely cared for his country and its problems. Unlike other Latin American dictators, Vargas generally practiced moderation rather than terror. He quickly banned new coffee plantings, though that hardly seemed necessary, since no sane farmer wanted to grow more coffee at such low prices.

Vargas also appointed a military governor in São Paulo who immediately alienated the Paulistas by decreeing a 5 percent wage hike and distributing some land to revolutionary veterans. Vargas infuriated coffeeshop owners by cutting the price of a cup of coffee in half. To conciliate the coffee growers and sellers, Vargas appointed José Maria Whitaker, a Paulista coffee banker, as his minister of finance. "It is absolutely necessary to return to unrestricted trading," Whitaker announced, "first removing the nightmare of the formidable coffee stocks." The government intended to burn the massive coffee surplus, but only so that the market could "revert to the time-honored law of supply and demand." In the first year, the Brazilians destroyed over seven million bags of coffee worth some $30 million–and they still had millions more bags clogging their warehouses.

Foreign journalist Heinrich Jacob first encountered the burning coffee from a low-flying airplane in the early 1930s. "An aromatic yet pungent odour was rising from beneath and permeated the cabin," he wrote. "It dulled the senses, and was at the same time actually painful. . . . The smell by now had become intolerable, and the fumes had produced a ringing in my ears. It seemed to sap my strength." Jacob subsequently met a distraught former coffee grower, now bankrupt, who declared, "Coffee is our national misfortune." He produced a small box with a glass cover containing the *broca do café*, the coffee borer, that had begun to attack beans about ten years earlier. "Nothing should be done to resist the onslaught of the *broca*," he said. "If the government really wants to save the country, it will take up loads of the eggs of this beetle in airplanes, and strew them far and wide over the plantations."

In this world of upside-down logic, in which planters were paid to harvest and process coffee only in order to destroy it, the Brazilians were desperate. Their scientists and inventors labored to find alternative uses for their surplus coffee. The minister of public works authorized a project to compress beans into bricks, to be used as fuel for the railroad. Other experiments sought to extract alcohol, oil, gas, caffeine, or cellulose by-products from coffee. A Rio newspaper suggested that nutritious bread "of excellent taste and appearance" could be made from flour milled in part from green coffee beans. Vintners made a passable white wine from the pulp, while perfume came from crushed coffee blossoms. A few years later one inventor created a new type of plastic from the beans.

The Brazilians also approached foreign governments with innovative coffee proposals. They would recognize Soviet Russia and trade coffee for Russian wheat or hides. They planned to open thousands of Brazilian coffeeshops throughout Asia, creating new markets for their beans. Little came of most such plans, but they did trade coffee for American surplus wheat, beginning in 1931.[1] Although the rich Brazilian *terra roxa* could have grown enough wheat for domestic consumption, the country grew only an eighth of its requirements—another result of the short-sighted devotion to coffee monoculture.

The coffee-wheat swap caused trouble, though. American shippers complained that the Brazilian shipping lines were carrying all of the wheat and coffee. The Argentineans, who had previously supplied wheat to Brazil, objected. American coffee men didn't like the idea of the government getting into the coffee market with cheap coffee that might lower the price. U.S. flour companies were upset when they learned that the deal involved an embargo on flour imports into Brazil.

In July 1932, just as the Grain Stabilization Board began to sell the coffee it had received in exchange for wheat, the frustrated Paulistas rebelled against Vargas, demanding a restoration of constitutional government. The port of Santos was closed. "Breakfast Without Its Cup of Coffee Looms," an August *New York Times* headline warned. Although

---

[1]The Brazilians also opened coffee bars in Great Britain, France, Denmark, Russia, and Japan.

the alternate ports of Rio and Victoria hastened to export more coffee, the huge supplies of better-grade beans from São Paulo were suddenly unavailable. In the United States the Grain Stabilization Board held over a million bags of coffee but was contractually restricted to sell only 62,500 bags per month. As a result, it looked as if there would be a coffee shortage, but the Paulista revolt fizzled after three months and coffee prices again declined.

"São Paulo warehouses full, refusing further consignments from interior," a cable from Brazil advised toward the end of November 1932. "Nowhere to deposit. Basements, houses being used for storage. Situation cannot continue. . . . Cannot cope with avalanche from interior. Burning going on rapidly."

Dictators and Massacres in Central America

The Great Depression and its low coffee prices also brought revolution, dictatorships, and social unrest to Central American countries. The crash of 1929 exacerbated already difficult conditions for laborers, and except in Costa Rica, the threatened coffee oligarchies hastened to install strong-arm leaders to restore "order and progress." All of the dictators continued to rely on foreign capital and support from the United States, while crushing any protests. In the wake of the 1929 crash the coffee elite gobbled up smaller farms through foreclosure and purchase, further widening the gap between haves and have nots.

In El Salvador the military ousted the elected president and installed dictator Maximiliano Hernández Martínez late in 1931. For the next twenty years he ruled El Salvador with an iron fist and increasingly bizarre policies. Known as *El Brujo* (the witch) owing to his belief in theosophy and the occult, Hernández Martínez shared his visions with the populace over the radio. "It is good that children go barefoot," he told his audiences. "That way they can better receive the beneficial effluvia of the planet, the vibrations of the earth." He claimed that he was protected by "invisible legions" in direct telepathic communication with the president of the United States. The dictator believed in reincarnation for human beings, but not insects. "It is a greater crime to kill an ant than a man, because a man who dies is reincarnated while an ant dies forever."

By the 1930s coffee accounted for over 90 percent of El Salvador's exports. Indians worked ten-hour days for 12 cents. They suffered, as a

Canadian observer wrote at the time, from "low wages, incredible filth, utter lack of consideration on the part of the employers, [under] conditions in fact not far removed from slavery."

Unable to meet mortgage payments and nominally in default, the plantation owners slashed wages, postponed routine maintenance, and fired many permanent workers. Coffee trees were left unharvested. "There came a time," one worker later told a journalist, "when we were not given land or work. . . . I had to abandon my wife and children. I did not get enough work to be able to give them food, still less clothing, or to educate them. I do not know where they are. Misery has separated us forever. . . . For this I became a Communist."

On January 22, 1932, urged on by charismatic Communist leader Agustín Farabundo Martí, Indians in the western highlands (where most of the coffee was grown) killed nearly 100 people, mostly overseers and soldiers.[2] Echoing the long-repressed rage of the oppressed workers, the nearby volcano Izalco erupted that same night. Armed only with clubs, slingshots, machetes, and a few rifles, the rebels stood no chance against encroaching government troops. Hernández Martínez authorized a brutal reprisal, while ordering the creation of Civic Guards, composed primarily of upper-class citizens.

The bloodbath that followed came to be known simply as *La Matanza*, The Massacre. The military, aided by the outraged and terrified ruling class, killed indiscriminately. Groups of fifty men were tied together by the thumbs and shot in front of a church wall. Others had to dig mass graves before machine guns dropped them into the holes. Bodies littered the roadsides. Anyone dressed in traditional Indian clothing was killed in what approached genocide in some regions. Putrifying bodies were left for pigs, dogs, and vultures to devour. Farabundo Martí died before a firing squad. Within a few weeks some thirty thousand people were dead.[3] The Communist party was virtually wiped out, along with any resistance for years to come. The memory of the massacre would influence Salvadoran history for the rest of the

---

[2]While the rebels committed some atrocities, their actions were greatly exaggerated later by the government, which also minimized the extent of the military massacre to follow.

[3]Estimates for the numbers killed in the *matanza* vary from two thousand to fifty thousand. In his classic 1971 book *Matanza* Thomas Anderson accepted an estimate of ten thousand, but many scholars now agree on thirty thousand.

century. "We were all born half dead in 1932," one of their poets would write.

In a July 1932 edition of its journal, the Coffee Association of El Salvador commented on the uprising and subsequent massacre. "There have always been two essential classes in every society: the dominators and the dominated. . . . Today they are called the rich and the poor." This division, they asserted, was inevitable, and efforts to end class divisions would "break the equilibrium and cause the disintegration of human society." Thus the Salvadoran coffee power elite justified the prolonged misery of the campesinos. Convinced that factories only provided fertile ground for Communists, Hernández Martínez passed laws discouraging industrialization. El Salvador turned even more firmly to coffee as its primary source of revenue.

In Guatemala, Nicaragua, and Honduras, dictators also came to power during the depression, clamping down on any signs of peasant unrest. When Jorge Ubico Castañeda took over in Guatemala in 1931, he quickly moved to squelch any opposition through imprisonment, assassination, execution, or exile. Recognizing the need to placate oppressed Indian laborers, he abolished debt slavery but instituted a vagrancy law that amounted to nearly the same thing. Nothing changed the appalling poverty of the Guatemalan peasant or the country's reliance on foreign capital and coffee exports. After 1933, when Ubico had a hundred trade union, student, and political leaders shot—and issued a subsequent decree allowing coffee and banana plantation owners to kill their workers with impunity—coffee peons didn't dare rebel.

General Anastasio Somoza García came to power in Nicaragua in 1934, following the assassination of guerilla leader Augusto César Sandino, which Somoza himself had arranged.[4] Officially elected in 1936, Somoza built a family dynasty based largely on massive coffee holdings, including forty-six plantations. Through intimidation and graft, Somoza became the largest property holder in the country. He too ordered massacres of suspected rebels.

In Honduras depression-era dictator Tiburcio Carías Andino proved less ruthless than his counterparts. He encouraged more coffee produc-

---

[4]Augusto César Sandino, the illegitimate son of a wealthy coffee planter and one of his harvest laborers, led a rebellion against the U.S. Marines who occupied his country, calling them "blond beasts" and "the enemy of our race and language."

tion, so that Honduras joined other Central American countries as a coffee power, though bananas remained its major export.

Meanwhile in Costa Rica and Colombia the Great Depression and its lower coffee prices also created problems, though legislative compromises through democratically elected governments helped resolve conflict. In Costa Rica, where predominant smallholders worked their own *fincas*, there were few labor issues; but the farmers were forced to sell their ripe cherries quickly to centralized processing centers that set very low prices during the depression. In 1933 the state finally intervened with regulations that forced processors to pay a decent price for the coffee berries.

Colombian farmers, who generally processed their own beans, struggled with high interest rates from financial institutions and a price squeeze from foreign exporters—A & P's American Coffee Corporation, Hard & Rand, W. R. Grace—who dominated the Colombian coffee industry.[5] Labor protests on the large *haciendas* escalated. *Colonos* and tenants refused to pay outstanding debts, contending that the land belonged to them. Squatters, known pejoratively as *parásitos*, claimed unused lands on *haciendas*. The Colombian legislature passed laws making vacant land subject to expropriation, leading to the decline of the large plantations. The wealthy coffee elite already were diversifying into industries such as cement plants, shoe factories, real estate, and transportation.

Colombian coffee continued to sell in ever greater amounts, however. The *Federación Nacional de Cafeteros* (FNC), the Colombian Coffee Federation, had been established in 1927 and quickly gained enormous political clout, becoming "a private State within a not-very-public State," as one observer put it. In the United States the Federation advertised Colombian beans as "Supreme Among Mild Coffees."

Brazil Opens the Floodgates

Although the United States per capita held steady around thirteen pounds of coffee a year in the thirties, the origins of those beans shifted as the depression continued. While Brazil burned more and more of its

---

[5]By 1927 A & P was buying one-tenth of Colombia's entire coffee production, roasting an average of four thousand bags of Colombian coffee per week.

crop, Colombia, Venezuela, and the Central American producers were able to sell in proportionately greater amounts. In desperation, Brazil called a multinational conference in Bogotá in 1936. The participating Latin American countries agreed to fund a Pan American Coffee Bureau that would promote coffee consumption in North America. Following the conference, Colombian and Brazilian representatives hammered out a price maintenance agreement: high-quality Colombian Manizales would sell for over 12 cents a pound, with mediocre Brazilian Santos at 10.5 cents a pound.

In 1937 Brazil burned an astonishing 17.2 million bags at a time when total world consumption was only 26.4 million bags. Only 30 percent of Brazil's coffee harvest reached the world market that year. Yet Colombia did not maintain the agreed-on price differential, announcing that it was "too burdensome"; Manizales sold for 11.6 cents a pound. With such a slim price premium over the inferior Santos, Colombia had no trouble selling its coffee.

The incensed Brazilians called yet another conference, held in Havana in August 1937. In his keynote address Brazilian representative Eurico Penteado told the other growers that "few of the resolutions voted at Bogotá have been carried out and nothing remains of the price agreement." Unlike Brazil, other countries continued to export their inferior grades. "As to price defense, only Brazil continues to bear the whole burden."

At the onset of the depression, Brazil had provided 65 percent of U.S. coffee imports. By 1937 it made up just over half, while Colombia had snared 25 percent of the market. At the same time, however, Brazil's dependence on coffee had lessened somewhat. In 1934 coffee had provided 61 percent of Brazil's exports, and two years later it was only 45 percent. "Therefore, gentlemen," Penteado concluded, "it will be seen that for the good of Brazil, while our capacity to go on destroying coffee has reached the point of exhaustion, we are really no longer confronted with the need of further sacrifice." Unless other countries agreed to stop new planting, cease export of inferior grades, and agree to some price support system, Brazil would, he threatened, drop its entire coffee support program.

Yet no one truly believed Brazil actually would end a practice it had begun over thirty years earlier with the first valorization. Nor were other Latin American producers eager to cease the exportation of their inferior grades, since cheaper African robustas were beginning to find their way to the United States and Europe. "A few years ago coffee brokers were loath to taste a cup of Robusta," one U.S. coffee expert observed in 1937. "After repeated sippings, however, one finds himself becoming accustomed to them." The growers at the Havana conference feared that robusta would simply replace the bottom-grade Latin American exports.

Indeed, a primary reason for the Latin American countries' willingness to consider a quota system was the increasing threat from the African colonies. During the depression the Kenyan growers of fine arabica beans established a Coffee Board and research bureau. They succeeded in establishing their own auction over the objections of London brokers, who previously had monopolized their trade. By the late 1930s the Kenyan plantations began to advertise extensively in American trade journals. Total African coffee production doubled in a decade, and Africa surpassed Asia to become the second largest continental coffee exporter. Little wonder then that Latin American producers were beginning to cast anxious glances across the Atlantic—and that they pointedly left the African, Indian, and Asian producers out of their conference plans.[6]

The Havana conference nonetheless ended without resolving the issue of overproduction, though the participating countries did agree on a U.S. advertising campaign to be funded with a 5 cent per bag export tax, which duly commenced the following year. Reluctantly, they also agreed to limit export of some inferior grades. They referred the intractable problem of price differentials and export quotas to the Pan American Coffee Bureau in New York, which was given sixty days to find a solution.

When the time limit expired without a resolution, Getúlio Vargas shocked the coffee world in November by simultaneously declaring himself a benign dictator of what he called the *Estado Novo*, or New State, and announcing Brazil's new policy of "free competition." He vowed to open the coffee floodgates just before Brazilian representative Eurico Penteado was due to speak in New Orleans at the annual meet-

---

[6]The British owned three prime coffee colonies: Kenya grew arabica, Tanganyika produced both arabicas and robustas, while Uganda specialized primarily in robusta. The French, Portuguese, and Belgians owned the African robusta coffee-growing colonies of French Equatorial Africa, French West Africa, Somaliland Coast, Ivory Coast, Cameroons, Madagascar, Angola, and the Belgian Congo. The Italians were about to take over Ethiopia, the birthplace of coffee.

ing of the Associated Coffee Industries of America (now renamed the National Coffee Association). Penteado defended his country's action, explaining that "Brazil was being displaced in an alarming manner from the world markets." The U.S. media reacted favorably, reporting that "Brazil is tired of holding the coffee bag for other countries which won't play ball."

At first the frustrated Brazilian growers cheered the $2 per bag tax reduction. The new free trade policy represented "a ray of light in the darkness of a long night," according to a São Paulo planter; but when prices plummeted to 6.5 cents a pound, the *fazenda* owners weren't so sure. And when their credit dried up, they were frantic. The burning program resumed, though in moderation. In 1938 Brazil exported over 300 million pounds more coffee to the United States than the previous year—but received $3.15 million *less* for the total than in 1937. In Brazil, as one observer noted the following year, "no longer is the coffee tree regarded as a 'Gift from Heaven.' The old glamour of coffee has departed."

Still the Brazilians continued to flood the world with coffee, with an eye to the future. They were determined to win back their fair share of the market. In addition, if that ever-elusive international coffee cartel ever set a firm quota system, they knew that it would be based on a country's market share over the last few years. Brazil's efforts seemed doomed, however, considering what had happened during the previous three decades. In 1906 Brazil had grown over 20 million bags of coffee, with the rest of the world contributing only 3.6 million. By 1938 Brazil produced nearly 22 million bags, but other coffee producers now grew 10.2 million bags, most of which were superior to the Brazilian beans.

While Latin American growers struggled for minimal profits in a world of low coffee prices, however, the Great Depression brought new selling opportunities to many U.S. coffee roasters, who had finally learned the virtues of selling an image—and a sound.

SHOWBOATING
THE DEPRESSION

Just around the corner,
There's a rainbow in the sky.
So let's have another cup o' coffee,
And let's have another piece o' pie.
                    —Irving Berlin, 1932

Although U.S. citizens endured hardships during the depression, their suffering certainly did not compare to that of Latin American peasants. North Americans generally had enough to eat and drink, even if some had to stand in bread lines for their food and coffee. To divert themselves in their homes they also had a miraculous new communication medium—the radio, which would provide another way to sell coffee.

Glued to Their Radios

In radio's infancy in the early twenties advertisers didn't dare make direct brand-specific appeals to consumers, as this would have appeared crassly commercial. Instead they sought an uplifting, educational tone. In 1923, for instance, John Watson of J. Walter Thompson put on his best professorial demeanor to discuss "Glands, the Mysteries of the Human Body," over WEAF. Although the announcer noted that the talk was given courtesy of Pebeco Tooth Paste, Watson did not mention the product. He concluded that "to keep the glands of the mouth active and healthy . . . it is advisable to brush your teeth after every meal with a tooth paste that cleanses and polishes the teeth without scratching the delicate enamel." Watson later observed that this talk "illustrates fairly well the technique of commercial advertising by radio. . . . The speaker does not have to say anything about the product being advertised."

Slowly advertisers became somewhat more aggressive, sponsoring entire shows. In 1924 A & P began advertising its three coffee brands on the radio with the "A & P Gypsies," soon to be followed by the "Everready Hour," "Lucky Strike Orchestra," "Wrigley Review," the "Jewel Tea Hour," and the "Maxwell House Hour." In the West, Folger's sponsored "Folgeria," with a marimba band theme, comic skits, and musical acts. Still the advertising was, as Erik Barnouw described it in his history of broadcasting, "brief, circumspect, and extremely well-mannered."

In 1929 all that changed. That year Americans spent $842 million on new radios, up well over 1,000 percent from seven years earlier. Early in 1929 virtually all of Chicago's radios were tuned into "Amos 'n' Andy," a show about two black men played by two white men, Freeman Gosden and Charles Correll. In May, William Benton, a young advertising man with the firm of Lord & Thomas, walked home to his Chicago apartment on a hot, muggy night when everyone had their windows open. "I heard these colored voices leaping out into the street, from all the apartments. I turned around and walked back up the street. There were nineteen radios on and seventeen were tuned to 'Amos 'n' Andy.'" The next morning Benton convinced agency chief Albert Lasker that Pepsodent, the firm's toothpaste client, should sponsor the show nationally. As a result, the radio program became a national obsession, and Pepsodent sales skyrocketed. As comedian Bob Hope recalled, "there wasn't a theater in the country that opened in the evening before 7:30. Why? Because they knew nobody was going to leave the house until after 'Amos 'n' Andy.' Nobody."[1]

Benton & Bowles Survive the Crash

On July 15, 1929, William Benton and Chester Bowles opened a new advertising firm in New York City. A few months later the market crashed, and the nascent firm struggled to survive the depression. The

---

[1]Gosden and Correll originated their Chicago show in 1926 as "Sam 'n' Henry," switching to "Amos 'n' Andy" in 1928. With Pepsodent sponsorship the show went national in 1929.

two Yale graduates were only twenty-nine and twenty-eight years old, respectively, but they were friends with Charles Mortimer, who worked in the advertising department of General Foods. Mortimer arranged for Benton and Bowles to meet with his boss, Ralph Starr Butler, a former marketing professor who headed General Foods' advertising. Impressed by the bright young partners, Butler gave them Certo and Hellman's Mayonnaise, two smaller accounts.

Bill Benton and Chet Bowles were unusual advertising men—intellectually insatiable, socially conscious, creative workaholics. Benton possessed a manic energy that allowed him to work insane hours under high pressure. Yet when he stepped back to contemplate his chosen profession, he was never satisfied. "As I sit at my desk turning out copy on oil ranges," he wrote his mother in 1924, "it all seems so futile. I am helping no one."

Chet Bowles, whose six-foot frame towered over the shorter Benton, lacked his partner's volatile energy. An affable, quiet, thoughtful man, Bowles wrote most of the firm's creative copy. "There was none of the huckster about him," an early associate observed. "He knew what he was talking about, and he said it simply and directly."

The two partners resolved to concentrate their advertising energies on food and drug products, which they correctly perceived as largely impervious to the depression. On Benton's thirty-second birthday, April 1, 1932, Ralph Starr Butler and Clarence Francis, the General Foods sales manager, summoned Benton to explain that they were unhappy with the sales of Maxwell House Coffee, then being handled by Erwin Wasey.[2] They asked him whether his agency could handle not only Maxwell House but also Baker's Chocolate, Post Toasties, Post Bran Flakes, Diamond Crystal Salt, and Log Cabin Syrup. Bill Benton answered, honestly, that he didn't think they were prepared to take on all of the accounts. The General Foods men then suggested that Benton and Bowles take on a third partner, Atherton Hobler, the restive account manager at Erwin Wasey.

---

[2]Erwin Wasey had taken over the Maxwell House account in 1929 when J. Walter Thompson had to give it up in order to take on Chase & Sanborn. In the twenties Fleischmann's Yeast and Maxwell House Coffee were two of the biggest JWT accounts. When Fleischmann's transmuted into Standard Brands, swallowing Chase & Sanborn, the JWT men had to choose between keeping the huge yeast account and switching coffee accounts or losing all of the Standard Brands business if they stuck with Maxwell House.

Benton, Bowles, and Hobler formed an equal three-way partnership. Hobler, ten years older than Benton, brought his added years of experience to the firm along with an aggressive, competitive edge. A large man with protuberant eyes that seemed to drill through people, Hobe, as he was usually called, drove himself and his subordinates hard. The partners quickly hired new staff, many coming from other agencies, eager to join the exciting young firm.[3]

Rancid Oils and Coffee Nerves

The admen's most urgent task was to revive Maxwell House sales. From net profits of nearly $3 million a year on sales of 50 million pounds before the crash, the brand generated virtually no profit on sales of only 39 million pounds three years later. The desperate General Foods management allotted a whopping $3.1 million to Benton & Bowles to advertise Maxwell House.

The depression had brought even fiercer competition to the coffee wars. In the twenties Maxwell House had been the only brand that could truly claim national distribution. Then Chase & Sanborn, with Standard Brand's aggressive distribution and advertising, claimed that its coffee was fresher than others. "Rancid Oil in Stale Coffee," a Chase & Sanborn headline announced, was "the cause of indigestion, headaches, sleeplessness." The company claimed that by avoiding other brands and sticking to its Dated Coffee, consumers could safely imbibe up to five cups of coffee a day. According to Standard Brands vice president Traver Smith, the coffee-as-a-fresh-food approach boosted sales over 300 percent in a little over a year.

Under the creative direction of Stanley Resor's JWT team, Chase & Sanborn had begun sponsoring a twenty-two-piece choral orchestra in 1929. After some floundering, in 1931 they settled on popular comedian–singer Eddie Cantor, who promoted the coffee effectively. As the elections neared, the host pretended to be running for president, and cries of "We Want Cantor, We Want Cantor" became a national joke.

On the packaging front many more competitors at long last were discovering the vacuum can, pioneered in 1900 by Hills Brothers. In 1931

---

[3]Novelist Sinclair Lewis applied for a job, but Benton turned him down, telling him, "I don't want to be the Babbitt or Gantry of your next work."

General Foods introduced its Vita-Fresh vacuum pack that purportedly removed 99 percent of the air—not just 90 percent, as with Hills Brothers, MJB, and Folgers. General Foods also installed a huge electric *spectacular* in Times Square. Designed by Norman Rockwell, it used seven thousand bulbs and showed a Southern gentleman drinking coffee, served by his seventeen-foot-tall black butler.

All Aboard for the Maxwell House Show Boat

Despite its new vacuum can and Times Square presence, Maxwell House continued to lose market share. In October 1932, after much discussion with his partners, Atherton Hobler met with the General Foods managers and leveled with them: Maxwell House Coffee was too expensive, it didn't taste good enough, and it needed a dramatic new advertising approach. He proposed what he called "the most startling recommendation I have ever known in advertising and marketing." Improve the blend by using less Brazilian and more high-grown mild beans. Cut the retail price by a nickel. And last, cut the advertising budget by $2 million, down to $1.1 million, but apply all of it to radio. It was a major gamble; sales would have to go up 20 percent just to break even, but the General Foods men were willing to try anything. Later that same month, the first weekly "Maxwell House Show Boat" went on the air at the unprecedented cost of $6,500 a show.

Inspired by the 1927 Jerome Kern musical (itself based on an Edna Ferber novel), the radio series reverted to the popular Dixieland Maxwell House theme, but with—quite literally—plenty of new bells and whistles.[4] "Come aboard, folks," production manager Tiny Ruffner announced as the steam whistle blew. "Your ticket of admission is just your loyalty to Maxwell House Coffee." Then jovial Cap'n Henry, played by Charles Winninger (who had created the same part on Broadway), took over for an hour of music, drama, and comedy. Dreamboat tenor Lanny Ross and his radio sweetheart, Mary Lou (sung by Muriel Wilson and acted by Rosaline Greene) crooned to one another. The Show Boat Four—Tubby, Scrappy, Len, and Bob—formed

---

[4]Through his lawyer, Jerome Kern at first objected to Maxwell House having stolen his theme, but Benton & Bowles's lawyer reported in May 1933 that Kern told him, "he is a regular listener to the *Maxwell House Radio Show Boat* hour, which he not only enjoys but considers the best program ever put on the air."

a harmonious quartet. Baritone Conrad Thibault sang earnestly, while Cap'n Henry's sister, Maria (played by Irene Hubbard), joined in dramatic skits. Blackface vaudevillians Pat Padgett and Pick Malone created the comic characters Molasses and January—typical of the racism of the era, but so were Amos 'n' Andy.

The radio show was an enormous hit. The sound effects—surging water from the paddlewheel, clatter of the gangplank—and acting were so convincing that many listeners believed the boat truly existed. Two thousand people waited in vain on the docks of New Orleans when the show's script was set there. The week before "Show Boat" supposedly played Pittsburgh a young General Foods salesman urgently requested tickets and received a return telegram: SHOW BOAT MYTHICAL. NO TICKETS AVAILABLE. The frustrated salesman called his district manager. "Look," he said, "I don't know about that damn 'mythical' stuff. I've got seventy people coming, and I've got to have those tickets!"

By the beginning of 1933 "Maxwell House Show Boat" was the top radio show in the country, a status it would maintain for the next two years. On the January 1 show Tiny Ruffner announced the 5-cent price cut and the improved blend. Within two months, sales increased 70 percent. Chase & Sanborn finally matched the price reduction in April. By year's end, Maxwell House sales had climbed by 85 percent. Under the creative direction of Chet Bowles and Hobe Hobler, the show featured several radio innovations. It was the first show with a live audience, complete with cue-card instructions to LAUGH or APPLAUD. Rather than presenting separate, easily ignored commercials, the Show Boat cast incorporated enjoyment of Maxwell House Coffee in the script itself, complete with the sounds of pouring, rattling coffee cups, and satisfied lip-smacking. Dozens of famous guest stars appeared on the program to sip their coffee, including Bob Hope, Robert Benchley, Gloria Swanson, George Jessel, Jackie Coogan, Amelia Earhart, Dale Carnegie, Lillian Gish, and Gertrude Lawrence.[5]

With the success of "Maxwell House Show Boat" Benton & Bowles quickly added two more radio shows, "Palmolive Beauty Box" and Fred Allen's "Town Hall Tonight." By 1934 their shows held three of

---

[5]Del Monte Coffee imitated the "Maxwell House Show Boat" with its own "Ship of Joy" program, starring Captain Dobbsie.

the top four positions in radio.[6] Other agencies scrambled to catch up. Although radio lacked the visual impact of traditional print advertising, it could reach the one in twenty American adults who could not read, as well as preliterate children. Radio advertising was marvelously unavoidable if one wished to listen to a particular show. While *Saturday Evening Post* readers could simply flip past a coffee ad, "Show Boat" listeners couldn't avoid the Maxwell House pitch unless they got up and turned the radio dial.

Benton & Bowles copywriters took advantage of the popularity of "Show Boat" by featuring photographs of the actors in character in print ads, which further enhanced the illusion of reality. In 1935 Maxwell House ads offered a new twist, offering little vignettes in the form of popular comic strips of the day.

As Bill Benton later observed, "Maxwell House didn't know there was a Depression. The chain stores were selling coffee that was almost as good–the difference was undetectable–for a much lower price. But advertising so gave glamour and verve to Maxwell House that it made everybody think it was a whale of a lot better. It doubled and quadrupled in sales." It also helped, Benton knew, that caffeine was addictive. "Every businessman wants a product that is habit-forming. That's why cigarettes, Coca-Cola and coffee do so well."

While Bill Benton and his partners were convincing the American public to drink more and more Maxwell House Coffee, Franklin D. Roosevelt was trying to sell his New Deal and instill hope in a demoralized country. Recognizing the unpopularity and impracticality of Prohibition, Roosevelt approved its repeal in 1933. Coffee, well-entrenched and well-advertised, did not suffer from renewed competition from legal liquor; rather, it continued, as it had in the speakeasies, to provide an illusory sobering effect for those who drank alcohol to excess.

The incredible success of the Benton & Bowles radio shows led to much more business. From billings just shy of a million dollars in 1931 the numbers leaped upward: $3.1 million in 1932, the year B & B secured the Maxwell House account; $4.5 million the following year; $7.1 million in 1934, and $10 million in 1935. By that year the staff had grown to 174. It was the middle of the depression and the three

---

[6]The same year they could have had the Coca-Cola radio account if they had agreed to merge with the D'Arcy agency. Coke boss Robert Woodruff, used to instant obedience, ordered the consolidation but the partners declined.

partners were rolling in money. Chet Bowles and Hobe Hobler bought huge yachts. Bill Benton built a Connecticut country estate.

At the height of the firm's popularity, with "Maxwell House Show Boat" cresting the waves of the air, Bill Benton resigned on his thirty-sixth birthday. He pursued a varied career in which, among other things, he made a fortune by buying and selling the Muzak Corporation, then purchasing the publisher of the Encyclopedia Britannica. Chester Bowles followed him out of advertising in 1941, taking a job with the Office of Price Administration, subsequently becoming the governor of Connecticut and U.S. ambassador to India. While he was governor, Bowles appointed his old partner Benton to fill out a term in the U.S. Senate, where he fought against the witch hunt of Senator Joe McCarthy.

Atherton Hobler was the only one of the original trio who remained in advertising. He was stuck with the well-recognized name of Benton & Bowles and became increasingly irritated as his former partners began to disparage advertising. Bill Benton later observed that "the Maxwell House Coffee program was, to my eternal regret, the stimulus that changed the commercials. . . . It inevitably led to the singing commercial and all the current excesses." He lamented that "I invented things that I now apologize for."

Arbuckles' and MacDougall Fade Away

While the depression didn't hurt Maxwell House or Chase & Sanborn, it ruined some U.S. coffee firms. In 1932 the two Jamison sisters hired C. King Woodbridge, the president of the Dictaphone Company and a noted "turnaround" expert, to supervise Arbuckle Brothers, the failing giant of the industry. In the next few years the venerable Arbuckle firm tried a number of different tactics, such as raising cash by selling its Yuban brand to another company. Without national advertising, however, Arbuckle was doomed. In 1937, with little fanfare, Woodbridge sold the business to General Foods, where Ariosa was allowed to die a quiet death. A few years later General Foods bought Yuban, which joined Maxwell House as a sister brand. By the time the two Jamison sisters died in the early 1940s the vast Arbuckle fortune had disappeared.[7]

---

[7]Even with enormous legal fees, it is difficult to understand how the estate that had been worth $40 million a few years earlier just evaporated. "To be told at this date," wrote one of the Arbuckle farm workers, "that there is nothing left ... to pay Miss Jamison's just debts and last bequests–it is a mystery for the Gods to solve."

When the depression hit, fewer carefree lovers sought the Italian atmosphere at Alice Foote MacDougall's elaborate coffeehouses. In 1930 she relinquished active control, and two years later the chain went into receivership, dragged down by the million-dollar lease. MacDougall, then sixty-five, resumed personal control. Within four months she increased business by 50 percent and repurchased the Cortile and Grand Central shops; but they never equaled their former glory, and the 1933 repeal of Prohibition proved the final straw. In place of expensive Italianate splendor, depression-era consumers now populated the Automat and small coffeeshops advertising "Nothing over 5¢." MacDougall's son Allan left the coffee business to join National Distillers, where he bought fine wines and liquors.

Lobbing Coffee Hand Grenades in Chicago

The Great Depression did not hurt the American coffee industry as a whole, though it promoted further consolidation and intensified competition. Comfortable profit margins, once the standard for the industry, disappeared. The big brand names such as Maxwell House, Chase & Sanborn, Eight O'Clock, and Jewel continued to add market share while regional coffee companies struggled to maintain their niches. Many small roasters went out of business.

In 1936, Herbert Delafield, the chairman of the national association lamented that while coffee had traditionally been a "gentlemen's business," it was being hijacked by "sharp shooting and scalping operators" who used coffee more than any other product as a "loss leader." The idea was to offer a popular staple at low prices—or even at a loss—in order to draw customers into the store, where they would buy other products. "Many medium and small sized companies depressed by four years' constant hammering are beginning to wonder whether or not continued effort is worth while." The more innovative regional roasters, however, managed to survive through clever advertising and loyal customers. They specialized in the restaurant–office institutional market, where local connections and special service still could compete successfully. Others roasted private label coffee, packing it under different names so that other businesses, such as chain stores, could resell it as their own. In addition there were "toll" or "trade" roasters, who roasted someone else's green coffee for a per-pound fee.

Two such regional roasters achieved the seemingly impossible—launching consumer brands. Joseph Martinson had built a thriving institutional business in the metropolitan New York area, supplying his high-grade Martinson Coffee to upscale hotels, restaurants, and steamship lines. In the late twenties he entered the packaged coffee field, offering only one top-grade blend for a premium price and advertising it steadily. Refusing to cut prices, he instituted a monthly mailing to ten thousand retailers and chain stores. Martinson's great rival was Sam Schonbrunn, who produced the high-quality Savarin brand ("the coffee served at the Waldorf Astoria"). Martinson and Schonbrunn demonstrated that quality coffees could rise above the fray of commoditized price-cutting firms—a lesson that had to be relearned periodically in the years to come. They survived and thrived during the depression.

The once-dynamic National Coffee Roasters Association found itself outmoded and outflanked by the wagon peddlers, chain stores, and green coffee importers. In 1932 the NCRA reluctantly bound together with all the other coffee men to form the Associated Coffee Industries of America, hoping to squeeze general promotional funds from the likes of Jewel, A & P, Standard Brands, and General Foods. Yet none of the coffee producers saw the wisdom of spending their money to promote someone else's brand. It was therefore "every man for himself," as a trade editorial lamented.

The San Francisco family businesses of Hills Brothers, Folger's, and MJB all expanded successfully west of the Mississippi River, with Hills Brothers commanding the greatest share of the market. In 1930 Hills Brothers boasted a cash hoard of $5 million. Having honed its approach to new markets in ninety other towns in the Midwest, the Hills Brothers sales force swung into action with military precision in Chicago in September 1930, nearly a year after the stock market crash. For a few months grocers were showered with oversized postcards previewing the campaign. Then beginning in February 1931 the company hired the Donnelley Corporation to mail half-pound vacuum-packed samples of Red Can Coffee to every Chicago telephone subscriber. They simultaneously mailed notices to over ten thousand independent grocers, announcing the sampling program. In the next few months over five hundred thousand families would receive a Hills Brothers coffee gift in the mail. "The battle is on," the Hills Brothers sales bulletin trumpeted. "To the victor belong the spoils." Within a year Hills Brothers surged past Maxwell House and Chase & Sanborn to become the best-selling coffee in Chicago, a position it would hold for the next two decades.

Despite its success in Chicago, however, Hills Brothers' overall sales slid during the early depression years. Advertising expenses had broken over $1 million for the first time, but sales dropped from 39 to 37 million pounds. E. E. Hills reiterated the family commitment to the firm, refusing to sell out to a conglomerate. "The spirit of our organization should not be dimmed by outside interference. . . . It is our intention to maintain our policies, our ideals, our ownership and our independence of thought and operations."

Yet sales figures continued to erode, falling to 25 million pounds in 1932. The company clung to its old campaign, "A Little at a Time," emphasizing the superiority of its "controlled roasting," vacuum packing, and high-quality beans. Yet consumers continued to slip away, attracted by the cheaper bargain brands. By 1933 they were also paying less attention to the Hills Brothers newspaper ads; instead they fiddled with their radio knobs to find their favorite show, which may no longer have been "Maxwell House Show Boat."

Getting the Gong and Trouble in Eden

In 1935 Standard Brands launched the "Major Bowes Amateur Hour" for Chase & Sanborn Coffee. Bowes, an unctuous master of ceremonies, introduced acts that would "get the gong" if they bombed. The J. Walter Thompson men soon modified this reliance on humiliation, stressing the positive aspects of the show and gonging fewer hopeful performers.

The "Amateur Hour" traveled from city to city, featuring aspiring local acts and attracting immense attention to Chase & Sanborn in those areas. The acts were varied, producing music from saws, jugs, bells, and toothbrushes. Tap dancers pounded the boards. Mimics tried to do FDR or movie stars. A young Frank Sinatra appeared on the show as part of the Hoboken Four, a winning quartet. The show allowed listeners to call in and vote to determine the talent contest winners; ads pleaded with viewers to purchase more Chase & Sanborn Coffee so that more amateurs might make good with Major Bowes. "THEIR

CHANCE DEPENDS ON YOU," headlines asserted. "Your purchases of Chase & Sanborn Dated Coffee help the Americans win fame, fortune." Civic organizations, retail grocers' associations, and other groups encouraged their members to buy Chase & Sanborn. Major Bowes was made Honorary Governor of Louisiana when the show appeared in that state. By the end of the year the "Amateur Hour" had passed "Show Boat" to become the number-one show on the air.

In May 1937, after Bowes defected to Chrysler for a higher salary, Edgar Bergen and his outspoken dummy, Charlie McCarthy, took over the pitch for Chase & Sanborn, consistently delivering high ratings in radio polls. Through Bergen's skill and wit the supposedly fourteen-year-old dummy often seemed more real than his master, as he sparred with guests. One annoyed critic called him "a little vulgarian, a brassy, blustering, sniggering blockhead." Yet it wasn't McCarthy who caused problems for the coffee sponsor, but Mae West. On Sunday, December 12, 1937, the sex queen flirted with the "short, dark and handsome" dummy, lasciviously calling him "all wood and a yard long." Despite the fact that his kisses gave her splinters, she invited him home with her. "I'll let you play in my woodpile," she cooed.

Such banter was merely the prelude to a racy Garden of Eden skit. Eve (Mae West) conned the "long, dark and slinky" snake (Edgar Bergen) into squeezing through the fence to get at the apple tree. It was quite clear that the snake—"my palpitatin' python," as West called him—was a phallic symbol, and that the struggle through the fence represented sexual intercourse.

SNAKE: I'll—I'll do it (hissing laugh).
EVE: Now you're talking. Here—right in between those pickets.
SNAKE: I'm—I'm stuck.
EVE: Oh—shake your hips. There, there now, you're through.
SNAKE: I shouldn't be doing this.
EVE: Yeah, but you're doing all right now. Get me a big one. . . . *I feel like doin' a big apple.* . . . Mmm—oh . . . nice goin', swivel hips.

When West delivered the line "*I feel like doin' a big apple*" in her inimitably sultry voice, the studio audience howled. Many listeners, however, were outraged. "Mae West Pollutes Homes," an editorial cried in the *Catholic Monitor*. Professor Maurice Sheehy from Catholic University fumed that Mae West, "the very personification of sex in its lowest connotation," had "introduced her own sexual philosophy" into the Bible. A politician read Sheehy's statement into the *Congressional Record*. Another senator called for a board of review "to prevent the recurrence of such broadcasts." Frank McNinch, the head of the Federal Communications Commission, declared that the skit was "offensive to the great mass of right-thinking, clean-minded American citizens."

Standard Brands executives hastened to apologize for Chase & Sanborn. Mae West was unrepentant. "Did they expect a sermon? Why weren't they in church if they were so religious? Forty million people listened to that broadcast." Edgar Bergen and the irascible Charlie McCarthy survived the flap, not least because ratings soared following the racy broadcast. They continued to sell Chase & Sanborn Coffee for years to come–especially after a survey showed that four times as many regular listeners used Chase & Sanborn as those who never tuned in.

Other major coffees also sponsored regional radio programs. Folger's first offered a detective serial, then "Judy and Jane," a daytime soap opera. G. Washington, the instant coffee, aired "Professor Quiz and His Brainbusters," featuring brainteasers. The various depression-era coffee-sponsored radio programs, combined with an onslaught of print ads, clearly got the message across. In 1933 some fifteen hundred housewives were asked to name the product with the "date on the can." Sixty-nine percent identified it as Chase & Sanborn, and by the end of the decade it was undoubtedly nearer 100 percent, along with an ability to name the coffee that was "good to the last drop."

By the end of 1937 the popularity of Edgar Bergen and Charlie McCarthy finally drove the now-venerable "Maxwell House Show Boat" off the air. In 1938 Maxwell House sponsored Fanny Brice as the hysterical Baby Snooks, along with an entire stable of MGM stars, twenty-two of whom appeared on the first show, including George Murphy, Buddy Ebsen, Sophie Tucker, Judy Garland, Jeannette MacDonald, and Allan Jones. The reciprocal nature of the radio–movie tie-in soon became apparent: the day after MacDonald and Jones appeared on the Maxwell House radio program their new movie opened nationwide. In addition to being good to the last drop, Maxwell House now boasted of its "Friendly Stimulation" and "Radiant Roasting."

Coffee Brutes and Bruises

The battle for coffee market share in the United States intensified in the mid-1930s, with combatants beginning to run attack ads against their opponents. Chase & Sanborn's print assaults on fellow coffee firms escalated. "Stale Coffee loses flavor . . . is nervously irritating," a *Ladies' Home Journal* ad proclaimed late in 1934. A cartoon strip provided a dramatic—and alarming—illustration: "Here's your coffee, dear," a wife says to her scowling businessman husband over the breakfast table. "I thought we were too old to play mud pies," he growls. Flinging the hot coffee at her, he yells, "What did you put in it this time? Bricks or gunpowder? See how you like it!" She cries, "Oh, you brute! I'm all black and blue." In the final two frames she wears a catcher's mask and holds a shield while offering him a cup of Chase & Sanborn. "The grocer said no husband would ever throw a cup of dated coffee," she observes anxiously. "I'll soon find out." Of course the husband loves it. "Take off the mask, darling. Your grocer knows his coffee. This is too fresh and good to waste a drop."

Ads such as this provide alarming evidence that wife battering was the stuff of comedy during the depression—especially if the husband didn't like his coffee. Terrified wives, hoped J. Walter Thompson admen, would purchase Chase & Sanborn in hopes of avoiding such confrontations; or perhaps the ad appealed to men—emasculated and powerless during the depression—who could at least feel that they were asserting themselves at home through their choice of coffee.[8]

Hills Brothers Coffee ads weren't quite so negative or violent, but they were equally sexist.[9] "Block That Kick," a 1933 ad headline read. "If His Royal Highness, the husband of your house, starts to kick about the coffee—block it at once with Hills Bros. Coffee." The ad went on to

---

[8]The life of the depression-era housewife clearly was not easy. On a popular 1932 radio show one commentator advised housewives to "keep a good big supply of coffee in the pantry. You'll find it something to cling to.... Otherwise, the day will surely come when you'll sit down in the middle of the kitchen floor and scream and yell at the ghastly, damnable futility of it all."

[9]The two original patriarchs, brothers Austin Herbert and Reuben Wilmarth Hills, died in 1933 and 1934, respectively, but their children carried on aggressively. Around the same time the second generation of Folger leadership passed on. Frank Atha died in 1935, followed by Ernest Folger in 1936, leaving third-generation Russell Atha and brothers Peter and James Folger III in charge.

assure the housewife that "there's nothing that soothes the savage mas-culine heart more quickly than steaming cups of this magnificent brew."[10] Trying to lure back fickle consumers who were buying bargain counter brands, the company instituted a Coffee Floaters campaign to stop "floating" from one brand to another. "I'm tired of this con-founded changing of coffees, Mary," a husband yells. The solution is to stick with Hills Brothers, which according to the ad, "actually made more delicious cups" than the cheaper brands.

To halt sliding sales—particularly after Maxwell House lowered its price by a nickel—Gray Hills (who preferred newspapers) reluctantly authorized spot radio ads in 1934, featuring an orchestral "hit of the day" and a human interest skit about Coffee Floaters. That same year the company established a beachhead in New York City in some two hundred stores, sending a half-pound sample to each customer on a grocer's list. They did not advertise in the papers or blanket the city as they had in Chicago, however, and Red Can failed to capture the East Coast market. Nonetheless total sales for the year came back up over 30 million pounds and continued to grow throughout the decade. By 1939 Hills Brothers was selling over 60 million pounds a year.

In the meantime General Foods' Postum ads reverted to their roots in the increasingly negative ad atmosphere. Roy Whittier of Young & Ru-bicam created a cartoon strip featuring "Mr. Coffee Nerves," a villain-ous character who twirled his long pointed mustache, wore a top hat, and caused innumerable problems until Postum banished him, foiled again. Ovaltine, another health drink made of eggs, barley, and malt extract, also sought to woo coffee drinkers.

The two major decaffeinated coffees, Kaffee-Hag and Sanka, had originated with the German inventor Ludwig Roselius earlier in the century but had gone their separate ways. Kellogg's Kaffee-Hag offered a cartoon strip with Artful Annie, a maid who couldn't stand her mis-tress's erratic performance at the wheel. "Please, Miss Mary, it's all that coffee that makes your driving so nervous." Without her knowledge

---

[10]Also in 1933 Hills Brothers took advantage of the jigsaw puzzle craze, giving away twenty thousand puzzles featuring a large coffeepot with cartoon characters. That same year Hills Broth-ers made much of its movie tie-in with *Eskimo*, showing pictures of the cast drinking coffee on the Arctic ice.

Annie substituted Kaffee-Hag. As a result, Miss Mary drove smoothly and still thought she was drinking regular coffee. Other Kaffee-Hag ads warned against "COFFEE HEART" "URIC ACID," "NEURITIS," and "COFFEE SLEEPLESSNESS." "Does your heart pound and act up? Better face the truth. See your doctor. But don't rebel when he says, 'No Coffee!'"

Sanka, owned by General Foods, didn't employ quite such overt scare tactics, but its advertising too was negative toward coffee. One ad featured an illustration of an apple. "In it, there are SEEDS. Nobody eats them. They do not make the apple taste better. . . . This is a COFFEE BEAN. In it, is CAFFEIN. Caffein has as little to do with the goodness of coffee as do the seeds with the goodness of the apple. So we take the caffein OUT of SANKA COFFEE. The PUNGENT AROMA remains." In 1939 General Foods bought Kaffee-Hag, giving it sole possession of the small American decaf market.

Negative advertising drove many coffee men wild. When the *Tea & Coffee Trade Journal* asked members of the trade for suggestions on increasing coffee consumption, over half answered the following year that false and misleading advertising should be stopped. "We feel that one large coffee firm, in particular, has said so much about the bad effects of coffee that many consumers have become disgusted and are giving up coffee in favor of other beverages," one respondent observed. He of course was referring to Chase & Sanborn.

Those other beverages were likely to be soft drinks. Coca-Cola, the "pause that refreshes," offered a gracious Southern appeal to match Maxwell House, and beginning in 1931 a red-clad Santa Claus began drinking Coke in tremendously popular ads. Pepsi-Cola, offering "twice as much for a nickel," grabbed market share as a cheaper depression-era alternative. Indeed "the competition feared most by coffee [is] Coca-Cola," wrote a *Business Week* reporter in 1936. "In the South Coca-Cola is sometimes a breakfast drink and now the practice of a 'coke' and a cruller in the morning is invading New York."

In addition, coffee was seasonal. "The drop in coffee sales from winter to summer is startling," a 1932 survey noted. "As a mid-morning and mid-afternoon drink," one speaker at a 1938 coffee convention admitted, "[coffee] has been almost completely replaced by other rapidly growing beverages."

For Better, For Worse

Even as soft drinks ate into market share, however, and while Chase & Sanborn, substitutes, and decafs slammed coffee, still there were hopeful signs. Due to the increasing popularity of the vacuum can and ads about stale coffee, more consumers were learning that fresh-roasted, fresh-ground coffee really was ideal, and that coffee should be kept in a cool, airtight container and used quickly. Most important, the percolator was increasingly displaced by the infinitely preferable drip method or the newly popular vacuum coffee maker. Glass Silex vacuum brewers appeared in upscale restaurants and kitchens, where the dramatic brewing method—in which water from a lower container boils into a higher one, only to be sucked back through the coffee when a partial vacuum ensued—could impress the bridge club.[11]

Surveys during the depression showed that a growing number of households were switching from perk to drip and vacuum methods. Still, 40 percent of those surveyed used an inadequate amount of coffee, regardless of their brewing habits. Many roasters, including Maxwell House, took advantage of the situation to advertise different grinds for different methods (coarse for percolator, medium for drip, and finer for vacuum), while others, such as Hills Brothers, advertised the "Correct Grind" for all methods.

The net effect, according to ex-advertising copywriter Helen Woodward, was simply to confuse the consumer. "The housewife experiments with percolators, with drip coffee, with Silex machines, and still most of the time the coffee isn't right," Woodward wrote in 1937. "She is battered and bewildered by new packages and new brands, by advertising."

In general the depression had a paradoxical effect on coffee quality in the United States. Due to lower prices and better education, consumers were developing an appreciation for the finer coffees of the world, such as Colombians and Kenyans. They also took greater care to avoid stale beans, utilize a proper grind, and brew by drip or

---

[11]In 1909 two sisters in Salem, Massachusetts, created the Silex brewer, based on the French vacuum maker created by Madame Vassieux in the 1840s. The Silex used fire-resistant Pyrex glass, however, making it far more durable, and soon was offered with an electric heating element.

vacuum pot. Yet nothing could beat fresh-roasted and fresh-ground coffee, regardless of beautiful packaging and hype. At the same time, fierce competition caused many roasters to cut corners in order to lower costs. They made their low-end blends with inferior beans, and after roasting intentionally added back the chaff to the grind.

Hammering the Chains

In the meantime Jewel Tea, A & P, and other chains were thriving. Due to Jewel's direct home delivery, promoted through advanced premiums that kept customers hooked, the firm rarely advertised other than through *Jewel News*, its newsletter. The company couldn't resist bragging in the Chicago papers when the depression-era popularity of negative ads reached its peak. "We have never joined the Coffee Knockers Circus," Jewel piously advised readers. "Frankly, we don't know of any coffee so poor that it will make a man desert his family, horsewhip his wife, or shoot his stenographer." But of course Jewel Coffee "will give you a new idea of just how good a cup of coffee can be."

Jewel had its share of troubles in the early 1930s, when retailers and roasters lobbied for local ordinances to keep the wagon men from stealing their coffee business. The first legislation banning out-of-town solicitation was passed in Green River, Wyoming, and such laws subsequently came to be known collectively as Green River Ordinances. To get around them the company arranged for customers to "invite" Jewel men into their homes. At the same time, fearing that the wagon routes might have to be abandoned, company president Maurice Karker diversified in 1932 by purchasing seventy-seven Loblaw stores in the Chicago area, along with four others from another chain. The company added more outlets to the newly named Jewel Tea chain of retail stores over the years.

As it turned out, Jewel successfully fought the ordinances in court, and national legislation never materialized. Supervised from new Jewel Park headquarters in Barrington, Illinois, the company added branches in San Antonio, Houston, and Sacramento. By 1936 Jewel operated a fleet of fifteen hundred delivery vehicles serving over a million customers in six thousand U.S. communities. The far-flung wagon men appeared like clockwork every two weeks, always at the same time on the same day of the week.

"Even when many businesses were retrenching and laying off people, Jewel continued to add employees," Karker noted with satisfaction. "Why worry about the competition of advertised brands," a Jewel executive told the wagon men, "when one can prove to his customer that she pays for the advertising—which goes into her waste basket; she pays for the can—which goes into her alley; she pays for the aroma—which goes into the air?" Instead, he asserted, Jewel offered fresh coffee for the same price and threw in a useful premium as well.

Yet the most serious competitor to Maxwell House and Chase & Sanborn was still A & P, whose brands accounted for 15 percent of all U.S. coffee consumption. A & P sold three brands of coffee, Eight O'Clock, Red Circle, and Bokar, increasing in quality in that order. Bokar offered a truly superior cup, "vigorous and winey," composed only of high-grown milds. Whole roasted beans were "ground before your eyes," as an ad asserted, right in the store. Moreover, all the A & P brands sold for 12 to 20 cents less per pound than most competitors. The company sponsored the fifteen-minute "Coffee Time" featuring Kate Smith belting out her hits three times a week, and advertised in local papers. The firm's entire $6 million-a-year advertising outlay was paid by kickback "advertising allowances" from other national brands. In fact the firm didn't need much promotion beyond its own stores and low prices.

In 1929, the year of the crash, company sales had topped a billion dollars for the first time, and A & P, sitting on nearly $41 million in cash and government bonds, was not affected. During the worst years of the depression, from 1929 through 1932, A & P earned over $100 million in after-tax profits.

The Hartford brothers nevertheless watched with concern as their sales slipped by the mid-thirties, challenged by the rise of the supermarket. Large, inexpensive spaces were readily available due to business failures. In 1930 Michael Cullen, a former A & P executive, opened a gigantic food store in Jamaica, Long Island, calling it King Kullen, the Price Wrecker, then added another outlet in an unused garage building. In 1933 the Big Bear Supermarket chain opened in an abandoned five-story factory building, offering at-cost groceries to attract shoppers to the other departments, such as a bakery, delicatessen, auto parts shop, shoe repair, and barber. Other grocery outfits quickly followed suit, including the Streamline markets of Pittsburgh.

These new supermarkets challenged the complacent A & P, Kroger, and Safeway chains, beating them at their own game. Whereas the older chains had thrived by offering discount goods without home delivery, the supermarkets slashed prices even further by giving shoppers baskets to pick their own purchases off shelves, then ringing them up at a register at the front of the store. They also offered free parking to the automobile-driving public. In 1936, with company sales dropping to $800 million, John Hartford of A & P finally convinced his conservative brother, George, to begin closing smaller, unprofitable stores while opening 100 new, big self-serve supermarkets. By 1938 the company had opened over 1,100 supermarkets, each designed to snare at least a 25 percent market share in its area, while the total number of stores had been whittled from nearly 16,000 to 10,800.

The real challenge to A & P and other grocery chains came from a different direction, however. The surge of chain store growth in the 1920s and 1930s brought howls of protests from independent grocers and druggists. Politicians were quick to smell a popular local issue. One Indiana legislator thundered that the chain stores were "sapping the life-blood of prosperous communities and leaving about as much in return as a travelling band of gypsies." A Montana senator prophesied that "this nation will soon be converted into a plutocracy where a few supremely rich men will rule." Anti-chain store legislation proliferated on the state level after 1931, when the U.S. Supreme Court ruled that special taxes against chains were constitutional. Thirteen states enacted such legislation in 1933 alone.

While the Roaring Twenties had crowned the American businessman king, the Great Depression dethroned him, at least in the public eye. A vociferous new consumer movement surfaced. In 1933, *100,000,000 Guinea Pigs* became a best-seller, with a subtitle warning against *Dangers in Everyday Foods, Drugs, and Cosmetics*. "In spite of the loud cries of rage and pain from small merchants," the authors wrote, "no action is taken to block the gradual displacement by A & P and Woolworth and other chain stores, of small retailers in America." Even *Business Week*, certainly pro-business, observed in the mid-1930s that "six years of abnormality have shaken the national admiration for bigness, both in men and in corporations."

To combat this anti-big business movement the chains and department stores formed the American Retail Federation in 1935 under the direction of a former Kroger executive. The new association backfired when it was labeled a "superlobby" for the chains, and a congressional investigation subsequently looked into chain store operations. Committee chairman Wright Patman of Texas, a former district attorney, launched a personal anti-chain crusade that would last for three decades. In an address to the Associated Coffee Industries of America, Patman called the chains "an unholy alliance of tremendous concentrated wealth and enormous influence."

Patman's congressional investigation uncovered the inner workings of A & P, which admitted to receiving $8 million annually in so-called advertising allowances and brokerage fees. To assure their products received prime shelf space, General Foods paid a total of $360,000 a year to A & P, without specifying how much applied to Maxwell House. Standard Brands paid nearly $100,000 annually for Chase & Sanborn's advertising allowance. In essence the testimony revealed that A & P extracted an extra 5 percent discount on top of the bulk discounts they already received.[12]

Largely as a result of the investigation, the Robinson-Patman Act, intended to eliminate such advertising allowances and other "discriminatory" price breaks for the chains, became law in 1936, though it proved difficult to interpret. Angered by what he perceived as unfair legislation, John Hartford announced that he was considering selling all of the A & P retail stores, concentrating only on manufacturing and wholesaling. General Foods and Standard Brands were terrified at the specter of Eight O'Clock Coffee challenging Maxwell House and Chase & Sanborn head to head in all supermarkets. They were relieved when Hartford backed off. Instead, his lawyers told him that the Robinson-Patman Act was so vaguely worded that he could safely resume demanding advertising allowances and brokerage fees. He did. In addition, he began to feature A & P's own brands of coffee and bread more prominently in advertisements. In 1937 the company published *Woman's Day*, a new monthly magazine that charged over a thousand dollars a page for a Maxwell House ad.

---

[12]Such practices are still common, with coffee firms paying slotting allowances to supermarkets for shelf placement.

Meanwhile, as a result of lobbying from small businessmen and the Anti-Monopoly League, in 1935 the California legislature passed an antichain act. The only way to avoid its implementation was to invoke a state referendum, which required over 115,000 signatures on a petition, or 5 percent of the voters. The chains banded together and hired the advertising firm Lord & Thomas. Through radio programs, newspaper ads, booklets, posters, speeches, and essay contests they spread the message that Proposition 22, the chain store tax, would increase food prices. The catchy slogan, "22 Is a Tax on You!" became the battle cry. As a result, the tax was defeated in 1936 by a narrow margin.

The public relations men again swung into action when Wright Patman sponsored even harsher federal anti-chain legislation in 1938. His bill proposed a progressive tax that for A & P would have totaled $471 million, dwarfing the company's earnings for the year, which were barely over $9 million. It truly was a "Death Sentence Bill," as the media promptly dubbed it. Patman campaigned hard for his tax, attacking the fortune amassed by brothers John and George Hartford. "Which will help our country more," Patman asked rhetorically, "a system that will build up huge fortunes in the hands of rich childless brothers . . . , or one that will distribute privileges and opportunities among all the people?"

The Hartfords struck back by hiring public relations counsel Carl Byoir and his firm. In 1939 A & P ran "A Statement of Public Policy," a two-page advertisement, in thirteen hundred papers. George and John Hartford could "retire without personal or financial inconvenience and live very comfortably if chain stores were put out of business," the lengthy ad explained. But eighty-five thousand A & P employees would lose their jobs. Consumers would be denied prices 25 percent lower than the average individual grocer offered. Such a loss would mean that "in millions of homes they would have to leave meat off the table another day a week," not to mention more expensive coffee. In addition, eight million farm families would be harmed, since 30 percent of their produce was sold through chain groceries.

The campaign succeeded. Carl Byoir organized A & P-funded false front organizations such as the National Consumers Tax Commission and Business Property Owners. During congressional hearings the public relations men orchestrated an impressive parade of one hundred fifty witnesses—farmers, manufacturers, organized labor, marketing authorities, consumers—to testify in favor of the chains. Patman's bill died in 1940.

The European Coffee Scene

During the 1920s and 1930s the European coffee industry developed along parallel lines to that in the United States, but with far less centralization, hype, or price wars. On the one hand, northern European consumers in general (in Germany, Sweden, Norway, Denmark, and Finland) drank even more coffee per capita than their American counterparts and demanded higher quality. On the other hand, the French, Italians, Portuguese, and Spanish enjoyed darker roasts that hid some of the bitter-tasting robustas they now added to the arabica beans. The farther south the darker the roast tended to be, so that southern Italians nearly turned their beans to charcoal, while northern Italians enjoyed a moderate roast. Throughout most of Europe the superior drip method predominated. "*Café bouillu, café foutu,*" the French adage warned ("Coffee boiled, coffee spoiled"). Many housewives still roasted green beans at home.[13]

In Italy and to a lesser degree in France the new *espresso* ("made on the spur of the moment") method increased in popularity during the thirties. Created initially at the turn of the century to meet the demand for an "instant" brew, espresso soon attracted devoted followers. Made by forcing hot water under high pressure through very fine grounds, espresso coffee, which takes less than thirty seconds to brew properly, is dark, rich, complex, concentrated, and satiny, with a rich hazel-colored crema on top and an overwhelming aroma.

In 1901 an Italian named Luigi Bezzera invented the first commercial espresso machine, an imposing, gorgeous, complicated affair with assorted spigots, handles, and gauges, all topped with a resplendent eagle.[14] Desiderio Pavoni bought the Bezzera patent, and along with other Italian inventors such as Teresio Arduino, soon produced steam pressure machines capable of spurting out a thousand cups of espresso in an hour. By the 1930s these had spread to cafés all over Europe and to Italian restaurants in the United States. One of the advantages of this

---

[13]Even so, the von Gimborn family continued to sell industrial coffee roasters in Emmerich, Germany, as it had since 1868, introducing the coke-burning, quick-roasting Probat line in 1893, followed in the twentieth century by a gas-heated drum roaster. By the depression era the firm had sold over twenty-five thousand roasters.

[14]Early pressure-brewers had been invented in nineteenth-century Europe.

quick, concentrated brew was that it hid all manner of inferior beans; in fact cheap robusta blends made a richer crema.

Coffee culture permeated Europe. In sidewalk cafés, fine restaurants, smoky subterranean coffeehouses, dining rooms and kitchens, Continentals enjoyed their coffee—either black or with varying amounts of milk, whipped cream, spices, sugar, or alcohol. From Vienna to Amsterdam they frequented their favorite coffeehouse to read the paper, play chess, or simply observe life over the rim of a coffee cup.

Thousands of regional family roasters, many going back generations, supplied the European coffee thirst, but none were owned by conglomerates as in the United States. A few were carving out large market shares, however. The Norwegian roaster B. Friele & Sons, founded in 1800, opened a new seven-story plant in 1938 in Bergen, featuring electric roasters and other modern refinements. The Dutch coffee firm Douwe Egberts had been in the same family since 1753. A hundred years later in 1853 young Victor Theodor Engwall began selling green coffee beans door to door in Gävle, Sweden, eventually founding the roasting firm Gevalia, purveyors of coffee to the royal family. In Finland, Gustav Paulig established Finland's first roasting plant at the turn of the century.

In Germany, Johann Jacobs had opened a small coffee shop in 1895, then began roasting his own coffee. In 1930 his nephew, Walther Jacobs, joined the firm, fresh from the United States, where he had learned the value of advertising. With aggressive salesmanship, slick packaging, and slogans such as "Jacobs Coffee—Satisfaction Down to the Last Bean," the company expanded during Hitler's Third Reich. Many Italian firms also boasted a long history, such as Caffé Vergnano, founded in 1882 by Domenico Vergnano, or Lavazza, begun in Turin in 1895. Founder Luigi Lavazza retired in 1936, but sons Mario, Beppe, and Pericle carried on the family business.

Other firms had begun more recently. In 1924 in Bremen, Germany—already the home of Jacobs Kaffee—Eduard Schopf created Eduscho (a combination of his first and last names) as a mail-order house—the only way at the time to achieve national distribution. By the end of the 1930s Eduscho was the largest roaster in Germany.

Despite their success during the depression, all European coffee firms feared for their businesses as war appeared more and more likely. In 1938, as part of a program to limit imports in preparation for war,

Hitler ordered the cessation of all coffee advertising. In January 1939 German coffee imports were reduced by 40 percent, and just before the war began the Nazi party confiscated the country's entire coffee stocks for use by the military.

At the end of the 1930s a long-established European firm entered the world of coffee. In 1867 Henri Nestlé, a German chemist who had settled in Vevey, Switzerland, had invented an infant feeding formula for women who couldn't nurse. By 1900 he had set up production facilities in several countries, including the United States, where he also made condensed milk. During the next thirty years the international beverage company added chocolate and confectionary products, while establishing factories and purchasing subsidiaries around the globe.

In 1938, after eight years of experimentation, Nestlé launched Nescafé, an improved powdered instant coffee destined to revolutionize the way many consumers around the world drank their coffee. Rather than using the drum method, in which brewed coffee was boiled down to crystals, Nestlé sprayed the liquid into heated towers, where the droplets turned to powder almost instantly. The manufacturers also added an equal amount of carbohydrates (dextrin, dextrose, and maltose), which they believed helped maintain flavor. The next year the company began marketing Nescafé in the United States.

The World of the Future

As the 1930s and the depression came to an end, the United States looked toward the future with much greater optimism than either Latin America or Europe. Now in his third term, Franklin Roosevelt represented stability and confidence as he opened the New York World's Fair in 1939. Life seemed good to the giants of the American coffee world, too; General Foods had just opened the largest coffee roasting facility in the world in Hoboken, New Jersey. The illuminated 182-foot Maxwell House Coffee sign, along with its 42-foot-high cup and nine-foot "last drop," lit the night sky.

At the World's Fair, Standard Brands had built the world's longest coffee bar to serve Chase & Sanborn, made from beans roasted and ground in a miniature demonstration plant nearby. In an open air theater, visitors could laugh while Edgar Bergen and Charlie McCarthy put on a live show, taking care to plug Chase & Sanborn appropriately, of course. "New swing bands at World's Fair are phenomenally popular; can't swing it too fast for the jitterbugs," an ad declared, illustrated by a girl flung high in the air by her partner. "Chase & Sanborn are popular, too, for thrilling, fast delivery." August 31 was set aside as Coffee Day at the fair.

Across the country, at the San Francisco Golden Gate International Exposition, Hills Brothers opened the Coffee Exposition Theater, where it showed its promotional film, *Behind the Cup*, and where tourists could sip coffee while viewing colorful murals depicting scenes from Hills Brothers' history. The company's ads tied in with the event while making a typically sexist appeal. "To a Woman, Every Day is EXPOSITION Day," the headlines read. "Where is the woman who doesn't take a quick glance at every mirror she passes–to 'check-up' and make sure she is looking her best?" asked the copy, while the illustration showed a woman checking herself out. "Is your coffee always at its best?"[15]

Things were indeed looking up for coffee in the United States. In 1939 a major national advertising campaign–funded by six Latin American countries that had formed the Pan American Coffee Bureau–spent $35,000 to encourage summer iced-coffee consumption.[16] They even crowned a buxom swim-suited Miss Iced Coffee. They sponsored a fall–winter marketing campaign, reaching 25 million families through newspapers and magazines, offering true–false quizzes such as "Coffee Makes Physical Work Easier" (True) and "Coffee Makes Your Brain Work Better" (True). The bureau also published *Coffee Facts and Fantasies,* a little booklet to combat the "health fetish" that branded coffee a drug. It reported on an experiment conducted at the University of Chicago in which two groups of college students were given coffee and milk, respectively. Not surprisingly the coffee group complained of disturbed sleep, while the milk group did not. The students did not know, however, that the coffee was decaffeinated, while

---

[15]The sexist Hills Brothers ads fit the times. Women were considered to be emotional, vain, insecure, and easily manipulated. "Woman clings to purchasable things more than her husband," advised Margaret Weishaar in a 1937 J. Walter Thompson publication. "They can be a prop for her. They can bolster her courage, help her keep up appearances."

[16]The six countries forming the Pan American Coffee Bureau were Brazil, Colombia, Cuba, El Salvador, Nicaragua, and Venezuela.

caffeine had been added to the milk. Thus, concluded the booklet, their reaction was clearly psychological rather than physiological.

Meanwhile coffee had taken not only to the radio airwaves but to the air. G. Washington advertised its availability on Eastern Air Transport flights: "Every Cup a Masterpiece Aboard These Giant 18-Passenger Planes"—and all in only three seconds to stir the instant brown crystals. Not to be outdone, Pan American Airways conducted a much-publicized "scientific experiment" to demonstrate that its drip coffee was satisfactory.

The American Can Company, which produced most of the vacuum cans for the nation's coffee, created its own Bureau of Home Economics designed to indoctrinate schoolchildren into the wonders of coffee. The company paid the famed photographer Margaret Bourke-White to spend a month in Brazil taking photographs of coffee cultivation and harvesting, then sent out educational coffee packets to over seven hundred thousand students.[17] The schools were delighted to get the free material as long as it didn't come directly from a coffee company. As a result, thousands of elementary school children penned coffee anthems and poems, such as the following effort from a young student who must have observed her parents:

> *It's a pick-me-up at breakfast,*
> *It's a stimulant at night.*
> *If you ever miss your coffee,*
> *You'll sure be apt to fight.*

National surveys revealed that 98 percent of the families in the United States drank coffee in one form or another, with 15 percent of children between six and sixteen years old partaking, and 4 percent of toddlers under age six. The A & P brands held the lead with 15 percent of the market, while Maxwell House and Chase & Sanborn had snared 13 percent and 11 percent respectively. The rest of the market was split among some five thousand other brands, all of which had managed to survive the depression. Annual U.S. coffee consumption finally had

---

[17]Bourke-White's powerful 1936 Brazilian portraits of black coffee laborers reflected her new-found social conscience. She returned from Latin America to photograph faces of the rural South for *You Have Seen Their Faces*, a collaboration with Erskine Caldwell.

topped fourteen pounds per capita. Seeking an explanation, a *Time* reporter felt that "high-pressure advertising plus cheap retail prices" had helped, along with "the nervous national tempo." He also surmised that "when depression nips an average man's buying power, he finds a 5¢ cup of coffee a sort of emotional ersatz for more expensive things."

To cap off the self-congratulatory year of 1939, grocers displayed a "Parade of Progress" of national brands, with coffee leading the list. In all this jitterbugging, promotional, bigger-and-better hubbub, the caffeinated nation paid scant attention to the gathering war clouds. The American coffee men were more concerned that Mussolini had declared war against coffee as an unhealthy drink. "Granting that the Nazis and the Fascisti are developing a race of supermen," an editorial in the *Tea & Coffee Trade Journal* stated, "the sure way to make them invincible, in the last analysis, is to feed them coffee in constantly increasing quantities and not to deny them the one drink that has ever been the indispensable beverage of strong nations."

∾ 12 ∾

CUPPA JOE

The United States, the leading coffee-drinking nation of the world, conform[s] in general to the coffee-pattern–non-conservative, self-assertive, dynamic. ... Coffee has ... expand[ed] humanity's working-day from twelve to a potential twenty-four hours. The tempo, the complexity, the tension of modern life, call for something that can perform the miracle of stimulating brain activity, without evil, habit-forming after-effects.

–Margaret Meagher, "To Think of Coffee" (1942)

On September 1, 1939, Hitler's *blitzkrieg* stormed across the Polish border. Europe was at war, and a market for some ten million bags of coffee–a little less than half the world's consumption at the time–snapped shut. As in the previous world war, Scandinavian countries initially bought heavily for resale to warring nations, but Germany's quick march through Europe early in 1940 soon closed off those ports. Besides, German U-boats made crossing the Atlantic–or even steaming from Santos to New York–extremely hazardous.

Suddenly the old Brazilian idea of a coffee agreement didn't seem so repugnant to other Latin American producers or to the United States government–at least not its foreign policy wing. Colombia, threatened by Brazil's open-the-floodgates policy and the wartime closing of the European markets, asked the U.S. State Department to help implement an accord. Meanwhile green coffee prices plummeted.

Goose-stepping in Guatemala

With startling German military successes early in the war, the prospect of nazified neighbors to the south seemed all too real. In many Latin

American countries Germans already held significant positions in the coffee industry. One contemporary map of Guatemala, for instance, identified German-owned coffee *fincas* with red swastikas, which dominated the cartography.

Many of the five thousand Germans in Guatemala were open Nazi sympathizers. In the northern province of Cobán, Germans owned 80 percent of all arable land and lived well, with sports fields, swimming pools, and private movie houses, while they paid their workers as little as 3 cents a day. In addition Germans controlled the prominent banking–export house of Nottebohm Brothers and many of the country's coffee export firms. According to contemporary Guatemalan journalist Mario Monteforte Toledo, the Germans "spoke chiefly their own language; sent their children to their own schools, [and] were sworn, almost to a man, to aid by every possible means Hitler's conquest of the world."

Monteforte Toledo probably overstated the case. There were a number of German Guatemalans who had no use for Hitler. Walter Hannstein, for instance, born in Guatemala in 1902, had grown coffee all of his adult life, while surviving pit vipers, army ants, and numerous revolutions. He cared only for his family plantation, not fascist megalomaniacs halfway around the globe.[1] Similarly, Erwin Paul Dieseldorff and his son, Willi, who inherited the huge Guatemalan coffee holdings in 1937, were opposed to the Nazi government. The outspoken Willi even publicized his Jewish ancestry, revealing that his great-grandfather, Salomon Lazarus Levy, had changed his name to Johann Heinrich Dieseldorff.

Local Gestapo members brought increasing pressure to bear on non-Nazi Guatemalan Germans, sometimes threatening them with violence if they did not comply. The Nazis compiled a secret list of forty "unpatriotic" Germans who were to be executed once Germany won the war and took over Guatemala.

Gerhard Hentschke, the commercial attaché to the German Embassy in Guatemala City, deluged Guatemalans with Nazi propaganda (in Spanish) through newspapers, radio, and libraries. Distributors of German goods enclosed Nazi literature in cases of merchandise. Otto

---

[1]See chapter 2 for background on Bernhard Hannstein, Walter's father, and Erwin Paul Dieseldorff. See also the Prologue and chapter 19 for contemporary information on the Hannstein *finca*, now run by Walter's daughter, Betty Hannstein Adams.

Reinebeck, the Nazi minister for all Central America, was headquartered in Guatemala. Tall, blond, and suave, Reinebeck invited groups of German coffee growers to parties, and soon the German Club flew the swastika alongside the flag of the old monarchy. "Germans in Guatemala began to act as if they had already conquered the republic," wrote Monteforte, "and were merely holding it until the Führer called for it." Nazi sympathizers marked the underside of strategic bridges with swastikas to let invading German forces know that these bridges were to be blown up.

Hammering Out a Coffee Agreement

Given this context it is easy to understand the alacrity with which the U.S. State Department hastened to assure coffee growers that they would support an agreement that would save the coffee industries and economies of Latin America. The United States was now the only market for their coffee. If the United States took advantage of the situation to extort ever-lower prices, it would virtually throw an embittered, impoverished Latin America to the Nazis or Communists.

On June 10, 1940, five days after Hitler invaded France, the Third Pan American Coffee Conference convened in New York City, with delegates from fourteen producing countries. After prolonged wrangling the conference assigned the task of quota divisions to a three-man subcommittee, which thrashed out a compromise. The Inter-American Coffee Agreement, which was to be renegotiated on October 1, 1943, allowed for 15.9 million bags to enter the United States—nearly a million over the estimated actual U.S. consumption at the time, which would ensure U.S. citizens of enough coffee while at least providing a quota ceiling so that prices would not decline to absurd levels. Brazil would get the lion's share of the quota—not quite 60 percent—with Colombia snaring just over 20 percent. The rest was divided between other Latin American producers, with a token 353,000 bags left for "other countries" that included Asian and African producers.

Although the conference closed on July 6, 1940, it took nearly five months to achieve an agreement that all of the participants would sign. Mexico and Guatemala were major holdouts, demanding a larger share of the pie. On July 9, Guatemalan dictator Jorge Ubico told John Cabot, the American chargé, that his country's proposed five hundred thousand bag quota was completely unacceptable. Given Nazi victories, the pro-German Ubico felt that he was negotiating from a position of strength. "The mere publication of the plan locally," he informed Cabot, "would result in driving this country commercially into the hands of Germany as soon as commercial relations with Germany can be resumed."

Meanwhile, as the pending quota agreement appeared in jeopardy, coffee prices continued their free fall, eventually reaching 5.75 cents a pound in September 1940, the lowest price in history.[2] Eurico Penteado of Brazil and Sumner Welles of the United States, working through the already-established Inter-American Financial and Economic Committee, agreed to tweak the quotas in a compromise that finally brought all of the signatories to the table.

Welles met on November 20, 1940, with representatives of fourteen Latin American coffee-producing countries to sign the agreement in English, Spanish, Portuguese, and French. The *New York Times* reported that it was "an unprecedented agreement" that would erect "economic bulwarks against totalitarian trade penetration." The agreement was perceived by many leaders to be the first step toward a grand economic union in the Western Hemisphere to counter a fascist European community.

1941: Surviving the First Quota Year

The first year of the agreement, which ran retrospectively from October 1, 1940 (when the new Brazilian harvest began to arrive in the United States) through September 30, 1941, was marked by controversy and uneasy compromise. In the first few months of 1941, coffee prices rose swiftly in response to the newly signed agreement. At first American coffee companies weren't unduly alarmed. W. F. Williamson, secretary of the National Coffee Association, put it succinctly: "The American consumer does not require, and will not insist on having coffee at prices which mean bankruptcy to Latin American producing countries." *Business Week* noted that higher coffee prices would "cushion

---

[2]In 1903 the price of Rio #7 beans fell to 5 cents per pound, but the dollar was worth more in those days, and the Rio bean was inferior to Santos #4, the standard in 1940.

the impact of the war on the economy of Latin American countries," while allowing them to purchase more goods from U.S. manufacturers.

The American consumer's generosity had its limits, however, and by June prices had nearly doubled from their lows of the previous year. At the Coffee Board meetings of the Inter-American Coffee Agreement the producing countries resisted the suggestion put forward by American representative Paul Daniels to increase the quotas. Both Brazil and Colombia flouted Daniels's request by increasing the official minimum price at which they would sell their coffees.

Leon Henderson, head of the newly created U.S. Office of Price Administration (OPA), took notice. Noted for his fierce temper and uncompromising opinions, the New Deal advocate had never approved of the coffee quota agreement and soon clashed publicly with the State Department over the issue. In July, when Brazil announced another minimum-price increase, Henderson blew up. "The unmistakable attitude of the producing countries to date," Henderson wrote, was: "'Here is a chance to make a killing.'" He threatened to suspend the quota agreement completely. Daniels subsequently invoked the right of the United States under the coffee agreement unilaterally to increase the various quotas, without the consent of the producers. On August 11 quotas were officially increased by 20 percent. The ploy worked, as prices began to subside.

In spite of numerous problems during the first year of the coffee agreement, it had clearly saved the Latin American coffee industry, and relations between the United States and Latin America seldom had been more amicable. "The commerce in coffee has been and is the great uniting force in this hemisphere," pronounced Roberto Aguilar of El Salvador. During 1941, per-capita coffee consumption in the United States had risen to sixteen and a half pounds–a new record.

In December six Latin American "coffee queens," funded by their governments, arrived in New York for a triumphant U.S. tour. Eleanor Roosevelt hosted them on her show, "Over Our Coffee Cups," which stressed the theme, "Get More Out of Life With Coffee," then appeared in White House photos with them at a December 5 reception. The coffee queens were scheduled to appear at the Waldorf Astoria a week later for a grand Coffee Ball and fashion show, resplendent in colors such as cafénoir, café conleche, and coffee blossom–but the Japanese upstaged them.

Coffee Goes to War—Again

Just as coffee prices and politics settled into an uneasy equilibrium and consumption was on the rise, the Japanese attacked Pearl Harbor on December 7, 1941. OPA czar Leon Henderson immediately froze coffee prices at their December 8 levels, explaining that the U.S. war entry "created a situation in which the inflationary tendencies in the price of coffee might again be intensified."

The war proved to be a boon for the coffee industry. The army requisitioned 140,000 bags a month, ten times as many beans as they had the previous year, to supply what would become a 32.5 pound annual per-capita military addiction. "The wharves of Santos may now be likened to the conveyor belts of Detroit," wrote one wartime journalist. "Both work for North American defense. Coffee is no luxury drink. It is essential in warfare." One governmental dispatch listed coffee as an essential raw material, "highly important to help maintain morale, both in the army and at home."

Although there were plenty of Latin American beans, shipping space was limited, with every available bottom devoted to the war effort. In addition, now that the United States had entered the war, German submarines posed more of a threat. On April 27, 1942, the War Production Board limited roasters to only 75 percent of the previous year's deliveries. The War Shipping Board took over the entire U.S. Merchant Marine fleet, and in June the Brazilians turned over their boats to the war effort as well, in return for promises that the U.S. Commodity Credit Corporation would buy all of the Brazilian coffee quota, even without available shipping. The War Production Board then took over control of all coffee entering the United States, effectively ending a free market.

By September 1942 the supply situation had reached crisis proportions, with the coffee quota to roasters cut to 65 percent. On October 26 Leon Henderson announced that coffee rationing for civilians would begin in a month, allotting one pound every five weeks to anyone over the age of fifteen. By giving a month's notice he created a wave of panic buying. Long lines of would-be coffee customers waited outside stores. *No Coffee* signs appeared in store windows, but for favored customers small bags of coffee were quietly slipped into grocery bags, almost like contraband drugs.

Henderson tried to assuage public fears by asserting that his coffee allowance meant 10.4 pounds for each adult—not much less than the per-capita consumption during the depression. Coffee men pointed out, however, that the official per-capita figures included children. Adjusted for adult consumption only, the figures revealed that rationing cut coffee allotments by half.

Rationing threatened to undo all of the brewing directives the roasters had been trying to teach American consumers. Articles instructing housewives in the fine art of diluting good coffee appeared. Jewel advertised that consumers could "get up to 60 fragrant cups per pound." President Franklin Roosevelt (who apparently didn't listen to his wife's radio program) horrified coffee men by suggesting that coffee grounds be used twice. "The newspapers are full of what to use instead of coffee," complained a Chicago coffee broker, "so we are getting malt, chick peas, barley, a concoction with molasses and cooked to a brown paste—anything to have a colored liquor." Postum experienced a renaissance. High-quality blends such as Hills Brothers and Martinson's also thrived. While Brazilian beans needed long transport, Colombian and Central American coffee had less distance to travel on ships and could also arrive by train across the Mexican border.

On February 2, 1943, the Germans lost at Stalingrad. From that point on the war clearly turned in favor of the Allies. German submarines no longer posed much of a threat to Atlantic freighters, and coffee flowed more freely from Brazil. On July 28 President Roosevelt announced the end of coffee rationing. While the period of enforced coffee curtailment helped inure Americans to a weak brew, it also reinforced the national craving, as scarcity often does. During the rationing period the poet Phyllis McGinley penned an eloquent lament in which she spoke of the "riches my life used to boast":

> *Two cups of coffee to drink with my toast,*
> *The dear morning coffee,*
> *The soul-stirring coffee,*
> *The plenteous coffee*
> *I took with my toast.*

Coffee at the Front

While civilians yearned for plenteous cups, the military supplied defense workers and troops with as much as they could drink. Production went up when factory workers were allowed time off for a cup of coffee. Jewel and Maxwell House converted part of their factories to manufacture "10-in-1" rations: waterproof, shockproof packages that included enough food and coffee for ten people for a day. The Quartermaster Corps, the military provision arm, roasted, ground, and vacuum-packed coffee at four facilities, in addition to subcontracting to nineteen commercial roasters.

After D-Day the military shipped green beans overseas. Army coffee men jury-rigged roasters from gasoline drums when they couldn't get industrial machines, roasting 12,000 pounds of coffee a day in an old Marseilles factory. Over fifty Mobile Units provided coffee and baked goods. In the Pacific theater of operations staff sergeant Douglas Nelson, a former Maxwell House employee, erected a plant in Noumea, the capital of New Caledonia, where he roasted locally grown coffee. In Europe three hundred Red Cross "clubmobiles" dispensed coffee and doughnuts to troops along with books, magazines, cigarettes, and phonograph records.

Coffee drinking became a competitive activity within branches of the military, with the U.S. Marines claiming the highest consumption level. "Many Marines drink five canteen cups full of coffee at one meal, or the equivalent of 20 regular cups, and think nothing of it," bragged one lieutenant. Far from the comforts of home the G.I. would do just about anything for a hot cup of coffee in a frigid foxhole, even if it was made from instant powder. The army provided lightweight aluminum foil packets of soluble coffee in K rations. By 1944 in addition to Nescafé and G. Washington there were ten other companies, including Maxwell House, making instant coffee, all of it requisitioned by the military. "Soldiers report that the capsules are easy to handle and the coffee simple to prepare," wrote *Scientific American* in 1943. "Where a fire is not available, the powder may be mixed with cold water."

But to the exhausted grunt at the front, warmth meant everything. Bill Mauldin, the war cartoonist and chronicler, described an infantry platoon stuck in the mud, rain, and snow of the northern Italian mountains. "During that entire period the dogfaces didn't have a hot meal. Sometimes they had little gasoline stoves and were able to heat packets of 'predigested' coffee, but most often they did it with matches—hundreds of matches which barely took the chill off the brew." The American soldier became so closely identified with his coffee that G.I. Joe gave his name to the brew, a "cuppa Joe." The military men also had quite a few other nicknames for coffee—depending on its strength or viscosity—including java, silt, bilge, sludge, mud, or shot-in-the-arm.

The American soldier may have had to settle for cold, instant coffee, but at least he had real coffee, unlike the Axis powers and occupied countries. By the summer of 1943 genuine coffee in Nazi-occupied Netherlands cost $31 a pound, when it was available at all. Many Dutch citizens were reduced to digging up, roasting, and grinding tulip bulbs to make a substitute. Even had they been able to get real coffee beans, however, many European roasters couldn't have done much with them. In Germany, France, the Netherlands, Belgium, and Italy bombs had reduced roasting plants to rubble.

To add insult to injury the British sent Royal Air Force squadrons that in mock bombardments dumped small bags of coffee beans over Nazi-occupied territory. The idea, a contemporary journalist wrote, was that "wherever the coffee beans fell, dissatisfaction would blossom." Although a diabolical way to taunt the deprived inhabitants, the coffee bombs failed to end the war.

Denazifying Latin America

Meanwhile, under United States coercion German, Italian, and Japanese settlers in Latin America—many of whom were coffee growers—were increasingly subjected to official blacklists. Their farms and businesses were confiscated, and in many cases they were actually deported and incarcerated. There has been a great deal of publicity about the internment camps for Japanese Americans, yet few people are aware that the U.S. government extradited coffee growers from Latin America to imprisonment in similar internment camps.

In Brazil, where there were sizable populations of all three nationalities, dictator Getúlio Vargas had been slow to side with the Americans. Before Pearl Harbor he repeatedly played Germany and the United States off against one another in masterful fashion. As German victories piled atop one another in the early part of the war, Vargas gave a proto-fascist speech in which he praised "nations imposing themselves by organization which is based on a sentiment of the Fatherland, and sustained by the conviction of their own superiority."

Pearl Harbor, however, swung Vargas decisively toward the U.S. side, and as German submarines sank Brazilian ships, public outrage burst forth. In March 1942 Vargas ordered the confiscation of 30 percent of the funds of all eighty thousand Axis subjects in Brazil, though only seventeen hundred or so were Nazi party members. In August Brazil officially declared war against the Axis powers.

In Guatemala, pragmatic dictator Jorge Ubico abandoned his German coffee friends in the wake of Pearl Harbor. With Ubico suddenly assuming a strong pro-American posture, a blacklist of German coffee concerns–prepared months before under pressure from the U.S. State Department–went into effect on December 12, 1941. "Interventors" took over farms owned by most native Germans and even some Guatemalan-born Germans. The government ran the German-owned export firms. Many Germans, even very old men, were arrested and shipped off to Texas internment camps beginning in January 1942. Germans were grabbed from all over Central America. Many were traded back to Germany (where they may never have lived) in return for American civilians interned behind enemy lines.

A total of 4,058 Latin American Germans were kidnaped, shipped to the United States, and interned largely to "hold them in escrow for bargaining purposes," as an internal U.S. State Department memo put it.[3] Another motivation may have been to eliminate business competition. Nelson Rockefeller, who headed the Office of the Coordinator of Inter-American Affairs and supervised counterintelligence efforts, emphasized the necessity of preventing German expansion in "America's backyard." Berent Friele, the coffee czar, left A & P to become Rockefeller's Brazilian agent, helping him survey the Amazon for future development.

In an extraordinary twist of logic the Latin American Germans were dragged into the United States, then imprisoned for illegal entry into the country.[4] Walter Hannstein nearly lost La Paz, his coffee *finca* in the San Marcos region in western Guatemala, even though he was born in Guatemala, was married to a U.S. citizen, and had pronounced anti-

---

[3]During World War II no Germans were taken to the United States from Brazil, since the program was perceived as an insult to Brazilian national sovereignty. In general only smaller countries, such as those of Central America, could be forced to agree to it. (Of course such governments also took advantage of the situation to grab land or get rid of political opponents who were conveniently labeled Nazis.) Vargas created his own wartime internment camp for Germans and Japanese in the Brazilian Amazon.

[4]In total over 31,000 so-called enemy aliens were interned during the war, taken from their homes in Latin America and the United States, including 16,849 Japanese, 10,905 Germans, and 3,278 Italians.

Nazi views. An FBI agent interrogated not only Hannstein and his wife, Marley, but their two terrified young daughters. "*Do you speak German? Do you know who Hitler is? Do you ever say Heil Hitler?*" Hannstein's farm and freedom were saved when he produced the list of forty Guatemalan Germans earmarked for elimination by the Nazis. Hannstein's was the thirty-sixth name on the list.

The U.S. Industry Survives the War

In the meantime the U.S. coffee industry adjusted to war conditions. With most of its male employees at the front, Jewel turned to women wagon route drivers for the first time, discovering that they could sell just as well as men. Myrtle Gutwein, for instance, won sales awards during the war. In addition to her sales savvy she was a humanitarian, occasionally paying for the coffee and rice of a single mother and her crippled son. Jewel even published *Women at Work*, a booklet with advice such as: "Certain ladies' fronts and backs are simply just not made for slacks." Women also proved their worth in coffee factories throughout the country, not only in routine, menial jobs but as roastmasters and supervisors.

In 1942 Maurice Karker joined the War Department (though remaining Chairman of the Board), leaving the Jewel presidency to Franklin Lunding. Due to Karker's influence and Jewel's contract to make 10-in–1 ration packs, the company received priority on restricted machinery parts and labor to keep their delivery trucks running. By the war period 65 percent of Jewel's sales volume came from its retail stores, but over 60 percent of its *profits* still derived from the lucrative wagon routes.

Maxwell House made patriotic appeals for its coffee. "Coffee's in the fight too! With the paratroopers . . . in the bombers . . . on board our Navy ships . . . the crews turn to a steaming cup of hot coffee for a welcome lift." General Foods urged housewives to put up fruits and vegetables in empty Maxwell House jars, doing "your bit for Uncle Sam."

The other coffee companies made similar albeit less strident patriotic appeals. The third-generation Folgers both went to war in their own ways. James Folger III was appointed to the War Production Board, while his brother, Peter, joined the marines. Meanwhile the Folger's plant manager found himself, according to a company history, "in a nightmare of coffee without containers, bottles without tops, mountains of ration stamps to be accounted for, and the whole normal chain of production and delivery broken down." Yet the war swelled California's coffee-drinking population, as many who had migrated to work in the war plants stayed. Veterans who had embarked from San Francisco for the Pacific theater of war returned to settle down. The state's population nearly doubled in a decade.

In 1940 Hills Brothers had opened an eight-roaster factory in Edgewater, New Jersey, from which it planned to supply the Midwest, and it hoped, eventually the entire East. Unfortunately for the company the war interrupted its expansion plans. Owing to shortage of manpower Hills Brothers let females into the cupping room, formerly a sacred male inner sanctum. Elizabeth Zullo and Lois Woodward, two Hills employees, learned to slurp, swirl, and spit with the best of them.

Chase & Sanborn had been struggling to maintain profits even before the war. Its parent company, Standard Brands, had traditionally been able to rely on Fleischmann's Yeast as its core moneymaker. But the American housewife had stopped baking bread by this time, the repeal of Prohibition ended the yeast market among illicit home brewers, and the patent medicine claims for yeast cures fizzled. The intensely competitive coffee market didn't offer the same profit margins. As a result, Edgar Bergen and Charlie McCarthy were cut to a half-hour, while Dorothy Lamour vanished from the show altogether. The Chase & Sanborn freshness claim, formerly based on twice-weekly deliveries along with yeast, were rendered moot by other brands' vacuum packs.

With profit margins dropping below 10 percent, and Chase & Sanborn's market share falling several percentage points behind that of Maxwell House, the company finally opted for vacuum cans in November 1941. The next month the company brought in James S. Adams from Colgate-Palmolive-Peet as president, just in time for Pearl Harbor. Adams completely reorganized the company, replacing key executives and suspending dividends. He tried to increase coffee sales by adopting a glass jar vacuum pack, but the war environment did not favor shifts in brand preference.

The war essentially put the U.S. coffee industry on hold, with roasters simply maintaining their positions, biding their time until the conflict and price controls ended. The major roasters such as Maxwell House dominated an industry that had seen considerable consolidation. In 1915 over thirty-five hundred roasters provided coffee to the

U.S. consumer. By 1945 there were only fifteen hundred roasters. Of those, only fifty-seven–less than 4 percent of the total–roasted more than fifty thousand bags a year.

Good Neighbors No Longer

As the war neared its end the price ceiling on coffee entering the United States–held at 13.38 cents a pound since 1941–became increasingly onerous for the producing countries. Although the Office of Price Administration (OPA) had allowed increases for consumer items grown domestically, it stubbornly refused to raise coffee prices. By fall 1944 the situation in Latin America had become critical. In the New York *Journal of Commerce*, El Salvador's Roberto Aguilar pled for a price rise for destitute growers. "They're making no profit today, they're not even holding their own." Because they couldn't pay better wages, the growers were losing workers to more remunerative industrial jobs. "The entire coffee industry is gravely ill, on the verge of collapse," he concluded.

On November 20, 1944, Brazil's Eurico Penteado wrote an open letter to George Thierbach, the president of the National Coffee Association, which the Pan American Coffee Bureau ran as a paid advertisement in over eight hundred U.S. newspapers. Penteado explained that the ceiling price was still 5 percent *below* the average price of the previous thirty years. "This state of affairs is already resulting in the abandonment of millions and millions of coffee trees throughout Latin America," he pointed out, the majority of which were Brazilian. São Paulo coffee production had declined to a third of its 1925 level. So had prices. Yet production costs had doubled. The Brazilian coffee-burning program, in which seventy-eight million bags had gone up in smoke since 1931, finally had ended, but now there was hardly any surplus left.

The Central American growers were equally hard-pressed. "Workers now pay $14 for shoes that formerly sold for $4.50," complained an El Salvador coffee grower. "Wages, already twice what they used to be, will have to go higher." Yet these realities did not appear to concern the American consumer. "The U.S. does nothing but talk about 5-cent-a-cup coffee as being something unalterable." The mild coffee-growing countries could not afford to ship their best coffee at OPA prices, so they began to send lower grades that had not been properly processed or sorted. Many growers withheld their crops entirely, waiting for better prices.

OPA turned a deaf ear to these anguished arguments—which is surprising, since Chester Bowles now headed the agency. Though he had made his fortune advertising Maxwell House, Bowles was now just another bureaucrat who apparently had lost his ability to write clear copy. "It is the view of this Government," he intoned, "that its decision not to increase the maximum prices of green coffee is essential to the maintenance of price controls that are adequate to withstand the inflationary pressures with which this country is now faced."

Bowles's heartless words reflected in part an overall shift in the government's attitude. Sumner Welles, the chief architect and promoter of the Good Neighbor Policy, had been forced from the State Department in 1943, and sympathetic Paul Daniels left the Coffee Board of the Inter-American Agreement shortly thereafter, replaced by Edward G. Cale, a functionary who worked against the coffee-growing countries even while serving on their board. As a former State Department man later recalled, "After the fall of France and during the dark days following Pearl Harbor, the United States had ardently courted Latin America." Now, however, "we had next to no time for [its] problems." U.S. officials regarded the Inter-American Coffee Agreement, begun as an altruistic venture to save the growers, as an embarrassing albatross.

Even when the war ended in 1945, the price ceilings remained in place. With the Brazilian economy in crisis, longtime dictator Getúlio Vargas was forced to resign by a dissatisfied military on October 29, 1945.[5] Though coffee prices were not directly responsible for the dictator's ouster, they added to the public's general discontent. During this crisis period, Brazil abolished its National Coffee Department and reduced its commitment to coffee advertising. Other members of the Pan American Coffee Bureau followed suit.

On October 17, 1946, OPA finally released its stranglehold and eliminated the price ceiling. "Liberated," the single-word headline in the *Tea & Coffee Trade Journal* announced. The first free contract for Santos sold at 25 cents a pound. In following years the price would rise steadily along with inflation.

---

[5]The age of the dictator appeared to be passing. The previous year, Maximilio Hernández Martínez and Jorge Ubico had been forced form power in El Salvador and Guatemala, respectively, as their restive citizens yearned for the freedom and democracy they had heard so much about during the war.

The Legacy of World War II

More than $4 billion in coffee beans were imported into the United States during World War II, accounting for nearly 10 percent of *all* imports. In 1946 U.S. annual per-capita consumption climbed to an astonishing 19.8 pounds, twice the figure in 1900. "Way down among Brazilians, coffee beans grow by the billions," crooned Frank Sinatra, the new teen idol, "so they've got to find those extra cups to fill. They've got an awful lot of coffee in Brazil." Moreover, according to the lyrics, in Brazil you couldn't find "cherry soda" because "they've got to fill their quota" of coffee.

During the war the U.S. civilian population had limited access to soft drinks because sugar rationing curtailed the major ingredient in Coke and Pepsi. But the ever-resourceful carbonated giants still found ways to promote their drinks. Pepsi opened Servicemen's Centers where soldiers could find free Pepsi, nickel hamburgers, and a shave, shower, and free pants pressing. But it was the Coca-Cola Company, through lobbying and insider contacts, that pulled off the major wartime coup: getting its drink recognized as an essential morale-booster for the troops. As such, Coke for military consumption was exempted from sugar rationing. Not only that, some Coca-Cola men were designated "technical observers" (T.O.s), outfitted in army uniforms, and sent overseas at government expense to set up bottling plants behind the lines. When a soldier got a bottled Coca-Cola in the trenches, it provided a compelling reminder of home, even more than a generic cup of coffee. "They clutch their Coke to their chest, run to their tent, and just look at it," one soldier wrote from Italy. "No one has drunk theirs yet, for after you drink it, it's gone."

Coffee men were well aware that Coke and Pepsi were preparing a postwar assault. "The existing carbonated beverage industry is counting on an immediate 20 percent increase in volume just as soon as the war is over," observed Jacob Rosenthal in 1944, observing that teenagers overwhelmingly preferred Coke to coffee. "Today to some 30 million school age youngsters a drink means milk, cocoa, soda or coke. We suffer from . . . anti-coffee propaganda with the youngster market despite the fact that cola drinks, cocoa and chocolate have about as much caffeine as coffee when served with cream and sugar."

"In thousands of drug stores, soda fountains, ice-cream parlors, and soft-drink stands," Rosenthal continued, "these boys and girls get together to talk, listen to music, and maybe to dance." Most of them bought something to drink. "How often is that sale—coffee? You know perfectly well—hardly ever." He urged coffee men to mount a campaign to match the soft drink appeal. "The fact is that as a group these adolescents like to think and act grown-up—and coffee is what the grown-ups drink." So why not capitalize on that yearning for adult status?

Unfortunately for them few coffee men were listening, and the baby boom generation, just then being born, would be devoted to Coke and Pepsi, while coffee itself would become increasingly poor in quality as companies used cheaper beans. A sad chapter in the coffee saga was about to begin, even as coffee appeared triumphant.

~ *Part Three* ~

BITTER BREWS

In the postwar diner, waitresses served up
bottomless cups of weak coffee.

13

COFFEE WITCH HUNTS AND INSTANT NONGRATIFICATION

Over second and third cups flow matters of high finance, high state, common gossip and low comedy. [Coffee] is a social binder, a warmer of tongues, a soberer of minds, a stimulant of wit, a foiler of sleep if you want it so. From roadside mugs to the classic demi-tasse, it is the perfect democrat.

—*New York Times*, 14 November 1949

There's every sign that coffee will remain the country's leading beverage forever.

—1952 *Coffee Annual*

By the end of World War II American coffee had become a standardized product like any other. Maxwell House, Chase & Sanborn, and the rest offered roasted ground coffee containing a blend based largely on average Brazilian beans, and they all tasted pretty much the same. The all-arabica cans weren't bad, but they weren't terribly good either. Despite the much-touted virtues of vacuum cans, the preground coffee gradually staled while sitting on the shelf. As the food writer M. F. K. Fisher wrote in 1945: "It comes in uniform jars, which we buy loyally according to which radio program hires the best writers, so that whether the label is green or scarlet the contents are safely alike, safely middling." And though the drip method was gaining in popularity, Americans came out of the war with a taste for weak, overextracted percolator coffee. "Our national taste," wrote one agonized coffee lover, "is still for pallid, grounds-specked, boiled slops."

From this state of mediocrity coffee went from "safely middling" to awful within the next two decades. What happened? A confluence of economic, political, and technological factors joined to produce the bitter cup.

Guy Gillette's Coffee Witch Hunt

Coffee prices climbed slowly but steadily after they were finally freed from price controls in 1946. By 1947 roasted coffee retailed for more than 50 cents a pound; yet economists and pundits expected a postwar recession any minute. "The popularity of the five-cent cup of coffee has made it an established institution that's here to stay," declared one newspaper prophet. The next year, when many restaurants began charging 7 cents, angry patrons broke mugs, stole silverware, and dumped cream and sugar on countertops in protest. Some coffee firms began to advertise that *their* brand required less grounds to brew a strong cup. One disgruntled coffee man concluded facetiously that if prices continued to rise, "we may yet see coffee so strong you won't have to use any at all to get a delicious aromatic, flavorsome cup."

The price rise stemmed primarily from legitimate free-market forces of supply and demand. After years of surplus coffee Brazil suddenly found itself without enough beans. The once-fertile São Paulo soil had lost its nutrients to coffee production, and the weakened trees were suffering from a broca (coffee bug) infestation. From its all-time high of 19.8 pounds just after the war, U.S. per-capita consumption fell slightly to 18.2 pounds in 1948, while European imports topped seven million bags, aided by the Marshall Plan—still below the prewar twelve-million-bag level, but significant and growing. To keep consumption up, the coffee growers boosted their self-imposed advertising tax from 2 cents to 10 cents to support the Pan American Coffee Bureau. Adventurous homesteaders, eager to capitalize on the pending coffee shortage, began to carve new *fazendas* out of the forest farther south in the Brazilian state of Paraná, but those new trees would take five years to begin producing.

The once warm feelings between Latin America and the United States deteriorated in the postwar world. In 1944 the Brazilians with great fanfare had donated four hundred thousand bags of green Santos beans to the U.S. military. Two years later the U.S. Army turned over five hundred thousand bags of "surplus" Brazilian coffee, along with two hundred thousand bags of Colombian beans, to the U.S. Department of Agriculture, which in turn sold them for an estimated $6 million profit. The Brazilian growers were infuriated. In 1948 the United States allowed the Inter-American Coffee Agreement to expire, and the group's advisory capacity was transferred to a toothless Special Commission on Coffee under the auspices of the Organization of American States.

By fall 1949 Brazil's surplus ran out just as a prolonged drought damaged the year's flowering in August and September. By October 19 green bean prices had crept up to 34 cents. Then prices rocketed to 51 cents a pound by mid-November. Roasters boosted prices to around 80 cents a pound. At restaurants the nickel cup of coffee died a permanent death, yielding to the dime. For the first time in history world coffee imports cost over a billion dollars. Predictably, U.S. consumers protested, while American politicians rumbled ominously.

Senator Guy Gillette, an Iowa Democrat, quickly directed his agricultural subcommittee to investigate coffee prices just before Christmas 1949, then took up the task again from March through May 1950. At seventy-one, the six-foot, silver-thatched Gillette had been raised on an Iowa farm and had grown corn and milked cows on his own farm for fourteen years. "I had the satisfaction of producing something I could see, smell, taste, and touch," he said. Given his background Gillette might have sympathized with the plight of the Latin American coffee farmer, but he manifestly did not. As a dairy farmer, he noted, he drank milk, not coffee.

Gillette stormed against the "manipulators" and "speculators" he held responsible for raising the price of coffee. His counsel, Paul Hadlick, interrogated witnesses with all the hostility of a murder prosecutor. Why had the price of coffee jumped so enormously in so short a time? "Could you explain," Hadlick asked a General Foods representative, "why large Brazilian interests were buying coffee in New York?"

Certainly, speculative interests, including Brazilians, had helped to drive up the price. But the fundamental reason for the price increase was legitimate: there just wasn't enough coffee. The most knowledgeable and passionate congressional witness was Andrés Uribe, the New York representative of Colombia's National Federation of Coffee Growers and chairman of the Pan American Coffee Bureau. Uribe explained the sudden price rise as a result of the "complacency" of the American trade, which never believed that the Brazilian stocks would run out. When they suddenly realized that the 1949 drought was all too real and that there were no surplus stocks, they panicked and began to buy. This resulted in a classic bull-market run for coffee, and as prices shot up, housewives began hoarding, creating an artificial scarcity.

"Latin Americans generally have been profoundly disturbed—even shocked," Uribe told the committee, "that the national integrity of their countries has been impugned; that they have been accused of gouging; of defrauding the American consumer, of engaging in plots and cabals." He pointed out that while the U.S. consumer had paid over $2 billion for roasted or brewed coffee in 1949, only 38 percent of that money had gone to the Latin American producing countries. The majority of the profits had been taken by U.S. roasters, retailers, and restaurants.

Uribe tried to make Gillette and his colleagues understand that while American consumers had to pay a little over 2 cents per cup for household coffee, those who tended the crop relied on it for a pitiful livelihood. If laborers in Latin America were paid U.S. wages, green coffee would cost $6 a pound. "Gentlemen," he said, "when you are dealing with coffee, you are not dealing only with a commodity, a convenience. You are dealing with the lives of millions of people." He paused for emphasis. "We in Latin America have a task before us which is staggering to the imagination—illiteracy to be eliminated, disease to be wiped out, good health to be restored, a sound program of nutrition to be worked out for millions of people. The key to all of this . . . is an equitable price for coffee." If they could secure a fair price, they could work a "miracle" similar to the thriving United States. "If coffee cannot receive an equitable price, then you cast these millions of persons loose to drift in a perilous sea of poverty and privation, subject to every chilling wind, every subversive blast."[1]

Uribe called on them to recognize the brotherhood of the Hemisphere, urging them to remember that the term *American* was not the exclusive province of U.S. citizens. "Gentlemen, I may be emotional about this—but I talk about my people, Americans all." His plea fell on deaf

---

[1] As a Colombian, Uribe must have been exquisitely aware of social problems, since his country had recently begun *La Violencia*, a decade of terror. Some two hundred thousand Colombians would die in the internal conflict.

ears. On June 9, 1950, the Gillette Committee finally issued its official 44-page report, a scathing document so offensive that fourteen Latin American countries lodged an official protest. The American politicians blamed the shortage on Brazilian growers, whom they accused of withholding huge stocks. Gillette suggested that the U.S. government "scrutinize most carefully" any loans to coffee countries, while encouraging coffee growth outside Latin America. The report not only recommended sweeping alterations in established methods of the coffee trade of the United States, but also told Brazil and Colombia that they should change their monetary exchange rates. No further coffee should be purchased through the Marshall Plan, and furthermore a U.S. Justice Department representative should attend future meetings of the Special Commission on Coffee—as if it needed legal watchdogging.

If the report's recommendations were implemented, it would be "tantamount to the bankruptcy of the coffee producing industry," said the Brazilian delegate to the Special Commission. Latin America then would become easy prey to Communists. A Rio newspaper called the report "a model of indelicacy, intimidation and revolting brutality." Colombia's foreign minister denounced the report as "an unwarranted act of interference" and "a tremendous blow to the Good Neighbor policy." In the midst of this outrage former dictator Getúlio Vargas made a stunning populist comeback and was elected Brazil's president later in the year, with a pledge to guarantee a minimum price to coffee growers and to strengthen rather than devalue the Brazilian *cruzeiro*.[2]

Trying to make amends, Assistant Secretary of State Edward G. Miller, Jr. scolded the full Agriculture Committee for not passing the report by the State Department before publication, noting that it was "deeply resented" not only by Latin American governments but by their citizens. He said that "no accusations of manipulation of markets, or collusion between producing interests, should be made unless and until there is clear evidence to substantiate such charges." Indeed there was no such evidence. He criticized the report's recommendations, noting that "little or no [background] information" supported them. Reluctantly, Gillette's committee revised the report somewhat, softening the tone and moderating its harsh recommendations. International feelings were temporarily soothed, just as the conflict in Korea intensified the

---

[2]In Brazil the Gillette razor company took out a full-page newspaper ad to disclaim any connection with Guy Gillette.

new cold war mentality and boosted the price of coffee once again to around 85 cents per pound retail.

Instant, Quick, Efficient, Modern—and Awful

In addition to negative publicity the era of high coffee prices provided the catalyst for profound changes in the coffee industry, including the increasing market share of cheap instant coffee, the dilution of the American cup, price and promotion wars, the widespread use of inferior African robusta beans, increased interest in fertilizers, pesticides, and hybrid varieties, and a new boom in coffee planting.

The instant coffee industry grew tremendously in the postwar period. At first Nescafé dominated sales in the United States through extensive advertising. The internationally powerful Swiss company also introduced its instant brand around the world in Europe, Latin America, Asia, Oceania, and South Africa.

The United States, however, provided the largest potential market by far. At the end of 1945 one commentator predicted the ever-increasing popularity of instant coffee in a "push-button, chromium-plated, begadgeted post-war world" in which consumers were "receptive to new developments and especially to new means to save time and trouble." The modern consumer willingly sacrificed quality for convenience, as new instant brands proliferated. When regular roasted coffee bumped up to 80 cents a pound in 1950, the real rush toward instant was on. Although soluble coffee required a gigantic capital outlay for the tall spraying towers and additional treatment processes, it cost 1.25 cents per cup, 1 cent *less* than regular.

The taste of instant coffee was so poor that it didn't much matter what kind of beans were used—including cheap robusta beans from African colonies eager for dollar infusions to their war-devastated economies. In addition the manufacturers could squeeze more solids out of each bean by overextracting the grounds—a process that produced a bitter regular brew. *Consumers' Research Bulletin* in 1950 noted that soluble crystals made a cup that was "hot and wet and looks like coffee," but that "any resemblance to coffee is purely coincidental." That year U.S. soluble sales increased 25 percent.

By the end of 1952 instant coffee accounted for 17 percent of all U.S. coffee consumption. Instant Maxwell House and Nescafé each were spending over a million dollars a year on advertising. "AMAZING

COFFEE DISCOVERY!" proclaimed Instant Maxwell House ads. "Not a powder! Not a grind! But millions of tiny 'FLAVOR BUDS' of *real* coffee, ready to burst instantly into that famous *GOOD-TO-THE-LAST-DROP* flavor!" The advertisements included a cartoon "magnified view" of the Flavor Buds looking something like asteroids, lending a scientific, modern appeal to the product.

Nestlé took a more down-to-earth, reason-why approach. "Easy to Vary the Strength to Suit Everyone in the Family," the Nescafé ads explained. "No Fussing with Pot or Percolator. No Tricky Parts to Clean. No Coffee Grounds." The pedestrian ads of the Swiss company failed to capture the imagination of the consumer, and in 1953 Instant Maxwell House jumped past Nescafé to become the undisputed leader in U.S. instant coffee sales. It held that position tenuously, however, through low prices and extensive advertising. Consumer surveys showed little brand loyalty for instant coffees.

To raise the enormous capital needed to produce instant coffee (a million dollars a plant), ten smaller roasters led by Joseph Martinson & Company (formerly noted for its high-quality coffee) banded together to form Tenco, a New Jersey cooperative that ran twenty-four hours a day to produce soluble coffee. Veteran coffee men who previously had scorned the inferior taste of instant coffee now took it seriously. Ed Aborn, Jr., who had championed proper brewing methods like his father before him, shocked members of the trade by selling the venerable family firm and joining Tenco. Berent Friele, who had dominated the coffee trade as head of A & P's American Coffee Corporation, convinced Nelson Rockefeller to invest in Tenco.

The new popularity of instant coffee accompanied and complemented the rise of the vending machine. Lloyd Rudd and K. C. Melikian, two army mechanical engineers, formed Rudd-Melikian, Inc. in 1947, introducing the Kwik Kafe vending machine that dispensed hot instant coffee into a paper cup in five seconds. They sold three hundred machines the first year. Other companies quickly went into competition with them. By the end of 1951 there were over nine thousand coffee vending machines in the United States, and by the middle of the decade over sixty thousand.

Invention of the Coffee Break

The vending machine helped facilitate the institutionalization of that most venerated American tradition, the coffee break. In fact the phrase was the 1952 invention of the Pan American Coffee Bureau. Supported by its $2 million a year budget, the bureau launched a radio, newspaper, and magazine campaign with the theme, "Give Yourself a Coffee-Break—And Get What Coffee Gives to You." The bureau gave a name and official sanction to a practice that had begun during the war in defense plants, when time off for coffee gave workers a needed moment of relaxation along with a caffeine jolt. The extraordinary ad blitz also was picked up as a straight news story. "Within a very short space," Charles Lindsay, the manager of the bureau, wrote late in 1952, "the coffee-break had been so thoroughly publicized that the phrase had become a part of our language."

While work time off for coffee had been virtually unknown before the war, 80 percent of the firms polled in 1952 had introduced a coffee break. The Pan American Coffee Bureau used ads and fliers to encourage the spread of the coffee break beyond factories and offices. Hospitals instituted them. After Sunday worship services congregations met for a coffee break with their pastors. The bureau launched a "Coffee Stop" campaign on the nation's roads to encourage motorists to pull over every two hours for coffee as a safety measure. The slogan "Make That One for the Road Coffee" created a furor in the South, where it was interpreted as encouraging drunk driving. Preachers sermonized against the "One for the Road" campaign, citing it as an example of deteriorating national moral fiber. The bureau responded by changing the slogan to "Stay Alert, Stay Alive—Make It Coffee When You Drive."

Even General Dwight Eisenhower's presidential campaign got into the act, using the coffee break idea for its Operation Coffee Cup, in which a "coffee party" introduced Ike to voters "on a cheerful, intimate basis." As *Look* Magazine noted, the coffee social trend was spreading. "Coffee and dessert boost attendance at town meetings; coffee parties raise funds for a symphony orchestra; coffees join teas as vehicles for parent-teacher conferences, spurred by the ease of serving instant coffee to large groups." Now they didn't have to bother with messy cream or milk. Instant Pream, a powdered milk product, provided the perfect tasteless mate to instant coffee. "No Waste, No Fuss," its ads proclaimed.

The Boob Tube

Along with instant coffee and cream came instant entertainment. Though television had made its shaky debut just before the depression, the new medium didn't become commercially viable until after World War II. By 1952 TV had invaded sixteen million homes, reaching 37 percent of the country's living rooms. By the end of the decade virtually everyone in America watched television an average of six hours a day. Although intellectuals sneered at the "idiot box" or "boob tube," it sold products, a fact that was not lost on the coffee industry.

General Foods, which employed over fifteen thousand people and garnered over $500 million in gross annual sales by the late forties, was one of the earliest television advertisers, pushed by Atherton "Hobe" Hobler, still in charge at Benton & Bowles. Hobler, who had seen what radio did for Maxwell House, was sure television, with sound *and* sight, would have an even greater impact. Hobler convinced General Foods advertising manager Charles Mortimer, who was soon to assume the presidency of the food conglomerate. "We want to be in the vanguard of knowledge and profitable use of television," the 1947 General Foods annual report stated. "Television offers us the first commercially feasible opportunity to picture and demonstrate our products and their uses to mass unseen audiences."

That same year Maxwell House Coffee sponsored "Meet the Press" in a changeover from radio to television. To advertise Sanka decaffeinated coffee General Foods sponsored a radio and TV version of "The Goldbergs," starring Gertrude Berg. In it Mrs. Goldberg and her clan provided an affectionate look at New York Jewish immigrant life in one of the first popular situation comedies. Looking out the window, Berg explained to the television audience that they could drink as much Sanka as they liked "because the sleep is left in."

A 1950 survey of forty-three hundred television owners showed that TV had a "far stronger effect on food sales than any other commodity." That same year Coca-Cola paid for a special with Edgar Bergen and Charlie McCarthy, who had defected from Chase & Sanborn to the soft drink. Coke also sponsored a Walt Disney program, and in 1951, "The Adventures of Kit Carson."

General Foods responded with "Mama," starring Peggy Wood, based on the popular Broadway play *I Remember Mama*. This gentle, old-fashioned family program appealed to nostalgia for a simpler time. At the end of each weekly show the cast gathered in Mama's kitchen for a cup of Maxwell House Coffee. That constituted the show's only commercial, which became an integral part of the program. "Mama" ran for eight years, until videotape brought an end to live television drama.

By 1953 it was clear to the coffee industry that in addition to newspaper, magazine, and radio advertising they now had to advertise on television, even though TV spots were significantly more expensive than other media. "High Response Convinces Roasters That T-V Is Their Best Ad Medium," a 1953 headline in the *Tea & Coffee Trade Journal* advised. The next year General Foods added "December Bride," starring Spring Byington, to its lineup of Maxwell House–sponsored shows. When Nestlé ran TV spots offering free samples of Nescafé, more than two million consumers responded over an eighteen-month period.

In the meantime the ailing Standard Brands couldn't afford extravagant television advertising, dooming it to a small market share. To make money in the 1950s you had to spend money. In comparison to General Foods' $27 million net profit in 1949, Standard Brands earned only $8 million. Maxwell House poured $2.5 million a year into advertising, while Chase & Sanborn spent just over $1 million.

Chase & Sanborn print ads claimed that their hand-selected coffee "puts you in a *heavenly* mood," but sales remained earthbound. The J. Walter Thompson admen were hamstrung not only by an inadequate budget but by Don Stetler, the short-sighted Standard Brands ad manager, who believed that coffee was strictly a local business. He canceled the Charlie McCarthy radio show and refused to run color ads in national magazines. In 1949 new president Joel S. Mitchell, a former Kellogg's executive, took over and promptly fired the J. Walter Thompson ad agency after a twenty-year association (though JWT held on to its Canadian account); but a new ad agency didn't help. "Competitive conditions in our industry are intensifying," the 1949 annual report lamented.

Hills Brothers also tried television in the early 1950s, with a blonde woman in an evening dress preparing coffee for guests in her kitchen. To schmaltzy music a female voice sang about Hills Brothers, "the friendliest of blends." Another commercial showed a stiff teenage couple. The boy, sporting a bow tie, opens a can of Hills Brothers and the girl smells it while the announcer intones: "Boy meets girl, girl makes coffee. Hills Brothers Coffee, of course." The boy picks up a tray and offers it to others sitting in the living room. "Hills Brothers Coffee, the life of the party." Even in 1951 such ads must have been perceived as fake and forced.

The Hills Brothers TV spots only ran in local markets. So far General Foods was the only coffee roaster with the funds and foresight to produce national television commercials. In addition to "Mama" and "The Gold-bergs" General Foods sponsored "Captain Video and His Video Rangers," starring handsome hero Al Hodge, who had been the super-hero Green Hornet on radio. Atherton Hobler eventually convinced General Foods to devote 80 percent of its advertising budget to television. In the live commercials for Instant Maxwell House, announcer Rex Mar-shall always showed the famed Flavor Buds under a magnifying glass and then made a cup. On one memorable occasion he intoned the familiar words, "Not a powder! Not a grind! But millions of tiny Flavor Buds of real coffee, ready to burst instantly–" at which point, just as he poured the hot water into a glass cup, it shattered spectacularly, as if on cue.

Price Wars, Coupons, and 14-Ounce Pounds

Due to high prices and the increasing popularity of instant coffee, roast-ers felt compelled to cheapen their brands, use price promotions, pre-miums, and money-back coupons, and cut quantity. The gracious ads of the past that emphasized quality and flavor disappeared. In 1951 Gray Hills announced that Hills Brothers would never resort to special promotions, deals, or coupons. Three years later, with sales slipping, the firm offered cents-off coupons. Some regional roasters who sup-plied the restaurants and institutions began to sell coffee in 14-ounce packages, claiming that their coffee produced the same results as a full pound. On its hundredth anniversary, Folger's advertised that con-sumers could use "one quarter less" of its blend because it was in some way richer. While one roaster denounced this trend as "disastrous," he admitted that he too had succumbed. The result? They were all selling less coffee, and the consuming public was getting a diluted cup.

In Europe economizing on coffee wasn't so much a matter of choice as necessity. As late as 1947 coffee had been so scarce that it was used instead of money on the European black market. By 1952 the French were importing 2.6 million bags of coffee, but over half were low-qual-ity robusta beans from French colonies in Africa. As a result, France's coffee, never known for its high quality, got worse. European home roasting declined as industrial roasters dominated the market. Still most Italians bought whole bean roasted coffee and ground it at home. Ital-ian advertising promised "Paradise . . . in the cup," but the blend con-sisted primarily of cheap Brazils and African robustas.

Neglecting a Generation

Even in destitute postwar Europe, however, a different American beverage was gaining popularity and stealing market share from coffee. On May 15, 1950, *Time* magazine's cover featured a painting in which a smiling red Coca-Cola disk with a skinny arm held a Coke bottle to the mouth of a thirsty globe. The legend beneath read "WORLD & FRIEND–Love that piaster, that lira, that tickey, and that American way of life." The editor of the National Coffee Association newsletter advised that the *Time* Coke article should be "required reading" for coffee men. He pointed out that while Guy Gillette and the consuming public fulminated against high coffee prices, a bottle of Coca-Cola cost over twice as much as a home-brewed cup of coffee. Yet soft drink sales were booming. Could coffee take a lesson from this carbonated caffeine delivery system?

A few months later, however, the same editor wrote complacently: "The coffee trade of the United States has never been interested in this group [under 15] as a market . . . because too many parents would prefer their children's beverage consumption to supplement their diet." It was clear that the stodgy coffee men were not getting the message. While they were busy cutting prices and one another's throats, diluting their beverage, and advertising coffee as a commodity, Coke and Pepsi were successfully promoting an image of youth, vitality, and as *Time* noted, the "American way of life."

In 1950 U.S. coffee per-capita consumption began to fall, as soft drink popularity rose.[3] That year the soft drink firms first reached parity with coffee in their advertising budgets: both beverages spent just over $7 million a year. But only two firms, Coke and Pepsi, dominated the fizzy drink industry, while coffee firms battled one another for their slowly dwindling share of the market. In 1953 tousle-haired, twenty-four-year-old crooner Eddie Fisher appeared in "Coke Time" on TV and radio. Meanwhile most coffee ads featured harried housewives or hurried businessmen. A few made feeble attempts to attract younger consumers, but most coffee firms simply fought it out in price wars, trying to lure housewives with coupons or deals.

---

[3]In 1950 Americans consumed an average of 177 soft drinks a year. By the end of the decade they would gulp 235 annually.

The Land That Smelled Like Money

High coffee prices in the meantime had spawned a worldwide resurgence of coffee growing. "New coffee trees are being planted in almost every producing country in the world," observed George Gordon Paton, the editor of *Coffee Annual,* at the end of 1950. "New land is being opened up to coffee." That was encouraging, but he added a cautionary note: "Will the world be ready to take this additional production?" As always, however, no one listened.

In the Highlands of Papua New Guinea, Australian Jim Leahy harvested his first coffee in 1952. While prospecting for gold in 1933, he and his two brothers, Mick and Dan, found not only gold, but a million New Guinea natives previously unknown to the outside world. Mick Leahy fathered Joe, a mixed-race child whom he abandoned when he returned to Australia, but Jim and Dan stayed on.[4] After the war Jim experimented with a small plot of coffee in the Highlands, where conditions turned out to be perfect for high-quality arabica beans. His first big harvest came in just as prices skyrocketed, and a New Guinea land rush commenced. By 1955 there were seventy-six coffee plantations in New Guinea, fifty-five of them owned by Europeans. Astonished by the wealth they saw around them, natives too began to plant small plots.

Meanwhile in Brazil a new speculative frenzy took hold. "In Paraná," other Brazilians observed with a shake of the head, "the craziness of the people is tremendous. It is a madness, a fever." The fights over disputed land were reminiscent of the California gold rush. In the gateway city of Londrina, prostitutes mingled with *picaretas* ("pickaxes"), swindlers who sold nonexistent or useless land to eager but unwary *jacús*, yokels who had rushed to Paraná to make their fortunes growing coffee.[5] Over the last six years, since the U.S. Office of Price Administration had freed coffee prices, over five hundred thousand settlers had descended on Paraná.

In 1952 the American journalist Harold Martin visited the frontier state of Paraná to research an article aptly titled "The Land That Smells Like Money." His introduction came by air. "Over Londrina and

---

[4]As an adult, Joe Leahy would become a wealthy New Guinea coffee planter (see chapter 15).

[5]A *jacú* is a Brazilian game bird notorious for flying directly toward hunters who whistle properly.

beyond it for 100 miles a dry fog hangs in the air so thickly that at times it obscures both the noonday sun and the earth beneath," Martin wrote. The destruction of Brazil's forests continued apace in the grand old tradition of slash-and-burn. Towns of fifteen thousand people sprang up in areas that only a few years earlier had provided homes for jaguars, tapirs, monkeys, snakes, and parakeets.

The Paraná lands produced up to five times more coffee per acre than the tired São Paulo soils. The rich rolling plateau, well-watered and 2,000 feet above sea level, appeared to provide perfect coffee growing conditions, with only one small problem. Periodic frosts posed a significant threat. No one worried about that in 1952, however. Life was good. The first wave of coffee trees, planted five or six years earlier, were being harvested, and millions more had been planted in the new lands.

Spurred by the much-heralded coffee shortage, the United States encouraged the establishment of experimental agricultural research stations in Latin America. For the first time scientific analysis of the soil and other methods applied for over a decade to U.S. corn, wheat, and fruit trees were suggested for coffee. Dr. William Cowgill, an agronomist with the U.S. Department of Agriculture, worked in Guatemala and traveled as a consultant throughout Central America, Colombia, Ecuador, and Peru.

In 1950 Cowgill coaxed one of his prize coffee trees to produce an astonishing fourteen pounds of cherries, compared to the average one pound per tree. The condescending specialist said that most coffee planters ("there are no coffee growers") simply followed tradition and didn't know what they were doing. "Coffee growing here is at about the same stage that apple growing was in the United States when Johnny Appleseed went around scattering seeds." Cowgill suggested eliminating shade trees, increasing fertilizer and pesticide applications, and planting coffee trees much closer together.

Coffee research stations also had begun in Colombia, Costa Rica, and Brazil, where Latin American scientists were studying crossbreeding to create hybrid strains as well as studying plant diseases and pests. The most promising Brazilian discovery, named *Mundo Novo*, was "found" rather than intentionally crossbred. A traditional arabica tree, it proved somewhat resistant to disease, matured in three rather than four years, and produced abundantly.

The Rockefellers threw the weight of their money into such ventures, determined to secure a place for U.S. business in Latin America. Nelson Rockefeller, who had served as the Coordinator of Inter-American Affairs during World War II, founded the International Basic Economy Corporation (IBEC) after the war and in November 1950 created the IBEC Research Institute (IRI). The following year young plant scientist Jerry Harrington moved to São Paulo, intent on discovering a cure for the decline in coffee production there. The IRI men brought the yields up somewhat, but something was missing. The trees still lacked the color and vigor of trees growing on the virgin soil of Paraná.

The Great Fourth of July Frost

As the cherries ripened on those vigorous young Paraná trees in June 1953 during Brazil's "winter," it appeared that the world would finally have a bumper crop. For seven previous years world production had lagged behind consumption. In March President Eisenhower lifted the coffee price ceiling imposed by the Korean War and the selling price edged up a few cents. Nervous U.S. coffee men hoped that a substantial crop finally would allow a price decline. Coffee growers in Latin America also had reason to be nervous. Any break in the coffee market might produce economic chaos for them.

On the night of July 4 an unusually cold air mass moved up from the Antarctic and fell on southern Brazil. By noon the next day many trees had been killed outright by the severe frost. In other cases the leaves had withered and the beans blackened on the branches. As it became apparent that the Brazilian harvest was several million bags short of predictions, and that the following year promised a poor harvest as well, coffee futures ratcheted up.

In January 1954 roasted coffee broke the crucial psychological barrier of $1 a pound, and once again housewives, politicians, and the media went into an accusatory frenzy. *Business Week* wrote of a "runaway market," while *U.S. News & World Report* reported that consumers wondered "why, when many kinds of farm products are going down in price, coffee prices are the highest in history and are shooting up further." Restaurants that had raised prices from a nickel a cup to 10 cents during the last crisis now boosted it to 15 cents or even a quarter. Coffee consumption in New York City dropped 50 percent in a matter of weeks. Movements for "coffee holidays" sprang up across the United States. "One New Yorker who stopped drinking coffee," a reporter noted, "said it was a traumatic experience he never wanted to relive even by discussing it." A Philadelphia hotel offered patrons a nickel if they did *not* order coffee. A sign in a Grand Central Station luncheonette urged customers to drink tea.

Again coffee quality suffered. Some coffee firms advertised that *their* product could produce one hundred cups of coffee per pound. Meanwhile Postum sales soared, instant coffee thrived, and chain stores began luring shoppers to their stores by using coffee as a loss leader. So did other enterprising entrepreneurs. A newspaper offered a pound of free coffee with each new subscription to raise readership, while a used car dealer with a sense of humor offered a free car with each package of $600-a-pound coffee.

As always, politicians quickly joined the fray. President Eisenhower ordered the Federal Trade Commission to investigate coffee prices. In February the U.S. House of Representatives commenced coffee hearings, while the Senate assigned *two* committees to look into the matter. Maine senator Margaret Chase Smith submitted a resolution suggesting that Communists must be behind the coffee price hike. She wanted to ban coffee imports from Guatemala, where, she asserted, "the Communist movement has gained such economic and political strength."

Gustavo Lobo, the new head of the New York Coffee & Sugar Exchange, defended himself in front of different committees throughout February 1954. "Today," he told Senator George Aiken's committee, "the very mention of the word 'coffee' is quite likely to bring about irrelevant discussions, hasty conclusions, and ill-considered action." Coffee was, he added, "subject to almost as many international problems as any product used by man." The exchange did not set prices, he explained. It only recorded them. Yes, there was speculation, but that was a necessary function of any commodity exchange. Lobo denied that anyone was reaping enormous profits from coffee. Veteran coffee brokers Chandler Mackay, Leon Israel, and Jack Aron agreed with Lobo. "I would say the jobber [wholesaler] tries to get 1 percent [profit]," Israel testified, "and is happy to get one-half of 1 percent."

The politicians remained skeptical, especially since the retail price kept climbing in the wake of the frost. By summer, roasted coffee cost $1.35 a pound. "It appears that the more we investigate the coffee situation, the higher the price becomes," one confused Congressman said.

A few commentators cautioned against hasty overreactions. In *Newsweek* Henry Hazlitt noted that Congressmen were happy enough to enjoy their 75-cent martinis and to seek ever higher butter prices by holding 264 million pounds off the market. "Could it be that this strange contrast has anything to do with the fact that coffee growers don't vote in [their] district, while dairy farmers do?" A *Christian Century* editorial added, "Americans who grumble may . . . presently begin to understand how our own agricultural policies look to poor and hungry people in the rest of the world." These quiet voices of reason were lost, however, in the screams of outrage over purported manipulation and speculation to drive up the cost of coffee.

The offended Latin Americans reacted bitterly. El Salvador advised the United States to stop demanding nickel coffee until it began selling thousand-dollar cars again. In Costa Rica President José Figueres noted that even in that coffee-growing country domestic coffee cost 90 cents a pound, while the average citizen's income was a tenth of his U.S. counterpart. The Brazilian government took a more creative approach, flying four U.S. housewives down to Paraná to see the frost damage for themselves. In March their pictures among the Paraná coffee groves appeared in the American media. There they were, dressed in middle-class fifties dresses, surrounding a very spindly, very dead coffee tree. The ladies were impressed with the destruction and promised to report back favorably to American housewives. "We are going to keep our friendship, and it is not going to dissolve in a cup of coffee." The FTC and congressional committees continued their investigations, determined to blame *someone* for high prices.[6]

A CIA Coup in Guatemala

Just after the housewives returned from Brazil, another Latin American drama was played out at a meeting of the Organization of American States (OAS) in Caracas, Venezuela. There U.S. Secretary of State John Foster Dulles was trying to force through a resolution aimed at Guatemala, where social reform threatened American business interests.

After the 1944 overthrow of Guatemalan dictator Ubico, new President Juan José Arévalo finally abolished "vagrancy" laws and other forms of forced labor, and the state assumed ownership of the coffee

---

[6]The FTC eventually published its 523-page report, blaming the 1954 price hike on poor crop estimates, speculation at the coffee exchange, and inventory hoarding by large U.S. roasters. By that time, however, coffee prices were dropping and the matter no longer seemed urgent.

plantations that had been expropriated from Germans during the war. Arévalo had not attempted any agrarian reform, however, even though plantations larger than 1,100 acres–accounting for only 0.3 percent of the number of farms–contained over half the country's farmland.

When former general Jacobo Arbenz Guzmán assumed the presidency in 1951, he vowed to transform Guatemala "from a dependent nation with a semi-colonial economy into an economically independent country." The following year Guatemala passed the Law of Agrarian Reform, which called for the redistribution of public lands, those not actively farmed by the owner, and property in excess of 90 hectares (222 acres). Those forced to sell land would be recompensed based on tax assessments. The Arbenz government began to hand over more than one hundred former German coffee plantations to peasant cooperatives. The United Fruit Company was the hardest-hit foreign corporation, since much of its potential banana land lay fallow.[7] Its land also had been undervalued to avoid taxation, so that the company was forced to sell land far below its fair market value.

In 1954 land-hungry peasants began to occupy coffee plantations illegally, with some Guatemalan Communists encouraging them. "The land reform program has practically been taken over by communist agitators who exhort peasants to 'invade' private property," the *Tea & Coffee Trade Journal* reported. "Owners have no recourse and objections only bring threats of fines and imprisonment on the grounds that they are 'hindering the land reform program.'" The writer concluded that "if the present trend continues, the days of large privately owned and operated coffee Fincas are numbered."

As a private lawyer, the new Secretary of State Dulles had represented the United Fruit Company. His brother, Allen Dulles, the head of the CIA, had served on the United Fruit board of directors for several years. Even more than concern for the banana company, however, the United States perceived Arbenz as a threat to American influence in Latin America. Communism provided a convenient excuse to attack radical nationalist regimes. In August 1953 they convinced President Eisenhower to approve Operation Success, a clandestine CIA plan to overthrow the Arbenz regime. They installed right-wing diplomat John Peurifoy as the U.S. ambassador to Guatemala, and they planned to

---

[7]United Fruit also was involved in the coffee trade. Its Great White Fleet offered weekly sailings that handled exported coffee from Colombia and Central American ports.

ram a resolution through the Caracas OAS meeting that would justify their planned intervention. This task would have been much easier if the coffee price crisis had not soured relations with Latin America, as journalist Patrick McMahon noted. He believed that the furor over coffee was "the greatest piece of sheer good luck that has fallen to the Communists since they opened their campaign to gain a firm foothold in the Western Hemisphere."

Like McMahon, most U.S. journalists accepted the cold war ideology that the Guatemalan government was communistic. In fact there were only four Communist deputies in the 1953–54 Guatemalan Congress, and Arbenz never appointed a Communist to his cabinet. True, the Communists did support his regime and even exerted considerable influence, but Arbenz was a nationalist who sought long overdue reforms, not an ideological Communist. "What is the real reason for describing our government as communistic?" asked Guillermo Toriello, Guatemala's foreign minister, on March 5 at the OAS meeting. "Why do they wish to intervene in Guatemala?" The answer, he said, was obvious. The Arbenz policy was adversely affecting "the privileges of foreign enterprises" such as United Fruit.

Though Toriello's speech received thunderous applause, John Foster Dulles prevailed, after two weeks of arm-twisting and threats to withhold aid. His resolution passed, though the only enthusiastic supporters were the worst Latin American dictators, such as Nicaragua's Somoza. Reporting on the conference, McMahon scoffed at the "typical Communist diversionary maneuver" in which Guatemala charged that the United States planned to "invade their country and unseat their 'democratic' government." Yet by the time his observations were published in the July issue of the *American Mercury* the CIA indeed *had* already sponsored an invasion of Guatemala and overthrown Arbenz.

Although Operation Success was indeed a success in the short term, it was a long-term disaster for Guatemala. The country's new president, General Carlos Castillo Armas, had been hand-picked by the CIA. He swiftly reversed the progressive tide. He canceled the agrarian reform legislation, disenfranchised illiterates, restored the secret police, and outlawed all political parties, labor groups, and peasant organizations. Within a year and a half Castillo Armas had driven most of the peasants off the land they had gained under Arbenz.

U.S. politicians resolutely turned a blind eye to the situation. The year after the coup a seven-man congressional delegation toured

Guatemala and met with Castillo Armas. Their report spoke glowingly of "the overthrow of the Communist-front government." Castillo Armas supposedly had "the overwhelming approval of the Guatemalan people." The U.S. politicians admitted that all political parties had been abolished and that Castillo Armas ruled by fiat. The Guatemalan president assured them, however, that "it was the avowed program of the Government to use democratic processes to the fullest extent." The report concluded: "Guatemala is the showcase of Latin America and has become a political, social, and economic laboratory."

Unfortunately, that laboratory would breed discontent, starvation, and dictatorship rather than happiness, economic boon, and democracy. Castillo Armas was assassinated in 1957. The country descended into three decades of repression, violence, and terror as governmental death squads and guerrilla bands roamed the countryside—a direct legacy of the U.S. intervention. The coffee elite continued to rely on cheap peasant labor, and even though many plantation owners deplored the violence and uncertainty under the repressive military regime, it allowed them to keep their land and status.[8]

Suicide in Brazil

Two months after the overthrow of Arbenz another dramatic Latin American shift of power occurred in Brazil. Again coffee economics lay at the heart of world-shaping events. Throughout the first half of 1954 the coffee price boom boosted Brazilian spirits. Through March, flush Brazilians bought 15 percent more American goods than in the same period the previous year. In June, Vargas raised the minimum coffee export price from 53 cents to 87 cents a pound. Then in July, coffee prices took a swift tumble. During the first half of 1954 the major U.S. coffee roasters—General Foods, Standard Brands, Hills Brothers, Folger's, A & P, Jewel—bought heavily in anticipation of a shortage; so did the American housewife. As a consequence, the overstocked U.S. market of July was hesitant to buy more at high prices.

---

[8]The United States poured over $100 million into Guatemala between 1954 and 1960, but most of it went toward highway construction and other programs designed to help U.S. businesses. "Of all the many millions that we have spent in Guatemala," noted a U.S. senator in 1958, "little has trickled down to the two million Indians of the country, who are the people who really need our help. They are still poor, while the businessmen are prospering."

To support the market the Brazilian government was forced to buy up some of its own coffee. Vargas sent his representatives to ask the Federal Reserve Bank of New York for a loan to pay off his country's growing debts, but the bank refused. Brazilian inflation threatened to spiral out of control, the free-market value of the *cruzeiro* having reached 60 to the dollar, which put increasing pressure on Vargas to officially devalue his currency. Brazil's single biggest import expense was for fuel oil; the country would require an estimated $200 million for oil in the next six months, even at the low official exchange rate. Brazil had plenty of its own crude oil, but Vargas was determined not to allow U.S. firms to develop and exploit his country's resources. *"O petróleo é nosso!"* ("The oil is ours!") was his battle cry the previous year when he had created Petrobrás, a state monopoly for petroleum exploration.

Over the weekend of August 14–15 Vargas attempted a stopgap measure, as some American roasters cut their prices by 10 cents a pound. The Brazilian government allowed coffee exporters to exchange 20 percent of their dollar receipts at the free exchange rate, effectively lowering the minimum export rate by 20 cents and unofficially devaluing the currency. The following week the U.S. coffee industry lowered prices by as much as 18 cents a pound.

As the Brazilian economy slid into chaos, a political crisis also hit Vargas. Since his election in 1951 opponents had been carping at him for his populist leanings and support of labor rights. On August 5 an assassination attempt against Carlos Lacerda—editor of the right-wing paper *Tribuna da Imprensa* and one of Vargas's most vocal critics—failed, although an Air Force major with him was killed. Lacerda had been running in a congressional race against Vargas's son Lutero, and a subsequent investigation linked the killer to the head of the president's personal guard. Cries for impeachment grew, just as the coffee situation became disastrous.

After a sleepless night, on the morning of August 24, 1954, Getúlio Vargas, seventy-one, shot himself through the heart in his bedroom. He left an eloquent, typed suicide note. "After decades of domination and plunder on the part of international economic and financial groups," he wrote, "I placed myself at the head of a revolution and won." Yet these unnamed international groups had joined his domestic enemies in an attempt to subvert his campaign to create national wealth and autonomy. When he took office in 1951, he wrote, "profits of foreign companies were reaching as much as 500 per cent per annum." Temporarily coffee came to the rescue. "Came the coffee crisis and the value of our main product rose." After this brief respite, however, "we tried to defend its price and the reply was such violent pressure on our economy that we were forced to give in. . . . There is nothing more to give you except my blood," Vargas concluded. "I have given you my life. Now I offer you my death. I fear nothing. Serenely I take my first step toward eternity and leave life to enter history."

It is not clear to what "international groups" Vargas attributed his downfall. One can hardly blame Vargas for his paranoia, however, since he must have been aware of the U.S. role in deposing Arbenz in Guatemala only two months earlier. Nonetheless he could not legitimately hold the United States responsible for the abrupt decline in coffee prices any more than U.S. politicians should have blamed the previous price hike on Brazilian machinations. In both instances the market price had responded—with a little help from speculators and panicky or angry consumers—to the basic laws of supply and demand.

Vargas died a tragic figure, his fate tied, as always, to coffee. He had risen to power in 1930 in large part because his country was in economic crisis following a collapse in coffee prices. A quarter century later he took his own life under similar circumstances. His political life as well as his beloved Brazil's history were intimately related to the coffee tree and its berry. "Coffee is such an important part of Brazil's economic life that it has become inextricably interwoven with politics," wrote an American journalist in October 1954. "Many feel that Brazil's capitulation on the coffee price was one of the things that led directly to President Vargas' suicide."

Tensions between the United States and Latin America remained high. In Latin America, with an average life expectancy of forty-seven, coffee prices meant life or death. "The anti-American riots and demonstrations which periodically sweep one or another of the twenty republics do not actually reflect a hatred of the United States," Andrés Uribe concluded in *Brown Gold*, his 1954 book about coffee. Rather they expressed "the exasperation of good neighbors with what they feel is United States indifference to their basic problems." That exasperation would grow in the next few years, as worldwide overproduction led to disastrously low coffee prices.

~ 14 ~

ROBUSTA
TRIUMPHANT

*There is hardly anything that some man cannot make a
little worse and sell it a little cheaper.*
—Comment at 1959
National Coffee Association convention

*In studying the position of the coffee industry today, it seems to me that our outlook
is exceedingly bright. I confidently expect that we are about to enter one of the periods of greatest growth in our history.*
—Edward Aborn, May 18, 1962

Since the late 1800s the boom-bust coffee cycle—too much coffee, then too little, then too much—had whipsawed Latin American economies. Though the cycle wasn't new, its consequences would be even more devastating in the cold war era, as more African and Asian countries came to rely on the fickle bean. The United States, which traditionally advocated unrestricted free trade, would gradually modify its views out of political fears; yet politics too experiences cycles, and the American support for fair coffee prices always would remain tentative. The international coffee drama never seemed destined to end.

Following the brief respite provided by the Paraná frost, a long-predicted coffee glut commenced in 1955. During the first half of the 1950s, as coffee prices had risen, hopeful growers in the tropics planted new trees. Arabica trees produce four years after they are planted.

Robusta trees, however, take only two years from seedling to harvest and produce more heavily. Encouraged by the popularity of instant coffee, many African colonies increased robusta growth dramatically.

Out of Africa

Africa underwent a major transition in the postwar period. With the European powers weakened by the war and natives eager to share the wealth around them, the traditional method of rule—white Europeans applying an iron-fisted *Bula Matari* ("rock crusher," in Kikongo)— clearly would not work anymore. As one African politician told the French National Assembly in 1946, "The colonial fact, in its brutal form . . . is impossible today. *This historical period of colonization is over.*" But it would take the European powers some time—and bloodshed—to realize that he was right.

In 1947 the British granted independence to India, and pressure grew for Britain, France, Portugal, and Belgium to release the colonies they had carved out of Africa in the late nineteenth century. In 1951 Britain gave Libya its independence, and the next year a military coup in Egypt severed its ties to England as well. As in Latin America, issues of economic inequities, forced labor, racism—and coffee—played a major role in the independence movement in countries such as Kenya, Uganda, the Ivory Coast, Angola, and the Belgian Congo.

In Kenya native laborers, called *boys* and *bibis* by the British, were forced to climb into the vats of fermenting coffee beans to loosen the mucilage with their feet. At first they reacted only by sabotaging crop harvests, but in 1952 many coffee workers joined other disenchanted Africans in what came to be called the Mau Mau Rebellion, which resulted in government suppression. By the end of 1954 detention camps and prisons held one hundred fifty thousand people.

At the same time, however, the British instituted land reforms and opened more coffee cultivation to African producers. By 1954 some fifteen thousand Kenyan natives grew coffee on tiny plots, totaling only 5,000 acres. Over the next few years Africans would come to dominate the Kenyan industry, producing some of the finest arabica beans in the world.

Other African countries also produced limited amounts of arabica, but the largest source remained Ethiopia, coffee's original home. Al-

though there were a few plantations where trees were grown scientifi-
cally—that is, severely pruned, some without shade—most coffee still
grew wild in the forests of the Kaffa provinces, as it always had. As a result, Ethiopian coffees varied wildly in flavor, from awful to sublime.

In 1954 Ethiopia exported 620,000 bags and Kenya 210,000 bags of
arabica beans, but over 80 percent of the nearly 6 million bags that left
Africa that year were robusta beans. Angola had always been the leading producer of robusta, with just over a million bags, but the tiny Ivory
Coast—about the size of New Mexico—surged past it that year to export
1.4 million bags of coffee. For the first time coffee provided more of
that country's income than cocoa.

In the Côte d'Ivoire, as the French colony then was known, coffee
had been harvested by forced labor since the 1920s. After World War
II African coffee grower Félix Houphouët-Boigny, elected to represent
the Ivory Coast in the French Assembly, sponsored a bill to abolish
forced labor in the French colonies. With its passage he became a hero.
Houphouët-Boigny saw gold in coffee. "If you don't want to vegetate in
bamboo huts," he said in a 1953 speech, "concentrate your efforts on
growing good cocoa and coffee. They will fetch a good price and you
will become rich." With such encouragement, and high prices, small
native coffee farms developed throughout the Ivory Coast. The French
colony's crop had always gone to France, where it was protected by favorable tax laws. With coffee prices up and U.S. roasters desperate for
cheap robusta, however, the Ivory Coast exported 215,000 bags to
North America (at 57 cents a pound) for the first time in 1954.

Aside from the Ivory Coast and Angola, other important robusta ex-
porters were Uganda, Madagascar, Tanganyika, and the Belgian
Congo. Asia also produced robustas in India, Indonesia, and French
Indochina (Vietnam), but an insignificant amount in comparison to
Africa. In 1951 African coffee had accounted for only 4.8 percent of
U.S. coffee imports; by 1955 the figure had risen to 11.4 percent.

Hot Coffee, Cold War

By February 1955 falling coffee prices had yet again panicked Latin
America. Following Vargas's suicide a group of U.S. banks loaned Brazil
$200 million, but the country was forced to devalue the coffee *cruzeiro*
anyway. Despite Brazil's attempt to bolster the market by holding back
nine million bags, prices continued to drop. American roasters allowed

their stocks to dwindle, anticipating even lower prices. The Colombian government slashed imports and ordered a partial devaluation.

The head of the Colombian Coffee Federation tried to convince other Latin American countries to hold coffee off the market to boost the price, or at least keep it from sinking further. By June 1956 nineteen Latin American countries had agreed, only another frost in Paraná put the quota plans on hold. A report from the Economic and Social Council of the Organization of American States (ECOSOC) to the Latin American heads of state predicted a growing surplus that threatened to bring a "disastrous slump" in coffee prices unless governments took "drastic action," setting quotas and stockpiling coffee.

The gloomy report contained no startling news. What *is* surprising is that Harold Randall, the U.S. State Department's representative on ECOSOC, signed it. Why did the State Department's stance against "cartels" suddenly soften? The cold war, rather than a warm heart, drove the shifting U.S. policy toward coffee. "A steep price fall might bring on dangerous economic and political crises," one journalist observed, "with tempting opportunities for local strongmen or Communist mischief-makers." But when unseasonable Colombian rains created a temporary shortage in mild coffees and prices spiked briefly in 1956, the State Department pulled back.

While the African share of the coffee market continued to swell, economists predicted that Brazil would owe a whopping $1.1 billion in debt and interest payments over the next few years. In October 1957 at a meeting in Mexico City the desperate Brazilians joined six other Latin American coffee-producing countries in an export quota scheme.

In January 1958 the United States sent an "observer" to a meeting in Rio de Janeiro, where Latin American and African growers joined in the 1958 Latin American Coffee Agreement with the ostensible aim of promoting increased consumption. Although the Africans were unwilling to limit their exports, Brazil agreed to withhold 40 percent of its crop, Colombia 15 percent, and other countries a smaller percentage.

In May, due to "evidence that the Soviet Union is intensifying its economic and political offensive in many parts of the world, including Latin America," according to a State Department official, Vice President Richard Nixon undertook a South American "good will" tour, but the State Department had underestimated the level of resentment against the "Colossus of the North." In Peru and Venezuela Nixon was booed, spit at, stoned, and nearly killed amidst cries of *"Muera Nixon!"* ("Death to Nixon!").

In the wake of the Nixon incidents State Department officials began to pay informal calls on Latin American embassies for coffee chats. Over fifty million bags were being processed for sale, while the world consumed only thirty-eight million bags. In the United States the price of roasted coffee fell below 70 cents a pound. "An economic setback [to Latin American coffee growers] may . . . topple governments friendly to the United States," warned Colombian coffee representative Andrés Uribe. "The forces dedicated to the overthrow of the entire free world would gladly take advantage of such a situation."

Regular Robusta

Even with falling prices the U.S. roasters locked themselves into a downward spiral of coupons-off deals, premium offers, and price wars. Robusta crept insidiously into regular blends, with new bargain brands selling 20 cents or even 30 cents below the leaders and containing 30 percent or more robusta. "One hesitates to speak of these poorer coffees as 'blends,'" wrote a coffee expert. "It seems almost like a form of deception to pack low-quality coffees in the expensive vacuum tins. It certainly is the lowering of a proud standard, the crumbling of a tradition." In response to the cheaper blends General Foods quietly began adding a small percentage of robusta to Maxwell House, and soon all of the other major brands followed suit. By the end of 1956 robustas accounted for over 22 percent of world coffee exports. In 1960 the New York Coffee & Sugar Exchange abrogated its long-standing ban on robusta.

By this time, offering a substantially less expensive product seemed the only way to break into the coffee industry. The five big roasters— General Foods, Standard Brands, Folger's, Hills Brothers, and A & P— now accounted for well over 40 percent of the market. Larger regional roasters, struggling to survive, gobbled others in order to compete. The thousand-plus wartime roasters dwindled to eight hundred fifty. Those who wanted to survive had to practice economies of scale and save labor through mechanization.

Size, speed, and efficiency seemed the only way to survive in the chain store business too. Ever-larger supermarkets offered ever-cheaper goods. Although A & P still predominated, reaching $5 billion in annual sales in 1958, it failed to adjust to this new reality. That year the heirs of John and George Hartford took the company public.[1] By that time other supermarket chains such as Safeway, Kroger, Winn Dixie, Food Fair, First National, Jewel Tea, and Grand Union were challenging the venerable leader. While A & P still accounted for a full third of the major chain sales, its smaller, older stores each sold an average $4,000 less per week than the competitors. In the mid-1950s General Foods passed A & P to become the largest U.S. coffee importer.

Meanwhile instant coffee manufacturers managed to make their product even worse. By 1958 most instant coffees contained at least 50 percent robusta beans, and many of the cheaper brands used 100 percent robusta. Moreover the manufacturers were squeezing the beans unmercifully. At first six pounds of green coffee were used to make one pound of instant. By overextracting every soluble component it then took only four pounds of raw beans. Through hydrolysis insoluble starch and cellulose were converted into soluble carbohydrates.

To fool the consumer into ignoring their coffee's ever-worsening taste, the instant manufacturers added back some smell. When subjected to enormous pressure—50,000 pounds per square inch—roasted coffee beans exuded an oil that, in tiny amounts, gave soluble coffee an illusory fresh-roasted scent. When a housewife opened a jar of instant coffee, it let off a brief burst of aroma; then it was gone. The cup of instant did not smell or taste any better.

Indeed with the growing popularity of "more economic" 10-, 12-, and 16-ounce jars, instant coffee was more likely to grow stale sitting in the pantry. Housewives also bought 2-pound cans of regular coffee. Though the vacuum cans kept the contents relatively fresh until they were opened, deterioration was rapid thereafter.

Coffee dispensed by vending machines was equally bad. Even though the machines now could brew fresh coffee on demand, the temptation to use more robusta was overwhelming. The vendors also economized by using dry powdered cream, which lent a slightly burnt taste to the brew. In order to compete successfully, a bitter roaster said, a vending machine firm "talks quality, thinks acceptability, and plans somehow to cut corners."

---

[1] John Hartford died in 1951 at seventy-nine, followed by ninety-two-year-old George Hartford in 1957.

The Chock Full Miracle

In the middle of this fierce competition, with its low quality standards and apparent market saturation, a New York nut vendor and restaurateur proved that a new brand stressing quality could triumph. William Black had begun life in 1904 as William Schwartz but changed his name, like many Jews in America eager to avoid the rampant anti-Semitism of the early part of the century. This was just about all the short, chunky, aggressive Black ever willingly changed to suit anyone.

In 1926, after graduating with an engineering degree from Columbia University, Black couldn't find a job. Noticing the crowds in New York City's theater district, Black opened a nut stand in a basement at Broadway and Forty-third Street, calling it Chock full o' Nuts. Within six years he owned a chain of eighteen such stores, all in Manhattan. When the depression hit, even shelled nuts seemed a luxury, so Black converted his stores to quick-order luncheonettes, offering a nutted cheese sandwich on whole wheat raisin bread, along with coffee, each for a nickel. Later he added soup and pie to the menu.

By the 1950s Black owned twenty-five restaurants in New York City. When coffee prices went up and quality began to decline, Black, a stickler for the freshest ingredients, was disturbed. At first, like other restaurant owners, he held to a 5-cent cup of coffee by watering the brew. He soon broke ranks, however, raising his price and announcing that he refused to compromise on quality.

Then in October 1953 he astonished the coffee trade by coming out with his own brand, Chock full o' Nuts, in the midst of the price crisis brought on by the great Brazilian frost. Everyone thought it would flop, particularly with such a stupid name. Maybe Chock full o' Beans—but nuts? In addition his cans were colored an ugly yellow and black. Furthermore when other coffees offered several grinds for different kinds of brewing devices, Black advertised his "All Method Grind." There was method to his madness, however—and his grind. With supermarket shelving at a premium his one can—one grind required less space.

Black understood the power of advertising. In radio spots, which blanketed the New York metropolitan airwaves, Black's second wife, Jean Martin, sang a hummable jingle:

> *Chock full o' Nuts is that heavenly coffee,*
> *Heavenly coffee, heavenly coffee.*

Chock full o' Nuts is that heavenly coffee—
Better coffee Rockefeller's money can't buy.

By August 1954, less than a year after its debut, Chock full o' Nuts had grabbed third place among vacuum-packed coffees in New York City. Nelson Rockefeller, who owned a number of Latin American coffee concerns, did not appreciate his family name being used to promote someone else's coffee. He sued. William Black simply changed the words of the jingle: "Better coffee a millionaire's money can't buy."

Black advertised Chock full o' Nuts as a premium coffee that was worth its high price. "Don't spend the extra money for this coffee," ads advised, "unless you're just plain *crazy* about good coffee."[2] Chock also resorted to a classic coffee advertising strategy. Ads showed a woman with an inverted cup on her head and coffee streaming down her face. "Men!" the ad proclaimed. "Don't let it come to this! Win your fight for a decent cup of coffee without losing your temper!"

A hands-on manager who wanted to control every aspect of his operation, Black drove his admen crazy, but his ideas worked. He insisted that his restaurant staff refuse tips (he considered tipping degrading and un-American) and keep the premises spotless. An intensely private man, he reported for work around noon, communicated primarily by handwritten memo, and worked late into the night. He took a certain pleasure in gruff bluntness. "I'm not as proud as I should be to announce that we're going into the instant coffee business," he confessed at the Chock Instant launch. "The very finest instant coffee is still a far cry from our regular coffee. Yet there are a lot of people who don't mind it."

The brand expanded into Connecticut, Massachusetts, and New Jersey. By the end of 1955 Chock full o' Nuts had nearly captured the lead in New York City. Black soon expanded northward throughout New England, upstate New York, and into Canada, and south into Delaware, Pennsylvania, Maryland, and Washington, D.C. An early advocate of

---

[2]Such counterintuitive advertising also worked for Wilkins Coffee, a regional Washington, D.C., roaster. In 1957 the firm commissioned local puppeteer Jim Henson to create seven-second television spots featuring Wilkins and Wontkins, two *Muppets* (from *marionette* and *puppet*). In the ads Wontkins, a gruff naysayer, always refuses to drink his coffee, with dire results. Wilkins shoots, brands, drowns, clubs, slashes, freezes, and blows up his buddy Wontkins. In a typical commercial Wilkins asks, "Have some Wilkins Coffee?" Wontkins hesitates, "Well, I ... I ...," so Wilkins hits him over the head a few times. "I'll take some," Wontkins growls. "Surprising how many are switching to Wilkins Coffee." Coffee sales soared, as did Henson's subsequent career.

racial equality, Black hired retired baseball star Jackie Robinson as his personnel director in 1957. Over half his employees were African Americans. In 1958 Black took the company public, selling 400,000 shares, while retaining 320,000 shares, and control, for himself.

The "poor boy from Brooklyn," as Black liked to describe himself, was now a millionaire many times over. In 1957 when his company auditor and lifelong friend contracted Parkinson's disease, Black created the Parkinson's Disease Foundation, funding it with an initial grant of $100,000. Three years later he gave an astounding $5 million to Columbia University for a medical research building. In doing so he challenged other wealthy men to give to worthy causes while they were still alive, thus avoiding the troubles inherited wealth caused. "My children won't be badly off," he said, "but I'm not going to leave them millions."

The Coffeehouse: A Saving Grace

A few other regional roasters also produced quality coffee during this period, particularly in San Francisco. Graffeo, founded by Sicilian immigrant John Graffeo during the depression, was purchased in 1953 by John Repetto, fresh from Italy. He eventually passed it on to his son, Luciano. In the same city Freed, Teller & Freed, founded by two brothers and a partner just before the turn of the century, was still a family company, passing down matrilineally. Still in their 1907 location, Freed, Teller & Freed roasted only arabica coffee in an ancient Burns Jubilee. Entering the store was, as one journalist put it, "like stepping into a time machine." Across the continent in Washington, D.C., the M. E. Swing Company, founded in 1916 by Marshall Edward Swing and his son, also survived as a charming anachronism, selling beans out of old oak bins to regulars and connoisseurs.

Another hopeful candle also lit the coffee gloom, and it came from Italy. With perfection of the modern espresso machine just after World War II the Italian coffee bar proliferated. In Milan in 1945 Achille Gaggia invented a spring mechanism that drove hot water at high pressure through finely ground roasted coffee. The art of espresso making then consisted of "pulling a shot" to each customer's satisfaction. "Its preparation," wrote an American postwar journalist, "partakes of the bravura of a tenor solo." While many of the monstrous old steam–valve machines with their gargoyles and dials still graced the counters, most bars now used the modern, low-slung versions.

The machines quickly found their way to Italian restaurants in New York and elsewhere. By the mid 1950s the Italian espresso craze had sparked a small coffeehouse revival, particularly in Greenwich Village, where bohemians, poets, artists, and beatniks could sip espresso at Reggio's, the Limelight, or the Peacock. Such coffeehouses gave birth, as one nostalgic customer put it, to "a generation that, for the price of an espresso, could imagine itself in the Europe that few of its members had ever seen." That fantasy included "an illusion of delicious wickedness, a hot breath of Continental amorality," observed a contemporary journalist, "from the safe distance of one marble-topped table away."

The allure of the coffeehouse reached the North Beach area of San Francisco when window washer Giovanni Giotta opened the Caffè Trieste in 1957.[3] In the back section, poets Allen Ginsburg and Bob Kaufman brooded over the faults of Eisenhower's America, while the Italians in the front laughed at them, wondering aloud, "When are they gonna work?" Soon more establishments appeared in San Francisco and other major cities.

A small market sprang up for home espresso, and specialty and department stores offered stovetop steam-pressure machines. New York regional coffee roaster Sam Schonbrunn, who already featured the high-quality Savarin, came out with Medaglia d'Oro, a dark-roasted, pulverized blend especially made for home espresso machines. Women's magazines offered numerous recipes for espresso-based drinks such as Caffè Borgia (equal parts espresso and hot chocolate, topped with whipped cream, sprinkled with grated orange peel), Caffè Anisette Royal (espresso with anisette, topped with whipped cream), or Café Brulot (espresso with spice and fruit peels, first flamed with brandy).

London Espresso

Espresso bars took London by storm in the early fifties. In 1952 an Italian immigrant named Pino Riservato, traveling the British countryside selling dental accessories, was appalled by what passed for coffee in the pubs and snack bars. Riservato formed a small company and imported five espresso machines, setting one up in his flat to demonstrate to caterers. They were unimpressed. Undeterred, Riservato opened the

---

[3]Actually Giotta purchased the Café Il Piccolo, revamping and renaming it.

COFFEE

"*Coffee An Aid to Factory Efficiency*"

As shown in this 1921 ad, coffee has always provided the pick-me-up that helps workers get through their day—providing a drug instead of rest, according to some critics.

G. Washington, the first major instant coffee, was so popular during the First World War that doughboys asked for "a cup of George."

Motorized vehicles revolutionized coffee delivery in the early 20th century.

By the 1930s, coffee was taking to the air.

Alice Foote MacDougall clawed her way to success in the man's coffee world, creating a chain of New York coffeehouses in the 1920s. "Fight, fight, fight until you win," she wrote. "It is this kind of determination that man has acquired through long generations, and the woman who is to conquer in the business world must acquire it too if she is to succeed." Still, she thought women should not be allowed to vote.

In the 1920s, Alice Foote MacDougall was inspired by a trip to Italy and replicated Italian decor in her elaborate New York coffeehouses.

In this 1934 cartoon ad, (only one panel shown here) Chase & Sanborn provide alarming evidence that wife-battering was apparently acceptable, understandable behavior during the Depression—especially if the husband didn't like the coffee. The company hoped that terrified wives would purchase Chase & Sanborn in hopes of avoiding such confrontations.

In Depression-era cartoons, "Mr. Coffee Nerves" created havoc, only to be "foiled again" by Postum.

This racist ad helped sell Maxwell House Coffee, just as the characters on the popular radio show did. The sound effects and acting were so convincing that many listeners waited hopefully on wharves for the mythical Show Boat.

New swing bands at World's Fair are phenomenally popular; can't swing it too fast for the jitterbugs. Chase & Sanborn are popular, too, for thrilling, fast delivery; speed rich, fine-quality *Dated* Coffee fresh from roasting ovens to grocer. It's speed that protects *Dated* Coffee's tempting, fragrant freshness.

Coming out of the Depression, Chase & Sanborn identified itself with the new jitterbug craze at the 1939 New York World's Fair.

In 1937, Mae West appeared on the "Chase & Sanborn Hour," lewdly calling dummy Charlie McCarthy "all wood and a yard long." But it was her Adam and Eve skit, in which she praised the serpent as a "palpitatin' python," that nearly got the show thrown off the air.

Coffee rediscovered its homeland in Africa during the 1930s, though in Kenya most of the coffee growers were white. Hence this racist ad from 1937.

In 1941, first lady Eleanor Roosevelt reached millions of listeners with her radio show, "Over the Coffee Cups," sponsored by the Pan American Coffee Bureau.

For exhausted GIs fresh from the front lines of World War II, coffee was essential. It is little wonder that U. S. per capita consumption peaked just after the war.

"Ya know, I ain't worth a dern in th' morning without a hot cuppa coffee."

U. S. soldiers would do almost anything for hot coffee during World War II, including wasting all their matches in the attempt.

AMAZING COFFEE DISCOVERY!

Not a powder! Not a grind! But millions of tiny "FLAVOR BUDS" of <u>real</u> coffee...ready to burst instantly into that famous MAXWELL HOUSE FLAVOR!

During the 1950s, instant coffee provided middle-class Americans a quick, convenient, cheap pick-me-up—without concern for quality.

The "coffee break"—as a phrase and concept—was invented in 1952 by the Pan American Coffee Bureau. It quickly became a part of the language, as evidenced by this cartoon book.

THE COFFEE BREAK

MORE WALL STREET JOURNAL CARTOONS

HURRY, YOU'LL MISS THE COFFEE BREAK!

SELECTED BY CHARLES PRESTON

In his early teen heartthrob days, Frank Sinatra sang "The Coffee Song," which immortalized "an awful lot of coffee in Brazil."

Chock full o' Nuts became a best-selling coffee in New York through such ads, once more playing the sexist theme.

During the fifties, coffee became an accepted part of American life, sanctioned by the police as an aid to safety.

In 1954, when outraged Americans blamed Brazil for artificially boosting coffee prices, the Brazilian government flew U. S. housewives down to Paraná to see the frost damage for themselves.

In a desperate attempt to compete with the bigger corporations, family-owned Hills Brothers stooped to ads in the 1960s claiming that its coffee could be reheated without damage.

Beginning in 1960, the mythical Juan Valdez sold Colombian coffee in the United States. Today, the actor who plays him owns a silk- screen t-shirt factory along with a coffee farm, where he pays others to grow his crop.

Muppeteer Jim Henson launched his career in 1957 with coffee ads for Wilkins Coffee in which puppet Wontkins, who refused to drink the right coffee, was shot, branded, drowned, clubbed, slashed, frozen, and blown up.

Moka Bar in a bomb-damaged laundry in Soho, renovating it with ultramodern Formica.

On opening day—and every day thereafter—the Moka Bar was mobbed, serving a thousand cups of coffee a day. Continental immigrants who had fled to England after the war were delighted to find straight shots of espresso again. The British customers preferred *cappuccino*, with its steamed, frothed milk. "It was so attractive that it hoodwinked the English, and particularly the teenagers, into drinking something which was against all their traditional tea-drinking instincts," British coffee and tea expert Edward Bramah observed. Within a year other espresso bars popped up in London, and by 1956 there were four hundred London espresso bars, with two new outlets opening every week. Others appeared in the provinces.

"People in this country are becoming *very* coffee conscious," one proprietor told a reporter in 1955. "Our business is 99 percent coffee individually made for each patron." At a shilling per demitasse—twice the going rate for regular coffee—it was a profitable undertaking. As in the United States, the espresso bars were distinctively decorated, often with neon lights, avant-garde artwork, huge potted plants, and even live parrots. "At the Rocola off Oxford Circus," a reporter noted, "a street musicians' band was blaring dance music outside. The place was packed with svelte young men and glamorous-looking females. It was nearly an hour before we could have word with the young woman in charge."

While espresso made inroads at the coffeehouses, however, it was instant coffee that found its way increasingly into the British home. Encouraged by tea rationing, which lasted over a decade beyond the war's end, Nestlé mounted a vigorous print and billboard campaign for Nescafé, and Maxwell House wasn't far behind. In 1956, when tea auctions finally resumed, everyone expected a British tea renaissance, but it never occurred.

The debut of English commercial television that same year had an unexpected impact. To steep a good, traditional cup of tea requires five minutes, and the commercial breaks in the TV programs weren't that long. With telly spots touting the simplicity and goodness of Nescafé and Instant Maxwell House, British consumers began to switch to soluble coffee, which soon accounted for over 90 percent of retail coffee sales. In desperation the tea companies abandoned the superior rolled tea, chopping it into bits for teabags that produced an inferior but quicker rust-red brew. Although tea remained the British drink, coffee was clearly on the rise. "Coffee is now socially superior to tea," the *Nottingham Evening Post* declared in 1955, "and the idea has caught on at all levels from the chain store's cafeteria to the exclusive restaurant."

European Coffee in the Fifties

In the meantime the continental European coffee industry, which survived the war mainly by producing coffee substitutes, had revived by the late 1950s. In 1956 European imports exceeded the twelve-million-bag prewar level, and by 1960 imports topped seventeen million bags.

The new espresso machines were popular in cafés in Paris, Vienna, Amsterdam, and Hamburg, though they simply fit into the preexisting coffee scene. Outside Switzerland (home of Nestlé) instant coffee had yet to attract many European consumers, although Nescafé, now manufactured in nineteen countries, dominated world soluble sales outside the United States.[4] In general a pattern had evolved in which the Continental markets eventually would follow the American lead, but with a significant lag time. Now, major European roasters began to dominate the scene as they had during the depression in America. European home roasting practically disappeared, but whole bean sales still exceeded the preground, canned product.

As West Germany got back on its economic feet, coffee consumption—mostly in the form of arabica—increased 15 percent annually. Bremen-based Jacobs Kaffee doubled its sales every two years. In 1949 Hamburg merchants Max Herz and Carl Tchilling-Hirrian founded the Tchibo company, supplying its Mocca Gold roasted coffee by mail.[5] Jacobs responded by delivering coffee in its yellow-and-black VW vans, nicknamed "Jacobs' Bumble Bees." In 1955 Tchibo opened specialty coffee shops selling whole beans and sample cups of coffee. An avuncular "coffee expert" helped establish the Tchibo image, while elderly *hausfrau* Sophie Engmann portrayed the "nation's grandmother" for Jacobs. The firms advertised primarily through magazines, radio, and cinemas, since television had yet to reach many consumers in Europe. The era of mass marketing clearly had arrived, with huge firms such as

---

[4]Ironically, Latin American countries exported their best beans and consumed cheap instant coffee, much to the chagrin of the growers, who coined the phrase, *"Nescafé, no es café,"* meaning "Nescafé is not coffee."

[5]The name *Tchibo* derived from Tchilling-Hirrian and *bohne*, the German word for bean.

Jacobs, Tchibo, and Eduscho dominating the field and smaller competitors disappearing. In 1950 there had been two thousand West German roasters. By 1960 there were only six hundred.

In the Netherlands, Douwe Egberts expanded its coffee, tobacco, and tea business after 1952, when coffee rationing finally ended. Its brands featured the "coffee lady," a woman in traditional Dutch costume pouring coffee for her guests. Douwe Egberts bought several smaller roasters and established offices in Germany, France, Belgium, and Scandinavia. By the end of the 1950s the old Dutch firm accounted for over 50 percent of its country's coffee exports.

In Italy three thousand roasters vied for local retail market share, trying to take advantage of the postwar coffee boom. Italians would drop into their favorite coffee bar several times a day, standing among friends for a few minutes while they downed their drink, then moving on. They ordered varieties of espresso: *ristretto* (short and dense), *macchiato* ("spotted" with a drop of milk), *corretto* (with a shot of brandy or grappa), and others. Most of the blends contained a great deal of robusta, though nothing compared to France, where robusta accounted for 75 percent of the beans in each cup.

Lavazza expanded from Turin, opening its first branch in Milan. The ambitious brand advertised with the lilting slogan *"Lavazza paradiso in tazza,"* meaning "Lavazza is paradise in a cup." In 1956 brothers Beppe and Pericle Lavazza ousted conservative older brother Mario.[6] They built a huge, new six-floor factory and introduced vacuum cans, which allowed national distribution. Illycaffè, a smaller company founded by Francesco Illy during the depression, produced the finest-quality espresso blend. Still the Italian industry remained primarily local, with over two thousand roasters in business by 1960.

Japan Discovers Coffee

Even the Japanese, with their elaborate tea ceremony, were discovering coffee in the postwar period. Coffee first came to Japan in the seventeenth century through a Dutch merchant trading at the island of Dejima, the only port opened to foreign trade. In 1888 the first *kissaten*

---

[6]Reflecting typical Italian sexist sentiment of the era, the Lavazza brothers signed an agreement that "only legitimate male heirs who are of age may take part in running the company."

(coffeehouse) opened in Tokyo, followed by many others, often frequented by artists and the literati.[7] A small coffee industry developed. In 1920 Bunji Shibata founded Key Coffee in Yokohama, opening offices in cities throughout Japan over the next fifteen years, then establishing branches in Korea, China, and Manchuria. Other roasters quickly sprang up after World War II. Tadao Ueshima, who had run a Kobe *kissaten* before the war, opened a Tokyo branch and incorporated Ueshima Coffee Company in 1951. All together there were some two hundred roasters, most of which were concentrated in Tokyo and Osaka.

After the war Shibata moved the main Key Coffee office to Tokyo, enticed by the influx of American occupation forces, who brought with them their taste for coffee. He could not yet legally import coffee, however, and had to resort to the thriving black market. After 1950, when official coffee imports were allowed, hundreds of *kissaten* appeared in Japanese cities, many with a special appeal. In some, customers could watch newsreels while sipping coffee. *Chanson* coffeehouses featured singers. In 1955 a six-story coffeehouse opened in Tokyo's fashionable Ginza district, featuring life-sized animated female dolls, several bands, and a purple décor. Some *kissaten* stayed open all night and offered private nooks favored by prostitutes and petty criminals.

The Japanese wanted to mimic the affluent Western lifestyle, sometimes with odd results. "In Tokyo," one writer observed in 1956, "waitresses do the mambo while carrying cups of Italian espresso to tables set against a Viennese décor." The *kissaten* frequently used English names: Dig was named to indicate that its owner did in fact "dig" jazz and American slang; he later opened a second coffeehouse called Dug.

Googie Coffee

The artsy beverage confections popular in international bohemian coffeehouses did not appeal to most U.S. consumers. An American roaster scoffed at the statement that "real coffee lovers haunt the café," sarcastically adding that the claim might be true if it referred to "the ghosts of Americans who dropped dead after the first cup" of espresso. For those

---

[7]In 1911 the first *café* opened, where exorbitantly priced coffee also bought a female companion. Such cafés were forerunners of the expensive Ginza bars and should not be confused with Japanese coffeehouses.

in search of *normal* coffee, indigenous U.S. coffee shops served a regular cuppa joe, usually in a paper cup and diluted to the tastes of the time, along with a hamburger and fries. These brash, plastic-and-chrome, neon-and-glass outlets served the car culture and possessed distinctly un-Italian names: Ship's, Chip's, Googie's, Biff's, Bob's Big Boy, Coffee Dan's, Dunkin' Donuts,[8] Herbert's, White Castle, Smorgyburger, McDonald's, Jack-in-the-Box. The soaring, garishly colored roofs signaled a new style called Coffee Shop Modern, or sneeringly, Googie Architecture. "Here Fred Flintstone and George Jetson could meet over a cup of coffee," wrote Alan Hess in *Googie*, his tribute to the genre. The only trouble was that all too often Flintstone and Jetson met over a Coke rather than coffee.

In Denial

During the late 1950s the U.S. coffee industry entered a period of what pop psychologists now would call "denial." Arthur Ransohoff, the chairman of the National Coffee Association, expressed a typical attitude in 1956. "How're we doing? Not too bad—I think," he wrote. "Some of the skeptics seem to have a way of comparing coffee consumption to some of the newfangled frozen drinks, and the like. Of course staid old coffee suffers by comparison. [But] coffee was here, on this earth, long before any of the 'colas.'" Ransohoff concluded that "good old coffee seems to be 'in there pitching' and gaining slightly if not sensationally compared to the population growth of the country."

Coffee *was* gaining, by the misleading statistics issued by the Pan American Coffee Bureau. Rather than expressing U.S. per capita in actual coffee pounds per citizen (the previous practice), the PACB now reported how many *cups a day* the average American *ten or over* consumed. Thus in 1955 it reported that the "average person of coffee drinking age consumes 2.67 cups a day," a 12.5 percent increase over the 1950 rate, while in fact the actual amount of ground coffee used had declined. Such rosy statistics camouflaged the truth in two ways. First, they ignored the swelling baby-boom generation, still under ten years

---

[8]Dunkin' Donuts began as the Open Kettle in 1948, but two years later Bill Rosenberg changed the name of the Quincy, Massachusetts, store to the catchier title. In 1955 he began to franchise the stores. Unlike its Googie brethren, Dunkin' Donuts prided itself on using whole-bean arabica, introducing middle-class Americans to decent, properly brewed coffee.

old. More fundamentally, they avoided acknowledging that the cups consisted of weak coffee, stretched to brew 64 cups per pound. "Americans are drinking more coffee than ever before," the PACB bragged, but the truth was that real coffee consumption in the United States had peaked in 1946. In addition, the unfortunate coffee-boiling percolator now accounted for 64 percent of all household brewing.[9]

In a 1956 address at the annual National Coffee Association meeting Judy Gregg of Gilbert Youth Research advised coffee men to "focus attention on the 15-to–19-year-old group," observing that they would increase by 45 percent in the next decade. "The soft drink companies have been aware of these trends," she said. "By examining what they have done to attract young people, perhaps you will be able to draw parallels for the coffee industry." She noted that Coke appealed to teens with popular singer Eddie Fisher. "The coffee manufacturer that decides to use the same personality technique and hires the services of one Elvis Presley could enjoy a strange success," Gregg continued. "Imagine Elvis sipping just one cup on TV."

None of the coffee men rushed to hire Elvis to appeal to the baby boomers. Even if they had, magazines such as *Seventeen* wouldn't have run the ads. Although willing to feature soft drink pitches, they still considered coffee unsuitable for teens. When the Pan American Coffee Bureau finally broke through that taboo in the late 1950s, it featured an insert, "How to Make a Good Cup of Coffee," aimed at the future housewife, which elicited only yawns. So did the preppy, clean-cut "Teen Mates" they used to promote coffee with donuts, or the roaster billboard saluting the "student of the month" at a local college.

The roasters didn't seem to understand that teenagers identified with rebels. They wanted action, energy, and adventure. As editor James Quinn observed in the *Tea & Coffee Trade Journal,* "coffee roasters and industry promotion groups appear willing to surrender the youth market by default." National Coffee Association president John McKiernan put the situation more graphically. "Today, the Pied Piper is . . . one giant cola bottle, and his limbs are formed of soft drink and beer cans,

---

[9]In 1942 the American inventor Peter Schlumbohm created an hourglass-shaped piece of Pyrex that he dubbed the Chemex, to match its laboratory appearance. The simple, functional drip brewer featured a wood and leather handgrip at its waist. It made good coffee, but it was difficult to clean. It never challenged the percolator, except among highbrows and purists. The simpler German Melitta cone drip system did not appear in the United States until 1963.

strung loosely so that he makes a lot of noise as he walks through the marketplace with our youth flocking after him."

In 1959 the Pan American Coffee Bureau hired BBDO, Pepsi-Cola's advertising firm, to counter another major problem: the diluted-coffee trend. In what the BBDO men termed a "sprightly and unconventional approach," the ads depicted a businessman gripping a broad sword atop a rearing horse, next to a woman on a motor scooter holding a banner with the motto, "More Coffee in Our Coffee or Fight." To join this "crusade" readers could send in a dime for a brewing leaflet and official membership certificate in the "League of Honest Coffee Lovers."

Predictably, the campaign failed to bring back decent coffee brewing. All it did was attract the satire of *Mad* magazine, which ran a parody about the "League of Frightened Coffee Growers," an organization that offered pamphlets telling "the whole miserable story of how the Pan-American coffee growers are losing their shirts." The headline screamed: *"Weak Coffee Sales Gives Us Growers Java Jitters!"*

Scared into Agreement

The 1960 *Mad* article did not amuse Latin American coffee producers, since it hit too close to the truth. A few years earlier, African growers would have laughed heartily, but now they too were suffering from overproduction and falling prices. Threatened with looming surpluses, the Africans bound together to form the Inter-African Coffee Organization. At the same time, they rushed to the negotiation table. Together with fifteen Latin American countries, Angola, the Ivory Coast, and Cameroon signed on to a one-year quota system in September 1959 in which each country agreed to export 10 percent less than its best year in the past decade.[10] Without any enforcement mechanism, however, the quota system was widely violated.

The new agreement was, everyone acknowledged, a stopgap measure, but at least it was a start. In 1960 the British African coffee colonies of Kenya, Tanganyika, and Uganda joined the agreement, which was extended for another year. "The biggest question," wrote Brazilian João Oliveira Santos early in 1961, "is how and when the

---

[10]Coffee production in India, Yemen, and Indonesia was of little concern, amounting to just over 3 percent of world production.

major coffee-consuming countries such as the United States will decide
to participate in a long-term agreement. Their support would be practically essential." He was optimistic, noting that "the ideological and political security of the Western World is directly dependent on its collective economic security." Clearly Santos was relying on the Communist menace to scare the United States into the agreement. As if to underline the threat, in 1960 the Brazilians sent a delegation to the Soviet Union to arrange a barter deal, trading coffee for Russian oil, wheat, airplanes, and drilling equipment.

In 1959 Fidel Castro's rebels had overthrown the Batista dictatorship in Cuba. In 1960 Castro aligned himself with the Soviets and began nationalizing American companies, throwing the United States into a panic over Communist influence in Latin America and further propelling the United States toward support for the coffee agreement.

The U.S. fear of communism focused not only on Latin America but also Africa. In 1960 the trickle toward inevitable African decolonization turned into a flood of newly independent countries, many relying primarily on coffee just when prices were nosediving. One coffee writer worried that the African nations might "become mere pawns in the economic warfare currently being fought by the mighty nations of the East and West"—in other words, would they be ripped apart by the cold war?

When Charles de Gaulle offered French African colonies a choice of independence or continued "interdependence," French Sudan (renamed Mali) and Madagascar (renamed the Malagasy Republic) chose independence while remaining in the French commonwealth. Their example prompted the Ivory Coast, which had first opted to remain a colony, to choose independence in August 1960, with Félix Houphouët-Boigny as president. The French continued to pump aid money into their former colonies, along with advisors. "Coffee is a political problem as much as an economic one," a French importer wrote. France had a duty, he said, to keep "millions of people within this side of the Liberty Curtain."

While the transition to independence proceeded smoothly in the Ivory Coast, it was disastrous in the Belgian Congo, the birthplace of robusta. Some seventy-five years earlier, when Africa had been artificially sliced up by the European powers, the countries' imposed national boundaries hid smoldering tribal rivalries that frequently erupted with independence. Nowhere was this more evident than in the

Congo.[11] Within a week of the Congo's June 30, 1960, independence the native army mutinied, looting, raping, and killing at random. The eastern province of Katanga attempted to secede, and the Belgian government sent troops. In the mounting chaos Prime Minister Patrice Lumumba, a former postal worker, appealed simultaneously to the United Nations and to Nikita Khrushchev in the Soviet Union for help.

By approaching the Communists, Lumumba sealed his fate. The United States ordained not only his overthrow but his death. With CIA air support Lumumba was captured by Mobutu Sese Seko, and was assassinated on January 17, 1961. The following years brought internecine warfare, attempted revolution, American intervention, and the long-term despotic rule of Mobutu, who renamed the country Zaire. "Production is declining," a Congo coffee man reported in 1965. "One of our merchant friends reports that 25 percent of his planter-clients have been killed. Others have left their plantations. On one *shamba*, the entire labor force of a hundred men were slaughtered."

Three days after Patrice Lumumba's assassination John F. Kennedy became the new President of the United States. Along with Cuba and the Congo, he worried about Angola. Determined to stymie Communist influence in Africa, Kennedy encouraged the Portuguese dictatorship to crush an Angolan rebellion rather than to allow independence. When unpaid coffee workers demanded back wages, planters panicked and fired on them. In the ensuing massacre hundreds of whites and thousands of blacks were killed in the coffee plantations. Finally, with American weapons, the Portuguese restored order and coffee cultivation.

The British delayed granting independence to Uganda, Kenya, and Tanganyika, hoping to provide a smooth transition. Late in 1960 Alan Bowler, a British coffee exporter, wrote from Nairobi, Kenya: "To millions in this Continent, coffee means the difference between too little to eat or enough." With tiny farms predominating, he doubted the efficacy of any scheme to reduce the surplus coffee harvest. "To any smallholder having three acres," he wrote, "it would take a great deal of filtered economics, plus a gun, to begin to persuade him to cut

---

[11]In densely populated Ruanda-Urundi (soon to become the separate countries of Rwanda and Burundi), where high-grown arabica coffee was the primary export, tribal tensions erupted in 1959 as the Hutu, poor farmers, rose up against their minority overlords, the Tutsi. The fall in coffee prices undoubtedly had made life even worse for the Hutu. After bloody fighting, the Tutsi king and over one hundred forty thousand members of his tribe fled, but violence recurred for decades to come.

production." By this point 80 percent of African coffee was grown by Africans.

The new coffee agreement thus was born out of the economic despair and political tension of this cold war world. In the United States in January 1961 John McKiernan of the National Coffee Association warned that in Africa Khrushchev could "exploit nationalism to ensnare emerging nations into Communist slavery." He concluded that, although the NCA traditionally had opposed quota schemes as limits on free trade, he now would support the International Coffee Agreement in this "atmosphere of international hypertension."

In 1961 President Kennedy sponsored the Alliance for Progress, designed to improve relations with Latin America through aid programs. In his March 13 speech introducing the Alliance, Kennedy acknowledged that "the prices of commodities are subject to violent change. A sudden fall can . . . sharply reduce the national income, upset the budget, and wreck the foreign exchange position. It is plain that no program of economic development can be effected unless something is done to stabilize commodity prices."

Secretary of the Treasury Douglas Dillon reiterated U.S. support for a coffee agreement. On July 9, 1962, the United Nations convened a UN Coffee Conference in New York City to negotiate a long-term agreement. The meetings ran virtually around the clock. "For me," U.S. delegate Michael Blumenthal later recalled, "the most amusing moment came at 4 A.M. one morning when I was still rushing around the smoke-filled rooms of the U.N., trying to break a deadlock. Two other members of the U.S. team were holding on to my coat-tails, begging me to maintain the dignity of my office. I think I replied that if I had any dignity, I would be home in bed."

After prolonged and bitter negotiations the participants finally reached a tentative quota agreement. The International Coffee Agreement (ICA) would come into full force, however, only when ratified by most of the importing and exporting countries.[12] The deadline for ratification was set for December 30, 1963. In the meantime the five-year agreement would go into effect informally.

---

[12]At first Guatemala, Cuba, Ethiopia, Yemen, Ecuador, and the USSR refused to sign, while Honduras, Nicaragua, and Haiti expressed reservations about the quota allotments. Most of these countries—with the exception of Yemen—eventually joined the ICA.

The basic quota was based on world exports of 45.6 million bags. Of that amount Brazil was allowed 18 million bags, Colombia just over 6 million, the Ivory Coast (now the world's third leading producer) 2.3 million, and Angola just over 2 million bags. The agreement called for quarterly quota adjustments requiring approval by two-thirds of both importing and exporting countries. Furthermore every coffee shipment was to be accompanied by a "certificate of origin," or reexport certificate. Countries with low coffee consumption, such as Japan, China, and the Soviet Union, were exempted from the quota system. Exporters therefore could ship as much coffee as they wished behind the Iron Curtain or to Japan. The agreement gave lip service to promotional efforts to increase worldwide consumption and to limit overproduction, but the provisions were all voluntary. Any country could withdraw from the agreement with ninety days' notice.

Stumbling Toward Ratification

At first, full United States participation in the International Coffee Agreement appeared to be a foregone conclusion, but the path toward ratification did not run smoothly. In March 1963 hearings were held before the Committee on Foreign Relations to discuss the agreement. Kansas senator Frank Carlson asked Under Secretary of State for Political Affairs George McGhee, "Is it not a fact that what you actually are doing is placing a burden on the coffee consumers of the United States to maintain a price level in a foreign country?" Another senator asked whether it were not really "an international cartel." Iowa senator Bourke Hickenlooper warned, "We had better start looking after American interests a little bit more rather than assuming that we are Lady Bountiful with an unlimited amount of resources to devote in a rather cavalier manner around over the world." In May the Senate ultimately ratified the agreement knowing that it still would have to pass "implementing" legislation that would allow U.S. Customs to reject coffee without a proper certificate of origin.

Then nature intervened in Paraná, first with an early August frost, then a devastating September fire, all in the midst of a prolonged drought. With Brazil's prospective crop severely damaged, coffee prices once again began to climb. After tortuous debate the House of Representatives nonetheless voted for implementing legislation on November 14, sending it back to the Senate for a final vote.

Eight days later, just after noon on November 22, 1963, President Kennedy was assassinated in Dallas. The coffee politics were so intense that the members of the ICA, engaged in a bitter debate over quotas at London headquarters, continued their all-day arguments late into the night, even after hearing of the U.S. president's murder. In the end, at 2:00 A.M. on November 23, they failed to increase quotas in response to rising prices.

In order to keep the ICA alive the United States deposited its instrument of ratification on December 27, four days before the deadline, still without implementing legislation. Coffee prices continued their steady climb, from 34 cents a pound up to 50 cents for Santos #4. On February 12, 1964, knowing that American politicians were likely to kill the agreement unless more coffee were released and prices moderated, the ICA Council voted overwhelmingly to increase quotas just over 3 percent, releasing another 2.3 million bags.

When the Senate Committee on Finance met two weeks later for three days of hearings, Averell Harriman of the State Department pointed out that the purpose of the ICA was to prevent the bankruptcy of producing countries. Delaware senator John Williams asked, "But it was a one-way protection, was it not? There was nothing in there that would protect the price of coffee from going to a dollar a pound."

The producing countries clearly had voted for a quota increase largely to placate U.S. politicians. "And once this implementing legislation has been approved by Congress and signed by the President," a senator observed, "they will not have the Senate to fear; isn't that true?"

Even liberal Democratic Senator Paul Douglas objected to the ICA implementation, on the grounds that higher coffee prices would not "trickle down" to peasant laborers. What had happened during the price spike in 1954? "Elaborate houses and plantation houses were built by the planters," Douglas observed, "and they sent abroad capital anonymously to be deposited in Swiss banks in numbered accounts. . . . Money was not used for the improvement of the condition of the people." If they did pass the legislation, Douglas noted, "we will be acclaimed for following out the good neighbor policy, but this is the superficial crust of Latin American life. The real volcano is underneath."

Wendell Rollason, who testified for a Miami anti-Castro organization, shared Douglas's concerns but drew a different conclusion: The campesinos of Latin America needed help. "They seek a piece of land, a steady job, a full belly, a child's education . . . It is going to be us or the Russians. It's that simple."

Averell Harriman told Senator Douglas that, at least in Brazil, which he had just visited, the government was attempting "social reform and social progress, improvements of the condition of the people." In Brazil huge *fazendas* still predominated, with 1.6 percent of the farms holding over half of the cultivated land.[13]

The ratification process ground on, delayed by a filibuster over civil rights legislation. The Senate finally passed the implementing legislation on July 31, 1964, but only after Republican Senator Everett Dirksen tacked on an amendment specifying that the United States would withdraw from the ICA upon a joint resolution of Congress. This meant that although the House already had approved the legislation, it now had to approve the amended version. By a narrow margin, in August, the House *rejected* it.

After the elections, in which Lyndon Johnson won a landslide victory, the Senate passed the amended bill on February 2, 1965, and the House once more held hearings in April. By this time Santos #4 had stabilized at 45 cents a pound, and in addition to the Dirksen amendment, there was reassuring language about protecting the interests of the U.S. consumer. "Coffee is not so much an economic problem as it is a political problem," Thomas Mann of the State Department testified, once again playing the Red Menace card. "The key question is whether it is in the U.S. interest to allow these countries . . . to go through the wringer," he said, "and take a chance that they would stay on our side of the curtain which divides the free and the Communist world." The House passed the implementing legislation, and the International Coffee Agreement went into full effect, with the United States monitoring certificates of origin.

Boomer Bust

While the politicians were arguing, the U.S. coffee industry continued to experience its own crisis. From a "peak" of 3.1 cups a day for U.S.

---

[13]He was speaking of the João Goulart regime. Goulart, who always had championed the poor and who tolerated Communists, came to power in 1961. Under his regime inflation raged out of control, with the government printing new money to pay its debts. Goulart did attempt to carry out agrarian land reform, however, which was his undoing. On March 31, 1964–a month after Averell Harriman's Senate testimony–Brazilian army units marched into Rio de Janeiro to oust Goulart. Within four hours President Lyndon Johnson sent a telegram congratulating the officers who executed the coup. Goulart fled into exile on April 4, and a twenty-year era of Brazilian military dictatorships commenced.

consumers age ten or over in 1962, per-capita coffee consumption began to fall, even using the overly optimistic cups-a-day statistics. By 1964 the average was 2.9 cups a day.

To appeal to the baby boomers, the Pan American Coffee Bureau introduced a series of campaigns such as "Mugmates," asking adolescents to decorate coffee mugs. "I go for coffee, you go for coffee, let's go for coffee together," a slogan urged. But these lame attempts did not woo teens. In fact, a survey revealed that "teenagers do not like the taste of coffee at all, and in many instances find it repulsive." Unlike soft drinks, coffee was not considered refreshing or beneficial in any way. At least there was some tiny solace: teens identified coffee as an adult beverage, and consumption of such a loathsome liquid signaled a rite of passage into the world of the businessman and housewife. "While the youngster is consuming hundreds and hundreds of bottles of pop, he is doing so with the full cognizance that in not too many years he will be a coffee drinker."

Unfortunately, just when additional coffee promotion appeared to be absolutely vital, even the small amount of support from the Pan American Coffee Bureau fizzled in anticipation that the London-based International Coffee Organization would take over. But the ICO members failed to appropriate promotional funds for three crucial years, from 1963 until 1966. At the same time, the Coffee Brewing Institute, that for over a decade had made valiant but ineffectual attempts to improve American brewing habits, lost its funding.[14]

Coca-Cola and Pepsi mounted ever-more sophisticated, expensive campaigns to entice youth. "Things go better with Coca-Cola," sang a cheerful folk group. "Food goes better with, Fun goes better with, You go better with Coke." The soft drink was portrayed as a "real live one" that put "extra fun" into everything. Pepsi countered with a brilliant attempt to snare—and even label—an entire generation. As television commercials showed frenetically active, happy young people on motorcycles or roller coasters, a woman sang "Come alive! Come alive! You're in the Pepsi Generation." In 1965 soft drink firms spent nearly $100 million on ads—*twice* the outlay for coffee.

---

[14]At first it appeared that European consumption would continue to climb. In 1963 Europe imported over twenty million bags for the first time. By 1965 consumption leveled off, and teenagers in Europe too found soft drinks more appealing than coffee.

A 1965 editorial in the *Tea & Coffee Trade Journal* summed up the problem succinctly: "Coffee has been engaged in a tough competitive struggle for a great many years and it has been losing that fight for at least a decade. Now, for the first time, the extent of the loss is becoming measurable and there is no reason to believe that the tide of battle is about to turn."

Merger Mania

Instead of mounting a truly effective campaign to attract the baby boomers, coffee roasters continued to battle one another for dwindling market share. As profit margins tightened, the process of industry concentration accelerated, with mergers and bankruptcies narrowing the field to just two hundred forty roasters by 1965. Of those the top eight companies accounted for 75 percent of sales. Chock full o' Nuts bought regional roasters in St. Louis, St. Paul, and Philadelphia. Houston-based Duncan Foods merged with firms in Nebraska, Tennessee, Missouri, Alabama, and California. Industrial giant Blaw-Knox swallowed roaster manufacturer Jabez Burns & Sons.

The most momentous merger was announced in September 1963. Consumer food conglomerate Procter & Gamble was buying Folger's, the oldest coffee firm in the West. P & G CEO Howard Morgens stated that "coffee would put Procter & Gamble into another highly competitive area." Up to that point Folger's and Hills Brothers had battled for coffee supremacy primarily in the West and Midwest. By the time Procter & Gamble paid $126 million for the company, Folger's had attained a slim lead over Hills Brothers in most of its markets. With roasting plants in San Francisco, Kansas City, New Orleans, Houston, Los Angeles, and Portland, it employed thirteen hundred people and held 11 percent of the U.S. coffee market.

The buttoned-down Procter & Gamble men, who had turned soap sales into a science, shook up the genteel coffee world. Everything now had to be documented with endless reports and memos. "We had always gone home at 5 P.M.," a veteran Folger's employee recalled. "These jerks from P & G didn't go home, and when they did, they carried fat briefcases." As Earl Shorris wrote in *A Nation of Salesmen*, the P & G men were "the Jesuits of marketing, rigorous thinkers, examiners, cold men."

With a major infusion of cash, sophisticated television ads now reached many more consumers, playing on their fears and desires. Mrs. Olson, an omniscient Swedish busybody played by actress Virginia Christine, magically appeared at the back door with a can of Folgers Coffee (P & G dropped the apostrophe), just in time to save a marriage and restore true love. The ads reinforced sexist images of petulant husbands incapable of making their own coffee and frantic wives whose worth was measured out in coffee spoons. Within Procter & Gamble it was known as the "There, There" campaign. The company conducted research to determine "how ugly and aggressive we could get," as one adman put it. They discovered that housewives would accept "all sorts of abuse" as reasonable, since they actually experienced it much of the time in their daily lives.

Only months after Procter & Gamble bought Folgers, archenemy Coca-Cola jumped into the coffee fray, announcing a merger with Duncan Foods in February 1964. The soft-drink firm already owned Tenco, the New Jersey instant coffee cooperative, which it got as a bonus when it bought Minute Maid orange juice in 1960. Now Coke suddenly was the fifth largest roaster in the United States, with brands such as Admiration, Butter-Nut, Fleetwood, Maryland Club, Huggins Young, and Blue Ridge, along with a healthy private label and institutional business. The announcement stunned and terrified the coffee world. "Is Coca-Cola *moving in?*" asked a trade journal correspondent. Just why the soft-drink titan would want to sell coffee, however, remained a puzzle, since colas offered a much higher profit margin. Many people suspected that Coke was more interested in acquiring aggressive managers such as Charles Duncan, Jr., and Don Keough, who had come onboard with Butter-Nut. Both men in fact would rise to the top at Coke.

The Maxwell Housewife

With the acquisition of Duncan Foods, however, Coca-Cola still commanded a mere 5 percent of the regular coffee market, and 1 percent of the instant. General Foods remained the real coffee behemoth, with a 22 percent share of regular coffee and a whopping 51 percent of instant. It owned Maxwell House, Sanka, and Yuban, and it practiced the most sophisticated, high-powered coffee marketing, appealing to slightly different segments of the market with each brand.

General Foods then took the merger phenomenon international. In the early 1960s it bought French, German, Swedish, Spanish, and Mexican roasters. Following liberalization of Japanese coffee imports, General Foods formed a joint venture with a local brewery and mineral water company in 1961 to produce instant coffee for the Japanese market. To solidify its new international image General Foods paid for Maxwell House to become the official coffee at the 1964 New York World's Fair, where it reminded visitors that it was good to the last drop on soaring 60-foot-high archways.

In 1960 viewers first saw the now-classic Maxwell House percolator ad, created by famed adman David Ogilvy and destined to run off and on for years as it entered the subconscious of a generation. As coffee began to spurt sporadically into the glass knob at the top of a percolator, a syncopated beat accompanied it, then as the percolator settled into full boil the tune broke into a sprightly, hummable melody that would forever signify the cheerful warmth of morning coffee preparation. It was a brilliant, evocative commercial, even though it celebrated a dreadful way to brew coffee, and Maxwell House commercials still bounce to its theme music.

In the first snob appeal to instant users, General Foods introduced instant Yuban the same year, with door-to-door sampling, advertising, and extensive sales promotion. Because it used all-arabica beans, this soluble product indeed was superior to other instants, although mediocre compared to regular coffee. Along with other coffee roasters General Foods switched to nonkey cans with plastic resealable lids. It coordinated a television campaign on "The Andy Griffith Show" with four-cup samples of Sanka bound into *Family Circle* and *TV Guide* magazines.

In 1964 the company introduced Maxim, the first freeze-dried coffee, a technological advance over spray-dried solubles that offered better flavor. "You are looking at something you've never seen before—the power to turn every cup in your house into a percolator," Maxim ads promised. "After years of research, ice is drawn off in a vacuum, forming concentrated crystals of real perked coffee." A spot for freeze-dried Sanka showed a man chipping away at an enormous ice block that contained a jar of Sanka.

In 1965 the company launched "the most powerful advertising ad promotion program in ground coffee history" for Maxwell House, featuring its first color-TV spots. Simultaneous print ads offered a 7-cents-off coupon and a free record, "12,000 Girl Scouts Sing America's National Favorites." The television minidramas, aimed at young married couples, urged women to "Be a Maxwell Housewife." A typical ad showed a pert young woman surrounded by packing boxes in a new apartment. "Wife," says the condescending husband in a voice-over, "pay attention, because I'm going to teach you to make coffee." The ad never shows the husband, only his hands, as he makes coffee. He orders her only to use Maxwell House coffee. "Smell it. Now taste it. See? Always good to the last drop. So—no experimenting with my coffee. Be a good little Maxwell Housewife and I think I'll keep you around." He pats her on the head and musses her hair. Intended to tap the insecurities of young wives, this spot also undoubtedly offended budding feminists.

The Decline of Hills Brothers

In the brave new world of coffee conglomerates Hills Brothers stubbornly held out as a traditional family firm. A 1958 opinion survey conducted for the firm showed that Hills Brothers suffered from an "old-fashioned" image, while Folgers was considered "modern and up-to-date." Worse, the survey found that "the belief that its quality has deteriorated is given as a reason for deserting Hills Brothers." The charge was true. Under immense competitive pressure Hills Brothers compromised the quality of the blend.

In 1960 consumer interviews revealed that the Hills Brothers Arab was perceived as a tired, old-fashioned patriarch. The best thing a consumer said was, "I kind of like him. He's a harmless old guy. Is that a nightshirt?" Worse, a Jewish woman thought him "a spy for the Arabs [who] is found out and hung." Marketing consultants concluded that "the figure is seen as hopelessly out-of-date," and called the Hills Brothers package "gutless" and "emasculated." The report only infuriated sixty-three-year-old Leslie Hills, R.W.'s son. "They throw the Arab off the label as though it were an old shoe." He refused to budge.

Although the Arab remained on the cans, the firm made valiant efforts to maintain market share, including the now-standard coupons and special deals. It offered free coffee urns to churches and clubs that sent in a sufficient number of coffee labels. Hills Brothers cosponsored the 1960 Squaw Valley Winter Olympics, but with a total annual ad budget of $5 million their TV spots appeared only in San Francisco,

Los Angeles, Portland, and Chicago. At the same time they sponsored local ads on "Shirley Temple's Storybook," "Bat Masterson," and "Walt Disney."

A new ad campaign urged consumers to "Head for the Hills!" asserting that the coffee was "just slightly richer, now—about 10 percent richer than other leading coffees." No one believed this irrational claim, any more than the absurd slogan, "Flavor so unbeatable, it's reheatable!" Television spots showed an auto body shop worker reheating his coffee over a blowtorch. The idea of "reheatable" coffee would have horrified the original Hills brothers, as it would any coffee expert.

In 1964 Gray Hills, A.H.'s son, died at age seventy. The next year an internal *Brand Image Study* stated: "Throughout the Western Zone, Hills Bros. was seen as a poor quality coffee or a brand that was declining in popularity." Folgers, with Procter & Gamble's marketing clout behind it, was seen as "*the* good quality coffee." Chicago, where Hills Brothers long had dominated, and the East, where it was newly introduced, provided the only bright spots, with a relatively favorable image. In hometown San Francisco, however, Hills Brothers was "a brand that wasn't used anymore, whose advertising claims were not believed, and which the man of the house did not like."

The Creation of Juan Valdez

While Hills Brothers market share and image declined, a South American initiative proved that quality *could* still sell. In 1960 the National Federation of Coffee Growers of Colombia invented Juan Valdez, a friendly, mustachioed coffee grower who, with his mule, trundled his hand-picked beans down from the Colombian mountains. Played by actor José Duval, dressed in traditional peasant garb and wearing a sombrero, the proud-yet-humble Juan Valdez captured the American imagination. For once advertising hype essentially matched reality; most Colombian coffee indeed was produced on small mountainside *fincas* by some two hundred thousand families headed by men such as Juan Valdez. Although railroads rushed coffee to freighters on the coast, the beans often did take the initial trip down the mountain on muleback. The Colombian beans really did make a fine cup of coffee, superior to most U.S. blends.

The initial ad campaign broke in January 1960 in ten major U.S. markets, using full-page newspaper spreads. "We don't know who's more stubborn–Juan Valdez or his mule," read the caption underneath a picture of the coffee grower, arms folded, in front of his pack animal. "Juan has a finca (coffee grove) 5,000 feet up in the Colombian Andes. The soil there is rich. The air is moist. Two reasons for the extraordinary coffee of Colombia. The third is stubbornness of growers like Juan." The copy went on to explain the importance of shade trees and hand harvesting. The ads demonstrated that coffee could be raised above the mere commodity level of coupon-off deals. As a trade journal editor observed, they made consumers aware of the "costly care and effort poured into a good cup of coffee."

The Juan Valdez campaign carved out a quality image for Colombian coffee and blends that contained it. Spending over a million dollars the first year, the federation brought Valdez to television viewers, who could actually see him picking the beans and leading his mule down the mountainside.

An *Advertising Age* writer praised the campaign for being "strikingly original without resorting to silly off-beat gimmicks and irrelevant stunts." Five months after the campaign began, there was a 300 percent increase in the number of consumers who identified Colombian coffee as the world's finest. Even the federation's ad agency, Doyle Dane and Bernbach, was astonished. "We [have] never achieved such rapid results," a DDB rep said. "When we began, we figured it would take at least two years to reach the percentage increase obtained in five months."

By 1962 the federation had taken the campaign to Canada and Europe. The campaign was so successful that many roasters not only bragged that their blends contained Colombian beans but also began marketing 100 percent Colombian cans. By creating a value-added product, the Colombian beans could command a premium price, rising above the price-cutting fray. In addition the federation provided free advertising support and the Juan Valdez logo on each can. A 1963 trade ad showed all-Colombian blends from around the world. "They're bringing in markkaa, francs, kroner, guilders . . . . and good old dollars too!" the copy bragged.

By the end of 1963 the television campaign had gone national, and Valdez now had a son. "See, Ramon," Valdez said, "we always shade our coffee trees from the sun–so the beans will ripen slowly. And we pick the coffee beans one by one." The federation called Juan Valdez their "coffee salesman supreme." In 1964 General Foods switched its high-end Yuban brand to 100 percent Colombian coffee, proving that the campaign had triumphed even in Maxwell House country. In 1965, only five years after the creation of the mythical Colombian coffee grower, over forty U.S. brands and over twenty European roasters featured all-Colombian brands.

In a Vortex

Aside from the Juan Valdez phenomenon, however, coffee had entered the vortex of a downward spiral. To stay in business you had to cut prices. To cut prices you had to narrow profit margins. To maintain profitability you had to cut quality. And so it went, in a seemingly vicious circle.

In 1963 one green coffee broker analyzed the contents of "one of the finest blends," probably Folgers. It contained 20 percent Brazilian beans, 40 percent Colombian, 30 percent Central American—and 10 percent African robusta. Only a decade earlier no self-respecting blend would have contained *any* robusta beans. In such a mass-market, bottom-line, loss-leader, robusta-blended world, was there any hope for decent coffee in the United States?

Surprisingly enough, the answer was Yes. But America's coffee savior would not be a General Foods or Procter & Gamble man, but a disgruntled Dutchman running away from his father.

~ *Part Four* ~

ROMANCING
THE BEAN

*The late twentieth century has witnessed a coffee revival. Much of Frasier, the
popular television show, takes place in the mythical Café Nervosa, where the
neurotic brother psychiatrists sip their lattes and cappucinos.*

～ 15 ～

A SCATTERED
BAND OF FANATICS

I believe that the American coffee industry is doing itself irreparable harm by mass marketing mediocre coffee at a low price. I think that what is happening today in the coffee business is just a foreshadowing of the eventual indifference of the total American public to the world of coffee drinking.

–Edward Bransten, 1969

The person who roasts coffee should continue his development not only with skill and judgment but with a measure of love and devotion.... The coffee roaster turns alchemist when he transforms an unappetizing seed into the makings of a delicious, invigorating drink. His magic is genuine; he must interpret the beans' secrets and reveal them to our senses.

–Joel, David, and Karl Schapira, 1975

When Henry Peet set up a business roasting coffee in the Dutch village of Alkmaar in the early twentieth century, he had no idea that he was beginning a chain of events that would pull America out of the coffee doldrums years later. A taciturn man, Peet did not consider the coffee business a calling. Like a butcher or barber, he practiced a trade, that was all. Henry Peet had hoped for better things for his middle child, Alfred, but the boy had disappointed him. Suffering from an undiagnosed learning disability, young Alfred did not do well in school–but he loved the smell and taste of his father's coffee.

After apprenticing with a large Amsterdam importer, eighteen-year-old Alfred Peet went to work for his father in 1938. During the early years of the war Alfred helped his father eke out a living with a faux coffee made from chicory, roasted peas, and rye drinks, since the Germans confiscated all their coffee beans. Alfred then was forced into a German labor camp, and after the war he returned to the family roasting business. In 1948, eager to escape his domineering father, Alfred Peet went to Java and Sumatra, where he learned to love full-bodied arabica beans. With Indonesian independence in 1950, Peet left for New Zealand, then eventually wound up in San Francisco in 1955.

For a few years he worked at E. A. Johnson & Company, a coffee importer for big roasters such as Hills Brothers and Folger's. Peet was appalled by what he had to sell. "Folgers bought lots of Brazils, Central American standards, and robustas. I couldn't understand why in the richest country in the world they were drinking such poor quality coffee." The public didn't seem to care. "People drank ten cups of that stuff a day. You knew it had to be weak. If you drank ten cups of strong coffee, you'd be floating against the ceiling."

In 1965 Peet was laid off. Forty-five years old and unable to land a new job, he decided to roast his own coffee–*good* coffee–and to sell it in his own store, using money he had inherited when his father died.[1] With a used 25-pound roaster and ten bags of Colombian beans, he opened Peet's Coffee & Tea on April 1, 1966, on the corner of Vine and Walnut Streets in Berkeley. Intent on selling whole-bean coffee for home consumption, he offered a small, inexpensive coffee bar with six stools to introduce his customers to good coffee. "I had an educational battle on my hands," he remembers. "If you are used to drinking Hills Brothers coffee and then try Peet's, roasted darker and brewed twice as strong, you wouldn't say it was terrific. It was written all over their faces. 'My God, is he trying to poison me?'" Expatriate Europeans, on the other hand, immediately thought they had found nirvana, a taste of home.

Because Peet sold his coffee with passionate authority, his women customers began to take it home and bring their husbands back the next weekend. Peet hired two young women and taught them to cup (smell, taste, and evaluate) coffees. "It takes a long time to understand

---

[1]Although Alfred Peet inspired a generation of coffee idealists, he was not the first in the tiny San Francisco vanguard. Graffeo and Freed, Teller & Freed (where Peet worked briefly) predated him. So did Hardcastle's, founded in 1963 by Jim Hardcastle, an academic historian, and Herb Donaldson, a criminal lawyer. In 1968 they changed the company name to Capricorn. In 1978 Jim Hardcastle died of bone marrow cancer. Donaldson, appointed a judge in 1983, eventually sold the business in 1990.

the language the bean uses to talk to you," he told them. It would take years, he said, before they could hear that secret language. Still, they could at least convey something of this knowledge to customers. Swept up in the excitement of their newfound expertise, they sniffed, sipped, swooned, and sold.

Within a year and a half there were lines stretching around the corner, waiting for Peet's Coffee. Peet's was hip. Peet's was groovy. Peet's was the place for hippies to hang out. Alfred Peet despised them. "Oh my God, I was trying to build a neat store, and they were disheveled." He took out the stools, and they sat on the floor. "I wanted an orderly business, and some of those guys were smelly."

Only the owner worried about the odor of his unwashed customers. Everyone else inhaled deeply, high on the smell of the wickedly dark fresh-roasted coffee. Burlap sacks full of green beans lined the back wall. In the middle of a sentence, Peet would jump up. "I have a roast!" he would exclaim, and rush over to let the rich brown beans tumble out. At this dramatic moment all conversation stopped. For Peet and his customers coffee was a religion. Peet could be a difficult guru, however. He did not suffer fools gladly. He would yell at customers who told him they planned to brew in a percolator. "Why spend all this money for good coffee and then boil the hell out of it?"

Zabar's Beans

In New York City, at about the same time that Alfred Peet opened his Berkeley coffee shop, Saul Zabar discovered the wonders of fresh-roasted beans. Zabar's father, Louis, had immigrated from Russia in 1925 and started a small smoked fish department in a local store. After Louis Zabar died in 1950 Saul gradually expanded the store at the corner of Broadway and Eightieth Street to serve the upscale Upper West Side community, with an emphasis on fresh produce. Around 1966 he decided to supply whole-bean coffee. After unsatisfactory experiences with several roasters he found the White Coffee Corporation in Long Island City, which supplied the institutional trade—primarily restaurants and hotels—with a high-quality all-arabica blend. Every day for a year Saul Zabar, then in his early forties, showed up for two hours of roasting and cupping sessions. Gradually, the pupil turned into the expert. Zabar got White to order Kenya AA, Tanzanian peaberry, Jamaican Blue Mountain, Hawaiian Kona, Guatemalan Antigua.

Zabar prided himself on producing a much lighter roast than Alfred Peet. "I think beans should be roasted just enough to bring out their unique flavor elements of body and acidity." Apparently, his customers agreed. Zabar's fame spread beyond New York City, up and down the East Coast, where his mail order business flourished.[2]

Mentors, Fathers, and Sons

Throughout the country a scattered, disparate band rediscovered or maintained the tradition of fresh-roasted, quality coffees. Many had roots in the old-style coffee business, before the Age of Robusta. Trained by Leon Cheek at General Foods, Peter Condaxis quit in disgust at the desecration of the Maxwell House blend. In 1959 he opened a small retail shop in Jacksonville, Florida, where customers could buy fresh whole-bean coffees from Costa Rica, Guatemala, and Colombia.

Donald Schoenholt grew up with the smells of Mocha & Java. His father, David, ran the New York–based Gillies Coffee Co., founded in 1840. In 1964 David Schoenholt had a massive heart attack, and Don, just shy of nineteen years old, took over the business. Throughout the rest of the 1960s the young Schoenholt struggled to maintain quality and keep the business going. "I developed this ideal that I was a lone craftsman, turning out fine coffee. I grew up in an age when the traditions of good coffee had been lost." He felt very much alone. At a coffee industry dinner, when Schoenholt told an executive for a large corporate roaster that he sold coffee from an open burlap sack, everyone laughed condescendingly. "I kept my composure, but inside I was shaking with rage and humiliation," he recalls. "I stuck it out, though. I was too stupid to quit."

Schoenholt's friend, Joel Schapira, also carried on a family coffee tradition begun by his grandfather, Morris Schapira, at the Flavor Cup on Tenth Street in Greenwich Village in 1903. At the same location Joel worked with his brother, Karl, and father, David, inviting favored customers to join them at the back room cupping table.

---

[2]McNulty's, a venerable Greenwich Village coffee outlet founded in 1895 by a New York judge, also experienced a renaissance in 1968, when Bill Towart rescued it from near oblivion, making it a vital part of the specialty coffee scene. Towart sold it to employee Tai Lee in 1980.

As one regional roaster put it, "We are the fungus that grows in the cracks between the big fellows." In Long Beach, California, young Ted Lingle, fresh from the war in Vietnam, joined Lingle Brothers, started by his grandfather and great-uncles in 1920. Lingle grew up listening to his father worry about the state of the business. "The whole trade was lamenting the trend away from quality, but no one seemed to know what to do about it."

Tourist Coffee and Other Problems

While a few coffee zealots mounted their quality crusade, the multi-billion-dollar world coffee trade tried to adjust to the International Coffee Agreement. Passed in 1962, the ICA was not fully implemented until 1965 and was due to be renegotiated in 1968. From the outset the agreement created as many problems as it solved. In order to encourage increased consumption in countries such as the Soviet Union and Japan ("new markets" or Annex B nations) the quota system did not apply to coffee sold there, nor did it restrict sales to nonmember countries. As a result, a two-tier pricing system developed in which beans were sold for less money to Annex B or nonmember countries. Unscrupulous dealers then turned around and resold the cheaper beans in West Germany, the United States, or other major consuming countries. In Germany trade experts estimated that "tourist coffee"—named for its circuitous travels—accounted for 20 percent of the country's imports in 1966. The same year, one expert estimated that $10 million worth of coffee was smuggled out of Colombia.

Overproduction was another unresolved issue, with 87 million surplus bags in 1966. Of those Brazil held 65 million in its warehouses, while robustas clogged government stabilization boards in Africa. Scientists made it possible to grow even *more* coffee. In a Brazilian lab Jerry Harrington and Colin McClung, Rockefeller's IBEC researchers, figured out that zinc and boron were essential micronutrients for coffee cultivation, and with the massive addition of lime and fertlizer, the barren Brazilian *cerrado* lands could support plantations. Agronomists made the situation even worse with new heavily producing hybrids. Their beans did not taste quite as good, but few noticed or cared. Capable of withstanding full sunlight, the new trees didn't require shade trees, but they did demand fertilizer to grow so prolifically without mulch.[3]

In 1968 the Brazilians instituted a drastic project to bulldoze or burn billions of older trees, and the International Coffee Organization (ICO) created a Diversification Fund to encourage coffee farmers to switch to other crops. Yet it was much easier for Brazil, with its gigantic *fazendas*, to cut back than it was for African countries where smallholders relied on their few trees for a livelihood. In Kenya, for instance, two hundred fifty thousand tiny farms grew coffee. As Uganda's Roger Mukasa, the chair of the ICO Council, asked, "Cut down whose trees and diversify to what?"

Other troubles plagued the agreement as well. Although India and Indonesia increased production, for instance, their quotas were not readjusted. "Even justifiable claims of small exporting countries are apt to be ignored and decisions forced upon them by powerful groups with overwhelming voting strength," wrote an anonymous Indian coffee grower.

Since votes to change quota levels were so strife-ridden, the agreement was revised to specify a target price range. If the price fell below the base level, it would automatically trigger a proportional quota decrease; if the price rose above the ceiling, quotas would increase. In addition, the *selectivity* principle was introduced, so that different price targets were set for robusta (primarily Africa and Indonesia), Unwashed Arabica (mostly Brazil), Colombian Milds (including Kenya), and Other Milds (primarily Central America). Yet no mechanism could satisfy everyone. Despite the required certificates of origin, many countries found ways to flout the quotas, while smuggling and mislabeling increased.

Another crisis soon surfaced. In a 1967 speech President Johnson encouraged Latin American countries to industrialize so that they could export processed agricultural products rather than merely selling raw produce. That same year, however, when Brazil took LBJ's advice and began to produce substantial quantities of soluble coffee for export to the United States, many in the U.S. coffee trade howled. "Brazilian powder," as the trade called it informally, produced a superior taste to

---

[3] *Caturra*, a mutant of *bourbon*, was discovered in the 1950s in Campinas, Brazil. *Catuai*, a cross between *Mundo Novo* and *caturra*, was created in the 1960s. "One after the other, the fine coffees carefully grown and harvested on the upper hills of America, Africa and Asia have become more scarce," wrote a lone voice in 1972.

the robusta-laden products that predominated in the United States. Because the Brazilian government did not tax soluble exports as it did green beans, domestic manufacturers could sell for a substantial discount to solubles produced in U.S. factories. In 1965 Brazilian powder accounted for only 1 percent of the U.S. market; by the end of 1967 it had snagged a 14 percent share.

The Brazilian powder crisis nearly derailed the new 1968 International Coffee Agreement, with Wilbur Mills, the powerful chairman of the House Ways and Means Committee, telling the press that he would not support the new ICA unless the "discriminatory" Brazilian practices ceased. With a temporary compromise, the ICA was renewed, but the issue wasn't resolved to anyone's satisfaction until 1971, when Brazil agreed to allow five hundred sixty thousand bags of cheap green beans—destined for soluble production in the United States—to be exported duty-free, thereby leveling the playing field somewhat.

The Brazilian soluble controversy left Latin American growers bitter. "Throughout the Hemisphere today there is a feeling of disappointment and frustration over the protectionist tendencies of the United States," wrote a Costa Rican coffee man. "Every time we try to produce something different we find that in the industrialized nations are strong vested interests . . . which close the markets."

Nevertheless, the ICA limped along. The agreement had been created to prevent average green coffee bean prices from declining below the 1962 level of 34 cents a pound, as well as to keep prices from climbing too high too quickly. By 1968, with the price hovering below 40 cents, it appeared that the system was working. The relative stability rendered the New York Coffee and Sugar Exchange a quiet, boring place. Futures contracts languished, since there was no point in hedging or speculating within a predictable price range.

Under the ICA, however, producing countries were hardly thriving. The glaring gap between the wealthy industrialized and poverty-stricken developing countries was widening. In 1950 the average income in consuming countries was three times that of coffee-growing nations. By the late 1960s it was five times greater. A U.S. laborer could earn more in four days than the average annual wage in Guatemala or Ivory Coast. "Malnutrition and gastroenteritis are endemic in these protein-starved regions, where one out of six children dies before the age of five," observed Penny Lernoux in *The Nation.* "Coffee has no nutritional value. For these peasants it is worth only as much as it can buy in food and clothing. And because it buys so little, it is a bitter brew, the taste of poverty and human suffering."

The Think Drink Thunks

Per-capita coffee consumption in the United States continued its gradual decline in the mid 1960s. The International Coffee Organization responded by voting a meager 15 cents per bag promotion allowance, which provided a 1966 worldwide advertising kitty of only $7 million, $3.5 million of which was allocated annually to the United States. The ICO promotion committee hired McCann-Erickson, Coke's ad agency, to create a campaign to seduce seventeen- to twenty-five-year-olds to drink coffee. The admen came up with the "Think Drink" slogan. Whenever a young adult had a difficult decision to make or serious studying to do, coffee would lubricate the brain cells.

The campaign was doomed. Its appeal to rationality was more appropriate to IBM, where THINK signs adorned every desk, than to a generation in open revolt against logic and reason. Another ad agency, in a special internal report on the under-thirty generation, identified "a downgrading of the importance of rationality and logic as the preferred ways of gaining 'understanding' and an upgrading of feeling and intuition." These young rebels experimented with drugs other than caffeine, looking for spontaneous enlightenment through LSD or marijuana. A Think Drink did not appeal. A Thrill Pill did.

In the meantime the National Coffee Association, with an even smaller budget, promoted youth-oriented coffeehouses on college campuses and in churches and civic organizations. The Pan American Coffee Bureau proudly noted that it was connecting with the "all-important youth sector" by serving coffee to the freshly scrubbed conservative teens in the Up With People program. These earnest efforts to induce young adults to drink more coffee lasted for a couple of years but failed to produce any significant results. "Coffee was always closely identified with the working man," lamented a 1968 trade editorial, "the lonely sailor on watch, the hard-working cop coming off his beat." Yet the new generation didn't identify with such characters. To them the policeman was a "pig," a member of the establishment.

During the 1968 presidential elections the National Coffee Association distributed fifty-eight thousand pamphlets, "Twelve Ways Coffee

Can Help You Win Elections." Instead of clinking cups at polite coffee parties, however, young Vietnam war protestors disrupted the Democratic National Convention in Chicago, and the police retaliated with a brutality that shocked the nation. In this era of the widely hailed generation gap, when Lyndon Johnson chose not to run for reelection in the face of mounting pressure to get U.S. troops out of Vietnam, another brand of coffeehouse sprang up—not the sort that the NCA or the Pan American Coffee Bureau ever envisioned.

The GI Coffeehouses

During a stint in the military at Fort Polk in 1963, Fred Gardner occasionally patronized bars serving watered-down, overpriced drinks in nearby Leesville, Louisiana. A few years later, in San Francisco, he had the idea to set up coffeehouses in army towns "for the hippies who couldn't avoid military service." In the fall of 1967, with Deborah Rossman and Donna Mickleson, Gardner opened the first GI coffeehouse in Columbia, South Carolina, near Fort Jackson. They named it the UFO—a play on USO, the United Servicemen's Organization, located one block away. On the walls they tacked up big black-and-white portraits of counterculture heroes such as Cassius Clay, Bob Dylan, Stokely Carmichael, Humphrey Bogart, and Marilyn Monroe—as well as one of Lyndon Johnson holding up a hound dog by the ears. The founders aspired to serve "the best coffee in South Carolina," says Gardner. They purchased a commercial espresso machine, a Chemex drip brewer, and arranged for a supply of high-quality beans.

Soon after the UFO opened its doors hundreds of soldiers found the new integrated hangout, where they could drink coffee, read, listen to music, play chess or cards, meet local college students, dance, flirt, and talk about the war. The coffeehouse was a magnet for antimilitary GIs.

Agents from Military Intelligence began interrogating soldiers who hung out at the UFO. "They invariably asked what we were putting in the coffee," Gardner recalls. "I was taken in by the State Law Enforcement Division one night and told by an agent that he could taste 'drugs' in it. He was absolutely convinced it was spiked. It wasn't, of course. It was just high-quality beans, well roasted and properly brewed."

Gardner relinquished leadership early in 1968, but over the next few years, with the support of Tom Hayden, Rennie Davis, and Jane Fonda, over two dozen GI coffeehouses sprang up outside army bases across the country. Drugs were banned. Jane Fonda organized shows of "political vaudeville" and music—featuring Donald Sutherland, Country Joe MacDonald, and Dick Gregory—to entertain soldiers at the coffeehouses as a kind of mirror image of Bob Hope's patriotic GI programs.

By October 1971 the coffeehouses had attracted the attention of Congressman Richard Ichord, chairman of the House Committee on Internal Security, who told his colleagues: "At many major military bases in the United States, GI coffeehouses and underground newspapers, reportedly financed and staffed by New Left activists, have become commonplace. The coffeehouses serve as centers for radical organizing among servicemen." A retired Marine Corps officer complained that "off-base antiwar coffeehouses ply GIs with rock music, lukewarm coffee, antiwar literature, how-to-do-it tips on desertion, and similar disruptive counsels."

Without consciously doing so, the GI coffeehouses replayed history. Ever since 1511, when Khair-Beg tried to close the coffeehouses of Mecca, these caffeinated meeting places served as brood chambers for seditious literature and revolt against authority. They fostered dissent against Charles II, the French monarchy, colonial masters. Now the antiwar coffeehouses served as hotbeds for resistance to LBJ, and after the 1968 elections, Richard Nixon. As in the past, the authorities tried to shut them down through intimidation and legal maneuvers. In several cases arsonists burned the coffeehouses. The Ku Klux Klan targeted one, while others were riddled with gunfire. The surviving establishments eventually disbanded, but not before leaving their mark on American history.

"Caution: Coffee May Be Hazardous to Health"

When Fred Gardner opened the first GI coffeehouse, another war resister scolded him. "Coffee is a poison," he said. By the late 1960s another round of health concerns had commenced. A 1963 survey of nearly two thousand factory workers seemed to implicate coffee in heart disease. Such epidemiological studies, which survey sample population groups, are difficult to evaluate, since they often don't (or can't) factor in other variables that may contribute to outcomes.[4] The next

---

[4]One such survey, for instance, concluded that blue-collar workers were 43 percent more likely to die of heart disease than sedentary white-collar workers. Does this mean that breathing factory air contributes to heart attacks? Or class differences? Or eating habits?

year Dr. D. R. Huene, a Naval Reserve flight surgeon, asserted that navy pilots who drank too much coffee "complained of frequent heart flip-flops while in the air." Such anecdotal reports weren't scientific, but they made headlines.

In 1966 Irwin Ross penned an outright attack on the drink in *Science Digest.* "Caffeine, the essential ingredient in coffee, is a poison. A drop injected into an animal's skin will kill it within a few minutes. An infinitesimal amount applied directly to your brain would send your body into uncontrollable convulsions." These observations, while true, are unfair, since coffee drinkers do not inject it or apply it directly through their skulls. Ross went on to blame coffee for stomach ulcers, coronary thrombosis, throat and stomach cancer, and nervous irritability, though he granted that the drink could help those suffering from migraines or asthma.

"A new problem for the coffee industry is rearing its ugly head," wrote Samuel Lee, the technical editor of the *Tea & Coffee Trade Journal* in 1966. "Serious scientific workers are trying to demonstrate that prolonged, continued or excessive consumption of beverage coffee may be deleterious, or even a serious health hazard." Two years later he worried that research into coffee's supposed ill effects could lead to a warning label similar to that forced on cigarettes: "Caution: Coffee May Be Hazardous to Health."

In 1969 the National Coffee Association created its Scientific Advisory Group (SAG), composed of scientists employed by the major roasters such as General Foods, Nestlé, and Procter & Gamble. They also hired the Arthur D. Little Company to conduct experiments they hoped would counter the negative information on coffee. Over the next fifteen years the NCA would fund over twenty studies at a cost of $3 million.

Yet the alarms over health continued. In 1971 Philip Cole, a Harvard researcher, reported that coffee might be linked to cancer of the bladder, particularly in women. In 1972 and 1973 Boston University's Hershel Jick and colleagues reported patient surveys reinforcing the link between heavy coffee intake and heart disease. Studies in which pregnant rats were injected with or fed caffeine conducted in Japan, Germany, France, and England showed that with heavy dosages, the offspring of the caffeinated rats had more birth defects than control groups.

Coffee soon was cleared on nearly all counts, as new studies failed to replicate earlier findings or conclusions were revised. Hans Falk, a doctor who evaluated caffeine studies for the National Institute of Environmental Health Sciences, admitted that he himself drank coffee in midafternoon for a little lift. "For many of us, this is one of the last sins left. We have lost our cigarettes, our pipes, our cigars. We never got to marijuana. And it may be that even sex is hazardous to your health. If coffee goes, there is really nothing left."

Like most scare stories, however, initial claims linking coffee to diseases made headlines and a huge impact on the public consciousness, whereas later qualifications slipped quietly to the back pages. In response to health concerns, sales of decaffeinated coffee surged, increasing 70 percent from 1970 to 1975, when it accounted for 13 percent of coffee consumed in U.S. homes.

General Foods triumphed with Sanka, whose dominant market share allowed larger profit margins than for regular coffee. In a stroke of genius General Foods hired actor Robert Young–the "Father Knows Best" star described by one critic as "tolerant, wise, benevolent, understanding, warm, compassionate"–to shill for Sanka in 1976, just as he was leaving a long stint as the kindly television doctor, "Marcus Welby, M.D." Now, in TV spots, Young explained that "many doctors tell millions of Americans to drink Sanka brand" if caffeine made them irritable. In one commercial, dinner guest Young witnesses young husband Phil explode angrily at his wife over something trivial, so he suggests Sanka, which "tastes just as good as regular coffee." A few weeks later all is well. "That's what happens when you fall in love–with Sanka brand," advised Phil, as Young nods approvingly.

In 1971 Nestlé came out with a freeze-dried Taster's Choice Decaffeinated, while General Foods created Freeze-Dried Sanka and Brim, virtually identical products. Because the Sanka brand already was firmly established with a medicinal image, Brim spots strove to attract the kind of health-conscious youth who shopped at natural foods stores. Other roasters quickly joined the fray. Tenco, owned by Coca-Cola, was delighted to provide decaffeinated coffee, putting the extracted caffeine into Coke. American capacity was overwhelmed, however, and many roasters sent their beans to Germany, where high-tech decaffeination plants worked around the clock.

Even decaffeinated coffee was plagued by health concerns. A 1975 National Cancer Institute study indicated that, in massive doses, the solvent trichloroethylene (TCE) caused cancer in rats. While TCE was used to decaffeinate green coffee beans, very little of the solvent remained in the beans, and that small amount was nearly all burned off during the roast. A frustrated General Foods executive pointed out that a human would have to consume 50 million daily cups of decaffeinated coffee for an entire lifetime to approximate the doses given the rats. Nonetheless, General Foods and other roasters abandoned TCE rather than suffer from the health scare. They switched to another chemical solvent, methylene chloride.

Gold Floats, Coffee Sinks

As world coffee prices drifted down to 35 cents in spring 1969, representatives of nine major Latin American and African coffee-producing countries—Brazil, Colombia, El Salvador, Ethiopia, Guatemala, Ivory Coast, Mexico, Portugal (Angola), and Uganda—gathered in Geneva to plot strategy and to demand a "realistic quota level" for the ICA. This "Geneva Group" was encouraged in July when another frost, followed by a drought, hit Paraná, damaging 10 percent of the current crop and about 30 percent of the following year's production. Prices rose 10 cents a pound by November, triggering the ICA's automatic quota increase. Even with larger quotas, prices climbed over 50 cents a pound for Santos #4 by the beginning of 1970. Brazil, which had been bulldozing trees, now reversed itself in its continuing love–hate relationship with coffee, preparing a three-year plan to *plant* two hundred million new trees. Though Brazil still held thirty-seven million surplus bags, its reserves were being drawn down year by year. With the U.S. Congress about to vote on implementing legislation again, the producing countries agreed to raise quotas in August.

In 1970 the dreaded leaf rust *hemeleia vastatrix* was discovered in Bahia, Brazil. Somehow—most likely on the clothing of African visitors—the spores had reached Latin America. A quick search revealed that the rust already had spread to parts of São Paulo and Paraná. Seeking to quarantine it, the Brazilians burned a scorched earth belt forty miles wide and five hundred miles long, but the disease jumped it. Throughout the decade *hemeleia vastatrix* would creep northward toward Central America. Brazil already had begun growing a small amount of disease-resistant robusta; now it increased acreage devoted to the inferior bean.

Matters rocked along through summer 1971. Then on August 15 Nixon shook the world economy by cutting the dollar loose from gold, while temporarily freezing wages and prices. In order to pay for huge defense budgets and growing welfare expenses, Nixon officially devalued the dollar on December 20 by about 8 percent. This lowered effective coffee prices, and the producing countries asked for a reasonable adjustment. Led by the United States, the consuming countries refused. Caught in a price squeeze, the producers reactivated the Geneva Group, announcing plans to undership ICA quotas in order to jack the price up, in imitation of OPEC, the oil cartel.

The United States deplored such a move, which raised "doubts about the continuing viability of the International Coffee Agreement," according to the National Coffee Association and the State Department. When prices *did* rise some 25 percent over the summer of 1972, the consuming countries blamed the Geneva Group. In August and December the ICA Council met to renegotiate the agreement, due to expire in 1973. Neither side would compromise, and after a week of late-night meetings the quota agreement lapsed on December 11, 1972.

One result of the agreement's suspension was the resurrection of the New York Coffee and Sugar Exchange. On August 24, 1972, as it became clear that the agreement would probably founder, the first real activity in months occurred in coffee futures contracts. Five lots–each signifying two hundred fifty bags of coffee–due for delivery in March 1973 sold at 53 cents a pound. By the end of 1972 they were worth 61 cents a pound. Suddenly, the coffee commodities market sprang to life, with enough open interest–several thousand contracts–to offer some liquidity to traders.

Coffee Inroads in Japan and Europe

As a "new market" under ICA regulations, Japan received relatively inexpensive beans. Without the quota system Japan now would pay the same as everyone else. Before 1973 Japanese coffee imports had grown dramatically, with General Foods and Nestlé each opening Japanese plants to produce instant coffee. Determined to westernize, many of the one hundred million Japanese embraced coffee–and Coca-Cola–as

symbolic American beverages. The Japanese *kissaten* (coffeehouses) proliferated at the rate of 20 percent annually. By the mid-1970s there were
twenty-one thousand in Tokyo alone. The drinks were pricey by American standards, but the Japanese were willing to pay for a status symbol.

In 1969 Ueshima Coffee Company introduced the first ready-to-
serve canned coffee to Japan. Five years later Coca-Cola introduced
Georgia Coffee, a canned sweetened coffee drink, with a commercial
spoof on *Gone With the Wind* in which the Rhett Butler character chose
the drink over Scarlett O'Hara. The canned beverages, dispensed hot
or cold from vending machines, quickly established a popular new coffee category in Japan. By 1975 the Japanese were consuming twenty
million cases a year, and total Japanese coffee sales swelled to more
than $100 million annually.

In Europe instant coffee sales grew to 18 percent of the market,
though its popularity varied by country. At home the British overwhelmingly favored instant coffee—much of it Nestlé's freeze-dried
Gold Blend—imbibing a regular brew only when dining out. Between
them Britain and West Germany consumed two-thirds of Europe's instant coffee. West German decaffeinated coffee—regular, instant, and
"specially processed" to remove acid—commanded 30 percent of the
market in that health-conscious country. The Scandinavians preferred
higher quality regular coffee, while the Italians stuck with espresso
and Neapolitan stovetop brewers. In France an instant–chicory mixture was popular, while this mix represented half of coffee consumption in Switzerland, home to Nestlé, the world's largest soluble manufacturer.

The large European roasters—Douwe Egberts, Jacobs, Eduscho,
Tchibo, Lavazza, and Gevalia (purchased by General Foods in 1970)—
expanded as the continent became more industrialized and urbanized,
while smaller roasters failed. Both Tchibo and Eduscho opened thousands of small retail outlets, where they sold whole arabica blends
along with gift items such as silverware, watches, handicrafts, and
clothing. Completely recovered from World War II, the European coffee industry reached a plateau in the 1970s, as per-capita growth stagnated. Since 1950, however, the consumption patterns of America and
Europe had reversed. By the 1970s Europe consumed approximately
half of the world's coffee, with the United States taking less than 40
percent.

The King of the Robustas and
the Burundi Massacres

In the early 1970s many coffee-growing African nations were still suffering from postindependence tribal friction and political corruption. In Zaire, under dictator Mobutu Sese Seko, coffee was sold through a centralized coffee board, the *Caisse de Stabilization*, from which Mobutu and his cronies took most of the profits. In 1970 Claude Saks, an ambitious young New York green coffee importer, visited the country. The brusque Kinshasa bureaucrats conveyed a "hate-the-white-man" attitude, and Saks was nearly shot by a local soldier. But he smelled cash. "Whenever there is chaos and disorganization," Saks observed, "that is the time to make money." With his father, founder of G. M. Saks Inc., he pushed the firm to become "king of the robustas, the low grades."

The younger Saks, in his mid thirties, chafed under the confining conservatism of his father and broke from him in 1972 to start Saks International with a partner. He lived only for coffee trading. "The trade people knew manners, wines, art, music, and politics," he noted approvingly. "They behaved as refined gentlemen, yet would not hesitate to cut your gizzard out or squeeze your balls if they could get the slightest advantage." Saks rose at four in the morning to telephone Africa before its lunch hour, then worked until seven at night, reviewing contracts, positions, and financing. He frequently flew to Africa or Indonesia to maintain contacts and swing deals, then merged with Multitrade, a Dutch commodities house.

In fall 1972 Claude Saks flew into the mountainous, landlocked former Belgian colony of Burundi, where the minority Tutsi ruled the Hutu majority. In April of that year, young Hutu intellectuals led an insurrection in which a small number of Tutsi were killed. In reprisal, the Tutsi engaged in a virtual Hutu genocide, lasting for four months. Saks learned that the government planned to nationalize all exporters, so he met with the minister of agriculture, a Tutsi, and cemented the relationship with an envelope stuffed with local currency. "I considered this practice no different than giving a tip to a maître d' to obtain a good table," he observed.

Over one hundred thousand Hutus were slaughtered in 1972, with some estimates ranging as high as two hundred fifty thousand. When the Tutsi army detachments ran out of ammunition, they killed civilian Hutus with hammers and nails. Other African states failed to intervene, since they had their own tribal tensions to worry about. Nor did the United Nations act, hesitant to interfere in a black-ruled country. The U.S. State Department did nothing, other than to suspend cultural exchanges.

The most effective action the United States could have taken would have been to boycott Burundi's coffee, since American importers bought 80 percent of the country's exported beans, on which the economy relied. The State Department's Herman Cohen told a congressional committee in 1973—when killings began anew—that a coffee boycott had been considered, but that it "would not have influenced the immediate problem of ethnic violence." Besides, it would have punished both Hutus and Tutsis, preventing them from purchasing bread, medicine, clothing, and other necessities. "In short, a coffee boycott would have been an inhuman response."

Roger Morris, a former White House staff member who represented the Carnegie Endowment for International Peace, vehemently disagreed. "Most of the ruling trade goes to the Tutsi," Morris said. "It is a main underpinning of the regime financially. About one-seventh get through to the Hutu family farmers." Because the United States had no strategic interest in Burundi and could easily do without its coffee, the situation provided the perfect opportunity, Cohen asserted, "for the United States to exercise its international morality, idealism, and commitment to human rights—that is what makes the case so tragic."

Importers such as Claude Saks were more interested in profits than human rights. Just before Thanksgiving in 1973, Saks lunched at the fancy St. Regis Hotel in New York City with the chairman and vice-chairman of the Burundi National Bank. "As you know," the well-dressed Tutsi chairman began over drinks, "there have been certain disturbances in our country." *Christ,* Saks thought, *100,000 dead and 100,000 fled, and he calls it "disturbances."* The banker explained that Hutu laborers had departed before picking all of the coffee, but the bank still held some one hundred sixty thousand bags. Saks purchased one hundred thousand of them.

Starbucks: The Romantic Period

While wheeler-dealers like Claude Saks made their fortunes, and General Foods, Procter & Gamble, Nestlé, and Jacobs fought for world supremacy in mass-marketed canned coffee, a renewed quest for quality was spearheaded by disaffected baby boomers. Many of them had hitchhiked through Europe or were stationed there while serving in the military, and they had discovered the joys of espresso, fine foods, specialty coffee shops, and the café. With heightened international tastes, they were also searching for community, for grassroots verities. They found them in aromatic fresh-roasted whole beans, tumbling from small roasters. Many had been directly inspired by a pilgrimage to Berkeley to inhale the atmosphere at Peet's.

Jerry Baldwin, Gordon Bowker, and Zev Siegl, three Seattle college students, had traveled through Europe together during a year off from college. By 1970, now in their late twenties, they all landed back in Seattle. Siegl wasn't thrilled to be teaching junior-high kids. Bowker wrote for a regional magazine and started an advertising company. Baldwin taught in a trade school.

In search of good coffee, Gordon Bowker periodically drove to Vancouver, British Columbia, to buy beans at Murchie's, a small gourmet outlet. On one such 1970 trip, "all of a sudden, I was blinded, literally, like Saul of Tarsus, by the sun reflecting off Lake Samish. Right then it hit me. Open a coffee store in Seattle!" Around the same time, a friend offered Jerry Baldwin a cup of coffee made from beans he had ordered from Peet's in Berkeley, and he experienced a similar revelation. This is what they would do. They would start a small, quality roasting business in Seattle.

Zev Siegl went down to the Bay Area to talk with Alfred Peet and other roasters such as Jim Hardcastle and Freed, Teller, & Freed. Peet agreed to supply them with his roasted coffee beans. "Alfred was very generous," Baldwin remembers. "We copied his store design, with his blessing." Over Christmas they took turns working in Berkeley at Peet's, learning the ropes. In Seattle, they ripped apart and refurbished an old secondhand store on Western Avenue where the rent was $137 a month. Baldwin took an accounting course. Each of the friends put up $1,500 and borrowed $5,000 from a bank. With Peet's help, they found suppliers for coffee grinders, brewers, other accessories, and bulk teas.

Nearly ready to open, they still lacked a name. "Bowker, Siegl, & Baldwin sounded too much like a law firm," Baldwin says, "but we wanted a family surname, so it would sound like it belonged to someone, and 'S' seemed like a good first initial. We came up with a bunch of names, including Steamers and Starbo. From Starbo, Gordon blurted out 'Starbuck.'" The name appealed to the literary trio, since characters in *Moby Dick* and *The Rainmaker* shared it. Besides, *Starbucks* had a strong ring to it. All the letters rested above the line, with tall letters framing either end.

With a bare-breasted, twin-tailed mermaid as a logo, Starbucks opened on March 30, 1971, and was an immediate hit, selling primarily whole beans and supplies. In the first nine months, the store grossed $49,000–not enough to live on, but encouraging. The partners opened another store the following year, and Alfred Peet told them they needed to buy their own roaster. "You're getting too big."

They added a third store in 1973. "I was happy," Baldwin reminisces. "I had employees making more money than I did, but it was an adventure. In retrospect, I would call this the Romantic Period, when so many young people caught the coffee bug. We were more interested in coffee than survival."

God's Gift to Coffee

In 1969 thirty-one-year-old former social worker Paul Katzeff dropped a tab of acid and then decided to move. "I realized I had to get out of New York City to find my spot, like Carlos Castaneda wrote in *The Teachings of Don Juan*." Having "tweaked" his mind with the acid, Katzeff bought an old Mack truck, put a wood-burning stove and waterbed in the back, and headed West. He wound up in Aspen, Colorado, where he decided to open the resort town's first coffeehouse.

In the "Thanksgiving Cafe," he served coffee in little individual Melitta drip pots. "Customers could see it brewed before their eyes." He soon supplied three grocery stores with packaged beans from what he named the Thanksgiving Coffee Company. The coffeehouse was a hit, but he could never turn a profit. "I gave my hippy friends jobs, and it turns out they were stealing from me."

In 1972 Katzeff cleared out, throwing his roaster and grinder on the back of the Mack truck and heading west to California, where he eventually wholesaled his beans to local bed-and-breakfasts, hotels, and businesses. In 1975, to reach beyond the "gourmet" consumer, he convinced a few local supermarkets to sell bulk Thanksgiving Coffee. Over time Katzeff developed a mail order business as well. While his coffee attracted loyal followers in California, Katzeff became a passionate, flamboyant advocate for quality coffee and liberal causes.

No one could accuse Paul Katzeff of false humility. "I don't want to sound self-serving, but I'm smart and eclectic. I had no baggage, no preconceived notions. When I came to coffee, the business consisted of a bunch of old people without much creativity. I was perhaps God's gift to coffee." He pauses, then laughs. "But at least I don't believe my own bullshit. I can laugh at myself."

A Coffee Love Affair

At the same time Paul Katzeff, Alfred Peet, and others were reintroducing consumers to quality coffees, Erna Knutsen was rediscovering coffee at origin, sourcing rare beans from special growing regions around the world. Knutsen, who had arrived in New York City from Norway when she was five years old, took a while to find her calling in life, working her way through three husbands and across the continent to California.

In 1968, already in her early forties, Knutsen (going by her married name, Erna Guerrieri) took a job as a private secretary to Bert Fullmer at B. C. Ireland, a long-established San Francisco coffee and spice importer. She not only took shorthand but kept a position book showing where the coffee was coming from and to whom it went. "We sold more Indonesian robusta to General Foods and Hills Brothers than any other green bean importer in the country," she recalls. "It was awful stuff. All you had to do was smell this robusta to know it was putrid."

In the early 1970s, with her boss's encouragement, Knutsen developed a little niche for herself, selling broken lots (less than a container of coffee, which holds two hundred fifty bags) of higher quality arabica beans to the "small trade," tiny roasting outfits that were beginning to pop up along the California coast. Eager to develop her palate, she told her boss that she wanted to learn the arcane art of cupping. If she really wanted to serve her clients, she needed to be able to speak from direct personal experience about the acidity, body, aroma, and flavor of a particular sample of beans. The men at B. C. Ireland objected. "If that cunt comes in here, we're quitting," Knutsen overheard one of them say.

Yet she persisted, and in 1973 she finally got into the cupping room. "They laughed at me and told me I didn't cup properly. I was too dainty at first." In time, however, she learned to slurp the coffee samples explosively, mixing the spray with oxygen in flavor blasts to her taste buds. "I have a very good palate and sense memory." She had commenced "the greatest love affair of my life," what she termed her "grand passion" for coffee.

Her enthusiastic expertise charmed roasters and earned her a reputation throughout the country as the doyenne of better beans, or "green jewels," as she called them. Knutsen developed exclusive relationships with buyers in Africa, Hawaii, Central America, Jamaica. For a time, she and Saul Zabar were the only U.S. importers of Jamaica Blue Mountain coffee, since Japanese coffee companies bought most of it. At a time when most U.S. green importers were pinching every penny in the low-quality price wars, Knutsen paid what seemed like exorbitant prices for the best beans that had been going only to Europe and Japan. In turn, her grateful customers willingly purchased them.

In 1974 the *Tea & Coffee Trade Journal* featured an interview with Knutsen, in which she coined the term *specialty coffees* to refer to the Celebes Kalossi, Ethiopian Yrgacheffe, and Yemen Mocha she sold. This term would come to define the nascent gourmet coffee movement. Knutsen lamented the poor quality of mass-marketed coffee but predicted a bright future for specialty coffee. "There is an emerging group, largely young people . . . who value good coffee, and I am certain that our end of the business will grow." Like those interested in fine wines, the coffee connoisseur would seek "those modest luxuries that most can still afford."

The Ultimate Aesthete

When George Howell moved from California to Boston in March 1974, he went through withdrawal. Having lived in the San Francisco Bay Area from 1968 to 1974, Howell was used to specialty coffees. Driving across the country with his wife and two small children, he ground his own fresh beans in the men's room of Howard Johnson's, ordered hot water, and brewed his own. In Boston, however, he ran out of beans and was unable to replenish his stock. "I couldn't get good coffee to save my life," he recalls. He tried the yellow pages. Nothing. He sought out expensive cheese shops that had bulk whole beans, but they had been sitting in bins so long that they were hopelessly stale. In desperation, he decided to start his own coffeehouse, buying his beans from Erna Knutsen.

Howell came at coffee as an aesthetic experience. He had studied art history and literature at Yale before opening an art gallery in California. "I saw the coffeehouse as a natural for me. It provided a place to exhibit art, and then there was the pleasure of the drink itself. I have always been a perfectionist, and I like to proselytize for the highest expression of whatever I'm doing."

With the help of his wife, Laurie, and partner, Michael Da Silva, Howell opened the Coffee Connection in Harvard Square in April 1975. They sold whole beans but also added a coffee bar with tiny press pots. After letting the coffee infuse for a few minutes, customers enjoyed pushing the plunger down, compressing the grounds to the bottom. "We were an overnight success," Howell recalls. He set up a small Probat roaster ten miles away in Burlington, Massachusetts, and stayed up every night, learning to roast–to perfection, of course. "We had to learn from scratch, but customer enthusiasm covered us. They were like parched people coming out of a desert and finding an oasis."

Specialty Proliferates

In the early 1970s specialty coffee roasters and coffeehouses began to appear with increasing frequency in the United States and Canada. In Juneau, Alaska, Grady Saunders opened Quaffs, later changing the name to Heritage Coffee Company. Paul and Kathy Leighton commenced business as the Coffee Corner in Eugene, Oregon, while Bob Sinclair served coffee in Pannikin Coffee & Tea in San Diego. Bill Boyer started Boyer Coffee Company in Denver, and Marty Elkin ran Superior Coffee (later renamed Elkin's) in New Hampshire. In Canada, there was Murchie's in Vancouver. In Toronto, Timothy Snellgrove founded Timothy's Coffees of the World, while Frank O'Dea and Tom Culligan opened the Second Cup in a Toronto mall.

Enthusiastic young men branched off from family coffee businesses when they caught the specialty bug. In tidewater Virginia, third generation Gill Brockenbrough founded First Colony, while Alan Rossman started Van Courtland Coffee, a specialty branch of Wechsler's, a longtime New York institutional roaster. With partner Hy Chabott, Don Schoenholt opened several Gillies specialty retail stores in Manhattan. In Pittsburgh, Nick Nicholas transformed Nicholas Coffee into a regional specialty company. Peter Longo carried on Porto Rico Importing, the family retail outlet in Greenwich Village. Mark and Mike Mountanos, brothers from a San Francisco coffee family, opened separate businesses as green coffee dealers and roasters, respectively, while Pete McLaughlin at Royal vied with Erna Knutsen to supply the specialty trade with the finest beans. Luciano Repetto followed the family tradition at Graffeo, roasting one arabica blend for fine local restaurants.

Several authoritative books about coffee appeared around this time, testifying to the renewed public interest in fine coffee. For a year, English professor Kenneth Davids owned a coffeehouse in Berkeley, then wrote *Coffee: A Guide to Buying, Brewing & Enjoying,* where readers could learn the fundamentals, including a country-by-country taste assessment, advice on grinders, and brewing instructions. Joel Schapira, with father David and brother Karl, wrote *The Book of Coffee & Tea.*

Another hopeful sign for coffee appeared in October 1972, with the introduction of the Mr. Coffee automatic electric drip brewer. Bunn-O-Matic and Cory had been making commercial versions for restaurants for nearly two decades, but this marked the first venture into the home brewing market. Promoted by baseball legend Joe DiMaggio, Mr. Coffee sales exploded. Competitors such as Braun, General Electric, Melitta, Norelco, Proctor-Silex, Sunbeam, and West Bend quickly jumped into the fray. By 1974 half of the ten million coffeemakers sold in the United States were electric drip. Although the new home brewers had their faults—insufficiently hot water, wrong brew times, hot plates that ruined coffee left too long—they were a huge advance over pumping percolators, and they encouraged the rise of better quality coffee, particularly among two-career families looking for simple automatic brewing.[5]

A few popular magazines discovered specialty coffees in the early 1970s. *Sunset* offered a simple explanation of acidity, body, roasts, and blends in a 1972 article. "Special coffee stores are worth searching out. One big reason is that there you can talk to someone whose business is coffee." Yet the *Tea & Coffee Trade Journal* largely ignored the nascent specialty coffee movement, continuing to report only on General Foods

---

[5]One unusual indication of America's newborn interest in quality coffee made the news in 1975 when a federal judge in Suffolk County, N.Y., asked a deputy sheriff to buy him a cup of coffee from a refreshment truck parked outside the courthouse. Outraged by the awful brew, the judge ordered the vendor handcuffed and brought to his chambers, where the judge screamed at him, releasing him only after he promised never again to serve poor coffee.

and its ilk. Nor did the big roasters pay much attention to the specialty fleas on their backs. "They thought it was a fad, like blue Jell-O, and that it would go away," Don Schoenholt recalls.

In 1972 General Foods did come out with flavored instants called Cafe au Lait ("deep French roast flavor"), Cafe Vienna (cinnamon), and Suisse Mocha (chocolate). The pricey "International" line, containing soluble coffee, nondairy creamer, sugar, and flavorings, claimed to possess "the same great coffee flavor you'd find abroad." Hills Brothers and Carnation followed with their own versions. Though these parodies of high-quality coffee, advertised as indulgences, garnered some market share, they were about as far from Alfred Peet's beans as they could get.

Mrs. Olson Slugs It Out with Aunt Cora

General Foods wasn't worried about the pipsqueak hippie specialty roasters. In the early seventies, its products accounted for over a third of all U.S. coffee sales. Its flagship brand, regular Maxwell House, held a 24 percent market share of roast–ground regular, while its instant coffees accounted for over half of that category's sales, nearly twice Nestlé's 27 percent instant share. Procter & Gamble offered no serious soluble competition, but its regular Folgers, with a 20 percent share, was creeping up on Maxwell House. Hills Brothers had slipped below 8 percent, while Standard Brands' Chase & Sanborn held only 4.3 percent, just above Coca-Cola's coffee share with Maryland Club and Butternut. Under inept management, A & P had dropped behind Kroger's in chain store coffee sales. None of the supermarket private label coffees fared well against the well-advertised, low-prices giants such as Maxwell House and Folgers.

With per-capita coffee consumption continuing its steady decline– from 3.1 cups a day in 1962 to 2.2 cups in 1974–the major roasters fought for ever-smaller pieces of an ever-shrinking pie. The roasters essentially had given up on the youth market, as their choice of middle-aged or older celebrity endorsers indicated.

General Foods and Nestlé spent the last years of the sixties vying for the freeze-dried instant market. It took General Foods nearly four years to roll out its Maxim brand nationally. The $18 million annual research expense represented the largest single capital investment the company had ever made for a new product. Nestlé countered with Taster's Choice. Both companies spent some $10 million a year marketing their new brands. About half of all American households received a freeze-dried sample in the mail.

According to its ads, Taster's Choice offered "all the deep, rich flavor and hearty coffee aroma you used to have to perk up a pot for." Of course, such boasts were more than a little exaggerated. While freeze-dried coffee certainly was better than spray-dried instant, it came nowhere near fresh-brewed flavor. These ads attempted to position Maxim and Taster's Choice against regular coffee to avoid cannibalizing their old instants' sales. Nestlé consciously distanced Taster's Choice from Nescafé by choosing a completely different name; few customers realized that the giant Swiss company even made the new brand. In contrast, the Maxim name clearly referenced Maxwell House. As a result, Maxim cut substantially into Instant Maxwell House sales, and Taster's Choice came out on top of the category.

Unwilling to match the huge capital expenditure required for freeze-dried coffee, Folgers and other instants responded by gluing their instant powder together in clumps in the process known as *agglomeration*, making it look more like regular coffee without changing the taste. Folgers advertised the product as "newer than freeze-dried." Rather than improving quality, all the major roasters pursued a strategy of technological innovation, gimmickry, and market segmentation during the early 1970s. General Foods created the Max-Pax, convenient rings of premeasured ground coffee in a filter. Using its Minute Maid orange juice technology, Coca-Cola offered a frozen coffee concentrate. Other firms sold coffee syrups in aerosol cans or freeze-dried coffee packaged in one-cup servings on a spoon, ready for stirring.

The real battle for U.S. coffee supremacy shaped up in the 1970s between consumer foods conglomerates Procter & Gamble and General Foods. Folgers's strength still lay primarily in the West, but Maxwell House strategists knew that it was only a matter of time before Folgers invaded the East. In 1971 Maxwell House executives formed a "Folgers Defense Team," asking Ogilvy & Mather, their advertising firm, for advice.[6] The food giant and the advertising gurus came up with a two-pronged response. General Foods created Horizon, in a red can similar to Folgers. While Folgers was "mountain grown," Horizon's beans were

---

[6]Ogilvy & Mather was the ad agency for Maxwell House. General Foods retained Young & Rubicam for Sanka. Nestlé hired Leo Burnett for Taster's Choice and Nescafé but chose Case & Mc-Grath for Decaf. Folgers employed Cunningham & Walsh.

"hand picked." Heavily couponed, Horizon would act, they hoped, as a diversionary tactic, allowing Maxwell House to sail on undisturbed.

General Foods's other tactic was the introduction of Aunt Cora, a plainspoken country storekeeper who extolled the old-fashioned virtues of Maxwell House—a direct counter to Folgers's Mrs. Olson. Veteran actress Margaret Hamilton seemed an odd choice for Aunt Cora, since she continued to terrify new generations of children in her 1939 role as the Wicked Witch of the West in the classic movie *The Wizard of Oz.* As the kindly, bespectacled Aunt Cora, Hamilton was hardly threatening, and she proved to be a good coffee promoter. She appeared on television just in time to go head-to-head with Mrs. Olson in Cleveland, where Folgers struck in fall 1971, before continuing a methodical drive into Philadelphia and Pittsburgh in 1973, then Syracuse in 1974. The "Battle of the Old Bags," as one analyst named it, had begun.

The Horizon brand flopped, but the Aunt Cora strategy worked just as Ogilvy & Mather executive Dave Maddox predicted. If Maxwell House could establish Cora as a familiar presence before Folgers launched locally, "Mrs. Olson could look like a second-rate imitation," Maddox advised. In Syracuse, where Aunt Cora had been praising Maxwell House for over two years before the Folgers onslaught, Procter & Gamble was forced to offer its coffee at a loss for 87 cents a can, well below the lowest normal retail price of $1.20. As one analyst observed, Folgers was "running like the devil just to stay in place." A Procter & Gamble spokesman acknowledged, "Coffee is not the easiest product to expand nationally."

The real losers in the titanic battle between Folgers and Maxwell House were regional roasters, forced to match the deep discounts of the two major brands. Some were forced into bankruptcy. As a result, the Federal Trade Commission sued General Foods (but not Procter & Gamble, inexplicably) for predatory pricing practices.[7]

Despite its success at stymieing the Folgers onslaught, the defense team at Maxwell House remained ill at ease. It was only a matter of time before Procter & Gamble made the big move into New York City, the coffee capital of the East. The Folgers men were preparing their battle plans when nature once more intervened in Brazil.

---

[7]In fact, the price war in the Syracuse area lasted for four years. As Paul De Lima, Jr., testified in 1979, Syracuse was a "profit wasteland for the period from October 1974 to at least mid–1978." The FTC suit was eventually dropped, however.

16

THE
BLACK FROST

The world's coffee trade ... may have been permanently altered by the frost. Few of the Paraná coffee bushes will recover, and many will not be replaced. The farmers have been frost-bitten too often in the past. They are planning to grow wheat and particularly soya beans.

—*The Economist*, 26 July 1975

Nature periodically outdoes herself. There are storms that occur once every hundred years that launch tidal waves over previously secure homes, volcanic eruptions that spew ash thick enough to block the sun, earthquakes that reshape the landscape—and there are frosts. Brazilian coffee farmers thought they had suffered through every kind of drought or frost, but 1975 brought snow to Paraná for the first time, and the ripples from this freak weather system would affect the global coffee industry for years to come.

The enormous frost hit Brazil on July 17 and 18 of that year. It was by far the worst of the century, virtually destroying the Paraná coffee lands, while inflicting terrible damage in São Paulo and elsewhere. Viewed from the air, the area looked burned over, so the event was named the Black Frost.[1] One and a half billion trees, well over half of Brazil's total growth, were killed. Most of the harvest was already complete, but world production had lagged consumption in eight of the

---

[1] The jubilant Colombians named it the "Holy Frost," however.

previous ten years, with Brazil's surplus making up the difference. Since new coffee plants required four years to come into production, it was likely that there would be a tight market for several years. In the frost's wake, coffee futures soared, and all producing countries halted exports in anticipation of ever-higher prices. Brazil too held on to its twenty-four-million-bag surplus, which it would have to ration carefully over the next few years. Coffee roasters, who had expected a surplus to bring down prices, were caught with low inventories. Within two weeks, the retail price of ground coffee rose by 20 cents a pound.

Several other factors combined to limit coffee production in 1975 and 1976. In Angola, tribal, regional, and political rivalries broke out in a violent civil war, in which the Movement for the Popular Liberation of Angola (MPLA) fought the Front for the National Liberation of Angola (FNLA) and the Union for the National Independence of the Totality of Angola (UNITA). In disarray itself after the fall of its military dictatorship, Portugal declared Angola independent in November 1975. The quarter million European settlers—many of them coffee farmers—fled the country, while the equivalent of three million bags of coffee rotted on the trees. When Cuban troops arrived to help the MPLA, the U.S. government rushed arms to the FNLA, with South Africa supporting UNITA. For another two decades, the cold war would be played out in Angola, and its once-thriving coffee industry died. Jungle creepers climbed the coffee trees, and swimming pools once used by the Portuguese coffee elite lay empty and cracked.

Elsewhere, civil war raged in Ethiopia, interfering with the harvest, while dictator Idi Amin's activities in Uganda were beginning to affect that country's coffee crop. A dock workers' strike stalled Kenyan exports. In Guatemala, a devastating earthquake early in 1976 missed the coffee regions but destroyed bridges and caused landslides that would delay shipments. Floods swept Colombia. Coffee leaf rust surfaced in Nicaragua. Moreover, speculators also took advantage of the situation, contributing to the size of the price hike.

Hesitantly, the United States agreed to join another International Coffee Agreement (the previous ICA having expired in 1973) in hopes that it would help to stabilize prices. For the time being, however, there was no quota system; it would kick in only when prices came down substantially. The 1976 ICA therefore was a formality, although it did encourage producers to export their coffees, because when quotas went into effect, they would be based largely on the amount each country had exported in recent years.

In March 1976 green coffee prices reached $1 a pound, a 100-percent hike in less than a year, prompting a congressional hearing before a House agricultural subcommittee. Julius Katz of the U.S. State Department assured the politicians that "no coffee-producing country is attempting to withhold coffee from the market" and that there had been no market manipulation. Prices continued to rise throughout the year. Consumers and retail chains began to stock up and hoard coffee in anticipation of even higher prices, driving the price up faster.

As coffee sales declined and market-share battles intensified, Hills Brothers, the only remaining major family-owned roaster, shocked the coffee world by selling out, in June 1976, to a Brazilian agricultural conglomerate. The Brazilian grandson of Lebanese immigrants, Jorge Wolney Atalla was the aggressive billionaire who arranged for the $38.5 million purchase of the ailing American roaster. Atalla and his brothers, the largest coffee growers in the world, owned their own freeze-dried soluble plant, an exporting agency, two Brazilian coffee roasting firms, and Copersucar, a huge sugar cooperative that also produced alcohol for use as a fuel. Atalla announced his intention to produce an all-Brazilian blend (primarily using his own beans), and to double Hills Brothers U.S. market share by 1980.

Machiavellian Market Manipulations

By the end of 1976, retail coffee averaged $2.55 a pound, and coffee once more created a crisis. Elinor Guggenheimer, New York City's Commissioner of Consumer Affairs, urged a much-publicized boycott. A 14-cup-a-day addict, Guggenheimer declared that she had gone "cold turkey," abandoning her favorite beverage in response to "scandalous" price increases.[2] As 1977 brought $3 a pound and over, other boycott movements sprang up around the country. Supermarket chains such as Stop & Shop joined the campaign, urging consumers not to buy coffee. The "MacNeil/Lehrer Report" devoted an entire show to the coffee crisis. "It's a bit ironic," observed Jim Lehrer, "that a nation that

---

[2]Guggenheimer relented within a few weeks and resumed drinking two cups of coffee a day.

started on its road to independence with a tea boycott should be kicking off its third century with a coffee boycott."

Conservative writer William Safire penned "Brazil's Coffee Rip-Off" in the *New York Times*, asserting that "the doubling of coffee prices has little to do with market forces"—it was all the fault of Brazil's military junta, who knew that "dopey Americans will pay anything for their coffee fix."

Disturbed by the storm he saw brewing, Jorge Wolney Atalla took out a full-page ad in the *Wall Street Journal* so that Hills Brothers could explain the price hike as a result of the frost and other natural and political disasters. Atalla invited three dozen U.S. consumer advocates and supermarket managers to come to Brazil as guests of Hills Brothers, to see the frost destruction for themselves. They also visited the four largest government storehouses to see that they were nearly empty. His efforts could not stem the tide of righteous indignation.

Once again, as in 1912 and 1950, a shrill political crusader led the charge of price manipulation. This time it was New York's Fred Richmond, the chair of the Domestic Marketing, Consumer Relations, and Nutrition Subcommittee of the Committee on Agriculture. Richmond expressed outrage when Brazil and Colombia repeatedly raised their export tax levies to take advantage of rising prices.

In February 1977 Richmond co-chaired joint hearings. "Coffee consumers in the United States and other nations are in the grip of one of the most Machiavellian market manipulations in modern memory," Richmond thundered in his opening remarks. He accused Brazil of conducting "a deliberate, pervasive campaign to inflate and artificially maintain coffee prices at record levels."

Elinor Guggenheimer brought along some of the three thousand encouraging letters she had received from consumers, along with a few from Germany, Switzerland, and Italy. "This is the first time I've ever written to protest anything," one Staten Island housewife wrote, protesting against "all the greedy coffee growers, companies, and dealers." The most heartfelt letter came from a veteran, who recalled "during World War II when a cup of coffee was the difference between misery and pleasure." He couldn't bring himself to abstain entirely, but he promised to cut his consumption.

Guggenheimer demanded to know what part speculators had played in pushing up the price. With satisfaction, she noted, "I am running the unpopularity contest of the year in Brazil and Colombia and Tanzania and the Ivory Coast." Jane Byrne, Chicago commissioner of consumer affairs (and future mayor), lamented the plight of the Brazilian laborers she had met on Wolney Atalla's plantation. "They work for $2 a day; they are allowed to plant a little bit of corn in their backyards, if they wish. Everything else which they make out of their $2 a day goes right back into the company store and goes for rent on the house."

Michael Jacobson, the head of the Center for Science in the Public Interest, testified in favor of a *permanent* boycott, or at least a severe cut in consumption, since he believed coffee could be harmful to health. He hoped that "the high price will have the beneficial effect of encouraging people to consume more healthful beverages."

Following this parade of critics, the State Department's Julius Katz asserted that the Brazilian and Colombian export taxes had no effect on coffee's cost to consumers. Rather, the export tax took a bite out of the price the farmer received. As prices rose, it was natural for the governments to increase their share in order to fund new plantings and the use of fertilizers and pesticides. Even so, the return to the Brazilian farmer had tripled. Katz ignored the plight of the laborers, however, since their wages remained minimal. Katz admitted that there was no coffee shortage, but "markets operate on the basis of anticipation." With Brazil gradually depleting its surplus stocks, another frost or unforeseen disaster could easily cause a real shortage.

Even at higher prices, coffee cost about 6 cents a cup when brewed at home. Soft drinks, which pushed past coffee in 1976 to become America's most widely consumed beverage, cost much more. What was it about coffee prices that invariably aroused U.S. citizens? It is difficult not to conclude that a xenophobic distrust of Latin Americans and Africans lay behind the uproar. "Where is it written," one coffee broker wrote to the *New York Times*, "that the rich industrial nations should always enjoy cheap commodities produced by dollar-a-day labor and at the same time pass on their higher wages and other costs to the poor countries in the form of ever-more-expensive manufactured goods?"

As such investigations inevitably did, the hearings ended without lowering coffee prices or accomplishing anything. Prices continued to climb, exceeding $4 a pound by May. In a moment of candor, Congressman Elliott Levitas observed, "We are really looking to see if we can tag the blame for this problem on someone, other than the frost, whether we can blame General Foods and other roasters, whether we can blame speculators on the commodity markets, whether we can blame Brazilian producers or the Brazilian government, or whether we can blame, maybe, the State Department."

Riding the Bull Market to Millions

While speculators may not have caused the price hike, some of them certainly profited from it. One veteran who prefers to remain anonymous—call him Mike—began trading in 1973, when the coffee market had just become viable again. As a "local," he traded for whatever brokerage firm hired him, but he also bought and sold futures on his own account. "I don't know anything about coffee," he cheerfully confesses. "I just know how to trade it. It wouldn't matter if I was trading lettuce. I can listen to the tone of the voices in the ring and tell what's going on."

In 1975 Mike took full advantage of the frost, then rode the price rises and shortfalls for all they were worth over the next few years. He jumped nimbly in and out of the market, sometimes taking a position only for a few minutes or even seconds. "I would just try to catch a move." A series of such small moves could add up, though. During the late 1970s, Mike made over a million dollars a year.

He had to work for it, though. "Every day before the opening bell, I would get butterflies. Then once it started, I would just automatically go. If my mother were standing next to me and I had to step on her to get an order off, I'd do it." The intense competition, the gesturing to bid or sell, and the screaming to be heard, made it a physically exhausting occupation. "It's a young man's job, and it's not an occupation for a deep thinker. A Phi Beta Kappa would study it too hard and not perform in time." It was the street-smart kids, those who could keep a level head under stress, who thrived.

"I used to put pebbles in my mouth, like that Greek guy, and practice shouting quotes and bids. The loudest guy does the most business." Trading hours were only 10:00 A.M. until 3:00 P.M., but no one left the floor, even to go to the bathroom, during that time. With a group of men—women were a rarity—screaming and sweating in close proximity, viruses thrived. "After I had two polyps removed from my throat from all the yelling, my doctor told me not to go on the floor and trade again. But I ignored him. It's in my blood."

At night, Mike would drink at Tom Brown's Pub in New York's financial district, with buyers and brokers. "We talked coffee all night."

Every three months, he rubbed shoulders at conventions—in Boca Raton, Florida, for the National Coffee Association, Bermuda with the Green Coffee Association, Pebble Beach, California, at the Pacific Coast Coffee Association, London for the European Coffee Association. "All these guys did very well, indeed. It was the high life."

Hot Coffee (Stolen) and High Yield (Awful)

As coffee prices spiraled in 1977, beans turned to gold for coffee thieves around the world. In San Francisco, a truck with $50,000 worth of coffee disappeared. Four men were arrested for stealing 17 tons in Miami. A rash of coffee hijackings off the New York City streets accounted for well over a million dollars.

In Brazil, coffee export earnings reached $4 billion, enough to match its whopping oil import bill, but rising prices caused problems there too. Greedy farmers broke fixed-price contracts with brokers. Smuggling out of countries with high export taxes, or low state-controlled prices to growers, increased dramatically, particularly from Colombia and Brazil. As one coffee expert observed, "Smuggling occurs almost everywhere. . . . If custom officials do not go along with the bribes, smugglers have been known to dispose of custom officials by beatings, intimidation and death."

In one daring swindle gone wrong, four men sold $8.7 million worth of mythical Dominican Republic beans to Cuba, intending to sink the ship en route. The scam was uncovered when the crew failed to scuttle the freighter, which arrived embarrassingly empty. In another case, New York's Citibank lost $28 million in loans to a fast-talking Colombian coffee broker. The Citibank agriloan officer turned out to be in business with the broker.

The higher coffee prices *did* filter down to smallholders (those with tiny coffee plots) in many countries around the world, including some in Brazil, where the number of large *fazendas* was declining. Those who benefited from the high prices realized that it was unlikely to last. "Coffee gives you a jacket," an old Brazilian aphorism has it, "and takes your shirt."

Still, these were boom times. In Mexico's Chiapas, some Indians could temporarily afford meat with their rice and beans. In the Papua New Guinea Highlands, while most white planters had abandoned their plantations during years of low prices and in fear of independence in 1975, natives found that their tiny plots, averaging five hundred trees, now provided a handsome income in their terms. Colombian smallholders were unhappy, though, since they received less than a third of the international price, due to high export taxes. Some growers burned their coffee in protest, threatening to grow marijuana instead.

The U.S. coffee industry responded, as it had to previous periods of high coffee prices, with substitutes and coffee-stretching claims. Nestlé introduced Sunrise, an instant coffee "mellowed with chicory," imported from its European plants, where the 46 percent chicory mix had long been a standard. General Foods came out with Mellow Roast, a coffee and cereal mixture that was easy enough to produce, since the firm simply added Postum to its regular roast. Procter & Gamble developed Folgers Flaked Coffee, specially cut into slivers with roller mill groovings, thus allowing overextraction in automatic drip machines. P & G sold it in full-size cans that held only 13 ounces, boasting that the flaked product made the same amount of coffee as a regular pound. Under its Brazilian management, Hills Brothers developed a "jet zone" roasting process in which beans were subjected to blasts of intense heat that overexpanded the cellular structure, resulting in a puffy product with more air, allowing Hills Brothers to pack *its* 13 ounces in a pound-size can of the new High Yield blend. General Foods followed with a similar high-yield product called Master Blend.

In 1977 food writers John and Karen Hess published *The Taste of America*, in which they lamented that "more than one-third of our coffee comes from West Africa, fit only to be made into instant, and most of the rest consists of the cheaper grades of Brazilian coffee. The finer grades are sold to affluent Europeans and, now, Japanese. Few young Americans have ever drunk a good cup of coffee."

Prices eventually leveled off in the summer of 1977, then fell sharply in August after a successful Brazilian harvest with no major frost. Determined to hold coffee prices up, Brazil refused to sell below $3.20 a pound, even as world prices tumbled below $2. Brazil sold little coffee, instead entering the world market to buy beans as far away as Madagascar in an effort to boost prices. Colombia, characterizing Brazil's stance as "suicidal," sold freely, afraid that North Americans would permanently lose their taste for coffee unless the price came down. Colombia itself was troubled by raging inflation fueled by too many dollars flowing into the country—not only from coffee, but from contraband in cocaine, marijuana, emeralds, and cattle. In November, Brazil finally succumbed, resuming sales at a 45 percent discount to the "official" price of $3.20 in order to save face, while arranging special deals with Maxwell House and Folgers for deeper discounts.

Although prices were coming down, they stayed over $3 a pound at retail, well above their prefrost levels. General Foods laid off workers from its four roasting plants because of declining demand, posting a 37 percent decline in earnings in the September quarter while taking a $17.5 million write-down on overpriced coffee inventories. On the whole, coffee sales were off 20 percent from preboycott levels.

Specialty Reaches the Heartland

One of the unforeseen consequences of the 1975 Black Frost and its aftermath was the boost it gave to specialty coffees. As prices rose, the percentage gap between inferior and quality coffees narrowed. "Really good coffee can be as overwhelming to the senses as a fresh truffle," food writer Raymond Sokolov advised. "Whatever other thoughts the current coffee shortage may provoke, when we pay more than $4 a pound for supermarket, canned, run-of-the-mill stuff, it is time to take a serious look at this curiously stimulating decoction of the fruit of *Coffea arabica*."

Across the country, consumers began to realize that for only a little more money they could buy a coffee that really tasted good. What's more, shopping for coffee in a clean, aromatic specialty store was *fun*. Customers could chat with the knowledgeable, enthusiastic owner–roaster, who delighted in telling them what all those different names, origins, and roasts meant, and who suggested different blends. "Try mixing the Kenya AA with a little French Roast to add beguiling dark tones." These guys spoke lovingly, poetically about their magic beans. Who would ever call Maxwell House or Folgers "beguiling"? And look at all those nifty exotic devices for sale—Melior pots from France, porcelain Melittas, grinders from Germany and Italy.

By 1980 specialty coffee was entrenched in the big cities on the East and West coasts of the United States and reaching further into the heartland. In Waitsfield, Vermont, Doug and Jamie Balne roasted coffee in their Green Mountain Coffee Shop. In Oregon, traveling tool salesman Gary Talboy started the Coffee Bean with a partner. Elsewhere in Oregon, Michael Sivetz bought an old church in Corvallis, installed a roaster, and opened a retail shop. A chemical engineer who once designed instant coffee plants for General Foods and Folgers, Sivetz invented a "fluid bed" roaster that tossed the beans in blasts of hot air, rather like a giant popcorn machine, and he became one of the loudest voices in the wilderness crying for a return to coffee quality.

In Orlando, Florida, former minister Phil Jones opened a Barnie's (his real first name), ordering his beans preroasted from Joel Schapira in New York. In Long Grove, a Chicago suburb, contractor Ed Kvetko bought a little coffee shop. "I didn't even drink coffee at the time." Within a few years he changed the name to Gloria Jean's Coffee Beans (named after his new wife), and he learned to love specialty coffee, adding a few more stores. Julius and JoAnne Shaw opened The Coffee Beanery in Flushing, Michigan. Phyllis Jordan founded PJ's Coffee & Tea in New Orleans. With Erna Knutsen having blazed the way, Jordan and Shaw represented the new female coffee entrepreneurs.[3]

Dominated by the huge roasters, the National Coffee Association ignored the tiny new entrants who sold their whole beans out of bags or barrels. So the neophyte enthusiasts began to congregate twice a year at the National Fancy Food & Confection Show hosted by the National Association for the Specialty Food Trade (NASFT). Every year their numbers swelled, along with their self-confidence. Gourmet roasters from the Atlantic to the Pacific began to get to know one another. Maybe the California crowd roasted their beans darker than the New Yorker would have preferred, but they shared the same dedication to quality.

Whole-bean coffees began to show up in selected supermarkets around the country as well. Starbucks offered its Blue Anchor brand in bulk supermarket bins throughout the state of Washington. Goodhost, a Canadian food supplier, pioneered whole bean in clear-plastic gravity feed bins in the Seattle area.

In the meantime, the great-granddaddy of whole-bean supermarket coffees, A & P, was in dire straits. In 1979, at A & P's Compass Foods, Paul Gallant's phone began to ring off the hook after A & P closed its

---

[3]By 1974 twenty-two Jewel home routes were operated by women, but with fewer housewives staying home, the door-to-door business declined throughout the decade and was sold off a few years later.

stores in the Pittsburgh, Cleveland, and Milwaukee divisions. Supermarket chains demanded to know, "Where can we get Eight O'Clock Coffee? Our customers want it." With company permission, Gallant began to sell Eight O'Clock and Bokar on an exclusive basis to selected markets. "In a brief period of time, these stores were doing more business in coffee than A & P was," he recalls. "Eight O'Clock Coffee was one of the triggers for the growth of the gourmet coffee movement. Our product was mostly Brazilian, but it was 100 percent arabica, which certainly made it better than most of the canned coffee out there."

One Big Slaughterhouse

Under many corrupt, repressive regimes in Africa and Central America, the high coffee prices of the late 1970s enriched government coffers and traditional oligarchies. In Uganda, the power-mad tyrant Idi Amin took virtually all of the coffee profits while murdering his countrymen. The semiliterate but shrewd Amin came to power in 1971, after helping to overthrow Milton Obote. He proceeded to ruin the economy, in part by persecuting and driving out the Asian business community. A Muslim, Amin then turned on the Christian majority, killing as many as three hundred thousand people. By 1977 the copper and cotton industries had been virtually destroyed, leaving coffee Uganda's only major export. Under Amin, coffee harvests declined by 35 percent, but due to the postfrost price hike, the beans provided cash to fund the dictator's luxurious lifestyle and to pay his army goons.

In March 1977 the *New York Times* reported that the United States was paying $200 million a year for Ugandan coffee to support the corrupt regime, while 80 percent of Ugandans survived only on subsistence garden plots. Most African leaders ignored or even supported Amin, but by the end of the year, concerned U.S. activists raised their voices. Freshman Ohio Congressman Donald Pease introduced a bill into the House of Representatives to force a boycott of Uganda's coffee, which accounted for about 6 percent of U.S. coffee imports, but a full third of Uganda's exports. General Foods, Procter & Gamble, Nestlé, and other major roasters jointly issued a statement through the National Coffee Association, calling the Ugandan massacres "abhorrent and morally repugnant," but asking for a "uniform national policy" for direction; in other words, they refused to implement a boycott until the government forced them to do so. Since the decline of Angolan production, Uganda, exporting mostly robusta, had become quite important to the major roasters of mediocre blends.

In February 1978 a congressional subcommittee held hearings on the Ugandan situation. The Congressmen heard horrendous firsthand testimony from several expatriate Ugandans. Remigius Kintu, the son of a coffee farmer, repeated a dark joke common among coffee farmers who had fled the country: "If one had a house in hell and a big farm in Uganda, he would sell that farm and rush to his house for safety." The official duties of the Amin death squads were to "terrorize, kill, rape, rob, and torture Ugandans," he said. Kintu spoke of prisoners forced to drink their guards' urine, of men made to crawl on broken glass with hands and legs cuffed, of the continual cries and groans rising from the Ugandan concentration camps. Amin, Kintu said, had turned Uganda into "one big slaughterhouse."

The testimony was riveting, and when Julius Katz from the State Department later temporized that "embargoes should be entered into only under extraordinary circumstances," Representative Stephen Solarz pointedly suggested that he and his State Department colleagues read the book *While Six Million Died*, documenting U.S. inaction during the Holocaust.

George Boecklin, president of the National Coffee Association, argued that if roasters acted on their own, they would face "serious antitrust risk." The chair of the hearing commented that this was a "self-serving" opinion, hardly a real possibility. "To me, American businessmen who would like to continue doing business with Idi Amin are merchants of death, more concerned with their bank balance than with human misery," a Ugandan exile testified. "Are American coffee companies prepared to do business with a genocidist like Amin or Hitler if the price is right?" asked Donald Pease.

Clearly, the answer was Yes, especially for importers like Claude Saks. "Our import statistics from Uganda were enormous," he recalls, "and this fact was picked up by a columnist at the *Washington Post*. We were lambasted for supporting Idi Amin's fascist and inhumane regime." Other papers picked up the story, and Saks soon received letters from the New York Archdiocese, Protestant churches, human rights groups, and citizens. Saks decided to "temper" his purchases and seek legal counsel on his "publicity problem." The lawyer advised him not to respond to the protest letters and articles and "see if the storm would pass."[4]

After the hearings ended the coffee roasters waited to see whether Congress would act. On Monday, May 15, Procter & Gamble learned that the House was on the verge of passing a resolution condemning Amin and urging President Carter to implement an embargo. The next day, without informing other members of the National Coffee Association, Procter & Gamble announced with a great flourish that Folgers would no longer buy any Ugandan coffee. Quickly, Nestlé issued a statement that it had stopped buying Ugandan beans the previous month, and General Foods said that it had ceased purchasing directly from the Ugandan Coffee Board in December–though General Foods still bought Ugandan beans through brokers.

Late in July 1978 Congress finally voted to impose an embargo on Ugandan coffee, but no other countries joined the boycott. It weakened Amin's support, however. In April 1979 Julius Nyerere of Tanzania sent troops into Uganda to oust Amin and, after several interim rulers, Milton Obote came back to power. The boycott was lifted in May, and business returned to normal. Unfortunately for Uganda, Obote was almost as ruthless and corrupt as Amin, and the terror and killings continued for years without any international outcry.

Repression and Revolution in Central America

Just as Idi Amin fell from power, the long-smoldering powder keg in Central America exploded. In Nicaragua, a small group of Marxist intellectuals, the Sandinistas, led the fight against longtime president Anastasio Somoza, Jr., with the entire country rallying behind them, eager to get rid of the dictator.[5] In July 1979 Somoza fled and the Sandinistas took over, promising a better life for all, including coffee growers and laborers. The Sandinistas faced a difficult task, however, with forty

---

[4]Claude Saks subsequently left the coffee business after suffering a massive heart attack. He discovered New Age spirituality and wrote advice such as, "Picture in front of your eyes a light golden mist which is gentle, warm, and full of unconditional love just for you." Perhaps Saks could have given these instructions to the Ugandans in their concentration camps.

[5]General Anastasio "Tacho" Somoza García had established his Nicaraguan dynasty in 1934. His son, Anastasio, Jr., "Tachito," had taken dictatorial control in 1967, but popular agitation against his regime increased, particularly after the 1978 murder of Pedro Joaquín Chamorro, the editor of *La Prensa*, the leading daily newspaper.

thousand dead, a million homeless, and a wrecked economy as the legacy of the civil war.

The key to the country's financial future, they believed, lay in coffee. Three months after the revolution, the government established ENCAFE (Empresa Nicaraghense del Café) as the sole buyer and seller of Nicaraguan coffee. The new government seized the vast Somoza family holdings, which included 15 percent of the coffee *fincas*, while dedicating itself to "renovating" selected farms, supposedly by applying the most progressive agricultural techniques. They would claim a $12 million prize—offered by the Pan American Coffee Bureau—for eliminating *roya*, the dreaded leaf rust, while upgrading the productivity of coffee farms. At first, Nicaraguan coffee workers and farm owners were enthusiastic about these programs; over the next few years, however, it became clear that the urban Marxists didn't know much about coffee.

At the same time, in El Salvador, the People's Revolutionary Army (ERP) challenged the repressive regime of General Carlos Humberto Romero. In October 1979 a junta took over, with moderate José Napoleón Duarte eventually rising to become Chief-of-State. The leftist rebels joined forces in 1980 to form the Frente Farabundo Martí para la Liberación Nacional (FMLN), dedicated to overthrowing the government by terror. At the same time, right-wing death squads roamed the countryside. The entire country descended into a bloodbath, with over fifty thousand people killed by one side or the other in the next few years. The coffee-growing oligarchy loathed the rebels but were split politically, with some supporting the death squads, others seeking moderate reforms. The chaotic violence inevitably reduced the coffee harvest, as many laborers were killed or joined the rebels. Other Salvadorans fled the country, sending money back from the United States to help support those who remained.

In Guatemala, the situation was just as bad. Since the CIA-sponsored overthrow of Arbenz in 1954, a series of corrupt, repressive military regimes had battled increasingly active guerrilla bands. In 1978, with the rigged election of General Romeo Lucas García, death-squad activity intensified, along with resistance in the countryside.

Until the late 1970s most Guatemalan Indians were merely trying to survive. Living in the *altiplano*, subsisting on their tiny *milpa* plots, they suffered from continual malnutrition. During harvest season, as activist Phillip Berryman wrote in 1977, "men, women, and children pile into labor contractors' rickety trucks and head to the plantations, where they are housed in sheds that are just roofs open on all sides. They get sick and have no medical attention. Besides their daily wage they are entitled to tortillas and perhaps beans—not even coffee."[6]

By 1977 Rigoberta Menchú's father, Vicente, had joined the revolutionary forces. The teenage Rigoberta soon joined the struggle too, which would bring her tremendous personal loss. In 1979 her sixteen-year-old brother was killed by the military. "My brother was tortured for more than sixteen days. They cut off his fingernails, they cut off his fingers, they cut off his skin." The following year, her father died with many others when soldiers set fire to the Guatemala City's Spanish embassy, which they were occupying at the time. Then her mother was kidnaped, raped, and murdered. Rigoberta eventually fled to Mexico but continued to make forays back to Guatemala to organize rebels. She grieved for her dead family and friends, but remained philosophical. "It was not only now we were being killed; they had been killing us since we were children, through malnutrition, hunger, poverty."[7]

El Gordo and the Bogotá Group

Even as his country of El Salvador drenched itself in blood, Ricardo Falla Caceres played the high roller in international coffee finance. Known as "El Gordo" ("The Fat One"), Falla was variously described as "a brilliant tactician," "someone I wouldn't buy a used car from," and a "formidable operator, admired and feared in the coffee market." As the head of the trading company Compania Salvadorena de Cafe SA, he had impressed coffee producers with his ability to drive up

---

[6] *Finca* laborers also were exposed to dangerous levels of pesticides by the late 1970s. During 1978 hearings on the U.S. export of banned products, the Food and Drug Administration revealed that DDT, DDE, BHC, chlordane, aldrin, dieldrin, endrin and heptachlor were among the pesticides used on coffee in Latin America that were illegal in the United States. Because the coffee bean was protected by the fruit, only traces of the chemicals were found in green beans, and those were burned off during the roast. There was, therefore, no health hazard for consumers. Yet the same was not true for unprotected campesinos.

[7] In 1992 Rigoberta Menchú won the Nobel Peace Prize for her work. Nonetheless, some of her stories are exaggerated. Anthropologist David Stoll, who interviewed Menchú's childhood neighbors, found that she did not spend most of her childhood picking coffee, but was sent away to a Catholic boarding school. "Her plantation stories may be poetically true but are not her own experiences," Stoll observes.

prices on the New York Coffee and Sugar Exchange in late 1977 and early 1978. The situation had so alarmed the watchdog Commodity Futures Trading Commission that it issued an emergency order on November 23, 1977, halting trade in the December coffee contracts—most of which were controlled by Falla—and allowing only their "liquidation," the fulfillment of preexisting contracts. In August 1978, on the heels of a mild Brazilian frost, coffee representatives from eight Latin American countries—Brazil, Colombia, Costa Rica, El Salvador, Guatemala, Honduras, Mexico, and Venezuela—met with Falla in closed session in Bogotá to plot a strategy.

The International Coffee Agreement's 77 cents per pound trigger price was woefully inadequate in the postfrost inflationary world, and the producers sought a way to boost the price of coffee. Quota restrictions without consumer country participation never worked in the past, since someone always cheated. Now, with green prices falling below $1 a pound, producers put together a $150 million fund and directed Falla to play the futures market. The infamous "Bogotá Group," named for its first meeting place, was born. With supply and demand roughly in balance, market manipulation stood a fair chance of succeeding, as people were more likely to react to false scarcity or fear of one. The coffee market was no place for the timid; thinly traded, compared to other commodities, coffee offered less liquidity, huge volatility, and high stakes, as one contemporary financial analyst pointed out. "Who's trading it?" he asked in 1978. "A few big speculators with brass-bound egos, some of the locals, and the trade—the producing countries certainly, and roasters, on occasion."

By September 1979 the Bogotá Group's activities were drawing fire in the American press. Syndicated columnist Jack Anderson wrote an article headlined "Price Gouging by the Coffee Cartel" in which he called the group a "gang of boardroom bandidos." Falla's activities also alarmed the U.S. State Department. Testifying before Congress, Julius Katz of the State Department accused the Bogotá Group of "acting collusively and unilaterally to try to support prices." Though he informed the group of the State Department's "serious concern," Falla snubbed him. "It may be your court," Falla said, "but it's our ball." In other words, without their coffee, there would *be* no exchange or futures market. At $1.85 a pound, coffee prices in fact were not unreasonable. Nonetheless, the New York exchange (now covering coffee, sugar, and cocoa) once again imposed "liquidation only" conditions on the December 1979 contract to prevent the Bogotá Group from performing a "market squeeze" in which they drove the price up by buying too many future contracts.

In spring 1980 Falla convinced the Bogotá Group to form its own trading house, Pancafe Productores de Cafe S.A., a Panamanian corporation based in Costa Rica, with a whopping $500 million to invest, bankrolled by his previous trades and new money from contributing countries. Falla now headed a "financial espresso machine to try to squeeze the last drop of value from their [producers'] beans," as one journalist put it. By incorporating as a Panamanian company, the speculators hoped to evade attempts by the Commodity Futures Trading Commission to make them divulge their trading position. To express its displeasure with Pancafe, Congress held up implementing legislation for the ICA, which had been renegotiated with a more reasonable trigger level of $1.68 a pound.

Then, according to informed insiders, U.S. Customs officials grabbed Falla out of a New York airport, where he was en route to London, and took him to a small room, where officials told him that he wasn't leaving the United States until he promised to disband Pancafe. If he agreed, they would push for full U.S. participation in the International Coffee Agreement. Falla succumbed to pressure, Pancafe dissolved, and Congress promptly passed implementing legislation. Coffee prices sagged in anticipation of oversupply. An observer from Merrill Lynch doubted whether Pancafe could have held prices up anyway. "The moral of the story," he said, "is that coffee may be black and liquid, but it is not oil."

Once again the United States agreed to resuscitate the ICA partly from cold war fears. The Sandinista revolution in Nicaragua, together with leftist guerrilla movements in El Salvador and Guatemala, heightened fears that communism would triumph in the troubled coffee countries of Latin America. With Brazilian production recovering and world consumption stagnant, another coffee glut loomed. Prices might drop to dismal levels again without a quota system. At the end of 1980, with prices down to the $1.20 a pound level, the ICA system kicked into gear again, with consuming and producing countries agreeing to cut world export quotas to 54.1 million bags for the coming year. Brazil was lucky to negotiate a 25 percent world quota share—down from the

40 percent it commanded in 1962, but better than its actual 18 percent bite of the 1979 market.

Grinding Out the Decade

For the big roasters, it was war as usual. As prices declined in 1978, Procter & Gamble finally rolled Folgers into New York City and the rest of the East Coast to complete its national expansion. By the end of the year, Folgers had grabbed 26.5 percent of the national market for regular coffee, surpassing Maxwell House, which held 22.3 percent. Because of its other regular brands—Sanka, Yuban, Max-Pax, Brim, and Mellow Roast—General Foods still edged Procter & Gamble out with 31.6 percent of the total roast and ground market, and it held a whopping 48.3 percent share of instant coffee. Even in that category, however, Nestlé's Taster's Choice was trouncing Maxim, the General Foods freeze-dried entry. The Folgers battle for supremacy hiked advertising expenditures for 1978, with the top ten coffee companies spending a total of $85.8 million, of which Procter & Gamble spent $25 million alone.

Abandoning Aunt Cora, General Foods switched to quick vignettes in which a cross-section of Americans—including young people—drink Maxwell House all day long. The ads attempted to rise above the fray to promote all coffee as a generally uplifting experience. Fighting back against Taster's Choice, General Foods brought out a new Maxwell House Freeze-dried Coffee, backed by a $20 million ad budget, though the company insisted it had no plans to phase out Maxim.

With high coffee prices no longer in the news, the new economy blends such as High Yield, Master Blend, and Folgers Flaked faltered, since they tasted even worse than the regular brands. Sanka provided the only real bright spot for General Foods, where it long had dominated the U.S. decaffeinated field—so much so that many restaurants listed "Sanka" on the menu instead of "decaf." Folgers launched High Point decaf in 1980 but barely dented the market. General Foods in the meantime bought Kaffee HAG from Ludwig Roselius, Jr., in Germany, where the longtime decaf leader (the sister brand of Sanka, both invented by the senior Roselius) had fallen to 25 percent of its segment, behind Tchibo's Sana brand, which held 40 percent of the decaf market. One German competitor scoffed at the new merger, calling General Foods and HAG "two drunks holding each other up."

If General Foods was a drunk, however, Hills Brothers and Chase & Sanborn were suffering from delirium tremens. Caught in the crossfire between Folgers and Maxwell House in the price wars, the second-string brands watched their market shares dwindle. Standard Brands' Chase & Sanborn had dropped to 0.6 percent of the market. Hills Brothers fared better, at 6.3 percent, but it too trended downward, despite a $6 million ad budget for its High Yield economy brand. Its Brazilian owners did not help much. During the price rise, Brazilian coffee magnate Jorge Wolney Atalla ordered Hills Brothers to stockpile his Brazilian beans, leaving the firm with high-cost inventory that produced a $40 million loss. Then, when Atalla sold his share in Copersucar (the firm that owned Hills Brothers), the Brazilians backed off and allowed the American managers to go their own way.

Regional roaster Chock full o' Nuts had to face the same price wars, though it held its ground relatively well in New York City, its home turf. In order to compete, Chock threw robusta into its blends too. Aging founder William Black, now in his seventies, was turning paranoid and reclusive, the Howard Hughes of the coffee business. In 1962 Black had divorced his second wife and remarried singer Page Morton, putting her on television to pitch the "heavenly coffee" for years to come. At a stockholders' meeting, someone from the audience asked why they didn't "get rid of that ugly broad." Black never attended another meeting. Communicating only by memo, he insisted on approving every communication that left the company.[8] Not surprisingly, Black ran through a string of presidents, none of whom he found satisfactory.

The elderly, paranoid executive provided an apt symbol for the stagnating traditional coffee industry. As the 1970s ended and a new decade began, the traditional roasters remained embattled, confused, and engaged in a myopic pursuit of market share through cheap, inferior products. They had no clue that specialty coffee represented coffee's hope for the future. In a January 1, 1980, speech in Boca Raton, where the coffee men met annually to socialize and bemoan their fate, NCA

---

[8]"If you misspelled one word, you were in deep trouble," longtime Chock employee Peter Baer recalls. One day, Baer left a memo stuck halfway through the letter-slot on Black's door, then realized it contained an error. Rushing back to retrieve it, he felt resistance at the other end. "I yanked it and heard a yell from the other side. I'd given Mr. Black a paper cut. I put my hand over the peephole, ducked, and scurried around the corner."

president George Boecklin reviewed the dismal seventies, with its frosts, record high prices, congressional hearings, civil wars, earthquakes, boycotts, health scares, and cutthroat competition. "Did I leave anything out?" he inquired.

Yes, he did. The little guys selling whole beans.

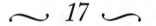

17

THE SPECIALTY REVOLUTION

[Frederic A. Cauchois] evolved his 'Private Estate' blend, which is a combination of the highest grades.... He firmly believes fresh-roasted coffee is as necessary as fresh bread.

—**William Ukers, 1905**

Our industry has the opportunity to stem the downward drift by paying attention to an industry phenomenon which has been labeled alternately 'specialty' or 'gourmet' bean coffees: the preparation and sale of whole beans blended, ground, and bagged right in front of the customer. It is an effort to bring the coffee business back to its roots.

—**Donald Schoenholt, 1981**

Specialty coffee proved to be the perfect drink for the go-go 1980s, which witnessed the triumph of yuppies—young urban professionals— willing to pay top dollar for life's luxuries. At the end of 1982 *Money Magazine* recognized its readers' new interest with an article entitled "Coffee to Your Taste: Rare Beans at $5 to $10 a Pound Resemble Wines in Their Richness," quoting specialty pioneers such as George Howell, Donald Schoenholt, and Nick Nicholas. *Glamour* magazine ran a similar article the following year. Flavored coffees such as Swiss chocolate almond introduced neophytes to gourmet beans. Specialty purists were horrified, but others argued that such customers would then "graduate" to straight varietal beans. Besides, flavored coffee sold, and few coffee men were too idealistic to make money when they could.

It was almost inevitable that the specialty roasters would form their own organization. Every time they met at the biennial Fancy Food Show, their numbers swelled. Primarily through the efforts of California's Ted Lingle and New York's Don Schoenholt, coffee idealists from both coasts met in San Francisco in October 1982, sitting cross-legged on the floor in the parlor of the little Hotel Louisa, and hammered out a national charter. In contrast to the National Coffee Association, dominated by the big companies and requiring huge dues, the new Specialty Coffee Association of America (SCAA) asked only $150 for membership. Forty-two charter members signed on.

"I call upon each of you, my heroes!" wrote Schoenholt in a January 1983 invitation to join the fledgling SCAA. "Rise up, my fine buckos, and assert your will." He likened the task before them to climbing Mt. Everest in sneakers, but urged them on. "We must throw ourselves into our task united, or we shall be hurled down into the massed elephantine corporations waiting to trample us alive."

Specialty coffee did not fit neatly into the corporate coffee statisticians' world of retail share, since usually it was sold in bulk or through direct mail. Yet by the end of 1983 even the stodgy *Tea & Coffee Trade Journal* took note. "Last year we said there was a general belief that specialties comprised about one percent or less of the coffee business in the U.S. market," wrote publisher James Quinn. "Today we have strong reason to believe that the gourmet market represents about three percent of the total market." The next year, three or four new specialty roasters entered the trade every month. By 1985 one expert estimated that specialty coffee accounted for 5 percent of all U.S. coffee retail sales, and now a new roaster set up shop every *week.* There were one hundred twenty-five wholesalers in the U.S. and Canada, with their numbers growing at a 25-percent annual clip.

To reach the upscale market through mail orders, specialty roasters such as Community Coffee in New Orleans—one of the venerable regional roasters—advertised in the *New Yorker, Gourmet,* and the *Wall Street Journal.* They now were able to package and ship their beans across the country because of the one-way valve, the most revolutionary packaging innovation since the Hills Brothers' vacuum can of 1900.

Built into an airproof, laminated plastic bag, the valve allowed fresh-roasted beans to "degas," letting out carbon dioxide, but it did *not* allow oxygen back into the bag. Together with inert gas flushing, the one-way valve prevented coffee beans from staling for up to six months. Invented by Italian Luigi Goglio in 1970, the one-way valve had been in use in Europe for over a decade by the time the U.S. specialty industry discovered it in 1982.[1]

Coffee's cachet among hyped-up computer nerds also swelled. "I can't even *talk* to anyone till I'm into my second cup," one Silicon Valley denizen told a writer for *Datamation* in 1985. "We're a small operation," another computer outfit explained, "yet we have a real nice [coffee] setup. We've got espresso as well as regular coffee." Another programmer scoffed at decaf drinkers, comparing them to cars with low-lead gasoline. "They go 'ping' when they walk upstairs after drinking it."

Good Till the Last Drop Dead

Whether they "pinged" or not, more consumers—specialty and mainstream—were switching to decaffeinated coffee as health concerns peaked in the early 1980s. From its earliest history, coffee had been accused of hurting people, from the London women of 1674 who thought it made their men impotent to C. W. Post, who asserted that the beverage attacked "the pneumogastric nerve." Now, however, health fears escalated, so that even the average coffee drinker worried about what his morning cup might be doing to him.

Throughout the late 1970s, Michael Jacobson of the Center for Science in the Public Interest (CSPI) had hammered away at the U.S. Food and Drug Administration to remove caffeine from the list of drugs "Generally Recognized as Safe" (GRAS). The FDA hesitated to take such a step, which would have disastrous economic consequences for the coffee, tea, and cola industries. In November 1979 Jacobson filed a petition with the FDA asking for warning labels on coffee and tea packages reading: "Caffeine May Cause Birth Defects." At the same time,

---

[1]Specialty coffee pioneer Joel Schapira introduced the one-way valve to the United States at the 1982 Fancy Food Show. Since then, he has become a virtual coffee hermit, withdrawing to his small roastery in Pine Plains, New York, where he services only selected customers.

he issued a press release and wrote letters to fourteen thousand obstetricians and midwives. At a press conference, he presented a woman who claimed that her heavy coffee consumption offered the only "reasonable explanation" for her child's deformities.

"Suddenly," as NCA president George Boecklin told fellow coffee men, "the issue which had been a scientific question . . . also became a legal and public relations matter." In an emergency meeting, the NCA funded a $250,000 program to counter the CSPI, hired public relations consultants, and lobbied the FDA not to remove caffeine from the GRAS list. The NCA pointed out that the rats were being forced to ingest the equivalent of 35 cups of coffee all at once. At that time the International Life Sciences Institute (ILSI), founded in 1978 with soft-drink money, joined the NCA to conduct epidemiological studies on caffeine. Coca-Cola was particularly concerned about saving caffeine's reputation, since it sold both coffee and Coke. Caught in the political riptide, the FDA waffled. "We're not saying caffeine is unsafe," Sanford Miller of the FDA said. "We're just not saying it's safe." The agency issued a warning against caffeine consumption by pregnant women, but it did not demand a warning label.

The next year, an epidemiological study appeared to link coffee to pancreatic cancer, triggering widespread media attention and sick jokes about coffee being "good till the last drop." One medical school student told a coffee-drinking classmate, "If you sign up now, I'll do your Whipple for you at today's prices," referring to an operation on the pancreas. Then a new study purported to link caffeine with the formation of benign breast lumps. Yet another claimed that coffee produced heart arrhythmia, while a Norwegian survey found higher cholesterol levels in heavy coffee drinkers.

The 1980 edition of the *Diagnostic and Statistical Manual of Mental Disorders*, bible of the American Psychiatric Association, included "caffeinism" as a diagnosis, making the consumption of too much coffee a bona fide psychiatric disorder. In 1981 Charles Wetherall published *Kicking the Coffee Habit*, a book dedicated "to the 15,000,000 coffee addicts in the U.S. who are hooked on a bum drug—and may not even know it." Those who drank coffee were "risking dozens of health hazards—many of them fatal." Wetherall wrote that the beverage, which he called "Public Health Enemy Number One," was waging "a pathological war on this country."

"As suspicions mount about the adverse health effects of caffeine," wrote health journalist Jane Brody in 1982, "millions of Americans are trying to diminish or eliminate entirely their dependence on this artificial mental and physical stimulant." Brody's husband, she noted, drank eight or more cups of coffee a day and was given to "moments of irritability, anxiety and depression." Without telling him, she mixed decaffeinated coffee with his regular in gradually increasing amounts, and his moodiness vanished.

The National Coffee Association moved vigorously to counter the calumnies against its drink, funding more studies and assembling a file of thousands of articles from the medical and scientific literature. Many other independent scientists and doctors also pointed out flaws in the anticoffee findings, and a 1982 study of twelve thousand pregnant women revealed no detectable ill effects from coffee consumption. Nonetheless, the damage was done. By 1984 two sociologists identified coffee drinking as an "emerging social problem" in the public mind. During the 1980s, coffee was associated with over one hundred diseases and disorders and, though subsequent studies threw every negative finding into question, the implanted fears led more consumers to decaffeinated alternatives or away from coffee completely. The number of Americans who drank coffee fell from 58 percent in 1977 to 50 percent in 1988.

Learning to Love Uncoffee

In 1979 a large Swiss manufacturing firm, Coffex, perfected a decaf process using only water. Although the methylene chloride method left virtually no chemical on the roasted beans, the new "Swiss Water Process" appealed to the yuppie health-conscious crowd, and many specialty roasters began to supply the beans. The decaffeinated variety would never taste as good as regular coffee, since essential flavor oils were removed along with the caffeine, but 1980s decaf offered a much better flavor than its predecessors. The processing had improved, and specialty roasters used higher quality beans to begin with. They also began to offer flavored decafs such as vanilla almond mocha to spice the denatured beans.

By the mid-1980s most restaurants offered decaf coffee. Royal Crown, Pepsi, and Coke created caffeineless soft drinks, while Seven-Up boasted that it was "crisp and clean with no caffeine." Nearly a quarter of all American coffee was decaffeinated, with some experts predicting that the segment would grow to 50 percent of the industry total within the next decade. One consumer groused: "We go out for a special meal, [followed by] a cup of uncoffee, with uncream and unsugar, to enjoy with an uncigarette."

While the overall coffee market continued to shrink, decaf swelled. In the early 1980s, everyone rushed to take advantage of the decaf craze. General Foods introduced decaffeinated versions of Maxwell House and Yuban to go along with Brim and Sanka. Nestlé added a new line of Nescafé decafs to go along with its Taster's Choice variety. Procter & Gamble sponsored a decaf Folgers instant to augment its High Point.

Ad budgets for decaf coffee increased. In 1982 General Foods recognized that Robert Young, still reprising his role as the fatherly doctor, had outlived his usefulness.[2] In his place, "real people" in active occupations—wildlife photographer, logger, white-water kayak instructor, tugboat captain, mountain climber—promoted Sanka. In a typical spot, rugged underwater welder Joe Zebrosky explains that "too much caffeine makes me tense. And down here, I can't afford that." After Sanka stopped using methylene chloride in favor of a carbon-dioxide process, its ads also touted its use of "pure mountain water." General Foods tried to stir Brim sales with an ad showing a young couple drinking coffee by fireplace. The only copy read: "The thunder was loud. The music was soft. The coffee was Brim."

Nestlé and Procter & Gamble followed suit with their decaf commercials, switching to emotional lifestyle appeals. Taster's Choice no longer proclaimed that it "looks like, smells like, tastes like ground roast coffee." Instead it featured romantic scenes with the tagline, "Times Like These Were Made For Taster's Choice." P & G's High Point abandoned its "Decaffeinate the One You Love" in favor of Lauren Bacall, featured in settings such as her chauffeur-driven limousine. In her throaty, sophisticated voice, Bacall explains, "Rushing for an eight o'clock curtain every night means giving up a lot of things. But coffee isn't one of

---

[2]It didn't help that Young recently had been hospitalized for "nervous depression." Young had a history of alcoholism and depression. In 1991, at the age of eighty-three, he attempted suicide. He had spoken of his guilt, portraying such all-knowing characters when he was often so unhappy himself.

them." She mixes a cup of High Point instant decaf at the coffee bar in her limo, praising the "deep-brewed flavor."

The Coffee Nonachievers

Aside from the decaffeinated and specialty segments, overall coffee consumption continued to dwindle throughout the early 1980s. The slugfest between Maxwell House and Folgers hadn't increased their sales materially; it only hurt smaller companies who couldn't compete. Beverage analyst John Maxwell blamed the decline on temperature and convenience level. "All hot drinks are going down," he observed in 1982. "People today are in a hurry. They want to slug something down and move on, particularly the younger ones." Indeed, U.S. coffee consumption had declined 39 percent in the twenty years since 1962, when nearly three-quarters of the population drank coffee. In 1982 only a little over half downed java.

At Maxwell House, young marketers such as Mary Seggerman, with a newly minted Wharton MBA, tried to change coffee's image. Seggerman pushed for bluesman Ray Charles to sing in lifestyle ads. "We needed to do hip, young, fun advertising. When I took over the Maxwell House trademark, their target was women over 45. You would have thought it was the riskiest thing in the world to include men in that target." At least the Ogilvy & Mather Ray Charles commercials tugged at the heartstrings, with swelling music, touching family scenes, and a tagline about "that good to the last drop feeling," appealing to emotions rather than taste. Although the ads obviously imitated upbeat soft-drink efforts, Seggerman complains that "General Foods never really understood that Maxwell House competed against Coke and Pepsi." She had to battle for the only 1983 ad to feature two teenagers, who worked on a beach boardwalk and met over a cup of coffee.

That same year, Seggerman and a few colleagues found relatively unknown stand-up comics at little clubs and made innovative, edgy Maxwell House spots in which they do their routine, including a reference to Maxwell House at the end. "What is the saucer for, what?" asks Jerry Seinfeld. "My mother says, 'That's what you put the cup on.' I thought that's what the table was for. I guess it's in case someone pulls the table out from under the coffee, you just go, 'Nice try, pal.'" Then he walks offstage to drink a cup. The comic ads aired only once, killed by conservative Maxwell House managers. Seggerman had to settle for

Hal, a hunky freelance photographer who roamed America with his dog Duke and drank coffee soulfully.

In the meantime, the generic "Coffee Achievers" campaign was launched by the National Coffee Association in 1983. Because of the small ad budget, they settled for third-string celebrities such as Ken Anderson (Cincinnati Bengals quarterback) and Allison Roe (former marathon winner), who supposedly represented the "new coffee generation." The announcer explains, "Coffee lets you calm yourself down. Coffee gives you the time to dream it. Then you're ready to do it. No other drink does it like coffee." Critics questioned how the drink could be simultaneously calming and invigorating. "Not a bad hype," observed *The Nation*, "for a product with no nutritional value, whose most important ingredient is an addictive drug that tends to make users nervous and irritable." The NCA modified the wording slightly to "Coffee is the calm moment." The short-lived ads did not increase coffee consumption.

No amount of advertising could move the shoddy products the major roasters offered. They introduced the "brick pack"—ground coffee vacuum-packed in skintight, laminated packages. The product had to be prestaled, since otherwise "degassing"—the carbon dioxide released from freshly roasted coffee—would ruin the brick. Cheaper than cans, the bricks could be stacked on shelves more compactly. For institutional use, fractional packages—"frac-paks"—containing just enough for one brewed pot became popular. They contained less and less coffee, however, and were often pinpricked to allow degassing and subsequent staling.

In their battle with Folgers, Maxwell House managers focused on trade deals and cost reduction. Every year they cut back a little more on their coffee's roast color, since there is less weight shrinkage with a lighter roast, and it saved on fuel to heat the beans. Unfortunately, underroasted coffee tastes bitter. They lowered the quality of the beans, using only cheap Brazilian and robusta. They introduced the "Fresh Lock," which allowed more weight-adding moisture before the ground coffee clumped together. They also pelletized and added back the chaff (silver skin blown off during the roasting process) to the blend.

The Little Big Guys Struggle

Smaller conventional roasters meanwhile struggled for survival, often becoming booty for investors who batted them about like shuttlecocks.

In 1982 tea company Tetley bought Schonbrunn, with its Savarin, Brown Gold, and Medaglia D'Oro brands, and Tenco, manufacturer of instant coffee, from Coca-Cola. Tetley already owned Martinson's and two Hispanic blends, Bustelo and Oquendo, which made it a player in the dark-roasted segment of the market. Unfortunately, Tetley downgraded the once-great blends of Martinson and Savarin, rendering them no better than Maxwell House or Folgers. It also cheapened Medaglia D'Oro, the only national espresso blend.

Chock full o' Nuts was still a powerful regional brand, but the company's fortunes declined as the aging William Black refused to relinquish power. After Black died in 1983, his physician, Leon Pordy, eventually took over the company. Chock could still claim first place in the New York coffee market, but only by cheapening its blend and selling 20 percent below the average price.

In the 1980s Nestlé decided it should expand its North American coffee business beyond its lackluster instant brands. In 1984 it bought Goodhost, a major Canadian roaster, and announced that it would exercise an option to buy Hills Brothers. The Brazilians at Copersucar sold the old family firm only four months earlier to a group of five investors, who then resold to Nestlé.

In quick succession, Nestlé bought two more coffee concerns–Chase & Sanborn and MJB.[3] "The sale of MJB is another indication of the difficulty small roasters face in staying independent in the face of industry domination by . . . very rich and aggressive companies," observed an *Advertising Age* commentator.

Whole Beans and Gorgeous Women

Even as they gobbled other companies, the big boys couldn't help noticing the growth of specialty bulk whole-bean coffees that had invaded grocery stores in the late 1970s, introduced by American hustlers such as Bernie Biedak, who bought all manner of things at U.S. Cus-

---

[3]In 1982 Standard Brands shed the ailing Chase & Sanborn to the General Coffee Corporation, a Miami organization headed by Alberto Duque Rodriguez, the flashy young son of a wealthy Colombian coffee grower. Duque had built his empire–complete with vast estates and yachts–entirely on fraudulent loans that collapsed spectacularly in 1983. Nestlé snapped up the tarnished Chase & Sanborn name the following year. In 1985 MJB, seeing the handwriting on the coffee wall, sold out to Nestlé as well.

toms auctions and sold them at his hip store in Ashland, Oregon. In 1978 he bought two bags of confiscated Guatemalan green coffee beans, had them roasted, then sold the beans for a huge profit out of his car in front of a local grocery store. He bought more beans from Gary Talboy at Coffee Bean International and installed his own clear-plastic gravity-flow bins in the produce aisle of Oregon supermarkets. He then hired gorgeous professional models to deliver the coffee and maintain the grinders. Biedak sold the beans at a uniform price of $3.99 a pound, providing the store managers a much larger profit than did canned coffee—and the beautiful delivery women didn't hurt either. By 1983 Biedak had expanded to San Francisco.

Meanwhile, Phil Johnson, working in Seattle, had the same idea. So did Starbucks's Jerry Baldwin, who sold bulk wholesale beans through his Blue Anchor division. Baldwin, a purist, didn't like the supermarket business, where he couldn't completely control quality. Johnson, who left Goodhost when Nestlé bought it, purchased Blue Anchor, making his company, now called Millstone, one of the largest whole-bean su-permarket players. In southern California, stores featured Sark's Gourmet Coffee. After founder Wally Sarkisian died in 1980, his widow, Rose, and daughter, Debra, continued to expand the business. In Fort Bragg, California, Paul Katzeff put Thanksgiving Coffee into bulk bins in supermarkets, while Steve Schulman did the same in northern California with his Hillside gourmet beans.

Across the country in rural New Hampshire, Marty Elkin and man-ager Mike Sullivan introduced the Café Du Jour brand in gravity-feed bins, one-way valve bags, and innovative 2-ounce miniature sample brick packs. Green Mountain Coffee Roasters was also expanding. Al-ready a millionaire from creating and selling EZ Wider papers for mar-ijuana smokers, Bob Stiller was blown away by the gourmet coffee he tried one day in 1981 in the Phoenix Restaurant in Waitsfield, a Ver-mont ski town. Stiller bought out the original small roasters and dra-matically expanded the business.

It was clear to the major roasters they were missing something. "The big boys began to show up at Fancy Food shows and crawl all over us," Don Schoenholt recalls. "These nicely dressed young executive types would come into your booth and kind of mill around. We were all out-raged. At the same time, we thought it was funny in a scary way. All you had to do was look at these people to see that even with the ideas right under their noses, they didn't get it."

Quotas and Quagmires

Even with new International Coffee Agreement quotas in place, the early 1980s witnessed substantial price volatility. In 1981, the first enforcement year, prices dropped below $1.15 a pound, triggering four successive quarterly quota cuts. Even so, the price briefly fell below $1 a pound for the first time in five years. The following year, it rose to a more reasonable $1.25 level and hovered there long enough to secure a new agreement, good until 1989. Under the Reagan administration, with its emphasis on free trade, the United States only reluctantly ratified the 1983 ICA.

"Tourist coffee" now sold to nonmember countries at discounts of 50 percent or more, and most consuming countries were not happy with the situation, though West Germany and France made a great deal of money from the tourist coffee that flowed in and out of the tax-free ports of Hamburg and Le Havre. Smuggling and counterfeit certificates of origin abounded. In 1983 U.S. Customs confiscated $26 million in illegal beans.

As the decade wore on, ICA regulations frustrated roasters who sought high-quality beans. The "other mild" countries (Kenya, Ethiopia, Central America, Peru) were not allowed to export more of their better beans to consumers with a taste for better blends and specialty coffee.

Rollinde Prager, the U.S. delegate to the annual quota renegotiation in 1985, objected strenuously to the two-tier price system and Brazil's deliberate undershipment of quotas. Failing to reach an agreement by the stroke of midnight on September 30, 1985, the negotiators stopped the clocks at the London ICO headquarters on Berners Street. Finally an agreement was struck, with the United States casting the only negative vote. "The outcome may not bode well for the future of the International Coffee Agreement or our participation in it," Prager said ominously.[4]

Guerrilla Wars, Coffee Disasters

Civil wars continued to inhibit coffee production in unstable countries around the world. In Angola, coffee exports had tumbled from 5.2

---

[4]The United States could have vetoed the agreement if one other consuming country had voted against it.

million bags in 1974 to less than 300,000 bags in 1984. "Stories from the surrounding countryside tell of fast-growing elephant grass coursing through neglected coffee fields," wrote a reporter. "These reports are hard to confirm. When this correspondent asked to visit a coffee plantation, local officials placed him under house arrest."

In Central America, three countries with a legacy of coffee oligarchies and poverty-stricken campesinos descended into prolonged internal struggle. "We are barefoot, but we are many," a Guatemalan peasant magazine declared in 1980. "We produce the riches that the landowners and all the powerful count, enjoy, and waste. Therefore, when we stop working, the wealth that they enjoy stops as well. Without us, they are nothing." While that may have been true, the military and oligarchy still held the true power.

In Guatemala, General Fernando Romeo Lucas García ruled with an iron fist and mounted a campaign against guerrillas that by 1981 amounted to genocide. "I saw the soldiers cut open the bellies of pregnant women and throw the unborn babies on the fire they had built," a fourteen-year-old witness recalled. While the guerrillas also committed their share of atrocities, the vast majority were committed by the army. Now that many Indians had joined the guerrillas, soldiers felt free to kill any Indian they met.

In 1982 a military coup ousted Lucas García, replacing him with General Efraín Ríos Montt, a born-again Christian. There was hope for peace when Ríos Montt first declared an amnesty, but he soon resumed the bloody war of extermination. In 1983 the Inter-American Human Rights Commission cited the Guatemalan army for the "very gravest violations of human rights, including the destruction, burning, and pillaging of entire villages."

Most coffee growers tried to avoid taking sides, praying that their *fincas* would be spared. Among them was Walter Hannstein, owner of *La Paz*, which meant "Peace." Whenever the military asked Hannstein for a truck, he always made an excuse that it was broken. Then the guerrillas insisted on talking to him. "My mother said that they might as well do it in a civilized manner," Betty Hannstein Adams recalls. "So they served coffee and pastries while they talked." When the military heard about the meeting, they decided that Hannstein was too friendly with the guerrillas, so they bivouacked three hundred men on the farm. Once the army left, the guerrillas concluded that Hannstein was too friendly with the army, so they burned his farm.

A coup replaced Ríos Montt with another military dictator in 1983, but the death squads continued to roam. Guns had become a way of life in Guatemala. "The blunt presence of armed men is everywhere," a visitor observed. Overhearing this comment, a bystander laughed. "If you think there are a lot of guns here, you ought to see El Salvador."

Indeed, violence and repression in tiny neighboring El Salvador were at least as bad as in Guatemala. About the size of New Jersey, El Salvador, with over four million people, was the most densely populated country in the Western Hemisphere. The life of the campesino in the countryside had become intolerable. "It is better to die quickly fighting than to die slowly starving," one guerrilla fighter said. Throughout Latin America, but particularly in El Salvador, liberal Catholic clergymen spoke out against the institutionalized violence. As a result, many priests were assassinated.

The United States did not take a firm moral stand against the killings. Fearful that all of Central America would fall to Communist influence (as had Nicaragua), the United States supported the repressive governments of El Salvador and Guatemala with helicopters and antiinsurgency training while trying to nudge them toward mild reforms. The U.S. Agency for International Development (AID) dumped money into ameliorative social programs while Congress authorized millions in military aid.

In 1980, under pressure from the Carter administration, a much-trumpeted land reform law was passed in El Salvador, but it barely touched the coffee oligarchy. At the same time, the reforms served as a cover for greater repression by the troops supposedly sent to enforce land division. "A circle of fire was lit around a village," reported Amnesty International, "to prevent local people from escaping; troops then entered the village, killing some forty people and abducting many others."

On March 23, 1980, Archbishop Oscar Romero delivered a powerful sermon. "We should like the government to take seriously the fact that reforms dyed by so much blood are worth nothing," he preached. "In the name of God, in the name of our tormented people who have suffered so much and whose laments cry out to heaven, I beseech you, I beg you, I order you, in the name of God, *stop the repression.*" The next day, as Romero celebrated a memorial mass, he was shot and killed.

Romero's death signaled the beginning of ever-more savage attacks by *escuadrones de muerte*, roving death squads that seemed intent on violating every human norm. "For the death squads, death was not punishment enough," wrote Tom Buckley in his 1984 book, *Violent Neighbors*. "Bodies often bore the marks of torture. It was nothing exquisite—fingers and joints crushed by hammerblows, flesh burned away by blowtorch, large areas of skin removed by the flayer's knife." Pushed to the wall, feuding guerrilla movements banded together to form the FMLN, a united rebel force, and open warfare began in 1981.

Right-wing Major Roberto D'Aubuisson, widely rumored to be associated with the death squads and the founder of the conservative ARENA (Alianza Republicana Nacionalista) party, led a coalition that won control of the Constituent Assembly in the 1982 elections. Even though Duarte's Christian Democrats technically ruled, it was clear that the repressive right wielded the real power. The pattern for years of bloodshed was set.

Having ceded power to the military years ago in order to maintain repressive order, the coffee oligarchy found that it had created a monster over which it had insufficient control. The coffee elite was now divided. None wanted major agrarian reform, of course, and all deplored the guerrillas. The majority favored peace negotiations, limited democracy, and free markets. A sizable minority of coffee growers, however, led by Orlando de Sola, lobbied for another *matanza* (massacre) to restore order. He dismissed the seventy-five thousand killed in the early 1980s by army terrorists and death squads as "Communist stooges" who deserved to die.

ARENA was closely identified with both coffee factions. Ricardo "Rick" Valvidieso, who cofounded the party with D'Aubuisson, was a coffee grower with a long Salvadoran pedigree. In 1985 Alfredo "Fredi" Cristiani, one of the country's largest coffee growers, replaced D'Aubuisson as the ARENA head. Even with a coffee man in a position of power, El Salvador's government continued to profit from IN-CAFE (Instituto Nacional del Café), the nationalized coffee monopoly that sold the country's beans at international prices in dollars, while paying producers in local currency equivalent to one-half or less of its real value. Dimayed by low domestic prices, coffee growers stopped applying fertilizer, and some abandoned their farms completely.

As in Guatemala, the farmers were caught between the guerrillas and the death squads, with the large producers more at risk. The rebels firebombed a coffee processing plant in 1983, causing $2 million in damage. Later, a documentary filmmaker followed guerrillas onto the Regalado Dueñas plantation. "They are multimillionaires," one rebel wearing a beret explained as he torched a building. "So we are burning this estate because they mistreat their workers." Many Salvadoran farmers came to an accommodation with the guerrillas, though, making secret deals agreeing to pay their workers more while reserving a small slice for the rebel FMLN, which controlled a quarter of the coffee-growing regions by 1985.

In neighboring Nicaragua, coffee growers were even more distressed. Most of them had supported the 1979 Sandinista revolution that overthrew the hated Somoza regime, but disillusionment set in quickly. As in El Salvador, the Nicaraguan government nationalized coffee exports through ENCAFE, a new government agency that paid the producers only 10 percent of the international market price. After taking all the profits, the Sandinistas supplied easy credit, but this only drove the farmers further into debt.

At the beginning of the revolution, the Sandinistas had taken over the vast Somoza coffee holdings, administering the farms as state-run enterprises. Unfortunately, the urban intellectual Sandinistas knew little about growing coffee. In an attempt to eliminate *roya*, the leaf rust disease, they cut down all the shade trees, selling them for lumber. They failed to fertilize or prune properly. At that time the government instituted the CONARCA program, in which they took over farms with the announced intention of "renovating" before returning them to the owners. Renovation meant ruination, timber harvesting, and neglect. Few farms were ever returned to their owners.

The Sandinistas called coffee farmers who cooperated with them "patriotic producers." Anyone who questioned their politics or policies was labeled a capitalist parasite. Throughout most of the 1980s, any farms that did not produce sufficiently, or whose owners were too vocal, were confiscated by the government. In May 1982 Roger Castellon Orué, one of the most enthusiastic Sandinista supporters, attended his son's graduation at a private Miami high school, where he got a call from a friend. "Don't come back. They have confiscated your farm and declared you an enemy of the people." Castellon had left over a million dollars' worth of processed coffee back in Nicaragua. All of it was gone, along with his house, *beneficio*, and personal possessions. He found work in K-Mart's plant department. "All I knew was coffee." His experience is far from unique. Another farmer's land was expropriated when he left the country for medical treatment.

Even those with the most impeccable Sandinista credentials became disillusioned. Horrifying her family, Luisa Maria Molina Icias disappeared into the mountains to join the guerrillas in 1971 and eventually was forced into exile in Costa Rica. She returned in 1979 with the successful revolution and joined the Ministry of Social Work. When her father's and brothers' land was confiscated, she told her family that all would be well in time. "It was a dream that many Sandinistas had," she explained years later, "but reality wasn't like the dream." In 1984 Molina finally left the party to fight for her family's lands.

Disaffected expatriates formed the Contra movement and supported by the U.S. government made incursions from bases just across the Honduran border. The Sandinistas did improve the lot of the urban poor, with literacy programs and medical services, but the plight of the campesino in the countryside worsened. The harried coffee growers could not afford to pay their workers decent wages. Those who allowed laborers to cultivate subsistence plots were afraid of their farms being confiscated because they were not using them "efficiently." Because they could make more money stealing than harvesting coffee, many campesinos turned to crime or joined the Contras. "Who are the real exploiters of the poor?" one farmer asked. "They [the government] only allow my workers four ounces of rice a day. I want to give them more, so who is exploiting the workers?"

In desperation, the Sandinistas recruited urban high school and college students to harvest the coffee, along with liberal volunteers from the United States and Europe. Enthusiastic pickers, they also were slow and inefficient. The farmers complained that their regular employees had been drafted or joined the Contras. The Contras in the meantime stepped up raids to disrupt the coffee harvest, killing not only Sandinistas but lowly harvesters, including women and children.[5] Both sides committed their share of atrocities.

There were no death squads in Nicaragua, however. One coffee grower suspected of aiding the Contras was arrested, stripped naked,

---

[5]Across the border in Honduras, coffee producers were also frustrated with the Contra military bases. "They have forced a war on us that doesn't interest us, that kills us," one grower said. While Honduras farmers resented the Sandinista artillery barrages and mined roadways, they also complained that the Contras were "cold-blooded killers."

and interrogated for hours, but he was not physically harmed. Compelled to relocate entire communities into "controlled zones," the Sandinista army forced two hundred thousand peasants off their land. Many fled across the border to Honduras, seeking protection from the Contras. Eventually, a half-million Nicaraguans—one-seventh of the population—lived in exile.

In response to the defections, the Sandinistas shifted their policy somewhat, giving individual pieces of land to campesinos. "We gave them land and a gun and said, 'This is yours. Now defend it,'" recalled General Joaquin Cuadra Lacayo, the Nicaraguan Army chief of staff. "We called it 'agrarian reform,' but the logic was strictly military. We wanted to stop them from joining the *contras*. I didn't give a damn if the farmer produced or not." With no management experience and little profit incentive, they let the coffee rot. Of course, the general's two coffee farms were not confiscated.

By 1986 most of the large coffee producers hung on simply from inertia. "We have no choice," observed one grower. "We have a huge investment tied up in the trees and can't leave them." Yet they were losing money, able to continue only through bank loans. Many farmers simply practiced minimal maintenance and harvesting to avoid confiscation. "One day the bell tolls for my neighbor, the next day for me," a farmer said fatalistically. "There isn't any future for private producers in Nicaragua. We are just subsisting."

Fair Trade Coffee

In April 1985 Paul Katzeff flew to Nicaragua at the invitation of UNAG, the pro-Sandinista coffee organization. For Katzeff, owner of Thanksgiving Coffee in Fort Bragg, California, the visit was a "life-changing event," reconnecting him to his social worker roots. "I hung out with the Sandinistas in the mountains, where they were fighting the *contras*. I met with three commandantes of the Revolution. I was educated about the relationship between coffee and revolution." Katzeff concluded that coffee could be the medium for his message. Back in California, he changed the company slogan to: "Not Just a Cup, But a Just Cup," and he packaged the Nicaraguan beans he roasted as "Coffee for Peace," donating 50 cents per pound to the Sandinistas.

One month later, the Reagan administration banned the import of all Nicaraguan goods. The flamboyant Katzeff sued Ronald Reagan, and he got around the embargo by having his Nicaraguan beans shipped and roasted through Canada. That year, Katzeff was co-chair of the Specialty Coffee Association of America, which convened in Anaheim. Without consulting Dan Cox, his co-chair from Green Mountain Coffee, Katzeff invited a Sandinista and two other activists to take part in a panel on coffee and human rights. Cox was not happy. "I told Paul, 'I like this country. I'm not against our government.' There was this nun crying. I'm at the podium thinking, 'What the hell's this all about?'"

Specialty coffee men had concentrated only on providing the "perfect cup," fighting the robusta blends of the big boys. Now they were challenged to consider the inequities built into the system of coffee cultivation, processing, and export. The beans that produced their high-priced cups were harvested by poverty-stricken campesinos. In 1986 three Massachusetts idealists who had worked in food co-ops formed Equal Exchange. "We aim to create a process," wrote cofounder Jonathan Rosenthal in 1986, "that allows people to reconnect with the people who grow much of the food and with the ecology from which it comes."

With help from investors—some had helped harvest the Nicaraguan crop—Equal Exchange got off the ground, providing "fair trade" Cafe Nica, their Nicaraguan coffee, primarily to food cooperatives. Their goals were to pay a guaranteed minimum price regardless of market fluctuations, buy directly from democratically run cooperatives of smallholders, help with credit, and encourage ecological farming practices. In Canada, Bridgehead, founded by two ministers and two social activists in 1984, also sold Sandinista coffee.

Around this time, two Dutchmen working in Latin America independently concluded that a better market mechanism was needed for fair trade coffee. In 1987 Franz van der Hoff, a priest who worked with UCIRI (a coffee cooperative in Oaxaca, Mexico) approached Solidaridad, a Dutch organization, asking for marketing help. At the same time, Bert Beekman, who had worked in Honduras and Nicaragua, returned to the Netherlands in frustration. "I concluded that over half of the development money was simply thrown away. There was no viable market for what these farmers had worked so hard to produce."

Supported by Solidaridad, Dutch churches, and the media, Beekman entered into a public debate with Douwe Egberts, the dominant Dutch roaster, owned since 1978 by the U.S. food firm Sara Lee. "They were quite open as long as it was just a debate," Beekman recalls. "But when it came to results and agreements, they delayed and delayed." The fair trade advocates decided to create their own collective brand. A survey revealed that 15 percent of the Dutch population would support a fair trade coffee mark. "In Holland, coffee is the center of social life," Beekman observes, "so it was the perfect product."

Having raised $4 million, the fair trade groups were prepared to launch their own brand when a group of smaller roasters—competitors of Douwe Egberts—approached Beekman. "Why don't we cut a deal? You create a certification label, and *we* will launch your coffee." Beekman agreed, and in November 1988 Max Havelaar Quality Mark coffee was introduced, taking its name from the 1860 Dutch novel that protested the inhumane treatment of Javanese coffee growers. The fair trade coffee garnered enormous publicity and a 1.6 percent market share during its first year, subsequently achieving a steady 2.5 percent level. Within a few years, the Max Havelaar seal appeared in Switzerland, Belgium, Denmark, and France. In Germany and Austria, where the Dutch name did not resonate, it became Transfair Coffee.

Blood in the Salvadoran Cups?

In the United States, late in 1989 concern over coffee and human rights shifted to El Salvador, where Robbie Gamble (great-great grandson of the founder of Procter & Gamble) had lived for two years. Deeply disturbed by the violence there, he felt personally implicated because Folgers purchased coffee beans from El Salvador. In protest, he gave away his inheritance. Then in November 1989, six Jesuit priests and two women workers were slain by death squads in El Salvador. Neighbor to Neighbor, a San Francisco–based activist group, immediately launched its long-planned boycott. Nestlé, which had endured a lengthy boycott because of its controversial infant formula sales in developing countries, quickly announced temporary suspension of purchases from the troubled Central American country. Robbie Gamble's younger brother, Jamie, announced his support of the boycott, and Neighbor to Neighbor narrowed its focus to Procter & Gamble.

When P & G CEO Ed Artzt refused to meet with the activists, they sponsored an inflammatory television spot. "Boycott Folgers Coffee," actor Ed Asner ordered viewers. "What it brews is misery and death."

As he spoke, blood oozed from under an inverted coffee cup. When a Boston station aired the spot, Procter & Gamble yanked its advertising, worth a million dollars a year to the station, restoring it only when the station declined to run the activists' spot again, saying that it made "unsubstantiated claims."

By this time the Specialty Coffee Association of America had come of age. Ted Lingle had become its full-time executive director in Long Beach, California, and the SCAA was holding its second independent convention at the Claremont Hotel in Oakland. With help from firebrand activist Paul Katzeff, Neighbor to Neighbor announced its intention to protest the convention. Dan Cox pointed out that few specialty roasters bought the mediocre Salvadoran coffee anyway. "But they didn't care," he recalls. "They just wanted to get publicity." Katzeff led a march through the meeting with banging drums and protest chants before dumping buckets of red-stained water on the steps.

More substantively, Neighbor to Neighbor formed an alliance with the International Longshoremen's and Warehousemen's Union (ILWU), whose dockworkers refused to unload Salvadoran coffee from a freighter when it docked in San Francisco, then Vancouver, Seattle, and Long Beach. Tipped off by the dockworkers, Neighbor to Neighbor organized impressive picket lines with signs denouncing "Death Squad Coffee." The freighter eventually turned back and unloaded the coffee in El Salvador. Under intense pressure, Red Apple, New York City's largest supermarket chain, temporarily agreed to suspend Folgers purchases and then to display Neighbor to Neighbor literature. Pizzeria Uno stopped using Folgers. The Evangelical Lutheran Church and the Commission on Social Action for Reform Judaism supported the boycott.

The campaign, waged by an underfunded grassroots organization, had an impressive effect, with huge media coverage. El Salvador's President Alfredo Cristiani, himself a coffee grower, called Neighbor to Neighbor a Communist organization. The CEOs for the major coffee roasters—Procter & Gamble, Nestlé, and Philip Morris—met with U.S. State Department officials, begging them to facilitate the Salvadoran peace process that the Bush administration had subverted. The U.S. coffee companies took out ads in Salvadoran papers favoring a negotiated settlement. Soon afterward, early in 1992, the twelve-year civil war that had killed eighty thousand people and sent over a million into exile finally ended. As part of the settlement, about 20 percent of El Salvador's coffee lands were given to campesinos in areas already controlled by the guerrillas anyway, providing at least a modicum of hope and reform.

The violence, social inequities, and land distribution problems of Central America were far from over, but at least for the time being, the worst of the atrocities had stopped. Coffee growers now could worry primarily about such mundane matters as producing quality beans and securing a decent price for them.

The Big Boys Try to Get Hip

During the late 1980s, North American roasters had more to worry about than boycotts. By mid-decade, they finally woke up to the fact that whole-bean specialty coffees represented a profitable, growing niche in the generally declining coffee industry, and that they were missing their chance to profit from it. In 1984 General Foods introduced the Swedish whole-bean Gevalia Kaffee to the United States through an ingenious direct-mail program. The company had bought Victor Theodor Engwall & Company, which produced Gevalia, still the dominant Swedish coffee, in 1970. Now, GF executive Art Trotman, with the help of direct-mail guru Lester Wunderman, supervised a marketing effort modeled after record clubs in which members were induced to join with a hefty premium gift, then automatically received new products on a regular basis. "The plan relies on people's basic inertia," Trotman observes. At first, Gevalia customers received a free canister. Then, in 1987, new members got an automatic electric drip coffeemaker. "That's when sales doubled in two years," Trotman recalls.

The advertisements for Gevalia, placed in upscale venues such as *Vogue* and *Bon Appetit,* emphasized the coffee's Swedish heritage, "the magnificent obsession that produced coffee favored by kings," and its preparation by a master roaster. Customers had no idea that they were buying a General Foods product, since that fact was carefully obscured. Fortunately for the quality of the product, the U.S. firm in fact had little influence over the coffee. The all-arabica blend was roasted in Sweden, hand-packed in one-way valve bags, shipped to a fulfillment service in the United States, and mailed out. General Foods never touched it, other than to take a sweet profit.[6]

---

[6]Art Trotman heard that in the 1970s, when General Foods wanted to bring robustas onto the floor in the Swedish factory, the workers went on strike. "They refused to roast it."

In 1985 General Foods decided to launch gourmet whole beans in U.S. supermarkets. Mary Seggerman put together a five-person "entrepreneurial attack team" that developed a line of seven whole-bean and ground coffees, including Kenya AA, Colombian, Breakfast Blend, French Roast, and several others. They wanted to set up kiosks in airports to sell espressos and cappuccinos, but that plan got nixed. Instead, they settled for gourmet beans sold in selected upscale supermarkets in one-way valve bags.

In the 1985–1986 Evanston, Indiana, test market, they named it the Maxwell House Master Collection and aired a television pitch featuring classical music and references to Bach's *Coffee Cantata*, asserting that this was "coffee even finer than that which inspired Bach." Focus groups showed that consumers confused it with Maxwell House Master Blend, the cheap, high-yield coffee. So they renamed it Maxwell House Private Collection and launched in high-income areas around the United States. The end-aisle display units featured shelves and a grinder.

Seggerman planned to have specialty food distributors deliver and supervise the beans. Just before the launch, however, General Foods president Phil Smith hired an outside consultant, who concluded they should use "direct distribution"—that is, the packaged beans would go to a supermarket chain's warehouse, where they would be treated like any other product.

"It was a big mistake," Seggerman laments. The French Roast and Colombian beans moved better than the Kenyan AA, which meant that grocers simply dropped the Kenyan product. With no one supervising the shelf space, it looked disheveled. Worse, local specialty roasters—who distributed their own products—placed their beans on the empty shelves, right next to the Maxwell House Private Collection.

Even so, the program was a moderate success, grossing $45 million the first full year in 1986. "But that wasn't enough for General Foods," Seggerman says. "Unless a new product garnered at least $200 million annually by the third year, they considered it too small to worry about." After three years, GF killed Private Collection. Seggerman transferred out of coffee in 1989 and left the company the following year. "I don't know how I lasted eight years without pulling my hair out and cutting my head off," she says. "If they had only let me do it properly, I really believe I could have saved the Maxwell House Coffee Company, which is deader than a doornail today." Others think that the name, not the distribution system, was the kiss of death. Few consumers believed that a true gourmet coffee product would have a "Maxwell House" preface.

The A & P was more successful in introducing its Eight O'Clock Royale Gourmet Bean Coffee in one-way valve bags. While in London, Paul Gallant, who headed Compass Foods, an A & P subsidiary, dropped in on H. R. Higgins Ltd., British coffee purveyors to the royalty. Entranced with the snob appeal, Gallant copied Higgins' elegant script, cribbed Loewenbrau Beer's lions, and produced a stunning product in a gold one-way valve bag. "I only steal from the best," Gallant explained. The A & P specialty product took off.

In line with its strategy of extension-by-acquisition, in 1987 Nestlé purchased California-based Sark's Gourmet Coffee and slowly began to expand that brand's whole-bean supermarket coverage.

For a while, Procter & Gamble, the classic low-end consumer goods marketer, ignored the upscale market while making other changes. P & G dumped the venerable Mrs. Olson and mounted one of its most effective lifestyle image campaigns, with the tagline, "The Best Part of Waking Up Is Folgers in Your Cup." The ads, which ran from 5:00 A.M. until noon, targeted both men and women.[7] P & G finally brought out Folgers Decaffeinated Instant Coffee, a long-overdue brand extension that quickly overtook its High Point Decaf.

As the specialty market swelled, Folgers played both ends of the quality spectrum. Procter & Gamble didn't go for whole beans, opting instead for Folgers Colombian Supreme, later changed to Folgers Gourmet Supreme. At the same time, however, it rolled out Folgers Special Roast Flaked Coffee, a new high-yield version that used even *less* coffee in an 11.5-ounce can claiming to match a regular pound's brewing capacity. The company also came out with Folgers Singles, "freeze concentrated" coffee in a bag, ready to brew in microwave ovens or boiling water in one minute, though marketers insisted it was not instant coffee.

Coffee and Cigarettes

Just as Mary Seggerman was test-marketing Maxwell House whole beans in fall 1985, Philip Morris, the behemoth multinational cigarette

---

[7]The Folgers ads were aimed at adults, though they test-marketed a few spots in which children drank coffee too. Irate customers called. "How dare you show kids drinking coffee?"

manufacturer, bought General Foods. By that time, it was clear that the U.S. tobacco business, while incredibly profitable, was a chancy proposition. Whether they would admit it publicly or not, the cigarette executives knew that their products contributed to lung cancer. Buying General Foods for $5.8 billion allowed Philip Morris to diversify while establishing itself as the largest U.S. consumer products company. The savvy tobacco executives soon became disenchanted with General Foods, however—especially the Maxwell House division, which accounted for a third of GF sales. The General Foods managers were "dead from their ankles up," complained a Philip Morris man. "Their arrogance was exceeded only by their sloth."

Shortly after the purchase, Philip Morris CEO Hamish Maxwell visited the Maxwell House wing of General Foods, in White Plains, New York, and asked for a cup of coffee. Certainly. Did he want Gevalia or Yuban? No, he wanted a cup of Maxwell House. Since no one drank the stuff, none was brewed. It took some time for someone to find a can opener and make a cup. "That was his first clue that there was a problem," Seggerman recalls.

Philip Morris was unhappy with its 1986 results, in which General Foods accounted for 40 percent of the corporation's gross sales but only 20 percent of the profits. With Folgers eating into Maxwell House market share with its "Wake Up" campaign, weren't they just pouring money down the drain with a $70 million annual coffee advertising budget? Declining coffee prices allowed ever narrower profit margins in the price war with Folgers. In April 1987 General Foods announced a 25-percent ad budget cut, lopping $17.5 million, then cut even more by year's end, putting more money into trade discounts and coupons than advertising. Bob Seelert, appointed senior vice president in charge of coffee and food service, focused strictly on the Maxwell House name, marketing all coffees as a brand extension. He saw no future in the whole-bean Private Collection.[8]

The slashed Maxwell House ad budget was a sure sign of troubled business in an era when the U.S. economy in general suffered from stagfation, soon to be followed by a recession and widespread unem-

---

[8]Maxwell House president Stephen Morris resigned in 1987, citing "philosophical differences" with Bob Seelert. "He believed in grinding out short yardage, winning inches of very expensive turf through promotion deals," Morris recalls.

ployment. Maxwell House had to beat retail prices in 1988 when it restored its ad budget but still lost 440 million that year. Folgers countered by entirely replacing its regular pound cans with a 13-ounce "fast roast," insisting that it was not a high-yield coffee, though even Alice in Wonderland wouldn't have believed that one. "The one-pound coffee container," one journalist noted, "is going the way of the Edsel." By 1989 Procter & Gamble's regular ground coffees had overtaken General Foods to claim the number-one spot.[9]

In 1988, anted up $13.1 billion for Kraft, Inc., an Illinois food conglomerate with a sterling record, and folded its two acquisitions into one unit called Kraft General Foods, placing Kraft executive Michael Miles in charge.

As the decade drew to a close, however, Maxwell House was clearly flailing to find direction. In a last-ditch effort, Ogilvy & Mather hired ex-TV news anchor Linda Ellerbee and TV weatherman Willard Scott to shill for Maxwell House. "In a national test, people said they liked Maxwell House better than Folgers Coffee," Ellerbee intoned at her news desk, then turned it over to Scott in the field, where a fireman told him he preferred Maxwell House for its "rich taste," then took the weatherman for a ride on his firetruck. In a scathing review, journalist Bob Garfield dismissed the ever-cheerful Willard Scott as a "human squirting-boutonniere" and lambasted Ellerbee for disguising advertising as real news. "It is misleading. It is cheap. It is wrong."

The jinxed ad aired during a controversial NBC drama, "Roe vs. Wade," about the landmark court decision to legalize abortions. As a result, right-to-life advocates threatened to boycott Maxwell House. A few days later, Maxwell House dumped Ogilvy & Mather in favor of D'Arcy Masius Benton & Bowles—the descendant of the firm that had created the enormously successful radio show, "Maxwell House Show Boat," during the depression.

The Collapse of the ICA

Even as Maxwell House struggled to regain ground in the American coffee wars, the fragile alliance of coffee producers and consumers dis-

---

[9] As a brand, regular Folgers had surpassed Maxwell House a decade earlier. Now, the combined P & G coffee brands beat *all* of the General Foods coffees, including Yuban, Sanka, and others.

integrated. In fall 1985, prices rose dramatically on news of a Brazilian drought that would affect the 1986 crop. Volatility was exacerbated by the growth of "hedge funds," mutual funds that traded in commodity futures and options. Controlling billions of dollars, the professional managers dramatically affected prices when buying or selling thousands of contracts. As green bean prices reached $2.30 a pound, Brazilian thieves began to hijack coffee trucks rather than robbing banks.

In February 1986 the ICA quota system was suspended automatically because the average price had stayed above $1.50 for forty-five market days. Coffee futures promptly plunged in anticipation that producers would dump their surplus stocks onto the world market, then firmed up when Brazil elected to restrict exports. Brazil announced that it would *import* African robusta beans, supposedly to supply domestic consumption and release higher quality beans for export. The Brazilians in fact were only trying to maintain high price levels. By the end of 1986, with forty-five million surplus bags overhanging the market and world consumption slumping, the price fell below $1.40 a pound, then drifted toward $1.20 by February 1987.

Technically, prices below $1.35 were supposed to trigger quotas again, but reaching an agreement proved difficult. The United States was angry that Latin American producers had formed a minicartel to limit exports, outside the ICA, an action that made the U.S. Trade Representative "seriously question the validity of our belief in international cooperation in coffee." Furthermore, the United States wanted a quota reallocation that would favor higher quality arabica beans. After March negotiations in London failed, prices sank to around a dollar a pound.

The United States agreed to a new International Coffee Agreement in October 1987, again for political reasons. With civil wars still raging in coffee-growing countries of Central America and Africa, the United States knew that economies devastated by low prices would exacerbate the misery and intensify the conflicts.

The new ICA was a stopgap, ad hoc measure that left all of the old issues unresolved. Brazil took a minuscule quota cut, from 30.55 percent to 30.48 percent of the total. Prices rose, generally hovering around the $1.20 ICA basement target. As tourist coffee reemerged in the two-tier market, the National Coffee Association abandoned its support of the ICA in February 1988, calling for "free and unrestricted trade in coffee." In April, the head of the U.S. delegation to the ICA announced that the government had not yet decided whether it would renew membership in the agreement when it expired in September 1989.

Rumors of the ICA's possible demise, then hopeful reports that a new agreement was near, sent coffee prices reeling up and down throughout the rest of 1988 and early 1989, but they sank gradually as Brazil and the United States squared off for a final confrontation over the two issues of tourist coffee and selectivity. With reformer Mikhail Gorbachev in the Kremlin and the Sandinistas recently voted out of power in Nicaragua, cold war fears no longer provided a compelling reason for the United States to support the agreement. By this time, Brazil's economy relied more on the export of soybeans, oranges, weapons, mahogany, and ballpoint pens than coffee. The deadlocked negotiations became so bitter that the ICA did not even survive until the September expiration date. When no coalition could summon the necessary votes to renew the quarterly quotas, the International Coffee Organization abruptly suspended all export limits on July 4, 1989.

All hell broke loose. By the end of July, prices had fallen to 85 cents a pound. Panicked producers rushed to the market with beans, hoping to sell before the price dropped lower, thereby driving prices down more steeply. In October, members voted to maintain minimal funding of the ICO, without quotas. With this news, prices collapsed again, down to 70 cents a pound. Only Maxwell House, Folgers, Nestlé, and the men screaming themselves hoarse in the futures pit were happy. The big roasters were slow to lower retail prices, taking a breather from the interminable price wars, while they built a gigantic stockpile of cheap beans.

The Coca–Coffee Connection and a Black Harvest

Under pressure from the Bush administration to crack down on cocaine processing and smuggling, Colombian President Virgilio Barco Vargas complained that the drop in coffee prices imperiled his fight against drugs. In 1988 Colombia had earned $1.7 billion from coffee exports, just over the estimated $1.5 billion in illegal cocaine sales. Now, Colombia stood to lose some $500 million from the coffee price decline, and many of its three million citizens who made a livelihood from coffee might well shift to growing coca.[10]

In January, the Colombian ambassador testified before a U.S. Senate subcommittee chaired by Joseph Biden that the Andean nations had lost nearly $750 million in revenue because of the ICA collapse. "How can we ask farmers in South America to grow coffee instead of coca leaves," Biden asked, "when the price they are getting for their coffee has been slashed in half over the past year?"

Despite the U.S. willingness to take another look, however, even the producers were ambivalent about another ICA. The Brazilians weren't willing to agree to a drastic reduction of their quota share. No one had been satisfied with the flawed system, which had limped through twenty-seven years from 1962 until 1989.

In the new free-market atmosphere of the 1990s, government control boards either were disbanded or radically weakened, allowing some farmers to keep a greater percentage of the market price. In 1990 the Brazilian Coffee Institute (IBC), with its staff of thirty-five hundred and a $15 million annual budget, was summarily abolished.[11] In Africa, the *caisse de stabilisation* boards fell by the wayside. By late 1993 last-gasp efforts to revive the ICA failed, and the United States officially withdrew from the lame-duck International Coffee Organization just as the growers in desperation created the Association of Coffee Producing Countries (ACPC) to initiate a retention scheme to boost prices again.

By then, coffee growers had suffered through four years of basement prices. Even for efficient plantations, prices remained below the cost of production.[12] As in previous bust cycles, many farmers stopped pruning or fertilizing. Others ripped up their trees to plant other crops. Although world coffee exports averaged 8.4 million bags a year more than in the late 1980s, average annual revenues *fell* from $10.7 billion to $6.6 billion—a staggering loss of over $4 billion a year. The dramatic price drop devastated small growers around the world.

---

[10]In fact, Colombia's drug lords already owned or controlled around 10 percent of the country's coffee crop.

[11]The demise of the IBC meant that Brazilian beans no longer needed to be lumped together for sale, allowing higher quality producers to form the Brazil Specialty Coffee Association. They faced an uphill battle to change the poor image of Brazilian coffee, however.

[12]In 1991 one coffee expert estimated that the break-even point for arabicas was between 80 cents and $1 a pound, and a bit over 60 cents a pound for robustas.

In the highlands of Papua New Guinea, for instance, the Ganiga tribe had staked its future on a new coffee plantation co-owned with Joe Leahy, the mixed-race son of an Australian gold prospector. In *Black Harvest*, a film documentary, Leahy told tribal leader Popina, "With good prices, you'll be up to your necks in money." Instead, the bottom dropped out of the market. The bewildered Popina observed, "I feel like selling my big pig and traveling to where they make these decisions. This affects all of us. We'll never be millionaires." The Ganiga refused to harvest for lower wages, and the berries blackened and rotted on the trees. Relations between Leahy and the tribe deteriorated. By the end of the film, the Ganiga had reverted in frustration to tribal warfare, and Leahy was considering a move to Australia.

Big Coffee: Ice Cold

In the consuming countries, few roasters thought much about the plight of growers. They were simply delighted to stockpile cheap beans, even as the merger mania continued in the industrial coffee world. In 1990 Philip Morris added to its coffee acquisitions by buying Jacobs Suchard, the dominant European coffee-chocolate conglomerate, for $3.8 billion. In one gulp, the global coffee business became even more concentrated. At the same time, Maxwell House announced the closing of its gigantic Hoboken roasting plant due to declining sales. All roasting would be shifted to a Jacksonville, Florida, facility. Showing its uncertainty, Maxwell House switched ad agencies again, back to Ogilvy & Mather. In 1991 Kraft General Foods barely managed to regain a slight lead in the ground-roast segment, holding 33 percent of the market vs. 32.7 percent for Procter & Gamble. Folgers as a brand still trounced Maxwell House.

In the first few years of the 1990s, the major roasters continued to battle one another without much to show for it, other than an innovative Taster's Choice campaign—and even that was cribbed from British commercials for Gold Blend, the Nestlé brand of freeze-dried coffee in the U.K.[13] The commercials featured mini soap operas in which Tony, a soulful bachelor, meets Sharon, his lovely British neighbor, when she

---

[13]In England, Gold Blend sales jumped 20 percent within eighteen months of the campaign's introduction in 1987. Actress Sharon Maughan regretted a television role in which she had said, "I hate coffee," but no one seemed to care.

knocks on his door to borrow Taster's Choice because of its "sophisti-cated taste." In serial episodes ranging over months and years, Tony and Sharon flirt over the freeze-dried coffee in commercials positively dripping with sexual innuendo, sensuality, and intrigue. Though Taster's Choice would appear an unlikely aphrodisiac, the advertise-ments catapulted the instant coffee to first place in market share by 1993, when Tony and Sharon finally kissed onscreen to great media hoopla. A romance novel based on the couple hit the best-seller list in England.

Other than the Taster's Choice lifestyle commercials, the big roasters continued to grind out traditional marketing efforts while throwing off new products. Maxwell House came out with a refrigerated liquid cof-fee concentrate, then tried Maxwell House 1892, purportedly the origi-nal slow-roasted formula. Both bombed. Next, it launched Cappio, one of many iced coffee drinks that were heralded as the new wave of caf-feinated beverages; it didn't do well either. Coca-Cola and Nestlé si-multaneously announced a joint worldwide venture to market cold cof-fee drinks—excluding Japan, where Coke already dominated the market with its Georgia Coffee. Nestlé came out with a Nescafé Mocha Cooler, followed by Chock O'Cinno from Chock full o' Nuts and a number of smaller specialty entrees such as the Cappuccino Cooler from Fairwinds in New Hampshire. None of the iced-coffee products caught on the way Snapple and other "New Age" drinks did.

By the mid-1990s it was clear to industry observers that the major roasters had lost their way, while gourmet small-scale coffees were booming. "Specialty coffees are the tail wagging the dog," noted one analyst. "The big companies in a sense have demythologized, decon-structed something very special." In 1995 *Forbes* summarized the fate of the big coffee merchants in a one-word headline: "Oversleeping." The message the business magazine conveyed to Maxwell House, Folgers, and Nestlé: "Wake up and smell the freshly ground coffee."

~ 18 ~

THE STARBUCKS
EXPERIENCE

According to legend, Merlin was born in the future and lived backward in time, moving toward the past. He must have often felt out of step with his contemporaries, filled as he was with unconventional notions of what might be. I'm no sage, but sometimes I think I know how he must have felt. My vision for the future, my aspirations for what kind of company Starbucks should be, are so easily misunderstood.
—**Howard Schultz, 1997**

By 1995 one specialty roaster had emerged as the definitive leader in the dynamic, fragmented market. Starbucks, the pioneering Seattle company begun in 1971 by Jerry Baldwin, Zev Siegl, and Gordon Bowker, had been transformed into a national phenomenon in an astonishingly short period of time. Without even paying for the publicity, the name *Starbucks* had become synonymous with fine coffee, hip hangouts, and upscale image. All this came about because in 1981 the coffee firm caught the attention of a curious plastics salesman named Howard Schultz. He wondered why this relatively small Seattle coffee company ordered so many drip-brewing thermoses from Hammarplast, the Swedish firm Schultz represented in the United States.

In 1980 original partner Zev Siegl sold out to pursue other interests, leaving only Jerry Baldwin and Gordon Bowker. By that time, Starbucks was the largest roaster in Washington, with six retail outlets. It also sold its beans to restaurants, other retailers, and supermarkets, and sold espresso machines, grinders, and brewers. Frustrated with so many enterprises, Baldwin shortly thereafter sold the Blue Anchor supermarket division to focus primarily on sales in his own stores. He also gave up the equipment accounts, but in 1982 he hired the visionary Schultz as his new head of marketing. "You've got a real jewel," Schultz told Baldwin. "Starbucks could be so much bigger." Though Baldwin didn't have such grandiose plans, he was impressed enough with the aggressive New York salesman to hire him.

Then in 1983 Baldwin got a call from Sal Bonavita, who had bought Peet's in 1979. Bonavita wanted to sell. "I was so excited I could hardly sit still," Baldwin recalls. Here was his chance to own the store that started it all. "In a young, dreamy, idealistic way, I wanted to see Peet's and Starbucks together." In 1984 Starbucks bought Peet's, putting the company deeply into debt. Baldwin found himself juggling two company cultures and commuting between Seattle and San Francisco.

Howard Schultz meanwhile was agitating to take Starbucks in another direction. In spring 1983 Starbucks sent Schultz to an international housewares show in Milan, Italy. There, like Alice Foote MacDougall sixty years earlier, he found a vibrant coffee culture. Milan, a city the size of Philadelphia, supported fifteen hundred espresso bars, and there were two hundred thousand in all of Italy. *"Buon giorno!"* a *barista* (bartender) greeted Schultz one morning, as he handed a tiny demitasse of espresso to one customer, then deftly created a perfect cappuccino. "The barista moved so gracefully that it looked as though he were grinding coffee beans, pulling shots of espresso, and steaming milk at the same time, all the while conversing merrily with his customers," Schultz recalls. "It was great theater." In nearby Verona, Schultz had his first caffè latte, a drink with more steamed milk than espresso.

Schultz was inspired. "It was like an epiphany. It was so immediate and physical that I was shaking." Why not take great Starbucks beans and brew such drinks? Why not create community gathering places like those in Italy? Back in Seattle, Schultz received a chilly reception. Jerry Baldwin wasn't keen to go into the restaurant business. He didn't want to dilute his mission, which was to sell whole beans.

When Starbucks opened a sixth store in April 1984, Baldwin let Schultz test a small espresso bar, tucked into a corner. It proved an immediate hit, but Baldwin didn't want customers to think of Starbucks as a place to grab a quick cup of coffee to go. At that point Schultz decided to branch out on his own, starting Il Giornale, a coffeehouse named after Italy's biggest newspaper that also means "daily."

Schultz, who grew up in relative poverty in a Brooklyn housing project, had the aggressive drive of a street kid determined to make it. Baldwin showed his goodwill and confidence by investing $150,000 of Starbucks money in Il Giornale, and Schultz convinced other Seattle businessmen to kick in seed money. He hired Dawn Pinaud, who had run the first test espresso bar, to train staff and supervise the retail stores. Then Dave Olsen joined the team. In 1975 Olsen opened the funky Café Allegro in Seattle's university district, where he roasted Starbucks beans to a dark finish for his espresso drinks. "I had been running my place for ten years by 1985, and I was beginning to think I should do more. Howard's dream matched mine."

The first Il Giornale store opened in April 1986. Within six months, a thousand people a day were buying espresso drinks there. A few gulped the concentrated beverage straight like the Italians, but most opted for the cappuccino (a little more espresso than steamed milk) and latte (a lot more milk). Italians drank such dilute beverages only in the morning but Schultz quickly adapted to American preferences. In Italy, most customers stand for their brief shot. Americans wanted to linger, so Schultz added chairs. Customers complained about the incessant opera, so he modified it to background jazz.

The essential elements worked, though. Dawn Pinaud and her staff created their own lingo. Although Il Giornale was essentially a fast-food outlet, the service people weren't soda jerks or flunkies. They were *baristas*, spotlighted as though on stage. A drink wasn't small, medium, or large. It was *short, tall,* or *grande.* A double espresso with a splash of milk was christened a *doppio macchiato.* "It's amazing to me that these terms have become part of the language," Pinaud says. "A few of us sat in a conference room and just made them up." Eventually, after Starbucks caved in to customer requests and offered skim milk and flavors, ordering became a poetic art form. A large decaf espresso with lots of milk and no foam was *an unleaded grande latte without.* A small iced hazelnut coffee with one shot of regular and one of decaf, skim milk, and a fair amount of foam, to go, was *an iced short schizo skinny hazelnut cappuccino with wings.*

Then, in March 1987, Howard Schultz learned that Starbucks was for sale. Gordon Bowker wanted to cash out to start a microbrewery. Baldwin sold off Caravali, the company's wholesale subsidiary, and was looking to spin off Starbucks itself. He and his chief roaster, Jim

Reynolds, would move to San Francisco to concentrate solely on Peet's. Within weeks, Schultz convinced his investors to contribute $3.8 million to buy the six Starbucks retail outlets and roasting plant. Schultz, then thirty-four, was poised to fulfill his vision, announcing plans to open one hundred twenty-five outlets in the next five years. At an employee pep rally, he promised, "I will not leave anyone behind." He abandoned the esoteric Il Giornale name in favor of Starbucks. He sanitized the logo's bare-breasted mermaid, reducing her to a wavy-locked goddess figure, while company brochures now proclaimed that Starbuck was the "coffee-loving first mate" in *Moby Dick*, although no one in the book drank coffee.

The Schultz enthusiasm was infectious, and he attracted a core group of devoted coffee people. Among them was Kevin Knox, the "coffee specialist" who supervised everything that happened from the time the beans tumbled from the roaster until the first sip. In October 1987 Howard Schultz sent Dawn Pinaud to open a Chicago Starbucks. "A consultant later said that I was parachuted into enemy territory with a Boy Scout knife and told to survive," Pinaud recalls. Over the next two years, she opened fifteen stores. Chicagoans, weaned on Hills Brothers and Folgers, did not take to the strong, dark-roasted Starbucks blend immediately. Still, the cappuccinos and lattes were tasty, and gradually the stores developed a loyal clientele.

In 1987 Starbucks lost $330,000. The next year, $764,000, and by 1989 the firm dropped $1.2 million. There were then fifty-five Starbucks locations in the Pacific Northwest and Chicago. Investors simply had to have faith, delivering repeated infusions of venture capital. In 1990 the company turned the corner, building a new roasting plant and showing a small profit. The following year, Dawn Pinaud took Starbucks into Los Angeles, where many feared the warm weather would deter hot coffee sales, but it was an immediate hit. "Almost overnight, Starbucks became chic," Schultz remembers. "Word of mouth, we discovered, is far more powerful than advertising."

Schultz began to hire MBAs and corporate executives with experience running chain franchises, creating complex computer systems, and training employees nationwide to deliver standardized consumer goods. He recruited many of them in the early 1990s from fast-food companies such as Kentucky Fried Chicken, Wendy's, McDonald's, Burger King, Pepsi, and Taco Bell, and they brought professional management to the preexisting coffee idealism—though the two did not always coexist comfortably. One former Taco Bell manager became infamous within Starbucks for saying, "I don't *do* creative, I *manage* creative," and for wondering aloud why the company didn't buy coffees according to what consumers would accept rather than seeking the very best beans. By the end of 1991, there were just over one hundred stores with $57 million in sales, and Schultz was preparing to take Starbucks public in order to finance even more rapid expansion.

Latte Land

"I became increasingly afraid of waking up the sleeping giants," Schultz admits, referring to Maxwell House, Folgers, and Nestlé. "If they had begun to sell specialty coffee early on, they could have wiped us out." Yet they never made a move into small retail stores. Several other regional specialty coffee outlets, however, were expanding rapidly.[1] Gloria Jean's Coffee Bean, owned by former construction worker Ed Kvetko, loomed as Starbucks' major competition. In 1985, when Kvetko owned eleven stores in the Chicago area, he began franchising, primarily in malls. While Starbucks projected a high-brow Italian image, Gloria Jean's was thoroughly middle-class, featuring a huge variety, including plenty of flavored beans and, eventually, a variety of coffee beverages. By 1991 Kvetko's wife's name graced one hundred twenty-four stores in over a hundred cities, considerably more than Starbucks'.

Sales of gourmet beans tripled in only six years, now accounting for 20 percent of home purchases. The specialty coffee revolution succeeded so well that it invited parody. Consumers were confronted with "beans from countries that college graduates cannot find on a map," one journalist groused. Once they settled on a nationality, they still had to decide on a flavor: "chocolate, amaretto, vanilla, Irish cream, sambuca, orange, cinnamon, hazelnut, macadamia, raspberry, even choco-

---

[1]By 1991 Joanne Shaw's Detroit-based Coffee Beanery had forty-eight franchised stores, primarily in the Midwest. In New Orleans, Phyllis Jordan owned four PJ's Coffee stores and had begun to franchise. California's Pasqua chain served Italian sandwiches along with its coffee in twenty stores. In Canada, Timothy's had expanded to forty locations, while Second Cup and Van Houte had both broken one hundred stores. In Boston, George Howell's Coffee Connection had expanded to six stores. There were eighty-one Florida-based Barnie's outlets, mostly in the Southeast. In Manhattan, however, Don Schoenholt and partner Hy Chabott closed their Gillies retail stores in order to concentrate on wholesale and spend more time with their families.

late raspberry. Will it be French, American or Italian roast? Decaffeinated or regular? Which grind?" In the 1991 movie, *LA Story*, comedian Steve Martin got a laugh by ordering a "half double decaffeinated half caf with a twist of lemon."

Martin may have ordered a nonsense decaf, but the health concerns of the previous decade were mostly tossed aside as the nation crested on a caffeine high. Coffee-lover Joan Frank described "a quivering bunch of quasi-homicidal crackpots" standing in line at Peet's in San Francisco. "*Don't mess with us*," their eyes seemed to warn, "*We haven't had our coffee.*" But who cared? "Bless every drop and granule of the stuff," Frank wrote. Yes, it was addictive, but what a lovely addiction. "Coffee's the vital juice that flows through the nation's veins, and on which floats its fragile morale." A darker aspect to this coffee surge was that many yuppies were recovering cocaine addicts by the early 1990s, and they turned to maximum-strength coffee as an alternative recreational drug that they could take along with their antidepressants, antipsychotics, and other prescriptions. These aging baby boomers had come full circle, back to the drink of their parents, after a childhood of Cokes and coming-of-age with cocaine.

If this java nation had a capital, it was Seattle, the home of Starbucks and many other coffee companies.[2] "It is hard to go anywhere," one visitor observed in 1991, "whether it be the local hardware store or shopping downtown, without coming across a sidewalk espresso cart, or passing the doorway of a sleek café with a gleaming espresso machine behind the bar." Truck drivers sipped lattes from drive-throughs. A dental office served espresso to waiting patients. The television show "Frasier" placed the pretentious psychologist in Seattle, where he and his friends drink cappuccinos at the Café Nervosa.

Starbucks: The (Very) Public Years

On June 26, 1992, Starbucks launched its initial public offering (IPO), going public at $17 a share with a market capitalization (the value of all

---

[2]Toronto, the most culturally diverse city in the world, rivaled Seattle as a coffee-mad metropolis that served up traditional Ethiopian and Greek coffee as well as espresso. John McHugh, who opened his first Toronto coffeehouse in 1960, kept his Chez Cappuccino open twenty-four hours a day, while Timothy's and Second Cups stood on every other corner, with funky, independent coffeehouses in-between. Founded in 1912, Mother Parker's Tea & Coffee supplied private-label coffee to Ontario.

shares) of $273 million. Howard Schultz had paid less than $4 million for the company only five years earlier. Within three months, the stock price had reached $33, making Starbucks worth $420 million. Schultz, Dave Olsen, and other high-powered executives—many recruited in the early 1990s from fast-food behemoths—were overnight millionaires. Schultz personally held 1.1 million shares, or 8.5 percent of the stock.

Some who had built the "Starbucks experience"—a favorite Schultz phrase—did not share in the booty, however. Dawn Pinaud quit in January 1992, before the IPO, to pursue other coffee ventures, eventually winding up in London working for a chain called the Seattle Coffee Company, trying to replicate Starbucks' success. Over the next year, other veteran Starbucks employees left. Kevin Knox, who had overseen the coffee quality, quit in January 1993. Knox is bitter that Schultz misled him. "One of his favorite lines was, 'We'll never grow at the expense of our people and our coffee.' We thought the commitment was there, but we were deceived. It used to be a product-driven company. Now it's clearly a marketing-driven company."

Knox owned 200 stock options. When he resigned, the inequity was so blatant that Dave Olsen offered to give Knox a substantial chunk of his own stock. "They were also willing to pay me $70,000 a year—a $30,000 raise. But I couldn't take Dave's stock or the salary boost. I would be perceived as a bought-off corporate guy, surrounded by all these fast-food people with no passion for coffee. The soul had gone out of it." He went back to Allegro Coffee in Boulder, Colorado, feeling "exploited, burned, and turned."

Sherri Miller, another coffee devotee, stuck it out at Starbucks until 1995. "When I first worked at Starbucks in 1990, I was excited to be carrying the torch for specialty coffee," she recalls. "But then it went from a flame to a flicker. There was less and less focus on coffee, and more and more focus on profits and the bottom line. Then they wanted me to sign a non-compete clause that would have kept me from ever working in coffee again if I left Starbucks. They wanted people to think there was no world outside Starbucks. It was sort of like a cult." She left soon afterward. "There's a lot of talk about treating employees with 'dignity' at Starbucks, but the reality often isn't there."

Knox and Miller maintain that Starbucks' bean quality has suffered, an inevitable consequence of growing so quickly. At least outwardly, however, Schultz and his team remained fanatical about maintaining freshness and quality. Mary Townsend (now Williams), a widely respected specialty coffee importer, replaced Knox in 1993. Roasted beans were shipped across country in one-way valve bags. Once opened, they had to be used within a week. Leftovers were donated to local food charities. All water used to brew Starbucks coffee was purified.

Starbucks employees were indoctrinated in twenty-five hours of course work that imprinted company rules. Among them: Thou shalt brew a double espresso shot between eighteen and twenty-three seconds and serve within ten seconds of brewing it, or throw it out. The courses, called Coffee Knowledge 101, Retail Skills, Brewing the Perfect Cup and Customer Service, were taught by ultra-earnest, peppy young instructors. "Lovely! Fabulous foam!" they would burble as students created lattes. Hip young Generation Xers had to remove studs and rings from nose, lip, or tongue, nor could any employee wear cologne or perfume that might interfere with the roast aroma.

Though Schultz could have quadrupled his rate of expansion by franchising Starbucks, he chose to open only company-owned stores, except in airports or other odd spots that demanded licensure. This way he could maintain strict control over quality and training.[3]

While Starbucks may have short-changed some pioneers, the chain paid slightly above minimum wage—better than most fast-food companies—and provided an innovative benefits package that included part-time employees who worked twenty hours a week or more. As a result, employee turnover at Starbucks was only 60 percent a year, compared to the industry average of 200 percent or more. In 1991 Schultz introduced his "Bean Stock" program, in which employees—now called "partners"—received stock options worth 12 percent of their annual base pay, to be vested in one-fifth increments over a five-year period. Every year, new options would be issued. Theoretically, each employee had a stake in the company's success. Since the average employee left after a year and a half, however, most options expired worthless. Still, for those who stayed with the company for several years, Bean Stock could provide a nice little nest egg if the stock kept climbing.

---

[3]Other specialty coffee insiders claim that Starbucks's quality control has slipped, particularly in licensed airport and bookstore locations. "I watched a Starbucks *barista* pull [brew] a three-second espresso recently at the Charleston airport," complains one coffee expert.

Starbucks also became the largest U.S. corporate donor to CARE, specifying that its contributions go to help coffee-producing countries such as Indonesia, Guatemala, Kenya, and Ethiopia, pledging $500,000 a year by mid-decade. The company sold a coffee selection package called a "CARE sampler," donating a portion of the proceeds. The grateful charity responded by giving Starbucks its International Humanitarian award. Cynics pointed out that the coffee chain garnered an immense amount of positive publicity quite cheaply, donating less than 0.2 percent of its net sales.

Indeed, Schultz appeared to be a master image builder. "He knows the jargon and the case for good coffee by rote now," veteran specialty roaster Don Schoenholt observed in 1994, "and [media people] seem to drink it up." A tall, slim, photogenic man, Schultz came across as a mild-mannered executive who preferred corduroy slacks and a checkered flannel shirt to a suit. One reporter described him as "soft-spoken [with] a timid, almost apologetic manner."

"I laugh when I see pictures of Howard looking casual," a Starbucks employee snorts. "He's not Mr. Casual Laid-Back Northwesterner." As Schultz himself has said, "My story is as much one of perseverance and drive as it is of talent and luck. I willed it to happen. I took my life in my hands, learned from anyone I could, grabbed what opportunity I could, and molded my success step by step." Schultz is, according to one acquaintance, "the most competitive person I have ever met." At an annual company picnic, Schultz became so fierce during volleyball games that he nearly came to blows over contested points.

In 1989 the sociologist Ray Oldenburg published *The Great, Good Place*, a lament over the passing of community meeting places like the old country store or soda fountain. The book contained an entire chapter on coffeehouses, concluding: "The survival of the coffeehouse depends upon its ability to meet present day needs and not those of a romanticized past." Schultz loved the book and adopted Oldenburg's academic term, christening Starbucks as a "third place" beyond home or work, "an extension of people's front porch," where people could gather informally. Modern coffeehouses such as Starbucks *do* arguably provide a much-needed space for friends and strangers to meet, especially as our cultural ethos becomes more paranoid and fragmented.

Schultz, however, was not in business primarily to provide community. He was in it to win. Starbucks mounted a blitzkrieg across the country following the initial public offering, growing to one hundred sixty-five stores in 1992, two hundred seventy-two in 1993, and four hundred twenty-five in 1994. By mid-decade, the company was opening an average of a store every business day, targeting appropriate locations by studying the demographics of mail-order customers. Schultz monitored the daily sales and profit numbers for each store, calling managers to congratulate or berate them.

As soon as the non-compete clause in the sales contract expired, Schultz wrote a letter to former boss Jerry Baldwin, offering to buy Peet's. When Baldwin refused, Schultz opened a Starbucks four doors down the street from a Peet's in San Francisco. "The typical approach has been, 'Why don't you sell out to us, or we'll crush you,'" Baldwin says.

In 1993 Starbucks established a beachhead on the East Coast in Washington, D.C. On National Public Radio, Susan Stamberg doubted whether the concept would work there. "I've lived in this town for thirty years. You are in workaholic central here. I mean, this is not a town where people want to hang out and take their time." Stamberg was wrong. Washingtonians flocked to Starbucks. *Fortune* featured Schultz on its cover as the CEO of one of America's 100 fastest-growing companies. "Howard Schultz's Starbucks grinds coffee into gold," the magazine noted.

Starbucks announced its intention of rolling into Minneapolis, Boston, New York, Atlanta, Dallas, and Houston in 1994. In Boston, the shock waves reverberated at Coffee Connection headquarters, where founder George Howell feared such a move. Schultz had appeared in Howell's Cambridge office in 1990 seeking to buy him out. The answer was No. Schultz repeated the offer over the next few years. Howell despised the dark Starbucks roast. He prided himself on nuanced roasting that brings out the delicate flavor of each bean. He didn't want to see the work of two decades destroyed, but he knew that Starbucks was coming. In preparation, Howell frantically opened new Coffee Connections, beginning in 1992. By the time Starbucks announced that it would roll into Boston in 1994, Howell had opened twenty-one outlets, with plans for six new stores that year.

The *Boston Globe* reported on the looming battle. "We don't like to get in coffee wars," Starbucks marketer George Reynolds told the *Globe*. But he added, "We want to dominate." Howell responded by calling his rival "Charbucks," referring to its roast style. Then in March, Howell shocked the specialty coffee world by agreeing to sell out to Starbucks for $23 million. He realized that he would have lost some quality control in the rapid expansion. He didn't enjoy financial management. The business wasn't fun any more. "Howard Schultz promised that the Coffee Connection would remain in business, that they would keep the concept and product unaltered," Howell recalls ruefully.

Former Coffee Connection employee Dave Tilgner remembers that Howard Schultz, along with Starbucks executives Orin Smith and Howard Behar, flew in the day after Howell told them of the sale. "They reassured us as a group that they were not buying us to shut us down or remove competition." Within two years, however, all of the Coffee Connections were converted to Starbucks outlets, many Coffee Connection employees were terminated, and the roast profile shifted toward the dark end of the spectrum. Requiring a centralized roasting plant on the East Coast, Starbucks opened a facility in York, Pennsylvania, shutting down the Boston Coffee Connection plant.

The Starbucks juggernaut appeared unstoppable, though some financial analysts worried about its high price-to-earnings ratio. Despite the occasional stock dip, however, Starbucks continued to confound critics. The enterprise moved at "warp speed," as *Business Week* observed, swiftly conquering New York City. In 1995 Starbucks opened in Pittsburgh, Las Vegas, San Antonio, Philadelphia, Cincinnati, Baltimore, and Austin for a total of six hundred seventy-six stores by year's end. The following year witnessed the thousandth Starbucks, one of which was an outlet in Tokyo. Howard Schultz was there, witnessing Japanese lined up in 95° weather for the Starbucks Experience. He cried.

Through shrewd joint partnerships, Starbucks spread its fame and logo while making even more money. With Pepsi, it created Mazagran, a carbonated coffee drink, its first flop, but followed that with Frappuccino, a cold milky coffee offering that took off in supermarkets. Teaming with Redhook Ale Brewery, the company came out with Double Black Stout, a coffee-flavored beer. Dreyer's produced a Starbucks coffee ice cream that swiftly became the best-selling brand of that flavor. Starbucks even issued its own music, *Blue Note Blend*, a jazz CD for easy listening and coffee sipping, and *Songs of the Siren*, a collection of women singers. It opened a slick web site. In Barnes & Noble superstores in the United States and in Chapters bookstores in Canada, customers could sip Starbucks coffee while reading in a comfortable café.

Starbucks seemed to be everywhere. It was in the air with United Airlines and Canadian Airlines, partnered with Oprah Winfrey to promote literacy, opened stores in Singapore, Hawaii, the Philippines, Taiwan, and Korea, made deals with hotel chains and cruise lines, bought a piece of a bagel chain, and entered test markets in supermarkets. *Starbucks* became a household word without mounting a national advertising campaign. Indeed, the company spent less than $10 million on advertising in its first twenty-five years. It was a veritable "word-of-mouth wonder," as a stunned *Advertising Age* reporter put it. Not only that, it *made* money while advertising itself, selling mugs, thermoses, and canisters with the emblazoned logo. In 1994 Dave Olsen wrote *Starbucks Passion for Coffee*, a coffee primer with recipes that was sold by Sunset Books, followed by *Starbucks Pleasures of Summer* the following year.

Two years later, Howard Schultz told his story (cowritten with a *Business Week* reporter) in *Pour Your Heart Into It: How Starbucks Built a Company One Cup at a Time*, donating the proceeds to the newly formed Starbucks Foundation. The book is a self-congratulatory Horatio Alger story in which Schultz writes, "What were the odds against me, a kid from the Projects?" But he succeeded because "I dared to dream big dreams, and then I willed them to happen." Despite his triumph, however, Schultz tells the reader, "I'm still running, chasing after something nobody else could ever see." He also claimed to "leave my ego at the door," though he couldn't resist adding, "I like to think of myself as a visionary."

On April 1, 1996, National Public Radio's "All Things Considered" reported: "Starbucks will soon announce their plans to build a pipeline costing more than a billion dollars, a pipeline thousands of miles long from Seattle to the East Coast, with branches to Boston and New York and Washington, a pipeline that will carry freshly roasted coffee beans." A coffee commentator observed, "the company really wants to go on to put tiny multimedia pipelines right into your house." It's a testament to Starbucks' ubiquity that many people initially believed that this April Fool's hoax was a real news story.

Deflecting the Critics

Starbucks' overwhelming success, with its aggressive tactics, inevitably brought criticism along with adulation. Specialty competitors complained that Starbucks used predatory retail tactics, frequently opening outlets directly across the street from their stores. In New York, for instance, Starbucks opened near Timothy's, Seattle Bean, Oren's Daily Roast, and New World Coffee outlets, prompting a *New York Times* reporter to call it "the Goliath of the country's coffee bars, the Big Bean, if you will." She quoted a city resident who complained, "I keep thinking of Starbucks as an elegant McDonald's."

When Starbucks sued Second Cup for allegedly copying the look and feel of its stores, the Canadian company countersued, accusing Starbucks of "bully tactics." Both suits were settled out of court. By 1996 the backlash against Starbucks forced it to abandon colonization plans in parts of San Francisco, Los Angeles, Toronto, and Minneapolis, following well-publicized community protests. In Vancouver, protesters greeted Starbucks with paint bombs and abusive graffiti. The company's dilemma was "how to get big and stay friendly at the same time," noted a *Newsweek* reporter.

It certainly didn't convey a friendly image when the landlord of Chicago's venerable Scenes Coffee House refused to renew its lease while simultaneously renting space in the same building to a new Starbucks. In Bethesda, Maryland, Starbucks offered to top Quartermaine Coffee Roasters' lease. When the landlord rejected its offer, Starbucks tried to buy the entire building.

Defensive Starbucks executives denied they were targeting competitors, though they refused to comment on specific cases. "It has never been Starbucks' intention to put anyone out of business, and we adhere to standard real estate practices when obtaining new locations," a public relations spokesman said. The company simply looked for optimal locations. Besides, "having competitors nearby does nothing but increase the awareness of coffee in general."

The *Utne Reader* complained that while Starbucks boasted of its communal nature, the acoustics produced by antiseptic tile floors, wood paneling, and plate-glass windows were "dismal," and that the uncomfortable short-backed chairs and tiny tables did not encourage customers to linger. "I hate this place," a man complained while standing in a Starbucks line. "It's expensive and crowded and I can't speak the language." Yet he waited for a latte and returned later for another.

Despite its critics' complaints, it was clear that Starbucks was doing something right. The average customer visited Starbucks eighteen times a month, and 10 percent came twice a day. "If you walk into any Starbucks store," Howard Schultz said, "you see little vignettes. Of business people having meetings. A mother and her child in a stroller. You see single people actually meeting there." He was right, though far more frequently, people came there seeking communal solitude. "The coffeehouse is the ideal place," as a Viennese wit once put it, "for people who want to be alone but need company for it."

Owing to its ubiquity, Starbucks perhaps has attracted an unwarranted amount of criticism. It certainly deserves credit for introducing many Americans to high-quality coffee and for rejuvenating the image of a bean that had been cheapened and commoditized. "It always has baffled me," Howard Schultz commented in 1997, "that in America for some reason, there are people who passionately root for the underdog to succeed, and when the underdog reaches a level of success, some of those same people find a need to tear it down." Specialty coffee veteran Dan Cox called for an end to "Starbucks bashing," pointing out that the brand has excellent management, provides consistent quality, treats its employees well, gives back to the community, and has been innovative within the industry.

Within a few short years, Howard Schultz built a coffee empire, a billion-dollar-a-year business with only the earth's boundaries as a limit. "Starbucks is going to be a global brand," Schultz predicts, "in the same genre as Coke and Disney." Comedian Jay Leno thinks it may go even farther. He showed his audience a satellite picture of life on Mars—where there was already a Starbucks.

Brothers Gourmet Coffee: A Cautionary Tale

As the Starbucks phenomenon unfolded, other specialty coffee entrepreneurs rushed to replicate its growth. In the free-for-all atmosphere, greed sometimes overwhelmed sound management decisions. Since 1992, most specialty coffee companies that have gone public—Green Mountain Coffee Roasters, Java Centrale, New World Coffee, Diedrich, Thanksgiving, and White Mountain—have seen their stock stagnate or decline. None provided a more disastrous example than Brothers Gourmet Coffee, a good idea gone bad.

Michael Chu, a young financial wheeler-dealer for conglomerate First Pacific, was attracted by the specialty coffee movement in the late 1980s when he served simultaneously on the boards of a boutique advertising firm, a commodity trading house, and a gourmet food store. "I saw the growth in 'affordable luxuries,'" Chu recalls. He realized that whole-bean sales were exploding, and that as supermarket chains expanded, they created a "demand pull" that was difficult for the small whole roasters to fulfill. "Typically, these multigenerational family businesses were not equipped with the financial or human capital to deal with rapid growth."

In 1989 Chu quit First Pacific and joined with other investors to form Specialty Coffee Holdings. In quick succession, they bought two regional family roasters—Pittsburgh's Nicholas Coffee in 1990 for just over $9 million, and New Hampshire's Elkin Coffee the following March for nearly $16 million. Wealthy from the sales, Nick Nicholas and Marty Elkin semiretired and took places on the board, while Mike Sullivan, a go-getter at Elkin, became the CEO.

At the time, Chu didn't see much future in retail coffee chains. "My favorite was Coffee Connection, but I didn't see it as a growth vehicle. Shame on me. Starbucks was on no one's radar screen." With East Coast strength established, Chu scoured the rest of the country, visiting dozens of regional roasters. "I came across Brothers out in Colorado. It was rapidly growing, run by an erudite guy, Dennis Boyer, and his younger brother, Sam."

Trained in coffee by their father, Bill Boyer, the two brothers split off to a separate facility in 1985 to specialize in whole bean supermarket sales. "My father wanted a good, solid, local, family business. The sky was the limit for me," Dennis Boyer recalls. "They were on the fast track," observes Jim Twiford, who still works for Bill Boyer and clearly is bitter at the sons' defection. The boys sued their father for possession of the Boyer name and, when they lost in 1988, they changed the name to Brothers Gourmet.

The Boyer brothers built their business quickly through innovative, imaginative approaches, creating attractive, spill-free store dispensers, a new method of flavoring freshly roasted coffee, and high-quality four-ply laminate packages. They were the first to put flavored coffee in a can, which gained entree to many new supermarkets. By the time Michael Chu approached them, Brothers was grossing $30 million a year, with a toehold in almost every state.

At the end of 1992, with backing from J. H. Whitney, a Connecticut private equity group, Chu's organization bought Brothers for over $29 million.[4] "With their inclusion, we were a substantial company," Chu says. "So the focus shifted from acquisitions to operations." Faced with a choice of Mike Sullivan or Dennis Boyer to head the enterprise, Chu chose Boyer. "He was the right age—early forties—and had the fire in the belly."[5] They changed the name to Gourmet Coffees of America, which had more of an "operating ring" to it, but Boyer soon changed it again to Brothers Gourmet Coffee, intending to create a national brand strategy. Chu disagreed, wanting to maintain strong regional identities, but by that time he was focusing on a new noncoffee venture. Having put the pieces together, Chu resigned from the board in May 1993, just before Brothers purchased California-based Hillside Coffee, which had spent a brief time under Chock full o' Nuts ownership, for $41.8 million.[6]

By now, Starbucks had appeared on *everyone's* radar screen, having gone public and declared its intention to rule the world. Every bit as aggressive as Howard Schultz, Dennis Boyer dreamed big too and decided that Brothers should launch into retail as well as wholesale. "In 1993 it was not a foregone conclusion that Starbucks would dominate," Boyer recalls. Howard Schultz was already selling his discount Meridian brand in the Costco chain, and the Starbucks 1993 annual report noted that "supermarkets offer customers the convenience of not having to make a separate trip to [our] stores." Schultz clearly had his eye on the grocery store shelf. Boyer knew this and was determined to mount a challenge to Starbucks.

Boyer cast his eye on Gloria Jean's, which had nearly as many outlets as Starbucks at the time. Owner Ed Kvetko wasn't planning to sell, though. "I owned 100 percent of the company and was looking to go public." He was franchising new stores at the rate of twenty-five a year, but franchisees didn't maintain quality, sometimes buying inferior beans. "It was like raising a child," recalls former Kvetko assistant Guy Wood. "After we educated them, they immediately became smarter

---

[4] Among the main investors were J. Peter Grace and J. P. Bolduc of W. R. Grace & Company, and William E. Simon, former U.S. Secretary of the Treasury.

[5] Mike Sullivan quit to form Comfort Foods, his own Massachusetts coffee company.

[6] Steve Schulman, the Hillside founder, had the same vision as Michael Chu back in 1989, but his venture on Wall Street ended in disaster and he was forced to sell to Chock full o' Nuts in 1991. "It was not a marriage made in heaven," is all he will say about the brief association. In 1993, when Chock sold Hillside (for a huge profit) to the Brothers consortium, Schulman hoped that his vision might at last come to pass.

than us." With the new trend toward cappuccinos and lattes rather than whole bean sales, the Gloria Jean mall locations were a liability, since malls were locked tight early in the morning and late at night—just when people descended on Starbucks and other coffeehouses.

Such was the situation when a group of investment bankers for Brothers visited Ed Kvetko in Illinois late in 1993. "We'd like to buy your company," the banker said. Kvetko stared him down sternly and said, "The company is not for sale." The banker said, "We'll give you $32.5 million." The flabbergasted Kvetko blurted out, "You just bought yourself a fucking company!" Now retired in Boca Raton, Florida, he says, "I kiss the Brothers Coffee displays every time I go by them."

A month after the Gloria Jean's purchase, Brothers went public with a splash at $20 a share. Oversubscribed, the stock lifted briefly to $22, when most of the institutional fund buyers took their profits and drove it back to $14 or so, where it languished, despite buy recommendations from experienced beverage analysts like Emanuel Goldman at PaineWebber. "There is only one company with a significant national presence in both the wholesale and retail (coffee house) sector," Goldman noted in February 1994, "namely, Brothers Gourmet Coffee."

The heady atmosphere of new acquisitions, media attention, rubbing shoulders with wealthy venture capitalists, and power appeared to go to Dennis Boyer's head. Having earned a Ph.D. in education, he insisted on being called Dr. Boyer. He uprooted the company base, moving to sumptuous quarters in Boca Raton, Florida, ostensibly for closer proximity to his investors and the port of Miami, and to avoid showing "favoritism" to Denver. Some cynics felt he just wanted to live there and take up sailing. Dan Cox, who joined Brothers as their coffee-quality expert, recalls that when they conducted a blind taste test to choose flavoring companies, the company Boyer favored lost, so he ordered another test. "This is a charade," Cox said. "Go ahead and pick the one you want." Cox left soon afterward to found Coffee Enterprises, his own consulting firm.

Marty Elkin, Ed Kvetko, and Nick Nicholas watched helplessly as their roasting facilities were shut down and years of brand loyalty were destroyed. While the Hillside plant never shut down, its output fell from 7 million to 2.5 million pounds. "Why take a successful company with fifteen years in the marketplace and destroy it?" asks an anguished Steve Schulman, who founded Hillside in 1977. "It was insane. I had a fantastic staff. They closed our office and fired nearly everyone. Just the cost of converting all of the packages, headers, trucks, and literature, all the way down the line, to say 'Brothers' was in the tens of millions of dollars. They ruined our distribution system. They had tremendous out-of-stock problems, unable to deliver product on time. Angry customers wanted to know where their favorite coffee had gone. Brothers made every mistake it was possible to make."

Brothers eventually sold the once-vibrant New Hampshire coffee service division to Superior, owned by Sara Lee. Dennis Boyer centralized Brothers' roasting in Houston in the old Maryland Club plant with its continuous roaster that did not allow for selective treatment of different types of beans.[7] The company had to ship all green coffee to Houston, roast it, then ship it all over the country again. Worse still, Brothers tried to cut corners by cheapening the blend, assuming customers wouldn't notice the difference.

Buoyant and brimming with confidence, Boyer announced that he would open a retail chain of Brothers coffeehouses, beginning in the new Denver airport, in addition to expanding the Gloria Jean's mall outlets. He furnished the new Brothers outlets sumptuously at an average cost of $350,000 per store. Every time he spoke to a reporter, his vision expanded. Brothers would have seven hundred retail outlets by 1997. "We're committed to being the biggest and best gourmet coffee company. We've got a compounded growth rate of 20 percent in annual revenues. I would not stand for anything less."

Boyer wrote *The Coffee Companion*, a disjointed, self-published book describing his "myriad dreams . . . of wealth enough to put poverty ever behind me and freedom always before me." He included an entire chapter describing his trek down the aisles of a supermarket with three of his seven children. "Why am I even here?" he wrote. "After all, I'm the 'president' of this big coffee business of ours. Are presidents supposed to buy groceries?" When Dennis Boyer shaved his mustache, Brothers changed the label on the bags (which featured the two brothers) to reflect his new look.

Throughout 1994, analysts and the media continued to praise Brothers, despite 1992 and 1993 net losses of $10.3 million and $7.2 million, respectively. Initial losses were to be expected. Boyer and his board plowed ahead, opening twenty-five Brothers retail stores. "This was the

---

[7]After Coca-Cola sold its Houston coffee plant in 1988, the plant bounced from one owner to another until it landed with Procter & Gamble, which dumped it on Brothers.

sexy, high-profile part of the business," Boyer recalls. Wall Street loved the one-brand concept, with fancy new Brothers outlets providing a visible presence. Brothers announced a deal with Randall's Food Markets in Houston, where they would not only sell beans but operate mini coffee bars, offering lattes and cappuccinos to shoppers. The company purchased Brio Coffees, a tiny Denver specialty chain, and made a deal with Publix Supermarkets to place their coffees in one hundred fifty Florida stores. *Inc.* magazine named Brothers one of its fastest-growing small companies. In August 1994 a *Miami Herald* headline boasted, "Brothers Gourmet Brews a 290 percent Leap in Income," based on second-quarter reports. Stock bounced up sharply at the end of February 1995 when Dennis Boyer let it be known that he had received inquiries from new outside investors and was exploring "strategic alliances and other possible transactions."

A month later, Brothers posted a $344,000 loss for the last quarter, and the stock tumbled below $12 a share. In May, with a reported loss of $3.5 million, the stock dropped again. "It came as a shock to me," Boyer recalls. "Only hours before the board meeting, we got the final numbers, and I saw how compromised we were." Finances were never Boyer's strong suit. "I hired good people and tried not to get in their way."

In June, the chairman of the board of directors announced the company's plan to sell all two hundred fifty coffee outlets. A month later, forty-four-year-old Dennis Boyer resigned. "I was not forced out," he insists. "I found myself in a less desirable situation, and life is too short for killing yourself." As the share price fell below $8, Boyer was "unavailable for comment," off sailing his sixty-five-foot catamaran.

Only after Boyer's departure did the extent of the disaster become apparent. New president David Vermylen, who came from Mother's Cookies, sold the two hundred twenty-four Gloria Jean's to Canada's Second Cup chain, then its other retail outlets to California's Diedrich Coffee. Brothers took a whopping $46.5 million second-quarter loss due to a "special charge" against earnings and soon closed its Denver roasting plant, laying off thirty-five employees. As the share price plummeted to $4, three class-action lawsuits filed by anguished stockholders tried to pry money out of the company.

In January 1996, after only six months as president, Vermylen deserted what appeared to be a sinking ship, going back to cookies at Keebler. Chief financial officer Donald Breen took over and has made a valiant effort to revive Brothers' fortunes. Late in 1996 he settled the shareholder suits for $8.5 million. Though Brothers remained a major player in whole-bean supermarket coffee, the stock drifted ever lower, down to 12.5 cents by August 1998, when Brothers filed for Chapter 11 bankruptcy and NASDAQ delisted its stock. That same year, Dennis Boyer was named director of Florida Atlantic University's Center for Entrepreneurship, a center he helped to fund.

In hindsight, Michael Chu and his investors perhaps should have heeded warning flags. "Dennis and Sam [Boyer] have no business plans or budgets because they want to be flexible in responding to changing market demands," wrote a reporter in *Colorado Business* in 1990. Chu certainly deserves credit for trying. His strategy was sound. He simply chose the wrong CEO, and the board of directors supported Boyer's mistakes.

A Maturing Market

By mid decade, there were signs that the specialty revolution had reached a plateau. While coffeehouses were still popping up—even a Mocha Joe's in Peoria—the number of espresso carts in Seattle actually declined somewhat, and analysts began to talk about "saturation." In rebuttal, the Specialty Coffee Association of America estimated that, while over four thousand specialty outlets existed in 1995, there would be ten thousand by the turn of the century.

From less than a hundred in 1985, SCAA membership had swelled into the thousands a decade later. Its annual convention turned into a gigantic marketing opportunity for suppliers of roasters, brewers, flavors, T-shirts with coffee messages, mugs, books, and every other conceivable device having anything remotely to do with coffee. Members listened not only to coffee experts but to slick motivational speakers who told them how to succeed with New Age hoopla. Veterans complained that neophytes had dollar signs in their eyes instead of coffee beans. Since it cost around $250,000 to open a coffee bar, perhaps that was understandable.

A new round of coffee books for the would-be connoisseur flooded bookstores.[8] Magazines devoted to coffee—*Coffee Journal, Cups, Café Olé,*

---

[8]In the 1990s Timothy Castle, Corby Kummer, Kevin Knox and Julie Huffaker, Kenneth Davids, Ian Bersten, Alain Stella, Francesco and Riccardo Illy, and others wrote books on coffee. (See bibliography.)

Coffee Culture, Fresh Cup, Literal Latte, and others—appeared in the 1990s. Most vanished as quickly as the morning cup of coffee, but a few survived with loyal readerships. Artists and writers parodied their own obsession. "I floated perpetually three feet above the floor and could telekinetically transport myself," wrote one Oregonian. "I was a tormented soul. I could never get enough of the stuff." Eventually he graduated to "Beelzebub's Black Bile." Another writer explained that he was a "reverse coffee snob," drinking terrible coffee at the local diner to avoid the pretentious Starbucks crowd.

Even the diner was likely to serve espresso. In California, McDonald's did. The 7-Eleven chain unveiled a Cafe Select line of eighteen flavored coffees, advertising that it was "Not the Same Old Grind." In Chicago, the White Hen Pantry advertised itself as "the coffee place." Dunkin' Donuts certainly didn't have the upscale panache or special drink jargon of Starbucks, but since its inception in 1948 as the Open Kettle, it always served excellent coffee. In 1983 it began to sell whole beans and by 1995, with over three thousand franchised outlets, it was actually a "coffee company disguised as a donut company," as one coffee expert described it. So was Tim Hortons, a similar Canadian chain.

The battle over whole beans in the supermarket was another sign of maturity. In the 1980s grocers were overjoyed to stock little-known specialty whole beans, since they offered a much larger profit margin than canned coffee. But as the competition mounted between Brothers, Millstone, Sark's–Nestlé, Hillside, Elkin, A & P, Green Mountain, Coffee Bean International, First Colony, Royal Cup, and others, the supermarkets began to demand discounts in the form of slotting allowances, gate fees, promotions, and free first-time bin fills—all trade practices that charged coffee roasters simply to get their beans onto shelves. "That's one of the reasons I was ready to sell," Marty Elkin admits. "It was becoming too competitive, with a lot of players, price-cutting, and deals."

By the mid 1990s business consultants were taking note of the specialty trend. In *Value Migration,* Adrian Slywotzky argues that "the customer was not driving decision-making at P & G, General Foods, or Nestlé," where coffee had become commoditized, while the smaller gourmet roasters were providing the value that had "migrated" from the big boys. Whole-bean gourmet coffee, and its associated beverages, provided identifiable status that mass marketers neglected. "A regional roaster launching a cafe design in 1991, staying one step behind Starbucks, could have built a national brand," Slywotzsky observes. "By

1994, it was too late." Procter & Gamble, which had introduced new brands "more skillfully than anybody else," missed the boat this time. "P & G could afford to invest $50–$100 million over two years to build a new national brand."

While *Value Migration* was at the printer, Procter & Gamble bought Millstone in December 1995 for an undisclosed sum.[9] By that time, founder Phil Johnson had grown Millstone to a seminational brand with roasting plants in Washington and Kentucky and its own truck fleet, selling 1.5 million pounds per month and grossing over $40 million annually. Disgusted with the slotting allowance extortion, Johnson approached all three major roasters offering to sell, and P & G bit. Johnson kept his Western roasting plant and continued to provide beans to Millstone.

It appeared that another business cycle was beginning. Just as the traditional coffee industry had gone through fragmented growth and merger, the specialty movement would, in its maturity, consolidate. In the process, would it also lose its soul?

---

[9]Business reporters guessed that Procter & Gamble paid anywhere from $20 million to $100 million for Millstone.

19

FINAL GROUNDS

Coffee is turning out to be quite a cosmic issue—and the way it's grown, marketed, and consumed has implications for the environmental health of the world.

–Russell Greenberg, Director,
Smithsonian Migratory Bird Center, 1996

"These are Coffee People. They pick coffee to buy food. They say the coffee price is bad. So the pay is too low to buy food. This village is fucked."

–*Men With Guns*, film by John Sayles (1997)

"Yes, it's excellent coffee, with a distinctive, mysterious taste. Would you like to try a cup?"

John Martinez is talking about Kopi Luwak, the rare Sumatran beans he sells for $300 a pound to mail-order customers. A Jamaican native, Martinez comes from a long line of coffee men, beginning with his great-grandfather, Pedro Martinez, a Spanish sea captain who traded coffee in the nineteenth century. In 1980 John Martinez set up shop in Atlanta, Georgia, and has been seeking out fine coffees for his mail-order customers ever since.

I have heard about Kopi Luwak, the unusual brew he is offering me. Like many fine beans, those that made this cup were processed by the "wet method," but in this case, removal of the pulp, mucilage, and parchment was all natural, performed as the cherry progressed through the gut of the palm civet, *paradoxorus hermaphroditus* (in Indonesian parlance, *luwak*), also known as a civet cat. Near its sexual organs, this mammal possesses a gland that secretes a musky oil long prized in the perfume industry. Indeed, Shakespeare's King Lear asked for some civet to "sweeten my imagination." A major dose isn't so sweet, however. Like a skunk, the palm civet uses it to spray enemies.

I am certainly curious and accept a cup, which I figure is worth more than $7. Bending over it, I catch a sweet, tantalizing aroma. Then I take a sip. A full-bodied coffee, it does indeed have an unusual taste—earthy? pungent? gutsy?—that lingers in the mouth long after the final sip. I don't think I would pay $300 a pound for the beans. In fact, I don't think I would pay anything.

But that's one thing I have learned through my coffee research: One consumer's poison is another's nectar. Harsh, fermented Rioy Brazilian beans, despised by most connoisseurs, are prized by the Greeks. The French love their coffee adulterated with chicory. Some consumers swear by Monsooned Malabar, Indian beans aged and humidified in those famed winds. Then there's the psychological factor. The rarer the bean the more expensive and desirable. Hence, Hawaiian Kona and Jamaican Blue Mountain command premium prices, even though most coffee experts consider them bland in comparison to Guatemalan Antigua or Kenya AA. Why the higher price then? In a good year, the Hawaiians and Jamaicans produce balanced, aromatic brews that appeal to just about any coffee lover. Primarily, however, the beans are scarce, and Japanese buyers have made them scarcer by buying most of the small production.[1]

John Martinez originally sold Kopi Luwak primarily "to show that my Jamaica Blue Mountain beans weren't so expensive at $40 a pound." For his efforts, he won the Ig Nobel Prize in Nutrition, a gag award created in memory of the mythical Ignatius Nobel. At the 1995 ceremony at Harvard University, Martinez recited his "Ode to the Luwak," which ended with the quatrain:

> Luwak! Luwak! After you've gorged,
> A new taste sensation has been forged.
> For all gathered here this is the scoop:
> We're drinking coffee made from your poop!

---

[1]Puerto Rican Yauco Selecto and Haitian Bleu are attempting to establish an upscale image for their Caribbean beans, ventures that could substantially boost their economies. In the case of Haiti, the poorest country in the Western Hemisphere, the project could save lives as well as trees.

Martinez specializes in fine, unblended estate coffees, likening them to wine. Indeed, the taste of coffee grown on a particular estate varies depending on the type of tree, soil, atmospheric conditions, and processing. "Some coffees bring with them the smells of the forests they grew near," rhapsodizes coffee expert Tim Castle, "the taste of the water that soaked their roots, the flavors of the fruits that grew near them. . . . Some coffees, when you taste them, transport you back to their birthplace."

The Kona Kai Scandal

Such romancing of the bean sounds nice, but in some cases it obviously isn't. Take the case of Michael Norton, owner of Kona Kai Farms, a California importer specializing in the costly Hawaiian beans. According to the company brochure, "the flavor is unique—full bodied, slightly acidic, mellow and straightforward." Well, maybe not all that straightforward. It turns out that for years Norton fooled just about everyone, buying cheap Panamanian and Costa Rican beans, rebagging them as Kona, and selling them at a huge profit.

When the story broke late in 1996, it sent shock waves through the specialty industry. Roasters knew that "Kona blend" had to contain only 10 percent Hawaiian beans, and that "Kona style" didn't necessarily have *any*, but Norton practiced outright deception. In addition, Mary Townsend (now Williams), a well-respected coffee broker, was at least indirectly involved. While working for Klein Brothers before going to Starbucks as the company's coffee buyer, Townsend had arranged for Norton to buy Panamanian beans from Grace Meña of Deli Café, a Central American exporter. It is unclear, however, whether Townsend or Meña knew that Norton was reselling the beans fraudulently. Many major roasters bought Kona Kai beans, including Peet's, Hills Brothers, Peerless, Brothers, Ueshima Coffee Company, and others, but they could hardly have been expected to know they were buying the wrong beans.

"They got what they bought—coffee," Norton told a former colleague in a secretly taped phone conversation. His lawyer was equally unrepentant. "The bottom line is that Michael Norton was selling high-quality coffee, and his customers were always happy with his product." Embarrassed coffee experts publicly admitted that even real Kona coffee didn't thrill them. "I must confess I didn't pay that much attention," Jim

Reynolds at Peet's told a reporter. "It tasted dull and uninteresting like Kona coffee, so I assumed it *was* Kona coffee."

To make sure the same thing doesn't happen to bona fide Jamaica Blue Mountain coffee, growers ship it in inscribed wooden barrels. After John Martinez has roasted the beans, he reduces the barrels to splinters to make sure they are not improperly reused.

La Minita: A Coffee City-State

John Martinez buys several of his estate coffees from Bill McAlpin, who grows coffee at La Minita, his showplace Costa Rican farm. McAlpin, an imposing man of six foot three whose considerable girth adds to his air of authority, has built a well-deserved reputation for delivering quality coffee. Though McAlpin is a U.S. citizen, he grew up in Latin America, where his financier father owned various businesses, including the land where his son now grows coffee. The younger McAlpin was educated in French-speaking Swiss schools, studying economics and philosophy, then worked on an Argentine cattle farm for a while before he began to grow coffee for his father in Costa Rica in 1974, buying him out a few years later.

Determined to set his beans apart from the common run, in 1987 Bill McAlpin, then thirty-six, culled the best of the best, shipped two hundred bags to Virginia, rented a U-Haul truck, and took to the road. With wife Carole Kurtz, he toured eastern U.S. specialty roasters to introduce them to his superb beans. His most important new customer was George Howell at Boston's Coffee Connection, where he met a soulmate. In the following years, Howell convinced McAlpin to seek out, improve, and sell special coffees from Guatemala and Colombia as well.

La Minita Tarrazu beans command a constant premium of $3.99 a pound, regardless of the gyrations of the price on the exchange. Only a small portion (around 15 percent) of the beans grown on the farm qualify, however. The rest are pegged to the market, albeit well above the regular price. In a way, McAlpin's extraordinary success mirrors Starbucks, since he too does not pay for most of his publicity. Customers are invited to visit La Minita, where they see the model farm in action, eat wonderful food along with their coffee, admire the 200-foot waterfall, visit the farm's medical clinic, and meet some of the apparently contented laborers. They can also take their own turn at harvesting.

La Minita was the capstone of my month-long coffee tour of Central America in January 1997. I got off to a rocky start. When McAlpin discovered I had picked up a few coffee beans from other countries along the way, he insisted that I conduct a strip search of myself and go through my luggage. *Broca,* little black bugs that eat coffee beans, have not reached Costa Rica, and I certainly didn't want to be the lethal carrier. Once at the farm, though, all cares fell away in the mountain paradise of the Tarrazu region, where I stayed in a guest house at 5,000 feet above sea level.

I woke at 6:00 A.M. to the sounds of workers laughing on the way to work. When I got up, the sunrise was just lighting the 9,500-foot mountain across the valley. After breakfast, the other guests and I hiked down to the river that forms one border of the plantation, passing the heavily laden coffee trees and the occasional orange tree, planted for the workers' refreshment. Then we took a turn at harvesting on the steeply terraced slopes. In an hour, I earned enough to buy two bags of peanuts at the commissary.

Then we joined the *real* harvesters, who were done by 2:00 P.M. I talked to Angel Martin Granados, a young man who told me, through a translator, that he had picked 122 *cajuelas* (66 gallons) that day, earning him around $15. After working at La Minita for three years, he had saved enough to buy a house and plant his own small coffee plot.

Bill McAlpin presides over his domain as a benign dictator, demanding obsessive attention to quality and detail. He spends the off-season at his summer home in Bar Harbor, Maine, but even from there, he directs the farm, which he considers a "classic city-state" that provides a model for the rest of the world—which is going straight to hell as far as he can see. He worries about overpopulation, crime, environmental degradation. "Perhaps we've passed our time," he told me over a gourmet dinner he had prepared. "Human beings are less than a pimple on the ass of history."

In a 1995 speech to his workers, McAlpin described La Minita as "a single living organism" where he tried to provide "a secure working and social habitat." Food, shelter, health, security, liberty, and spiritual activity were what the farm offered, he said, in contrast to the rest of the world. McAlpin's idealism extends to his coffee. Rather than use herbicides, his workers weed the 800 acres of coffee with machetes. Except in extraordinary circumstances, he avoids insecticides. Instead, the trees are regularly sprayed with a "coffee aphrodisiac" of boron, zinc, and copper. The soil is tested twice a year. Shade trees help by fixing nitrogen and shedding leaves for mulch, but fertilizer is also dispensed regularly.

Despite McAlpin's concern for social and environmental issues, he insists that over the long haul, he is simply being pragmatic. He treats his workers well because it is good business. He scorns fair trade coffee, which he believes asks people to purchase coffee out of guilt. "I don't want anyone to buy La Minita because of the way we grew it. I want them to buy it because it is superior coffee." He accuses the well-intentioned folks at Equal Exchange and Max Havelaar of "cultural imperialism," blasting those who blend "suffering, pain and humiliation" into the beans they sell to "the affluent but guilt-ridden, Birkenstock shod, politically correct, myopically naive creature known as the 'huppy'" –whom he defines as a combination hippie–yuppy.

Coffee Kids and the Coyotes

Bill McAlpin wishes that *all* coffee growers could command the same premium as La Minita. Then the social inequities built into the system could solve themselves. Unfortunately, the realities of the marketplace make this almost impossible. When I visited Betty Hannstein Adams at her *Finca Oriflama* in western Guatemala, we discussed social issues at length. Her father and grandfather had farmed the same land.

Yes, it was true that she paid her laborers about $3 a day. She couldn't pay them more than other coffee farmers without pricing her beans out of the market. The profit margin was narrow, and the volatile price swings made planning difficult. After the 1989 collapse of the International Coffee Agreement, for instance, the farm lost money for years, until declining worldwide production and a Brazilian frost drove the price up again briefly in 1994. When we talked early in 1997, the price was heading up again. As Adams figured it, coffee would have to fetch about $4.50 more per pound to enable farmers to pay their workers the U.S. minimum wage of $5.15 an hour. That wouldn't be unreasonable. Even at $15 a pound for roasted specialty beans, consumers could enjoy a cup of properly brewed coffee for about 37 cents–not much when you consider the cost of a soft drink.

Alfred Peet, a Dutch immigrant, fathered the U. S. specialty coffee movement at his Berkeley coffee shop, which opened in 1966. He is shown here cupping coffee in Kenya.

Despite this 1970 effort to attract the baby boom hippies, the coffee industry lost out to the Pepsi Generation.

In 1971, partners Jerry Baldwin, Gordon Bowker, and Zev Siegl (*left to right*) founded Starbucks in Seattle, selling fresh-roasted whole beans to local customers.

In the early 1970s, Erna Knutsen fought her way into the male-dominated cupping room and became the doyenne of specialty coffee importers, seeking out her "green jewels."

In the 1970s, conscience-stricken liberals began to worry more about the plight of the *campesino,* who often received starvation wages while middle-men and roasters profited. This cartoon appeared in 1976.

After starring in *Father Knows Best* and *Marcus Welby, MD,* actor Robert Young was the perfect pitchman for Sanka decaf, dispensing fatherly medical advice to avoid caffeine—even though in real life he suffered from depression and alcoholism.

Folger's Mrs. Olson, played by actress Virginia Christine, gave motherly advice to save coffee and marriages.

In 1977, following the Black Frost in Brazil, coffee prices rose quickly, bringing consumer protests and congressional hearings.

BRING PRICES DOWN DON'T DRINK COFFEE

COFFEE
The Backbone of Uganda's Economy

"EMMWANYI ZANGE NNUNGI NNYO!!"

These may be strange words to you but in Uganda it is our way of saying, "Mine is an excellent crop of coffee." Uganda is situated at the base of the mighty river Nile and offers ideal climatical conditions for growing coffee. It is the largest coffee producer in the Commonwealth with a production of almost 180,000 tons of carefully nurtured coffee, mainly robusta, every year. Estimated production for the current year is 188,000 tons.

further details from:

The Secretary,

COFFEE MARKETING BOARD
P. O. Box 2853,
KAMPALA (Uganda)

Ugandan coffee was indeed the country's economic mainstain. Unfortunately, dictator Idi Amin relied on coffee earnings to fund his genocidal regime.

When Folger's rolled East to challenge Maxwell House in the 1970s, a clever cartoonist portrayed Mrs.Olson duking it out with Aunt Cora, the Maxwell House busybody.

THE FAR SIDE By GARY LARSON

That settles it, Carl! . . . From now on, you're getting only decaffeinated coffee!

In this Far Side cartoon, Gary Larson lampooned health concerns over caffeine, which peaked in the early 1980s.

Young coffee idealists like Don Schoenholt, shown here in 1981, led the specialty revolution. "Rise up, my fine buckos, and assert your will," Schoenholt advised.

Fair trade coffee organizations urge consumers to buy coffee that has been grown by well-paid workers, often using guilt-inducing tactics such as this Equal Exchange ad.

By the early 1990s, caffeine addicts were loud and unrepentant.

In serial episodes ranging over months and years, Sharon flirted with her neighbor Tony over the freeze-dried coffee in commercials positively dripping with sexual innuendo, sensuality, and intrigue.

In Starbucks modern incarnation, the original mermaid logo *(left)* has been sanitized as a demure New Age coffee maiden.

Not everyone loved Starbucks. Critics accused the chain of using aggressive, predatory tactics to put smaller coffeehouses out of business, as in this 1996 cartoon.

Inspired by a trip to Italy, Howard Schultz spread the espresso/cappuccino/latte gospel through the Starbucks Experience, taking over the company in 1987 and taking it global.

Those concerned about preserving habitat for migratory birds can buy shade-grown coffee offered by several companies.

During the 1990s, environmentalists and birders created a market for "bird-friendly" coffee" grown in shaded plantations that provide important habitat for migratory birds and other rain forest animals.

Bill Clinton used political coffees to raise funds for his 1996 presidential re-election bid, brewing a scandal for himself.

Staten Island restaurant owner Joe McBratney drinks the equivalent of 50 cups of Colombian coffee a day. "I believe at any point in time I could slow down if I wanted to. Well, maybe I need that first cup…"

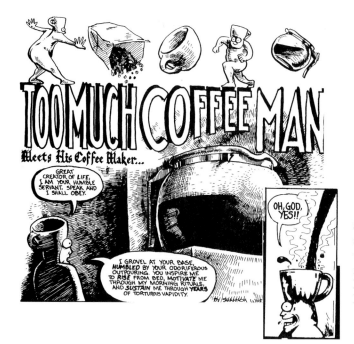

Some think that coffee addiction is no joke, though "Too Much Coffee Man" cannot endure his banal and meaningless existence without it.

Fat chance, though. Through the years, U.S. citizens and politicians have made it clear that they consider inexpensive coffee a birthright. A few good Samaritans don't mind paying extra for "fair trade" beans every now and then, but even they might squawk if *all* coffee provided a decent living for those who produce the crop.

Nor are we likely to see another International Coffee Agreement in our lifetime. The Association of Coffee Producing Countries (ACPC) has predictably failed to raise prices consistently, and major producers such as Mexico and Vietnam (a huge source of robusta in the last few years) refuse to join. The major roasters are still battling it out in price wars. The only way for coffee growers to get more for the crop is to find some value-added method. La Minita, Jamaica Blue Mountain, and Hawaiian Kona have risen above the pack, but few others have been able to duplicate their success. The only other way appears to be through the appeal to conscience that Bill McAlpin so harshly disparages.

There are several alternate pathways into the "huppy" pocketbook, and in general all are commendable, if limited. In 1988 Rhode Island coffee retailer Bill Fishbein visited small coffee farmers in Guatemala, looking for ways to help them. "I was filled with enthusiasm and naiveté," he recalls. While appalled by their living conditions, he found that "they were living vibrant lives in poverty, with a sense of community and a spirit that is absent in our own lives. Every time I visit, I wonder which side is more impoverished. They have no sanitation and are in poor health, but they are rich in spirituality. There seems to be far more life where coffee is grown than here where it's sold, despite all our economic advantages."

Nonetheless, Fishbein wanted to do something to help. At first, he worked with established nongovernment organizations (NGOs) but soon became disillusioned. Too often, the NGOs simply threw money at communities, then declared projects successful even without long-term improvements. "It amounts to a network to move money around, to pull the heartstrings of donors," he complains. In frustration, Fishbein created Coffee Kids, an organization that works *with* communities, providing seed money to create community banks that offer low-interest loans. Throughout Latin America, Coffee Kids has helped children primarily by helping their parents. In particular, the organization encourages women to create alternative businesses to bring in money to supplement the coffee harvest. Some coffee roasters donate money directly to Coffee Kids. Other retailers collect voluntary coin donations from customers.[2]

Working with inventor Raul Raudales, Coffee Kids is developing a solar drier that, if sufficiently cheap and effective, would offer small farmers a better chance to secure a decent price. When coffee cherries are harvested, they must be processed within twenty-four hours or they start to ferment. Without access to their own driers, the farmers must sell to the *coyotes*, opportunistic middlemen who pay cash for underpriced beans. A solar drier would provide a way to dry processed beans in the parchment stage. Then farmers could bide their time, waiting to sell at the best price.

Mending the Heart with Organic

Another way for farmers to sell their coffee at premium prices is to go organic. Gary Talboy of Coffee Bean International (CBI) pioneered the certification and marketing of organic coffee in the mid 1980s, working with Tom Harding of the Organic Crop Improvement Association (OCIA) to certify coffee from Mexican and Guatemalan cooperatives.

Organic coffee now has grown to 3 percent of the specialty market, though many coffee experts remain skeptical of its quality. At first, most organic coffee was pretty bad; it came from poverty-stricken smallholders whose coffee had always been organic by default, since they could not afford fertilizer or pesticide. They also took little care with proper pruning or processing. Over the years, however, organic coffee improved dramatically, thanks largely to the efforts of people such as San Diego businesswoman Karen Cebreros.

In 1989 Cebreros, who had married into a large Mexican family, was diagnosed with a rare heart disease and told she would eventually need a transplant. Her doctor told her not to travel far from a major hospital and to carry a beeper at all times. Instead, determined to live life to the fullest, she flew to South America to visit her brother-in-law George in the remote Peruvian village of Tamborapa. "There was no running water, no electricity, but the people were so loving and happy and giv-

---

[2]Readers may contact Coffee Kids by calling 1–800–334–9099.

ing," Cebreros recalls. They grew coffee, for which they received 8 cents a pound.

Wanting to help, Karen Cebreros convinced the villagers to scrape together a 100-pound bag of roughly processed beans, took it down the mountainside on a donkey, and eventually cleaned it on her backyard picnic table, removing the rocks, sticks, and black beans. When roasted, the beans unfortunately tasted like the dirt on which they had been dried. Working with Gary Talboy at CBI and Tom Harding of the OCIA, Cebreros helped the Peruvians to improve their coffee and get it certified as organic. Today, with the premiums from organic coffee sales, Tamborapa has electricity, running water, telephones, bridges, roads, a school, and a laboratory to study coffee quality. "But they are still loving, happy, and giving," Cebreros reports. Miraculously, her heart has healed itself.

Over the years, Cebreros greatly expanded her business. "We now source killer cups of coffee," she claims. Her company—first called Elan International, then Eco Coffee Company—acts as a facilitator, working with local growers to improve quality and to help fill out the mountain of paperwork to become certified.

"When we began, the questionnaires weren't even available in Spanish, let alone indigenous languages." Many of the growers were illiterate, and they didn't have the survey maps the OCIA and other certification agencies demanded. Nor did they have the hefty application fees, which Elan initially paid. To be certified, coffee must be inspected for three consecutive years to make sure it is chemical-free. The entire process costs about $30,000. Still, the effort has been worth it for cooperatives that produce El Salvador's Pipil Organic Coffee, Mexico's Aztec Harvest, and others in Latin America. There are also a few certified organic coffees from Indonesia and Africa.

It is certainly ironic that most truly organic coffees (e.g., the majority of Ethiopia's and Indonesia's beans) can't be sold as such, since they aren't certified. Yet rumor has it that many coffees that *are* sold as "organic" in fact are not—they cheat. They have to, according to cynics like Bill McAlpin. "There is no such thing as viable organic coffee," he insists. At La Minita, he emphasizes ecological practices and minimal chemical application, but he scorns the organic bureaucracy. His coffee trees certainly look a lot healthier than the organic trees I saw at another Costa Rica farm. Those were sad, spindly specimens.

Pesticides pose no threat to consumers, since they are applied to the cherries, which protect the inner seed. Then the heat of the roast drives off any chemical residue. Coffee is, however, the third most heavily sprayed crop on earth, after cotton and tobacco. It is doubtful whether soil cares whether its nutrients come from chemical or natural fertilizers, but the artificial variety are made primarily from fossil fuels such as petroleum. For coffee drinkers concerned about the environment and the health of campesino laborers, organic coffee makes sense, and it assures growers a decent price for their product.

Even certified organic coffee can cause terrible water pollution, however. For years, in the wet process, the fermented mucilage floated downstream, where its decomposition robbed the water of oxygen, killed fish and other wildlife, and smelled horrible. Two-thirds of the river pollution in Costa Rica's Central Valley stemmed from coffee wastes until recently, when stringent national legislation changed *beneficio* practices. Even today, some processors there violate the law.

Fortunately, there are viable alternatives, three of which I witnessed on my Central American tour. At Guatemala's *Oriflama*, coffee is depulped without water, the red-skinned pulp piled up in a huge pit and sprinkled with lime. There, it slowly decomposes without the stench that accompanies the water-soaked variety. After the controlled fermentation, the water used to loosen the mucilage is recycled until it makes a thick soup, then discharged into a pit that creates some of the best fertilizer imaginable. Even the parchment is recycled, burned to fire the dryers.

Later, at a Honduran coffee research facility, I saw what California red worms can do to coffee pulp, transforming it in three short months to rich soil. I also squinted to see the tiny African parasitic wasps that provide biological control for the dreaded *broca*, the coffee borer. Next I stayed at an ecological coffee resort in Matagalpa, Nicaragua, run by Eddy and Mausi Kühl. Selva Negra, named for the Black Forest of Kühl's German ancestors, is a 2,000-acre farm (much of it virgin cloud forest) where visitors eat at a central Swiss-style chalet and sip the sun-dried coffee. The coffee mucilage, along with cow and pig manure, undergoes anaerobic decomposition in an underground tank, producing enough methane to cook the food. Electricity for the coffee mill is produced by a Pelton water turbine.

Befriending the Birds

Walking through Selva Negra, you might spot a resplendent quetzal, a toucan, or one hundred seventy-five other varieties of birds. I didn't see a quetzal during my brief hike there, but I heard a constant chorus of birdsong and the occasional cry of a monkey. Like me, most rain forest visitors actually see little of the wildlife around them, but they can hear the thrumming chorus. These birds lie at the heart of a recent controversy over coffee cultivation techniques. Should coffee always be grown under overarching trees that provide shade? Or is this just a politically correct crusade against modern agricultural practices?

Shade-grown coffee provides an important habitat for migratory birds. "Thousands of birds fill the air with song—pert green parakeets, big gray mockingbirds, brilliant bluebirds and little yellow canaries," wrote a 1928 visitor to Guatemala. "It is difficult to imagine anything more delightful than a ride through the long avenues of trees heavy with green coffee berries. . . . When new ground is to be planted in coffee, shade is the most important consideration." This description is still true of plantations such as Selva Negra, but their number is dwindling. Within the last few years, "bird-friendly coffee" has provided one more value-added way to sell beans.

Prompted by the invasion of leaf rust into Latin America—arriving in Brazil in 1970 and spreading to Central America six years later—researchers urged coffee growers to "technify" their plantations, switching from traditional arabica beans such as *bourbon* and *typica* varieties that require shade to "modern" arabica varieties such as *caturra, catuai,* or *catimor,* which can be grown in full sun.[3] The Colombian Coffee Federation pushed hardest for the change, while creating a new hybrid

---

[3]Many specialty roasters vilify the modern strains of coffee used in technified production, including *catuai, caturra, catimor, Colombia,* and the Kenyan *Ruiru 11.* Coffee expert Kenneth Davids, who hosts a blind cupping panel Web site (www.coffeereview.com) cautions against such stereotypes. For regular coffee, he disdains robustas and *catimor* (a robusta-arabica hybrid) but refrains from generalizing about the others. "The finest old arabicas have been growing in particular microclimates for years. It isn't so much the variety per se as the way a botanical variety interacts with growing conditions to affect the taste. The challenge is to find the right variety for a given set of growing conditions." Davids even points out that a small amount of a good robusta can add body to an espresso blend.

strain named *Colombia* that is even more disease resistant. The U.S. Agency for International Development provided funds for the switch to technified sun coffee as well.

As a result, by 1990, 69 percent of Colombian and 40 percent of Costa Rican coffee was grown in closely-packed rows in full sun. When I visited a sun plantation in Costa Rica, the trees were so tightly packed that I could not easily walk through them. They stretched up the hillside in solid, silent, low-slung ranks. There were no birds, only morning glory vines climbing the squat trees in search of the sun.

Like the Green Revolution that was supposed to provide a miracle cure through new strains of rice, wheat, and corn, the sun coffee revolution has failed to fulfill its promise. Instead, it has contributed to ecological degradation and loss of important habitat. Various species of swallows, swifts, warblers, vireos, orioles, raptor, thrushes, and hummingbirds are neotropical migrants. Up to ten billion birds summer in the temperate forests of North America, then fly south to winter in Latin America. During the decade 1978–1987, the U.S. Fish and Wildlife Services' Breeding Bird Survey showed a decline in neotropical migrants, ranging from 1 to 3 percent annually. Although there may be other factors involved, it is alarming that shade-grown coffee was declining at precisely the same time.

"Throughout the Latin American wintering grounds of migratory birds," wrote Russell Greenberg of the Smithsonian Migratory Bird Center in 1991, "the natural landscape is undergoing massive changes at phenomenal rates." By 1983, he observed, 80 percent of Costa Rica's original forest had been destroyed. The world's rain forest belt once covered five billion acres, 14 percent of the earth's land surface. Humans have destroyed over half of it, and the destruction continues at the rate of 80 acres a minute, according to some estimates. Species are disappearing at the rate of three per hour. In the 1830s Charles Darwin observed: "The land is one great wild, untidy luxuriant hothouse, made by nature herself." Unfortunately, much of the land he saw has now been deforested for cattle, soybeans, or other uses.

Coffee itself is an Ethiopian tree–shrub that has displaced local vegetation and dramatically altered the habitat. Yet "traditional" shade-grown coffee at least provides a relatively benign habitat, encouraging more biodiversity than many other agricultural alternatives. "Traditional" is in quotation marks because much coffee of the eighteenth and nineteenth century was grown in full sun. Arguments over shade versus sun are long-standing.

By the turn of the last century, most agronomists came down on the side of shade. In 1901 the U.S. Department of Agriculture published *Shade in Coffee Culture*, in which O. F. Cook pointed out the multiple benefits of nitrogen-fixing leguminous shade trees. "[They] hold the soil in place, and seldom require replanting or other care; their shade discourages the growth of weeds, diminishes the cost of cultivation, and lessens the bad effects of drought." They also protected coffee from high winds and provided mulch in the form of falling leaves. Cook observed that two indigenous Latin American products, cacao and coca, were also grown under shade prior to the European invasion.

By eliminating shade trees, modern technified coffee plantations can produce more beans but must support hastened photosynthesis through heavy applications of oil-based fertilizers. Perhaps due to the high growing altitudes, leaf rust has not caused as many problems as feared. The coffee borer has thrived instead in the monoculture of sun coffee, though other wildlife cannot survive there. Birds, insects, and other animals abandon coffee grown in the open as an "ecological desert," according to Russell Greenberg. In countries such as El Salvador, shaded coffee plantations account for 60 percent of the remaining "forest" cover. Billions of migratory birds fly south into the narrow funnel of southern Mexico and Central America, where loss of the coffee canopy could prove disastrous.

Turf Battles over Politically Correct Coffee

The ecological controversy surrounding coffee production brought me to the National Zoo in Washington, D.C., in September 1996, where I attended the first Sustainable Coffee Conference sponsored by the Smithsonian Migratory Bird Center. For the first time, academics, conservationists, and development experts came together with coffee growers, importers, exporters, roasters, and retailers to discuss and debate coffee *sustainability*, a buzzword that was never clearly defined.

Biological researchers at the conference made a compelling case for shade coffee's support of biodiversity. "What is surprising here is the large numbers of species of insects that are found in the canopy of single trees in the traditional farm," Professor Ivette Perfecto reported.

Russell Greenberg noted that his Mexican survey found one hundred eighty different bird species in shaded coffee, second only to the number found in undisturbed tropical forests.

Greenberg then launched into a pragmatic pitch for bird-friendly coffee's commercial potential. Of the fifty-four million Americans who consider themselves birders, twenty-four million actually traveled in 1991 to observe their avian friends. In the process, they spent $2.5 billion—and who knows how much of that went for strong predawn coffee? The demographics for serious birders—well-educated, well-heeled, and interested in conservation—dovetailed nicely with those who drank specialty coffees. Not only that, aging baby boomers spending all this money would swell the coffee-swilling ranks. From 1990 to 2010, the forty-five-year-old-and-older bracket is projected to grow 225 percent faster than the general population.

As Chris Wille of Rainforest Alliance told the audience, it seemed an open-and-shut case. "We can tell people to drink more coffee and better quality coffee—just make sure it is certified eco-friendly. The birds win. The bees win. Everybody here wins." Yet turf battles loomed over how to label and market bird-friendly coffee. Organic retailers couldn't agree with fair traders. The Rainforest Alliance wanted to stamp the coffee with its Eco-OK seal, while Conservation International representatives planned a slightly different set of criteria. Unwilling to wait for a consensus, Paul Katzeff unveiled his own point verification system for Thanksgiving Coffee's shade-grown brand.

Even if they could agree on a shade-coffee seal, what would constitute sufficient shade? At Selva Negra, I climbed up the mountain into an abandoned coffee grove where a huge strangler fig had grown completely around the original host. Though secondary forest, it seemed utterly wild. With the shade so thick that little sun filtered to the ground, I barely recognized the spindly coffee trees with their scant berries. On the other hand, at La Minita, the *poro* shade trees were kept uniformly trimmed and provided minimal shade or bird habitat. It was only when I walked out of the coffee groves and into the La Minita forest preserve that birdsong drenched me. Also, all the attention to shade-grown coffee centered on Latin America, ignoring Africa and Asia, while the promoters didn't discuss areas in which shade is unnecessary because of cloud cover and climate.

Bert Beekman, the Dutch founder of Max Havelaar, gave the most pragmatic advice to the bird-loving coffeephiles gathered at the National Zoo: create a uniform, recognizable high-quality product, avoiding fragmentation of the message. Make it readily available at reasonably competitive prices in supermarkets by forming joint ventures with major roasters. Refrain from one-upsmanship, turf wars, and ego tripping. Convey a simple, clear message, and get tons of free publicity through church groups and the press. Begin the campaign intensively in one regional test market, then expand.

Unfortunately, no one heeded Beekman's message. True, the SCAA added *sustainability* to its mission statement, and its Sustainable Coffee Criteria Group created a document urging minimal agrochemical use, cessation of habitat destruction, biodiversity preservation, and other fine-sounding phrases. Yet without a concrete agenda, little has been accomplished. Consumers who want to purchase certified shade-grown coffee can do so, but from a fragmented industry. Even so, bird-friendly coffee now accounts for 1 percent of the specialty coffee market.[4]

Chiapas, Congo, Rwanda, Haiti, Colombia . . .
Again, Again, Again

At the Smithsonian conference, I took part in a working group that included both coffee growers from Central America and U.S. specialty roaster–retailers. In translation, I heard a grower ask a question that hung like a storm cloud over the proceedings. "We are shocked and confused that specialty roasters sell our coffee for $8 or $10, when we only receive a little over a dollar a pound. How is that just?" While their U.S. colleagues made sympathetic noises, no one really answered the question, so I asked point-blank for a breakdown of costs along the line from tree to cup. Resounding silence.

Later, a specialty roaster gave me an answer. Let us say he pays $1.30 a pound for Colombian Supremo green beans (and remember that this price can fluctuate wildly). Add 11 cents for freight-in, storage, and handling, then factor in another 31 cents for the 18 percent weight loss during roasting, 12 cents a pound for the fuel for roasting, 25 cents to

---

[4]Thanksgiving Coffee sells the Songbird brand in conjunction with the American Birding Association. In North Carolina, Counter-Culture Coffee offers the Sanctuary brand by mail order and through outlets of the Wild Bird Centers of America. Karen Cebreros has created Café Audubon, which is both organic and shade-grown and helps support the National Audubon Society and the Smithsonian Migratory Bird Center. Rainforest Alliance sells Eco-OK coffee, while Conservation International sponsors E-Coffee.

hand-pack in 5-pound valve bags for wholesale shipments, and 30 cents for shipping costs. That brings the total to $2.39. Add $2.15 to cover overhead for the roaster and distributor (overhead includes everything from mortgages and machinery loans to sales commissions, repairs, and rubbish removal). Then tack on 24 cents profit (about 5 percent), and it costs $4.78 to deliver roasted coffee to a specialty retailer. Depending on the retailer's size, rent, and other overhead costs, he or she must then charge between $8 and $10 a pound to make a reasonable profit.

Taking the beans one step further, to a coffeehouse outlet, the proprietor converts the $4.78 per pound beans into regular coffee at $1 or cappuccino or latte for $2 or more. If the proprietor gets 40 cups to the pound, that translates to an outrageous $40 to $80 a pound for coffee in beverage form, minus the cost of the milk, stirrer, and sweetener. On the other hand, coffeehouse owners have to pay astronomical rents and allow customers to hog a table for long, philosophical conversations or solitary reading over their single cup of coffee.[5]

It appears, then, that the higher costs are probably justified, at least in terms of the U.S. economy and lifestyle. Nonetheless, there remains the glaring disparity between the affluence of the United States and the relative poverty of Central America and other coffee-growing regions, and all the talk about migratory birds seemed dilettantish to some participants at the Smithsonian conference. "If people in a wealthy country, where obesity is a major health problem, want to focus upon their own birds and trees, I have no complaint," wrote Price Peterson, a Panamanian coffee grower I met at the conference. In a country where the average annual income is $1,500, however, there is less concern about the environment. "If you are hungry, you shoot birds to eat—you do not protect them. If you are homeless in Panama, where no one cares for the homeless, you cut down trees to build a house—you don't conserve them."

---

[5]Everyone in the coffee industry appears to envy everyone else. Growers object to the brokers making a commission just by picking up the phone to sell their beans to exporters. The brokers think the exporters have it made, but exporters feel at the mercy of importers, who sell to rich Americans. Importers, caught in savage price swings, feel pinched with a tiny profit margin, but they think the roasters make millions. Roasters see retailers doubling the price of their roasted beans, while coffee bars convert the beans to expensive beverages. Yet the coffeehouse owner is working fifteen-hour days, six days a week, fighting the health inspector and the Starbucks that just opened down the street.

At the conference, a Mexican speaker complained, "Coffee communities which produce wealth for the country live in poverty without the benefit of social policies. . . . The coffee growing areas are a powderkeg waiting to explode." Although he was talking about Mexico, he also described conditions in many other coffee-producing nations around the world.

In the last few years, the evening news has brought these same countries into our living rooms with depressing regularity. For the student of coffee history, it's *déjà vu.*

In 1994 in Rwanda, the Hutu massacred nearly a million Tutsi, who then retaliated, the violence spreading to Burundi.

In Ethiopia, coffee's birthplace, the hated Soviet-backed leader, Mengistu Haili Mariam, was overthrown in 1991, but new president Meles Zenawi has encouraged ethnic divisions and imprisoned critics.

In Kenya, corrupt president Daniel arap Moi turned a blind eye as Kikuyu tribesmen were driven off their farms.

In troubled Uganda, the "Lord's Resistance Army," led by self-proclaimed messiah Joseph Kony, forced abducted teenage soldiers to kill one another.

In Zaire, longtime dictator Mobutu was overthrown in 1997 and the country renamed the Democratic Republic of Congo, but the new leader, Laurent Kabila, doesn't appear to be much better. Meanwhile, in Zimbabwe, President Robert Mugabe threatened to confiscate coffee farms owned by white citizens.

In Colombia, violence escalated as the paramilitary and guerrillas kidnap and murder with near impunity.

In Haiti (which supplied over half the world's coffee before the 1791 slave revolt), the United States intervened to force restoration of order and a shaky democracy, which quickly slid into disarray.[6]

In Indonesia, Suharto was finally forced to abdicate amidst increasing civil unrest.

In Mexico's coffee-growing Chiapas region, the Zapatistas led a revolt demanding land reform, setting off a chain of violent reprisals by paramilitary groups. In the December 1997 massacre at the village of Acteal, forty-six men, women, and children—members of a local coffee

---

[6]After years of decline, the Haitian coffee industry is struggling to revive with Haitian Bleu, value-added specialty beans.

cooperative—were killed. "Coffee has a long and bloody record here," Mexican historian John Ross wrote to me a few months before that massacre. "The map of poverty and armed insurrection follows the route of coffee."[7]

As if that weren't enough, coffee-growing regions seemed plagued with more than their fair share of natural disasters, because many lie atop grinding tectonic plates. As this book neared completion, two hurricanes, George and Mitch, devastated the Caribbean and Central America, and an earthquake rocked the Colombian coffee-growing region. Hurricane Mitch alone killed an estimated eleven thousand people and cut coffee production nearly in half in Honduras and Nicaragua.

Guilt Tripping in Guatemala

All is not utterly dismal, however. I flew into Guatemala City in January 1997, only days after the signing of the historic peace accord that ended four decades of bloody civil war, in which more than one hundred thousand people died. There was an air of cautious optimism in this beautiful country, and though the violence has not completely ended—nor has the occupation of coffee farms by the landless—at least there is some hope for the future.

During part of my visit, I was hosted by a gracious older *ladino* woman whose family has long owned a huge coffee plantation near Antigua. Afraid of kidnappers, she requested that I not use her real name, so I will call her Luisa. The perfect cone of Volcan Agua looms over the traditional shaded farm, where Luisa lives part time in a baronial house built by a nineteenth-century Guatemalan president. Her servants brought us fine coffee at a huge old mahogany table. I also visited Luisa's luxurious homes in Guatemala City and Antigua. While I was at the plantation, the Mayan Indians came down from the hills to begin the harvest. They stayed in rough huts provided by the farm. Wearing traditional clothing, they washed their clothes in a *pila*, a community basin. Few spoke Spanish. They smiled and nodded when approached.

---

[7]Businesses for Human Rights and Fair Trade in Chiapas (BETHRIC)—an organization comprised primarily of concerned coffee roasters—has sent two fact-finding delegations to Chiapas.

I asked Luisa how her workers related to her. "They treat me with great respect." As an example, she explained that she was forbidden to watch while her cows were bred in mounting stations. "They consider me too delicate to witness this event," she laughed. I asked her whether she didn't feel guilty, having three beautiful homes while her Indians lived in huts. "Of course," she replied, but did not elaborate.

Luisa is a gentle, kind person. She has encouraged one of her literate Indian laborers—a rare person—to write his autobiography. She keeps her eighty-six-year-old foreman on the payroll. He was born on the farm and has lived there all his life. His father worked for Luisa's grandfather. She was pleased that the peace accord had finally been signed. "But after thirty-six years, what did the guerrillas accomplish?" she asked me. "Nothing is any better. They paid them about the same wages in 1980 as now."

There are no simple answers to the inequities built into the system in Guatemala and elsewhere. I interviewed Charlie and Ruth Magill, who spent four years building houses with Habitat for Humanity in rural Guatemala. Charlie is a retired IBM engineer and Ruth is a former school librarian. "I went to Guatemala a flaming liberal, filled with outrage over injustice to the poor," Ruth told me. "Charlie went as a conservative. We came back with me calming down and him becoming more liberal. Things are not all black-and-white. You can't paint an extreme picture and lay a guilt trip on everyone. But there really are some disturbing issues."

In recent years, the U.S. Guatemala Labor Education Project (US/GLEP) *did* lay a guilt trip on Starbucks. In December 1994 the Chicago-based organization launched a protest campaign, embarrassing the company at outlets across the country. Their brochures pointed out that the amount customers paid for a pound of roasted Starbucks beans was equivalent to a week's wages for the average Guatemalan coffee laborer. Starbucks spokesmen noted that the company had no control over the Central American pay scale. Compared to the major roasters, Starbucks was a minor Guatemalan coffee buyer. The US/GLEP activists knew that, but they picked Starbucks for its high profile. The strategy worked. In less than a year, Starbucks released a "Framework for a Code of Conduct," calling for its overseas suppliers to pay decent wages and benefits and to provide "safe housing, clean water, and health facilities and services."

Then nothing happened until February 1997, when Starbucks announced that it would donate $75,000 to Appropriate Technologies International (ATI), a nonprofit research organization, to help Guatemalan coffee cooperatives build processing facilities. US/GLEP wasn't impressed, pointing out that this campaign addressed only bean quality, not living quality, and did not affect large plantations at all. In March 1998 Starbucks announced that it was giving $500,000 that year to growers who agreed to improve working and living conditions. US/GLEP hailed this as a "major step," though it asked Starbucks to find a way to verify that the money was getting through to the campesinos. The activists implied that they would go on to target other coffee companies.

The effect of the US/GLEP campaign was salutary. Starbucks probably would not have drafted its Code of Conduct or instituted the Guatemalan program had it not been pushed. But the premise that most Guatemalan coffee laborers are oppressed and mistreated is inaccurate. "I won't say that oppression isn't happening anywhere in Guatemala, but things are vastly different from what they used to be," Dave Olsen of Starbucks told me. "We deal in the area between the simple lie and the complex truth." Similarly, Guatemalan coffee grower Betty Hannstein Adams bridles at the suggestion that her laborers are unhappy. Though she acknowledges Guatemalan social inequities, she is infuriated by the condescending superiority of some U.S. activists. "Consider the sweatshops for illegal immigrants in New York," she says. "Their workers are virtual slaves, not allowed any freedom whatsoever until they have paid back the debt they owe the employer. People picking coffee are happier and freer than their cousins in New York."

Certainly, some activists, such as environmentalist Alan Durning, go over the top in trying to induce guilt. "Growing these [coffee] trees required several doses of insecticides, which were manufactured in the Rhine River Valley of Europe," Durning writes; hence, coffee growers are responsible for polluting European rivers. "The beans were shipped to New Orleans in a freighter constructed in Japan, of steel made in Korea. The steel was made of iron mined on tribal lands in Papua New Guinea." Then of course the beans were roasted (using fossil fuel) and packaged in bags made of polyethylene, nylon, aluminum foil, and polyester. "The plastics were fabricated in factories in Louisiana's 'Cancer Corridor,' where toxic industries have been disproportionately concentrated in areas where the residents are black." The bauxite to make the aluminum came from Australia, "the ancestral land of aborigines." Durning goes on and on, complaining about the car that carries the consumer to a coffeehouse, the gold filter used to brew the coffee, even the cream that came from a cow whose stream walks "muddied the water and made life difficult for native trout."

Betty Adams believes that guilt tripping coffee drinkers is ridiculous. "Do you feel guilt when you eat a tomato that was picked by a Mexican field hand's child in California, where the good citizens have refused the workers access to schools and social services?" she asks. "Does Bill Gates feel guilt when he wears a shirt made in a New York sweatshop?" She also emphasizes that her own life as an owner is not easy. "I never fully realized the enormous risk involved in producing coffee until I started to run the *finca* myself. I never realized how much damage a wind could do, or a prolonged rain, or a bad bookkeeper—not to mention the vulnerability to a capricious and unstable market."

Coffee—Part of the Matrix

Coffee is inextricably bound up in a history of inequity in which the haves took from the have nots. The drink, primarily a stimulant that helps keep the industrialized world alert, is grown in regions that know how to enjoy a *siesta*. There is no question that coffee laborers have been oppressed in the past; even now they are being murdered by paramilitary groups in Chiapas.

On my trip to Central America, the close connection between coffee, power, and violence was brought home repeatedly. In Nicaragua, I met Alvaro Peralta Gedea, a young man who came back to reclaim his family's *finca* located near the Honduran border. The farm had been confiscated by the Sandinistas in the early 1980s.[8] Before he could prune the neglected trees, however, he had to remove the mines planted throughout his land. Fortunately, he had been trained by the U.S. Navy to re-

---

[8]Roger Castellon Orué, whose farm confiscation story is told in chapter 17, was my driver in Nicaragua. Now he has his farm back, but he remains bitter. At a cupping session, I met Luisa Maria Molina Icias, whose story is also told in that chapter.

move mines and he taught his campesinos. On his uncle's farm, however, an incautious worker was blown up.

During my time in Honduras, Nicaragua, and El Salvador, I joined a trip organized by the Specialty Coffee Association of America. Naturally, the coffee powers-that-be rolled out the red carpet for the SCAA. Thus, I found myself at a cocktail party hosted by General Joaquin Cuadra Lacayo, the current head of the Nicaraguan army, on *Esperanza*, his beautiful coffee estate. He explained how, as a Sandinista general, he had given land and guns to peasants and told them to defend it, while his government confiscated other coffee *fincas*. His own farms, he explained, were not suitable for confiscation.

The next day, we crossed the border into El Salvador, where our genial guide was Ricardo "Rick" Valvidieso, the cofounder with Roberto D'Aubuisson of the right-wing ARENA party. Raised in the United States, he resembled a wholesome camp leader, yelling from the front of the bus, "Are you having fun?" It was difficult to imagine that he, like D'Aubuisson, might have been associated with death squads—an allegation he denied when I asked him about it. Yet when we visited his family coffee plantation, there were guards with submachine guns behind every tree. He told me how he had been shot and nearly killed in El Salvador just before the 1982 elections. He had stayed in the hospital only one day, then was spirited away to a "safe house" to avoid assassination.

The coffee economy itself is not directly responsible for social unrest and repression; we should not confuse a correlation with a cause. Inequities and frustrations built into the economic system nonetheless exacerbate conflicts. Compared with many other products developed countries demand in cheap quantity, however, coffee is relatively benign. Laboring on banana, sugar, or cotton plantations or sweating in gold and diamond mines and oil refineries is far worse. The vast majority of coffee is grown on tiny plots by peasants who love their trees and the ripe cherries they produce.

As the anthropologist Eric Wolf observed in his classic 1982 work *Europe and the People Without History*, "the world of humankind constitutes . . . a totality of interconnected processes." Coffee provides one fascinating thread, stitching together the disciplines of history, anthropology, sociology, psychology, medicine, and business, and offering a way to follow the interactions that have formed a global economy.

While this history has concentrated solely on coffee, similar stories could be told for other products. The European countries extracted furs, silver, gold, diamonds, slaves, spices, sugar, tea, coffee, cocoa, tobacco, opium, rubber, palm oil, and petroleum from Asia, Africa, and the Americas. As North America, taken over by white Europeans, developed industrially, it too joined the conquest, particularly of Latin America.

Caffeine, the Drug of Choice

Developed countries are not the only place people drink coffee. Over 22 percent of the world's production is consumed where it is grown. Brazilians have grown so fond of the beverage that some experts predict Brazil will eventually become a net importer of coffee. Caffeine is the most widely taken psychoactive drug on earth, and coffee is its foremost delivery system. "Today, most of the world's population, irrespective of geographic location, gender, age, or culture consumes caffeine daily," writes Jack James, author of two books on caffeine. "Global consumption has been estimated to be 120,000 tons of caffeine per annum. This is the approximate equivalent of one caffeine-containing beverage per day for each of the globe's five billion or more inhabitants." In the United States, around 90 percent of the population habitually takes caffeine in one form or another—including plain caffeinated water.

Is this bad? Humans clearly crave stimulating concoctions, drinking, chewing, or smoking some form of drug in virtually every culture in the form of alcohol, coca leaves, kava, marijuana, poppies, mushrooms, qat, betel nuts, tobacco, coffee, kola nuts, yoco bark, guayusa leaves, yaupon leaves (cassina), maté, guaraná nuts, cacao (chocolate), or tea. Of those in the list above, caffeine is certainly the most ubiquitous—appearing in the last nine items. Indeed, caffeine is produced by more than sixty plants, although coffee beans provide about 54 percent of the world's jolt, followed by tea and soft drinks. As cartoonist Robert Therrien has a character proclaim, "Coffee Is My Drug of Choice!"

What is caffeine and what does it do to you? Is it safe? Experts disagree. Caffeine is one of the alkaloids: organic (carbon-containing) compounds built around rings of nitrogen atoms. Alkaloids are the pharmacologically active chemicals produced by many tropical plants in self-defense. Because they have no winter to provide relief from predators, tropical plants have evolved sophisticated methods of protecting themselves. In other words, caffeine is a natural pesticide. Although some bugs and fungi adapt to any chemical, it is quite likely that plants contain caffeine because it affects the nervous system of would-be consumers, discouraging them from eating it. Of course, that is precisely the attraction for the human animal.

Caffeine, $C_8H_{10}N_4O_2$, is a white, odorless powder with a bitter taste, first isolated from green coffee beans in 1820. It consists of three methyl groups (H_3C) attached around a xanthine molecule—one of the common building blocks of plants and animals—making caffeine (a trimethylxanthine) a knobby molecule that bumps about in the bloodstream, though it readily passes through biological membranes such as the gastrointestinal tract. The human liver treats caffeine as a poison and furiously attempts to dismantle it, stripping off methyl groups. It can't cope with all of them, so quite a few whole caffeine molecules make it past the liver and eventually find a docking place in the brain.

The caffeine molecule mimics the neurotransmitter adenosine, which decreases electrical activity in the brain and inhibits the release of other neurotransmitters. In other words, adenosine slows things down. It lets us rest and probably helps put us to sleep once a day. When caffeine gets to the receptors first, however, it doesn't let the frustrated adenosine do its job. Hence, caffeine doesn't keep us awake in a positive sense—it just blocks the natural mental brake, preventing adenosine from making us drowsy.

The brain isn't the only place caffeine affects. There are adenosine receptors throughout the body, where the hormone apparently performs varied functions. Thus, caffeine causes the heart to beat more rapidly, constricts some blood vessels, and causes certain muscles to contract more easily. At the same time, however, it can relax the airways of the lungs and *open* other types of blood vessels. Caffeine is a diuretic, and small amounts of calcium float away in the urine, leading to concern over possible bone loss. The latest research indicates that this is a potential concern only for elderly women with low calcium intake, however.

As we have seen, coffee and caffeine have been implicated in an enormous array of ailments, but subsequent studies failed to confirm most of the negative findings. As Stephen Braun concludes in his 1996 book *Buzz:* "The effects of caffeine on such things as breast cancer, bone loss, pancreatic cancer, colon cancer, heart disease, liver disease, kidney disease, and mental dysfunction have been examined in . . . detail and, to date, *no* clear evidence has been found linking moderate consumption of caffeine . . . with these or any other health disorder."

After reviewing the same data, Jack James, in his 1997 book *Understanding Caffeine*, agrees that there is no unequivocal linkage, but he feels that caffeine *probably* contributes to heart disease. In addition, he points out that boiled or unfiltered coffee has been linked to higher serum cholesterol levels. "Even the equivalent of one cup of coffee produces modest increases in blood pressure lasting 2 to 3 hours," James argues. "Experienced over a lifetime, these daily elevations of blood pressure probably contribute to cardiovascular disease." His conclusion is that there is *no* safe level of caffeine consumption, and that the drug should be avoided completely.

Few doctors would go so far, though all authorities agree that people with high blood pressure, as well as those with insomnia and anxiety disorders, should consult their physician about their caffeine intake. They also recommend that patients taking other drugs ask their doctor about possible interactions with caffeine. In the stomach, caffeine stimulates gastric acid secretion. Thus, while it helps some people digest food, it gives others an acid stomach. For years, doctors thought coffee drinking might cause ulcers, but this appears to be a myth.

Like Stephen Braun, most authorities recommend "moderate consumption." There are many anecdotal and clinical reports that drinking too much caffeine can cause problems. The likely lethal dose for humans is about 10 grams, though it would be virtually impossible to consume that much quickly by drinking coffee. Initial signs of toxicity include vomiting, abdominal cramps, and a racing heartbeat. The *Diagnostic and Statistical Manual of Mental Disorders* (DSM-IV) includes *caffeine intoxication* as a bona fide ailment. A psychiatrist may legally diagnose you if you display five or more of the following twelve symptoms during or shortly after caffeine ingestion: restlessness, nervousness, excitement, insomnia, flushed face, diuresis, gastrointestinal disturbance, muscle twitching, rambling flow of thought and speech, tachycardia or cardiac arrhythmia, periods of inexhaustibility, and psychomotor agitation.

While *caffeinism* has long been recognized as a real ailment for those who consume excessive amounts of the drug, the symptoms of *caffeine intoxication* are rather similar to those of a panic attack. The only difference is that someone must have recently drunk coffee, tea, or soft drinks, which appears to have a circular diagnostic logic. At various times while writing this book, I have exhibited five of these symptoms, including restlessness, excitement, insomnia, periods of inexhaustibility, and particularly, rambling flow of thought. I drink only one or two daily cups of coffee, in the morning.

Moderate caffeine intake has its benefits, though most doctors recommend alternative drugs. As Harry Hollingworth found in his 1911 double-blind studies, caffeine can minimally improve motor skills and reaction time while leaving sleep patterns relatively unaffected.[9] Coffee boosts athletic performance (perhaps through stimulation of more adrenaline) to the point that the International Olympic Committee has called caffeine a "doping agent"–too much caffeine in the bloodstream means expulsion from the games. Caffeine can help those who suffer from asthma and is given to infants suffering from neonatal apnea (cessation of spontaneous breathing). Some adults with allergies find that caffeine allays symptoms. It can mitigate the pain of migraine headaches (though withdrawal from caffeine *causes* other headaches). For those who need a diuretic or laxative, coffee provides relief. Some studies even commend the drink's use as an antidepressant to prevent suicide.

Far from being the antierotic that British women of 1674 complained about, caffeine has been shown to increase sperm motility, so it may prove useful in artificial insemination programs (though others fear it may harm the sperm while speeding it on its way). Combined with analgesics such as aspirin, caffeine appears to help alleviate pain. It may have therapeutic potential for some cancers, though evidence is weak. While coffee often is accused of providing no nutrition, it provides minute traces of potassium, magnesium, and manganese. Because it raises the metabolic rate, it may help with dieting, but the effect is slight. Like ritalin, caffeine has a paradoxical effect on hyperactive children with attention-deficit disorder: letting such children drink coffee seems to calm them down.

---

[9]There is no proof that coffee is a brain tonic. Still, one professor coined a definition: "*mathemetician*: a machine for turning coffee into theorems."

Surprisingly, there is little evidence that caffeine harms children, despite widespread belief that it stunts growth, ruins health, and so on. Like adults, however, children are subject to withdrawal symptoms—from soft drink deprivation more frequently than from coffee. Many doctors have expressed concern about pregnant and nursing women who drink coffee. Caffeine readily passes through the placental barrier to the fetus, and it turns breast milk into a kind of natural latte. Because premature infants lack the liver enzymes to break down caffeine, it stays in their systems much longer. By the time they are six months old, most children eliminate caffeine at the same rate as adults, with a bloodstream half-life of around five hours.

Research has failed to prove that caffeine harms the fetus or breastfed infant, but recent studies appear to implicate caffeine in lower birthweights. Jack James urges pregnant women to abstain completely from drinking caffeine beverages. In *Protecting Your Baby-to-Be* (1995), Margie Profet agrees. "It's prudent for first-trimester women to consciously halt or at least strictly limit their intake of coffee . . . if pregnancy sickness does not do it for them." On the other hand, the National Coffee Association (which certainly has a vested interest in the matter) asserts that "most physicians and researchers today agree that it's perfectly safe for pregnant women to consume caffeine." For those who choose to "err on the side of caution," the NCA recommends one or two cups daily.

Experts in fact don't agree on much when it comes to coffee and caffeine intake, partly because individuals exhibit remarkably different reactions. Some people are wired for hours with a mere sip; others can drink a double espresso right before falling into a sound sleep. Thus, every coffee lover should determine his or her level of comfortable consumption, preferably no more than two or three cups a day.[10]

Are You Addicted?

Then there's Joe McBratney, the thirty-six-year-old chef and owner of Staten Island's Kreisher Mansion restaurant, where you can dine under

---

[10]The three-cup limit is based on an average 100 milligrams of caffeine per 6-ounce cup, but this amount will vary depending on cup size, brew strength, and blend. Robusta blends will have substantially more caffeine than pure arabicas. Those who quit smoking may find that their normal coffee intake suddenly affects them more, since smoking lessens the effect of caffeine.

chandeliers, listen to soothing classical music, and enjoy fabulous seafood dishes, followed by rich Colombian coffee. I saw McBratney on a 1995 television program talking about his extraordinary daily coffee intake, the equivalent of fifty regular cups, or 5,000 milligrams of caffeine. I paid him a visit and found a seemingly calm, happy host. "I feel like a changed person after my first cup every morning," he told me. "I feel great." At the restaurant, he drinks all day out of a soup bowl–sized cup.

McBratney is convinced that his habit doesn't hurt his health, even though he admits it keeps him awake if he drinks it near bedtime. "But it doesn't make me jumpy or shaky." His blood pressure is in the normal range. What happens if he doesn't get enough coffee? "I won't allow myself to be in a situation where I can't get coffee." At Disneyland once, he had a hard time finding a cup. "Let's stop and get Joe a cup of coffee, please," his wife said. "He's driving me crazy." Still, he says, "I believe at any point in time, I could slow down if I wanted to."

McBratney is probably fooling himself. He's hooked. The reason he can drink so much without bouncing off the walls is that he has developed a caffeine tolerance. If he quit cold turkey, he would probably suffer exquisitely, like Cathy Rossiter, who took part in a 1993 Johns Hopkins study on the effects of caffeine withdrawal. Rossiter favors Mountain Dew, chugging the heavily caffeinated lemon-lime soft drink all day. Her need was so intense that she found herself standing in a supermarket line holding a Mountain Dew in either hand while she was in labor with her second child.

For the study, Rossiter agreed to abstain from caffeine for two days. "It felt like a migraine, just right behind your eyes. It was like someone had a little knife digging out your brains." She nearly threw up–not surprising, since caffeine withdrawal symptoms include headaches, drowsiness, fatigue, decreased performance, and, for extreme cases, nausea and vomiting. Rossiter made it through the two days but refused the offer to help her kick the habit permanently. With relief, she went back to her Mountain Dew.

"There is a real withdrawal syndrome," caffeine researcher John Hughes emphasizes, "even for those who consume as little 100 milligrams (one cup of coffee) a day. Many people who believe that caffeine helps them are probably fooling themselves. In reality, taking more caffeine simply relieves their withdrawal symptoms and brings them back to the norm." Hughes considers it ridiculous that coffee, tea, and cola containers do not currently have to specify the amount of caffeine they contain, though the FDA has mandated minute revelations about riboflavin and vitamins. He would like to see a warning label: "Abrupt cessation of caffeine can cause headache, drowsiness, and fatigue."

Despite the pain of caffeine withdrawal, however, it only lasts a week or so. As addictions go, it is a relatively harmless one. "Addiction has lost whatever vestige of clear scientific definition it ever had," caffeine researcher Peter Dews says. "Most people are addicted to caffeine-containing beverages, just as most are addicted to showers and regular meals. That is not a bad thing. It is a habit that can be indulged for a lifetime without adverse effects to health."[11]

Maybe. The habit has such a hold on us as we approach the twenty-first century that there are innumerable Web sites, chat rooms, and newsgroups on the Internet devoted to coffee. Indeed, one can log on at a cybercafe and sip coffee while reading about it online. Perhaps it isn't just the caffeine. There are two thousand other chemicals in the roasted bean—oils, caramels, carbohydrates, proteins, phosphates, minerals, volatile acids, nonvolatile acids, ash, trigonelline, phenolics, volatile carbonyls and sulfides—making it one of the most complex of food products. Still, I suspect it's the caffeine that binds most of us to coffee. I found an anonymous joke floating in cyberspace with seventy-five different sentence completions for "You know you're drinking too much coffee when . . ." Among my favorites:

You chew on other people's fingernails.
You go to AA meetings just for the free coffee.
People get dizzy just watching you.
You can jumpstart your car without cables.
You don't sweat, you percolate.
When someone says, "How are you?" you say, "Good to the last drop."

---

[11]Peter Dews, a Harvard professor emeritus, conducted research funded by what Jack James calls "the caffeine lobby": organizations such as the International Life Sciences Institute (ILSI), the International Food Information Council (IFIC), and the National Coffee Association, that portray caffeine as "an enjoyable, benign, and even beneficial substance."

You introduce your spouse as your coffeemate.
You want to be cremated just so you can spend the rest of eternity
    in a coffee can.

A joke? Not according to the main character in Mark Helprin's quirky
1995 novel *Memoir from Antproof Case*. For him, coffee is a sin. "It's the
devil's nectar. It's filthy and unhealthy." It has "vanquished the human
soul, spoiled innocence, and destroyed childhood. . . . All over the world,
people drink it, blindly, by the millions, by the hundreds of millions, by
the *billions*. And they must have it, they think they cannot do without it."
Before reading Helprin's tome, I never considered that coffee could ob-
sess anyone as thoroughly as it did this man who didn't even drink it.

The Lions and the Lambs

Despite such apparent coffeemania, world consumption–people spend
approximately $80 billion annually for coffee in all forms–is growing
only at a modest rate as we enter a new century. The steady decline in
the United States has been arrested by the specialty revolution, but per-
capita intake remains static at around 10 pounds a year. At least we are
drinking better coffee, in general. Specialty coffee now accounts for approximately 20 percent of U.S. home coffee consumption. Even the big
roasters have improved the quality of their blends, with arabica content
growing. It is becoming increasingly difficult to find reliable sources,
since the supply of true "specialty" high-end beans–10 percent of the
world's arabica at best–is getting tight.

Still, Procter & Gamble is now telling restaurant managers to buy its
"Folgers Ultra Roasted Coffee" frac-packs, claiming that this ultra-high-
yield blend will brew 196 cups per pound rather than the standard 40
cups per pound. Little wonder that specialty pioneer Don Schoenholt is
worried that the big boys such as Procter & Gamble, Philip Morris, and
Nestlé may infiltrate the SCAA, seducing the small fry with cash infusions. Schoenholt objected to a $75,000 P & G–Millstone donation to the
newly formed Specialty Coffee Institute (SCI), which will conduct scientific research on proper brewing methods, cupping profiles, and so forth.

At the 1998 annual SCAA convention, Schoenholt made an impas-
sioned speech. "We happy few have borne the burden of lifting half a continent's taste and half a continent's hopes and aspirations on our shoulders
for a generation," he declared. He called the National Coffee Association

the "tool of Big Coffee," and warned against "making nice-nice" with the NCA. "If we snuggle up too close, we will in time be devoured whole and alive, kicking and screaming. Beware the beasts in the forest. The lion may lie down with the lamb, but the lamb won't get much sleep."

It appears that Schoenholt faces an uphill battle. SCAA executive director Ted Lingle wants to work with the NCA, which funds research on caffeine and lobbies to protect U.S. coffee interests. "I believe in constructive engagement," Lingle says. "We need to raise the quality of the bottom end to get overall coffee consumption back where it was just after World War II." The real issue isn't between big or small, Lingle believes, but between those who advocate high standards—for bean quality, freshness, and brewing—and those who don't. "The Specialty Coffee Institute is part of that quest to develop scientific standards. Millstone is just helping to fund it."

When current NCA director Robert Nelson took the helm from long-time president George Boecklin in 1996, the NCA was a moribund organization with a dwindling membership. Since then, Nelson has increased membership, lowered dues rates, and actively reached out toward the specialty sector for members and support.

Only time will tell whether the Big Three have learned any real lessons about quality, or whether the specialty movement will be able to keep its youthful idealism in the face of its own consolidations and mergers. With Procter & Gamble's Millstone and Nestlé's Sarks, the line between specialty and mass-marketed coffee has been blurred. Late in 1998 Starbucks stunned the specialty world by making a deal with Kraft Foods (Philip Morris), owner of Maxwell House, for the giant multinational to distribute Starbucks in more than twenty-five thousand grocery stores nationwide. At the same time, Starbucks shocked followers by introducing a lighter roast in addition to its traditional dark offering. Some specialty insiders think it is only a matter of time before Maxwell House—a failure at its own whole-bean attempt—swallows Starbucks whole.[12]

---

[12]Coffee mergers and consolidations continue. AFC Enterprises—owner of several fast food chains—purchased Seattle's Best Coffee in 1998 and is taking its coffee franchise to the Middle East. Starbucks gobbled the forty-eight-store Pasqua chain in 1999. Under the direction of Michael Bregman and Randy Powell, Canada's Second Cup has emerged as the runner-up to Starbucks. In the United States, Second Cup bought Gloria Jean's, Coffee People, and Coffee Plantation. In 1998 it spun them off under the corporate heading of Coffee People, though Second Cup still owns 69 percent of the U.S. company. President Alton McEwen is pursuing an aggressive franchising effort in the United States. Minnesota-based Caribou Coffee, begun in 1992 by John and Kim Puckett, is rapidly expanding. Meanwhile, Germany's Probat purchased Jabez Burns roasters.

In response to Don Schoenholt's 1998 Denver manifesto, then-SCAA president Linda Smithers said, "Ten years ago, I stood before this organization and I kicked the can"–that is, she had denigrated supermarket coffee that came in a vacuum can. "I am embarrassed. I am humiliated at that, and I will never forget that I did that," she continued. "A consumer who likes Maxwell House deserves to have a good cup of Maxwell House coffee." Schoenholt, who finds nothing good in cans of supermarket coffee, must have been apoplectic.

The old-fashioned can acquired its poor reputation because of the inferior beans that went into the blends in the first place. This could be remedied. There is nothing inherently wrong with the vacuum can. Sure, it is better to buy fresh-roasted whole beans, then grind and brew them soon afterward; but for those who prefer the convenience of a can, there are encouraging options. At least two roasters–Comfort Foods and Gloria Jean's–are now putting one-way valves into can tops, which means that fresh-ground coffee can be canned without previous degassing and staling.

State of the Coffee World

"We have led not just the U.S. coffee market, but the world coffee market," Linda Smithers boasted in her SCAA Denver speech. "We are the example, we are the model, we have changed the view of coffee." Consumers in Finland would certainly dispute that claim. With a 28-pound annual per-capita consumption, the Finns drink more coffee than anyone in the world. They use *no* robusta beans and consume a token 2 percent of instant coffee.[13] For years, northern Europeans set the standard for coffee quality while the mass-market barbarians in the United States drank coffee swill.

Yet Smithers was right, in a way. Coffee inspiration has a way of flowing from one continent to another. Starbucks CEO Howard Schultz brought Italian espresso to North America, where he improved the quality of the beans, using all arabica, then drowned the result in milk for lattes and cappuccinos. In the 1995 foreword to his book on coffee,

---

[13]Inviting a woman for coffee in Finland is a sure sign of romantic interest. Finnish personal ads seeking a "day-coffee companion" are understood to be ads for casual sex. In nearby Norway, distances used to be measured by the number of "coffee boils"–the number of times someone had to stop to prepare coffee along the way.

Joel Schapira took a swipe at the new trend. "Coffee bars proliferate and landlords salivate as major metropolitan areas are saturated with . . . milk. Yes, the much vaunted coffee renaissance often looks very much like a large glass of hot milk, stained by carelessness." As much as the purist may denigrate such beverages, however, they have seduced many consumers back to coffee. So have all the flavors.[14]

The U.S. specialty movement is now spreading *back* to Europe and the rest of the world. Starbucks has opened stores throughout the Pacific Rim and in 1998 bought the Seattle Coffee Company (SCC), a sixty-three-store British chain founded by Seattle natives Scott and Ally Svenson. The British are clearly learning to love lattes, with specialty coffeehouses in Great Britain increasing by almost 850 percent from 1993 to 1997. Costa Coffee, founded in 1971 by brothers Sergio and Bruno Costa, is the leading chain, with one hundred seventeen coffee bars in the United Kingdom; Whittards is close behind. Incredibly, coffee has now overtaken tea as the beverage for which Brits spend the most money annually. Starbucks will use England as a springboard to invade the Continent, where it plans to open five hundred retail locations by 2003. C-Day should arrive soon.

The French, who still consume bitter cups brewed with a 45:55 robusta to arabica mix, certainly need Starbucks, even though their culinary pride may be offended. The Italians use almost as much robusta as the French, so the Americans may well succeed even in Milan, where Howard Schultz had his 1983 coffee epiphany. "Going back to Italy has been my dream," Schultz says. "It will be our greatest challenge. . . . But I am convinced we can succeed." Slowly, Europeans also are learning to drink flavored coffees. The United States, which bought half the world's coffee just after World War II, now consumes about 20 percent, with a united Germany close behind.

Japan, of course, is a coffee success story. That country now accounts for 11 percent of worldwide coffee sales (by value), and the Japanese appreciate high quality, buying some of the world's best beans. Although the number of *kissaten* has declined to one hundred thousand, quick-serve coffee shops, fast-food outlets, and family restaurants are

---

[14]Coffeehouses are popping up in surprising places throughout the United States. To lure readers, some public libraries are serving coffee, for instance, while the Legal Grind in California offers legal advice along with lattes. Car washes, doctors' offices, barbershops—all have opened coffee bars in various locales.

offering coffee too. Japan is unique in its devotion to vended canned coffees, with Coca-Cola's Georgia brand accounting for nearly half of all canned sales. The rest of the market is controlled largely by Ueshima Coffee Company, Key Coffee, and Art Coffee, while Nestlé dominates the instant sector with a 66 percent market share.

Indeed, every year Swiss-owned Nestlé sells over $6.4 billion in coffee around the globe, generating an operating profit of $1.3 billion. That makes it the world's largest and most profitable coffee company. While Nestlé owns several regular coffee firms—including Hills Brothers, Chase & Sanborn, MJB, and Sarks in the United States—it is still primarily a soluble-coffee company, selling over half the world's instant coffee, which puts it in good position to expand in the developing markets of Eastern Europe and Asia, where instant coffees tend to thrive. If Asian citizens drank three daily cups of Nescafé, Nestlé would double its current global sales. In developed markets such as Western Europe, North America, and Japan, finer-quality regular coffee is slowly gaining on instant, however. Worldwide, instant coffee accounts for 25 percent of all coffee sales by volume, but 40 percent by value.

As the twentieth century draws to a close, the coffee market already has undergone considerable consolidation. U.S. tobacco giant Philip Morris owns 14 percent of the world coffee market and is the world's leader in roast and ground coffee, while supplying 20 percent of the global soluble-coffee market.[15] Sara Lee, through its Dutch subsidiary Douwe Egberts and Superior in the United States, bites off another 11 percent of the world market, putting it in third place. Procter & Gamble is next with 8 percent, almost all of it in North America. Italy's Lavazza, which has expanded aggressively in Europe and the United States, now holds 2 percent of the world's coffee business, which may sound small but represents nearly $1 billion in annual sales.

That still leaves plenty of room for strong regional roasters, which account for over half of the world's regular coffee sales. In Spain, to take just one example, there are still two hundred forty roasting companies, most of which are very local businesses. Other roasters have an international presence. Illycaffè, the high-quality family Italian espresso

---

[15]Philip Morris owns Kraft (Maxwell House) in the U.S., Gevalia in Sweden, Nabob in Canada, Jacobs in Germany, Grand Mère, Carte Noire, and Jacques Vabre in France, Splendid and Mauro in Italy, and Saimaza in Spain, among others.

firm, now has subsidiaries in France, Germany, the Netherlands, and the United States. Tchibo recently swallowed Eduscho to become the largest German roaster–retailer with 38 percent of the national market, while Aldi, a German retail chain, supplies 15 percent of the country's households. Bremen-based Melitta is doing well not only in Germany, where it holds a 10 percent market share, but has expanded around the world.

In North America, where specialty retailers such as Starbucks, Second Cup, and the Coffee Beanery garner all the attention, Dunkin' Donuts in the United States and Tim Hortons in Canada sell a lot more coffee in their middle-class fast-food bakery outlets. In addition, many unheralded coffee roasters provide private-label and office coffees while innumerable coffeehouses and restaurants sell coffee as a beverage around the world.

A few large multinational green bean importers supply most of the world coffee trade, buying the raw beans at origin and selling them to roasters. Because of extremely narrow profit margins, these firms must rely on volume and speculation to stay in business. During the last decade, a number of traditional importers were closed or went bankrupt, caught in volatile price swings. Some guessed market movements incorrectly; others couldn't supply contracted coffee to roasters because producers defaulted on *their* contracts; and still others were plagued by mismanagement or fraud. A few simply concluded there are better ways to use their money with less risk. As a result, bankers have become more cautious about extending money for coffee.

The biggest suppliers now are Neumann Kaffee Gruppe (incorporating Bernhard Rothfos), Volcafe, Cargill, and the Esteve group (including Atlantic USA). Many smaller importers supply the specialty market with finer beans, however. In the United States, Knutsen, M. P. Mountanos, Royal, and Atlantic Specialty are located on the West Coast, while Paragon, Amcafe, and American Coffee Company are located on the East Coast. There are many other niche players throughout the continental U.S. and Europe.

By the turn of the century, world coffee production and consumption should exceed one hundred million bags a year. With more sophisticated machinery, mechanized harvesting will become somewhat more common, but hand picking will still predominate. Scientists may create genetically altered trees that produce decent-tasting "naturally" decaffeinated coffee beans, and chemists may come closer to replicating the magical coffee aroma and even the taste.

Even with new science and technology, however, the coffee industry will remain essentially unchanged. The boom-bust cycle will continue to send prices reeling up and down, exacerbated by frosts, droughts, speculative hedge funds, and the major roasters' just-in-time inventory practices, which leave them more vulnerable to shortages. The world-wide trend toward higher-quality coffee, for which consumers are willing to pay premium prices, gives some grounds for hope that small farmers and laborers may someday break out of poverty, though that day is certainly far in the future. Vietnam's booming robusta production, for instance, has driven the price down, and there is always a market for the inexpensive robusta known as *triple Bs*–blacks, brokens, and bits, the worst of the worst–that can show up in instant coffee, espresso, or cheap blends.

The Coffee Tour in Costa Rica

Eventually, consumers in coffee-growing areas may even be able to buy a decent cup of coffee in their own country. Historically, the best beans have been exported, but as domestic markets become more sophisticated, and as tourists flood the tropical paradises where coffee thrives, there will be an increasing demand for better quality in the producing countries.[16]

In Costa Rica, Steve Aronson sells Café Britt, his Strictly Hard Bean (meaning high-grown, high-quality) specialty offering. Aronson, a Brooklyn native, has spent his entire career in coffee trading or roasting. By the early 1990s, with Costa Rican tourism booming, he saw an opportunity. For years, Costa Rican law forced all coffee exporters to sell 10 percent of their beans at a government auction for domestic use. The prices were so low that exporters could have gotten more money abroad for even their blackest beans. As a result, the exporters often would sell 2 percent of their beans, buy them back, resell them, and continue this recycling until they had sold 10 percent in volume, but not in fact.

---

[16]There is even a Denver travel agency, Café Away, devoted to arranging tours in coffee-producing regions.

To counter such subterfuge, the government dumped beans to be auctioned into a vat of blue dye, to prevent their being resold, thus making them even less palatable. By law, it was *illegal* to sell high-quality beans in Costa Rica. Aronson successfully lobbied to change the law and to do away with the blue-dye fiasco. He now sells his Café Britt beans in upscale Costa Rican supermarkets, hotels, restaurants, and offices. It is consequently much easier to find a decent—indeed, superior—cup of coffee. I can testify that the regular brew is horrific. I had perhaps the worst coffee of my life—weak, bitter, and tasting faintly of ammonia—with my black beans and rice one morning in Heredia, a town in Costa Rica's Central Valley and the center of the coffee industry.

Taking advantage of the one-way valve, Aronson is pioneering in another way as well. He roasts, bags, and sells his beans worldwide through an 800 number and air courier service, cutting out all middlemen. U.S. consumers pay about $11 a pound (including shipping) for their specially delivered beans. Aronson attracts most of these customers through the Coffee Tour show at his roasting plant in Heredia. There, tourists pay $20 to watch attractive, energetic young actors present a whirlwind history of coffee in English and Spanish. The Pope blesses a coffee plant, French doctors vilify it and eventually it comes to Costa Rica, where the actors pick the coffee before your eyes. And what better way to end the tour than to buy some Café Britt? Some forty thousand people annually troop through the Coffee Tour, making it Costa Rica's third-biggest tourist attraction—and 10 percent of them become regular customers back home.

As entrepreneurs like Aronson make the world a smaller place, allowing us to dial 800-GO-BRITT and talk to someone in Costa Rica, perhaps the profits from coffee will be distributed somewhat more evenly.

Winged for Posterity

Only one thing is certain about coffee, though. Wherever it is grown, sold, brewed, and consumed, there will be lively controversy, strong opinions, and good conversation. "The best stories [are told] over coffee," wrote a wise commentator in 1902, "as the aroma of the coffee opens the portals of [the] soul, and the story, long hidden, is winged for posterity."

Author Mark Pendergrast (left) looks down at his half-filled canasta, which he picked in the same time it took his caporal Herman Gabriel Camel (right) to harvest a full basket on Finca Oriflama in Guatemala.

APPENDIX:
HOW TO BREW THE
PERFECT CUP

Despite all the mystique and hoopla, brewing a good cup of coffee is relatively simple. Grind recently roasted whole beans of a high-quality arabica blend. Bring cold, pure water to a near boil. Let the not-quite-boiling water remain in contact with the ground coffee at the proper ratio—2 tablespoons of coffee per 6 ounces of water—for four or five minutes.[1] Pour the filtered coffee into your cup. Add sugar or cream if you prefer it that way. Drink immediately. Sigh contentedly.

That really is all there is to it. Having said that, however, I have to admit there are finer points that true coffee *aficionados* can (and do) discuss endlessly. What is the best grind for what kind of brewing method? Which is the best brewing device? How dark should the beans be roasted? Is it preferable to store roasted coffee in the freezer or the refrigerator? Which are the best beans for after-dinner enjoyment? Are paper filters OK to use? Many other books on coffee cover these issues in much greater detail (see notes this section). God help you if you want to read about espresso, which is treated as if it were an esoteric art best performed by Leonardo da Vinci on speed. Though these matters are not of earth-shattering importance compared to global warming or world poverty, they *do* warrant answers. I'll try to be succinct.

I must admit that I am something of a nut on the subject myself. Coffee is truly addictive, in every way imaginable. When I began writing this book, I thought I appreciated good coffee. Now I've slurped, swirled, and spat at cupping sessions, tried beans from Antigua to Zimbabwe, and own five brewing systems. For $6, I bought a baby coffee tree from Melitta and hope it will grow

---

[1] An "approved coffee measure," available from some roasters, holds 2 tablespoons. If you like your coffee weaker, brew to the proper ratio and then add more hot water. To make iced coffee, brew it much stronger, since the ice will dilute it. Better, make coffee ice cubes and use regular-strength coffee.

to a lovely house tree that gives me my very own coffee cherries to process in another four or five years.

Sometimes I even roast my own beans in my kitchen oven at 450° F. using a Palani Plantation roasting pan—an aluminum pie plate with holes punched regularly in the bottom that set me back $21.50, including a supply of green beans.[2] In my oven, it takes about 7 minutes until the *first pop*, when I can hear the beans crackling and expanding. With the oven fan on, I take them out at 11 minutes for a medium roast, then toss them outdoors in a colander to cool them quickly. I blow on them to remove most of the brown chaff—the silver skin that pops off during the roast. It's magic. I put in the hard green beans that look something like peanuts, and when they come out, they have doubled in size and look like roasted coffee.

They taste like it too. The heat has caused a chemical alchemy inside the beans, carmelizing sugars and carbohydrates, producing chlorogenic acids, and releasing volatile aromatic oils. I grind my fresh-roasted beans in a cheap blade grinder, shaking it up and down for a minute or so. Then I measure the right amount into my preheated press pot (sloshing hot water around in it does the trick). In the meantime, I have put a tea kettle on the stove until it's whistling. I take it off the burner and let it sit for a few seconds, then pour the water in. Because the beans are so fresh, they still have a lot of carbon dioxide, and they foam up. I stir them down, add more water until it's full, cover it with the little piston, and go read the paper for five minutes. Then I slowly press the plunger to the bottom and pour my cup.

I like the press pot because it is so basic—it makes a real infusion, just the coffee and hot water. The drawback is that it's annoying to clean, and the coffee cools off pretty quickly. Regardless of your brewing method, you should pour it into a thermos to keep it warm once it's made. I also use a gold filter sometimes, pouring the hot water over the coffee, which filters directly into my thermos. And, of course, you can always use a paper filter system, which makes cleanup easier. (Unbleached filter papers may be better for the environment, but coffee passing through them picks up a slightly off flavor.) For a superb, dramatic brew, use a vacuum system, if you can find one in a specialty shop. If you insist, use an automatic electric brewer, but beware—only a few models get the temperature (should be 195° F.) and brew time right. And don't leave the coffee on the hotplate, where it will turn bitter quickly. You can even make a decent cup of coffee in a pumping percolator if you carefully regulate time, temperature, and grind, but I don't advise it.

---

[2]Fax Palani orders to 650–327–5660. In *Home Coffee Roasting,* Kenneth Davids also covers more expensive home roasters that use the "fluid bed" roasting principle. These are essentially modified popcorn poppers.

If you're not keen on coffee smoke in your kitchen (or setting off your smoke detector), and if you want professionally roasted coffee, you should find a local specialty roaster. Ask questions, and you'll get suggestions for different blends and roast styles. For that bright wake-up cup, try a high-grown Guatemalan Antigua. For after-dinner coffee, how about a rich, full-bodied bean like Sumatra? I cannot advise whether or not to purchase dark-roasted beans, since this is a matter of preference. I don't like beans roasted just this side of charcoal, but many people love them. The main point, regardless of what roast or origin you choose, is to get freshly roasted coffee at frequent intervals, buying only what you plan to use in the coming week or so. Otherwise, your coffee will get stale, no matter how great it was to start with.

If you don't have a local roaster, order through the mail. I can't recommend specific suppliers, but there are plenty of them. Some advertise; some are recommended in other books. Edward Behr, who writes a newsletter called *The Art of Eating*, is rather finicky and dislikes overly dark roasts. See his fall 1997 issue for sources.[3] At any rate, you can get terrific coffee through the mail.

If all else fails, try your local supermarket. The choices are getting better. If you buy bulk whole beans, ask the manager how frequently they are rotated. You don't want to buy beans that have been staling for a couple of weeks. If you buy packaged beans, make sure they are all-arabica and that they come in a one-way valve bag. While the valve won't guarantee freshness, it's better than nothing.

If you have to store your beans, put them in your freezer in an airtight container (with as little air in it as possible). You can grind and brew them straight from the freezer. Unless you're rich, don't bother buying a superior burr grinder—one of the blade whackers will do. The longer you let it whine, the finer your grind will be. Generally, the grind is determined by how long the grounds remain in contact with the hot water. For drip methods, a medium grind allows the flavorful solubles to be dissolved in five minutes. Longer contact with water just extracts bitterness. For my press pot, I use a slightly coarser grind, since the water remains in full contact with all of the grounds for the entire brewing time. For espresso or vacuum brewing, you want a fine, powdery grind owing to a very short period of contact.

If you're into espresso, there are all kinds of expensive machines. I bought one for $5 at a garage sale that works quite well. It even has a wand that steams the milk. And if you *really* want great espresso, go to your favorite coffeehouse and buy it there.

---

[3] *The Art of Eating*, Box 242, Peacham, VT 05862.

If you want to flavor your coffee, try easy-to-find natural additives first. The Ethiopians and Arabs used cinnamon, cardamom, nutmeg, citrus rinds, or ground nuts. They didn't know about cocoa or vanilla. Various forms of liquor work well. Whipped cream is nice. If you must, use flavoring syrups *after* you've brewed the coffee, or buy preflavored beans. Remember—whatever you like is OK.

NOTES

Due to space constraints and numerous sources, notes have been shortened and combined for each subsection within chapters. Individual citations are separated by semicolons. Citations are given in the order in which information is cited. For full citation of sources, see the bibliography. Newspaper and magazine articles with bylines are listed by author, and certain feature articles are listed by short title only. Other sources are cited by publication title and date.

Chapter One

3–4   **"Coffee makes us severe":** Swift quoted in Ukers, *All About Coffee*, 681; Lewin quoted in McKenna, *Food of the Gods*, 185; Jacob, *Saga of Coffee*; Castle, *Perfect Cup*; Kummer, *Joy of Coffee*; *Culturgram '97: Ethiopia*; Morris, *Road*; Roden, *Coffee*; Ukers, *All About Coffee*; Ted Lingle interview; Thomas, *Slave Trade*, 27; Steven Topik E-mail, April 1998.

4–5   **"The Puzzled Boy":** Schapira, *Book of Coffee*, 5; Jacob, *Saga of Coffee*, 30; Haarer, *Modern Coffee Production*, 1–2; Bersten, *Coffee Floats*, 34–39, Ukers, *All About Coffee*, 265; Heise, *Coffee and Coffee Houses*, 10–12; Morris, *Road*, 85; Aregay, "Early History"; Sherri Miller interview; Knox, "Coffee Safari."

6–7   **"Coffee Goes Arab":** Davids, *Coffee*, 21–22; Castle, *Perfect Cup*, 15–17; Ellis, *Historical Account*; Schapira, *Book of Coffee*, 6; Jacob, *Saga of Coffee*, 26–29, 55–58, 72; Hattox, *Coffee and Coffeehouses*, 6; Roden, *Coffee*, 12; Haarer, *Modern Coffee Production*, 3–5; Wrigley, *Coffee*, 1–60; *Coffee: Botany, Biochemistry*, 10; Heise, *Coffee and Coffee Houses*, 7–14, 107; Wellman, *Coffee*, 8–15; Ukers, *All About Coffee*, 12–19; *Tea & Coffee Trade Journal*, February 1933, 172.

7–10   **"Smugglers, New Cultivation":** Jacob, *Saga of Coffee*, 105–14, 155, 161; Haarer, *Modern Coffee Production*, 5–11, 400; Tannahill, *Food in History*, 314–15; Wrigley, *Coffee*, 1–60; Ukers, *All About Coffee*, 1–2, 21–23, 29, 33, 87–95; Heise, *Coffee and Coffee Houses*, 15–24, 37–43, 91–97, 127, 172–73; Bersten, *Coffee Floats*, 41; Wellman, *Coffee*, 16–18, 27–31; *Indonesia*, 15–19; Ellis, *Historical Account*; Thomas, *Slave Trade*, 159–61; Schoenholt, "Myth"; Jean Leclant, "Coffee and Cafés in Paris, 1644–1693," in *Food and Drink in History*, 92, 97; Visser, *Much Depends*, 207; Bramah, *Coffee Makers*, 26–28; Balzac, "Pleasures and Pains of Coffee."

10–11 **"Kolschitzsky and Camel Fodder":** Ukers, *All About Coffee*, 45–48; Jacob, *Saga of Coffee*, 67–69; Bersten, *Coffee Floats*, 39–42; Davids, *Espresso*, 11–12; Heise, *Coffee and Coffee Houses*, 96–100.

11–12 **"Lovlier Than a Thousand Kisses":** Ukers, *All About Coffee*, 41–43; 713–15; Heise, *Coffee and Coffee Houses*, 40–59, 89, 153–54; Bach, *Coffee Cantata*, modern slang translation by Metcalfe et al.

12–14 **"The British Coffee Invasion":** Ukers, *All About Coffee*, 50, 53–54, 68–79; Robinson, *Early English Coffee House; Old English Coffee Houses*,9–13, 16, 20–22; Uribe, *Brown Gold*, 14, Ellis, *Penny Universities*, viii, xiii, 10–11; Heise, *Coffee and Coffee Houses*, 104, 108, 130–33, 186; Bramah, *Tea & Coffee*, 48, Jacob, *Saga of Coffee*, 141–45; Mintz, *Sweetness and Power*, 111–14, 138; Bersten, *Coffee Floats*, 45, 49–54; Uribe, *Brown Gold*, 14; Wellman, *Coffee*, 22–26; Dobranski, "Where Men"; Pelzer, "Coffee Houses"; Smith, "Accounting for Taste."

14–15 **"The Legacay of the Boston Tea Party":** Furnas, *Americans*, 189; Ukers, *All About Coffee*, 101–26; Fugate, *Arbuckles*, 14; Heise, *Coffee and Coffee Houses*, 171–72.

15–16 **"Coffee Goes Latin":** Ukers, *All About Coffee*, 3–4; Haarer, *Modern Coffee Production*, 5–11, 16–17, 439–42; Jacob, *Saga of Coffee*, 189–92, 291–92; Wellman, *Coffee*, 18–38; Heise, *Coffee and Coffee Houses*, 15–24.

16–17 **"Coffee and the Industrial Revolution":** Heise, *Coffee and Coffee Houses*, 46–50.

17–19 **"Of Sugar, Coffee, and Slaves":** Ukers, *All About Coffee*, 15; James, *Black Jacobins*, ix, 4, 10–11, 16–23, 28, 55, 88; Jacob, *Saga of Coffee*, 163–64, 193–94; Trouillot, "Motion in the System"; Mintz, *Sweetness and Power*, frontispiece, 19–50, 110, 248; Bersten, *Coffee Floats*, 40, 60; Heinl and Heinl, *Written in Blood*, 26–27, 44, 94–95, 122, 151, 299, 679; Multatuli, *Max Havelaar*, 73–74; 123; *Indonesia*, 20–30; Bacha and Greenhill, *150 Years of Coffee*,19.

19–20 **"Napoleon's System":** Ukers, *All About Coffee*, 70; Jacob, *Saga of Coffee*, 220–33, 265–68; Tulard, *Napoleon*, 153–55, 198, 287; Ludwig, *Napoleon*; Bersten, *Coffee Floats*, 44, 60; Hewitt, *Coffee*, 63; Thurber, *Coffee*, 184.

Chapter Two

21–22 **"You believe perhaps":** Galeano, *Open Veins of Latin America*, 77; Steven C. Topik in *Second Conquest*, 37–84; Roseberry, *Coffee and Capitalism*, Burns, *History of Brazil*, 151–75; Jacob, *Saga of Coffee*, 298–99; Bushnell, *Emergence of Latin America*, 147.

22–24 **"Brazil's *Fazendas*":** Burns, *History of Brazil*, 1–2, 192–95, 270–71; Galeano, *Open Veins of Latin America*, 71–75; Bushnell, *Emergence of Latin America*, 148–51, 177–79; Thomas, *Slave Trade*, 571, 598–99, 611, 629–36, 730–33, 739–47, 787, 804; Haarer, *Modern Coffee Production*, 413–22, 453–58; Ukers, *All About Coffee*, 149–51; Curtin, *Atlantic Slave Trade*, 240–69; Isola, "Rediscovering the Legacy," 42; Freyre, *Masters and the Slaves*, xlii, 336, 428; Stein, "Negro Slavery in Brazil," in *Century of Brazilian History*, 64–67; *Documentary History*, 251–67; Jacob, *Saga of Coffee*, 296–97; Burns, *Latin America*, 143–44; Dean, *Rio Claro*, 34–87; Stein, *Vassouras*, 44–173; Bacha, *150 Years of Coffee*, 18–22, 131–95.

24–25 **"War Against the Land":** Dean, *With Broadax and Firebrand*, 178–90; 216–25, 234–35.

25–27 **"How to Grow and Harvest Brazilian Coffee":** Dinesen, *Out of Africa*, 8; Lago, *From Slavery to Free Labor*, 44; Jacob, *Saga of Coffee*, 293–94; *Culturgram '97 Brazil*, Ukers, *All About Coffee*, 133–52; Wellman, *Coffee*, 93–112, 370–73; Burns, *History of Brazil*, 191; Cameron, "Second International Coffee Conference," 907; "Brazil's Hidden Wealth."

27–28 **"From Slaves to *Colonos*":** "Brazil's Hidden Wealth"; Galeano, *Open Veins of Latin America*, 111; Dean, *With Broadax and Firebrand*, 210–11, 220; Burns, *History of Brazil*, 198–201; Ybarra, "Old King Coffee," 48, 50; Stolcke, *Coffee Planters*, 171–73, 185; Levi, *Prados of São Paulo*; Baer, *Brazilian Economy*, 16–20; Dean, *Rio Claro*, 88–197; Stein, *Vassouras*, 258–61.

28–29 **"The Brazilian Coffee Legacy":** Arnold, *Coffee*, 252–53; Dean, *With Broadax and Firebrand*, 217; Muniz, "What It Costs," 1231; Burns, *History of Brazil*, 209–12, 273, 285, 300–301; Dean, *Industrialization of São Paulo*, 3–66; Evans, *Dependent Development*, 80.

29–32   **"Guatemala and Neighbors":** *Culturgram '97: Guatemala*; Stephens, *Incidents of Travel*, 277–78; Woodward, *Central America*, 97–105; Williams, *States and Social Evolution*, 18–20, 28–31, 56; Burns, *Eadweard Muybridge in Guatemala*, 5–12, 28–30; Handy, *Gift of the Devil*, 35–74; McCreery, *Rural Guatemala*; Perez-Brignoli, *Brief History of Central America*, 84–87; *Guatemalan Indians and the State*; Haarer, *Modern Coffee Production*, 430–36; Wilson, *Maya Resurgence*, 34–37; *Indian in Latin American History*, xxiii–vi; Brockett, *Land, Power, and Poverty* 21–24; Conrad, *Nostromo*, 344.

32–33   **"Guatemala–A Penal Colony?":** McCreery, *Rural Guatemala*, 82; 175–80, 187–90, 226–32, 265–78, 282, 289, 293, 301; Williams, *States and Social Evolution*, 61–62, 121; McCreery and Munro, "Cargo of the Montserrat"; Cambranes, *Coffee and Peasants*, 153; Sanborn, *Winter in Central America*; Paige, *Coffee and Power*, 87; Richard Adams E-mail, February 1998.

34–36   **"The German Invasion":** McCreery, *Rural Guatemala*, 195–15, 232–33; Williams, *States and Social Evolution*, 59, 119, 154, 165–69, 196; Sanborn, *Winter in Central America*; Adams, *Crucifixion by Power*, 138–39; King, *Coban and the Verapaz*, 29–35, 95–99; Hannstein, *Early Twentieth-Century Life*, 11–27; Betty Adams E-mail, February 1998; Falcón, *Erwin Paul Dieseldorff*, 36–66, 302–48.

36–37   **"How to Grow and Harvest Coffee in Guatemala":** Ukers, *All About Coffee*, 144–47; Williams, *States and Social Evolution*, 150; Wellman, *Coffee*, 373–80.

37–38   **"Women and Children as Laborers":** William Dinwiddie quoted in Stone, "Puerto Rico's Needs," 1023; McCreery, *Rural Guatemala*, 278–80, 331; Perez-Brignoli, *Brief History of Central America*, 107; Conrad, *Nostromo*, 103; Buckley, *Violent Neighbors*, 13.

38–39   **"Stealing the Land":** Turner, *Barbarous Mexico*, 8–13, 58–79, 92–93, 112–13, 224–26; Ross, *Annexation of Mexico*, 49–80; Woodward, *Central America*, 171; Perez-Brignoli, *Brief History of Central America*, 87–88; Williams, *States and Social Evolution*, 69–79, 84–91, 123–26; Paige, *Coffee and Power*, 18–19, 154–62; Burns, *Latin America*, 148–52; North, *Bitter Grounds*, 17–28; White, *El Salvador*, 80–90; *El Salvador*, 3–14, 49–58, 120–22; Anderson, *War of the Dispossessed*, 14–18; Brockett, *Land, Power, and Poverty*, 25–26.

40–41   **"Coffee in Costa Rica":** Williams, *States and Social Evolution*, 9, 39, 44–53, 127–30, 161–62, 197; Gudmundson in *Coffee, Society, and Power*, 112–50; Seligson, *Peasants of Costa Rica*, 14–48; Winson, *Coffee and Democracy*, 1–36; Samper Kutschbach in *Coffee, Society, and Power*, 151–80; Mario Samper interview; Carolyn Hall interview; Brockett, *Land, Power, and Poverty*, 26–27.

41–43   **"Indonesians, Coolies":** Thurber, *Coffee*, 66–69; Haarer, *Modern Coffee Production*, 6–7; Arnold, *Coffee*, vi, 35–46, 117–29, 225; Weatherstone, *Pioneers*, 90–117, 146–78; Kooiman, "Plantations in Southern Asia"; Barron, "Science and the Nineteenth Century."

43–44   **"*Vastatrix* Attacks":** Arnold, *Coffee*, 129–32, 232, 268; Haarer, *Modern Coffee Production*, 1–7, 17–18, 296–99, 400–402; Wellman, *Coffee*, 80–87, 250–60; Thurber, *Coffee*, 78–79; Schapira, *Book of Coffee*, 37; McDonald, *Coffee Growing*, 7–22.

Chapter Three

45–46   **"We have joined":** Beecham, *Gettysburg*, 117; Lender, *Drinking in America*, 9; Langdon, *Everyday Things*, 188; Ukers, *All About Coffee*, 399–400; Powell, *Bring Out Your Dead*, x–xi, 11–27, 47, 72; Root, *Eating in America*, 127–29; Fugate, *Arbuckles*, 15, 20–22; Uribe, *Brown Gold*, 31–32; Thurber, *Coffee*, 247; Furnas, *The Americans*, 464–66; Taylor, *Writer's Guide*, 86–87.

46–47   **"Home Roasting, Brewing, and Ruination":** *Spice Mill*, July 1879, 77; Uribe, *Brown Gold*, 34–36; Hewitt, *Coffee*, 77; Davids, *Home Coffee Roasting*, 19; Bramah, *Coffee Makers*, 48–51, 59–68, 82–96, 118; Heise, *Coffee and Coffee Houses*, 54–58; Bersten, *Coffee Floats*, 55–98; Delbanco, "Rumford"; Orton, *Observations*, 15–24; Hess, *Taste of America*, 66–67, 104.

47–48   **"The Antebellum Coffee Industry":** Bacha and Greenhill, *150 Years of Coffee*, 317; Thurber, *Coffee*, 23, 59, 184–85; Ukers, *All About Coffee* 400, 596; Davids, *Home Coffee Roasting*, 26; Fugate, *Arbuckles*, 37; *Spice Mill*, November 1880, 326–27.

48–50   **"The Union (and Coffee) Forever":** Thurber, *Coffee*, 187–88, 201; Uribe, *Brown Gold*, 32–33; Wiley, *Life of Billy Yank*, 224–41; Billings, *Hardtack and Coffee*, 111–30; Crane, *Great Short Works*, 268; Fugate, *Arbuckles*, 16, 18, 24–25; Ukers, *All About Coffee*, 682–83; Root, *Eating in America*, 185; Thurber, *Coffee*, 188; Bacha and Greenhill, *150 Years of Coffee*, 150; DiBacco, *Made in the U.S.A.*, 135–45.

50–51   **"Jabez Burns, Inventor":** "Burns, Jabez," *Dictionary of National Biography*, v. 7, 423–24; Ukers, *All About Coffee*, 454, 595–96; Donald Schoenholt interview; Burns, *Notes of a Tour*, 107–8, 175; *Spice Mill*, October 1880, 29; Davids, *Home Coffee Roasting*, 24.

51–53   **"Arbuckle's Ariosa":** Fugate, *Arbuckles*, 29–30, 38–44, 66, 118, 192; Ukers, *All About Coffee*, 403; Arbuckle vs. Blackburn, 27–28; Chase & Sanborn, *Coffee*, 19; NYC, v. 273, 1054, 1100J, 1100WW, Dun Collection; *Spice Mill*, April 1917, 391–92; Dobie, "Good Coffee," 173; Moffett, "John Arbuckle," 542–44; Hardwick Report, 2311, 2317; "Arbuckle, John," *National Cyclopedia*, v. 15, 24–26.

53–55   **"Mr. Chase Meets Mr. Sanborn":** Standard Brands, "History of Chase & Sanborn," 1–8, 13–14; Chase & Sanborn, *Coffee*, 5–11, 24–28, 37, 40–49; Chase & Sanborn file, Warshaw Collection; Pancoast, *Trail Blazers in Advertising*, 41.

56–57   **"Jim Folger and Gold Rush Coffee":** Melville, *Moby-Dick*, 158; Newhall, "Folger Way," 1–16; CA, v. 15, 279, Dun Collection; "Schilling Lays Food Standard," *SF Bulletin*, May 1922, HB Scrapbook, Hills Brothers Collection.

57–61   **"Jabez Burns, Editor":** *Spice Mill*, January 1878, 5–7, 15, 23; Thurber, *Coffee*, 20, 26, 162–70; Bersten, *Coffee Floats*, 97-98, 255–56; *Spice Mill*, October 1878, 102–3, July 1878, 76, July 1879, 76–77; Pancoast, *Trail Blazers of Advertising*, 39–40; *Spice Mill*, June 1880, 165–66; "Artificial Coffee Beans"; Fugate, *Arbuckles*, 71, 148; "A Cup of Coffee," 244; *New York Times*, 3 June 1875, 12; Furnas, *The Americans*, 693; Jacob, *Saga of Coffee*, 230; Hewitt, *Coffee*, 88–90; Walsh, *Coffee*, 138-43, 201–17; Kains, *Chicory Growing*, 10–11, 44–45; *Spice Mill*, April 1879, 50; January 1880, 5, 10; "Poison in Every Cup," *New York Times*, 3 May 1884, 8; Schoenholt, "Shall We Talk"; idem, "Myth."

61–62   **"The Indispensable Beverage":** Hewitt, *Coffee*, vii, 37, 43–44; "A Cup of Coffee," 237; Thurber, *Coffee*, 204, 221–22; *Spice Mill*, April 1878, 52; Chase & Sanborn, *Coffee*, 7.

Chapter Four

63–65   **"Speculation seeks to discount":** Wheatley, "Coffee Exchange," 435, 442; Ukers, *All About Coffee*, 412, 455; "The Coffee Trade," *New York Times*, 25 April 1876, 8; Thurber, *Coffee*, 193–94; Michael Jimenez in *Coffee, Society, and Power*, 52; Hewitt, *Coffee*, dedication; *Coffee Annual* 1950, 45; NY, v. 202, 600E, NY, v. 276, 1317, 1390, 1398, 1395, 1400N, Dun Collection.

65–66   **"A Coffee Suicide?":** *New York Times*, 8 December 1880, 1, 9 December 1880, 5; MA, v. 86, 185, NY, v. 276, 1400N, Dun Collection; Wakeman, *History and Reminiscences*, 135–41; Ukers, *All About Coffee*, 455–56; Thurber, *Coffee*, 194.

66–67   **"Creating the Coffee Exchange":** Wakeman, *History and Reminiscences*, 146–48; 174–80; Wheatley, "Coffee Exchange," 436, 442; Ukers, *All About Coffee*, 456–57.

67–69   **"The Most Speculative Business":** Wheatley, "Coffee Exchange," 435–36; Ukers, *All About Coffee*, 457; *New York Times*, 5 April 1895, 2; Wakeman, *History and Reminiscences*, 180–81; Lexow Committee, 194; Brady, *Corner in Coffee*, 15–16; 146–48; 168–70.

69–70   **"The Great Coffee–Sugar War":** Fugate, *Arbuckles*, 57; Industrial Commission, 105–18; Lexow Committee, 119–20, 133–38, 145–47; United States v. American Sugar Refining, 7 June 1912, 1736–43.

70–73   **"Cutting the Thing Wide Open":** Lexow Committee, 195; Hardwick Report, 2306, 2309, 2316–17, 2321, 2324; *New York Times,* 19 December 1886, 14; Kuhn vs. Woolson; Mullins, *Sugar Trust,* 116; Arbuckle v. Blackburn, 17, 25–29.

73–74   **"The Arbuckle Signatures":** Fugate, *Arbuckles,* 107–12, 123–25; Warshaw Collection; Pancoast, *Trail Blazers of Advertising,* 52–53.

74–76   **"Coffee–Sugar Ceasefire":** Hardwick Report, 2320, 2323, 2329–32, 2336–37; Mullins, *Sugar Trust,* 21–28, 124; United States vs. American Sugar, 1757–65.

Chapter Five

77–79   **"Planters and producers have been lulled":** *Production and Consumption of Coffee,* 99; Sielcken in Sloss, "New York Coffee Party," 772; Holloway, *Brazilian Coffee Valorization,* 8–35; Dean, *With Broadax and Firebrand,* 231; Bacha and Greenhill, *150 Years of Coffee,* 23–34, 176–91.

79–80   **"The First International Coffee Conference":** *Production and Consumption of Coffee,* 3–31, 39–40, 61–62, 128; 61–62; *Tea, Coffee & Sugar,* 21 January 1903, 2; *Tea, Coffee & Sugar,* 11 February 1903, 6; Bergad, *Coffee and the Growth of Agrarian;* Goto, "Ethnic Groups," 112–13.

80–82   **"São Paulo Goes It Alone":** *Tea, Coffee & Sugar,* 4 February 1903, 5, 35–41, Holloway, *Brazilian Coffee Valorization,* 50–57; Rohr, *Inter-American Coffee Agreement,* 10–22; *Documentary History,* 325–29; Bacha and Greenhill, *150 Years of Coffee,* 35–42; 196–206.

82–85   **"Hermann Sielcken to the Rescue":** Holloway, *Brazilian Coffee Valorization,* 56–58, 64–69; Ukers, *All About Coffee,* 449; *Tea & Coffee Trade Journal,* December 1911, 472; *Essays on Coffee,* 86–87; "Penniless Immigrants," 12; *Money Trust Investigation,* 36, 52–62; Rohr, *Inter-American Coffee Agreement,* 16–17; Wellman, *Coffee,* 420–21.

85–87   **"The United States Howls":** Valorization file, Dept. of Justice, 1911–1913; *Congressional Record,* 2 March 1911, 3916, 26 April 1911, 635–42; Norris, *Fighting Liberal,* 154; *Tea & Coffee Trade Journal,* October 1911, 279, December 1911, 471–81; National Archives, Dept. of Justice Microfilm, 832.6133/82; Holloway, *Brazilian Coffee Valorization,* 73.

87–90   **"Sielcken Snaps His Fingers":** *Money Trust Investigation,* 52–53.

93–94   **"The Lawsuit Against Sielcken":** Valorization file, Dept. of Justice, 1911–1913; Sloss, "New York Coffee Party," 203; *Tea & Coffee Trade Journal,* June 1911, 470–71, September 1911, 204, October 1911, 289; "Sielcken Sees Flaw in Anti-Coffee Bill," *New York Times,* 22 February 1913; Holloway, *Brazilian Coffee Valorization,* 74–75, 82–84.

95–97   **"Hermann Sielcken's Final Years":** "Sielcken's Partner Leaves Him $1,000,000," *New York Times,* 5 February, 1913; "Sielcken Rumors Denied," idem, 23 May 1915; "Senators Consider Offer by Rumely," idem, 13 July 1918; "Visited Germany," idem, 25 November 1920, 16; "Dr. Rumely on the Stand," idem, 4 December 1920; "Recover Sielcken Wealth," idem, 6 April 1921; "Mrs. Roberts Wins Case," idem, 27 September 1919; "Halts Sielcken Payments," idem, 30 May 1922; "Mrs. Clara Sielcken Weds," idem, 12 February 1922; "Sielcken Executor Settles Big Suit," idem, 2 February 1923.

Chapter Six

97–99   **"The drug, caffeine":** "Sleep Nights," Postum ad, Post Family Papers; Paxson, *Charles William Post,* 20–40, 105–17; Carson, *Cornflake Crusade,* 43–83, 147–99; Bruce, *Cerealizing America,* 24–35; Deutsch, *New Nuts,* 57–109; Hubbard, "Two Live Men," 5; *Tea & Coffee Trade Journal,* March 1906, 129; *Spice Mill,* December 1912, 1107; Pendergrast, *For God, Country and Coca-Cola,* 10–11; Kellogg quoted in Post letter, 13 January

1913, Box 1, Post Family Papers; *Tea, Coffee & Sugar,* 4 February 1903, 11; Kellogg, "Nervousness, A Coffee Drunkard," Box 10, Kellogg Papers.

97–99 **"Mind Cure and Postum":** Paxson, *Charles William Post,* 40–46, 51–55, 73, 186–87; Bruce, *Cerealizing America,* 25–26, 28; Boyle, *Road to Wellville,* 118; "Mental Suggestion in Your Dietetics"; Carson, *Cornflake Crusade,* 15, 151–61; Francis Bellamy, "The Reason of Postum," manuscript, 1, Box 3, Post Family Papers.

99–100 **"Post's Fierce Attacks":** Bruce, *Cerealizing America,* 28–30; Paxson, *Charles William Post,* 74, 190–92; *Literary Digest* letter, 22 July 1921, Trigg Collection, Series 1, Box 2; Bellamy, 6, 10, Box 3, Post Family Papers; Collins, "There's a Reason," 4; "Turkey Threatens Libel Suit," *Battle Creek Journal,* 7 January 1913, Post Family Papers, Box 7; Deutsch, *New Nuts,* 104; Scott, *Psychology of Advertising,* 125; Post Family Papers, Box 1; Pendergrast, *For God, Country and Coca-Cola.*

100–1 **"Tapping the Paranoia":** Deutsch, *New Nuts,* 99, 111–20; Pendergrast, *For God, Country and Coca-Cola,* 109–24; *Tea & Coffee Trade Journal,* July 1906, 371; Paxson, *Charles William Post,* 73, 76–91.

101–3 **"Monk's Brew":** *Tea & Coffee Trade Journal,* June 1906, 303–4, 357, July 1910, 488–89, November 1912, 480; Hawk, "What We Eat"; Crothers, "Coffee and Tea Drunkenness," 740; Osborne, "Children Should Not Drink Coffee"; *Spice Mill,* November 1913, 1060.

104–6 **"The Coffee Merchants React":** *Tea, Coffee & Sugar,* 23 July 1902, 6, 4 February 1903, 6; *Tea & Coffee Trade Journal,* May 1906, 129, 237–40, November 1907, 252, October 1907, 206–7, June 1906, 304, July 1906, 369–70, July 1910, 45; Roden, *Coffee,* 34; Ukers, *All About Coffee,* 496; *Spice Mill,* December 1916, 1374, December 1912, 1156; Dwinell-Wright copy, 1914, Hills Brothers Collection; "Grandma Hedin," *The Coffee Club,* January 1923, Hills Brothers Collection; Collins, "There's a Reason," 4–5.

106–7 **"The *Collier's* Libel Flap":** "Colliers Sue Post"; Collins, "There's a Reason," 6; "Mental Suggestion in Your Dietetics"; Paxson, *Charles William Post,* 207–11; Post letter, 29 June 1910, Post Family Papers, Box 3.

107–10 **"Dr. Wiley's Ambivalence":** *Tea & Coffee Trade Journal,* May 1906, 129, October 1910, 734, November 1907, 253, December 1907, 304, November 1910, 806–8, April 1910, 276; Pendergrast, *For God, Country and Coca-Cola,* 109–22; Ukers, "Better Teas and Coffees"; Harris, "Some Coffees," 264–65; *Spice Mill,* January 1910, 50; McMakin, "Influence of Coffee"; Wiley speech, *Tea & Coffee Trade Journal,* December 1912, 33–38; Hollingworth speech, idem, December 1912, 52–56.

110–12 **"Post's Last Act":** Paxson, *Charles William Post,* 271–98, 310–31; *Tea & Coffee Trade Journal,* February 1914, 159–60; Hubbard, "Two Live Men," 5; Bellamy, 3, Box 3, Post Family Papers; Bruce, *Cerealizing America,* 25.

Chapter Seven

115–17 **"[By 1915], the sheer excitement":** Schlereth, *Victorian America,* 302; *Tea & Coffee Trade Journal,* October 1907, 217, October 1920, 423; *Spice Mill,* November 1909, 704, December 1911, 1077, May 1915, 465, December 1915, 1262, 1285–86, 1336, 1340, 1352, January 1916, 14, February 1916, 180; Carson, *Old Country Store,* 14; Bramah, *Coffee Makers,* 120, 134–35; Melitta North America company material; Ukers, *All About Coffee,* 477, 618.

117–19 **"A & P Grinds Its Own":** "Coffee Department," *Sears Roebuck Catalog,* unpaged; Tedlow, *New and Improved,* 188–211; *International Directory of Company Histories,* v. 2, 636–38; Walsh, *Rise and Decline;* Hoyt, *That Wonderful A & P!;* Adelman, *A & P: A Study; FTC Decisions,* v. 1, 163–72.

119–20 **"The Premium Peddlers":** Lunding, *Sharing a Business,* 19–21; Jewel Tea Co., *Merchandising Plans and History,* 3–4; *First Thirty Years,* 9; *Spice Mill,* September 1908, 570,

August 1915, 802, November 1915, 1204–5, October 1917, 1228–29, December 1916, 1391–99, September 1916, 1051; Paul Haserodt, "Our Retail Distributor."

120–21 **"The Institutional Niche":** *Spice Mill,* November 1904, 413–14; *Tea & Coffee Trade Journal,* April 1905, 149–52, May 1960, 21; Schoenholt, "Frederic A. Cauchois"; Donald Schoenholt E-mail; Bowman, *More Than a Coffee Company,* 1–14; "90 Years"; Earl Lingle interview.

121–24 **"Sexy Coffee?":** *Tea & Coffee Trade Journal,* January 1907, 696, July 1911, 38, September 1912, 267; *Tea & Coffee Trade Journal* Suppl., December 1912, 80, October 1914, 1018–19, December 1914, 1306, January 1910, 60, February 1907, 751, July 1907, 38, October 1912, 367, January 1911, 78; *Spice Mill,* December 1914, 1244–45, March 1914, 328–29, December 1915, 1298–1304, March 1916, 236–48, April 1916, 416, June 1916, 594, May 1916, 531; Scott, *Psychology of Advertising,* 74–75; 210–11.

124–26 **"Hills Brothers Fills a Vacuum":** Broussard-Simmons and Shay, *Register of the Hills Bros.*; Wilson, *Background Story of Hills Bros.,* 26; Wellman, *Coffee,* 386–91; *Tea & Coffee Trade Journal,* October 1920, 425–27; *Coffee Annual* 1950, 49; "Vacuum Cans"; "The Wreck of the Pomona," reprint from the *Press Democrat,* August 2, n.d., Hills Brothers Collection; Frank B. Veirs, Jr., "Notes and Informal Memoirs," idem; HB Scrapbook, 1910–1912, Series 3, Box 6, idem; 1912 HB salesman's book, Series 8, Box 1, idem; Rules for exhibitors, Universal Exposition, Series 14, Box 1, idem; Convention at San Francisco Commerce Club, 17 August 1917, idem; Reuben Hills to A. H. Hills, 10 December 1922, Series 1, Box 1, idem; T. Carroll Wilson interview.

126–28 **"MJB: Why?":** Sherrell, "Coffee Roasting California Style"; McDougall, *Coffee, Martinis,* 11–16, 25–26, 55–70, 100–104; Fox, *Mirror Makers,* 40–77; *Tea & Coffee Trade Journal,* April 1906, 201; *Spice Mill,* June 1909, 302.

128–30 **"The Great San Francisco Earthquake":** Newhall, *Folger Way,* 7–11; *Tea & Coffee Trade Journal* May 1906, 260–61, November 1906, 572, September 1907, 151; Veirs, "Notes," Hills Brothers Collection; McDougall, *Coffee, Martinis,* 1–10.

130–31 **"Chase & Sanborn: Tally-Ho":** Standard Brands, "History," 9, 13; *Spice Mill,* January 1909, 47; *How Can I Get Good Coffee?* (1898), *After Dinner Tricks* (1900) pamphlet, Chase & Sanborn, Warshaw Collection; *Tea & Coffee Trade Journal,* October 1907, 208, January 1906, 35, January 1907, 705, March 1909, 176, April 1912, 323.

131–35 **"Joel Cheek Creates Maxwell House":** "History of Maxwell House Coffee"; "Cheek-Neal Coffee Company, Account History," Box 3, Hartman Center, J. Walter Thompson Inc. Files; Kraft Foods, "Maxwell House Coffee: A Chronological History"; Kraft Foods, "Maxwell House Coffee Company: Corporate Backgrounder"; Davis, "Good Since the First Drop"; West, "Good to the Last Drop"; "Joel O. Cheek," *Tea & Coffee Trade Journal,* November 1921, 704, October 1907, 206, July 1910, 48, February 1911, 114–15, 125, September 1964, 59; *Coffee Annual* 1950, 48; *Nashville City Directory* 1908; Robert S. Cheek to General Foods, 31 October 1939, Kraft Foods Archives; Bill Bateman E-mail, September 1997; Fox, *Mirror Makers,* 6; *Spice Mill,* December 1915, 1335, January 1914, 65, December 1914, 1235, 1242–44, 1268–70, 1296–98, December 1915, 1293, 1368, 1384–86, December 1916, 1336, 1381.

135–38 **"Gift, Guest, or Yuban?":** MacDougall, *Autobiography,* 145; *Coffee Annual* 1950, 53; *Tea & Coffee Trade Journal,* April 1912, 306–8, 320, June 1910, 406; "John Arbuckle Is Dead," *Baltimore Sun,* 28 March 1912; "No Arbuckle Will Found," *Baltimore Sun,* 2 April 1912; "Arbuckle Floating Hotel to Be Closed," *New Paltz Times,* October 1913, property Stanley Newkirk; JWT Info Center, Box 2, Hartman Center, J. Walter Thompson Inc. Files; "Can a Coffee Be Nationally Standardized?" 9 November 1912 letter, Arbuckle Brothers, Box 2, Hartman Center, J. Walter Thompson Inc. Files; Fox, *Mirror Makers,* 79–94; Sid Bernstein, Box 5, 7, Hartman Center, J. Walter Thompson Inc. Files; Fugate, *Arbuckles,* 48; *Spice Mill,* December 1913, 1269, April 1915, 343, August 1915, 803, December 1915, 1323, April 1916, 354, July 1916, 770;

New York Evening Journal, 26 February 1914; "Yuban Coffee Campaign," *Independent Advertising,* 1916, Howard Henderson, Box 5, J. Walter Thompson Inc. Files.

138–42   **"The (Slow) Rise of Women":** Helen Resor affidavit, 20 March 1924, U.S. Treasury Dept., "In the Matter of J. Walter Thompson Co.," No. 2112, 68–70, Bernstein, Box 9, Hartman Center, J. Walter Thompson Inc. Files; Fox, *Mirror Makers,* 86–94; interview with James Webb Young, 11 November 1963, Bernstein, Box 1, 5, 8, Hartman Center, J. Walter Thompson Inc. Files; *Spice Mill,* October 1913, 969; Frank Veirs Notes, Hills Brothers Collection; *Tea & Coffee Trade Journal,* October 1910, 296, September 1911, 168; *Spice Mill,* October 1913, 994, February 1915, 211, October 1915, 1097; Arbuckle Bros., "Can a Coffee Be Nationally Standardized?" Box 2, 2–5, Hartman Center, J. Walter Thompson Inc. Files; MacDougall, *Autobiography,* 2–5, 42–43, 51–97, 144–57, 186–87; Rella MacDougall interview; "Alice Foote MacDougall Dies."

Chapter Eight

143–41   **"Take a carefully blended":** 2 October 1917 letter, Series 1, Box 2, Trigg Collection; *Spice Mill,* December 1914, 1300, 1336o–1336p, 1354–55, June 1917, 675, December 1915, 1263–64, 1403–6, August 1916, 832, 855, August 1914, 806, September 1914, 966, 1022–23, November 1914, 1136–37, October 1914, 1070, 1075, January 1915, 4, October 1915, 1058, July 1917, 774, January 1917, 67, February 1917, 184, May 1917, 513, June 1915, 585, January 1918, 60, July 1916, 770, December 1916, 1337, April 1913, 348c, June 1913, 511–12, 541, July 1913, 616–20d, 650–51, August 1913, 726, 748; Clayton, *Grace,* 335–36; Rohr, *Inter-American Coffee Agreement,* 23–25; "Germany Finds Substitutes"; Jacob, *Saga of Coffee,* 323–24; Shaw, "Civil War in Brazil," 63; *Tea & Coffee Trade Journal* August 1919, 147–48; Perez-Brignoli, *Brief History of Central America,* 103; Brockett, *Land, Power, and Poverty,* 59–60; White, *El Salvador,* 90–96; Bacha and Greenhill, *150 Years of Coffee,* 40–41, 202–5.

146–47   **"Coffee and the Doughboy":** *Spice Mill,* April 1917, 418, 428, July 1917, 767, 808, June 1918, 708, August 1918, 972, December 1917, 1413, 1461, 1489, February 1918, 207, 209–10, April 1918, 418, 444–45; *Tea & Coffee Trade Journal,* January 1919, 32, 36; 54–55; September 1919, 254–55; *Coffee Annual* 1950, 56.

147–49   **"A Cup of George":** *Tea & Coffee Trade Journal,* January 1919, 54–55, March 1919, 237, May 1919, 418, June 1919, 527, September 1919, 254, July 1921, October 1945, 18–20, 39–40, April 1946, 57; Finley, "St. Louis Coffee," 27; Martin, "History of Coffee Prices," 767; Bramah, *Tea & Coffee,* 51; Nicolle, "Coffee"; *Spice Mill,* April 1916, 370, July 1915, 745, March 1918, 299, June 1918, 677, October 1918, 1185, November 1918, 1398a–98b, December 1918, 1459, 1478g–78i; W. W. Krag Memo, Series 1, Box 2, Trigg Papers; Bond, "Coffee," 160; Driver, "Soluble Coffee," 19; Bersten, *Coffee Floats,* 257–58; Trigg letter, 13 August 1918, Series 1, Box 2, Trigg Papers; E. Montgomery letter, Dept. of Commerce, 16 November 1921, idem; Gladwell, "Dead Zone," 52; "Epidemic Delays Coffee Shipments," *New York Times,* 28 October, 1918, 8.

149–50   **"Meanwhile, Back on the *Fazenda* . . .":** Burns, *History of Brazil,* 352–60; Rohr, *Inter-American Coffee Agreement,* 25–27; Topik, *Political Economy,* 74; *Tea & Coffee Trade Journal,* January 1919, 33–34; Hannstein, *Early Twentieth-Century Life,* 28–29; Ramos articles, *Spice Mill,* April 1909, 229–30; May 1909, 298–99; Bacha and Greenhill, *150 Years of Coffee,* 40–41.

150–52   **"Colombia Comes of Age":** Beyer, *Colombian Coffee Industry,* 135, 140, 157–233; Palacios, *Coffee in Colombia,* 68–120, 198–223; Uribe, *Brown Gold,* 102–4; *Colombia: A Country Study,* 22–32; Jiménez, "Traveling Far"; Gudmundson, "Peasant, Farmer"; *Spice Mill,* September 1914, 912, February 1909, 96–97, July 1910, 489–90; Mario Samper Kutschbach, "In Difficult Times," and Michael F. Jiménez, "At the Banquet of Civilization," in *Coffee, Society and Power,* 151–80, 262–93; Schapira, *Book of Coffee & Tea,* 69–70; *Tea & Coffee Trade Journal,* August 1919, 148, January 1920, 47–49; *New*

York Times, 1 February 1920, sec. 2, 6, 18 July 1920, sec. 2, 13; Parsons, "Why Coffee Is High"; Bacha and Greenhill, *150 Years of Coffee*, 41, 291–375.

152–53 **"Robusta or Bust":** *Spice Mill*, June 1909, 366, January 1911, 28–30, December 1911, 1020–24, February 1912, 143, April 1912, 343, September 1914, 908, March 1914, 255; *Tea & Coffee Trade Journal*, March 1912, 227, April 1912, 323, September 1920, 299, March 1921, 325–26, April 1921, 461; Haarer, *Modern Coffee Production*, 1.

153–54 **"Between Cancer and Capricorn":** *Spice Mill*, September 1914, 897–98, October 1914, 1014–15, June 1917, 638; *Tea & Coffee Trade Journal*, May 1911, 351–54, March 1921, 313; *New York Times*, 24 February 1924, 12, 29 June 1924, 4; Huxley, *Flame Trees of Thika*; idem, *Out in the Midday Sun*; Dinesen, *Out of Africa*; McDonald, *Coffee Growing*; Wellman, *Coffee*, 38–40; Beyer, *Colombian Coffee Industry*, 167.

Chapter Nine

155 **"Professor Prescott speaks":** "Solid Benefit," *Boston Transcript*, 18 October 1923, in 1924 *Coffee Club*, Hills Brothers Collection.

155–58 **"Prohibition and the Roaring Twenties":** *Spice Mill*, January 1917, 67, April 1917, 362; Coffey, *Long Thirst*; *Tea & Coffee Trade Journal*, March 1919, 224–25, May 1919, 432, 441, April 1919, 332, June 1919, 524, July 1919, 56, September 1919, 266, December 1919, 547, 565–65e; January 1920, 58, March 1920, 323, April 1920, 443, June 1920, 689, 696, December 1920, 710–11, May 1921, 570, 612–13, September 1921, 326–27, October 1921, 462–63; "The Coffee Den," *San Francisco Call*, 16 October 1919, in HB Scrapbook, Hills Brothers Collection; *New York Times*, 9 July 1922, sec. 9, 14; Series 3, Box 12, Hills Brothers Collection; February 1924 *Coffee Club* newsletter, idem; "How to Use the Coffee Exhibit," 1921, Hills Brothers Misc. Collection; Joint Coffee Trade Publicity Committee, "The Most Helpful Coffee Advertisement Ever Published," 1924, "American Press Hails Prescott's Coffee Vindication," 1923, Hills Brothers Collection; Johnson, "Scientific Research"; Young, *Adventures in Advertising*, 44–49; Ukers, *All About Coffee*, 306–13; Ewen, *Captains of Consciousness*, 41, 80, 202–3.

159–61 **"The Coffeehouse Resurgence":** *Tea & Coffee Trade Journal*, March 1919, 221, December 1919, 565e–65f; *New York Times*, 4 January 1920, sec. 2, 1, 13 November 1920, 10, 2 February 1921, 15, 2 September 1923, 11; "Coffee-Drunken New York," idem, 16 September 1923, sec. 4, 12; "More Coffee Drunk," idem, 24 February 1924, 12; "Bids for Coffee Prize," idem, 19 February 1925, 2; "Drinks 85 Cups," idem, 12 January 1927, 1; "Tea and Tension," idem, 9 August 1928, 18; "A Cup of Coffee, A Sandwich and You," Billy Rose and Al Dubin, 1925, "Hot Coffee," Bartley Costello, 1926, "You're the Cream in My Coffee," B. G. De Sylva et al., 1928: all songs in Box 145, DeVincent Collection; Nan Schwab Pendergrast interview, December 1996; MacDougall, *Autobiography*, 112–43, 168–70, 203–5; "Alice Foote MacDougall Dies."

161–62 **"Eight O'Clock Rocks":** Hoyt, *That Wonderful A & P!*, 112–23, 135–36; Ukers, *All About Coffee*, 386–87, 467; Adelman, *A & P*, 265; Walsh, *Rise and Decline*, 34–44; *Coffee Annual 1950*, 58; "Venezuela's Coffee," 15; Taylor, "Once Around the Clock"; Jewel Tea Co. publications; Roseberry, *Coffee and Capitalism*; Barnard, *Dividends*, 7; "Premium Men on Strike," *Tea & Coffee Trade Journal*, September 1919, 278, April 1921, 522; Allen, *Only Yesterday*, 163–67; Taylor, "Once Around the Clock."

163–64 **"The West Coast Brands":** HB 1921 Scrapbook, Hills Brothers Collection; Wilson, *Background Story*; "Playing the Favorite," *Pacific Retail Adviser*, August 1920, HB Scrapbook, Hills Brothers Collection; "Coffee Trade Loses Good Friend," HB Scrapbook, 1921, idem; Misc. ads, HB Scrapbook, 1921–1922, idem; Twitchell, *Adcult USA*, 52;

Edward Hills to A. H. Hills, 26 September 1921, E. M. Cofer memo to A. H. Hills, 12 October 1922, Series 1, Box 1, Hills Brothers Collection; *Federal Trade Commission Decisions*, vol. 11, 163–69, vol. 9, 180–91; Piggly Wiggly, "No Hills Coffee," December 1920; "A Fight to the Finish," *Retail Grocers Advocate*, 7 January 1921; "No Coffee Margins," idem, 31 March 1922; Charles Bain address to Pacific Coast Grocers Ass., 10 June 1925, Hills Brothers Misc. Collection; "Hills' 'Red Can' Hypocrisy," *Duncan's Trade Register*, January 1922, "With the Editor," *Grocer's Journal*, 7 April 1922, H. G. Hills to J. Herbert Smith, 12 April 1922, all in HB Scrapbook, Hills Brothers Collection; "Brief of Hills Bros.," No. 4493 in the U.S. Circuit Ct. of Appeals for the Ninth District, 1925, and other FTC documents; "Decision of U.S. Supreme Court"; *Federal Trade Commission Decisions*, v. 8, 351–60; San Francisco, Getz Bros. Exporters 1925 catalog, Series 14, Box 1, Hills Brothers Collection; 1925 HB ads, Series 3, Box 60, idem; Ayer estimate, 6 December 1926, idem; Ayer, "Coffee Data in Towns in Illinois, Indiana, Iowa, Michigan, Wisconsin," December 1927, idem; "Coffee Peddler Makes His Last Call," 1928, Series 3, Box 68, idem; Series 3, Box 66, idem; "The 1929 Campaign" and Chicago folder, idem; Series 3, Box 74, idem; "Chicago Bulletin for Salesmen," 28 September 1928, Series 7, Box 1, idem; "Chicago Bulletin for Salesmen," 9 June and 10 September 1930, "Service Betterment," 3–5 February 1926, Series 7, Box 1,idem; McDougall, *Coffee, Martinis*, 94, 116–18, 130–35; Newhall, *Folger Way, Printer's Ink*, 25 May 1915, quoted in Twitchell, *Adcult USA*, 229; B. W. Harrison, *Tea & Coffee Trade Journal*, October 1920, 504; Hoyt, *That Wonderful A & P!*, 105–8; Link, *New Psychology of Selling*, 22.

167–68 **"The Decline of Arbuckles":** Goetzinger, "Arbuckle Brothers"; "Report Prepared for Arbuckle Brothers," 30 April 1921, 1–33, Howard Henderson, Box 5, J. Walter Thompson Inc. Files; "Arbuckle Brothers (Yuban Coffee)," undated, Information Center, Box 1, idem; "In the Orphans' Court," 3–6.

168–72 **"The Corporate Monsters":** "Let Them Eat Cake," 132; Fox, *Mirror Makers*, 89, 93, 97, 101–12; Goodrum and Dalrymple, *Advertising in America*, 38, 101; "Great American Drink" ad for Chase & Sanborn, 1923, *FTC*, December, v. 9, 184, HB Scrapbook, Hills Brothers Collection; Standard Brands, "History of Chase & Sanborn"; Florance, "Food," 36; Standard Brands 1929 annual report, in Historical Collections, Baker Library; Kraft Foods, "Maxwell House Coffee: A Chronological History," 2; "Maxwell House Is Instant Hit," Hills Brothers Collection; "Account History, Cheek-Neal Coffee Co.," 23 December 1925, Box 3, J. Walter Thompson Inc. Account Files; Buckley, *Mechanical Man*, 4, 123–47; Watson, "What Is Behaviorism?" 728; Watson, "Feed Me on Facts"; Lewis, *Babbitt*, 13, 16, 95; Larson, "Highlights," 3; MacGowan, "Profiles"; Rorty, *Our Master's Voice*, 284–85, 350; Allen, *Only Yesterday*, 179–81; Twitchell, *Adcult USA*, 33, 192–93; Burnham, "John Broadus Watson," 671; James W. Young memo, 6 January 1959, Sid Bernstein, Box 6, J. Walter Thompson Inc. Files; Buckley, "Selling of a Psychologist," 14; Pancoast, *Trail Blazers in Advertising*, xii, 42; Chase, *Your Money's Worth*, 9; Paxson, *Charles William Post*, 346, 352–53; General Foods 1930 annual report, 19, in Historical Collections, Baker Library; "Prominent Chicagoans Extend Welcome," Chicago *Daily News*, 14 December 1927, 7, Sid Bernstein, Box 7, J. Walter Thompson Inc. Files; "Let Them Eat Cake," 124–26; "Edward F. Hutton . . . Dies"; Davis, "Good Since the First Drop."

173–78 **"The Great Stock Market–Coffee Crash":** Rohr, *Inter-American Coffee Agreement*, 27–41, 46–50; Rowe, *Studies*; Welman, *Coffee*, 421–23; Beeson, "American Coffee Drinker"; "Defends Brazil in Coffee Policy," *New York Times*, 2 January 1925, 28; "Federal Aid Asked in Coffee Situation," idem, 20 December 1924, 17; "International Drama of a Cup of Coffee," *New York Times Magazine*, 11 January 1925, 7; "Gov't. Behind Bar on Coffee Loans," *New York Times*, 13 November 1925; "Hoover Warns World," idem, 10 January 1926, 1; U.S. Congress, House, *Crude Rubber, Coffee*, 1–3; 23–27; 298–99; *New York Times*, 5 January 1926, 29, 7 January 1926, 42; "Where Coffee Is King"; "Brazilians Firm on Coffee Prices," *New York Times*, 10 September 1928,

30; Burns, *History of Brazil,* 389; Muniz, "What It Costs," 1232–34; Allen, *Only Yesterday,* 303; Naylor, "Coffee Price Crisis"; "Says Coffee Trade Is in Good Condition," *New York Times,* 28 October 1928, pt. 3, 1; "Coffee Restriction Defended," idem, 21 January 1929, 6; Dean, *With Broadax and Firebrand,* 240–48, 258; "Brazil Inaugurates Coffee Warehouse," *New York Times,* 17 February 1929, 3; "Lower Prices Urged," idem, 19 May 1929, pt. 3, 7; Naylor, "Brazil's Coffee Plan"; "Brazilian Exports Better," *New York Times,* 15 August 1929, 31; Boyle, "Black Coffee," 43; Ybarra, "Old King Coffee," 48; Moon quoted in Jones et al., *American Policies Abroad,* 172–94; Handy, *Gift of the Devil,* 77; *New York Times,* 23 November 1928, 24; Paige, *Coffee and Power,* 105, 157–68; Buckley, *Violent Neighbors,* 63; LaFeber, *Inevitable Revolutions;* Gilmore, "In the Mountainous Kingdom"; *Tea & Coffee Trade Journal,* December 1936, 424; Masferrer quoted in Barry, *Roots of Rebellion,* 21; "Big Coffee Crop Forecast," *New York Times,* 28 July 1929, sec. 2, 18; "Big Coffee Movement," idem, 9 September 1929, 33; "Britons on Way to São Paulo," idem, 21 September 1929, 4; Kindleberger, *Manias, Panics, and Crashes,* 92; Baer, *Brazilian Economy,* 32–36; Bacha and Greenhill, *150 Years of Coffee,* 41–54, 218–28; "Failure to Get Loan for Coffee," *New York Times,* 16 October 1929, 40; Allen, *Only Yesterday,* 321, 323; Kindleberger, *Manias, Panics, and Crashes,* 126, 149–51, 235–42.

Chapter Ten

179   **"Coffee is our national":** Jacob, *Saga of Coffee,* 356.

179–82   **"The Coffee Inferno":** Burns, *History of Brazil,* 395–404; "Coffee and Revolution in Brazil"; Shaw, "Civil War in Brazil"; "Coffee and Politics Disrupt Brazil"; Rohr, *Inter-American Coffee Agreement,* 65; Wellman, *Coffee,* 422–23; Proni, *Coffee,* 46; "Dr. Vargas Depicts Plight of Brazil," *New York Times,* 28 December 1930, sec. 3, 6; "Brazilian Coffee Developments"; *New York Times,* 9 December 1930, 7, 10 December 1930, 10, 11 October 1931, 31, 18 October,1931, sec. 2, 8; *Tea & Coffee Trade Journal,* September 1931, 250–53, 280, December 1931, 627–29, August 1932, 138; Ybarra, "Old King Coffee," 48; "Make Coffee Plastic"; "Coffee Plastic"; "Coffee Plastics"; Marden, "Coffee Is King," 575; Moore, "As São Paulo Grows," 660, 673; Ukers, "Santos, São Paulo and Coffee," 30; "Big Wheat-Coffee Swap"; Dulles, *Vargas of Brazil,* 14–79; Skidmore, *Politics in Brazil,* 10–43; Jacob, *Saga of Coffee,* 334–57; Friele letter, 12 September 1931, Coffee-Wheat Swap Files; Rohr, *Inter-American Coffee Agreement,* 65; Baer, *Brazilian Economy,* 36–37, 240–41; Dean, *Industrialization of São Paulo,* 83–180; *New York Times,* 3 February 1931, 20, 8 March 1931, sec. 3, 8, 9 March 1931, 10, 1 June 1931, 26, 3 June 1931, 24, 21 June 1931, sec. 3, 8, 29 June 1931, 33, 2 August 1931, sec. 2, 14, 21 August 1931, 3, 6 September 1931, sec. 9, 1, 24 October 1931, 1, 5 December 1931, 12, 26 December 1931, 14, 1 January 1932, 21, 9 January 1932, 4, 28 February 1932, sec. 3, 8, 2 June 1932, 7, 12 June 1932, sec. 4, 1; Cameron, "Second International Coffee Conference"; "Rise and Fall of Coffee"; "This Coffee Maneuvering"; "Brazil Just Can't Afford"; "Coffee Men Nervously Watch"; Friele cable, 22 August 1932, Lawrence letters, 9 and 16 September 1932, Anon. cable, 28 November 1932, Coffee-Wheat Swap Files; *New York Times,* 13 August 1932, 15, 14 August 1932, 20, 16 August 1932, 32, 21 August 1932, sec. 4, 10, 21 August 1932, sec. 8, 12, 22 August 1932, 14, 25 August 1932, sec. 4, 8; 28 August 1932, sec. 4, 8, 30 August 1932, 31, 1 September 1932, 33, 2 September 1932, 21, 3 September 1932, 27, 20 September 1932, 34, 23 September 1932, 34, 30 September 1932, 8; Bacha and Greenhill, *150 Years of Coffee,* 55–60, 229–34.

182–85   **"Dictators and Massacres":** Woodward, *Central America,* 186, 209–23; Perez-Brignoli, *Brief History of Central America,* 98–126; Buckley, *Violent Neighbors,* 81–83; McCreery, *Rural Guatemala,* 316–22; Handy, *Gift of the Devil,* 94–100; Adams, *Crucifixion,* 174–84; Galeano, *Open Veins of Latin America,* 124–27; El Salvador Media Project,

Doble Cara; Armstrong and Shenk, *El Salvador*, 21–32; Anderson, *Matanza*, 1–21, 83–146; North, *Bitter Grounds*, 29–42; Perez-Brignoli, "Indians, Communists and Peasants," in *Coffee, Society, and Power*, 232–61; Barry, *Roots of Rebellion*, 26; Cambranes, *Coffee and Peasants*, 321; Paige, *Coffee and Power*, 102–26, 153–83; "Coffee-Cup Crisis"; "Asserts Coffee Price Caused Haiti Strikes," *New York Times*, 4 January 1930, 36; Mario Samper Kutschbach, "In Difficult Times," and Michael F. Jiménez, "At the Banquet of Civilization," in *Coffee, Society, and Power*, 151–80, 262–93; McCue, "Where Coffee Is King"; Paige, *Coffee and Power*, 127–52; Beyer, *Colombian Coffee*, 236–39; *Tea & Coffee Trade Journal*, September 1933, 237; Bulwer-Thomas, *Political Economy of Central America*, 48–86; White, *El Salvador*, 97–103; *El Salvador*, 16–18; Anderson, *War of the Dispossessed*, 20–51.

185–88   **"Brazil Opens the Floodgates":** *Tea & Coffee Trade Journal*, September 1936, 187, February 1937, 118, November 1937, 273, 284, 322; Dinesen, *Out of Africa*, 7; Stella, *Book of Coffee*, 56; "Colonial Coffee Areas," *Tea & Coffee Trade Journal*, February 1931, 153, August 1931, 151–52, October 1931, 367, November 1931, 534–35, July 1932, 24, February 1933, 172, December 1933, 490, January 1937, 30, May 1937, 281, June 1937, 375, 349, July 1937, 11, 36, August 1937, 79–80, 94, 96, 123, 127, September 1937, 156, 160, October 1937, 205, 220, 228, February 1938, 18, August 1938, 14, October 1938, 26, December 1938, 58; Rohr, *Inter-American Coffee Agreement*, 65–96; *Tea & Coffee Trade Journal*, January 1935, 6, December 1936, 407, 422, June 1937, 329, September 1937, 139, 154, 184–85, December 1937, 333, 350, January 1938, 34, February 1938, 26, June 1938, 9, September 1938, 15; Penteado speech, Associated Coffee, *Excerpts*, 1937, 57–58; "Another Cup"; "Coffee and the Bogotá Conference"; "3¢ a Cup?"; "Brazil Cuts Coffee Export Tax"; "Brazil Tires of Coffee Control"; New York Coffee, *Annual Coffee Supplement*, 1939; Dean, *Industrialization of São Paulo*, 207–42; *Documentary History of Brazil*, 346–52.

Chapter Eleven

189–90   **"Glued to Their Radios":** Irving Berlin, "Let's Have Another Cup O' Coffee," 1932, DeVincent Collection; J. A. Hawkins to HB, 9 May 1922, HB Scrapbook, Hills Brothers Collection; Jt. Coffee Trade Publicity Committee, 7 June 1922, Series 3, Box 12, idem; Watson, "Advertising by Radio," J. Walter Thompson Bulletin no. 98, May 1923, JWT Papers, J. Walter Thompson Inc. Files; Kraft Foods, "Maxwell House Coffee: A Chronological History," 2; Newhall, Folger Way, 12; *The Jewel*, 1 December 1995, 1; Allen, *Only Yesterday*, 164–67; Fox, *Mirror Makers*, 150–62; Sobel, *Manipulators*, 126–43; Hope quoted in Campbell, *Golden Years*, 10; Barnouw, *Tower in Babel*, 158–91; Benton interview in Terkel, *Hard Times*, 79–84; Ely, *Adventures of Amos 'n' Andy*.

190–92   **"Benton & Bowles Survive":** Bowles, Promises to Keep, 19–24; Hyman, *Lives of William Benton*, 96–153; Hobler, *Triangle of Marketing*, 59–102; Webber, *Our Kind*, 20–40; Smith, Manuscript.

192–93   **"Rancid Oils":** "Consumers Get Less Air"; "September 1929 Chase & Sanborn Report," Box 17, Reel 233, J. Walter Thompson Inc. Files; *Tea & Coffee Trade Journal*, August 1933, 158; "Urge to Excess"; Smith, "Policies"; Webber, *Our Kind of People*, 31–33; McPhee, "Competitors Roasted"; "Story Behind 'Dated Coffee' Success," *Tea & Coffee Trade Journal*, May 1931, 497, August 1931, 127, September 1932, 245–46; Chase & Sanborn material, Box 17, J. Walter Thompson Inc. Files; "General Foods Corp," Harvard Business School, 1934, 5, Historical Corporate Reports Collection; "Maxwell House Back"; "Two More Products"; "New Process."

193–96   **"All Aboard":** Bowles, *Promises to Keep*, 19–24; Hyman, Lives of William Benton, 3–6, 96–169; Hobler, *Triangle of Marketing*, 59–104; Webber, *Our Kind of People*, 20–42; "Hot Dated Coffee," *Tea & Coffee Trade Journal*, October 1934, 357; Smith, Manuscript, 46, 205–7; Campbell, *Golden Years of Broadcasting*, 46–47; Bill Fleming to

Atherton Hobler, 8 May 1933, Box 16, Kraft Foods Archives material; Benton letters to mother, Box 4, Maxwell House ads, 1932–1935, Box 71, Benton & Bowles Collection; "Del Monte Radio Program," *Tea & Coffee Trade Journal*, March 1934, 213; Fox, *Mirror Makers*, 150; Maxwell House ads, 1932–1935, Box 71, Benton & Bowles Collection; Benton quoted in Terkel, *Hard Times*, 81–83; Benton letters to mother, 30 October 1932, 27 June1933, 13 August 1933, 3 December 1933, Box 4, Benton & Bowles Collection; Pendergrast, *For God, Country and Coca-Cola*,351; Barnouw, *Golden Web*, 7; Sobel, *Manipulators*, 147–54; Allen, *Big Change*, 150–57; "Brewery Bequeaths"; *Tea & Coffee Trade Journal*, May 1933, 434, December 1933, 463; Benton & Bowles Billing, Benton & Bowles Collection; Benton quote in Mayer, *Madison Avenue*, 11.

196–97   **"Arbuckles's and MacDougall Fade Away":** Bergreen, *As Thousands Cheer*, 308–9; *Tea & Coffee Trade Journal*, January 1936, 58, July 1932, 97, October 1932, 398, April 1934, 322, June 1934, 479; "Arbuckle Markets New Brand," idem, April 1935, 314, October 1936, 318; "To Buy Arbuckle Properties," *New York Times*, 5 January 1937; J. R. Lewis to C. K. Woodbridge, 21 June 1950, property of Stanley Newkirk; Martha Jamison to Havemeyer, 13 November 1938, property of John Jeanneney; John Jeanneney interview; Stanley Newkirk interview; Kraft Foods Archives material; Kevan, "Many of Miss Jamison's Legatees"; "Alice Foote MacDougall Dies"; Caroline MacDougall letter, 16 October 1997; Rella MacDougall interview; "The Five Cent Coffee House," *Tea & Coffee Trade Journal*, July 1932, 35.

197–99   **"Lobbing Coffee Hand Grenades":** T*ea & Coffee Trade Journal*, September 1933, 205, November 1936, 345, February 1937, 81, May 1937, 270; Herbert Delafield speech, Associated Coffee Industries, *Excerpts*, 1936, 1–2, 15; "Another Cup," 22; Weiss, "Selling Quality in a Price Market"; Zimmerman, "Can Branded Staples Compete?"; "Coffee Forces Unite"; "All Factors in Coffee Trade"; *Tea & Coffee Trade Journal*, May 1931, 512–13, 534, October 1931, 359, November 1931, 465, 490–93, May 1933, 414–15, September 1933, 220–21; Associated Coffee Industries, *Report of Board of Directors Meeting*, 1932; "Hills Brothers to Cut Stock Melon," *San Francisco Examiner*, 1 April 1930; Tea & Coffee Trade Journal, January 1938, 50; HB Scrapbook, Hills Brothers Collection; "Conquest of Chicago," HB Misc., idem; "Outline of Merchandising," Series 3, Box 78, idem; "Chicago Bulletin for Salesmen," 1930–1931, idem; H. G. Hills letter, 2 January 1930, Series 3, Box 70, idem; "Addresses at the 1931 Sales Convention," idem; Quinn, *Scientific Marketing*, 38..

199–202   **"Getting the Gong":** "Bowes Inc."; Chase & Sanborn material, Bernstein, Boxes 6–8, 17, J. Walter Thompson Inc. Files; Barnouw, *Golden Web*, 6, 98, 112–13; Sobel, *Manipulators*, 171; Standard Brands, "History of Chase & Sanborn"; *Tea & Coffee Trade Journal*, April 1936, 301, September 1936, 199; "Sinatra, Frank," *Current Biography*; "Bowes, Edward," idem; "Bergen," idem; "FCC on Mae West"; Leider, *Becoming Mae West*, 339–42; R. Colwell interview, 8 November 1963, Bernstein, Box 6, J. Walter Thompson Inc. Files; H. G. Hills memo, 18 September 1939, Hills Brothers Collection; Rorty, *Our Master's Voice*, 244–46; Newhall, *Folger Way*, 12; *Tea & Coffee Trade Journal*, August 1936, 154, January 1937, 69, January 1938, 50, October 1938, 61; Interview with Mrs. Morse in Smith, Manuscript, additional material; Maxwell House ads, 1937–1939, Box 72, Benton & Bowles Collection.

202–205   **"Coffee Brutes":** Chase & Sanborn ad, *Ladies' Home Journal*, November 1934, 46; Chase & Sanborn article, Series 3, Box 71, Hills Brothers Collection; *Tea & Coffee Trade Journal*, July 1932, 38, January 1934, 20, February 1934, 115D, May 1934, 403, June 1934, 479, December 1934, 573, January 1935, 12–13, February 1935, 125, April 1935, 300–301, May 1936, 390–91, November 1937, 268, December 1937, 340; Newhall, *Folger Way*, 13; Hills Brothers ads, January 1935 HB memo, Hills Bros. ad summary, Box 71, Hills Brothers Collection; Fox, *Mirror Makers*, 134; Kraft Foods, "Maxwell House Coffee"; Kaffee-Hag ad, *Time*, 11 May 1936, 51; Pendergrast, *For*

God, Country and Coca-Cola, 176–98; "Another Cup," 22; Associated Coffee Industries, *Retail Market*, 4; J. W. Millard speech, idem, *Excerpts*, 1938, 26–27.

205–6　　**"For Better, For Worse":** Williamson speech, Associated Coffee Industries, *Report*, 1932, 13; Schapira, *Book of Coffee*, 123–24; Bramah, *Coffee Makers*, 120, 133; *National Consumer Survey*, 1939; January 1940 survey, Box 17, J. Walter Thompson Inc. Files; "We Make All Kinds"; Woodward, "About Coffee"; "I Love Coffee," 74; Egmont Arens speech, Associated Coffee Industries, *Excerpts*, 1938, 82–101.

206–11　　**"Hammering the Chains":** *Tea & Coffee Trade Journal*, October 1933, 317, January 1934, 82, March 1935, 215, February 1936, 108, February 1937, 80; "Arrests," reprint, *The Jewel*, 1 June 1995, 6; Miller, *Jewel Tea Grocery*, 8–41, 211–13; Norm Storkel interview; Jewel Tea Co., *Story of Jewel*, "Solid Trainload," *Jewel News*, 1937; "A & P's New Coffee Packages"; Zimmerman, "Can Branded Staples Compete?"; Hoyt, *That Wonderful A & P!*, 134–97; Walsh, *Rise and Decline*, 44–64; Lebhar, *Chain Stores*, 142–293; *International Directory of Company Histories*, 604–6, 633–84; Kallett and Schlink, *100,000,000 Guinea Pigs*, 294; "Chester Points," 12; "Let Them Eat Cake," 73; Barnouw, *Tower in Babel*, 282; Rorty, *Our Master's Voice*, 70–71; "Public Is Not Damned," 112–14; Patman speech, Associated Coffee Industries, *Excerpts*, 1937, 10; "Patman."

211–13　　**"The European Coffee Scene":** *Tea & Coffee Trade Journal*, December 1931, 702, January 1937, 38, February 1937, 118, August 1937, 94, December 1937, 341, 372, January 1938, 13, 28, February 1938, 48, April 1938, 12, October 1938, 18, November 1945, 48, August 1958, 22, 56–58; Stella, *Book of Coffee*, 150–219; Illy, *Book of Coffee*, 168–69; Schapira, *Book of Coffee*, 126–28; Bramah, *Coffee Makers*, 138–43; Spitzer, "Coffee"; Fumagalli, *Coffeemakers*; Hoffmann, *That Fine Italian Hand*, 36–37; Rotthauwe, *Heavenly Inferno*, 30–36; Schmidt, "Presentation on Probat's"; Illy et al., *Espresso Coffee*, 164–65; Davids, *Espresso*, 15–26; Bersten, *Coffee Floats*, 99–146; Lavazza, *Lavazza*, 3–13; Gevalia company literature; Paulig company literature; Eduscho web site; Nestlé corporate information; Kraft Jacobs Suchard, *100 Years of Jacobs Café*, 11–36; "Jacobs Suchard AG," *International Directory of Company Histories*, 520; "Nestlé S.A.," idem, 545–49; Heer, Nestlé, 194–200.

213–16　　**"The World of the Future":** Taylor, "Victuals and Vitamins"; "World's Largest Coffee Plant Opens"; *Tea & Coffee Trade Journal*, July 1938, 20, 60, March 1939, 45, May 1939, 22; Chase & Sanborn ad, *Collier's*, 15 June 1940, 27; Series 3, Box 71, Hills Brothers Collection; Weishaar, "Psych-Ing Mrs. Smith"; *Tea & Coffee Trade Journal*, January 1938, 60, August 1938, 9, 18; February 1939, 12–13, April 1939, 20–21, June 1939, 15; G. Washington ad, November 1931, *Ladies' Home Journal*, 107; Isabel Young speech, Associated Coffee Industries, *Excerpts*, 1937, 19–24; Box 6, American Can file, Margaret Bourke-White Papers; MBW Prints, Box 49, Folder 388, idem; Goldberg, *Margaret Bourke-White*, 152–71; Sharpe speech, Millard speech, Associated Coffee Industries, Excerpts, 1938, 4–5, 25–41; "Chase & Sanborn Nationwide Consumer Survey," January 1940, Reel 377, Box 17, J. Walter Thompson Inc. Files; Woodward, "About Coffee," 718; "Plan $500,000 Coffee Drive"; *Coffee Facts and Fantasies*, "Emotional Ersatz."

Chapter Twelve

217–19　　**"The United States, the leading coffee-drinking nation":** Meagher, "To Think of Coffee"; Rohr, *Inter-American Coffee Agreement*, 94–99; "Coffee Pickup"; Chuck Jones interview; Hannstein, *Early Twentieth-Century Life*, 43–103; Falcón, *Erwin Paul Dieseldorff*, 426–30; Monteforte, "Bean of Contention"; Martin, "Nazi Intrigues"; Colby, *Thy Will Be Done*, 125; Betty Hannstein Adams E-mail, January–February 1998; Adams, *Crucifixion*, 139, 180; King, *Coban and the Verapaz*

217–19   **"Hammering Out a Coffee Agreement":** *Coffee Annual* 1950, 45; Rohr, *Inter-American Coffee Agreement,* 99–126; "Inter-American Coffee Quota Agreement"; Wellman, *Coffee,* 423; Woodward, *Central America,* 230; *Guatemala,* 22; *Tea & Coffee Trade Journal,* November 1941, 34; Krammer, *Undue Process,* 89.

220–21   **"1941: Surviving":** "Coffee Pickup"; Rohr, *Inter-American Coffee Agreement,* 127–58; "Henderson, Leon," *Current Biography;* "Coffee: Stimulant"; *Tea & Coffee Trade Journal,* August 1941, 28–29, September 1941, 11, 28, November 1941, 46, March 1942, 46, December 1942, 16–18, November 1969, 15, December 1941, 26–30, January 1942, 16, 18–19.

222–23   **"Coffee Goes to War":** Rohr, *Inter-American Coffee Agreement,* 154–84; HB files, 1942–1944, Hills Brothers Collection; Behrendt, "Coffee Goes to War," 28–29; "Coffee Freeze"; "Commodity Notes" ; "Black Coffee Outlook"; *Tea & Coffee Trade Journal,* August 1942, 24, November 1942, 39, December 1942, 28, 31, March 1944, 23, February 1945, 11; "Half-Ration Coffee"; "Coffee Rationing"; "Coffee by Coupon"; "Coffee Stretchers"; "Lumps with the Coffee"; Modell, "Coffee à la Mode"; "Coffee Stabilized"; Driver, "Stretching"; "Coffee Shipment"; "No Coffee Ration"; WW II Jewel folder, property Bill Hamilton;B & B Files, Box 85, Benton & Bowles Collection; "Boomerang"; Daniels, "Inter-American Coffee Agreement," 12; "Off the Editor's Chest"; Darrock, "What Happened to Price Control?"; George Thierbach letter, July 1943, Hills Brothers Collection; "Staples Paradox"; McGinley, "They Also Serve."

223–25   **"Coffee at the Front":** *Tea & Coffee Trade Journal,* October 1941, 38–39, 44, October 1942, 11, January 1944, 9, March 1944, 10–18, May 1944, 24, August 1944, 11, March 1945, 11, July 1945, 34, August 1945, 22; Kent, "Cuppa Coffee, Chum?" 151, 238; "Packaged Coffee"; *History of Jewel Companies,* 13; *The Jewel,* January 1997, 1; General Foods Annual Report, 1944, 13, Historical Corporate Reports Collection; Berner, "Future of Soluble Coffee"; "Soluble Coffees"; Mauldin, *Up Front,* 168–69, 175; Wynn, "About"; Rohr, *Inter-American Coffee Agreement,* 184; DiChario, "Soldier," 365; Eduscho company literature; Van der Zee, *Van Winkelnering,* 278–79; Lavazza, *Lavazza,* 13–14; Kraft Jacobs Suchard, *100 Years,* 36; Jacques Louis-Delamare, *Coffee Annual* 1950, 82; Behrendt, "Coffee Goes to War," 29.

225–27   **"Denazifying Latin America":** Dulles, *Vargas,* 195–235; Bourne, *Getulio Vargas,* 100–105; *Brazil,* 43–44; Rout and Bratzel, *Shadow War,* 106–222; Krammer, *Undue Process,* 89–174; *Guatemala,* 22; Rohr, *Inter-American Coffee Agreement,* 139–40; Monteforte, "Bean of Contention," 46; Colby, *Thy Will Be Done,* 107–80; Hannstein, *Early Twentieth-Century,* 39, 103; Falcón, *Erwin Paul Dieseldorff,* 430–31; Max Paul Friedman (U.C. Berkeley) E-mails, March 1998; Betty Hannstein Adams E-mails, January–February 1998; *Tea & Coffee Trade Journal,* August 1941, 24; Adams, *Crucifixion,* 139; King, *Coban and the Verapaz.*

227–29   **"The U.S. Industry Survives":** *History of Jewel Companies,* 12–14; Miller, *Jewel Tea Grocery Products,* 205; *The Jewel,* 1 September 1995, 4; *Tea & Coffee Trade Journal,* March 1944, 24; General Foods *Family Album,* 1948, 20, Kraft Foods Archives; B & B Files, Box 72, Benton & Bowles Collection; Newhall, *Folger Way,* 13–14; HB Box 71, Ad Summaries, 1940–1949, Hills Brothers Collection; Wilson to Hills, 9 September 1940, idem; "Procedure for Sampling Campaign," HB Files, Box 68, idem; *Tea & Coffee Trade Journal,* November 1944, 18, December 1944, 15; "Pennies from Leaven"; Standard Brands, address by James S. Adams, 5 May 1942, 5 May 1943, 2 May 1944, Kidder Peabody 1947 report, "Standard Brands Inc.," Historical Corporate Reports Collection; *Tea & Coffee Trade Journal,* July 1941, 33, December 1941, 30, June 1942, 42, June 1945, 9.

229–30   **"Good Neighbors No Longer":** Aguilar, "Flexibility of Wartime Coffee"; Penteado, "Declares Coffee"; Penteado, "Facts"; "Bouças Coffee Plan," 43; *Tea & Coffee Trade Journal,* May 1944, 14, July 1944, 14, January 1945, 42–43; Jiménez, "Coffee in Costa Rica," 88; Driver, "Coffee Supplies," 20; "Coffee Prices," 305; Rohr, *Inter-*

American Coffee Agreement, 184–259; *Brazil*, 45; Dulles, *Vargas of Brazil*, 252–74; Woodward, *Central America*, 232–33, 249–50; *Colombia*, 34–35; *Latin America in the 1940s*, 15–35, 141–61; Winson, *Coffee and Democracy*, 50–92; Seligson, *Peasants of Costa Rica*, 122–72; White, *El Salvador*, 103–5; *El Salvador*, 18.

231–32 **"The Legacy of World War II":** National Coffee Association newsletter, March 1947; Mark L. McMahon, "Changes Ahead," *Coffee Annual* 1944, 35–36; "The Coffee Song," *Coffee*, January 1947, 2; Pendergrast, *For God, Country and Coca-Cola*, 199–217; *Tea & Coffee Trade Journal*, November 1944, 18–22, March 1947, 28, January 1959, 66; Redbook Magazine Marketing Research Dept., "Regular and Instant," 12.

Chapter Thirteen

235–36 **"Over second and third cups":** *Coffee Annual* 1949, 86; *Coffee Annual* 1952, 53; Fisher, "Coffee," 114; de Goût, "Strong Coffee," 119.

236–40 **"Guy Gillette's Coffee Witch Hunt":** *Coffee*, March 1947; *Tea & Coffee Trade Journal*, March 1948, 9, 18; National Coffee Association (NCA) *News Bulletin*, 28 March 1947; *Tea & Coffee Trade Journal*, January 1948, 9, June 1948, 10, September 1948, 53, October 1948, 16, March 1949, 13, 18, 22, May 1949, 13; NCA newsletter, 12 September 1947, 5 December 1947; *Coffee Annual* 1950, 88–92; Rohr, *Inter-American Coffee Agreement*, 254–66; Redbook Magazine Marketing Research Dept., "Regular and Instant," 12; *Tea & Coffee Trade Journal*, November 1949, 58, December 1949, 13, 20–28, December 1950, 9–10; *Colombia*, 37–44; Baer, *Brazilian Economy*, 50–60; "Gillette, Guy"; "Ex-Senator Guy Gillette Dead"; "Cup That Agitates"; U.S. Congress, Senate, *Utilization of Farm Crops*, 33, 813, 983, 1036, 1168, 1185–86, 1210–37, 1334–38; *Tea & Coffee Trade Journal*, February 1950, 20; NCA newsletter, 30 June 1950; Hoyt, *That Wonderful A & P!*, 192–217; Walsh, *Rise and Decline*, 64–68; *Tea & Coffee Trade Journal*, January 1950, 16d–26, February 1950, 18–20, June 1950, 11, 15–18, December 1950, 9; "Racket in Coffee"; NCA newsletter, 7 July 1950, 20 October 1950, 3 November 1950; *Tea & Coffee Trade Journal*, July 1950, 9, 22, August 1950, 15, March 1951, 13; NCA newsletter, 9 and 16 June 1950; "Grounds for Discipline?"; "Coffee Nerves"; "Tempest in a Percolator"; Uribe, *Brown Gold*, 185; Skidmore, *Politics in Brazil*, 114–37; "Getulio Voltará"; Miller, "Clarification"; Acheson, "Department"; *Latin America in the 1940s*.

240–41 **"Instant, Quick, Efficient":** Heer, *Nestlé*, 199–200; Driver, "Soluble Coffee," 19; "New Coffees"; "Soluble Coffees," August 1950; "Instant Coffee–Coming Up"; 1954 Instant Maxwell House ad, Box 75, Benton & Bowles Collection; Webber, *Our Kind*, 114–15; *Tea & Coffee Trade Journal*, February 1949, 10, April 1949, 12, December 1950, 9, June 1951, 12, 34, July 1951, 14, 72, 111, August 1951, 30, March 1952, 20, April 1952, 16–17, 44–45, August 1952, 17, 32–33, October 1952, 22, 28, March 1953, 18, July 1953, 32, September 1953, 22, November 1953, 70, December 1953, 83, January 1954, 31, April 1954, 66, May 1954, 24–26, July 1954, 23, August 1958, 57–58, January 1962, 24; "Story of the Instants"; "Instants Band Together"; Nescafé ad, October 1951; *Coffee Annual* 1953, 67; Talbot, "Struggle," 119–22; *Tea & Coffee Trade Journal*, April 1947, 11, May 1947, 18, December 1947, 42–44, January 1952, 63, February 1953, 57, October 1953, 43, February 1954, 31, November 1954, 128, February 1955, 30, April 1956, 80; NCA newsletter, 11 April 1947; "Dial K for Koffee"; NCA newsletter, 31 March 1950, 29 September 1950; "Coffee Fragrance"; *Coffee Annual* 1953, 44, 54; *Tea & Coffee Trade Journal*, January 1959, 64, January 1960, 29; Neville, "Coffee"; Hess, *Taste of America*, 66–69.

241–42 **"Invention of the Coffee Break":** *Tea & Coffee Trade Journal*, April 1952, 19, November 1952, 40–42, May 1953, 44, July 1953, 22, July 1954, 22, 61; NCA newsletter, 22 August 1952; "Coffeeman's on the Job"; "293,884,843 Cups of Coffee"; Pream ad, April 1953; Quinn, *Scientific Marketing*, 159–62.

242–43 **"The Boob Tube":** Bogart, *Age of Television*, 10; *This Fabulous Century, 1950–1960*, 250; Barnouw, *Golden Web*, 272–77; Miller, *Fifties*, 346–71; Webber, *Our Kind of People*, 115–38; General Foods Annual Report, 1944, 1947, 1959, Standard Brands Annual Report, 1948, 1949, Historical Corporate Reports Collection; Chase & Sanborn, Box 17, Sid Bernstein, Box 7 & 8, Howard Henderson, Box 5, Samuel Dobbs in HH, Box 6, J. Walter Thompson Inc. Files; Pendergrast, *For God, Country and Coca-Cola*, 261; Land, "Hobler"; Smith, manuscript, 8–11, 21; Richards, "Television"; "Goldbergs" Sanka ad, 1949, Museum of Television and Radio; "Television Boost"; Hills Brothers 1951 video 395.3, Hills Brothers Collection; *Tea & Coffee Trade Journal*, September 1947, 80, October 1947, 68, October 1950, 9, 39, November 1953, 19, March 1954, 13, June 1954, 15, 74, October 1955, 19.

245 **"Price Wars":** *Tea & Coffee Trade Journal*, March 1947, June 1947, 9, April 1950, 11, March 1952, 20, August 1953, 22, July 1954, 61, January 1962, 104–5; *Coffee Annual* 1952, 56–58, 62, 69, 84, 93–94; *Coffee Annual* 1953, 66; HB Chicago Bulletin for Salesmen, 9 August 1951, 10 December 1952, 8 October 1954, Hills Brothers Collection; "The Art of Coffee-Making," 1952, idem; Quinn, *Scientific Marketing*, 143, 166–67.

246 **"Neglecting a Generation":** Pendergrast, *For God, Country, and Coca-Cola*, 181–82, 239, 261–62, 268; "Sun Never Sets"; NCA newsletter, 19 May 1950, 17 November 1950; *Tea & Coffee Trade Journal*, April 1947, 11, September 1949, 22, December 1949, 29, 36, March 1953, 35.

247–49 **"The Land That Smelled":** *Coffee Annual* 1950, 31, 39–40; *Coffee Annual* 1951, 52–53; Stewart, *Coffee*, 4–23; *Black Harvest*; Martin, "Land That Smells"; "Coffee Klondike"; Wilson, "What's Happened," 4; McMillen, "All of Us"; "Packaged Plantations"; *Coffee Annual* 1951, 43, 59; *Tea & Coffee Trade Journal*, January 1951, 16a, 42–44; *Coffee Annual* 1953, 53–54; "Coffee Woes Just Starting"; "Modern Methods"; Cotton, "Research"; McMillen, "All of Us," 16; Uribe, *Brown Gold*, 166–67; Jerry Harrington interview; Baer, *Brazilian Economy*, 347; Adams, *Crucifixion*, 339; Bacha and Greenhill, *150 Years of Coffee*, 66–74, 238–52.

249–51 **"Great Fourth of July Frost":** *Tea & Coffee Trade Journal*, August 1953, 23, 34–35, September 1953, 14–15, November 1953, 44, 118–19; "With Lid Off"; "Too Many Beans"; *Coffee Annual* 1953, 61; "Cost of Coffee"; "Coffee Growers Blame"; Szulc, "About Coffee"; "Coffee Growers Blame"; "Why Coffee Keeps Costing More"; "What's Really Brewing?"; "Coffee Jitters"; "No Coffee, Thanks"; "Cup That Agitates"; "U.S. Coffee Nerves"; "Is the High Price"; "Coffee Nerves" (1954); "Coffee Holidays"; Nickerson, "Thriftier Cup"; Farbstein, "Coffee on the Side"; Margaret Chase Smith resolution, *Congressional Record*, 8 February 1954, 1475; U.S. Congress, Senate, *Regulation of Coffee Futures Trading*, 1–4, 29–45; idem, *Study of Coffee Prices*, 10–20, 46, 81, 139; U.S. Congress, House, *Include Coffee*, 11–15; Hazlitt, "Coffee, Butter"; 31 July 1954 letter to HB, Hills Brothers Collection; "Meditation on the Price of Coffee"; "Just the Facts"; "Getting a Few Things Clear"; "Year More"; Tea & Coffee Trade Journal, April 1954, 14, July 1954, 33; JWT newsletter, 19 April 1954, Box 6, J. Walter Thompson Inc. Files; Friele to Rockefeller, 28 January 1954, Rockefeller Family Archives; HB Series 7, Box 20, Hills Brothers Collection; Kluger, Ashes to Ashes, 160–70; Uribe, *Brown Gold*, 160; Federal Trade Commission, *Economic Report*; U.S. Congress, Senate, Study of Coffee Prices, 360–73; "Old Coffee Grounds."

251–54 **"CIA Coup in Guatemala":** *Guatemala: A Country Study*, 22–38; Schlesinger, *Bitter Fruit*, 39–61, 132–46, 162–235; Handy, *Revolution*; Immerman, *CIA in Guatemala*; Stephen Rabe, "Dulles, Latin America," in *John Foster Dulles*, 159–87; Gleijeses, *Shattered Hope*; McMahon, "Tempest"; "What They Want"; Carnahan, Report of the Special Study Mission; *Tea & Coffee Trade Journal*, January 1952, 62, May 1954, 34–36;

Stephen M. Streeter E-mail, April 1998; Adams, *Cultural Surveys*, 261–412; LaFeber, *Inevitable Revolutions; Guatemalan Indians and the State; Community Culture*, 1-54, 131–206; Bulwer-Thomas, *Political Economy*, 130–49; Adams, *Crucifixion by Power*, 139–41, 184–205, 341, 393, 404; Forster, "Time."

254–56 **"Suicide in Brazil":** "Year More of Costly Coffee"; "Brazil Feels the Squeeze"; "Buyers Get a Break"; "Coffee Prices: Can the Jumping Bean Be Tamed?"; "Year on a Roller Coaster"; *Coffee Annual* 1954, 86, 122, 126; Dulles, *Vargas of Brazil*, 309–48; Bourne, *Getulio Vargas*, 166–226; Burns, *History of Brazil*, 426–56; *Tea & Coffee Trade Journal*, September 1954, 20–21; *Brazil*, 48–51; "FTC on Coffee"; "Coffee Cornered"; "Coffee Roasted"; "Coffee Growers Are Still Bogged"; *Coffee Annual* 1954, 49; Uribe, *Brown Gold*, xii–xiv, 180–89; Skidmore, *Politics in Brazil*, 134–37.

Chapter Fourteen

257–58 **"There is hardly anything":** *Tea & Coffee Trade Journal*, January 1960, 33, June 1962, 22–23.

258–59 **"Out of Africa":** Lucier, *International Political Economy*, 31, 247–81; *Tea & Coffee Trade Journal*, December 1954, 19–56, December 1955, 20, 64, August 1956, 50, October 1957, 24–70, January 1962, 104–5; Haarer, *Modern Coffee Production*, 349–85; Young, *African Colonial State*, 1–2, 182–84; Birmingham, *Decolonization*, 9–15, 32, 39–53, 94; *Decolonization and African Independence*, 12, 347–80, 401–26; Mbapndah, "French Colonial"; *Coffee Annual* 1955, 133; Redbook Magazine Marketing Research Dept., "Regular and Instant," 18; Hedlund, *Coffee, Co-operatives*.

259–61 **"Hot Coffee, Cold War":** "Prices Grind"; "Coffee Growers Are Still Bogged"; "Coffeeplot"; Cale, "Coffee in Inter-American Relations"; "Ever-Normal Coffee Muddle"; "Coffee Growers Seek Ways"; *Coffee Annual* 1955, 51, 133–43; "Coffee, Black"; "Coffee Break," *Business Week*; "Surplus & Shortage"; *Coffee Annual* 1956, 57, 148–52; *Coffee Annual* 1957, 63–65; *Tea & Coffee Trade Journal*, November 1949, 9, June 1955, 30, July 1955, 18, August 1955, 30, May 1956, 32–33, January 1958, 164, February 1958, 19, 22–24, October 1958, 21, 23, 67; "Brazil and Portugal Growers:; Lucier, *International Political Economy*, 119–24; Rubottom, "Quarter-Century"; idem, "Basic Principles"; Nixon, *RN*, 186–93; Wicker, *One of Us*, 207–12; "Time to Rebuild"; "Coffee Switch"; "Smash the Demitasses?"; "Coffee Nerves–A Cure?"; Redbook Magazine Marketing Research Dept., "Regular and Instant," 13, 21; "Coffee Smiles"; Palacios, *Coffee in Colombia*, 224–26; Wellman, *Coffee*, 425–27; Bacha and Greenhill, *150 Years of Coffee*, 75–81, 311.

261–62 **"Regular Robusta":** National Coffee Asssociation (NCA) newsletter, November 1947; Driver, "Quality of Vacuum-Packed Coffees"; Redbook Magazine Marketing Research Dept., "Regular and Instant," 2; Walsh, *Rise and Decline*, 74–93; Lebhar, *Chain Stores*, 368; *Tea & Coffee Trade Journal*, April 1956, 81; January 1957, 30, 36, October 1957, 20, 48, August 1958, 23, March 1960, 73, November 1960, 60–63, January 1962, 30, 34, 36, 72–74, 78–87, February 1962, 13, June 1962, 17, October 1965, 14, 40; Peter Condaxis interview, January 1997.

263–65 **"The Chock full Miracle":** Finch, *Jim Henson*, 22; Wilkins Coffee ads, Museum of Television and Radio; *Tea & Coffee Trade Journal*, July 1958, 15, 99, March 1961, 44; Quinn, *Scientific Marketing*, 40, 71, 98–99, 109, 178–80; Peter Baer interview; Gary Fischer interview; Andrea Bass interview; *Tea & Coffee Trade Journal*, July 1951, 8, January 1954, 31, August 1954, 66, October 1954, 62, December 1954, 109, May 1955, 82, August 1955, 20, February 1956, 54, August 1956, 11, August 1957, 88, December 1957, 19, September 1958, 82, April 1959, 81, July 1959, 73, January 1960, 124, February 1960, 17, October 1960, 64, November 1960, 93, April 1961, 81, May 1962, 65;

Redbook Magazine Marketing Research Dept., "Regular and Instant," 4; "Black, William."

265–66   **"The Coffeehouse: A Saving Grace":** Driver, "Which Kind," 13; "San Francisco's Oldest"; "Washington's M. E. Swing"; Spitzer, "Coffee"; Illy, *Book of Coffee*, 169–72; Powell, "Espresso"; Heise, *Coffee and Coffee Houses*, 201–2; Gee, *Limelight*; Davids, *Espresso*, vii, 37; Cantwell, "Village Voice"; Gianfranco Giotta interview; Luciano Repetto interview; Di Ruocco, "Specialty Coffee"; Kamiya, "North Beach"; Nickerson, "Come for Coffee"; Mitgang, "New York's Caffe"; Gee, *Limelight*, 5, 35, 56; "Coffee News for Coffee Lovers"; "Café Espresso"; "Coffee, Café, Caffè"; Donald Schoenholt interview.

266–68   **"London Espresso":** Mitgang, "New York's Caffe"; *Coffee Annual* 1954, 121; *Tea & Coffee Trade Journal*, March 1948, 20, April 1948, 10, March 1955, 28, December 1955, 22, November 1957, 25, 62, May 1961, 22; Bramah, *Tea & Coffee*, 51, 67–74; Edward Bramah interview, February 1997; David Higgins interview, February 1997.

268–69   **"European Coffee":** *Tea & Coffee Trade Journal*, December 1955, 20–36, March 1957, 59–60, November 1957, 21–64, August 1958, 57–58, October 1958, 69, November 1958, 27, January 1959, 136–37, May 1961, 20–24, December 1964, 19; Heer, *Nestlé*, 492; *Coffee Annual* 1957, 88–89; Kraft Jacobs Suchard, *100 Years*, 37–54; Tchibo Group, *All About Tchibo*; Letter from Tchibo, 6 February 1998; Van der Zee, *Van Winkelnering*, 280–84; Lavazza, *Lavazza*, 14–23; Hoffmann, *That Fine Italian Hand*, 36–40.

269–70   **"Japan Discovers Coffee":** NCA newsletter, September 1947; *Coffee Annual* 1952, 89; Mitgang, "New York's Caffe"; Shūhei, "Tokyo Kissaten"; Stinchecum, "Japan's Other Ritual"; Seidensticker, *Low City*, 104, 201; idem, *Tokyo Rising*, 189–90; Key Coffee Inc. material and correspondence; Ueshima Coffee Co. material and correspondence.

270–71   **"Googie Coffee":** NCA newsletter, 5 December 1947; Hess, *Googie*, 7, 15, 41–99; Dunkin' Donuts company literature.

271–73   **"In Denial":** Kummer, "Untroubled Brewing"; Lasker, "High Style"; *Coffee Annual* 1956, 65; *Coffee Annual* 1957, 65, 70, 93; *Tea & Coffee Trade Journal*, July 1955, 17, October 1956, 24, February 1957, 24, 38–42, 46, March 1957, 13, August 1957, 15, 17, 48, 89, June 1958, 23, July 1958, 26, January 1959, 66, 94, February 1959, 19, June 1959, 19, August 1959, 65, September 1959, 19, 23, January 1960, 29, June 1960, 12, September 1960, 17, November 1960, 58; Redbook Magazine Marketing Research Dept., "Regular and Instant," 12, 30; Froman, "Coffee"; "Giving Coffee More Zest"; "Bane of the Bean"; Quinn, *Scientific Marketing*, 4–29, 67–78, 105, 149–50, 162–64.

273–77   **"Scared into Agreement":** Vicker, "African Agriculture"; "Coffee Cause & Effect"; Neville, "Coffee"; Santos, "Right Amount"; "Coffee for Comrade K"; *Tea & Coffee Trade Journal*, January 1960, 78, June 1960, 36, July 1960, 44, November 1960, 30, January 1961, 16, June 1962, 39; U.S. Congress, Senate, *Executive Sessions*, 195–200, 207; Lucier, *International Political Economy*, 123, 254–72; Birmingham, *Decolonization*, 49–50, 60–69, 93–98; Johnson, *Modern Times*, 506–43; Young, *African Colonial State*, 201–2; Ilunga Kabongo, "The Catastrophe of Belgian Decolonization," in *Decolonialization*, 381–98; Brooke, "Angolan Coffee Trade"; *Tea & Coffee Trade Journal*, September 1960, 32, November 1960, 11, 15, 20–44, December 1960, 12, 46, January 1961, 56, 110, 115, 117, February 1961, 24–28, March 1961, 13, 15, 57–58, January 1962 76–78, February 1962, 22, 37, March 1962, 24, 41–48, April 1962, 24, May 1962, 25–30, June 1962, 15, 20–21, 36, 39–41, July 1962, 16–17, August 1962, 17, September 1962, 13, 26–27, 36–37, November 1962, 12, 43, January 1963, 28, 66–72, October 1965, 24; NCA Special Bulletin, 10 July 1962, 25 August 1962; "Soothing the Coffee Nerves"; "Coffee Break," *Newsweek*; "International Coffee Agreement Is Approved"; Blumenthal, "World Coffee Agreement," 221; Eisenhower, *Wine Is Bitter*, 101–5.

277–79 **"Stumbling Toward Ratification":** U.S. Congress, Senate, *International Coffee Agreement*, 3, 45–47, 56, 62, 75–76, 81–93; Lucier, *International Political Economy*, 132; NCA Special Bulletin, 23 November 1963, 12 February 1964, undated NCA parody; U.S. Congress, Senate, *Coffee*, 3–10, 21, 99–103, 123, 146–47, 172–84; Woodward, *Central America*, 250–51; Burns, *History of Brazil*, 447–504; *Documentary History*, 384–86; Skidmore, *Politics in Brazil*, 270–75; *Century of Brazilian History*, 193–95; Julius Kahn interview; U.S. Congress, House, *International Coffee Agreement: Executive Hearings*, 9–16; *Tea & Coffee Trade Journal*, April 1963, 15, 32, June 1963, 13, September 1963, 12, 32, 65, November 1963, 24, January 1964, 42–46, 60–70, February 1964, 17, 30–32, 35, 40, March 1964, 17, 20–22, 26–34, 44–46, 63, June 1964, 22–23, July 1964, 11, 22, 32–35, August 1964, 13, September 1964, 13, November 1964, 13, 22–27, December 1964, 36–39, February 1965, 22; "Wind Without Pity"; *Coffee Annual* 1963, 41–50, 55–66, 163; "High Cost of Coffee."

279–81 **"Boomer Bust":** *Tea & Coffee Trade Journal*, January 1960, 32, March 1961, 17, 18, January 1961, 62, June 1961, 15, January 1962, 65, 90, March 1962, 38, April 1962, 59, December 1962, 91, March 1963, 13, 18, 31–36, June 1963, 13, November 1963, 69, January 1964, 21, March 1964, 16, April 1964, 47, June 1964, 15, October 1964, 13, 30, December 1964, 19, 44–46, 49–53, January 1965, 12, 17, 24, 42–44, 65–66, February 1965, 15, March 1965, 19, 32–40, July 1965, 13, December 1965, 54; Pendergrast, *For God, Country and Coca-Cola*, 279–80; Quinn, *Scientific Marketing*, 148–52; "It's Like Wild"; *Coffee Annual* 1964, 41–43, 51–52, 67–68, 74–76; *Coffee Annual* 1965, 41–42, 49–51, 61–63, 81–82; *Coffee Drinking* (1966).

281–82 **"Merger Mania":** Federal Trade Commission, *Cents-Off Promotions*; *Tea & Coffee Trade Journal*, November 1960, 92, February 1961, 58, February 1962, 13, 55, April 1962, 59, May 1962, 65, October 1962, 75, November 1962, 65, December 1962, 91, September 1963, 28, December 1963, 69, February 1964, 47, 49, March 1964, 11, 61–62, August 1964, 39; "Folger"; Newhall, *Folger Way*; Schisgall, *Eyes on Tomorrow*, 230–32; Swasy, *Soap Opera*, 91, 117–18; Donald Atha interview, May 1998; Pendergrast, *For God, Country and Coca-Cola*, 278, 289, 307–10, 315–24.

282–84 **"The Maxwell Housewife":** Federal Trade Commission, *Cents-Off Promotions*, 12; *Tea & Coffee Trade Journal*, October 1955, 19, February 1960, 17, July 1960, 11, 42–47, August 1960, 65, September 1960, 16, February 1961, 58, June 1961, 16, July 1962, 57, January 1963, 62, March 1963, 57, June 1963, 22, 54, April 1964, 17, May 1964, 15–16, 43–45, 63, 67, August 1964, 39, December 1964, 70, April 1965, 49, July 1965, 54, October 1965, 45, 57, November 1965, 61; "Perking Pot," Jared Scott E-mail; Maxim ad, Sanka ads, "The First Day" Maxwell House ad, Museum of Television and Radio; Kraft Foods, "Maxwell House Coffee: A Chronological History"; Center for Research in Marketing, "Study of Hills Bros.," 18–20; Quinn, *Scientific Marketing*, 92, 182–84, 229–31.

284–85 **"The Decline of Hills Brothers":** *Tea & Coffee Trade Journal*, March 1960, 76, April 1960, 13, 60, September 1964, 59, April 1965, 49; Opinion Research Corporation, "Coffee Preferences"; Center for Research in Marketing, "Study of Hills Bros."; L. W. Hills letter, 9 June 1960, 1960 Adv. Budget, Series 3, Box 71, 1960–1964 Rumors file, HCCI Print Adv, 1962–1965, 1963 Management Letters, Series 7, Box 19, "Brand Image Study," December 1965, Hills Brothers Collection; Quinn, *Scientific Marketing*, 137.

285–87 **"Creation of Juan Valdez":** Eduardo Libreros interview; *Tea & Coffee Trade Journal*, January 1960, 24, February 1960, 17, April 1960, 12, June 1960, 12, November 1960, 10, January 1961, 40, March 1961, 12, January 1962, 14, 48, January 1962, 119, March 1962, 14, January 1963, 2–5, 19, 75, May 1963, 60, October 1963, 14–15, December 1963, 69, Juan Valdez insert, January 1964, 25–36, February 1964 49, March 1964,

64, April 1964, 9–10, July 1964, 10, January 1965, 19, 73–76, May 1965, 10–11, June 1965, 28–30, December 1965, 10; Quinn, *Scientific Marketing,* 165, 173.

287   **"In a Vortex":** *Tea & Coffee Trade Journal,* February 1963, 14, October 1963, 25.

Chapter Fifteen

291   **"I believe that the American":** *Coffee Annual* 1969, 42; Schapira, *Book of Coffee and Tea,* 47–48; Alfred Peet interview; Jerry Baldwin interview; Katherine Archer speech, 1976, property Alfred Peet; Schoenholt, "Starbucks," 26–28; Davids, "Peet's California Coffee Cult"; "Capricorn Coffees"; Herb Donaldson interview; *Indonesia,* 31–51.

293–94   **"Zabar's Beans":** Saul Zabar interview; David Dallis interview; Jonathan White interview; George Howell interview; "92 Year-Old McNulty's."

294–95   **"Zabaris Beans":** Peter Condaxis interview; Donald Schoenholt interview; Menzies, "Why Folger's Is Getting Creamed," 76; Ted Lingle interview; Schapira, *Book of Coffee and Tea,* 1–2.

295–98   **"Mentors, Fathers, and Sons":** Saul Zabar interview; David Dallis interview; Jonathan White interview; George Howell interview, "92-year-old McNulty's.

298–99   **"Tourist Coffee and Other Problems":** *Coffee Annual* 1965, 71–73, 103–4; *Coffee Annual* 1966, 51, 60–87, *Coffee Annual* 1967, 47–49, 63–67; *Coffee Annual* 1968, 43–50, 61–63, 73–74, 77; *Coffee Annual* 1971, 42–45, 146; *Coffee Annual* 1972, 61; *Coffee Annual* 1973, 106; National Coffee Association (NCA) Special Bulletin, 18 August 1965, 15 September 1965, 22 August 1966, 30 June 1966, 6 September 1966, 5 June 1967, 5 December 1967, 16 and 23 January 1968, 20 February 1968, 3 March 1969, 1 April 1971; Maidenberg, "Smaller Tree"; Haarer, *Modern Coffee Production,* 41–47; Wellman, *Coffee,* 74; Jerry Harrington interview; Evans, *Dependent Development,* 80–94; Colin McClung interview; "Cure for Coffee"; "Instant Coffee Brews"; Talbot, "Struggle for Control"; "U.S. Battles Brazil"; Solomon, "United States Policy," 389; Lucier, *International Political Economy,* 134–45; "United States and Brazil Conclude"; *Tea & Coffee Trade Journal,* September 1965, 17, October 1965, 15, February 1966, 17, April 1966, 28–30, July 1966, 18–20, August 1966, 33, September 1966, 12–13, 16, 20, 27–29, October 1966, 24, February 1967, 22, 46, May 1967, 35–36, August 1967, 18–19, September 1967, 16, 24, October 1967, 25–26, November 1967, 30, February 1968, 18–22, June 1968, 16–17, November 1969, 23, August 1970, 30, November 1970, 20, December 1970, 45; Ted Lingle interview; Lernoux, "World Politics"; Bacha and Greenhill, *150 Years of Coffee,* 82–86.

298–99   **"The Think Drink Thunks":** *Coffee Annual* 1966, 72–74, 91–93; Maidenberg, "Frost in Brazil"; NCA Special Bulletin, 20 August 1965; Pendergrast, *For God, Country and Coca-Cola,* 294; "The Seventies, A Marketing View," 1 February 1971, Box 17, J. Walter Thompson Inc. Files; *Coffee Annual* 1967, 42, 70–71, 79–83; *Coffee Annual* 1968, 34, 67–68, 93–95; *Coffee Annual* 1973, 29–31; *Tea & Coffee Trade Journal,* December 1965, 59, January 1966, 24, 34, 52, March 1966, 26, April 1966, 23–24, August 1966, 26, October 1966, 26, February 1967, 24, March 1967, 30–34, May 1967, 53, June 1967, 26, 36, August 1967, 16–18, September 1967, 41, October 1967, 25, June 1968, 38, September 1968, 15, January 1969, 24, 56, May 1970, 15, November 1970, 17.

299–300   **"The GI Coffeehouses":** Gardner, "Hollywood Confidential"; Fred Gardner interview; Reed, "'Fayettenam'"; Schutts, *We Say No to Your War!,* 1–49, 79–87, 127–31; Moser, *New Winter Soldiers,* 98–100.

300–303   **"Caution: Coffee May Be Hazardous":** "Coffee and Your Heart"; "Coffee and the Job"; "Break with Coffee?"; Ross, "What Coffee Really Does to You"; *Tea & Coffee Trade Journal,* August 1966, 14, 29–32, April 1968, 14–15, 24; Kluger, *Ashes to Ashes,* 164, 210; NCA Special Bulletin, 31 March 1980; George Boecklin interview; *Coffee Drinking,* 1969; "Heavy Coffee Drinkers"; "Coffee and Your Health";

"What–Coffee, Too?"; "Heavy Coffee Drinkers"; Maugh, "Coffee and Heart Disease"; Bassler, "Long-Distance Runners"; Dempewolff, "Truth About Coffee"; Malcolm Manber, "The Medical Effects of Coffee," in U.S. Congress, House, Joint Hearings, *Rising Coffee Prices*, 63–70; Servaas, "Medical Mailbox"; Altman, "Perils of Caffeine"; Maitland, "Coffee Decline"; Barmash, "General Foods Changing Sanka"; Kaufman, "Sanka Knows Best"; Copulsky, "Cannibalism"; Schoenholt, "Decaffeinated"; *New York Times*, 14 June 1976, 37; Robbins, "Robert Young"; Kanner, "Coffee Nerves"; Pace, "Last Cup of Sanka"; Sanka commercials in Museum of Television & Radio.

303–4   **"Gold Floats, Coffee Sinks":** "Iced Coffee Chills"; "Why Coffee Prices"; Lucier, *International Political Economy*, 147–50; Yergin, *Prize*, 589–92; *Coffee Annual* 1969, 83; *Coffee Annual* 1971, 134, 137, 148, 153; *Coffee Annual* 1972, 29–40, 52–60, 66, 69–71; *Coffee Annual* 1972, 25, 35–60; *Coffee Annual* 1973, 43–44, 48; NCA Special Bulletin, 16 March 1970, 5 April 1971, 18 April 1972, September 1972, 12 December 1972; "Bitter Brew for the Economy"; "Coffee Nerves in Brazil"; Cameron, "How the U.S."; Lernoux, "World Politics of Coffee"; *Tea & Coffee Trade Journal*, May 1969, 28, June 1969, 43, July 1969, 41, October 1969, 25, December 1969, 24–27, July 1970, 34, August 1970, 31, November 1970, 22–23, 38–40; Bacha and Greenhill, *150 Years of Coffee*, 86–89.

304–5   **"Coffee Inroads in Japan and Europe":** Malcolm, "In Tokyo,"; Pendergrast, *For God, Country and Coca-Cola*, 282, 314, 392; Kilburn, "Canned-Coffee Market"; *Tea & Coffee Trade Journal*, June 1967, 38, September 1967, 25; *Coffee Annual* 1969, 49, *Coffee Annual* 1971, 74, 161; *Coffee Annual* 1972, 68; *Coffee Annual* 1974, 33–34, 45–46; *Coffee Annual* 1975, 49–50, 63–64; "Instant Profits"; *Coffee Annual* 1963, 97; *Coffee Annual* 1964, 91–93, 169; *Coffee Annual*, 1965, 64–65; *Coffee Annual* 1966, 109–10, 113–18; *Coffee Annual* 1973, 35–40; *Coffee Annual* 1974, 30–37; *Coffee Annual* 1975, 51–53; *Tea & Coffee Trade Journal*, December 1964, 52–53, December 1965, 42, April 1966, 51, January 1968, 49–50, September 1969, 25–26, August 1969, 37; December 1969, 12, December 1970, 12–13; Proni, *Coffee: Voltaire's Friend*, 48–81; Lavazza, *Lavazza*, 24–28; Tchibo Group, *All About Tchibo*; *Eduscho*; Kraft Jacobs Suchard, *100 Years*, 50–60; "GF Freeze-Dried."

306–7   **"The King of the Robustas and the Burundi Massacres":** Saks, *Strong Brew*, 33, 60–71, 74, 131, 134–36, 173; U.S. Congress, House, *International Protection*, 64–90, 974–81.

307–9   **"Starbucks: The Romantic Period":** Jerry Baldwin interview; Jim Reynolds interview; Schoenholt, "Starbucks," 26; idem, "We Owe a Debt," 42; 1998 Starbucks brochure.

309   **"God's Gift to Coffee":** Paul Katzeff interview.

309–11   **"A Coffee Love Affair":** Erna Knutsen interview; *Tea & Coffee Trade Journal*, November 1974, 18–19, 35–36; "Coffee's First Lady"; "A Visit with Erna Knutsen"; Shore, "Erna Knutsen"; Sinnott, "Erna Knutsen"; Knutsen speeches, courtesy Erna Knutsen; Hewitt, "For Coffee Buffs"; Quimme, *Signet Book*, 93.

311–12   **"The Ultimate Aesthete":** George Howell interview; Rifkin, "Delicate Balance."

312–13   **"Specialty Proliferates":** Grady Saunders interview; Kenneth Davids interview; Peter Longo interview; Luciano Repetto interview; Frank O'Dea interview; Donald Schoenholt interview and E-mail, May 1998; Schoenholt, "We Owe a Debt"; Davids, *Coffee*; Quimme, *Signet Book*; Schafer, *Coffee*; Kolpas, *Coffee Lovers' Companion*; Schapira, *Book of Coffee & Tea*; Hewitt, "Drip Coffee Makers"; O'Connor, "Coffee Brands Perk"; "Discovery of Coffee"; Smith, "Stirring News"; "Nestle Waits"; "Hills Bros., Carnation Move"; *Tea & Coffee Trade Journal*, January 1962, 38, March 1964, 63; Seigel, "Judge Sued on Outburst"; Dougherty, "Coffee Makers Expand"; "How to Get Coffee Prices."

313–14 **"Mrs. Olson Slugs It Out with Aunt Cora":** "Coffee Market Share"; *Coffee Drinking*, 1974; Leezenbaum, "Coffee Makers Ignore"; "Bit of Good News"; Federal Trade Commission, *Cents-Off Promotions*; "Bonus Jars"; *Tea & Coffee Trade Journal*, January 1966, 21, March 1966, 55, September 1966, 14, July 1967, 22, January 1968, 79, April 1968, 41, October 1968, 39, December 1968, 47, April 1969, 14, 25, October 1969, 51, June 1970, 43; Copulsky, "Cannibalism"; O'Connor, "Coffee Brands Perk"; Edwards, "Marketer of Coffee Bags"; "F/f/s"; "Square Closure"; Ward, "Marketing Mix"; "Premeasured Coffee"; "Coffee Makes Like Tea"; "Coca-Cola's Coffee"; "Wards Foods Campaign"; Blum, "Big Gamble"; "Maxim Carves"; "How Good Is Freeze-Dried"; "Is There a Market?"; O'Connor, "GF Countering Folger's"; Gordon, "FTC Files"; U.S. Congress, Senate, *Mergers and Economic Concentration*, 350; "Procter & Gamble's Wary Eye"; "GF Defense Against P&G"; Levine, "Drip," 198; "What Killed Coffee?" 20; U.S. Congress, House, *Coffee Price Review*, 95–96; "FTC Judge Drops General Foods Case."

Chapter Sixteen

317–19 **"The world's coffee trade":** "Coffee Frostbite"; Maidenberg, "Frost in Brazil"; "Bitter Cup"; "Coffee Nerves" (1975), "Brazil's Coffee Frost"; Birmingham, *Decolonization*, 64–69; Maidenberg, "Coffee Supplies Cut"; Jones, "Others' Misfortune"; Maidenberg, "Higher Coffee Prices"; U.S. Congress, House, *Coffee Price Review*, 4–30; Howe, "Angolan Asserts Cuba Is Main Ally"; Brooke, "Angolan Coffee Trade"; *Coffee Annual 1976*, 65, 131; "Coffee Prices: First," 135–36; 1975 HB "Advertising Rationale," Hills Brothers Collection; Louis, "Brazil's Coffee (With Sugar) Billionaire"; Wheeler, *Coffee to 1995*, 19–21; Bacha and Greenhill, *150 Years of Coffee*, 90–92.

319–22 **"Machiavellian Market Manipulations":** Maidenberg, "Coffee Futures"; O'Connor, "Nestle Launches"; "Jumping Beans"; Cerra, "Grocery Chains Join in Boycott"; Lucier, *International Political Economy*, 1–14; "MacNeil/Lehrer Report"; Cerra, "Rep. Richmond Says"; Cherry, "From Grower to Table"; Kandell, "Brazil's Coffee Exporters"; "Coffee: An Awful Little"; "Trying to Apply a Coffee Brake"; Safire, "Brazil's Coffee Rip-off"; Maidenberg, "There's Worse to Come"; "A Storm Brews"; "The Coffee Boycott"; Oduber, "'Hasty and Shortsighted'"; "Liquid Consumption Trends"; "Coffee Prices: First"; Louis, "Brazil's Coffee (with Sugar) Billionaire," 88; *Coffee Annual 1976*, 43–44; U.S. Congress, House, Joint Hearings, *Rising Coffee Prices*, 2–82, 91–100, 126–28, 135–38, 150–67, 184, 203–41, 268–78; Talbot, "Regulation of the World Coffee Market," in *Food and Agrarian Orders*, 139–68.
Interview with anonymous coffee trader.

323–25 **"Hot Coffee (as in Stolen)":** *New York Times*, 23 February 1977, B6, 20 March 1977, 30, 5 April 1977, 55, 16 April 1977, 29, 18 April 1977, 67, 31 May 1977, 39, 29 June 1977, D7, 10 October 1977, 46, 27 October 1977, D12; Ferrante, "Cracking"; "Cuban Coffee Caper"; Sherrid, "Citibank's Adventures"; Cummings, "Soaring Price"; Geld, "Brazil," 8–9, 12; Kandell, "Coffee Again King"; "Take That"; Stewart, *Coffee*, 5, 15; *Tea & Coffee Trade Journal*, August 1937, 80, 94; "Colombian Coffee: Smuggling Pays"; "Zaire's Coffee Percolates Abroad"; Sivetz, *Coffee Quality*, 42; "Coffee Alternates"; O'Connor, "GF Pits New Coffee"; HB High Yield script, 19 January 1978, Hills Brothers Collection; O'Connor, "Hills Out to Roast"; Bernstein, "Extra Measure"; O'Connor, "GF Tries Economy Area"; Hess, *Taste*, 68; "Coffee Breaks" (1977); Maidenberg, "Coffee Futures Prices Level"; Armbrister, "Behind Those Soaring"; "Coffee Simmers Down"; "Finally, a Coffee Brake"; "About Wild Swings"; "Brazil's Exports"; "Falling Out"; "Shaky Price Floor"; Vidal, "Colombia"; "Brazil Cuts and Runs"; "Bean Bagged"; "Coffee Producers Try Salvaging"; "Coffee Perplex"; "Coffee Tries"; "Tight-Fisted."

325–27   **"Specialty Reaches the Heartland":** Carlson, "Confessions"; Sokolov, "Grounds for Delight"; Donald Schoenholt E-mail; Schoenholt, "Present at the Creation"; *New York Times*, 31 January 1977, 37, 14 April 1978, B3; Phil Johnson interview; Norm Storkel interview; Edward Kvetko interview; Phyllis Jordan interview; Prial, "Club Alters"; Kneeland, "Secretary Who Spurned"; Miller, *Jewel Tea Grocery Products*, 16; Paul Gallant interview; Jerry Baldwin interview; Sivetz, *Coffee Quality*, 76; Walsh, *Rise and Decline*, 171–204.

327–29   **"One Big Slaughterhouse":** Birmingham, *Decolonization*, 48–49; Johnson, *Modern Times*, 533–37; *Coffee Annual* 1977, 127, 133, 153, *Coffee Annual* 1978, 67, 139–43, 153, *Coffee Annual* 1979, 113–19, *Coffee Annual* 1980, 119–20, 148; Kaufman, "Coffee Drinks"; Darnton, "Coffee Airlift"; *New York Times*, 19 August 1977, B4, 29 September 1977, 22; 18 May 1978, D4; Wall, "Death and Coffee"; U.S. Congress, House, *United States-Uganda Relations*, 32–44, 61, 69, 94, 107, 117, 132–37, 147, 232–37, 283–84; Ullman, "Human Rights"; "Another Cup of Coffee" (1978); De St. Jorre, "Ugandan Connection"; Saks, *Strong Brew*, 199, 222; George Boecklin interview.

000–000   **"Repression and Revolution in Central America":** Woodward, *Central America*, 219–23, 241–67; Armstrong, *El Salvador*, LaFeber, *Inevitable Revolutions*; Colburn, "Class, State, and Revolution"; *Coffee Annual* 1980, 148; Berryman, "Cost of Coffee"; Barry, *Roots of Rebellion*, 28, 140–41; Menchú, *I, Rigoberta Menchú*, 22–24, 34–39, 114–16, 139, 150, 172–99, 223, 242–47; Handy, *Gift of the Devil*, 246–47; U.S. Congress, House, *U.S. Export of Banned Products*, 201–9; David Stoll interview and E-mail; Stoll, *Between Two Armies; Guatemalan Indians and the State; Harvest of Violence*; Stoll, "Life Story"; idem, *Rigoberta*; North, *Bitter Grounds*, 61–98; Anderson, War; Bulwer-Thomas, *Political Economy*, 200–229; *El Salvador*, 26–36; *Campesino*; Brockett, *Land, Power*.

331–34   **"El Gordo and the Bogotá Group":** *Coffee Annual* 1977, 152–53; *Coffee Annual* 1978, 147, 154; *Coffee Annual* 1979, 133–53, *Coffee Annual* 1980, 107–26, 148; *New York Times*, 1 December 1978, D12; "Coffee Exporters Try"; Anderson, "Price Gouging"; Wheeler, *Coffee to 1995*, 21–24; *Congressional Record*, 25 September 1979, 26123–24, 6 February 1980, 2235–36, 2 December 1980, 31580–81; Ginsberg, "Into the Grinder"; "Starting Their Own Café"; Donnelly, "Commodities Corner" (1978); Gross, "Coffee Comeback"; Maidenberg, "Coffee Futures Curbed"; Maritza Midence interview; Steve Aronson interview; "Brazil's Full of Beans"; "Coffee Producers' Precarious Quota"; Barry, *Roots of Rebellion*, 81; Talbot, "Regulation of the World Coffee Market," in *Food and Agrarian Orders*, 139–68; Bacha and Greenhill, *150 Years of Coffee*, 92–95.

334–36   **"Grinding Out the Decade":** O'Connor, "P&G Tops Off"; Menzies, "Why Folgers"; O'Connor, "Folgers Eastern Invasion"; Luxenberg, "Folgers Scores"; Maxwell, "Folgers Takes First Place"; "Coffee Market Shares" (1979); *New York Times*, 4 May 1979, D13, 15 June 1979, D11; Fanelli, "GF Sets $20 Million"; "Coffee Ads Target Youth"; Rozen, "Coffee Prices"; Fanelli, "GF Sends Master Blend"; Mussey, "Uphill Battle"; "Coffee Market Shares" (1981); Pendleton, "Hills Bros. Bets"; Revett, "Coffee Share Dip"; Powle, "Hills Bros. May Grab"; Bullock, "Hills Bros.' Brazilian Sleighride"; U.S. Congress, Senate, *Mergers and Economic Concentration*, 322–44; Peter Baer interview; "Black, William"; *Tea & Coffee Trade Journal*, March 1963, 57, January 1964, 99, February 1965, 42–43, October 1965, 56, January 1966, 93–94, August 1966, 50, October 1968, 39, March 1969, 53, November 1969, 41; "Chock Full O' Presidents"; Boecklin speech, 1 January 1980.

Chapter Seventeen

337–39   **"[Frederic A. Cauchois] evolved":** *Tea & Coffee Trade Journal*, April 1905, 151; Schoenholt, "Coffee Culprits," 27; idem, "Staling Common"; Dreyfus, "Coffee to

Your Taste"; "Consumer's Guide to Coffee"; Ted Lingle interview; Donald Schoenholt interview; Schoenholt, "Present at the Creation"; idem, "Gourmet Trade Is New York Bound"; idem, "1982, The Year It All Began"; diem, "New Year"; "Specialty Roasters Make Headway"; "New Association Brewing"; Cohen, "On the Trail"; "Quality Coffee Catalog"; "Regular, No Sugar, Please"; Carty, "Savor the Flavor"; *Tea & Coffee Trade Journal*, November 1983, 9; Schoenholt, "Gourmet Zone," September 1984; idem, "Specialty Coffee Progress."

339–41   **"Good Till the Last Drop Dead":** "If Coffee Is Bad"; *New York Times*, 4 February 1976, 10, 10 April 1979, C3, 18 November 1979, 32, 1 June 1980, 41, 5 September 1980, 16, 30 June 1981, C2, 8 April 1983, A14, 16 June 1983, A10, 19 July 1983, C6; Abrams, "Beware of Coffee"; "An Industry Confronts"; Thomas, "Morning Cup"; "Coffee and Cancer"; "Coffee Nerves: Is There Cancer in the Cup?"; "Cancer and Coffee"; "Drug Break Time?"; Wetherall, *Kicking the Coffee Habit*, 20–21; Brody, "Weaning the Body"; Burros, "Caffeine Conflict"; Taulbee, "Study Links Coffee"; Konner, "Caffeine High"; Eisenberg, "Looking"; National Coffee Association (NCA) Special Bulletin, 31 March 1980; Sullivan, "Coffee, Cancer, Reporting"; "Trouble Brewing"; Schmeck, "Coffee Drinking"; NCA Coffee Update, June 1982, August 1984; National Coffee Association, *U.S. Coffee Consumption*, 6.

341   **"Learning to Love Uncoffee":** Lecos, "More Cups Lifted"; Reed, "Coffees You Can Sleep On"; Hollie, "Big Word"; "P & G's Campaign"; Jervey, "Decaf-Coffee Marketers"; "After-Dinner UnCoffee"; "Great Decaf Wars"; Kapoor, "Decaf Process"; Davids, *Espresso*, 64–68; Fabricant, "Decaffeinated Coffee"; Kanner, "Coffee Nerves"; Sanka ads, Robert Young file, High Point ads, Museum of Television and Radio; *New York Times*, 26 August 1982, D19; "What Killed Coffee?"; Jervey, "GF to Pour Out"; Maxwell, "Coffee Market Still Cool"; "Coffee Companies Pitch"; Kaufman, "Sanka Knows Best"; Jervey, "P & G Rushes"; Winters, "Sanka Going Natural."

343–44   **"The Coffee Nonachievers":** *Tea & Coffee Trade Journal*, November 1981, 9; Jervey, "Coffee Marketers Brew"; Angrist, "Weak Coffee?"; Mary Seggerman interview; Maxwell House ads, Museum of Television and Radio; Kanner, "Coffee Nerves"; *New York Times*, 29 August 1982, D23; "What Killed Coffee?" 60; "All Eyes"; Schaeffer, "Exercise in Futility?"; "Coffee and Tea Cup Runneth Under"; Schreiber, "Hal's a Hit"; Jervey, "Coffee Group"; "Coffee Market's Ups and Downs"; "Richness"; "Coffee Companies Pitch."

344–45   **"The Little Big Guys Struggle":** Tetley corporate information; Peter Baer interview; Marshall, "Chock Full"; Jervey, "Nestlé, Hills"; Bonner, "Downfall"; Stroud, "Chase & Sanborn"; Jervey, "Nestlé's Big Bite"; McCabe, "Look into Nestlé"; Mary Seggerman interview.

345–47   **"Whole Beans and Gorgeous Women":** Bernie Biedak interview; Gary Talboy interview; Phil Johnson interview; Jerry Baldwin interview; Michael Slater interview; Paul Katzeff interview; Donald Schoenholt interview and E-mail; *Tea & Coffee Trade Journal*, December 1992, 20; Bird, "Regional Roasters"; Marty Elkin interview; Bob Stiller interview.

347–53   **"Guerrilla Wars, Coffee Disasters":** Brooke, "Angolan Coffee Trade"; Tuckman, "Healing Painful"; Russell, "Unearthing Guatemala's Disappeared"; Woodward, *Central America*, 305–7; Handy, *Gift of the Devil*, 11–14, 206–81; Betty Hannstein Adams interview; Smith, "Guatemala," 789; Petras and Morley, *US Hegemony Under Siege*, 132; Newhagen, "Now Coffee Threatens"; *New York Times*, 12 May 1983, A12; Armstrong, *El Salvador*, 75–190; El Salvador Media Project, *Doble Cara*; Task Force, *Central America*, 13–14, 111, 113; Barry, *Roots of Rebellion*, 52, 122–37, 170; Paige, *Coffee and Power*, 189–218, 272–312; Kinzer, "Nicaragua's Bitter Harvest"; "Peace Corps for Nicaragua"; Kinzer, "Nicaraguan Rebels"; Kinzer, "Sandinista Says"; Russell, "Coffee Caper"; Ricardo Valvidieso interview; Buckley, *Violent Neighbors*, 19, 32, 86, 95, 133, 188, 204–24; Colburn, "Class, State, and Revolution"; Roger Castellon Orué interview; Luisa Maria Molina Icias interview; Sklar, "Bringing the War Home"; LeMoyne, "Rid Us of the Contras"; Joaquin Cuadra Lacayo interview;

Berman, "In Search"; LaFeber, *Inevitable Revolutions*; *Guatemalan Indians and the State*; *Harvest of Violence*; Stoll, *Between Two Armies*; North, *Bitter Grounds*, 99–120; Bulwer-Thomas, *Political Economy*, 230–94; Annis, *God and Production*; Danner, *Massacre*; *Campesino*; Schwantes, *Guatemala*; *Dream Compels Us*; *El Salvador*, 36–45; Falla, *Massacres*.

354–55 **"Fair Trade Coffee":** Barry, *Roots of Rebellion*, 122, 133; Buckley, *Violent Neighbors*, 138; Paul Katzeff interview; Dan Cox interview; *Java Jive* (Equal Exchange newsletter), November 1996, April 1997; "Development of Fair Trade"; Bert Beekman interview; Jonathan Rosenthal interview; Van der Zee, *Van Winkelnering*, 285; Multatuli, *Max Havelaar*, 73–74; 123; Bolscher, "Speech"; *Max Havelaar: Fair Trade Practices*.

355–57 **"Blood in the Salvadoran Cups?":** *New York Times*, 25 March 1987, C6; Swasy, *Soap Opera*, 193–97; *New York Times*, 12 December 1989, D2, 4 January 1990, A22, 12 May 1990, A1, A8, 21 September 1990, D3; 14 December 1990, A20; Greenwald, "Bitter Cup of Protest"; Dagnoli, "Coffee Boycott Boils"; Liberman, "Salvadoran Coffee, Go Home"; Youman, "Red Apple Chain"; Larsen, "Java Jive"; "Coffee Boycott," *Christian Century*; Alva, "Trouble's Brewing"; Dan Cox interview; Rob Everts interview; "Ceremony in El Salvador"; Cheney, "Struggling Back"; Neighbor to Neighbor, *International Boycott*; idem, *History*; *United Nations and El Salvador*.

357–59 **"The Big Boys Try to Get Hip":** Walsh, "General Foods' Coffee Achievement"; "All Eyes"; Wunderman, *Being Direct*, 193–202; Art Trotman interview; Mary Seggerman interview; Donna Neal interview; Dunkin, "Maxwell House Serves"; Paul Gallant interview; Jervey, "Folger's Perks Minus Mrs. Olson"; Jervey, "P & G Rushes Folger's"; Mark Upson interview; Alter, "WRG Will Brew"; Winters, "New High-Yield Folgers"; idem, "Coffee Leaders"; Talbot, "Regulating," 120–22.

359–62 **"Coffee and Cigarettes":** Mary Seggerman interview; Steve Morris interview; Kluger, *Ashes to Ashes*, 597–99, 607–13; Dagnoli, "GF Exec Out"; idem, "Maxwell House Ads Lose"; idem, "Coffee Battle Boils"; "Ground Coffee," 529; Freeman, "Coffee Price War"; Maxwell, "Coffee Consumption"; Levine, "Drip, Drip, Drip"; Garfield, "Ellerbee Grounds Out"; Graham, "Maxwell House May Face Boycott"; Rothenberg, "Maxwell House Lost By Ogilvy"; Dagnoli, "Maxwell House Lands"; idem, "Maxwell House Gets Reheated."

362–63 **"The Collapse of the ICA":** *New York Times*, 11 January 1986, A48, 13 January 1986, D6, 21 January 1986, D24, 14 February 1986, D13, 17 February 1986, D6, 25 February 1988, D6; 7 July 1986, D8, 17 September 1986, D2, 13 October 1986, D6, 7 July 1987, D15, 8 October 1987, D14, 25 February 1988, D6, 3 August 1988, D1, 4 August 1988, D14, 19 September 1988, 1 October 1988, A36, 5 November 1988, D17; 19 November 1988, A42, 23 December 1988, D13, 29 December 1988, D13, 30 December 1988, D13, 20 February 1989, D5, 23 February 1989, D15, 25 February 1989, A47, 8 April 1989, A45, 29 May 1989, A32, 4 July 1989, A41, 7 July 1989, D13, 28 July 1989, D14, 3 October 1989, D17, 3 December 1989, F8, 14 December 1989, D18; "Bitter News"; "Bitter Harvest"; "Coffee Calamity"; Beltrão, "Statement"; "Not an Awful Lot"; "Coffee Nerves That May Not Last"; Donnelly, "Money Worries"; idem, "No Joy in Geneva"; Weiss, "Coffee Growers"; "Greatly Strained"; Donnelly, "Coffee: Let's Sell Grandma"; "Has Beans, Will Travel"; "Terrible Twins"; Vesilind, "Brazil," 368; Baer, *Brazilian Economy*, 346–47; Stainer, "International Coffee Review 1987/88"; Cavill, "OPEC"; Raffaelli, *Rise and Demise*, 67–72; Donnelly, "No Bottom in Coffee?"; Fuhrman, "Another Cartel"; Donnelly, "Offal Truth"; Talbot, "Regulating," 123, 128–33; idem, "Regulation of the World Coffee Market," in *Food and Agrarian Orders*, 139–68; Wheeler, *Coffee to 1995*, 26–40; Bacha and Greenhill, *150 Years of Coffee*, 98–103.

364–64 **"The Coca–Coffee Connection":** Treaster, "Coffee Impasse"; Fuhrman, "Another Cartel," 42; Passell, "Fighting Cocaine, Coffee"; "One Way to Help"; *New York Times*, 22 September 1989, D6; U.S. Congress. Senate, *U.S. International Drug Policy*, 55–186; George Boecklin copy of testimony; Brooke, "King Coffee"; Warren, "Coffee Jitters";

Ahlfeld, "Coffee in 1990/91"; Wheeler, *Coffee to 2000*, 6–11, 26–30; Talbot, "Regulating," 133–44; Weiss, "When You Bet"; Ahlfeld, "Coffee in 1991/92," C31; Garcia, "Reality in the Campo"; Reerink, "Stockpiles and Shortages"; Marcelo Vieira interview; Ahlfeld, "Coffee in 1992/93"; *Black Harvest.*

365–66 **"Big Coffee: Ice Cold":** Dagnoli, "Suchard Buy"; Bird, "Philip Morris Brews"; De-Palma, "Hoboken Loses"; Maxwell, "Morning Report"; Lev, "Soap Opera from Britain"; Dagnoli, "Brewing Romance"; Allis, "Sex by the Cupful"; Lippert, "Coffee Break"; Medcalf, "Nestlé: We Don't Kiss"; Bowes, "Coffee Couple's Story"; Garfield, "One More Cup"; Rickard, "Taster's Choice Rolls"; Irwin Warren interview; Susan Irwin interview; Dagnoli, "GF Brews"; idem, "GF Brings Back"; idem, "Iced Coffee Next"; idem, "GF Ices Cappuccino"; McMath, "Iced Cappuccino"; Friedman, "Get Your Iced"; McMath, "Coffee Fights"; Jabbonsky, "Ready to Go"; Zweig, "Chock Full O' Potential"; Masterson, "Top 100"; Moukheiber, "Oversleeping."

Chapter Eighteen

367–71 **"According to legend, Merlin":** Jerry Baldwin interview; Schultz and Yang, *Pour Your Heart*, 22–116, 145, 154, 330; Dawn Pinaud interview; Dave Olsen interview; Melville, *Moby-Dick*; Kevin Knox interview; Jim Reynolds interview; Frederick, "Java Jive"; Davids, *Espresso*, 36–44.

371–72 **"Latte Land":** Schultz and Yang, *Pour Your Heart*, 114; Joanne Shaw interview; Phyllis Jordan interview; Jim Stewart interview; Becky McKinnen interview; Sandy McAlpine interview; Edward Kvetko interview; Underwood, "Place-Based Coffee"; *New York Times*, 19 March 1990, 18; 12 April 1991, 28; Fader, "What's Happening"; Frank, "Achieving"; Loomis, "City"; Yang, "Fewer Cups"; Johnson, "Coffee Reconquers"; Scarpa, "Gourmet Coffee"; Harvey, "Gourmet Coffees"; Kummer, "Before the First Sip," 117; Radovanovic and Hanney, *Coffee Lover's Guide to Toronto*, 29–43; "Toronto's Coffee Culture"; "Brew-Ha Ha"; Knapp, "Damn"; Guy Wood interview; Jim Twiford interview.

372–78 **"Starbucks: The (Very) Public Years":** Schultz and Yang, *Pour Your Heart*, 7–20, 85, 107, 118, 125–39, 185–296 ; Smith, "Wanted"; Dawn Pinaud interview; Kevin Knox interview; Sherri Miller interview; Jerry Baldwin interview; Murphy, "More Than Coffee"; Liddle, "Starbucks Looks"; Rothman, "Into the Black"; Reese, "Starbucks"; Clark, "Friendly Coffee War"; National Public Radio, 27 March, 1993; Scherreik, "Getting the Most"; Oleck, "Tap Won't Cut It"; Russ Kramer interview; Nolan, "Starbucked!"; Schoenholt, "Starbucks"; Brammer, "Grounds"; Craig, "Investors"; Witchel, "By Way of Canarsie"; Anonymous Starbucks employee interview; Oldenburg, *Great, Good Place*, 160–61, 183–99, 226, 237; Morrison, "Howard's Trend"; Model, "Pouring"; Raimy, "Caffeine Nation"; Biddle, "Coffee Connection"; Rosenberg, "Battle Brews"; George Howell interview; Dave Tilgner interview; Kahn, "Sniffing"; Rifkin, "Delicate Balance"; Kindleberger, "Starbucks Buys"; Gelston, "Ex-Coffee Connection Chief"; Cobb, "Bean Stalk"; Gelston, "Suit Brews"; Reidy, "Boston Area"; McDowell, "Bean Counters"; idem, "Starbucks"; Kugiya, "Seattle's Coffee King"; Olsen, *Starbucks Passion*; National Public Radio, 1 April, 1996.

378–80 **"Deflecting the Critics":** Liddle, "Howard Schultz"; Gerloff, "Clean, Well-Lighted"; Witchel, "By Way"; Pogrebin, "Starbucks Pours"; Oren Bloostein interview; McCabe, "Woman Sues"; Hamlin, "Customer"; Schultz and Yang, *Pour Your Heart*, 121; Morrison, "Howard's Trend"; Olsen, *Starbucks*, 8; Morrison, "All Alone Together"; Solomon, "Not in My Backyard"; Nolan, "Starbucked!"; Reese, "Starbucks"; Murphy, "More Than Coffee"; McDowell, "Bean Counters"; Cox, "Enough"; Davids, "Starbucks Paradox"; Francis, "Starbucks"; Pressler, "Brains"; "New Starbucks"; Slywotzky, *Value Migration*, 157–78.

380–85 **"Brothers Gourmet Coffee":** Michael Chu interview; Dennis Boyer interview; Jim Twiford interview; Steve Schulman interview; Jay Isais interview; Slywotzky, *Value Migration*, 171; Edward Kvetko interview; Guy Wood interview; Dan Cox interview; Marty Elkin interview; Don Breen interview; Specialty Coffee Holdings, *Confidential Information*; Brothers Gourmet Coffee, 31 December 1993, Notes to Consolidated Financial Statements; Goldman, "Brothers"; Esterberg, "It's Now Brothers"; "Brothers Gourmet to Open"; McCash, "Brews Brothers"; Ferraro, "Brothers Coffee Business"; "Bros. Coffee"; Boyer, *Coffee Companion*, ix, 38; "Boca Coffee Roaster"; Antosh, "Maryland Club"; Jones, "Brothers"; Ferraro, "Brothers Coffees Plans"; "Brothers Gourmet Brews"; "Brothers Sells Unit"; "Coffee Firm"; Leib, "Coffee-shop Losses"; Conklin, "Brothers Selling"; idem, "One Brother Bows"; Leib, "Brothers to Take Earnings Charge"; Conklin, "Brothers Is Closing"; "Coffee Executive"; Barron, "Diedrich Buys"; McCash, "Roaster Shedding"; Pounds, "Company to Settle"; idem, "Brothers"; *Tea & Coffee Trade Journal*, October 1998, 123; Don Breen interview; "People on the Move"; Bronk, "Boyer Brothers."

386–88 **"A Maturing Market":** "Trendy Coffee Bars"; Levine, "Java News"; Brumback, "Grounds for Expansion"; Johnson, "Lure"; Dan Cox interview; Castle, *Perfect Cup*; Kummer, *Joy of Coffee*; Davids, *Home Coffee Roasting*; Bersten, *Coffee Floats*; Stella, *Book of Coffee*; Illy, *Book of Coffee*; Bohnaker, "Haunts"; Piro, *Caffeinated Cartoons*; Ferguson, "Coffee Thing"; Dunkin' Donuts corporate history; Whalen, "Gourmet Coffee"; Lubove, "Coffee Versus"; Brown, "Who's Tending"; Marty Elkin interview; Phil Johnson interview; Segal, "So You're Thinking"; Slywotzky, *Value Migration*, 157–78; Alexander, "Millstone Expansion"; Sturdivant, "Two Volume Movers"; Buck, "P&G Buys."

Chapter Nineteen

389–91 **"Coffee is turning out to be":** Greenberg quote in *Proceedings, Memorias*, 131; *King Lear*, act 4, sc. 6, line 133; John Martinez interview; Cook, *Shade*, 16; Davids, *Espresso*, 77; McKenna, "It's Good"; Mirsky, "You May Already"; Gomez, "One Great Cup"; Jaime Fortuño interview; Gary Talboy interview; Castle, *Perfect Cup*, 35, 86.

391–92 **"The Kona Kai Scandal":** Kona Kai Farms 1996 brochure; Chao, "Is Kona Coffee Good"; Craig Thurber, affidavit in USA v. Michael L. Norton; Amended Request, USA v. Michael L. Norton; Fimrite, "Coffee Fans Abuzz"; Golden, "U.S. Accuses."

392–94 **"La Minita: A Coffee City-State":** Bill McAlpin interview; Russ Kramer interview; Castle, "La Minita Hangs On"; Daniels, "Passion for Taste"; Vogel, "Carriage Trade Coffee"; McAlpin, "La Minita News"; idem, "Coffee and the Socially Concerned"; McAlpin, "Speech."

394–96 **"Coffee Kids and the *Coyotes*":** Betty Hannstein Adams interview; Wheeler, *Coffee to 2000*, 59–60; Bill Fishbein interview; David Abedon interview; Schoenholt, "Oz"; Fishbein, "Coffee Kids."

396–98 **"Mending the Heart with Organic":** Gary Talboy interview; Karen Cebreros interview; Cebreros, "Socially"; Lane, "Coffees with Conscience"; "Organic Coffees"; Cheney, "Struggling Back"; Pollock, "Organic Coffee"; Davids, *Espresso*, 74–76; Murphy, "La Selva"; "Green, as in Greenbacks"; Kenworthy, "Campaign"; Eddy and Mausi Kühl interview.

399–401 **"Befriending the Birds":** Gilmore, "In the Mountainous Kingdom"; Perfecto "Shade Coffee"; Brown, *Seeds of Change*; Pearse, *Seeds of Plenty*; Shiva, *Violence*; Greenberg, *Birds over Troubled Forests*; *Lessons of the Rainforest*; Forsyth and Miyata, *Tropical Nature*, xii, 1; Caufield, *In the Rainforest*, 37; Vandermeer and Perfecto, *Breakfast of Biodiversity*, 136–46; *Green Revolution Revisited*, 6–9, 79–99; Kenneth Davids interview; Davids, *Espresso*, 80–81; Rice, *Coffee, Conservation*; Nowell, "Durham Coffee Roaster";

Haarer, *Modern Coffee Production*, 59–60, 77–96; McDonald, *Coffee Growing*, 42–49; Cook, *Shade in Coffee Culture*, 7–25; Wellman, *Coffee*, 37, 57–59, 327–46.

401–3 **"Turf Battles":** *Proceedings, Memorias*, 131–35, 143–55, 191–93, 321–25; Wille, "Birds and the Beans"; Greenberg, "Phenomena"; Fred Houk interview; Silver, "Coffee's Shady Side."

403–6 **"Chiapas, Congo, Rwanda, Haiti, Colombia":** *Proceedings, Memorias*, 98, 255; Price Peterson 1996 correspondence, Donald Schoenholt E-mails, Skip Blakely interview; Carrie MacKillop interview; Jeanne Kail interview; Purvis, "Roots of Genocide"; Berkeley, "Encore for Chaos"; "Ethiopia: Federal Sham"; "Horn of Africa"; Connell, "Africa's New Bloc"; Heller, "Out of the Heart"; Parker, "From Mobutu to Kabila"; Rosenberg, "Teenage Nightmare"; Omona, "Uganda: Stolen Children"; Tyson, "Grounds of Contention"; Larmer, "Tears of a Nation"; Robinson, "Is Colombia Lost?"; Dettmer, "Drug War"; Nares, "Colombia Faces"; Rohter, "Political Feuds Rack Haiti"; Gary Talboy interview; Bocage, "Declining"; Wilson, "Haitian Bleu"; Rick Peyer E-mail, 1 September 1998; Aspin, "Rebels"; "Massacre in Mexico"; Padgett, "Laws of the Jungle"; McCaughan, "Bloodbath in Chiapas"; Appel, "Report on Chiapas"; John Ross E-mail, 27 August 1997; Ross, *Annexation*; BETHRIC statement; "Aftermath Hurricane Mitch."

406–9 **"Guilt Tripping in Guatemala":** Charlie and Ruth Magill interview; *Report on Guatemala*; Entine, "Blowing"; U.S. Guatelmala Labor Education Project (US/GLEP), *Justice*, 1996; Zachary, "Starbucks Asks"; Dave Olsen interview; Starbucks press releases; US/GLEP press releases; Betty Hannstein Adams E-mail; Barnes, "Slaves"; Durning, "History"; idem, "Coffee."

409–11 **"Coffee–Part of the Matrix":** Wolf, *Europe*, 3, 22, 310.

411–15 **"Caffeine, the Drug of Choice":** Roland Veit interview; James, *Caffeine and Health*, 3–86, 219–38, 280–83; idem, *Understanding Caffeine*, 1–14, 114–32, 156–58; Gilbert, *Caffeine*; "Truth About Damage"; "Coffees Are Good"; Rehak, "To Drink or Not to Drink"; Ott, *Pharmacotheon*, 30, 67–68, 171, 213–14, idem, *Cacahuatl Eater*, 73–96; Roland Veit interview; Therrien, *Give Us*; Braun, *Buzz*, 107–95; Massey, "Caffeine and the Elderly," 46; *Diagnostic and Statistical Manual*, 212–15, 708–9; *New York Times* 22 April 1877, 4; Paul Erdos; Profet, *Protecting*, 141; National Coffee Association web site; International Food web site.

415–18 **"Are You Addicted?":** Joe McBratney interview; "Addicted to Caffeine"; IFIC web site, http://ificinfo.health.org; National Coffee Association web site, http://www.coffeescience.org; Hughes, "The Ability of Low Doses"; idem, "Behavioral Effects"; idem, "Clinical Importance"; Strain, "Caffeine Dependence"; John Hughes interview; Marsha Nagley-Moody interview; Peter Dews E-mail; Sivetz, *Coffee Technology*, 254, 558–67; *Coffee International*, 77; Helprin, *Memoir*, 8–9, 54, 82–83.

418–20 **"The Lions and the Lambs":** Anthony Bucalo interview; Datamonitor, *U.S. Coffee*; Cox, "One Perspective"; Folgers ad in *Nations Restaurant News*, 11 May 1998; SCAA 1998 Denver conference tape; Ted Lingle interview; Moriwaki, "Starbucks Coffee"; Poole, "Coffee and Buns"; Starbucks press releases; Mike Sullivan interview; Second Cup press releases; Alton McEwen interview; Jay Isais interview; Caribou brochure; Fiedler, "Riding Herd."

420–24 **"State of the Coffee World":** SCAA 1998 Denver conference tape; Specter, "Coffee Clash," 42; *Coffee International*, 64–89, 153–268, 308–22; Anu Suomela E-mail, April 24, 1998; Bjorn Heggset correspondence; Starbucks press releases; Dawn Pinaud interview; "Coffee Overtakes Tea"; Clairmonte, *Merchants of Drink*, 107–18; Schapira, *Book of Coffee*, Foreword; "Beverages," *Sun Sentinel*; Steve Colten interview; Jaime Polit interview.

424–25 **"The Coffee Tour in Costa Rica":** Doug Mitchell interview; Steve Aronson interview; Philip Aronson interview; Café Britt literature; Carolyn Hall interview; Edgar Rojas interview.

425   **"Winged for Posterity":** *Over the Black Coffee,* 108.

Appendix

427–30   Castle, *Perfect Cup*; Davids, *Home Coffee Roasting*; Davids, *Coffee: A Guide*; Knox, *Coffee Basics*; Kummer, *Joy of Coffee*; McCoy, *Coffee and Tea*, Schapira, *Book of Coffee and Tea*; Palani Plantation; Behr, "Gentle Manifesto."

BIBLIOGRAPHY

"A & P's New Coffee Packages." *Printer's Ink Monthly*, October 1933, 17, 65.

"About Wild Swings in Coffee Prices." *U.S. News & World Report*, 8 August 1977, 61.

Abrams, H. Leon, Jr. "Beware of Coffee, Tea, and Cola Beverages If You Value Good Health." *Consumers' Research Magazine*, May 1977, 21–24.

Acheson, Dean G. "Department Expresses Regrets on Revised Senate Coffee Report." *Department of State Bulletin*, 4 September 1950, 388.

Adams, Richard N. *Crucifixion by Power: Essays on Guatemalan National Social Structure, 1944–1966*. Austin: University of Texas Press, 1970.

_____. *Cultural Surveys of Panama, Nicaragua, Guatemala, El Salvador, Honduras*. Washington, DC: Pan American Sanitary Bureau, 1957.

_____. "Guatemalan Ladinization and History." *The Americas* (April 1994): 527–43.

"Addicted to Caffeine." *ABC News*, "20/20," 18 August 1995, Transcript no. 1533.

Adelman, M. A. *A & P: A Study in Price-Cost Behavior and Public Policy*. Cambridge, MA: Harvard University Press, 1966.

"After-Dinner Uncoffee." *New York Times*, 17 May 1984, A26.

"Aftermath Hurricane Mitch." *Specialty Coffee Chronicle* (January–February 1999): 2.

Aguilar, Roberto. "Flexibility of Wartime Coffee Controls Urged." *Journal of Commerce and Commercial* (25 October 1944): 14.

Ahlfeld, H. "Coffee in 1990/91." *F. O. Lichts International Coffee Yearbook 1991*. Ratzeburg, Germany: F. O. Lichts, 1991, C27–35.

_____. "Coffee in 1991/92." *F. O. Lichts International Coffee Yearbook 1992*. Ratzeburg, Germany, 1992, C31–46.

_____. "Coffee in 1992/93." *F. O. Lichts International Coffee Yearbook 1993*. Ratzeburg, Germany, 1993, C30–45.

Alexander, Karen. "Millstone Expansion Plans Are Perking Up." *Seattle Times*, 9 February 1993, F2.

"Alice Foote MacDougall Dies; Won, Lost Restaurant Fortune." *New York Herald Tribune*, 13 February 1945.

"All Eyes on Decaffeinated." *Progressive Grocer*, July 1985, 113.

"All Factors in Coffee Trade Join in Program to Aid Consumption." *Sales Management*, 15 August 1932, 152.

Allen, Frederick Lewis. *The Big Change: America Transforms Itself, 1900–1950*. New York: Harper & Brothers, 1952.

_____. *Only Yesterday: An Informal History of the Nineteen-Twenties*. New York: Harper & Brothers, 1931.

Allis, Tim. "Sex by the Cupful." *People*, 20 May 1991, 94–95.

Allon, Janet. "Son of Coffee Bar: The Java-Steeped Magazine." *New York Times*, 20 August 1995, 8.

Alter, Stewart and Judann Dagnoli. "WRG Will Brew Ads for New P & G Coffee." *Advertising Age*, 13 April 1987, 1, 98.

Altman, Lawrence K. "The Perils of Caffeine." *New York Times*, 15 March 1975, 12.

Alva, Marilyn. "Trouble's Brewing over Coffee Beans." *Restaurant Business*, 1 January 1992, 18.

"America's Coffee Renaissance Explodes with Excitement as Specilaty Coffee Trade Booms." *World Coffee & Tea*, August 1981, 10–15.

Anderson, Jack. "Price Gouging by the Coffee Cartel." *Washington Post*, 20 September 1979.

Anderson, Thomas P. *Matanza: El Salvador's Communist Revolt of 1932*. Lincoln: University of Nebraska Press, 1971.

_____. *The War of the Dispossessed: Honduras and El Salvador, 1969*. Lincoln: University of Nebraska Press, 1981.

Angrist, Stanley W. "Have Another Cup–Please." *Forbes*, 9 September 1985, 156.

_____. "Help! Call the Cartel." *Forbes*, 3 August 1981, 106.

_____. "Weak Coffee?" *Forbes*, 20 December 1982, 178.

Annis, Sheldon. *God and Production in a Guatemalan Town*. Austin: University of Texas Press, 1987.

"Another Cup." *Business Week*, 4 April 1936, 20–22.

"Another Cup of Coffee." *New Republic*, 13 May 1978, 7–8.

Antosh, Nelson. "Maryland Club Coffee Plant Sold." *Houston Chronicle*, 4 May 1994, 1.

Appel, Kerry. "Report on Chiapas Massacre." E-mail from Mexican cybercafe, 6 January 1998.

Arbuckle v. Blackburn [John Arbuckle et al. vs. Joseph E. Blackburn]. U.S. 350 (October 1902).

Aregay, Merid, W. "The Early History of Ethiopia's Coffee Trade and the Rise of Shawa." *Journal of African History 29*, 1 (1988): 19–25.

Arévalo, Juan José. *The Sharks and the Sardines*. New York: Lyle Stuart, 1961.

Armbrister, Trevor. "Behind Those Soaring Coffee Prices." *Reader's Digest*, May 1977, 65–68.

Armstrong, Robert and Janet Shenk. *El Salvador: The Face of Revolution*. Boston: South End Press, 1982.

Arnold, Edwin Lester. *Coffee: Its Cultivation and Profit*. London: W. B. Whittingham & Co, 1886.

"Artificial Coffee Beans." *Scientific American*, 21 November 1891, 321.

Aspin, Chris. "Rebels, Nature Cut Mexico Coffee Crop." *Washington Post*, 21 January 1994, D2.

Associated Coffee Industries of America. *Excerpts from Proceedings, Annual Convention*, 1936, National Coffee Association Files.

_____. *Excerpts from Proceedings, Annual Convention*, 1937, National Coffee Association Files.

_____. *Excerpts from Proceedings, Annual Convention*, 1938, National Coffee Association Files.

_____. *Report of Board of Directors Meeting*, 1932, National Coffee Association Files.

_____. *The Retail Market for Coffee*. New York: ACIA, 1932..

Bach, Johann Sebastian. *Coffee Cantata*. Modern slang trans. William Metcalfe, Larry Rudiger, Jill Levis, Shelburne Farms, VT, 26 July 1997.

Bacha, Edmar, and Robert Greenhill. *150 Years of Coffee*. Rio de Janeiro, Brazil: Marcellino Martins & E. Johnston Exportadores, 1992.

Baer, Werner. *The Brazilian Economy: Growth and Development*. 3d ed. New York: Praeger, 1989.

Balzac, Honoré de. "The Pleasures and Pains of Coffee." *Michigan Quarterly Review* (Spring 1996): 273–77.

"Bane of the Bean." *Newsweek*, 27 April 1959, 90–91.

Barmash, Isadore. "General Foods Changing Sanka and Brim Solvent." *New York Times*, 17 July 1975, 37.

Barnard, Ignatius. *Dividends on Jewel Common*. Chicago: Jewel Tea Co., 1923.

Barnes, Edward. "Slaves of New York." *Time*, 2 November 1998, 72–75.

Barnouw, Erik. *The Golden Web: A History of Broadcasting in the United States*. Vol. 2, *1933 to 1953*. New York: Oxford University Press, 1968.

_____. *A Tower in Babel: A History of Broadcasting in the United States*. Vol. 1, *to 1933*. New York: Oxford University Press, 1966.

Barron, Kelly. "Diedrich Buys 17 Locations in Denver Market." *Orange Country Register*, 29 February 1996, C2.

Barron, T. J. "Science and the Nineteenth Century Ceylon Coffee Planters." *Journal of Imperial and Commonwealth History 16*, 1 (1987): 5–23.

Barry, Tom. *Roots of Rebellion: Land & Hunger in Central America.* Boston: South End Press, 1987.

Bassler, Thomas J. "Long-Distance Runners." *Science,* 12 October 1973, 113.

Bates, Robert H. *Open-Economy Politics: The Political Economy of the World Coffee Trade.* Princeton, NJ: Princeton University Press, 1997.

"Bean Bagged." *Forbes,* 15 April 1977, 28.

Beecham, R. K. *Gettysburg: The Pivotal Battle of the Civil War.* Chicago: A. C. McClurg, 1911. Reprint. Stamford, CT: Longmeadow Press, 1994.

Beeson, Emmet. "American Coffee Drinker at the Mercy of Brazil." *New York Times,* 29 June 1924, 4.

Behr, Edward. "A Gentle Manifesto on the Craft of Roasting Coffee." *Art of Eating* (Fall 1997): 13–17.

Behrendt, Ernst. "Coffee Goes to War." *Travel* (March 1942): 28–31, 39.

Beltrão, A. F. "Statement." 11 February 1986, Boca Raton, FL, National Coffee Association Files.

Benson & Benson. "Survey of Consumer Attitudes on Coffee for National Coffee Association." 12 October 1955, National Coffee Association Files.

Benton & Bowles Collection. D'Arcy Masius Benton & Bowles Archives, Hartman Center, Duke University.

"Benton, William." *Current Biography* (1945), 40–42.

Bergad, Laird W. *Coffee and the Growth of Agrarian Capitalism in Nineteenth Century Puerto Rico.* Princeton, NJ: Princeton University Press, 1983.

"Bergen, Edgar." *Current Biography* (1945), 42–45.

Bergreen, Laurence. *As Thousands Cheer: The Life of Irving Berlin.* New York: Viking, 1990.

Berkeley, Bill. "An Encore for Chaos? Ethnic Battles in Kenya." *Atlantic Monthly* (February 1996): 30.

Berman, Paul. "In Search of Ben Linder's Killers." *The New Yorker,* 23 September 1996, 58–80.

Berner, Frederic G. "The Future of Soluble Coffee." *Coffee Annual* 1944, 37–39.

Bernstein, Henry R. "Extra Measure Puts Coke Unit Deeper into Hot Coffee Area." *Advertising Age,* 14 August 1978, 3.

Berryman, Phillip. "The Cost of Coffee." *Environment* (August 1977): 12–15.

Bersten, Ian. *Coffee Floats, Tea Sinks: Through History and Technology to a Complete Understanding.* Sydney, Australia: Helian Books, 1993.

Bess, Alan. *Googie: Fifties Coffee Shop Architecture.* New York: Chronicle Books, 1985.

BETHRIC (Businesses for Human Rights and Fair Trade in Chiapas) statement from Judy Wicks, White Dog Cafe, Philadelphia, PA, judy@whitedog.com.

"Beverages." *Sun-Sentinel,* 30 April 1998, 3D.

Beyer, Robert Carlyle. *The Colombian Coffee Industry: Origins and Major Trends, 1740–1940.* Ph.D. diss., University of Minnesota, 1947. Ann Arbor, MI: UMI, no. 76–8130.

Biddle, Frederic M. "Coffee Connection on the Defensive as Starbucks Comes to Town." *Boston Globe,* 2 January 1994, 29.

"The Big Wheat-Coffee Swap." *Literary Digest,* 5 September 1931, 40.

Billings, John D. *Hardtack and Coffee, or the Unwritten Story of Army Life.* Boston: George M. Smith & Co., 1887.

Bird, Laura. "Philip Morris Brews Coffee Wars with Nestlé in Europe." *Adweek's Marketing Week,* 25 June 1990, 4.

_____. "Regional Roasters Keep Coffee Brewing." *Adweek's Marketing Week,* 18 February 1991, 5.

Birmingham, David. *The Decolonization of Africa.* Athens: Ohio University Press, 1995.

"A Bit of Good News on 'Cents-Off'." *Consumer Reports,* February 1966, 52.

"A Bitter Brew for the Economy." *Business Week,* 25 July 1970, 27.

"Bitter Cup." *Newsweek,* 11 August 1975, 60.

"Bitter Harvest." *Time,* 27 January 1986, 38.

"Bitter News for the World Coffee Market." *Business Week,* 13 January 1986, 50.

"Black Coffee Outlook." *Newsweek,* 7 September 1942, 66.

Black Harvest. A film by Bob Connolly and Robin Anderson. VHS, 90 min. Santa Monica, CA: Direct Cinema Ltd., 1992.

"Black, William." *Current Biography* (1964), 45–47.

"Black, with No Sugar." *Economist*, 2 June 1984, 78–79.

Blum, Ernest. "The Big Gamble at General Foods." *International Management*, December 1969, 26–28.

Blumenthal, W. Michael. "The World Coffee Agreement and U.S. Foreign Economic Policy." *Department of State Bulletin*, 11 February 1963.

Boadle, Anthony. "CIA in Latin America Showed Less Heroic Side to Cold War." *Reuters*, 18 September 1997.

"Boca Coffee Roaster Posts Loss for Year." *Miami Daily Business Review*, 28 February 1994.

Bocage, Ducarmel. "The Declining Importance of Coffee in the Haitian Economy." *Journal of Third World Studies 6*, 1 (1989): 124–46.

Boecklin, George. Speeches. Property of George Boecklin, Long Island, NY.

Bogart, Leo. *The Age of Television*. 3d ed. New York: Frederick Ungar, 1972.

Bohnaker, Will. "Haunts of the Aardwolf." *Willamette Week*, 25–31 January 1995, 17–19.

Bolscher, Hans. "Speech in Sweden." 1996. Property of Bolscher, Stichting Max Havellar, Utrecht, The Netherlands.

Bond, R. S. "Coffee, the Smiling Drink." *Outing* (July 1921): 158–60.

Bonner, Raymond. "Downfall of an Entrepreneur Raises Questions on His Rise." *New York Times*, 25 June 1983, A1, 38.

"Bonus Jars, Coupons Push Coffee; Price Cut Better?" *Advertising Age*, 30 June 1975, 18.

"Boomerang." *Business Week*, 25 July 1942, 99.

"Bouças Coffee Plan." *The Inter-American*, February 1945, 42–43.

Bourne, Richard. *Getulio Vargas of Brazil, 1883–1954: Sphinx of the Pampas*. London: Charles Knight, 1974.

"Bowes, Edward." *Current Biography* (1941), 96–98.

Bowes, Elena. "Coffee Couple's Story to Percolate in Book." *Advertising Age*, 14 December 1992, 6.

"Bowes Inc." *Time*, 22 June 1936, 63.

Bowles, Chester. *Promises to Keep: My Years in Public Life, 1941–1969*. New York: Harper & Row, 1971.

Bowman, Jim. *More Than a Coffee Company: The Story of CFS Continental*. Chicago: CFS, 1986.

Boyer, Dennis, with John O. Davies. *The Coffee Companion*. Denver, CO: Entreper Press, 1992.

Boyle, James E. "Black Coffee, Raw Silk." *World's Work* (April 1931): 40–43.

Boyle, T. Coraghessan. *The Road to Wellville*. New York: Viking, 1993.

Brady, Cyrus Townsend. *The Corner in Coffee*. New York: G. W. Dillingham Co., 1904.

Bramah, Edward and Joan. *Coffee Makers: 300 Years of Art & Design*. London: Quiller Press, 1989.

_____. *Tea & Coffee: A Modern View of Three Hundred Years of Tradition*. London: Hutchinson, 1972.

Brammer, Rhonda. "Grounds for Caution." *Barron's*, 15 August 1994, 20.

Braun, Stephen. *Buzz: The Science and Lore of Alcohol and Caffeine*. New York: Oxford University Press, 1996.

Brazil: A Country Study. Edited by Richard F. Nyrop. Washington, DC: Government Printing Office, 1982.

"Brazil and Portugal Growers Talk About Banding Together in Coffee." *Business Week*, 13 July 1957, 67.

"Brazil Cuts and Runs on Coffee Prices." *Business Week*, 7 November 1977, 28.

"Brazil Cuts Coffee Export Tax." *Business Week*, 6 November 1937, 60–61.

"Brazil Feels the Squeeze." *Business Week*, 24 July 1954, 112–13.

"Brazil Just Can't Afford a Coffee Famine." *Business Week*, 24 August 1932, 8.

"Brazil Tires of Coffee Control." *Literary Digest*, 20 November 1937, 31.

"Brazilian Coffee Developments." *Bulletin of the Pan American Union*, August 1932, 586–88.

"Brazil's Coffee Frost Has an Instant Bite." *Business Week*, 8 September 1975, 21.

"Brazil's Exports: Bluffing with Beans." *Economist*, 22 October 1977, 96.

"Brazil's Full of Beans." *Economist*, 11 October 1980, 84–87.

"Brazil's Hidden Wealth." *New York Times,* 26 January 1890, 17.

"Break with Coffee?" *Newsweek* 17 February 1964, 68–71.

"Brew-Ha Ha." *Glamour,* January 1991, 162–63.

"Brewery Bequeaths Dry Era Outlet to Competitor." *Printer's Ink Monthly,* 6 July 1933, 10–11.

Brockett, Charles D. *Land, Power, and Poverty: Agrarian Transformation and Political Conflict in Central America.* Rev. ed. Boulder, CO: Westview Press, 1991.

Brody, Jane E. "Weaning the Body from Dependence on Caffeine." *New York Times,* 21 April 1982, C6.

Bronk, Janet. "Boyer Brothers Brew Up Success Through Excellence." *Colorado Business,* October 1990, 76.

Brooke, James. "Angolan Coffee Trade in Shambles." *New York Times,* 14 January 1985, D4.

_____. "King Coffee Bean vs. King Coffee." *New York Times,* 27 May 1991, A33, 35.

"Bros. Coffee." *Reuters,* 25 February 1994.

"Brothers Gourmet Brews a 290% Leap in Income." *Miami Herald,* 10 August 1994, C1.

"Brothers Gourmet to Open Coffee Bars at Denver Airport." *Bloomberg Business News,* 15 February 1994.

"Brothers Sells Unit to Sara Lee Corp." *Miami Herald,* 1 November 1994, C1.

Broussard-Simmons, Vanessa, and Wendy Ann Shay. *Register of the Hills Bros. Coffee, Inc. Collection ca. 1856–1988.* Washington, DC: Archives Center, National Museum of American History, 1996.

Brown, Lester R. *Seeds of Change: The Green Revolution and Development in the 1970's.* New York: Praeger, 1970.

Brown, Suzanne J. "Who's Tending the Beans?" *Tea & Coffee Trade Journal* (May 1994): 46.

Bruce, Scott, and Bill Crawford. *Cerealizing America: The Unsweetened Story of American Breakfast Cereal.* Boston: Faber & Faber, 1995.

Brumback, Nancy. "Grounds for Expansion." *Restaurant Business,* 20 May 1995, 112–30.

Buck, Richard. "P & G Buys Millstone Coffee," *Seattle Times,* 1 December 1995, D1.

Buckley, Kerry W. *Mechanical Man: John Broadus Watson and the Beginnings of Behaviorism.* New York: Guilford Press, 1989.

_____. "The Selling of a Psychologist." 1980 paper in J. Walter Thompson Inc. Files.

Buckley, Tom. *Violent Neighbors: El Salvador, Central America, and the United States.* New York: Times Books, 1984.

Bullock, Jane Elise. "Hills Bros.' Brazilian Sleighride." *Fortune,* 17 July 1978, 70.

Bulwer-Thomas, Victor. *The Political Economy of Central America Since 1920.* Cambridge, UK: Cambridge University Press, 1987.

Burnham, John C. "John Broadus Watson." *Dictionary of American Biography.* Suppl. 6. New York: Scribner's, 1980, 670–73.

Burns, E. Bradford. *Eadweard Muybridge in Guatemala, 1875: The Photographer as Social Recorder.* Berkeley: University of California Press, 1986.

_____. *A History of Brazil.* 2d ed. New York: Columbia University Press, 1980.

_____. *Latin America: A Concise Interpretive History.* 6th ed. Englewood Cliffs, NJ: Prentice Hall, 1994.

Burns, Jabez. *Notes of a Tour in the United States and Canada in the Summer and Autumn of 1847.* London: Houlston & Stoneman, 1848.

Burros, Marian. "The Caffeine Conflict–Where Does It Stand?" *New York Times,* 21 April 1982, C1, 6.

Bushnell, David, and Neill Macaulay. *The Emergence of Latin America in the Nineteenth Century.* New York: Oxford, 1988.

"Busted Robusta." *Economist,* 29 March 1975, 102.

"Buyers Get a Break on Coffee." *Business Week,* 21 August 1954, 48.

"Café Espresso." *Sunset* (March 1955): 150–51.

Cale, Edward G. "Coffee in Inter-American Relations." *U.S. Dept. of State Bulletin,* 6 June 1955, 941–42.

Cambranes, J. C. *Coffee and Peasants: The Origins of the Modern Plantation Economy in Guatemala, 1853–1897.* South Woodstock, VT: CIRMA, 1985.

The Cambridge History of Latin America. Vol. 4, *1870–1930.* Edited by Leslie Bethell. Cambridge, UK: Cambridge University Press, 1986.

Cameron, C. R. "Second International Coffee Conference." *Bulletin of the Pan American Union,* September 1931, 901–15.

Cameron, Juan. "How the U.S. Got on the Road to a Controlled Economy." *Fortune,* January 1972, 74–77, 156–65.

Campbell, Robert. *The Golden Years of Broadcasting: A Celebration of the First 50 Years of Radio and TV on NBC.* New York: Charles Scribner's Sons, 1976.

Campesino: The Diary of a Guatemalan Indian. Translated and edited by James D. Sexton. Tucson: University of Arizona Press, 1985.

"Cancer and Coffee: Concern Percolates." *Science News,* 4 July 1981, 6.

Cantwell, Mary. "Village Voice." *New York Times Book Review,* 30 November 1997, 34.

"Capricorn Coffees: Specialty Coffee Is Their Specialty." *World Coffee & Tea,* September 1975, 24–25, 38.

Carlson, Peter. "Confessions of a Coffee Addict." *Newsweek,* 16 May 1977, 13.

Carnahan, A. S. J. *Report of the Special Study Mission to Central America on International Organizations and Movements,* 12 July 1955, Union Calendar no. 343, Report no. 1155, 1–20, in *House Reports,* vol. 4. Washington, DC: Government Printing Office, 1955.

Carson, Gerald. *Cornflake Crusade.* New York: Rinehart & Co., 1957.

_____. *The Old Country Store.* New York: Oxford University Press, 1954.

Carty, Winthrop P. "Savor the Flavor." *Américas* (March–April 1985): 2–7.

Castle, Tim. "La Minita Hangs on Despite Plunging Producer Prices," *Tea & Coffee Trade Journal* (November 1992): 63–66.

_____. "Pacific NW Hosts Expansive Growth." *Tea & Coffee Trade Journal* (March 1988): 18–19.

_____. *The Perfect Cup: A Coffee-Lover's Guide to Buying, Brewing and Tasting.* Reading, MA: Addison-Wesley, 1991.

Caufield, Catherine. *In the Rainforest.* Chicago: University of Chicago Press, 1991.

Cavill, John. "A Coming Crisis in Coffee?" *Barron's,* 31 May 1982, 49.

_____. "OPEC: Before the 'Lapse Back Into Cheating' . . . the Coffee Arbitrage." *Barron's,* 25 July 1988, 54.

Cebreros, Karen. "Socially, Environmentally, and Economically Delicious: Is There Such a Thing as Organic Coffee?" *In Good Taste* (March–April 1992): 12.

Center for Research in Marketing. "A Study of Hills Bros. Instant Coffee Packaging and Coffee Drinker Attitudes." May 1960, in Hills Brothers Collection.

A Century of Brazilian History Since 1865: Issues and Problems. Edited by Richard Graham. New York: Alfred A. Knopf, 1969.

"Ceremony in El Salvador Marks Formal End to 12-Year Conflict." *UN Chronicle* (March 1993): 67.

Cerra, Frances. "Grocery Chains Join in Boycott of Coffee." *New York Times,* 4 January 1977, 12.

_____. "Rep. Richmond Says Major Coffee Producers Exploit Shortage and Calls for Congressional Investigation." *New York Times,* 5 January 1977, sec. 4, 1.

Chao, Julie. "Is Kona Coffee Good to the Last Drop? That's All You Get." *Wall Street Journal,* 24 August 1995, A1, 6.

Chase & Sanborn. *Coffee: Presented with Compliments of.* Boston: Chase & Sanborn, ca. 1892.

Chase, Stuart, and F. J. Schlink. *Your Money's Worth: A Study in the Waste of the Consumer's Dollar.* New York: Macmillan, 1927.

Cheney, Glenn Alan. "Struggling Back: El Salvador's Coffee Industry." *Tea & Coffee Trade Journal* (July 1994): 16ff.

Cheney, Ralph Holt. *Coffee: A Monograph.* New York: New York University Press, 1925.

Cherry, Rona. "From Grower to Table, Coffee Will Cost More." *New York Times,* 12 January 1977, sec. 4, 1, D7.

"Chester Points the Way." *Business Week,* 7 March 1936, 12–13.

"Chock Full O' Presidents." *Dun's* (February 1972): 63–64.

Clairmonte, Frederick, and John Cavanagh. *Merchants of Drink: Transnational Control of World Beverages*. Penang, Malaysia: Third World Network, 1988.

Clark, Charles. "The Friendly Coffee War." *Tea & Coffee Trade Journal* (August 1994): 18–25.

Clayton, Lawrence A. *Grace: W. R. Grace & Co., The Formative Years, 1850–1930*. Ottawa, IL: Jameson Books, 1985.

Cobb, Nathan. "The Bean Stalk: Deal Leaves Coffee Mavens Uneasy." *Boston Globe*, 31 March 1994, 1.

"Coca-Cola's Coffee Freezes Out Competition." *Marketing Magazine*, 1 July 1970, 51.

"Coffee Ads Target Youth." *Advertising Age*, 11 February 1980, 24.

"Coffee Alternatives: The Tastes Without the Cost?" *Consumer Reports*, August 1977, 478.

"Coffee: An Awful Little in Brazil." *Economist*, 15 January 1977, 81.

"Coffee and Cancer: A Brewing Concern." *Science News*, 21 March 1981, 181.

"Coffee and Politics Disrupt Brazil." *Literary Digest*, 1 November 1930, 9.

"Coffee and Revolution in Brazil." *New Republic*, 22 October 1930, 245–46.

"Coffee and Tea Cup Runneth Under." *Marketing and Media Decisions* (October 1983): 179–88.

"Coffee and the Bogotá Conference." *Bulletin of the Pan American Union*, January 1937, 39–45.

"Coffee and the Job: Heartfelt Insults?" *Science News*, 23 November 1985, 327.

"Coffee and Your Health." *Consumer Bulletin*, April 1971, 22.

"Coffee and Your Heart." *Science Digest* (October 1963): 55.

"Coffee Aroma Chemicals: Over 300 Are Identified." *Oil, Paint and Drug Reporter* (January 1971): 5.

"Coffee, Black." *Time*, 23 January 1956, 30.

Coffee: Botany, Biochemistry and Production of Beans and Beverage. Edited by M. N. Clifford and K. C. Willson. London: Croom Helm, 1985.

"Coffee Boycott." *Christian Century*, 15–22 May 1991, 544.

"The Coffee Boycott." *Newsweek*, 17 January 1977, 62–63.

"Coffee Break." *Business Week*, 12 May 1956, 98.

"Coffee Break." *Newsweek*, 10 September 1962, 76.

"Coffee Breaks." *Time*, 30 May 1977, 68.

"Coffee by Coupon." *Business Week*, 28 November 1942, 14.

"Coffee, Café, Caffè, Koffie." *Sunset* (May 1959): 201–6.

"Coffee Calamity." *Fortune*, 3 February 1986.

"Coffee Cause & Effect." *Time*, 5 October 1959, 39.

"Coffee Companies Pitch to a More Discerning Drinker." *Business Week*, 28 May 1984, 72–73.

"Coffee Cornered." *Time*, 9 August 1954, 70–71.

"The Coffee-Cup Crisis." *Literary Digest*, 22 February 1930, 67–68.

Coffee Drinking in the United States, Winter 1966. New York: Pan American Coffee Bureau, 1966.

Coffee Drinking in the United States, Winter 1969. New York: Pan American Coffee Bureau, 1969.

Coffee Drinking in the United States, Winter 1974. New York: Pan American Coffee Bureau, 1974.

"Coffee Executive Going to Cookies." *Sun-Sentinel*, 20 January 1996, 14C.

"Coffee Exporters Try to Perk Up Prices." *Business Week*, 27 March 1978, 44–45.

Coffee Facts and Fantasies. New York: Pan American Coffee Bureau, 1939. Hills Brothers Collection.

"Coffee Firm Posts Loss." *Sun-Sentinel*, 30 March 1995, 3D.

"Coffee Firm Posts Loss." *Sun-Sentinel*, 17 May 1995, 3D.

"Coffee for Comrade K." *New Republic*, 20 June 1960, 6.

"Coffee Forces Unite for Sales Campaign." *Business Week*, 5 October 1932, 8.

"Coffee Fragrance More Stimulating Than Onion." *Science News Letter*, 29 August 1953, 135.

"Coffee Freeze." *Business Week*, 2 May 1942, 82.

"Coffee Frostbite." *Economist*, 26 July 1975, 85–86.

"Coffee Growers Are Still Bogged Down." *Business Week*, 5 March 1955, 88–90.

"Coffee Growers Blame Frost." *Business Week*, 16 January 1954, 72.

"Coffee Growers Seek Ways to Perk Up Falling Prices." *Business Week*, 6 August 1955, 112.

"Coffee Holidays." *Commonweal*, 19 February 1954, 488.

Coffee International File 1995–2000. London: Market Tracking International, 1996.

"Coffee Jitters." *Time*, 25 January 1954, 98.

"Coffee Keeps Brazilians Awake." *Business Week*, 19 October 1957, 133.

"Coffee Klondike." *Life*, 13 November 1950, 17–20.

"Coffee Makes Like Tea in Wesco's New Bag." *Sales Management*, 15 April 1971, 54–55.

"Coffee Market Shares," *Advertising Age*, 13 April 1981, 74.

"Coffee Market Shares by Company." *Advertising Age*, 21 October 1974, 70.

"Coffee Market Shares by Company." *Advertising Age*, 30 April 1979, 70.

"The Coffee Market's Ups and Downs." *Newsweek*, 30 January 1984, 63.

"Coffee Men Nervously Watch Course of Revolt in Brazil." *Business Week*, 21 September 1932, 6.

"Coffee Nerves." *Time* 26 June 1950, 30.

"Coffee Nerves." *Time*, 15 February 1954, 34–36.

"Coffee Nerves." *Time*, 11 August 1975, 56.

"Coffee Nerves–A Cure?" *Newsweek*, 18 August 1958, 73–75.

"Coffee Nerves in Brazil." *Time*, 19 October 1970, 46.

"Coffee Nerves: Is There Cancer in the Cup?" *Time*, 23 March 1981, 73.

"Coffee Nerves That May Not Last Long." *Business Week*, 8 September 1986, 40.

"Coffee News for Coffee Lovers." *Look*, 29 May 1956, 94–95.

"Coffee Overtakes Tea in England." *The Coffee Reporter* (NCA), February 1999, 6.

"The Coffee Perplex." *Newsweek*, 15 November 1977, 91.

"Coffee Pickup." *Business Week*, 14 February 1941, 41–44.

"Coffee Plastic, a New Achievement of Science." *Bulletin of the Pan American Union*, October 1939, 594–95.

"Coffee Plastics." *Business Week*, 29 March 1941, 59–60.

"Coffee Prices." *Bulletin of the Pan American Union*, May 1945, 304–5.

"Coffee Prices: Can the Jumping Bean Be Tamed?" *Time*, 30 August 1954, 68.

"Coffee Prices: First the Bad News and Then the *Bad* News." *Consumer Reports*, March 1977, 134–36.

"Coffee Producers' Precarious Quota Plan." *Business Week*, 20 October 1980, 47.

"Coffee Producers Try Salvaging Their Prices." *Business Week*, 8 August 1977, 25–26.

"Coffee Rationing." *Life*, 30 November 1942, 64, 66.

"Coffee Roasted." *Business Week*, 16 October 1954, 32.

"Coffee Shipment." *Scientific American* (July 1943): 26–27.

"Coffee Simmers Down." *Time*, 27 June 1977, 63.

"Coffee Smiles." *Time*, 23 March 1959, 40.

Coffee, Society, and Power in Latin America. Edited by Roseberry, Gudmundson, and Kutschbach. Baltimore, MD: Johns Hopkins University Press, 1995.

"Coffee Stabilized." *Business Week*, 23 January 1943, 50.

"Coffee: Stimulant to Good Neighborliness." *Scholastic*, 30 March 1942, 26.

"Coffee Stretchers." *Business Week*, 8 November 1942, 62–63.

"Coffee Switch." *Time*, 16 June 1958, 28–30.

"Coffee Tries to Regain Its Lost Consumers." *Business Week*, 26 December 1977, 33–34.

Coffee-Wheat Swap Files, 1931–1933, Boxes 1–8, NC 28, Entry 55, U.S. National Archives.

"Coffee Woes Just Starting." *Science News Letter*, 13 February 1954, 102.

"The Coffeeman's on the Job." *Business Week*, 10 February 1951, 104–8.

"Coffeeplot." *Time*, 18 April 1955, 46–48.

"Coffees Are Good for Business: Sipping Java with the President." *Boston Herald*, 1 March 1997, 3.

"Coffee's First Lady." *Coffee International*, 3 (1977): 33.

Coffey, Thomas M. *The Long Thirst: Prohibition in America, 1920–1933*. New York: Laurel, 1976.

Cohen, Steve. "On the Trail of Blue Mountain Coffee." *Américas* (March–April 1985): 8–11.

Colburn, Forrest D. "Class, State, and Revolution in Rural Nicaragua: The Case of *Los Cafetaleros*." *Journal of Developing Areas* (July 1984): 501–18.

Colby, Gerald, with Charlotte Dennett. *Thy Will Be Done: The Conquest of the Amazon: Nelson Rockefeller and Evangelism in the Age of Oil.* New York: HarperCollins, 1995.

"Colliers Sue Post for Alleged Libel." *New York Times*, 7 September 1907.

Collins, James H. "There's a Reason." *Printer's Ink*, 12 August 1908, 3–9.

Colombia: A Country Study. Edited by Dennis M. Hanratty and Sandra W. Meditz. Washington, DC: Government Printing Office, 1988.

"Colombian Coffee: Smuggling Pays Better." *Economist*, 9 April 1977, 82.

"Commodity Notes." *Inter-American Monthly* (June 1942): 43.

Community Culture and National Change. Edited by Richard N. Adams. New Orleans: Middle American Research Institute, 1972.

Conklin, Michele. "Brothers Is Closing Local Plant." *Rocky Mountain News*, 12 January 1996, 51A.

_____. "Brothers Selling Coffee Shop Chain." *Rocky Mountain News*, 23 June 1995, 60A.

_____. "One Brother Bows Out of Coffee Firm." *Rocky Mountain News*, 21 July 1995, 58A.

Connell, Dan, and Frank Smyth. "Africa's New Bloc." *Foreign Affairs* (March 1998): 80.

Conrad, Joseph. *Nostromo: A Tale of the Seaboard*. New York: Penguin Books, 1987.

"Consumers Get Less Air." *Printer's Ink*, 30 July, 1931, 75.

"Consumer's Guide to Coffee." *Glamour*, October 1983, 288.

Cook, O. F. *Shade in Coffee Culture*. U.S. Dept. of Agriculture, Bulletin No. 25. Washington, DC: Government Printing Office, 1901.

Copulsky, William. "Cannibalism in the Marketplace." *Journal of Marketing* (October 1976); 103–5.

"Cost of Coffee." *Business Week*, 17 October 1953, 152–54.

Cotton, C. Marden. "Research on Coffee." *Science News Letter*, 10 April 1954, 234–35.

"Coup of Coffee." *Newsweek*, 8 July 1974, 59.

Cox, Daniel C. "Enough Starbucks Bashing." *Gourmet Retailer* (July 1997); 140–42.

_____. "One Perspective: The Future of Coffee Purchasing in the U.S." *Tea & Coffee Trade Journal* (September 1998): 74.

Craig, David, and Donna Rosato. "Investors Check Out Hot Retailing Stocks." *USA Today*, 27 October 1994, 3B.

Crane, Stephen. *Great Short Works of Stephen Crane*. New York: Harper & Row, 1965.

Crothers, T. D. "Coffee and Tea Drunkenness." *Current Literature* (June 1902): 740–41.

"The Cuban Coffee Caper." *Time*, 12 February 1979, 22.

Culturgram '97: Federal Republic of Brazil. Provo, UT: Brigham Young University, 1997.

Culturgram '97: Federal Democratic Republic of Ethiopia. Provo, UT: Brigham Young University, 1997.

Culturgram '97: Republic of Guatemala. Provo, UT: Brigham Young University, 1997.

Cummings, Judith. "Soaring Price of Coffee Inspires Protesters and a Wave of Thefts." *New York Times*, 6 March 1977, 36.

Cuneo, Alice Z. "Starbucks' Word-of-Mouth Wonder." *Advertising Age*, 7 March 1994, 12.

"A Cup of Coffee." *Harper's New Monthly Magazine*, January 1872, 237–44.

"The Cup That Agitates." *Time*, 8 February 1954, 16–17.

"Cure for Coffee." *Time*, 3 February 1967, 75.

Curtin, Philip D. *The Atlantic Slave Trade: A Census*. Madison: University of Wisconsin Press, 1969.

Dagnoli, Judann. "A Brewing Romance." *Advertising Age*, 8 April 1991, 22.

_____. "Coffee Battle Boils." *Advertising Age*, 24 August 1987, 3, 50.

_____. "Colombian Arrival." *Advertising Age*, 3 April 1989, 60.

_____. "'Fast Roast' Turns into Weighty Issue." *Advertising Age*, 3 October 1988, S2, S4.

_____. "GF Brews New Coffees." *Advertising Age*, 16 April 1990, 3, 70.

_____. "GF Brings Back Slow-Roast Coffee." *Advertising Age*, 18 June 1990, 20.

_____. "GF Exec Out as Coffee Ad Fund Slashed." *Advertising Age*, 20 April 1987, 2, 97.

_____. "GF Ices Cappuccino." *Advertising Age*, 23 July 1990, 49.

_____. "Iced Coffee Next for Coke, Nestle." *Advertising Age*, 21 May 1990, 4.

_____. "Maxwell House Ads Lose Out to Promotion." *Advertising Age*, 27 April 1987, 3, 80.

_____. "Maxwell House Gets Reheated." *Advertising Age*, 27 November 1989, 1, 116.

_____. "Maxwell House Lands at D'Arcy." *Advertising Age*, 29 May 1989, 1, 47.

_____, and Laurie Freeman, "Coffee Boycott Boils." *Advertising Age*, 21 May 1990, 6.

_____, and Dagmar Mussey. "Suchard Buy Brings PM Close to Nestle." *Advertising Age*, 25 June 1990, 2, 60.

Daniels, Jim. "A Passion for Taste." *Cigar Aficionado*, (Fall 1995): 290–99.

Daniels, Paul C. "The Inter-American Coffee Agreement–A Year of Adjustment." *Coffee Annual* 1942, 11–12.

Danner, Mark. *The Massacre at El Mozote.* New York: Vintage, 1993.

Darnton, John. "Coffee Airlift from Uganda to a Thirsty Market Is Flying a Route to Instant Riches." *New York Times*, 25 May 1977, A3.

Darrock, Michael. "What Happened to Price Control?" *Annals of America.* Chicago: Encyclopedia Britannica, 1976. Vol. 16, 140–48.

Datamonitor. *U.S. Coffee: Quantifying Emerging Markets.* New York: Datamonitor, 1999.

Davids, Kenneth. *Coffee: A Guide to Buying, Brewing & Enjoying.* 4th ed. Santa Rosa, CA: 101 Productions, 1976, 1991.

_____. *Espresso: Ultimate Coffee.* New York: Cole Group, 1993.

_____. *Home Coffee Roasting: Romance & Revival.* New York: St. Martin's Press/Griffin, 1996.

_____. "Peet's California Coffee Cult." *Coffee Journal* (Autumn 1997): 42–47, 76.

_____. "The Starbucks Paradox." *Coffee Journal* (Autumn 1998): 48–53, 70–72.

Davis, Louise, "Good Since the First Drop," *The Tennessean*, January 4, 1976, F1.

De Goût, Q. "Strong Coffee." *Atlantic Monthly* (June 1945): 117–20.

De St. Jorre, John. "The Ugandan Connection." *New York Times Magazine*, 9 April 1978, 27–28, 82–88.

Dean, Warren. *The Industrialization of São Paulo 1880–1945.* Austin: University of Texas Press, 1969.

_____. *Rio Claro: A Brazilian Plantation System, 1820–1920.* Stanford, CA: Stanford University Press, 1976.

_____. *With Broadax and Firebrand: The Destruction of the Brazilian Atlantic Forest.* Berkeley: University of California Press, 1995.

Decolonization and African Independence: The Transfers of Power, 1960–1980. Edited by Prosser Gifford and William Roger Louis. New Haven, CT: Yale University Press, 1988.

Delbanco, Nicholas. "Rumford." *American Heritage* (September 1993): 67–77.

Dempewolff, Richard F. "The Truth About Coffee and Your Health." *Science Digest* (June 1975): 30–36.

DePalma, Anthony. "Hoboken to Lose a Symbol of Industrial Era." *New York Times*, 28 June 1990, B1.

Dettmer, Jamie. "Drug War on U.S. Streets Is Fought in Colombia." *Insight*, 24 November, 1997, 36–44.

Deutsch, Ronald M. *The New Nuts Among the Berries.* Palo Alto, CA: Bull, 1977.

"The Development of Fair Trade in the Netherlands." Fair Trade Organisatie web site, September 1996, www.web.net/fairtrade/fair645.html.

DeVincent Collection. Archives Center, Smithsonian, National Museum of American History, Washington, DC.

Di Ruocco, John. "Specialty Coffee in the United States." Speech at XXX Giornate Internazionali del Caffè, Trieste, Italty, 28 June 1996.

Diagnostic and Statistical Manual of Mental Disorders. 4th ed. Washington, DC: American Psychiatric Association Press, 1994.

"Dial K for Koffee." *Fortune*, October 1955, 202.

DiBacco, Thomas V. *Made in the U.S.A.: The History of American Business.* New York: Harper & Row, 1987.

DiChario, Nicholas A. "The Soldier and His Dead Companion." In *Crime Through Time*, edited by Miriam Grace Monfredo and Sharan Newman. New York: Berkley Prime Crime, 1997.

Dinesen, Isak. *Out of Africa.* New York: Random House, 1938.

"The Discovery of Coffee by Playing the Blending Game." *Sunset* (November 1972): 199–202.

Dobie, J. Frank. "Good Coffee Is a State of Mind." *Vogue*, 1 April 1954, 173–75.

Dobranski, Stephen B. "'Where Men of Differing Judgements Croud': Milton and the Culture of the Coffee Houses." *Seventeenth Century 9*, 1 (1994): 35–56.

A Documentary History of Brazil. Edited by E. Bradford Burns. New York: Alfred A. Knopf, 1966.

Donnelly, Richard A. "Coffee: In the Grip of a Cartel That Really Works." *Barron's*, 21 March 1983, 70, 72.

———. "Coffee: Let's Sell Grandma." *Barron's*, 16 March 1987, 92–93.

———. "Commodities Corner." *Barron's*, 12 June 1978, 53–54.

———. "Crashing Coffee." *Barron's*, 9 March 1987, 93.

———. "In Currencies, The Cry Is Banzai! In Coffee, Buy!" *Barron's*, 5 March 1984, 76–78.

———. "Money Worries . . . Coffee's Ups and Downs." *Barron's*, 29 September 1986, 84–86.

———. "No Bottom in Coffee?" *Barron's*, 16 October 1989, 66.

———. "No Joy in Geneva . . . Coffee's Ups and Downs." *Barron's*, 22 December 1996, 54.

———. "The Offal Truth . . . Trading Coffee Takes Nerve." *Barron's*, 11 December 1989, 71.

Dougherty, Philip H. "Coffee Makers Expand TV Spots." *New York Times*, 12 May 1975, 43.

A Dream Compels Us: Voices of Salvadoran Women. Edited by New Americas Press. Boston, MA: South End Press, 1989.

Dreyfus, Patricia A. "Coffee to Your Taste." *Money*, December 1982, 193–96.

Driver, James. "Coffee Supplies and Quality." *Consumers' Research Bulletin*, February 1945, 19–20.

———. "The Quality of Vacuum-Packed Coffees." *Consumer Bulletin*, September 1957, 10–11.

———. "Soluble Coffee: Not the Best Breakfast Beverage." *Consumers' Research Bulletin*, December 1945, 18–21.

———. "Stretching Your Coffee Supply." *Consumers' Research Bulletin*, January 1943, 5–6.

"Which Kind of Coffee, for Good Flavor and Aroma?" *Consumers' Research Bulletin*, August 1958, 13–14.

"Drug Break Times?" *Current Health* (November 1981): 12–13.

Dulles, John W. F. *Vargas of Brazil: A Political Biography.* Austin: University of Texas Press, 1967.

Dun, R. G. & Co. Collection. Baker Library, Harvard University Graduate School of Business Administration.

Dunkin, Amy. "Maxwell House Serves Up a Yuppie Brew." *Business Week*, 2 March 1987, 62.

Durning, Alan Thein. "Coffee." *Adbusters Quarterly* (Winter 1995): 72–74.

Durning, Alan Thein, and Ed Ayres. "The History of a Cup of Coffee." *World Watch* (September–October 1994): 20–22.

E D & F Man Coffee Limited. *World Coffee Situation.* September 1993, London.

Eduscho: Documentation 1993/94. Bremen, Germany: Eduscho, 1994.

"Edward F. Hutton, Financier, 86, Dies." *New York Times*, 12 July 1962.

Edwards, Bob. "Truth About Damage Awards." National Public Radio, "NPR Morning Edition," 8 September 1998.

Edwards, Larry. "Marketer of Coffee Bags Dips into Louisiana Test." *Advertising Age*, 23 September 1974, 2.

Eisenberg, Steve. "Looking for the Perfect Brew." *Science News*, 16 April 1988, 252–53.

Eisenhower, Milton S. *The Wine Is Bitter: The United States and Latin America.* Garden City, NY: Doubleday, 1963.

El Salvador: A Country Study. Edited by Richard A. Haggerty. Washington, DC: Government Printing Office, 1990.

El Salvador Media Project. *Doble Cara (Two Faces).* Video. El Salvador Media Project, 1989. Distributed by AFSC Film and Video Library, Cambridge, MA.

Ellis, Aytoun. *The Penny Universities: A History of the Coffee-Houses.* London: Secker & Warburg, 1956.

Ellis, John. *An Historical Account of Coffee.* London: Ellis, 1774.

Ely, Melvin Patrick. *The Adventures of Amos 'n' Andy: A Social History of an American Phenomenon.* New York: Free Press, 1991.

"Emotional Ersatz." *Time*, 16 January 1939, 50.

Entine, Jon and Martha Nichols. "Blowing the Whistle on Meaningless 'Good Intentions'." *Chicago Tribune*, 20 June 1996.

"Ersatz Brews." *Newsweek*, 30 May 1977, 76.

Essays on Coffee and Economic Development. Edited by Carlos Manuel Pelaez, translated by Magnolia Maciel Pelaez. Rio de Janeiro: Instituto Brasileiro do Cafe, 1973.

Esterberg, Don. "It's Now Brothers . . . Coffee, That Is!" *Florida Grocer*, February 1994.

"Ethiopia: Federal Sham." *Economist*, 16 August 1997, 36.

Evans, Peter. *Dependent Development: The Alliance of Multinational, State, and Local Capital in Brazil.* Princeton, NJ: Princeton University Press, 1979.

"Ever-Normal Coffee Muddle." *Fortune*, June 1955, 95.

Ewen, Stuart. *Captains of Consciousness: Advertising and the Social Roots of the Consumer Culture.* New York: McGraw-Hill, 1976.

"Ex-Senator Guy Gillette Dead." *New York Times Biographical Edition*, March 1973, 424.

Fabricant, Florence. "Decaffeinated Coffee: A New Brew." *New York Times*, 25 October 1989, C1, 6.

Fader, Liz. "What's Happening in Flavored Coffees?" *Tea & Coffee Trade Journal* (December 1991): 28.

Falcón, Guillermo Nañez. *Erwin Paul Dieseldorff, German Entrepreneur in the Alta Verapaz of Guatemala, 1889–1937.* Ph.D. diss., Tulane University, 1970. Ann Arbor, MI: UMI no. 70-24,543.

Falla, Ricardo. *Massacres in the Jungle: Ixcán, Guatemala, 1975–1982.* Translated by Julia Howland. Boulder, CO: Westview Press, 1994.

"A Falling-Out Among the Coffee Exporters." *Business Week*, 17 October 1977, 40–41.

Fanelli, Louis A. "GF Sends Master Blend into Battle." *Advertising Age*, 26 January 1981, 1, 75.

_____. "GF Sets $20 Million Effort." *Advertising Age*, 15 December 1980, 2, 69.

Farbstein, W. E. "Coffee on the Side." *New York Times Magazine*, 7 March 1954, 57.

"FCC on Mae West." *Time*, 24 January 1938, 51–52.

Federal Trade Commission. *Cents-Off Promotions in the Coffee Industry.* Bureau of Economics, April 1966. Property of Colombian Coffee Federation, New York office.

_____. *Economic Report of the Investigation of Coffee Prices.* Washington, DC: Government Printing Office, 30 July 1954.

Federal Trade Commission Decisions. Vol. 1- , 1920- .Washington, DC: Government Printing Office.

Ferguson, Andrew. "A Coffee Thing." *National Review*, 21 November 1994, 80.

Ferrante, Angela. "Cracking the Cuban Coffee Connection." *Maclean's*, 26 February 1979, 24–25.

Ferraro, Cathleen. "Brothers Coffee Business Perking." *Rocky Mountain News*, 31 March 1994, 62A.

_____. "Brothers Coffees Plans More Stores in Mexico." *Rocky Mountain News*, 23 June 1994, 49A.

"F/f/s, Five-Material, Square Coffee 'Can'." *Modern Packaging* (October 1974): 29–31.

Fiedler, Terry. "Riding Herd on Caribou." *Minneapolis Star Tribune*, 22 June 1997, D1.

Fimrite, Peter. "Coffee Fans Abuzz over Kona Brew-haha." *San Francisco Chronicle*, 9 November 1996, A1.

"Finally, a Coffee Brake." *Time*, 8 August 1977, 68.

Finch, Christopher. *Jim Henson: The Works the Art, the Magic, the Imagination.* New York: Random House, 1993.

Finley, Ann. "St. Louis Coffee." *St. Louis Memories 6* (1996): 23–32.

Fishbein, Bill and Dean Cycon. "Coffee Kids." *World Coffee & Tea* (October 1992): 14–15, 28.

Fisher, M. F. K. "Coffee." *Atlantic Monthly* (May 1945): 114–15.

Florance, Howard. "Food: A Giant Industry." *Review of Reviews* (February 1933): 34–37.

"Folger, James Athearn III." *National Cyclopedia of American Biography.* Vol. 59. Clifton, NJ: James T. White, 1980, 177.

Font, Mauricio A. *Coffee, Contention, and Change in the Making of Modern Brazil.* London: Basil Blackwell, 1990.

Food and Agrarian Orders in the World-Economy. Edited by Philip McMichael. Westport, CT: Praeger, 1995.

Food and Drink in History. Vol. 5. Edited by Robert Forster and Orest Ranum. Baltimore: Johns Hopkins University Press, 1979.

Foot, Frederick N. *Coffee: The Beverage.* New York: Spice Mill, 1925.

Forster, Cindy. "The Time of 'Freedom': San Marcos Coffee Workers and the Radicalization of the Guatemalan National Revolution, 1944–1954." *Radical History Review 58* (1994): 35–78.

Forsyth, Adrian, and Ken Miyata. *Tropical Nature: Life and Death in the Rain Forests of Central and South America.* New York: Scribner's, 1984.

Fowler, Elizabeth M. "Brazil Drought Buoys Coffee." *New York Times*, 16 December 1985.

Fox, Stephen. *The Mirror Makers: A History of American Advertising and Its Creators.* New York: William Morrow, 1984.

Francis, Mike. "Starbucks CEO Pours Heart into Growing Company." *Oregonian*, 21 September 1997.

Frank, Joan. "Achieving Legal Liftoff." *Utne Reader* (May–June 1991): 114–16.

Frederick, Jim. "Java Jive." *New York Times Magazine*, 31 July 1994, 10.

Freeman, Laurie, and Judann Dagnoli. "Coffee Price War Brews." *Advertising Age*, 7 March 1988, 2.

Freyre, Gilberto. *The Masters and the Slaves.* Translated by Samuel Putnam. Berkeley: University of California Press, 1933. Reprint. 1986.

Friedman, Dorian. "Get Your Iced, Cold Java." *U.S. News & World Report*, 29 April 1991, 59.

Froman, Robert. "Coffee, This Instant Upstart." *Reader's Digest* (April 1959): 152–56.

"FTC Judge Drops General Foods Case." *New York Times*, 4 February 1982, D4.

"FTC on Coffee." *Business Week*, 7 August 1954, 66–68.

Fugate, Francis L. *Arbuckles: The Coffee That Won the West.* El Paso: Texas Western Press, 1994.

Fuhrman, Peter. "Another Cartel Bites the Dust." *Forbes*, 30 October 1989, 41–42.

Fumagalli, Ambrogio. *Coffeemakers: Macchine da Caffè.* San Francisco: Chronicle Books, 1990.

Furnas, J. C. *The Americans: A Social History of the United States 1587–1914.* New York: Putnam, 1969.

Galeano, Eduardo. *Open Veins of Latin America: Five Centuries of the Pillage of a Continent.* New York: Monthly Review Press, 1973.

Garcia, Arturo. "Reality in the Campo." *Business Mexico* (August 1993): 30–31.

Gardner, Fred. "Hollywood Confidential: Part I." *Viet Nam Generation Journal & Newsletter 3*, 3 (November 1991): 1–7, http://jefferson.village.edu/sixties/html.

Garfield, Bob. "Ellerbee Grounds Out with Maxwell House." *Advertising Age*, 22 May 1989, 74.

———. "One More Cup of Coffee for That Perky Couple." *Advertising Age*, 26 July 1993, 40.

Gee, Helen. *Limelight: A Memoir.* Albuquerque: University of New Mexico Press, 1997.

Geer, Thomas. *An Oligopoly: The World Coffee Economy and Stabilization Schemes.* New York: Dunellen, 1971.

Geld, Ellen Bromfield. "Brazil: Letter from a Coffee Planter." *Atlantic* (August 1977): 6–12.

Gelston, Steff. "Ex-Coffee Connection Chief: Daily Grind Behind Sales Decision." *Boston Herald*, 25 March 1994, 34.

———. "Suit Brews Against Coffee Connection." *Boston Herald*, 22 June 1994, 28.

Gerloff, Robert, and Mark Schapiro. "A Clean, Well-Lighted Place." *Utne Reader* (November–December 1994): 66–67.

"Germany Finds Substitutes for Coffee." *American Review of Reviews* (September 1915): 368.

"Getting a Few Things Clear." *Newsweek*, 1 March 1954, 59.

"Getulio Voltará." *Newsweek*, 3 July 1950, 32.

"GF Defense Against P & G Coffee Triggers FTC Monopoly Charge." *Advertising Age*, 26 July 1976, 1, 66.

"GF Freeze-Dried Coffee Launched in West Germany." *Advertising Age*, 8 September 1969, 36.

Gilbert, Richard J. *Caffeine: The Most Popular Stimulant.* New York: Chelsea House, 1986.

"Gillette, Guy Mark." *Current Biography* (1946): 207–10.

Gilmore, Mildred Haskin. "In the Mountainous Kingdom of Coffee." *Travel* (March 1928): 12–16.

Ginsberg, Stanley. "Into the Grinder." *Forbes*, 2 February 1981, 33–34.

"Giving Coffee More Zest." *Business Week*, 11 April 1959, 48.

Gladwell, Malcolm. "The Dead Zone." *The New Yorker*, 29 September 1997, 52–65.

Gleijeses, Piero. *Shattered Hope: The Guatemalan Revolution and the United States, 1944–1954*. Princeton, NJ: Princeton University Press, 1991.

Goetzinger, M. E. "Arbuckle Brothers, a Sketch of Their History and Activities." *The Percolator* (February 1921).

Goldberg, Vicki. *Margaret Bourke-White: A Biography*. New York: Harper & Row, 1986.

Golden, Tim. "U.S. Accuses Coffee Supplier of Selling Fraudulently Marked Beans." *New York Times*, 13 November 1996.

Goldman, Emanuel. "Brothers Gourmet Coffees, Inc." PaineWebber, 16 February 1994, 1–27.

Gomez, Matthew R. "One Great Cup." *Coffee Journal* (Summer 1998): 26–27, 77.

Goodrum, Charles, and Helen Dalrymple. *Advertising in America: The First 200 Years*. New York: Harry N. Abrams, 1990.

Gordon, Richard L. "FTC Files Reveal GF's Plan to Make Cora a Star." *Advertising Age*, 3 April 1978, 3.

Goto, Baron. "Ethnic Groups and the Coffee Industry in Hawaii." *Hawaiian Journal of History 16* (1982): 112–24.

Graham, Judith. "Maxwell House May Face Boycott." *Advertising Age*, 22 May 1989, 3, 6.

"The Great Decaf Wars." *Newsweek*, 19 July 1982, 64.

"Greatly Strained." *Economist*, 7 February 1987, 61.

"Greek Coffee Shops Fall Victim to Pace of City Life." *New York Times*, 10 August 1980, 9.

"Green, as in Greenbacks." *Economist*, 1 February 1997, 42.

The Green Revolution Revisited: Critique and Alternatives. Edited by Bernhard Glaeser. London: Allen & Unwin, 1987.

Greenberg, Russell. "Phenomena, Comments and Notes." *Smithsonian* (November 1994): 24–27.

——————, and Susan Lumpkin. *Birds Over Troubled Waters*. Washington, DC: Smithsonian Migratory Bird Center, 1991.

Greenhill, Robert G. "Investment Group, Free-Standing Company or Multinational? Brazilian Warrant, 1909–52." *Business History 37*, 1 (1995): 86–111.

Greenwald, John. "Bitter Cup of Protest." *Time*, 28 May 1990, 52.

Gross, Stephen M. "The Coffee Comeback." *Commodities* (May 1979): 28–29.

"Ground Coffee." *Consumer Reports*, September 1987, 527–33.

"Grounds for Discipline?" *Time*, 19 June 1950, 88–89.

Guatemala. Edited by Susanne Jonas and David Tobis. Berkeley, CA: North American Congress on Latin America, 1974.

Guatemala: A Country Study. Edited by Richard F. Nyrop. Washington, DC: Government Printing Office, 1983.

Guatemalan Indians and the State: 1540 to 1988. Edited by Carol A. Smith. Austin: University of Texas Press, 1990.

Gudmundson, Lowell. "Peasant, Farmer, Proletarian: Class Formation in a Smallholder Coffee Economy, 1850–1950." *Hispanic American Historical Review 69*, 2 (1989): 221–57.

Haarer, A. E. *Modern Coffee Production*. 2d ed. London: Leonard Hills, 1962.

"Half-Ration Coffee." *Business Week*, 31 October 1942, 14.

Hamlin, Suzanne. "Customer Is Always Right, Right?" *New York Times*, 14 June 1995, C1.

Handy, Jim. *Gift of the Devil: A History of Guatemala*. Boston: South End Press, 1984.

——————. *Revolution in the Countryside: Rural Conflict and Agrarian Reform in Guatemala, 1944–1954*. Chapel Hill: University of North Carolina Press, 1994.

Hannstein, Walter B. *Early Twentieth-Century Life in Western Guatemala: Personal Narratives of Walter B. Hannstein*. Introduction and Epilogue by Betty Hannstein Adams. South Woodstock, VT: Plumsock Mesoamerican Studies, 1995.

(Hardwick Report), U.S. Congress. House. *Hearings Held Before the Special Committee on the Investigation of the American Sugar Refining Co.* Vol. 1. Washington, DC: Government Printing Office, 1911.

Harris, William B. "Some Coffees of Today." *Good Housekeeping*, August 1913, 264–68.

Harvest of Violence: The Maya Indians and the Guatemalan Crisis. Edited by Robert M. Carmack. Norman: University of Oklahoma Press, 1988.

Harvey, Jane. "Gourmet Coffees Perk Up in Popularity." *USA Today*, 6 July 1992, 4D.

"Has Beans, Will Travel." *Economist*, 25 April 1987, 64, 67.

Hattox, Ralph S. *Coffee and Coffeehouses: The Origins of a Social Beverage in the Medieval Near East.* Seattle: University of Washington Press, 1985.

Hawk, Philip B. "What We Eat: and What Happens to It." *Ladies' Home Journal*, December 1916, 37.

Hazlitt, Henry. "Coffee, Butter, and Politics." *Newsweek*, 22 February 1954, 90.

"Heavy Coffee Drinkers Get More Heart Attacks." *Science News*, 28 July 1973, 55.

Hedlund, Hans. *Coffee, Co-operatives and Culture: An Anthropological Study of a Coffee Co-operative in Kenya.* Nairobi: Oxford University Press, 1992.

Heer, Jean. *Nestlé: 125 Years, 1866–1991.* Vevey, Switzerland: Nestlé, 1991.

Heinl, Robert Deb, Jr., and Nancy Gordon Heinl. *Written in Blood: The Story of the Haitian People 1492–1971.* Boston: Houghton Mifflin, 1978.

Heise, Ulla. *Coffee and Coffee Houses.* Translated by Paul Roper. West Chester, PA: Schiffer, 1987.

Heller, Henry. "Out of the Heart of Darkness: Rebellion in Zaire." *Canadian Dimension* (May 1997): 49.

Helprin, Mark. *Memoir from Antproof Case.* New York: Harcourt Brace, 1995.

"Henderson, Leon." *Current Biography* (1940): 377–79.

Hess, Alan. *Googie: Fifties Coffee Shop Architecture.* San Francisco: Chronicle Books, 1986.

Hess, John L., Karen Hess. *The Taste of America.* New York: Penguin, 1977.

Hewitt, Jean. "For Coffee Buffs, Clues on Labeling." *New York Times*, 11 February 1975, 44.

_____. "Drip Coffee Makers." *New York Times*, 14 June 1975, 20.

Hewitt, Robert, Jr. *Coffee: Its History, Cultivation, and Uses.* New York: D. Appleton & Co., 1872.

"The High Cost of Coffee." *Time*, 28 August 1964, 80.

"Hills Bros., Carnation Move into Flavored Coffee Market." *Advertising Age*, 9 December 1974, 73.

Hills Brothers Collection. Archives Center, Smithsonian, National Museum of American History, Washington, DC.

Historical Corporate Reports Collection. Historical Collections, Baker Library, Harvard University, Boston, MA.

History of Jewel Companies, Inc., 1899–1977. Jewel Tea, 1977. Property of Bill Hamilton, Pontiac, MI.

"History of Maxwell House Coffee: Romance of South." *Jersey Observer*, 13 October 1939.

Hobhouse, Henry. *Seeds of Change: Five Plants That Transformed Mankind.* New York: Harper & Row, 1986.

Hobler, Atherton W. *The Triangle of Marketing Success.* Typescript, 1971. Benton & Bowles Collection, Box 19, Hartman Center, Duke University.

Hoffmann, Paul. "Hail to the Ancients for Rome's Espresso." *New York Times*, 23 April 1980, C1, 4.

_____. *That Fine Italian Hand.* New York: Henry Holt, 1990.

Hollie, Pamela G. "Big Word in Coffee Is Decaffeinated." *New York Times*, 21 January 1985, D1, 4.

Holloway, Thomas H. *The Brazilian Coffee Valorization of 1906: Regional Politics and Economic Dependence.* Madison: State Historical Society of Wisconsin, 1975.

"The Horn of Africa Begins a New Era of Conflict." *Defense & Foreign Affairs' Strategic Policy* (April 1997): 5.

"How Good Is Freeze-Dried Coffee?" *Consumer Reports*, August 1969, 434–35.

"How to Get Coffee Prices for Sugar and Vegetable Oil." *Consumer Reports*, April 1977, 184–85.

Howe, Marvine. "Angolan Asserts Cuba Is Main Ally." *New York Times*, 20 May 19761, 13.

Hoyt, Edwin P. *That Wonderful A & P!* New York: Hawthorn Books, 1969.

Hubbard, Elbert. "Two Live Men of Battle Creek." *Human Life* (August 1908): 5–6.

Hughes, John R. "Clinical Importance of Caffeine Withdrawal." *New England Journal of Medicine* (15 October 1992): 1160–61.

_____., Alison H. Oliveto, Warren K. Bickel et al. "The Ability of Low Doses of Caffeine to Serve as Reinforcers in Humans: A Replication." *Experimental and Clinical Psychopharmacology 3*, 4 (1995): 358–63.

_____., and Kelly L. Hale. "Behavioral Effects of Caffeine and Other Methylxanthines on Children." *Experimental and Clinical Psychopharmacology 6*, 1 (1998): 1–9.

Huxley, Elspeth. *The Flame Trees of Thika: Memories of an African Childhood.* London: Chatto & Windus, 1982.

_____. *Out in the Midday Sun: My Kenya.* New York: Viking, 1985.

Hyman, Sidney. *The Lives of William Benton.* Chicago: University of Chicago Press, 1969.

"I Love Coffee." *House and Garden*, November 1938, 62, 74.

"Iced Coffee Chills a Pact on Prices." *Business Week*, 14 February 1970, 44.

"If Coffee Is Bad for Your Health." *U.S. News & World Report*, 2 February 1976, 48.

Illy, Andrea, and Rinantonio Viani. *Espresso Coffee: The Chemistry of Quality.* London and San Diego: Academic Press, 1995.

Illy, Francesco, and Riccardo Illy. *The Book of Coffee: A Gourmet's Guide.* New York: Abbeville, 1989. Reprint. 1992.

Immerman, Richard H. *The CIA in Guatemala: The Foreign Policy of Intervention.* Austin: University of Texas Press, 1982.

In the Orphan's Court of Allegheny County, PA, no. 10595 (1943). The Union Trust Co. of Pittsburgh v. Martin E. Goetzinger et al.

The Indian in Latin American History: Resistance, Resilience, and Acculturation. Edited by John E. Kicza. Wilmington, DE: Scholarly Resources, 1993.

Indonesia: A Country Study. Edited by William H. Frederick and Robert L. Worden. Washington, DC: Government Printing Office, 1992.

(Industrial Commission), U.S. Congress. House. Industrial Commission, *Preliminary Report on Trusts and Industrial Combinations.* Washington, DC: Government Printing Office, 1900.

"An Industry Confronts the Issues." Panel Discussion, National Coffee Association, Boca Raton, FL, 11 February 1981. Property of NCA.

"Instant Coffee Brews a Quarrel." *Business Week*, 30 September 1967, 180.

"Instant Coffee–Coming Up." *Changing Times* (November 1953): 23–24.

"Instant Profits for Coffee." *Business Week*, 1 May 1971, 40.

"Instants Band Together to Keep Up." *Business Week*, 21 March 1953, 142–44.

"International Coffee Agreement Is Approved." *United Nations Review* (September 1962): 10–12.

"Inter-American Coffee Quota Agreement." *Bulletin of the Pan American Union*, January 1941, 56–57.

International Directory of Company Histories. Edited by Lisa Mirabile. Vol. 2. Chicago: St. James Press, 1990.

International Food Information Council web site: http://ificinfo.health.org.

"Is the High Price of Coffee Driving Them Away?" *Business Week*, 13 February 1954, 56–58.

"Is There a Market for Frozen Coffee?" *Quick Frozen Foods* (December 1969): 33–34, 121.

Isola, Marina. "Rediscovering the Legacy of Brazil's Coffee Barons." *New York Times*, 17 March 1996, 42.

"It's Like Wild." *Seventeen*, March 1962, 120–21, 150–52.

Jabbonsky, L., and A. E. Wolf. "Ready to Go." *Beverage World* (September 1991): 58.

Jacob, Heinrich Eduard. *The Saga of Coffee: The Biography of an Economic Product.* London: George Allen & Unwin, 1935.

James, C. L. R. *The Black Jacobins: Toussaint L'Ouverture and the San Domingo Revolution.* 2d ed. rev. New York: Vintage, 1963.

James, Jack E. *Caffeine and Health.* London: Academic Press, 1991.

_____. *Understanding Caffeine: A Biobehavioral Analysis.* Thousand Oaks, CA: Sage, 1997.

Jervey, Gay, "Coffee Group Lines Up Sports Stars for Drive." *Advertising Age*, 14 February 1983, 1, 63.

_____. "Coffee Marketers Brew Generic Campaign." *Advertising Age*, 16 August 1982, 34.

_____. "Decaf-Coffee Marketers' Cup Runneth Over." *Advertising Age*, 6 May 1985, 52.

_____. "Folger's Perks Minus Mrs. Olson." *Advertising Age*, 27 September 1984, 2, 63.

_____. "GF Stands Its Ground." *Advertising Age*, 8 April 1985, 1, 90.

_____. "GF to Pour Out Maxwell Decaf." *Advertising Age*, 13 February 1984, 3, 70.

_____. "P & G Rushes Folger's to Perky Decaf Field." *Advertising Age*, 23 August 1984, 2, 54.

Jervey, Gay, and Jennifer Pendleton. "Nestle, Hills Coffee Deal Good News, Bad News." *Advertising Age*, 16 April 1984, 1, 82.

_____. "Nestle's 'Big Bite' Gobbles MJB." *Advertising Age*, 13 May 1985, 1, 118.

Jewel Tea Co. *The First Thirty Years, 1899–1929*. Chicago: Jewel Tea Co., 1929. In Baker Library, Harvard Business School, folder.

_____. *Merchandising Plans and History*. Chicago: Jewel Tea Co., 1923. In Baker Library, Harvard Business School, folder.

_____. *The Story of Jewel*. Chicago: Jewel Tea Co., 1935. In Baker Library, Harvard Business School, folder.

_____. *Working for Jewel*. Chicago: Jewel Tea Co., 1927. In Baker Library, Harvard Business School, folder.

Jiménez, Manuel F. "Coffee in Costa Rica." *Bulletin of the Pan American Union*, February 1945, 88–89.

Jiménez, Michael F. "Traveling Far in Grandfather's Car: The Life Cycle of Central Colombian Coffee Estates." *Hispanic American Historical Review 69*, 2 (1989): 185–219.

Jobin, Philippe. *The Coffees Produced Throughout The World*. Le Havre, France: Jobin & Cie., n.d. (ca. 1992).

John Foster Dulles and the Diplomacy of the Cold War. Edited by Richard H. Immerman. Princeton, NJ: Princeton University Press, 1990.

Johnson, Elaine, and Christine B. Weber. "Coffee Reconquers the West." *Sunset* (February 1992): 70–75.

Johnson, Helen Louise. "Scientific Research in Coffee Brewing." *Journal of Home Economics* (April 1925): 199–205.

Johnson, Kirk. "The Lure of the Coffee Bar, the Smell of the Grounds." *New York Times*, 13 August 1995, C10.

Johnson, Paul. *Modern Times: The World from the Twenties to the Eighties*. New York: Harper & Row, 1983.

Jones, Brendan. "Others' Misfortune Helps Ivory Coast." *New York Times*, 30 December 1975, 31.

Jones, Chester Lloyd et al. *American Policies Abroad: The United States and the Caribbean*. Chicago: University of Chicago Press, 1929.

Jones, Jeanne. "Brothers Coffee Bars Opening in Randall's." *Houston Post*, 15 April 1994.

"Jumping Beans." *Economist*, 23 October 1976, 101–2.

"Just the Facts, Senhor." *Time*, 1 March 1954, 33–34.

J. Walter Thompson Inc. Files. Hartman Center, Duke University.

Kahn, Joseph P. "Sniffing Out a Good Cup of Joe." *Boston Globe*, 8 May 1993, 21.

Kains, Maurice G. *Chicory Growing as an Addition to the Resources of the American Farmer*. U.S. Dept. of Agriculture, Bulletin No. 19. Washington, DC: Government Printing Office, 1898.

Kallett, Arthur, and F. J. Schlink. *100,000,000 Guinea Pigs: Dangers in Everyday Foods, Drugs, and Cosmetics*. New York: Vanguard Press, 1933.

Kamiya, Gary. "North Beach at Twilight." *Image*, 27 June 1993, 11–15.

Kandell, Jonathan. "Brazil's Coffee Exporters Pressed to Keep Prices High." *New York Times*, 12 January 1977, D7.

_____. "Coffee Again King in Brazil as Prices Prime Economy." *New York Times*, 8 March 1977, 41, 52.

Kanner, Bernice. "Coffee Nerves." *New York*, 13 September 1982, 18–23.

Kapoor, Sandy. "The Decaf Process." *Restaurant Business*, 10 August 1988, 70.

Kaufman, Joanne. "Sanka Knows Best." *Madison Avenue* (May 1984): 83–88.

Kaufman, Michael T. "Coffee Drinkers of U.S. Help Keep Amin's Treasury Well Provided." *New York Times*, 11 March 1977, 2.

Keable, B. B. *Coffee: From Grower to Consumer*. London: Sir Isaac Pitman & Sons, ca. 1915.

Kellogg Papers. Bentley Historical Library, University of Michigan, Ann Arbor.

Kent, John L. "Cuppa Coffee, Chum?" *Popular Mechanics*, March 1946, 148–51, 238–40.

Kenworth, Sidon. "Campaign for LA-Grown Organic Coffee." October 1997, Web site.

Kevan, S. McKean. "Many of Miss Jamison's Legatees Will Receive Nothing." *New Paltz Times*, 26 April 1945, courtesy of Stanley C. Newkirk, Ulster Park, NY.

Kilburn, David. "Canned-Coffee Market Is Steaming in Japan." *Advertising Age*, 26 October 1992, Suppl., I–4.

Kindleberger, Charles P. *Manias, Panics, and Crashes: A History of Financial Crises*. Rev. ed. New York: Basic Books, 1989.

Kindleberger, Richard. "Starbucks Buys Coffee Connection." *Boston Globe*, 16 March 1994, 43.

King, Arden R. *Coban and the Verapaz: History and Cultural Process in Northern Guatemala*. New Orleans: Middle American Research Institute, 1974.

Kinzer, Stephen. "Cracks in World Coffee Pact." *New York Times*, 18 July 1983, D7.

_____. "Nicaraguan Rebels Step Up Raids in Coffee Areas as Harvest Nears." *New York Times*, 23 November 1984, A1, 4.

_____. "Nicaragua's Bitter Harvest: War in the Coffee Fields." *New York Times*, 23 December 1983, A2.

_____. "Sandinista Says Rebels Fail to Block Coffee Crop." *New York Times*, 3 January 1985, A9.

Kirschen, Leonard. "International Coffee Developments in 1981." *F. O. Lichts International Coffee Yearbook*. Ratzeburg, Germany: F. O. Lichts, 1981.

Kleinfeld, N. R. "A Cold War over Coffee." *New York Times*, 29 October 1989, C1, 11.

Kluger, Richard. *Ashes to Ashes: America's Hundred-Year Cigarette War, the Public Health, and the Unabashed Triumph of Philip Morris*. New York: Alfred A. Knopf, 1996.

Knapp, Caroline. "Damn, That's Good Coffee!" *Mademoiselle*, February 1991, 62.

Kneeland, Douglas E. "A Secretary Who Spurned the Coffee Detail." *New York Times*, 28 October 1977, 10.

Knox, Kevin. "Coffee Safari." *Coffee Chronicles* (Allegro Coffee Co.), Fall–Winter 1996.

_____, and Julie Sheldon Huffaker. *Coffee Basics: A Quick and Easy Guide*. New York: John Wiley, 1996.

Kohn, Alfie. "Hooking America on Caffeine." *Nation*, 19 May 1984, 604–6.

Kolpas, Norman. *The Coffee Lovers' Companion*. New York: Quick Fox, 1977.

Konner, Melvin. "Caffeine High." *New York Times Magazine*, 17 January 1988, 47.

Kooiman, Dick. "Plantations in Southern Asia: Indigenous Plants and Foreign Implantations." *South Asia 15*, 1 (1992): 53–79.

Kraft Foods Archives. 6350 Kirk Street, Morton Grove, IL 60053.

Kraft Foods. *Maxwell House Coffee: A Chronological History*. White Plains, NY, 1996.

Kraft Foods. "Maxwell House Coffee Company: Corporate Backgrounder." White Plains, NY, 1995.

Kraft Jacobs Suchard. *100 Years of Jacobs Café*. Bremen, Germany: Kraft Jacobs Suchard, 1995.

Krammer, Arnold. *Undue Process: The Untold Story of America's German Alien Internees*. London: Rowman & Littlefield, 1997.

Kroll, Stanley. "Coffee and Copper." *Financial World*, 15 June 1983, 42.

Krug, C. A. *World Coffee Survey*. Rome, Italy: FAO, 1959. Property of National Coffee Association.

Kugiya, Hugo. "Seattle's Coffee King." *Seattle Times*, 15 December 1996, 20–24.

Kuhn v. Woolson Spice Co., 10 Ohio Dec. 292; XI Ohio Circuit Decisions, Arbuckle v. Woolson Spice Co., 18 February 1901.

Kummer, Corby. "Before the First Sip." *Atlantic* (May 1990): 117–23.

_____. *The Joy of Coffee: The Essential Guide to Buying, Brewing and Enjoying.* Shelburne, VT: Chapters, 1995.

_____. "Untroubled Brewing." *Atlantic* (June 1990): 107.

LaFeber, Walter. *Inevitable Revolutions: The United States in Central America.* New York: W. W. Norton, 1983.

Lago, Luiz Aranha Correa do. *From Slavery to Free Labor: The Brazilian Coffee Economy in the Nineteenth Century.* N.d. Property of International Coffee Organization, Berners Street, London.

Land, Herman. "Hobler of Benton and Bowles." *Television Magazine,* October 1958, 56–59, 88–92.

Lane, Hilary. "Coffees with Conscience." *E Magazine,* January–February 1994, 40–42.

Lang, Tom. *Coffee: A Story.* Portland, OR: Boudelang Press, 1995.

Langdon, William Chauncy. *Everyday Things in American Life, 1776–1876.* New York: Charles Scribner's Sons, 1941.

Larmer, Brook, and Steven Ambrus. "The Tears of a Nation." *Newsweek,* 22 June 1998, 22.

Larsen, Elizabeth. "Java Jive, the Politics of Coffee." *Utne Reader* (November–December 1990): 20–21.

Larson, Cedric A. "Highlights of Dr. John B. Watson's Career in Advertising." *Industrial Organizational Psychologist 16,* 3 (May 1979): 3–4.

Lasker, David. "High Style Around Home, Chemex Coffee Makers." *Los Angeles Times,* 8 January 1989, 36D.

Latin America in the 1940s: War and Postwar Transitions. Edited by David Rock. Berkeley: University of California Press, 1994.

Lavazza, Notizie. *Lavazza: 100 Years of Lavazza History.* Turin, Italy: Notizie Lavazza, 1995.

Lebhar, Godfrey M. *Chain Stores in America, 1859–1962.* 3d ed. New York: Chain Store Publishing Corp., 1963.

Lecos, Chris. "More Cups Lifted Sans Caffeine." *FDA Consumer* (May 1980): 23–25.

Leezenbaum, Ralph. "Coffee Makers Ignore Warning Signals." *Marketing/Communications* (May 1970): 18–27.

Leib, Jeffrey. "Brothers Gourmet Buying Brio Coffee Chain." *Denver Post,* 6 May 1994, C1.

_____. "Brothers to Take Earnings Charge." *Denver Post,* 15 August 1995, C3.

_____. "Coffee-shop Losses Grind for Brothers." *Denver Post,* 17 May 1995, C2.

Leider, Emily Wortis. *Becoming Mae West.* New York: Farrar, Straus & Giroux, 1997.

LeMoyne, James. "Rid Us of the Contras, Farmers in Honduras Ask." *New York Times,* 16 November 1985, A2.

Lender, Mark Edward, and James Kirby Martin. *Drinking in America: A History.* Revised and expanded. New York: Free Press, 1987.

Lernoux, Penny. "The World Politics of Coffee." *Nation,* 2 August 1975, 75–81.

Lessons of the Rainforest. Edited by Suzanne Head and Robert Heinzman. San Francisco: Sierra Club Books, 1990.

"Let Them Eat Cake, or the Story of General Foods." *Fortune,* October 1934, 68–75, 122–35.

Lev, Michael. "Soap Opera from Britain Fans Taster's Choice Flame." *New York Times,* 19 March 1991.

Levi, Darrell E. *The Prados of São Paulo, Brazil: An Elite Family and Social Change, 1840–1930.* Athens: University of Georgia Press, 1987.

Levine, Joshua. "Drip, Drip, Drip . . . Drip." *Forbes,* 17 April 1989, 196–98.

_____. "The Java News." *Forbes,* 22 May 1995, 234.

Lewin, Lewis. *Phantastica: Narcotic and Stimulating Drugs.* New York: E. P. Dutton, 1931.

Lewis, Sinclair. *Babbitt.* New York: Harcourt, Brace, 1922.

(Lexow Committee), *Report and Proceedings of the Joint Committee of the [New York] Senate and Assembly Appointed to Investigate Trusts,* 9 March 1897. Albany, NY: Wynkoop Hallenbeck Crawford, 1897.

Liberman, Andrew. "Salvadoran Coffee, Go Home." *Progressive,* May 1990, 15.

Liddle, Alan. "Howard Schultz." *Nation's Restaurant News,* 1 January 1995, 183.

———. "Starbucks Looks to IPO to Perk Up Expansion." *Nation's Restaurant News*, 22 June 1992, 14.

Lingle, Ted R. *Avenues for Growth: A 20-Year Review of the U.S. Specialty Coffee Market.* Long Beach, CA: SCAA, 1993.

———. *The Coffee Brewing Handbook.* Long Beach, CA: SCAA, 1996.

———. *The Coffee Cupper's Handbook.* 2d ed. Washington, DC: Coffee Development Group, 1986.

Link, Henry C. *The New Psychology of Selling and Advertising.* New York: Macmillan, 1932.

Lippert, Barbara. "A Coffee Break from Taster's Choice." *Adweek's Marketing Week,* 6 May 1991, 29.

"Liquid Consumption Trends in U.S. from 1967 to 1976." *Advertising Age,* 11 July 1977, 164.

Loomis, Susan Herrmann. "A City in the Espresso Lane." *New York Times,* 25 August 1991, E14, 19.

Louis, Arthur M. "Brazil's Coffee (with Sugar) Billionaire." *Fortune,* July 1977, 82–88.

Lubove, Seth, "Coffee Versus Gazebo Blend." *Forbes,* 20 June 1994, 112.

Lucier, Richard L. *The International Political Economy of Coffee: From Juan Valdez to Yank's Diner.* New York: Praeger, 1988.

Ludwig, Emile. *Napoleon.* Translated by Eden and Cedar Paul. New York: Horace Liveright, 1926.

"Lumps with the Coffee." *Time,* 9 November 1942, 22.

Lunding, Franklin J. *Sharing a Business: The Case Study of a Tested Management Philosophy.* Scarsdale, NY: Updegraff Press, 1951.

Luxenberg, Stan. "Folger's Scores in the Coffee Wars." *New York Times,* 28 January 1979, C1, 5.

McAlpin, William. "Coffee and the Socially Concerned." *World Coffee & Tea* (July 1994): 6–7.

———. "La Minita News." San Jose, Costa Rica: Hacienda La Minita, October 1995.

———. "Speech." Specialty Coffee Association of America convention, Minneapolis, MN, 20 April 1996.

McAlpin, William J., with photos by Jim Daniels. *Hacienda La Minita: Photographs and Essays of the Renowned Coffee Farm.* Portland, ME: Pie Hole Productions, 1997.

McCabe, Jane. "A Look into Nestle Beverage Company." *Tea & Coffee Trade Journal* (December 1992): 16ff.

McCabe, Michael. "Woman Sues over Coffee Spill." *San Francisco Chronicle,* 25 January 1995, A18.

McCash, Vicki. "The Brews Brothers." *Sun Sentinel,* 13 February 1994.

———. "Roaster Shedding Some Bean Dreams: Brothers Wakes Up and Smells the Coffee." *Sun-Sentinel,* 3 November 1995, 1D.

McCaughan, Michael. "Bloodbath in Chiapas." *In These Times,* 8 February 1998, 5.

McCoy, Elin, and John Frederick Walker. *Coffee and Tea.* 4th ed. Redwood City, CA: G.S. Haly, 1998.

McCreery, David. *Rural Guatemala, 1760–1940.* Stanford, CA: Stanford University Press, 1994.

McCreery, David, and Doug Munro. "The Cargo of the Montserrat: Gilbertese Labor in Guatemalan Coffee, 1890–1908." *Americas 49,* 3 (1993): 271–95.

McCue, Ed Lew. "Where Coffee Is King in Colombia." *Pan American Magazine,* May 1927, 20–23.

McDonald, J. H. *Coffee Growing: With Special Reference to East Africa.* London: East Africa Journal, 1930.

MacDougall, Alice Foote. *The Autobiography of a Business Woman.* Boston: Little, Brown, 1928.

McDougall, Ruth Bransten. *Coffee, Martinis, and San Francisco.* San Rafael, CA: Presidio Press, 1978.

McDowell, Bill. "The Bean Counters." *Restaurants & Institutions,* 15 December 1995, 40–55.

———. "Starbucks Is Ground Zero in Today's Coffee Culture." *Advertising Age,* 9 December 1996, 1, 49.

McGinley, Phyllis. "They Also Serve Who Only Stand in Line." *Ladies' Home Journal,* April 1943, 115.

MacGowan, Kenneth. "Profiles: The Adventure of a Behaviorist." *The New Yorker,* 6 October 1928. McKenna, M. A. J. "It's Good to the Last Dropping." *Atlanta Journal/Constitution,* 9 October 1995, C1.

McKenna, Terence. *Food of the Gods: The Search for the Original Tree of Knowledge.* New York: Bantam, 1992.

McMahon, Patrick. "The Tempeste in the Coffee Pot." *American Mercury* (July 1954): 133–36.

McMakin, A. L. "The Influence of Coffee on Brain Workers." *Good Housekeeping,* March 1912, 381–82.

McMath, Robert. "Coffee Fights That Run-Down Feeling." *Adweek's Marketing Week,* 17 June 1991, 25.

———. "Iced Cappuccino in a Can, Please." *Adweek's Marketing Week,* 3 September 1990, 32.

McMillen, Wheeler. "All of Us." *Farm Journal* (May 1954): 15–16.

"MacNeil/Lehrer Report." "Coffee Prices," Show no. 2087, 4 January 1977.

McPhee, Douglas G. "Competitors Roasted–a Little at a Time." *Western Advertising,* 5 November 1931, 32–33, 88.

Maidenberg, H. J. "Coffee Futures Curbed to Prevent a Squeeze." *New York Times,* 22 November 1979, D8.

———. "Coffee Futures Prices Level After Long Rise." *New York Times,* 9 May 1977, 43, 48.

———. "Coffee Futures Soaring; Brokers Cite Hoarding." *New York Times,* 18 August 1976, 55.

———. "Coffee Supplies Cut by Weather and Warfare." *New York Times,* 23 November 1975, sec. 3, 7.

———. "Frost in Brazil Sending Coffee Prices Up." *New York Times,* 4 August 1975, 29.

———. "Higher Coffee Prices Are Expected." *New York Times,* 12 February 1976.

———. "Smaller Tree, More Beans." *New York Times,* 23 November 1975, sec. 3, 7.

———. "There's Worse to Come in Coffee." *New York Times,* 16 January 1977, C3.

Maitland, Leslie, "Coffee Decline–Fewer Drinkers, Fewer Cups." *New York Times,* 15 March 1975, 12.

"Make Coffee Plastic." *Business Week,* 28 January 1939, 33.

Malcolm, Andrew H. "In Tokyo, Things Go Better with Coffee." *New York Times,* 2 October 1976, 27.

Marden, Luis. "Coffee Is King in El Salvador." *National Geographic* (November 1944): 575–84.

Margaret Bourke-White Papers. Syracuse University, Syracuse, NY.

Marshall, Christy. "Chock Full Full of New Marketing Plans." *Advertising Age,* 19 September 1983, 4, 62.

Martin, Francis H. "History of Coffee Prices in the United States, 1840–1954." *Monthly Labor Review* (July 1954): 765–67.

Martin, Harold H. "The Land That Smells Like Money." *Saturday Evening Post,* 22 November 1952, 28–29, 86–93.

Martin, Lawrence, and Sylvia Martin. "Nazi Intrigues in Central America." *American Mercury 53* (July 1941): 66–73.

"Massacre in Mexico." *Economist,* 3 January 1998, 37.

Massey, Linda K. "Caffeine and the Elderly." *Drugs and Aging 13,* 1 (July 1988): 43–50.

Masterson, Peg. "Top 100 Succumbs to Specialty Coffees' Aroma." *Advertising Age,* 29 September 1993, 30.

Maugh, Thomas H. II. "Coffee and Heart Disease: Is There a Link?" *Science,* 10 August 1973, 534–35.

Mauldin, Bill. *Up Front.* 1945. Reprint. New York: W. W. Norton, 1995.

Max Havelaar: Fair Trade Practices with the Third World Countries. Utrecht, The Netherlands: Stichting Max Havelaar, 1995.

"Maxim Carves 13% Niche in Instants." *Advertising Age,* 22 September 1969, 36.

"Maxwell House Back in Magazines." *Printer's Ink Monthly,* 2 February 1933, 67.

Maxwell, John C., Jr. "Coffee Consumption Continues to Cool Off." *Advertising Age,* 13 June 1988, 34.

———. "Coffee Market Still Cool." *Advertising Age,* 30 April 1984, 14.

———. "Folgers Takes First Place as Prices Drop." *Advertising Age,* 30 April 1979, 70.

_____. "Morning Report." *Advertising Age*, 24 June 1991, 24.

Mayer, Martin. *Madison Avenue, U.S.A.* New York: Harper & Brothers, 1958.

Mbapndah, Ndobegang M. "French Colonial Agricultural Policy, African Chiefs, and Coffee Growing in the Cameroun Grassfields, 1920–1960." *International Journal of African Historical Studies 27*, 1 (1994): 41–58.

Meagher, Margaret. "To Think of Coffee." *Catholic World* (September 1942): 712–20.

Medcalf, Laura, "Nestlé: We Don't Kiss and Tell." *Marketing*, 16 September 1991, 3.

"Meditation on the Price of Coffee." *Christian Century*, 10 February 1954, 165.

Melville, Herman. *Moby-Dick, or, The Whale.* 1851. Reprint. Boston: Houghton-Mifflin, 1956.

Menchú, Rigoberta. *I, Rigoberta Menchú: An Indian Woman in Guatemala.* Edited and Introduced by Elisabeth Burgos-Debray. Translated by Ann Wright. New York: Verso, 1983. Reprint. 1984.

"Mental Suggestion in Your Dietetics." *New York Times*, 3 December 1910.

Menzies, Hugh D. "Why Folger's Is Getting Creamed Back East." *Fortune*, 17 July 1978, 68–76.

Miller, C. L. *The Jewel Tea Company: Its History and Products.* Atglen, PA: Schiffer, 1994.

_____. *Jewel Tea Grocery Products.* Atglen, PA: Schiffer, 1996.

Miller, Douglas T., and Marion Nowak. *The Fifties: The Way We Really Were.* Garden City, NY: Doubleday, 1977.

Miller, Edward G. "Clarification Asked on Senate Coffee Report." *Department of State Bulletin*, 24 July 1950, 140–44ff.

Mintz, Sidney. *Sweetness and Power: The Place of Sugar in Modern History.* New York: Penguin, 1985.

Mirsky, Steve. "You May Already Be a Wiener." *Scientific American* (December 1995): 24.

Mitgang, Herbert. "New York's Caffe (Espresso) Society." *New York Times Magazine*, 14 October 1956, 27.

Model, Betsy. "Pouring His Heart into It." *Washington CEO* (December 1997): 17–21.

Modell, Merriam. "Coffee à la Mode." *The New Yorker*, 28 November 1942, 69–70.

"Modern Methods Could Double Coffee Production." *Science News Letter*, 20 February 1954, 120.

Moffett, Samuel E. "John Arbuckle." *Cosmopolitan*, September 1902, 542–44.

"Money-Saving Tips for Coffee Lovers." *Good Housekeeping*, April 1977, 197.

Money Trust Investigation. Subcommittee of the Committee on Banking and Currency. Vol. 1. Washington, DC: Government Printing Office, 1913.

Monteforte Toledo, Mario. "Bean of Contention." *The Inter-American* (March 1943): 22–24, 46.

Moore, Alexander. *Life Cycles in Atchalán: The Diverse Careers of Certain Guatemalans.* New York: Teachers College Press, 1973.

Moore, W. Robert. "As São Paulo Grows." *National Geographic* (May 1939): 657–88.

Moriwaki, Lee. "Starbucks Coffee Crafts Deal with Kraft." *Seattle Times*, 28 September 1998, 1.

Morris, James. *The Road to Huddersfield: A Journey to Five Continents.* New York: Pantheon Books, 1963.

Morrison, Jim. "All Alone Together." *New York Times*, 30 July 1995, 37.

_____. "Howard's Trend." *Spirit*, 37–38, 102–13.

Moser, Richard R. *The New Winter Soldiers: GI & Veteran Dissent During the Vietnam Era.* New Brunswick, NJ: Rutgers University Press, 1996.

Moukheiber, Zina. "Oversleeping." *Forbes*, 5 June 1995, 78, 82.

Mullins, Jack Simpson. *The Sugar Trust: Henry O. Havemeyer and the American Sugar Refining Company.* Ph.D. diss., University of South Carolina, 1964. UMI no. 69–3010.

Multatuli. *Max Havelaar: Or the Coffee Auctions of a Dutch Trading Company.* Translated with notes by Roy Edwards. 1860. London: Penguin, 1987.

Muniz, J. C. "What It Costs to Grow Coffee in São Paulo." *Bulletin of the Pan American Union*, December 1929, 1231–40.

Murphy, Ellen Contreras. "La Selva and the Magnetic Pull of Markets: Organic Coffee-Growing in Mexico." *Grassroots Development 19*, 1 (1995): 27–34.

Murphy, Kim. "More Than Coffee, a Way of Life." *Los Angeles Times*, 22 September 1996, 8.

Museum of Television and Radio. New York, NY.

Mussey, Barrow. "Uphill Battle Ahead for GF After Buy into HAG." *Advertising Age*, 8 October 1979, 18.

Nares, Peter. "Colombia Faces Labor Shortages." *Tea & Coffee Trade Journal* (July 1998): 24.

National Coffee Association. *U.S. Coffee Consumption Trends and Outlook: 1995 Winter Coffee Drinking Study.* New York: NCA, 1995.

A National Consumer Survey of Coffee Consumption. New York: Pan American Coffee Bureau, 1939, National Coffee Association Files.

National Coffee Association web site: http://www.coffeescience.org.

National Cyclopedia of American Biography. Vol. 15. 1916.

Naylor, Douglas O. "Brazil's Coffee Plan Insures Farm Profits." *New York Times,* 9 June 1929, sec. 9, 11.

———. "Coffee Price Crisis Menaces São Paulo." *New York Times,* 7 October 1928, sec. 3, 1.

Neighbor to Neighbor. *The History of the Salvadoran Coffee Boycott.* San Francisco: Neighbor to Neighbor, 1992.

———. *International Boycott of Salvadoran Coffee: Report on the Campaign's First Hundred Days.* San Francisco: Neighbor to Neighbor, 1990.

"Nestle Waits as Others Battle GF Int'l Coffees." *Advertising Age,* 16 December 1974, 82.

Neville, Tove. "Coffee: Natural or Synthetic?" *Science News Letter,* 21 November 1959, 346–47.

"New Association Brewing for Specialty Coffee Industry." *Gourmet Today* (September–October 1982): 18–19.

"New Coffees." *Business Week,* 7 July 1945, 81–82.

"New Process Keeps Coffee Fresh in High Vacuum Cans." *Popular Science,* October 1931, 59.

"New Starbucks Opens in Rest Room of Existing Starbucks." *The Onion,* 27 May 1998.

New York Coffee and Sugar Exchange. *Annual Coffee Supplement 1882 to 1939 Inclusive.* July 1939. In Baker Library, Harvard Business School.

Newhagen, John. "Now Coffee Threatens Stability in Central America." *Business Week,* 10 August 1981, 42.

Newhall, Ruth Waldo. *The Folger Way.* Cincinatti, OH: Folger Coffee Co., ca. 1962.

Nickerson, Jane. "Come for Coffee." *New York Times Magazine,* 30 January 1955, 48–49.

———. "A Thriftier Cup of Coffee." *New York Times Magazine,* 22 August 1954, 38–39.

Nicolle, Edgar A. "Coffee in an Instant." *Américas* (February 1975): 25–28.

"90 Years of 'Superior' Coffee." *Midwest Foodservice News,* May–June 1998, 3.

"92-Year-Old McNulty's Gears Up for Its Greatest Period of Growth." *Specialty Food Merchandising,* March 1987, 22–25.

Nixon, Richard. *RN: The Memoirs of Richard Nixon.* New York: Grosset & Dunlap, 1978.

"No Coffee Ration." *Business Week,* 27 May 1944, 88–90.

"No Coffee, Thanks." *Newsweek,* 1 February 1954, 20.

Nolan, Nicole. "Starbucked!" *In These Times,* 11 November 1996, 14–17.

Norris, George W. *Fighting Liberal: The Autobiography of George W. Norris.* New York: Macmillan, 1945.

North, Lisa. *Bitter Grounds: Roots of Revolt in El Salvador.* 2d ed. Westport, CT: Lawrence Hill, 1985.

"Not an Awful Lot." *Economist,* 30 August 1986, 60–61.

O'Connor, John J. "Coffee Brands Perk to Needs of Drip Filter Units." *Advertising Age,* 1 March 1976, 3, 64.

———. "Folger's Eastern Invasion Making Progress, P & G Says." *Advertising Age,* 7 August 1978, 3.

———. "GF Countering Folger's Expansion with Horizon." *Advertising Age,* 16 December 1974, 82.

———. "GF Pits New Coffee Against P & G, Nestle." *Advertising Age,* 11 April 1977, 1, 108.

———. "GF Tries Economy Area with Master Blend Brew." *Advertising Age,* 29 January 1979, 1, 82.

———. "Hills Out to Roast Rivals with High Yield Coffee." *Advertising Age,* 23 January 1978, 1, 77.

———. "Nestle Launches Coffee with Chicory." *Advertising Age,* 20 September 1976, 1, 98.

———. "P & G Tops Off Coffee Rollout with Attack on GF Turf." *Advertising Age,* 20 February 1978, 86.

Oduber, Daniel. "The 'Hasty and Shortsighted' Coffee Boycott." *New York Times*, 30 January 1977, D16.

"Off the Editor's Chest." *Consumers' Research Bulletin,* January 1943, 2, 13–14.

"Old Coffee Grounds." *Time*, 25 October 1954, 78.

Old English Coffee Houses. London: Rodale Press, 1954.

Oldenburg, Ray. *The Great Good Place.* New York: Paragon House, 1989.

Oleck, Joan. "The Tap Won't Cut It at Starbucks." *Restaurant Business*, 1 January 1994, 32.

Olsen, Dave. *Starbucks Passion for Coffee: A Starbucks Coffee Cookbook.* Menlo Park, CA: Sunset Books, 1994.

Omona, George. "Uganda: Stolen Children, Stolen Lives." *Lancet*, 7 February 1998, 442.

"One Way to Help Colombia." *World Press Review* (November 1989): 28.

Opinion Research Corporation. "Coffee Preferences and Brand Images Among West Coast Consumers: A Survey for Hills Bros. Coffee, Inc." May 1958. In Hills Brothers Collection.

"Organic Coffees: A Growing Segment of the Specialty Coffee Market." *World Coffee & Tea* (October 1994): 19–24.

Orton, Vrest. *Observations on the Forgotten Art of Building a Good Fireplace: The Story of Sir Benjamin Thompson, Count Rumford, an American Genius.* Dublin, NH: Yankee, 1969.

Osborne, Oliver T. "Children Should Not Drink Coffee or Tea." *Good Housekeeping*, October 1924, 284–86.

Ott, Jonathan. *The Cacahuatl Eater: Ruminations of an Unabashed Chocolate Addict.* Vashon, WA: Natural Products Co., 1985.

_____. *Pharmacotheon: Entheogenic Drugs, Their Plant Sources and History.* Kennewick, WA: Natural Products Co., 1993.

Over the Black Coffee. Compiled by Arthur Gray. New York: Baker & Taylor, 1902.

"P & G's Campaign to Unseat Sanka." *Business Week*, 26 January 1981, 65.

Pace, Eric. "Last Cup of Sanka for Dr. Welby." *New York Times*, 26 August 1982, D19.

"Packaged Coffee." *Scientific American* (June 1943): 268.

"Packaged Plantations: Bonanza on Frontier?" *Business Week*, 26 June 1954, 152–56.

Padgett, Tim. "Laws of the Jungle." *Time*, 12 January 1998, 58.

Paige, Jeffrey M. *Coffee and Power: Revolution and the Rise of Democracy in Central America.* Cambridge, MA: Harvard University Press, 1997.

Palacios, Marco. *Coffee in Colombia, 1850–1970.* Cambridge, UK: Cambridge University Press, 1980.

Palani Plantation. 430 Nevada Ave., Palo Alto, CA 94301, 650–327–5774. Fax: 650–327–5660.

Pancoast, Chalmers Lowell. *Trail Blazers in Advertising: Stories of the Romance and Adventure of the Old-Time Advertising Game.* New York: F. H. Hitchcock, 1926.

Parker, Frank J. "From Mobutu to Kabila: An Improvement?" *America*, 8 November 1997, 18.

Parsons, F. W. "Why Coffee Is High." *Saturday Evening Post*, 14 February 1920, 36–38.

Passell, Peter. "Fighting Cocaine, Coffee, Flowers." *New York Times*, 20 September 1989, D2.

"Patman, (John William) Wright." *Current Biography* (1946): 461–64.

"Paul Erdos, an Eccentric Titan of Mathematical Theory, Dies." *Washington Post*, 24 September 1996, B7.

Paxson, Peyton. *Charles William Post: The Mass Marketing of Health and Welfare.* Ph.D. diss., Boston University, 1993. Ann Arbor, MI: UMI no. 9319980.

"A Peace Corps for Nicaragua." *Economist*, 7 January 1984, 22.

Pearse, Andrew. *Seeds of Plenty, Seeds of Want: Social and Economic Implications of the Green Revolution.* Oxford: Clarendon Press, 1980.

Pelzer, John, and Linda Pelzer. "The Coffee Houses of Augustan London." *History Today 32* (October 1982): 40–47.

Pendergrast, Mark. *For God, Country and Coca-Cola: The Unauthorized History of the Great American Soft Drink and the Company That Makes It.* New York: Scribner's, 1993.

Pendleton, Jennifer. "Hills Bros. Bets Big on High Yield." *Advertising Age*, 23 June 1980, 2, 90.

"Pennies from Leaven." *Time*, 11 March 1940, 69–70.

"Penniless Immigrants Who Have Made Millions." *New York Times*, 2 November 1913, sec. 5, 12.

Penteado, Eurico. "Declares Coffee Problems Reflect Lack of Cooperation." *Journal of Commerce and Commercial* (25 October 1944): 15.

———. "The Facts on the Coffee Situation." *Bulletin of the Pan American Union*, February 1945, 115–18.

"People on the Move." *Sun-Sentinel*, 27 July 1998, 11.

Perez-Brignoli, Hector. *A Brief History of Central America*. Translated by Ricardo B. Sawrey and Susana Stettri de Sawrey. Berkeley: University of California Press, 1989.

Perfecto, Ivette, Robert A. Rice, and Martha E. Van der Voort. "Shade Coffee: A Disappearing Refuge for Biodiversity." *BioScience 46*, 8 (September 1996): 598–608.

Petras, James, and Morris Morley. *US Hegemony Under Siege: Class, Politics and Development in Latin America*. London: Verso, 1990.

Piro, Stephanie. *Caffeinated Cartoons: Cartoons About Coffee and Tea*. Bala Cynwyd, PA: Laugh Lines Press, 1996.

"Plan $500,000 Coffee Drive." *Business Week*, 9 September 1939, 33.

Pogrebin, Robin. "Starbucks Pours It On." *New York Times*, 25 June 1995, 4.

Political Changes in Guatemalan Indian Communities: A Symposium. Compiled by Richard N. Adams. New Orleans: Middle American Research Institute, 1972.

Pollock, Elizabeth. "Organic Coffee: Quality with a Conscience." *Fresh Cup* (December 1994): 16–19, 49.

Poole, Shelia M. "Coffee and Buns to Go: AFC to Franchise in Middle East." *Atlanta Journal/Constitution* (18 December 1998).

Post Family Papers. Michigan Historical Collections, Bentley Historical Library, University of Michigan, Ann Arbor.

Pounds, Marcia H. "Brothers Coffee Files Chapter 11." *Sun-Sentinel*, 29 August 1998, 16C.

———. "Company to Settle Shareholders' Suits." *Sun-Sentinel*, 26 October 1996, 13C.

Powell, J. H. *Bring Out Your Dead: The Great Plague of Yellow Fever in Philadelphia in 1793*. Philadelphia: University of Pennsylvania Press, 1949. Reprint. 1993.

Powell, William. "Espresso, Increasingly Popular in Europe, in America." *Vogue* 15 August 1954, 152–53.

Powle, Brian. "Hills Brothers May Grab Share of Thinning Coffee Profits." *Advertising Age*, 13 February 1978, 86.

"Premeasured Coffee Doesn't Measure Up." *Consumer Reports*, June 1968, 290.

Pressler, Margaret Webb. "The Brains Behind a Coffee Empire." *Washington Post National Weekly Edition*, 13 October 1997, 17–18.

Prial, Frank J. "Club Alters Its Nonrules for Women." *New York Times*, 5 August 1979, 44.

"Prices Grind Coffee Growers." *Business Week*, 26 February 1955, 139–41.

Proceedings, Memorias: 1st Sustainable Coffee Congress, September 1996. Edited by Robert A. Rice, Ashley M. Harris, and Jennifer McLean. Washington, DC: Smithsonian Migratory Bird Center, 1997.

"Procter & Gamble's Wary Eye on New York." *New York Times*, 9 February 1975, sec. 3, 17.

Production and Consumption of Coffee, Etc. Senate Document no. 35, 57th Congress, 2d Session. Washington, DC: Government Printing Office, 1902.

Profet, Margie. *Protecting Your Baby-to-Be: Preventing Birth Defects in the First Trimester*. Reading, MA: Addison-Wesley, 1995.

Proni, Giampaolo. *Coffee: Voltaire's Friend*. Translated by Chanan Zass. Milan, Italy: Lupetti Editori di Comunicazione, 1994.

"The Public Is Not Damned." *Fortune*, March 1939, 83–88, 109–14.

Purvis, Andrew. "Roots of Genocide: Why Hutu and Tutsi Cannot Live in Peace." *Time*, 5 August 1996, 57.

"Quality Coffee Catalog Increases Sales 25 Percent." *Direct Marketing* (November 1983): 90–91.

Quimme, Peter. *The Signet Book of Coffee and Tea*. New York: New American Library, 1976.

Quinn, James P. *Scientific Marketing of Coffee*. New York: Tea & Coffee Trade Journal, 1960.

"Racket in Coffee." *New Republic*, 2 January 1950, 7.

A Racketeer. "The Inside of the Testimonial Racket." *Advertising & Selling*, 7 January 1931, 20–21, 57–58.

Radovanovic, Vida, and Gail Hanney. *The Coffee Lover's Guide to Toronto*. Toronto, ON: V & G Communications, 1995.

Raffaelli, Marcelo. *Rise and Demise of Commodity Agreements: An Investigation into the Breakdown of International Commodity Agreements*. Cambridge, England: Woodhead, 1995.

Raimy, Eric. "Caffeine Nation." *Human Resource Executive*, (March 1996).

The Reason for Higher Coffee Prices. National Coffee Association, March 1941. In Hills Brothers Collection, Misc. File.

Redbook Magazine Marketing Research Dept. "Regular and Instant Coffee, Substitutes and Other Coffee Beverage Products: Notes on Consumption and the Household Market." January 1957, National Coffee Association Files.

Reed, Adolph, Jr. "'Fayettenam,' 1969: Tales from a GI Coffeehouse." *The Objector* (Spring 1996): 4–5, 12.

Reed, J. D. "Coffees You Can Sleep On." *Money*, August 1986, 93–98.

Reerink, Jack. "Stockpiles and Shortages." *Futures*, December 1993, 52–54.

Reese, Jennifer. "Starbucks: Inside the Coffee Cult." *Fortune*, 9 December 1996, 190–200.

"Regular, No Sugar, Please." *Datamation*, 15 January 1985, 148–50.

Rehak, Melanie. "To Drink or Not to Drink." *New York Times Magazine*, 14 March 1999, 20.

Reidy, Chris. "Boston Area Coffee Connection Shops Set to Brew Under Starbucks Name." *Boston Globe*, 17 January 1996, 38.

Report on Guatemala. Washington, DC: Network in Solidarity with the People of Guatemala, Winter 1994.

"Reports Perk Up Brothers' Stock." *Sun-Sentinel*, 25 February 1995, 1B.

Revett, John. "Coffee Share Dip Challenges Hills and WRG Shop." *Advertising Age*, 10 March 1980, 2, 84.

Rice, Robert A., and Justin R. Ward. *Coffee, Conservation and Commerce in the Western Hemisphere*. Washington, DC: Smithsonian Migratory Bird Center, 1996.

Richards, Art. "Television: An Autobiography." 3 May 1963 shooting script, Benton & Bowles Collection.

"Richness." *The New Yorker*, 19 March 1984, 40–41.

Rickard, Leah. "Taster's Choice Rolls Love Potion No. 9." *Advertising Age*, 12 June 1994, 70.

Rifkin, Glenn. "A Delicate Balance for a Coffee Chain." *New York Times*, 18 January 1994, D2.

"Rise and Fall of Coffee." *Barron's*, 24 October 1932, 16.

Robards, Terry. "Coffee Producers End Talks Without Reaching an Accord." *New York Times*, 26 April 1975, 39.

Robbins, Jack. "Robert Young: Now Doctor Knows Best." *New York Post*, 1 October 1969.

Robinson, Edward. *The Early English Coffee House*. 1893. Reprint. Christchurch, New Zealand: Dolphin Press, 1972.

Robinson, Linda. "Is Colombia Lost to Rebels?" *U.S. News & World Report*, 11 May 1998, 38.

Rockefeller Family Archives. Tarrytown, NY, R. G. 4 (Nelson A. Rockefeller Paper, Personal), Series: AIA-IBEC, Box 2.

Rockefeller, Nelson. *The Rockefeller Report on the Americas*. Chicago: Quadrangle Books, 1969.

Roden, Claudia. *Coffee: A Connoisseur's Companion*. New York: Random House, 1994.

Rohr, Mary A. *The Inter-American Coffee Agreement of 1940*. Toledo, OH: University of Toledo, 1981 (University Microfilms no. 8127773).

Rohter, Larry. "Political Feuds Rack Haiti: So Much for Its High Hopes." *New York Times*, 18 October 1998.

Rolnick, Harry. *The Complete Book of Coffee*. Hong Kong: Melitta, 1982.

Root, Waverley, and Richard de Rochemont. *Eating in America: A History*. New York: Ecco, 1976.

Rorty, James. *Our Master's Voice: Advertising*. New York: John Day, 1934.

Roseberry, William. *Coffee and Capitalism in the Venezuelan Andes.* Austin: University of Texas Press, 1983.

Rosen, Diana. *The Coffee Lover's Companion: The Ultimate Connoisseur's Guide to Buying, Brewing, and Enjoying Coffee.* Secaucus, NJ: Carol, 1997.

Rosenberg, Debra. "A Battle Brews in Beantown." *Newsweek,* 7 March 1994, 47.

Rosenberg, Merri. "A Teenage Nightmare." *Scholastic Update,* 8 December 1997, 4.

Ross, Irwin. "What Coffee Really Does to You." *Science Digest* (July 1966): 79–83.

Ross, John. *The Annexation of Mexico, from the Aztecs to the IMF: One Reporter's Journey Through History.* Monroe, ME: Common Courage Press, 1998.

Rothenberg, Randall. "Maxwell House Lost by Ogilvy." *New York Times,* 27 May 1989, 29–41.

Rothman, Matt. "Into the Black." *Inc.,* January 1993, 59–65.

Rotthauwe, Helmut. *The Heavenly Inferno: On the Hundredth Anniversary of Probat-Werke Emmerich.* Emmerich, Germany: J. L. Romer, 1968.

Rout, Leslie B., Jr., and John F. Bratzel. *The Shadow War: German Espionage and United States Counterespionage in Latin America During World War II.* Frederick, MD: University Publications of America, 1986.

Rowe, J. W. F. *Studies in the Artificial Control of Raw Material Supplies: No. 3, Brazilian Coffee.* London: Royal Economic Society, 1932.

Rozen, Leah. "Coffee Prices Hurt Economy Blends." *Advertising Age,* 11 February 1980, 3, 24.

Rubottom, Roy R., Jr. "Basic Principles Governing United States Relations with Latin America." *Department of State Bulletin,* 14 April 1958, 608–14.

———. "A Quarter-Century of Inter-American Cooperation on Coffee." *Department of State Bulletin,* 10 February 1958, 212–17.

Russell, George. "Coffee Caper." *Time,* 14 January 1985, 41–42.

Russell, Grahame. "Unearthing Guatemala's Disappeared." *Nonviolent Activist* (January–February 1997): 3–4.

Safire, William. "Brazil's Coffee Rip-off." *New York Times,* 13 January 1977, 35.

Saks, Claude. *Strong Brew: One Man's Prelude to Change.* Charlottesville, VA: Heartsfire Books, 1996.

Samper, Mario. *Generations of Settlers: Rural Households and Markets on the Costa Rican Frontier, 1850–1935.* Boulder, CO: Westview Press, 1990.

"San Francisco's Oldest Bean Coffee Retailer Sticks to Traditional Methods." *Specialty Food Merchandising,* September 1982, 33–40.

Sanborn, Helen J. *A Winter in Central America and Mexico.* Guatemala City: Popol Vuh Museum, 1996.

Santos, João Oliveira. "The Right Amount of Coffee." *Americas* (March 1961): 26–29.

Scarpa, James. "Gourmet Coffee Is Piping Hot." *Restaurant Business,* 10 February 1992, 24.

Schaeffer, Larry. "An Exercise in Futility?" *Progressive Grocer,* July 1986, 83.

Schafer, Charles, and Violet Schafer. *Coffee.* San Francisco: Yerba Buena, 1976.

Schapira, Joel, David Schapira, and Karl Schapira. *The Book of Coffee & Tea.* 2d ed. New York: St. Martin's Griffin, 1996.

Scherreik, Susan. "Getting the Most Out of Stock Options." *New York Times,* 30 April 1994, 37.

Schiller, Zachary, and Mark Landler. "P & G Can Get Mad, Sure, but Does It Have to Get Even?" *Business Week,* 4 June 1990, 65.

Schisgall, Oscar. *Eyes on Tomorrow: The Evolution of Procter & Gamble.* Chicago: J. G. Ferguson, 1981.

Schivelbusch, Wolfgang. *Tastes of Paradise: A Social History of Spices, Stimulants, and Intoxicants.* New York: Pantheon, 1992.

Schlereth, Thomas J. *Victorian America: Transformations in Everyday Life, 1876–1915.* New York: HarperPerennial, 1991.

Schlesinger, Stephen, and Stephen Kinzer. *Bitter Fruit: The Untold Story of the American Coup in Guatemala.* Garden City, NY: Anchor, 1983.

Schmeck, Harold M., Jr. "Coffee Drinking in Pregnancy Is Not Found to Harm Fetus." *New York Times,* 20 January 1982, 14.

Schmidt, Karl. "Presentation on Probat's Roasting Equipment." National Coffee Association meeting, Phoenix, AZ, 28 February 1997.

Schoenholt, Donald N. "Coffea Canephora: The 'R' Word." *Tea & Coffee Trade Journal* (February–May): 1992.

_____. "The Coffee Culprits Are Ourselves." *Tea & Coffee Trade Journal* (September 1981): 26–27, 52–54.

_____. "Decaffeinated–Not Decapitated." *Tea & Coffee Trade Journal* (February 1993): 32–35.

_____. "Frederic A. Cauchois and the 'Private Estate' Brand." *Tea & Coffee Trade Journal* (September 1985): 35.

_____. "Gourmet Trade Is New York Bound." *Tea & Coffee Trade Journal* (June 1982): 38.

_____. "The Gourmet Zone." *World Coffee & Tea* (September 1984): 62–63.

_____. "A Myth Is as Good as a Mile: The Mocha & Java History Mystery." *In Good Taste* (March 1994): 7–8.

_____. "A New Year, a New Idea." *Tea & Coffee Trade Journal* (January 1983): 20.

_____. "1982, the Year It All Began." *In Good Taste* (November 1997): 6–9.

_____. "Oz and the Speciality Coffee Adventure." *Tea & Coffee Trade Journal* (January 1992): 99–100.

_____. "Present at the Creation." *In Good Taste* (November–December 1992): 7.

_____. "Shall We Talk a Bit of 'Old Gov't Java'." On alt.coffee Newsgroup, 21 May 1997.

_____. "Specialty Coffee Progress Report." *Tea & Coffee Trade Journal* (November and December 1985).

_____. "Staling Common Retail Problem." *Tea & Coffee Trade Journal* (July 1982): 22.

_____. "Starbucks, Metaphor for Specialty Coffee." *Tea & Coffee Trade Journal* (February 1994): 26–29.

_____. "Top Quality Coffee Opens Door." *Tea & Coffee Trade Journal* (November 1981): 10–11, 32–33.

_____. "We Owe a Debt to the 'Flower Children'." *Tea & Coffee Trade Journal* (January 1982): 42–43, 61.

Schreiber, Norman. "Hal's a Hit." *Popular Photography* (March 1984): 35.

Schultz, Howard, and Dori Jones Yang. *Pour Your Heart Into It: How Starbucks Built a Company One Cup at a Time*. New York: Hyperion, 1997.

Schutts, Jeff Richard. *We Say No to Your War!: The Story of the Covered Wagon GI Coffeehouse, Mountain Home Air Force Base, Idaho, 1971*. Master's thesis, Boise State University, 1994.

Schwantes, V. David. *Guatemala: A Cry from the Heart*. Minneapolis: Health Initiatives Press, 1990.

Scott, Walter Dill. *The Psychology of Advertising*. Boston: Small, Maynard, 1913. 5th ed. Reprint. New York: Arno Press, 1978.

Sears Roebuck Co. *1897 Sears Roebuck Catalogue*. Reprint. Introduction by S. J. Perelman. New York: Chelsea House, 1976.

The Second Conquest of Latin America: Coffee, Henequen, and Oil During the Export Boom, 1850–1930. Edited by Steven C. Topik and Allen Wells. Austin: University of Texas Press, 1998.

Segal, Troy. "So You're Thinking of Opening a Coffee Bar." *Executive Female* (March–April 1995): 38–41, 76.

Seidensticker, Edward. *Low City, High City: Tokyo from Edo to the Earthquake*. San Francisco: Donald S. Ellis, 1985.

_____. *Tokyo Rising: The City Since the Great Earthquake*. New York: Alfred A. Knopf, 1990.

Seigel, Max. "Judge Sued on Outburst over 'Terrible' Coffee." *New York Times*, 2 October 1975, 43.

Seligson, Mitchell A. *Peasants of Costa Rica and the Development of Agrarian Capitalism*. Madison: University of Wisconsin Press, 1980.

Servaas, Cory. "Medical Mailbox." *Saturday Evening Post*, December 1974, 92.

"A Shaky Price Floor Under Coffee Beans." *Business Week*, 10 October 1977, 52–57.

Shaw, Roger. "Civil War in Brazil." *Review of Reviews* (November 1930): 63–64.

Sheldon, Mary Boardman. *Coffee and a Love Affair: An American Girl's Romance on a Coffee Plantation*. New York: Frederick A. Stokes, 1908.

Sherrell, Jean. "Coffee Roasting California Style: Three San Francisco Pioneers." *California Historical Society Newsletter*, August 1982.

Sherrid, Pamela. "Citibank's Adventures in the Coffee Trade." *Fortune*, 19 May 1980, 134–38.

Shiva, Vandana. *The Violence of the Green Revolution*. London: Zed Books, 1991.

Shore, Teri. "Erna Knutsen: Coffee Importer, World Traveler," *Café Olé Magazine*, May 1994, 22–24.

Shorris, Earl. *A Nation of Salesmen: The Tyranny of the Market and the Subversion of Culture*. New York: W. W. Norton, 1994.

Shūhei, Sakurai, "Tokyo Kissaten." *The East* (January–February 1996): 6–13.

Silver, Sara. "Coffee's Shady Side." *Associated Press*, 15 December 1998.

"Sinatra, Frank." *Current Biography* (1943): 700–702; *Current Biography* (1960): 384–86.

Sinnott, Kevin. "Erna Knutsen: Queen of Green (Coffee That Is)." *Coffee Companion* (March 1994): 4–5.

Sivetz, Michael. *Coffee Quality Primer*. Corvallis, OR: Sivetz Coffee, 1996.

Skidmore, Thomas E. *Politics in Brazil, 1930–1964: An Experiment in Democracy*. London: Oxford University Press, 1967.

Sklar, Zachary. "Bringing the War Home in Nicaragua." *Nation*, 8 February 1985, 136–38.

Sloss, Robert. "The New York Coffee Party." *Everybody's Magazine*, June 1913, 772–83.

_____. "Why Coffee Costs Twice as Much." *World's Work* (June 1912): 194–205.

Slywotzky, Adrian J. *Value Migration: How to Think Several Moves Ahead of the Competition*. Cambridge, MA: Harvard University Press, 1996.

"Smash the Demitasses?" *Fortune*, June 1958, 86–93.

Smith, Frank. Typescript, history of Benton & Bowles, 1968. In Benton & Bowles Collection, Hartman Center, Duke University.

Smith, Griffin, Jr. "Guatemala: A Fragile Democracy." *National Geographic* (June 1988): 768–803.

Smith, M. J. Sebastian. "Stirring News About Exotic Coffees." *Saturday Evening Post*, October 1976, 102–4.

Smith, Orin C. "Wanted: The Right Investment Banker." *Financial Executive* (November–December 1994): 14–18.

Smith, S. D. "Accounting for Taste: British Coffee Consumption in Historical Perspective." *Journal of Interdisciplinary History* (Autumn 1996): 183–214.

Smith, Traver. "Policies That Made Chase & Sanborn a National Leader." *Sales Management*, 9 April 1932, 34–35, 55.

Sobel, Robert. *The Manipulators: America in the Media Age*. Garden City, NY: Anchor Press/Doubleday, 1976.

Sokolov, Raymond. "Grounds for Delight." *Natural History* (January 1978): 8–14.

Solomon, Anthony M. "United States Policy Toward International Efforts to Improve Conditions of Commodity Trade." *Dept. of State Bulletin*, 18 March 1968, 387–92.

Solomon, Jolie. "Not in My Backyard." *Newsweek*, 16 September 1996, 65–66.

"Soluble Coffees." *Consumers' Research Bulletin*, June 1942, 14.

"Soluble Coffees." *Consumers' Research Bulletin*, August 1950, 24–25.

"Soothing the Coffee Nerves." *Time*, 31 August 1962, 58.

Specialty Coffee Holdings, Inc. *Confidential Information Memorandum*. September 1992. Property of the author.

"Specialty Roasters Make Headway in Forming Association." *World Coffee & Tea* (August 1982): 38–39.

Specter, Michael. "Coffee Clash." *The New Yorker*, 19 October 1998, 40–43.

Spitzer, Silas. "Coffee." *Holiday*, September 1949, 65–68.

"Square Closure on a Square Jar." *Modern Packaging* (September 1974): 30–31.

Stainer, Robin. "International Coffee Developments in 1983." *F. O. Lichts International Coffee Yearbook*. Ratzeburg, Germany: F. O. Lichts, 1983.

_____. "International Coffee Review 1987/88." *F. O. Lichts International Coffee Yearbook*. Ratzeburg, Germany, 1988.

_____. "International Coffee Year 1985." *F. O. Lichts International Coffee Yearbook.* Ratzeburg, Germany, 1985.

Standard Brands. "The History of Chase & Sanborn Coffee." Hartman Center, Duke University.

"Staples Paradox." *Business Week,* 1 May 1943, 22.

Starbird, Ethel. "The Bonanza Bean: Coffee." *National Geographic* (March 1981): 388–405.

"Starting Their Own Café." *Economist,* 24 May 1980, 98–99.

Steif, William. "Squeezing out the Last Drop." *Progressive,* February 1990, 17–18.

Stein, Stanley J. *Vassouras: A Brazilian Coffee Country, 1850–1900.* Cambridge, MA: Harvard University Press, 1957.

Stella, Alain. *The Book of Coffee.* Paris, NY: Flammarion, 1997.

Stephens, John L. *Incidents of Travel in Central America Chiapas and Yucatan.* Vol. 1. 1841. Reprint. New York: Dover, 1969.

Stewart, Randal G. *Coffee: The Political Economy of an Export Industry in Papua New Guinea.* Boulder, CO: Westview Press, 1992.

Stinchecum, Amanda Meyer. "Japan's Other Ritual: A Coffee Ceremony." *New York Times,* 17 November 1991, sec. 5, 6.

Stolcke, Verena. *Coffee Planters, Workers and Wives: Class Conflict and Gender Relations on São Paulo Plantations, 1850–1980.* New York: St. Martin's Press, 1988.

_____, and Michael M. Hall. "The Introduction of Free Labour on São Paulo Coffee Plantations." *Journal of Peasant Studies 10,* 2–3 (1983): 170–200.

Stoll, David. *Between Two Armies: In the Ixil Towns of Guatemala.* New York: Columbia University Press, 1993.

_____. "Life Story as Mythopoesis." *Cultural Survival Website, Active Voices.* 1998. http://www.cs.org/.

_____. *Rigoberta Menchú and the Story of All Poor Guatemalans.* Boulder, CO: Westview Press, 1999.

Stone, Roy. "Puerto Rico's Needs: A Practical Suggestion." *Outlook* (30 December 1899): 1023–25.

"A Storm Brews over Coffee Prices." *U.S. News & World Report,* 17 January 1977, 58.

"The Story of the Instants." *Business Week,* 28 February 1953, 50–51.

Strain, Eric, and Roland Griffiths. "Caffeine Dependence: Fact or Fiction." *Journal of the Royal Society of Medicine* (August 1995): 437–40.

_____, G. K. Mumford, K. Silverman et al. "Caffeine Dependence Syndrome." *Journal of the American Medical Association* (5 October 1994): 1043–48.

Streeter, Stephen M. *Managing the Counterrevolution: The United States and Guatemala, 1954–1961.* Ph.D. diss., University of Connecticut, 1994.

Stroud, Ruth. "Chase & Sanborn Gets Back in the Chase." *Advertising Age,* 25 February 1985, 12.

Sturdivant, Shea. "Two Volume Movers in Supermarket Distribution." *Tea & Coffee Trade Journal* (May 1993): 44.

Sullivan, Philip R. "Coffee, Cancer, Reporting." *America* (5 September 1981): 93–94.

"The Sun Never Sets on Cacoola." *Time,* 15 May 1950, 28–32.

"Surplus & Shortage." *Time,* 10 September 1956, 51.

Swasy, Alecia. *Soap Opera: The Inside Story of Procter & Gamble.* New York: Times Books, 1993.

Szulc, Tad. "About Coffee." *New York Times Magazine,* 10 January 1954, 60–61.

"Take That, El Exigente." *Time,* 28 March 1977, 79–80.

Talbot, John M. "Regulating the Coffee Commodity Chain." *Berkeley Journal of Sociology 40* (1995–1996):113–49.

_____. "The Struggle for Control of a Commodity Chain." *Latin America Research Review 32,* 2 (1997): 117–35.

Tannahill, Reay. *Food in History.* New York: Stein and Day, 1973.

Task Force Report on Central America. *Central America in Crisis: A Program for Action.* Washington, DC: Washington Institute for Values in Public Policy, 1983.

Taulbee, P. "Study Links Coffee to High Cholesterol." *Science News,* 25 June 1983, 406–7.

Taylor, Dale. *The Writer's Guide to Everyday Life in Colonial America.* Cincinnati: Writer's Digest Books, 1997.

Taylor, Herbert J. "Once Around the Clock: Processing Coffee, a Swift Production Job." *Factory and Industrial Management* (April 1930): 801–3.

Taylor, Kiley. "Victuals and Vitamins: Coffee." *New York Times Magazine*, 4 August 1940, 14.

Tchibo Group. *All About Tchibo.* Hamburg, Germany: Tchibo, n.d., ca. 1992.

Tedlow, Richard S. *New and Improved: The Story of Mass Marketing in America.* New York: Basic Books, 1990.

"Television Boost." *Business Week*, 7 July 1945, 82.

"Tempest in a Coffee Pot." *Time*, 23 June 1941, 76.

"Tempest in a Percolator." *Newsweek*, 3 July 1950, 32.

Terkel, Studs. *Hard Times: An Oral History of the Great Depression.* New York: Washington Square Press, 1970.

"The Terrible Twins." *Economist*, 10 October 1987, 70.

Therrien, Robert, Jr. *Give Us This Day Our Daily Brew.* East Haven, CT: Long River Books, 1994.

"This Coffee Maneuvering Is Just Shrewd Strategy." *Business Week*, 31 August 1932, 20.

This Fabulous Century: 1950–1960. Vol. 6. New York: Time-Life, 1970.

Thomas, Fred B. "Morning Cup of Coffee and Heartburn." *USA Today*, August 1980, 4.

Thomas, Hugh. *The Slave Trade: The Story of the Atlantic Slave Trade, 1440–1870.* New York: Simon & Schuster, 1997.

Thomson & Taylor Spice Co. *Coffee: Its History and Also Its Remarkable Growth in the World of Commerce.* Chicago: Thomson & Taylor, 1898.

"3¢ a Cup?" *Time*, 15 November 1937, 75.

Thurber, Francis B. *Coffee: From Plantation to Cup.* New York: American Grocer Publishing Assn., 1881.

"Tight-Fisted Coffee Lovers: There's Still Some Hope." *Consumer Reports*, February 1978, 65.

"Time to Rebuild." *Time*, 16 June 1958, 28.

"Too Many Beans in One Basket?" *Business Week*, 4 July 1953, 96.

Topik, Steven. *The Political Economy of the Brazilian State, 1889–1930.* Austin: University of Texas Press, 1987.

"Toronto's Coffee Cultures." *Coffee Culture* (Spring 1998): 12, 30.

Treaster, Joseph B. "Coffee Impasse Imperils Colombia's Drug Fight." *New York Times*, 24 September 1989, A20.

"Trendy Coffee Bars Even Play in Peoria." CBS, "CBS This Morning," 20 July 1994.

Trigg, Charles W. Papers. Archives Center, Smithsonian, National Museum of American History, Washington, DC.

"Trouble Brewing." *Technology Review* (November–December 1981): 54–55.

Trouillot, Michel-Rolph. "Motion in the System: Coffee, Color, and Slavery in Eighteenth-Century Saint-Domingue." *Review 3* (Winter 1982): 331–88.

Troyer, Ronald J., and Gerald E. Markle. "Coffee Drinking: An Emerging Social Problem?" *Social Problems 31*, 4 (April 1984): 403–16.

"Trying to Apply a Coffee Brake." *Time*, 17 January 1977, 46–47.

Tuckman, Jo. "Healing Painful in Guatemala." *Burlington Free Press*, 9 December 1996.

Tulard, Jean. *Napoleon: The Myth of the Saviour.* Translated by Teresa Waugh. London: Weidenfeld & Nicolson, 1984.

Turner, John Kenneth. *Barbarous Mexico.* 1910. Reprint. Austin: University of Texas Press, 1969.

Twitchell, James B. *Adcult USA: The Triumph of Advertising in American Culture.* New York: Columbia University Press, 1996.

"293,884,843 Cups of Coffee a Day." *Look*, 21 April 1953, 122–23.

"Two More Products Pass the General Foods Tests." *Business Week*, 1 May 1932, 10.

Tyson, Remer. "Grounds of Contention." *Time*, 22 December 1997, 27.

Ukers, William H. *All About Coffee.* 2d ed. New York: Tea & Coffee Trade Journal, 1935.

_____. "Better Teas and Coffees." *Good Housekeeping*, October 1911, 495–98.

_____. "Santos, São Paulo, and Coffee." *Bulletin of the Pan American Union*, January 1935, 19–30.

Ullman, Richard H. "Human Rights and Economic Power: The United States versus Idi Amin."
Foreign Affairs (April 1978): 529–43.
Underwood, Elaine. "Place-Based Coffee." *Adweek's Marketing Week*, 24 February 1992, 12.
The United Nations and El Salvador, 1990–1995. New York: United Nations, 1995.
"United States and Brazil Conclude Agreement on Soluble Coffee." *Dept. of State Bulletin*, 10 May
1971, 627–28.
United States v. American Sugar Refining Company, U.S. District Court, Southern District of New
York, 7 June 1912.
"The Urge to Excess." *Journal of the American Medical Association* (19 November 1932): 1784.
Uribe C., Andrés. *Brown Gold: The Amazing Story of Coffee*. New York: Random House, 1954.
"U.S. Battles Brazil to a Coffee Break." *Business Week*, 8 August 1970, 15.
"U.S. Coffee Nerves." *Scholastic*, 10 February 1954, 30.
U.S. Congress, House, Committee on Agriculture. *Coffee Price Review*. 16 and 18 March 1976.
Washington, DC: Government Printing Office, 1976.
U.S. Congress, House, Committee on Agriculture. *Include Coffee Under Commodity Exchange Act*.
Washington, DC: Government Printing Office, 1954.
U.S. Congress, House, Committee on Foreign Affairs. *International Protection of Human Rights*.
Washington, DC: Government Printing Office, 1974.
U.S. Congress, House, Committee on Government Operations. *U.S. Export of Banned Products*.
11–13 July 1978. Washington, DC: Government Printing Office. 1978.
U.S. Congress, House, Committee on International Relations. *United States–Uganda Relations*. 1, 2,
9 and 22 February, 6 and 28 April 1978. Washington, DC: Government Printing Office, 1978.
U.S. Congress, House, Committee on Interstate and Foreign Commerce. *Crude Rubber, Coffee, Etc.:
Hearings*. Washington, DC: Government Printing Office, 1926.
U.S. Congress, House, Committee on Ways and Means. *International Coffee Agreement: Executive
Hearings*. Washington, DC: Government Printing Office, 1965.
U.S. Congress, House, Joint Hearings, Subcommittees of the Committee on Government Opera-
tions and the Committee on Agriculture. *Rising Coffee Prices and the Federal Response*. 22 and 23
February 1977. Washington, DC: Government Printing Office, 1977.
U.S. Congress, Senate, Committee on Agriculture and Forestry. *Regulation of Coffee Futures Trading*.
Washington, DC: Government Printing Office, 1954.
U.S. Congress, Senate, Committee on Agriculture and Forestry. *Utilization of Farm Crops: Price
Spreads–Coffee: Report*. 10 July 1950. *Senate Reports*, Misc. Vol. 5. Washington, DC: Government
Printing Office, 1950.
U.S. Congress, Senate, Committee on Finance. *Coffee: Hearings*. Washington, DC: Government
Printing Office, 1964.
U.S. Congress, Senate, Committee on Foreign Affairs. *International Coffee Agreement, 1962: Hearing*.
Washington, DC: Government Printing Office, 1963.
U.S. Congress, Senate, Committee on the Judiciary. *Mergers and Economic Concentration: Hearings*. 8,
23 and 30 March, 25 April 1979. Washington, DC: Government Printing Office, 1979.
U.S. Congress, Senate, Joint Hearings, Committee on the Judiciary and Caucus on International
Narcotics Control. *U.S. International Drug Policy, Multinational Strike Forces, Drug Policy in the An-
dean Nations*. 6 November 1989, 18 January, 27 March 1990. Washington, DC: Government
Printing Office, 1991.
U.S. Congress, Senate, Senate Foreign Relations Committee. *Executive Sessions of the Senate Foreign
Relations Committee (Historical Series)*. Vol. 11. Washington, DC: Government Printing Office,
1982.
U.S. Congress, Senate, Special Subcommittee of the Committee on Banking and Currency. *Study
of Coffee Prices*. Washington, DC: Government Printing Office, 1954.
U.S. Congress, Senate, Subcommittee of the Committee on Agriculture and Forestry. *Utilization of
Farm Crops: Price Spreads–Coffee: Hearings*. Parts 2 and 3. Washington, DC: Government Printing
Office, 1950.

U.S. Guatemala Labor Education Project (US/GLEP). *Justice for Coffee Workers Campaign.* Chicago, 1996.

USA v. Michael L. Norton, U.S. District Court of California, Criminal no. 96–40173-DLJ. Original and amended public documents.

"Vacuum Cans: Pivot for Coffee's Half Century." *World Coffee & Tea* (April 1961): 25–26.

Valorization File, Dept. of Justice, 1911–1913. Box 132 in General Departmental Files, 1917–1930, U.S. National Archives.

Van der Zee, P. R. *Van Winkelnering Tot Wereldmerk: Douwe Egberts Van 1753 Tot 1987.* Utrecht: Douwe Egberts, 1987.

Vandermeer, John, and Ivette Perfecto. *Breakfast of Biodiversity: The Truth About Rain Forest Destruction.* Oakland, CA: Institute for Food and Development Policy, 1995.

"Venezuela's Coffee." *Pan American Magazine,* December 1920, 15–16.

Vesilind, Priit J. "Brazil: Moment of Promise & Pain." *National Geographic* (March 1987): 348–85.

Vicker, Ray. "African Agriculture." *American Mercury* (April 1959): 134–39.

Vidal, David. "Colombia: Coffee Bonanza Boomerangs." *New York Times,* 16 October 1977, C3.

Vieira, Marcelo. "Brazil: Producing Country Profile." *World Coffee & Tea* (December 1993): 22–25.

_____. "An Overview of the Brazilian Coffee Market." *In Good Taste* (August 1994): 8–9.

"A Visit with Erna Knutsen." *Gourmet Retailer* (May 1994): 40–42.

Visser, Margaret. *Much Depends on Dinner: The Extraordinary History and Mythology, Allure, and Obsessions, Perils and Taboos of an Ordinary Meal.* New York: Collier, 1986.

Vogel, Jason. "Carriage Trade Coffee." *Financial World,* 25 April 1995, 62–65.

Wakeman, Abram. *History and Reminiscences of Lower Wall Street and Vicinity.* New York: Spice Mill, 1914.

Wall, James M. "Death and Coffee in Uganda." *Christian Century,* 26 October 1977, 971–73.

Walsh, Doris L. "General Foods Coffee Achievement." *American Demographics* (March 1985): 18, 47.

Walsh, Joseph M. *Coffee: Its History, Classification and Description.* Philadelphia: Henry T. Coates & Co., 1894.

Walsh, William I. *The Rise and Decline of The Great Atlantic & Pacific Tea Company.* Secaucus, NJ: Lyle Stuart, 1986.

Ward, William Knox. "Marketing Mix." *Modern Packaging* (May 1971): 12–14.

"Wards Food Campaign Backs Its Cuppa Coffee." *Advertising Age,* 12 January 1970, 24.

Warren, William J. "Coffee Jitters." *American Shipper* (June 1991): 78.

Warshaw Collection. Archives Center, Smithsonian, National Museum of American History, Washington, DC.

"Washington's M. E. Swing Is Monument to Coffee Quality and Service." *Specialty Food Merchandising,* October 1987, 22–32.

Watson, John B. "Advertising by Radio." *J. Walter Thompson Bulletin* no. 98, May 1923. In J. Walter Thompson Inc. Files, Hartman Center, Duke University.

_____. "Feed Me on Facts." *Saturday Review of Literature,* 16 June 1928.

_____. "Lecture to Standard Brands Class." 27 April 1931. In J. Walter Thompson Inc. Files, Hartman Center, Duke University.

_____. "What Is Behaviorism?" *Harper's Monthly Magazine,* May 1926, 723–29.

"We Make All Kinds of Coffee in All Kinds of Ways." *Business Week,* 3 August 1932, 23.

Weatherstone, John. *The Pioneers 1825–1900: The Early British Tea and Coffee Planters and Their Way of Life.* London: Quiller Press, 1986.

Webber, Gordon. *Our Kind of People.* Typescript history of Benton & Bowles, n.d., Benton & Bowles Collection, Box 22, Hartman Center, Duke University.

Weishaar, Margaret. "Psych-Ing Mrs. Smith." *People,* October 1937, 5–7. House periodical, in J. Walter Thompson Inc. Files, Hartman Center, Duke University.

Weiss, E. B. "Selling Quality in a Price Market." *Printer's Ink Monthly,* April 1932, 24, 53.

Weiss, Gary. "Coffee Growers Are in for Lots of Sleepless Nights." *Business Week,* 2 February 1987, 67.

_____. "When You Bet on Coffee, Use the Old Bean." *Business Week,* 13 July 1992, 148.

Wellman, Frederick L. *Coffee: Botany, Cultivation, and Utilization.* London: Leonard Hill, 1961; New York: Interscience, 1961.

West, Phil. "Good to Last Drop Coffee Celebrates 100 Years." *Nashville Banner,* 26 October 1992, D17.

Wetherall, Charles F. *Kicking the Coffee Habit.* Minneapolis: Wetherall, 1981.

Whalen, Jeanne. "Gourmet Coffee Perks Up Fast-Food." *Advertising Age,* 24 January 1994, 12.

"What–Coffee, Too?" *Newsweek,* 12 July 1971, 82.

"What Is Driving Prices Down?" *Business Week,* 6 July 1981, 22–23.

"What Killed Coffee?" *Marketing Communications* (March 1983): 19–22, 60.

"What They Want." *Time,* 1 March 1954, 33.

"What's Really Brewing?" *Newsweek,* 25 January 1954, 73.

Wheatley, Richard. "The Coffee Exchange of the City of New York." *Harpers Weekly,* 13 June 1891, 433–36, 442.

Wheeler, Michael. *Coffee to 1995: Recovery Without Crutches.* London: Economist Intelligence Unit, 1990.

_____. *Coffee to 2000: A Market Untamed.* London: Economist Intelligence Unit, 1995.

"Where Coffee Is King." *Pan American Magazine,* January 1926, 13–16.

White, Alastair. *El Salvador.* New York: Praeger, 1973.

"Why Coffee Keeps Costing More." *U.S. News & World Report,* 22 January 1954, 40.

"Why Coffee Prices Are Percolating." *Business Week,* 27 September 1969, 124.

"Why Thousands Die." *Washington Post,* 4 November 1998.

Wicker, Tom. *One of Us: Richard Nixon and the American Dream.* New York: Random House, 1991.

Wickizer, V. D. *The World Coffee Economy with Special Reference to Control Schemes.* Stanford, CA: Food Research Institute, Stanford University, 1943.

Wiley, Bell Irvin. *The Life of Billy Yank: The Common Soldier of the Union.* Indianapolis: Bobbs-Merrill, 1952. Reprint. 1971.

Wille, Chris. "The Birds and the Beans." *Audubon* (November–December 1994): 58–64.

Williams, Franklin H. "Idi Amin's Achilles' Heel." *New York Times,* 14 August 1977, D17.

Williams, Robert G. *States and Social Evolution: Coffee and the Rise of National Governments in Central America.* Chapel Hill: University of North Carolina Press, 1994.

Wilson, Betty. "What's Happened to Coffee?" *Américas* (April 1954): 3–5, 41.

Wilson, Jason. "Haitian Bleu." *Coffee Journal* (Autumn 1998): 16–19, 69.

Wilson, Joan Hoff. *American Business & Foreign Policy, 1920–1933.* Lexington: University Press of Kentucky, 1971.

Wilson, Richard. *Maya Resurgence in Guatemala: Q'Eqchi' Experiences.* Norman: University of Oklahoma Press, 1995.

Wilson, T. Carroll. *A Background Story of Hills Bros. Coffee, Inc.* Presented at the Philadephia District Sales Meeting, 9 September 1966. In Hills Brothers Collection.

"Wind Without Pity." *Time,* 23 August 1963, 67.

Winson, Anthony. *Coffee and Democracy in Modern Costa Rica.* New York: St. Martin's Press, 1989.

Winters, Patricia. "Coffee Leaders Perking Up Instants." *Advertising Age,* 15 December 1986, 28.

_____. "New High-Yield Folgers Battles Coffee Price Rise." *Advertising Age,* 17 March 1986, 1, 104.

_____. "Sanka Going Natural: Decaf War Perks Up." *Advertising Age,* 12 January 1987, 1, 56.

Witchel, Alex. "By Way of Canarsie, One Large Hot Cup of Business Strategy." *New York Times,* 14 December 1994, C1, 8.

"With Lid Off, How High Can They Go?" *Business Week,* 21 March 1953, 148–50.

Woodward, Helen. "About Coffee." *Nation,* 25 December 1937, 717–18.

Woodward, Ralph Lee, Jr. *Central America: A Nation Divided.* 2d ed. New York: Oxford University Press, 1985.

"World's Largest Coffee Plant Opens." *Jersey Observer,* 13 October 1939.

Wrigley, Gordon. *Coffee.* Essex, UK: Longman Scientific & Technical, 1988.

Wunderman, Lester. *Being Direct: Making Advertising Pay.* New York: Random House, 1996.

Wynn, Read W. "About–A Cup of Joe." *New York Times,* 11 April 1954, 59.

Yang, Dori Jones. "Fewer Cups, but a Much Richer Brew." *Business Week*, 18 November 1991, 80.

Ybarra, T. R. "Old King Coffee." *Collier's*, 14 April 1934, 28, 48, 50.

"A Year More of Costly Coffee." *U.S. News & World Report*, 23 July 1954, 32.

"A Year on a Roller Coaster." *Business Week*, 9 October 1954, 186–87.

Yergin, Daniel. *The Prize: The Epic Quest for Oil, Money, and Power*. New York: Simon & Schuster, 1991.

Youman, Nancy. "Red Apple Chain Joins Folgers Protest." *Adweek's Marketing Week*, 25 June 1990, 6.

Young, Crawford. *The African Colonial State in Comparative Perspective*. New Haven, CT: Yale University Press, 1994.

Young, John Orr. *Adventures in Advertising*. New York: Harper & Brothers, 1948.

Zachary, G. Pascal. "Starbucks Asks Foreign Suppliers to Improve Working Conditions." *Wall Street Journal*, 23 October 1995.

"Zaire's Coffee Percolates Abroad." *Economist*, 9 May 1981, 92.

Zimmerman, M. M. "Can Branded Staples Compete with the Chains' Private Brands?" *Printer's Ink Monthly*, 28 May 1931, 3–6, 116–19.

Zweig, Jason. "Chock Full O' Potential." *Forbes*, 22 June 1992, 52–54.

LIST OF INTERVIEWS

The following interviews were conducted between 1 December 1995 and 15 March 1999.

David Abedon
Betty Hannstein Adams
Richard N. Adams
Walter Adams
Pamela Aden
Mané Alves
Dominic Ammirati
Tommy Ammirati
Jose Julio Arivillaga
José Armado Cheves
Philip Aronson
Steve Aronson
Donald Atha
Peter Baer
Albert Baez
Lamar Bagby
Jerry Baldwin
Gonzalo Barillas
Stephen Bauer
Andrea Bass
Bert Beekman
Ed Behr
Frank Bendaña
Ian Bersten
Bernie Biedak
Jack Binek
G. Barry "Skip" Blakely
Oren Bloostein
George Boecklin
Jim Bowe
Dennis Boyer
Kathy Brahimi
Edward Bramah
Don Breen
Anthony Bucalo
Ray Bustos
Gabriel Cadena Goméz

Jim Cannell
Anthony Caputo
Roger Castellon Orué
Karen Cebreros
Andrea Chacón
Esperanza Chacón
Tom Charleville
Joe Charleville
Holly Chase
Michael Chu
Stephen Coats
Bob Cody
Jerry Collins
Steve Colten
Paul Comey
Peter Condaxis
Neal Cowan
Dan Cox
Paul Crocetta
Joaquin Cuadra Lacayo
David Dallis
Kenneth Davids
Stuart Daw
María del Carmén Cálix
David Donaldson
Herb Donaldson
Pablo Dubois
Mike Ebert
Laura Edghill
Craig Edwards
Marty Elkin
Rob Everts
Francis Miles Filleul
Gary Fischer
Bill Fishbein
Victoria Fisichelli
Jaime Fortuño

Hideko Furukawa
Paul Gallant
Fred Gardner
Patrice Gautier
Gianfranco Giotta
Miguel Gomez
Jorge Gonzalez
Larry Gorchow
Sterling Gordon
Angel Martin Granados Gonzales
Carolyn Hall
Doug Hall
Tom Harding
Jerry Harrington
Barbara Hausner
Adalheidur Hedinsdottir
Carmen Hernandez Melendez
David Higgins
Eirikur Hilmarsson
Will Hobhouse
Fred Houk, Jr.
John J. Hourihan
George Howell
John Hughes
Richard von Hunersdorff
Ernesto Illy
Susan Irwin
Jorge Isaac Mendez
Jay Isais
Stephen Jaffe
Michael Jimenez
Phil Johnson
Chuck Jones
Phil Jones
Phyllis Jordan

Julius Kahn
Jeanne Kail
Elizabeth Kane
Paul Katzeff
Frederick S. M. Kawuma
Jim Kharouf
Trina Kleist
Kevin Knox
Erna Knutsen
Suryakant Kothari
Russ Kramer
Stanley Kuehn
Eddy Kühl
Edward Kvetko
David Latimer
Gerardo Leon-York
Eduardo Libreros
Earl Lingle
Jim Lingle
Ted Lingle
Celcius Lodder
Peter Longo
Bill McAlpin
Sandy McAlpine
Joe McBratney
Jane McCabe
Colin McClung
Rella MacDougall
Alton McEwen
Becky McKinnon
Carrie MacKillop
Charlie Magill
Ruth Magill
Mitchell Margulis
Oscar Marin
John Martinez
John Mastro
Tom Matzen
Maritza Midence
Sherri Miller
Bruce Milletto
Doug Mitchell
Melissa Maria Molina Icias
Raul Molina Mejia
Klaus Monkemüller

Fernando Montes
Dave Moran
Steve Morris
Steve Moynihan
Kerry Muir
Marsha Nagley-Moody
Donna Neal
Robert Nelson
Stanley Newkirk
Frank O'Dea
Toshi Okamoto
Kate Olgiati
Samuel Olivieri
Dave Olsen
Simeon Onchere
Carlos Paniagua Zuñiga
Alfred Peet
Humberto Peña
Tony Pennachio
Alvaro Peralta Gedea
Hector Perez Brignoli
Price Peterson
Rick Peyser
Dawn Pinaud
Ruben Pineda Fagioli
Jaime Polit
Joanne Ranney
Luciano Repetto
Jim Reynolds
Dory Rice
Paul Rice
Robert Rice
Stefano Ripamonti
Mark Ritchie
Claudia Roden
Connie Roderick
Oscar Rodriguez
Edgar Rojas
Jonathan Rosenthal
Neil Rosser
Steve Sabol
Mario Samper
Luz Maria Sánchez
Grady Saunders
Donald Schoenholt

Steve Schulman
Mary Seggerman
Jo Shannon
Joanne Shaw
Elise Wolter Sherman
Roberio Silva
Michael Slater
Julio C. Solozano
Jim Stewart
Bob Stiller
William Stixrud
David Stoll
Dana Stone
Norm Storkel
Mike Sullivan
Alecia Swasy
Gary Talboy
Karen Techeira
Dave Tilgner
Steven Topik
Art Trotman
Timothy Tulloch
Jim Twiford
Mark Upson
Ricardo Valvidieso
Jerry Van Horne
Matt Vanek
Pablo Vargas Morales
Roland Veit
Marcelo Vieira
Carter Vincent
Patty Vincent
Bill Walters
Irwin Warren
Craig Weicker
Jon Wettstein
Jonathan White
Robert L. White
Elizabeth Whitlow
T. Carroll Wilson
Guy Wood
Jeremy Woods
Saul Zabar
Cecelia Zarate-Laum

ACKNOWLEDGMENTS

Researching and writing *Uncommon Grounds* took three years, which included much travel and archival research. I should have kept better records of the many people who helped me along the way. If anyone feels left out, please put it down to my memory rather than my intent.

The path toward publication illustrates the perils of today's book world. To my conversations with my former editor Hamilton Cain (among others), I owe the genesis for the idea of a social and business history of coffee—even though the publisher with whom he was then associated did not jump at the subsequent proposal. My ever-patient agent, Lisa Bankoff, sold it to Basic Books, then part of HarperCollins, where editor Paul Golob acquired it. Subsequently, HarperCollins announced that it was killing the Basic imprint, and Paul Golob departed to another publisher, leaving me without an editor.

A few months later, Basic Books was sold to the Perseus Books Group, thanks to owner Frank Pearl, a "white knight" of quality publishing. There, I was relieved when my book was assigned to Tim Bartlett, who immediately grasped the scope and importance of the project, and his assistant, Caroline Sparrow. In addition, my freelance editor, Regina Hersey, helped me prune over a third of the manuscript to produce the volume you hold in your hands. Michael Wilde, copyeditor, also provided constructive comments on the contents.

Many other people read portions of the manuscript and made helpful suggestions, including Betty Hannstein Adams, Rick Adams, Mané Alves, Irene Angelico, Mike Arms, Mané Alves, Ian Bersten, Dan Cox, Kenneth Davids, Margaret Edwards, Max Friedman, David Galland, Roland Griffiths, Marylen Grigas, John Hughes, Jack James, Wade Kit, Russ Kramer, Liz Lasser, Ted Lingle, Jane McCabe, Chris and Penny Miller, Bill Mitchell, Betty Molnar, Alfred Peet, Britt and Nan Pendergrast, John and Docie Pendergrast, Scott Pendergrast, Joanne Ranney,

Larry Ribbecke, Don Schoenholt, Steve Schulman, Tom Stevens, David Stoll, Steve Streeter, Steven Topik, Blair Vickery, and K K Wilder. Of course, I alone am responsible for the contents.

I must single out Betty and Rick Adams from that list. Betty appears as a character in the book, particularly in the final chapter. She was also a thoughtful reader of the manuscript. In this book's bibliography, Rick appears as Richard N. Adams, the anthropologist. In Guatemala, he was my part-time chauffeur as well as guide, and his criticism of some oversimplifications in the original manuscript helped keep me honest. Both were gracious hosts when I visited *Finca Oriflama* in Guatemala.

I also want to thank the many E-mail correspondents who helped brainstorm the book title. Coincidentally, *Uncommon Grounds* is also the name of a fine coffeehouse in Burlington, Vermont, where I sat on bags of coffee beans for the author photo that appears on the jacket.

I could not have completed this book without the help of research assistants William Berger, Brady Crain, Jan DeSirey, Erica De Vos, Chris Dodge, Shad Emerson, Sherecce Fields, Meg Gandy, Denise Guyette, Margaret Jervis, John Kulsick, Liz Lasser, and Dhamma Merion. Many thanks to Chris Dodge, Peter Freyd, Henry Lilienheim, my parents, and others who acted as my "coffee clipping service."

Helena Pasquarella took photos from old periodicals that appear in the illustrations, and I am grateful to Greg Arbuckle, Brad Becker, and Jerry Baldwin for help with other illustrations. In conjunction with his film on coffee, David Ozier shared archival music and video footage. Jane McCabe, editor of the *Tea & Coffee Trade Journal*, generously granted permission to reprint illustrations from that publication's pages.

Librarians and archivists helped me at the Hartman Center at Duke University, the Rockefeller Archives (Tarrytown, NY), the Underhill Public Library (VT), the Brownell Library (Essex Junction, VT), Bailey-Howe Library at the University of Vermont, the National Archives, the Library of Congress, the New York Public Library, the South Street Seaport Museum, the Archives Center at the National Museum of American History (Smithsonian), CIRMA (Antigua, Guatemala), Syracuse University Special Collections, Stanford University Special Collections, and the International Coffee Organization in London. I am particularly indebted to librarians/archivists/curators Anne Dornan, Ellen Gartrell, Bill Gill, Steven Jaffe, Tab Lewis, Ginny Powers, Tom Rosenbaum, Allison Ryley, and Martin Wattam.

In general, I found members of the coffee industry to be passionate about their product and eager to help with this project. See the bibliography for the long list of interviewees who shared their time and memories. In particular, I want to single out a few coffee people. Don Schoenholt generously shared his vast knowledge of coffee history and meticulously reviewed the manuscript. T. Carroll Wilson, who joined Hills Brothers in 1924 and is now in his nineties, took me through eight decades of his life in coffee. Dan Cox gave me hours of his time and expertise. Russ Kramer shared his wonderful private coffee library. Coffee exporter Klaus Monkemüller, who runs Unicom, hosted me on my initial forays in Guatemala. Bill McAlpin put me up at La Minita and shared his firmly held convictions. Doug Mitchell, the travel agent who runs Café Away, made the three-week SCAA visit to Honduras, El Salvador, and Nicaragua a well-planned pleasure. Ted Lingle shared with me his knowledge and the resources of the Specialty Coffee Association of America, just as Robert Nelson allowed me to rummage through the National Coffee Association files and helped me in other ways as well. Starbucks executive Dave Olsen granted a lengthy interview. Otherwise, Starbucks cooperated by sending numerous press releases.

Other coffee experts who unselfishly helped were Jerry Baldwin, Ian Bersten, Kenneth Davids, George Howell, Fred Houk, Kevin Knox, Erna Knutsen, Sherri Miller, Alfred Peet, Rick Peyser, and Gary Talboy. Thanks to Green Mountain Coffee Roasters for allowing me to be a student for a day at the company's Coffee College.

Like most writers, I couldn't afford standard accommodations during my research forays. I was fortunate to stay with varied and interesting hosts—Sue Taylor in Fairfax, Virginia (near Washington, D.C.), Dan McCracken, Roz Starr and Grace Brady in New York City, Esperanza "Chice" Chacón and her daughter, Andrea, in Guatemala City, Rick and Betty Adams at *Finca Oriflama* and their home in Panajachel, Guatemala, Bill McAlpin's La Minita in Costa Rica, Philip and Jessica Christey in London, Sheila Flannery in Chapel Hill, Brent and Janie Cohen in Oakland, and Britt and Nan Pendergrast (my parents) in Atlanta.

The three largest coffee corporations—Philip Morris (Kraft–Maxwell House), Procter & Gamble (Folgers–Millstone), and Nestlé (Hills Brothers–MJB–Chase & Sanborn–Nescafé–Taster's Choice–Sarks)—chose not to participate in this project, other than in a minimal way, so I had to rely primarily on interviews with former employees. Becky Tousey of the Kraft Archives provided background material about Maxwell House, however, and Nestlé headquarters at Vevey, Switzerland, sent me a fine published corporate history. Procter & Gamble provided a 1962 history of Folgers. Ogilvy & Mather (Maxwell House) and McCann-Erickson (Taster's Choice) personnel were helpful.

INDEX